THE UNITED STATES
MILITARY AVIATION
DIRECTORY

THE UNITED STATES
MILITARY AVIATION
DIRECTORY

Tom Kaminski
Mel Williams

A Special Publication from

AIRtime Publishing Inc.

Published by AIRtime Publishing Inc.
120 East Avenue, Norwalk, CT 06851 USA

Copyright © 2000 AIRtime Publishing Inc.

ISBN 1-880588-29-3

Editors
 Tom Kaminski
 Mel Williams

Author
 Tom Kaminski

Contributing Authors
 Margaret Bone, Robert F. Dorr
 Don Logan, Mel Williams

Artists
 Zaur Eylanbekov, Mark Styling
 Walter Wright

Designer
 Zaur Eylanbekov

Production & Distribution
 E. Rex Anku, Leslie Davis III
 Najwa Deeb, Natalie Klinger
 Shannon Walsh

Controller
 Linda DeAngelis

Publisher
 Mel Williams

Color Reproduction
 Chroma Graphics, Singapore

Printing
 KHL Printing, Singapore

This book was compiled by the *Combat Aircraft* editorial team. *Combat Aircraft* is published eight times per year and provides in-depth reports on the world's air forces and their aircraft, plus the latest military aviation news and developments. It is written and illustrated by many of the world's best aviation authors and photographers, and printed in full color throughout.

Subscriptions are available from:
AIRtime Publishing Inc.
120 East Avenue, Norwalk, CT 06851
USA

Call toll free within the United States 1-800-359-3003
Tel (203) 838-7979 • Fax (203) 838-7344

Some of the material in this book has also appeared in *Combat Aircraft* magazine.

Acknowledgements

Preparation of **The United States Military Aviation Directory** would not have been possible without the assistance of many individuals from within the military, aerospace and aviation publishing communities. We express our sincere gratitude to everyone who has helped ensure the material in this book is as timely and accurate as possible. Some of those to whom we are indebted include:

SFC David Abrams	Lt. j.g. Barbara Kelly
Mike Anselmo	Jon Lake
Christie Anderson	Doris Lance
Capt. Don Arias	Maj. Dave Lapan
Capt. Aisha Bakkar Poe	CW3 Kurt Lawrence
Lt. Col. Kimo Bacon	Bob Leder
Bill Barto	Ellen Lemond-Hollman
Pete Becker	Don Linn
Ned Beddessem	Rick Llinares
Lt. Lisa Braun	Dave Mason
Troy Brown	Angela Miccinello
Dennis Buley	Riccardo Niccoli
Rick Burgess	Sherry O'Connor
Piotr Butowski	JOC Brian O'Rourke
Ted Carlson	Susan L. Paruch
Maj. Michael Copes	Lt. Col. Eric Peck
Lt. Col. Michael Courts	Maj. Ken Pippin
JO2 Brianna Dandridge	Maj. Alain Pirrone
Jim Dunn	Chick Ramey
Norris Graser	Tom Ring
Stephen Harding	Brian C. Rogers
Rob Harris	Capt. Shillcutt
Paul Hart	Don Spering
Bill Hayes	Bill Tuttle
Debbie Heathers-Stiteler	Maj. Rick Sims
Eric Hehs	Troy Snead
Ted Herman	Warren E. Thompson
John Hoffman	Mike Tull
E.S. Holmberg	Terry L. Turner
Randy Jolly	Lt. Col. Scott Wagner
Susan Junkins	Zoë Williams
Ken Kaimann	Dick Ziegler

AIRtime Publishing is the source for a number of high quality military aviation journals and books. To receive a free copy of our latest catalog, please send your details to the address shown on this page.

Distributor and retailer inquiries are welcome.

INTRODUCTION

The *United States Military Aviation Directory* profiles the current aviation assets of the US Air Force, US Navy, US Marine Corps, US Coast Guard and US Army, and includes details of all commands, units, air bases, aircraft carriers and assault ships, along with descriptions of every serving aircraft. Within each of the air arm sections, aircraft types are arranged alphabetically by company. However, recent consolidations within the aerospace industry mean some types are not shown under the name of the original manufacturer. In instances where a program has been acquired or is now managed by another contractor, that aircraft is listed under the most current company. Comprehensive indices to all serving aircraft, units and military organizations are included.

CONTENTS

Holloman AFB, New Mexico, is home to Air Combat Command's two operational F-117A Stealth Fighter units. The 'Black Sheep' of the 8th Fighter Squadron (FS) and the 'Flying Knights' of the 9th FS belong to the 12th Air Force's 49th Wing.

SENIOR COMMAND STRUCTURE OF THE US ARMED SERVICES

In addition to the United States Air Force, America possesses powerful naval and army air forces equipped with large fleets of aircraft. Operating as fully independent organizations, each headed by a civilian secretary, the USAF, United States Navy and United States Army report to the Department of Defense (DoD), a cabinet agency set up in 1947 and headed by a civilian secretary of defense. The status of the United States Marine Corps is somewhat different, however. This service is a department of the US Navy and its commandant thus reports to the secretary of the Navy. For the United States Coast Guard, the situation is different again. Although a full-time military organization, the Coast Guard reports to the secretary of transportation during peacetime but is attached to the Department of the Navy in the event of a national emergency.

Representing the military leadership of the DoD are the military heads of their respective services plus two additional appointees. The three chiefs of staff, commandant of the Marine Corps, and two four-star generals who occupy the posts of chairman and vice chairman, comprise the Joint Chiefs of Staff (JCS). This office reports directly to the secretary of defense. Likewise, the nine unified commanders who have control of elements of all military branches, whenever such forces are deployed within their geographical areas, also report directly to the secretary of defense.

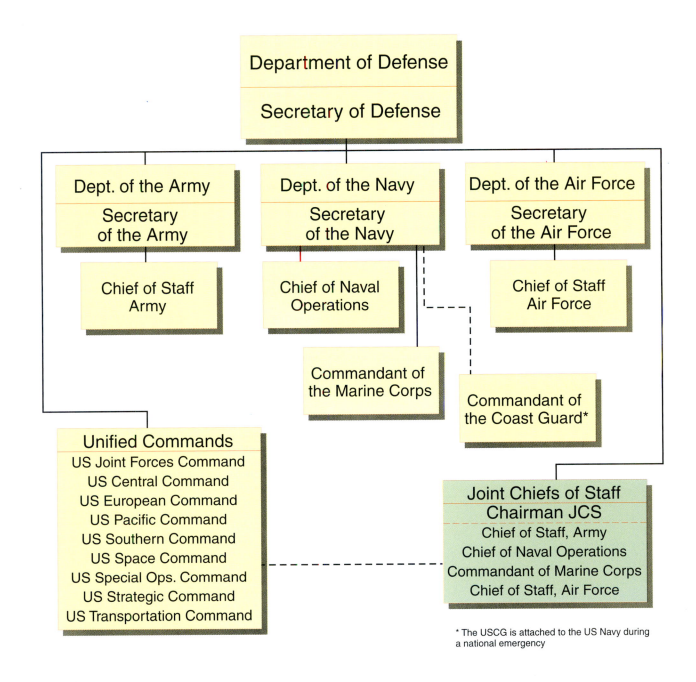

* The USCG is attached to the US Navy during a national emergency

US AIR FORCE

OVERVIEW

The United States Air Force traces its roots back to 1 August 1907, when the Aeronautical Division of the US Signal Corps was formed to develop military ballooning and explore the use of flying machines for warfare. It was subsequently redesignated the Aviation Section and the Division of Military Aeronautics, respectively, during the 11 years that followed. Absorbed by the newly formed Air Service in 1918, the latter was succeeded by the Air Corps following passage of an act of Congress in 1926.

The Air Corps remained in existence for more than 20 years but became a subordinate arm of the US Army Air Forces (USAAF) when this was established on 20 June 1941. Although the United States officially had not yet been drawn into World War II, the conflict had been raging in Europe for almost two years.

The first commanding general of the USAAF was Gen. Henry Harley "Hap" Arnold whose early vision and guiding hand subsequently led to a fully independent air arm. He laid the groundwork for today's USAF, which came into existence officially on 18 September 1947. However, it fell to one of his key officers, Gen. Carl A. Spaatz, who succeeded him in early 1946, to continue the process during the difficult period immediately after the war. The rapid and chaotic demobilization that followed the victory over Japan left the US military desperately short of skilled personnel and dangerously vulnerable to the possibility of aggression by the Soviet Union. With a fleet of obsolescent warplanes and too few qualified airmen under his command, Spaatz became the first chief of staff of the USAF.

With the world having entered the nuclear age in the final months of World War II, US

An F-15E Strike Eagle belonging to the 'Bold Tigers' of the 391st FS, 366th Wing. Based at Mountain Home AFB, Idaho, the wing is pioneering the Expeditionary Aerospace Force (EAF) concept the Air Force will implement for overseas deployments.

security now rested largely on the deterrence value of the nation's nuclear weapons stockpile. In reality, however, only a handful of such weapons existed. The Air Force's Strategic Air Command had a very limited number at its disposal and barely the means to deliver them against Soviet targets had it been called upon to do so. The USAF was in dire need of a fleet of modern aircraft and a bigger nuclear "stick" to properly address ever present threats posed by the highly confrontational atmosphere of the Cold War. In fact, within just a few years the USAF found itself fighting a new war in Asia, after the communist forces of North Korea invaded its southern neighbor, the Republic of Korea, in June 1950. In the late 1960s the USAF again was called upon to fight in another superpower surrogate conflict in the region, this

time the long and disastrous Vietnam War.

Such conflicts illustrated the need for and hastened the development of more sophisticated jet aircraft and missiles to counter the technological advances made by the Soviet Union. They also taught the United States valuable lessons as to the ways it might prosecute future wars.

Turning the focus of its attention in the 1980s to the means by which it could better fight in limited-theater situations, the USAF invested heavily in developing new tactics, electronic battlefield intelligence and precision weapons. The payoff was dramatically illustrated during the 1991 Gulf War against Iraq. That brief conflict represented a watershed for the United States by demonstrating how its military, and the USAF in particular, had the means to deliver a stunning victory

by employing advanced technology against an enemy's communications system, and the infrastructure upon which its warfighting capabilities depended. Using a limited number of guided weapons against such targets, the Air Force left Iraq's large military forces incapable of functioning within a matter of days. Not only was it a significant battlefield victory but its implications were far larger.

The outcome of the war demonstrated to the leaders of the Soviet Union that the West had made significant technological advances in warfighting, many of which were far ahead of their own. With Russia already teetering economically, there is no doubt this realization helped push the former superpower to its final collapse. Equally important for the United States, the war proved that in the hands of a relatively small number of well-trained personnel, operating under joint-service conditions even, such technologies could be employed decisively.

With the end of the Cold War and many of the perceived threats gone, the 1990s brought more dramatic changes to America's military services. As was the case for the nation's other air arms, the USAF experienced major fleet and personnel reductions as a result of budgetary constraints linked largely to a reassessment of the country's security needs.

Two years after the Gulf War the USAF had a fleet of some 7,600 aircraft and employed close to one million active-duty, reserve and civilian personnel. Now, the fleet size is closer to 6,000 aircraft and the overall personnel count is less than 800,000. Reductions in hardware and manpower are likely to continue for the foreseeable future.

Today's Air Force comprises some 370,000 active-duty personnel, which is similar to the active-duty strength of the US Navy and is slightly fewer than the number serving 50 years ago. Eighty-seven percent are assigned to one of the nine major commands around which the USAF is primarily structured and which are described in the pages that follow. Some 17,000 personnel currently serve as aircrews and, for the past three years, the service has averaged close to 2.2 million flight hours annually.

With many of its aircraft receiving new upgrades and enhancements to extend their useful lives, the fleet continues to age. At the end of Fiscal Year 1998 the average age of the active-duty fleet was reported to be 19.7 years, compared with 18.7 years and 22.0 years for the fleets respectively serving the two reserve elements: the Air National Guard and Air Force Reserve.

Among several new aircraft projects under development, two are designed to replace fighter assets early in the 21st century. However, in the summer of 1999 Congress deleted from the defense appropriations bill further funding for the Lockheed Martin F-22 Raptor air dominance fighter, just as the aircraft was about to enter its initial production phase. Key to the USAF's future fleet planning, the F-22 decision stunned senior military officials at the Pentagon and aerospace contractors alike. Meanwhile, the Joint Strike Fighter (JSF) program is currently being contested by rival aerospace companies Boeing and Lockheed Martin. Development of one of these designs is supposed to lead to the fielding of an affordable, single-platform fighter during the next 15 to 20 years, which will be used by the Air Force, US Navy and US Marine Corps. The new warplane is described in the *Military Aircraft Programs Under Development* section of this book.

ORGANIZATION

REPORTING STRUCTURE OF THE UNITED STATES AIR FORCE
MAJOR COMMANDS AND AIR NATIONAL GUARD

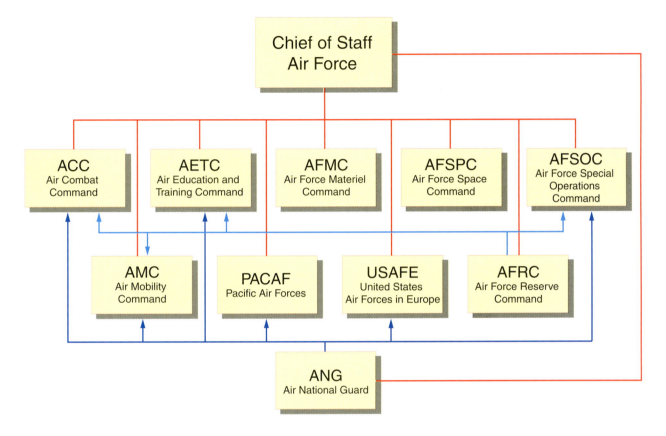

The United States Air Force is organized largely around nine major commands that report directly to the Air Force chief of staff. These comprise:

- Air Combat Command (ACC)
- Air Education and Training Command (AETC)
- Air Force Materiel Command (AFMC)
- Air Force Space Command (AFSPC)
- Air Force Special Operations Command (AFSOC)
- Air Mobility Command (AMC)
- Pacific Air Forces (PACAF)
- United States Air Forces in Europe (USAFE)
- Air Force Reserve Command (AFRC)

Several of these commands also report to a specific unified commander in chief (CinC) in operational situations, as is the case with the other military services. The commander is usually a four-star general, although the AFRC and AFSOC are each led by a two-star major general.

Most of the units within the USAF are assigned to one of these commands, which are typically made up of individually numbered air forces. The latter are led either by a three-star lieutenant general or a two-star major general, and organized into wings commanded by a one-star brigadier general or colonel.

Within the wing, aircrews and intelligence units typically are assigned to its operations group, whereas maintenance, supply, security and other personnel report to such groups as logistics, support or medical.

Each wing has one or more flying squadrons, and the number of aircraft assigned to each is referred to as the Primary Aircraft Inventory (PAI). This number varies by command and type of mission flown by the unit. Fighter squadrons within ACC, PACAF and USAFE are nominally assigned 18 or 24 aircraft each but fighter squadrons within the AFRC, as well as the Air National Guard (ANG), which is not part of this command structure, are each equipped with only 15 aircraft. In the case of B-1B and B-52 reserve units, just eight bombers are assigned whereas 12 bombers are assigned for an ACC squadron. Active-duty air refueling and airlift squadrons within AMC each have 12 aircraft, compared with as few as eight for non-active-duty units.

Outside of this command structure are several organizations that report directly to the Air Force chief of staff. These include the ANG, mentioned above, and the United States Air Force Academy (USAFA), along with units responsible for communications, doctrine, security and other matters.

While the AFRC and ANG are entities distinct and separate from each other and from the commands listed, their assets (air forces and aircraft) are tasked operationally by specific elements of ACC, AETC, AFSOC, AMC or PACAF. Referred to as gained units, these numbered air forces are listed with appropriate gaining commands in the "Commands and Units" section.

The collapse of the Soviet Union a decade ago signaled an end to the Cold War and an urgent need to reassess US security needs. Significant cutbacks in personnel, operational aircraft and active facilities followed, driven by budgetary pressures and the perception that many of the old threats had gone. Like its sister services, the USAF has had to find new and more efficient ways of meeting its force-readiness obligations with the aircraft at its disposal.

During the last 10 years the United States has experienced the largest peacetime economic expansion in its history and this has had a negative impact on USAF manpower. Whereas it was necessary to reduce the number of personnel and create a leaner force, the USAF has suffered a serious drain of its most experienced personnel. In particular, many of its best pilots and maintenance crews continue to be drawn away to better paid jobs in the civil sector that also do not require them to spend extended periods overseas and away from their families. Aircrews and maintainers from the Airborne Warning and Control

System (AWACS) community, for instance, are required to spend as much as 225 days away from home, annually. This has become a serious issue in light of the fact that 73 percent of current USAF airmen are married, compared with just 23 percent in 1952.

In an effort to better meet the realities of warfighting in the 21st century and to address the needs of its personnel, the service is turning to the concept of the Expeditionary Aerospace Force (EAF), a deployment method that was routine before the advent of the Cold War.

Expeditionary Aerospace Force (EAF): New Deployment Thinking

During the last 40 years the policy has been to deploy large numbers of Air Force personnel overseas for extended periods of time at permanent bases in Europe, Asia or elsewhere. However, the current thinking is that such forces primarily will be deployed abroad only when necessary. In essence, the new policy is an acknowledgment that it is no longer necessary for the country to have half of its air force stationed at bases encircling the former Soviet Union. Instead, they will be garrisoned stateside in peacetime and deployed abroad (termed an "expedition") only as situations require.

The fighting components that make up an EAF are known as Air Expeditionary Forces (AEFs) and will include, among other elements, Air Expeditionary Wings (AEWs). Under the EAF, force deployment "packages" will be called upon that comprise combat, mobility and space forces on alert for approximately 90 days, roughly every 15 months. On average, two AEFs will be on call at any one time to meet contingencies. The concept went into effect on 1 October 1999, and now means that airmen will have much longer notice of when they might be required to travel overseas.

Announced in July 1998, not only is the EAF an acknowledgement of how the USAF intends to fight its future wars but the hope is it will slow the drain of skilled personnel who are abandoning the service in

midstride. It should mean Air Force personnel will be able to spend more time with their families because it will cap the length of each deployment, and allow them to plan for their time away with more certainty.

The aircraft in service today were conceived and built largely for nuclear war against the Soviet Union. Now, the service is faced with quite different mission taskings, including what is termed military operations other than war (MOOTW). For the purpose of developing strategies and tactics necessary to make the EAF an effective warfighting system, the USAF has charged the 366th Wing based at Mountain Home AFB, Idaho, with finding ways to deploy warplanes in scenarios that were never imagined by their designers. As such, the wing represents the vanguard of the program.

Not only that, the 366th Wing, and the 4th Fighter Wing (FW) at Seymour Johnson AFB, North Carolina, will act as backup (or "on call") AEWs whereas most of the Air Force including the Reserve and ANG, will be divided into 10 AEFs. According to Air Force Secretary F. Whitten Peters, such structuring has been developed from computer modeling of world events since the 1991 Gulf War. Analysis has been made of the past and projections made for the future, to look at how often and where troops most likely will have to deploy. The 10 "expeditionary" groups will rotate responsibility for foreign deployments to areas of conflict while five separate mobility groups will be called upon specifically to handle humanitarian missions and provide AEF support.

It should be noted that although the 366th Wing is composite in nature, that is, it flies more than one mission type aircraft from the same base, EAF and composite units are very different concepts. The fact that this wing is both a composite unit and spearheading the EAF is coincidental.

Charged under the EAF with being ready to deploy anywhere in the world within 48 hours, each AEF will comprise approximately 175 aircraft to include fighters, heavy bombers, reconnaissance, electronic warfare, transport and refueling platforms. Approximately 20,000 personnel will also be assigned to each AEF and, although aircraft will be stationed at different bases, aircrews will train together and cooperate in developing skills and tactics during regular exercises and competitions like Red Flag and Gunsmoke. The EAF will also bring 125,000 AFRC and ANG personnel into the rotation system.

Although the EAF represents the blueprint for addressing future conflicts and humanitarian assistance efforts, the USAF's current garrisons at overseas bases, including Europe, South Korea and Japan, will not be affected. The first AEFs on call will be those headquartered at Hill AFB, Utah, and Dyess AFB, Texas. For humanitarian missions, however, the unit at Pope AFB, North Carolina, will be the first to enter the rotation. Short of a global war, the EAF will be the USAF's deployment system for the foreseeable future.

The list of AEFs, their headquarters and rotation order is included as an appendix.

The 1st FW at Langley AFB, Virginia, is composed of three fighter squadrons. One unit, the 'Hat-in-the-Ring Gang' of the 94th FS, traces its roots back to World War I and the First Pursuit Group, which operated from small airfields across France. Today, the unit and its sister squadrons, the 27th FS and 71st FS, operate 54 F-15C/D MSIP Eagles.

COMMANDS AND UNITS

AIR COMBAT COMMAND (ACC)
Headquarters: Langley AFB, Virginia

Established on 1 June 1992, ACC operates all USAF bombers along with continental United States (CONUS)-based combat-coded fighter, attack, reconnaissance and combat rescue aircraft. The command is responsible for organizing, training and equipping air combat–ready forces and charged with providing nuclear forces for US Strategic Command (USSTRATCOM). ACC provides theater air forces for US Joint Forces Command (USJFCOM), US Central Command (USCENTCOM), US Southern Command (USSOUTHCOM), US European Command (USEUCOM) and US Pacific Command (USPACOM), as well as air defense forces for North American Air Defense Command (NORAD).

Reporting directly is the USAF's Air Warfare Center (AWC), which comprises the operational test and evaluation (OT&E) organization that is the 53d Wing at Eglin AFB, Florida, and the 57th Wing at Nellis AFB, Nevada, which focuses on advanced training and operational missions. The latter includes the USAF Air Demonstration Squadron better known as the 'Thunderbirds.'

Four numbered air forces are assigned to ACC. The First Air Force is composed entirely of ANG wings, which the command gains in operational situations, whereas the Eighth, Ninth and Twelfth Air Forces comprise gained ANG as well as active-duty units. Additionally, elements of the Tenth Air Force are gained from the AFRC. Such units have been integrated into the ACC tables that follow.

ACC has approximately 90,000 active-duty personnel and employs 11,000 civilians. Additionally, 63,000 airmen come under its operational control from ANG and AFRC elements.

First Air Force (1 AF)
Hqtrs: Tyndall AFB, Florida

In October 1997, the First Air Force became exclusively an ANG numbered air force tasked with ensuring the air sovereignty and air defense of CONUS. It forms the continental US component of the binational NORAD and comprises 10 ANG fighter wings and three regional air defense sectors. The latter include the Western Air Defense Sector (WADS), located at McChord AFB, Washington; the Northeast Air Defense Sector (NEADS), located in Rome, New York, at the former Griffiss AFB; and the Southeast Air Defense Sector (SEADS), at Tyndall AFB, Florida. The CONUS Regional Operations Control Center is also located at Tyndall AFB.

Under the Quadrennial Defense Review, the number of wings assigned to air defense missions was reduced to just six with operations undertaken at seven "alert" sites. The remaining wings are general purpose units which can be called upon for alert duties.

AIR COMBAT COMMAND (ACC)
Langley AFB, Virginia

Direct Reporting Units

Component	Unit	Base	Aircraft	Tail Code	Color
Air Warfare Center - Nellis AFB, Nevada					
53d Wing		**Eglin AFB, Florida**			
53d TEG		Nellis AFB, Nevada			
	85th TES 'Skulls'	Eglin AFB, Florida	F-15A/B/C/D/E, F-16A/B/C/D	OT	Black/White
	Det. 2*	Ellsworth AFB, S.D.	(B-1B)	EL	
	72d TES*	Whiteman AFB, Missouri	(B-2A)	WM	
	49th TESTS*	Barksdale AFB, Louisiana	(B-52H)	LA	
	422d TES 'Green Bats'	Nellis AFB, Nevada	A-10A, F-16C/D (Block 42/52), F-15C/D/E	OT	Black/Green
	Det. 1	Holloman AFB, N.M.	F-117A	HO	
53d WEG	82d ATRS	Tyndall AFB, Florida	E-9A, QF-4E/G	WE	
	Det.1	Holloman AFB, N.M.	QF-4E/G		
57th Wing		**Nellis AFB, Nevada**			Black/Yellow
	USAFADS	Nellis AFB, Nevada	F-16C/D (Block 32)		
57th OG	11th RS	Indian Springs AFAF, Nevada	RQ-1A	WA	
	15th RS	Indian Springs AFAF, Nevada	RQ-1A	WA	
	66th RQS	Nellis AFB, Nevada	HH-60G	WA	
	414th CTS	Nellis AFB, Nevada	F-16C/D (Block 32)	WA	
USAFWS	F-16 Div.	Nellis AFB, Nevada	F-16C/D (Block 42/52)	WA	
	F-15 Div.	Nellis AFB, Nevada	F-15C/D	WA	
	F-15E Div.	Nellis AFB, Nevada	F-15E	WA	
	A-10 Div.	Nellis AFB, Nevada	A-10A	WA	
	HH-60 Div.	Nellis AFB, Nevada	HH-60G	WA	
	(Det. 4) B-1 Div.*	Ellsworth AFB, S.D.	(B-1B)	EL	
	(Det. 5) B-52 Div.*	Barksdale AFB, Louisiana	(B-52H)	LA	

* Unit utilizes aircraft borrowed from host wing

AIR COMBAT COMMAND (Continued)					
Component	Unit	Base	Aircraft	Tail Code	Color

First Air Force (ANG) - Tyndall AFB, Florida
The First Air Force is composed entirely of gained ANG units

102d FW — **Otis ANGB, Massachusetts**
102d OG ....101st FS 'Eagle Keepers' F-15A/B

119th FW — **Hector IAP, Fargo, North Dakota**
119th OG........178th FS 'Happy Hooligans' ....F-16A/B (ADF)
          Det. 1 ....Langley AFB, Virginia ....F-16A (ADF)

120th FW* — **Great Falls IAP, Montana**
120th OG.......186th FS ....F-16A/B (ADF)

125th FW — **Jacksonville IAP, Florida** — FL
125th OG.......159th FS 'Jaguars'.......................................C-26B, F-15A/B
          Det. 1 ....Homestead ARS, Florida........F-15A

142d FW — **Portland IAP/ANGB, Oregon**
142d OG ....123d FS 'Red Hawks'......................................F-15A/B

144th FW — **Fresno-Yosemite IAP/ANGB, California**
144th OG........194th FS 'Griffins' ....C-26B, F-16C/D (Block 25)
          Det. 1 ....March ARB, California F-16C

147th FW* — **Ellington Field/ANGB, Houston, Texas** — EF
147th OG.......111th FS 'Ace in the Hole'................................C-26B, F-16C/D (Block 25)

148th FW — **Duluth IAP/ANGB, Minnesota**
148th OG........179th FS 'Bulldogs' ....F-16A/B (ADF)
          Det. 1 ....Tyndall AFB, Florida ....F-16A (ADF)

158th FW* — **Burlington IAP, Vermont** — (VT)
158th OG.......134th FS 'Green Mountain Boys'....................................F-16C/D (Block 25)

177th FW* — **Atlantic City IAP/ANGB, New Jersey** — AC
177th OG........119th FS 'Jersey Devils' ....F-16C/D (Block 25)

* Unit tasked with a general purpose mission

USAF adversary training is provided by Block 32 F-16C/Ds from the 414th Combat Training Squadron (CTS), a unit of the 57th Wing, which is part of ACC's Air Warfare Center (AWC) at Nellis AFB, Nevada.

13

US Air Force

AIR COMBAT COMMAND (Continued)

Component	Unit	Base	Aircraft	Tail Code	Color
Eighth Air Force - Barksdale AFB, Louisiana					
2d BW		**Barksdale AFB, Louisiana**		LA	
2d OG	11th BS(FTU) 'Mr Jiggs'		B-52H		Gold
	20th BS 'Buccaneers'		B-52H		Blue
	96th BS 'Red Devils'		B-52H		Red
5th BW		**Minot AFB, North Dakota**		MT	
5th OG	23d BS 'Bomber Barons'		B-52H		Red/Yellow
7th BW		**Dyess AFB, Texas**		DY	
7th OG	9th BS 'Bats'		B-1B		Black
	28th BS(FTU) 'Mohawk Warriors'		B-1B		Blue/White
27th FW		**Cannon AFB, New Mexico**		CC	
27th OG	428th FS 'Buccaneers'*		F-16C/D (Block 52)		Black
	522d FS 'Fireballs'		F-16C/D (Block 30)		Red
	523d FS 'Crusaders'		F-16C/D (Block 30)		Blue
	524th FS 'Hounds'		F-16C/D (Block 40)		Yellow
28th BW		**Ellsworth AFB, South Dakota**		EL	
28th OG	37th BS 'Tigers'		B-1B		Black/Gold
	77th BS 'War Eagles'		B-1B		Maroon/Yellow
85th Group		**NAS Keflavik, Iceland**		IS	
	56th RQS		HH-60G		
	TDY Units		TDY F-15, F-16. HC-130P		
509th BW		**Whiteman AFB, Missouri**		WM	
509th OG	325th BS		B-2A		
	393d BS 'Tigers'		B-2A		
	394th CTS		T-38A		
Eighth Air Force–gained ANG units					
110th FW		**W.H. Kellogg Airp./Battle Creek ANGB, Mich.**		BC	
110th OG	172d FS 'Mad Ducks'		A-10A, OA-10A		
115th FW		**Dane County RAP-Truax Field, Madison, Wisconsin**		WI	
115th OG	176th FS 'Badgers'		C-26B, F-16C/D (Block 30)		
122d FW		**Fort Wayne IAP, Indiana**		FW	
122d OG	163d FS 'Marksmen'		F-16C/D (Block 25)		
127th Wing**		**Selfridge ANGB, Mount Clemens, Michigan**		MI	
127th OG	107th FS 'Wolves'		F-16C/D (Block 30)		
131st FW		**Lambert–St Louis IAP, Missouri**		SL	
131st OG	110th FS		F-15A/B		
159th FW		**NAS New Orleans JRB, Louisiana**		JZ	
159th OG	122d FS		C-130H, F-15A/B		
181st FW		**Terre Haute IAP/Hulman Field, Terre Haute IAP, Indiana**		TH	
181st OG	113th FS 'Racers'		F-16C/D (Block 30)		
183d FW		**Capital Airport, Springfield, Illinois**		SI	
183d OG	170th FS 'Fly'N Illini'		F-16C/D (Block 30)		
184th BW		**McConnell AFB, Kansas**			
184th OG	127th BS 'Jayhawks'		B-1B		
187th FW		**Montgomery RAP-Dannelly Field, Alabama**		AL	
187th OG	160th FS 'Snakes'		C-26B, F-16C/D (Block 30)		
188th FW		**Fort Smith RAP/Ebbing ANGB, Arkansas**		FS	
188th OG	184th FS 'Flying Razorbacks'		F-16A/B		

* Squadron provides training for the Republic of Singapore Air Force
** Wing controls squadrons assigned to ACC and AMC

Eighth Air Force (8 AF)
Hqtrs: Barksdale AFB, Louisiana

Until 1 June 1992, the Eighth Air Force was assigned to the former Strategic Air Command (SAC). When that command was inactivated, the Eighth was transferred to the newly formed ACC and is now responsible for eight active-duty wings and groups, including all of the active-duty manned bomber units. It is also the ACC component of USSTRATCOM. Additionally, the Eighth Air Force is responsible for the operational readiness of 11 ANG and three AFRC units, and for USAF operations at Portugal's Lajes Field in the Azores.

Ninth Air Force (9 AF)
Hqtrs: Shaw AFB, South Carolina

One of two numbered air forces originally assigned to the old Tactical Air Command (TAC), the Ninth Air Force is tasked as the US Central Command Air Force (USCENTAF). In addition to controlling seven CONUS-based active-duty wings and groups and a provisional wing in southwest Asia, the Ninth Air Force supports 13 ANG and two AFRC wings and groups. The structure of its 347th Wing at Moody AFB, Georgia, will be revised as the unit becomes the USAF's only dedicated combat search and rescue (CSAR) wing, and it will ultimately lose two F-16C squadrons and its directly assigned A-10A/OA-10A Thunderbolt II squadron as additional CSAR assets join the unit. However, it is likely a separate fighter group will be retained, equipped with Thunderbolt IIs.

AIR COMBAT COMMAND (Continued)

Component	Unit	Base	Aircraft	Tail Code	Color
Ninth Air Force - Shaw AFB, South Carolina					
1st FW		**Langley AFB, Virginia**		FF	
1st OG	27th FS 'Fighting Eagles'		F-15C/D		Yellow
	71st FS 'Ironmen'		F-15C/D		Red
	94th FS 'Hat-in-the-Ring'		F-15C/D		Blue
4th FW		**Seymour Johnson AFB, North Carolina**		SJ	
4th OG	333d FS(FTU) 'Lancers'		F-15E		Red
	334th FS(FTU) 'Eagles'		F-15E		Blue
	335th FS 'Chiefs'		F-15E		Green
	336th FS 'Rocketeers'		F-15E		Yellow
20th FW		**Shaw AFB, South Carolina**		SW	
20th OG	55th FS 'Fighting 55th'		F-16C/D (Block 50)		Blue
	77th FS 'Gamblers'		F-16C/D (Block 50)		Red
	78th FS 'Bushmasters'		F-16C/D (Block 50D)		Yellow/Red
	79th FS 'Tigers'		F-16C/D (Block 50D)		Yellow/Black
33d FW		**Eglin AFB, Florida**		EG	
33d OG	58th FS 'Gorillas'		F-15C/D		Blue
	60th FS 'Fighting Crows'		F-15C/D		Red
93d ACW		**Robins AFB, Georgia**		WR	
93d OG	12th ACCS		E-8C		Green
	16th ACCS		E-8C		Red
	93d TRS		TE-8A		Yellow
347th Wing		**Moody AFB, Georgia**		MY	
347th OG	68th FS 'Lancers'		F-16C/D (Block 40)		Red
	69th FS 'Werewolves'		F-16C/D (Block 40)		Black
	70th FS 'White Knights'		A-10A, OA-10A		Blue
	41st RQS 'Jolly Green'		HH-60G		Green
	71st RQS 'Kings'		HC-130P, C-130E		Blue
23d FG	74th FS 'Flying Tigers'	Pope AFB, North Carolina	A-10A, OA-10A	FT	Blue
	75th FS 'Sharks'	Pope AFB, North Carolina	A-10A, OA-10A	FT	Black/White
363d AEW		**Prince Sultan AB, Al Kharj, Saudi Arabia**			
363d EOG	Rotational ACC Units				
	363d ERS	Prince Sultan AB, Saudi	U-2S		
	363d EAACS	Prince Sultan AB, Saudi	E-3B/C		
	363d EARS	Prince Sultan AB, Saudi	KC-135E/R		
	363d EAS	Prince Sultan AB, Saudi	C-130E/H		
	763d ERS	Prince Sultan AB, Saudi	RC-135V/W		
	763d EARS	Al Dhafra AB, UAE	KC-135E/R		
	763d EAS	Al Seeb AB, Oman	C-130E/H		
332d AEG	332d EFS	Ahmed Al Jaber AB, Kuwait	A-10A, OA-10A, F-16C		
	332d ERQS	Ahmed Al Jaber AB, Kuwait	HH-60G		
9th EOG	9th ERQS	Ali Al Salem AB, Kuwait	HC-130P		
	9th EAS	Ali Al Salem AB, Kuwait	C-130E/H		

Heading out for a practice mission from Pope AFB, North Carolina, this A-10A Thunderbolt II from the 75th FS is carrying AGM-65 Maverick missiles on its inboard underwing pylons, and a pair of AIM-9 Sidewinders on its outboard stations.

US Air Force

The ANG provides ACC with one-third of its tactical fighter strength. These F-16Cs belong to the 138th FS, 174th FW, based at Syracuse IAP, New York. The wing recently transitioned from Block 30 to Block 25 jets.

The 'Black Hogs' of the ANG's 103d FS, 111th FW, operate A-10As and OA-10As from NAS Willow Grove JRB, Pennsylvania.

AIR COMBAT COMMAND (Continued)

Component	Unit	Base	Aircraft	Tail Code	Color
Ninth Air Force–gained ANG units					
103d FW		Bradley IAP/ANGB, Windsor Locks, Connecticut		CT	
103d OG	118th FS 'Flying Yankees'		A-10A, OA-10A		
104th FW		Barnes MAP/ANGB, Westfield, Mass.		MA	
104th OG	131st FS		A-10A, OA-10A		
106th RQW		Francis S. Gabreski Airport/ ANGB, New York		LI	
106th OG	102d RQS 'ANG's Oldest Unit'		HC-130N/P, HH-60G		
111th FW		NAS Willow Grove JRB, Pennsylvania		PA	
111th OG	103d FS 'Black Hogs'		A-10A, OA-10A		
113th Wing*		Andrews AFB, Maryland		DC	
113th OG	121st FS 'Capital Guardians'		F-16C/D (Block 30)		
116th BW		Robins AFB, Georgia		GA	
116th OG	128th BS		B-1B		
169th FW		Columbia Metropolitan Airport/ McEntire ANGS, South Carolina		(SC)	
169th OG	157th FS 'Swamp Foxes'		C-130H, F-16C/D (Block 52D)		
174th FW		Syracuse IAP-Hancock Field, New York		NY	
174th OG	138th FS		F-16C/D (Block 25)		
175th Wing*		Martin State Airport/Warfield ANGB, Baltimore, Maryland		MD	
175th OG	104th FS		A-10A, OA-10A		
178th FW		Springfield-Beckley MAP, Ohio		OH	Red
178th OG	162d FS		F-16C/D (Block 30)		
180th FW		Toledo Express AP, Ohio		OH	Green
180th OG	112th FS 'Stingers'		F-16C/D (Block 42)		
192d FW		Richmond IAP-Byrd Field, Virginia		VA	
192d OG	149th FS		F-16C/D (Block 30)		

* Wing controls squadrons assigned to ACC and AMC

This Lockheed U-2S is from the 99th Reconnaissance Squadron (RS), 9th Reconnaissance Wing (RW), at Beale AFB, California. The wing operates two squadrons in that state, another at Osan AB, South Korea, plus a detachment at Akrotiri AB in Cyprus.

Twelfth Air Force (12 AF)
Hqtrs: Davis-Monthan AFB, Arizona

The Twelfth Air Force is tasked as USSOUTHCOM, responsible for USAF missions throughout Central and South America. In all, it commands seven active-duty wings and oversees the operational readiness of nine ANG and six AFRC units from the Tenth Air Force.

AIR COMBAT COMMAND (Continued)

Component	Unit	Base	Aircraft	Tail Code	Color
Twelfth Air Force - Davis Monthan AFB, Arizona					
	Coronet Oak ....Luiz Munoz Marin IAP, P.R.....TDY ANG/AFRC C-130 Units				
	Coronet Nighthawk ....Hato IAP, Curaçao,				
		Netherlands Antilles ....TDY ANG F-15/F-16 Units			
9th RW		**Beale AFB, California**		BB	
	Det.1	Akrotiri AB, Cyprus U-2S			
9th OG	1st RS(FTU)	Beale AFB, California T-38A, U-2S, TU-2S			
	5th RS	Osan AB, Korea....................U-2S			
	99th RS	Beale AFB, California T-38A, U-2S			
49th FW		**Holloman AFB, New Mexico**		HO	
49th OG	7th CTS 'Screamin' Demons' T-38A			Yellow
	8th FS 'Black Sheep' F-117A			White
	9th FS 'Flying Knights' F-117A			Red
	20th FS 'Silver Lobos'* F-4F			Silver
55th Wing		**Offutt AFB, Nebraska**		OF	
55th OG	1st ACCS E-4B			
	38th RS 'Fighting Hellcats' ....RC-135U/V/W, TC-135W ....Green			
	45th RS 'Sylvester' OC-135B, WC-135W,			
			RC-135S, TC-135B/S ....Black		
	Det. 1 ....Eielson AFB, Alaska RC-135S			
	82d RS ....Kadena AB, Okinawa, Japan ..RC-135U/V/W			
	95th RS ....RAF Mildenhall, England RC-135V/W			
	Det. 1 ....Souda Bay, Crete RC-135V/W			
355th Wing		**Davis-Monthan AFB, Arizona**		DM	
355th OG	41st ECS 'Scorpions' EC-130H			Blue
	42d ACCS 'Axe' EC-130E			Gray
	43d ECS 'Bats' EC-130H			Red
	354th FS 'Bulldogs' A-10A, OA-10A			Blue
	357th FS(FTU) 'Dragons' A-10A, OA-10A			Yellow
	358th FS(FTU) 'Lobos' ....A-10A, OA-10A ....Black/White			
366th Wing		**Mountain Home AFB, Idaho**		MO	
366th OG	22d ARS 'Mules' KC-135R			Gray
	34th BS 'Thunderbirds' B-1B			Black/Red
	389th FS 'Thunderbolts' ....F-16C/D (Block 52) ....Red/Yellow			
	390th FS 'Wild Boars' F-15C/D			Blue
	391st FS 'Bold Tigers' F-15E			Orange/Black
388th FW		**Hill AFB, Utah**		HL	
388th OG	4th FS 'Fightin Fuugins' ....F-16C/D (Block 40)......................Yellow			
	34th FS 'Rude Rams' ....F-16C/D (Block 40).........................Red			
	421st FS 'Black Widows' ....F-16C/D (Block 40)........................Black			
552d ACW		**Tinker AFB, Oklahoma**		OK	
552d OG	963d AACS 'Blue Knights' E-3B/C			Black
	964th AACS E-3B/C			Maroon
	965th AACS E-3B/C			Yellow
	966th AACS(FTU) E-3B/C, TC-18E**			Blue

* *Luftwaffe* training squadron
** TC-18E not operational currently

355th Wing

US Air Force

AIR COMBAT COMMAND (Continued)

Twelfth Air Force–gained ANG units

Component	Unit	Base	Aircraft	Tail Code	Color
114th FW		**Joe Foss Field, Sioux Falls, South Dakota**			
114th OG	175th FS 'Lobos'		F-16C/D (Block 30)		
124th Wing		**Boise Air Terminal-Gowen Field, Idaho**		ID	
124th OG	189th AS		C-130E		
	190th FS		A-10A, OA-10A		
129th RQW		**Moffett Federal Airport/ANGS, California**		CA	Blue
129th OG	129th RQS		HH-60G, MC/HC-130P		
132d FW		**Des Moines IAP, Iowa**		IA	
132d OG	124th FS 'Hawkeyes'		F-16C/D (Block 42)		
138th FW		**Tulsa IAP, Oklahoma**		OK	
138th OG	125th FS		F-16C/D (Block 42)		
140th Wing*		**Buckley ANGB, Aurora, Colorado**		CO	
140th OG	120th FS 'Cougars'		F-16C/D (Block 30)		
149th FW		**Kelly AFB, Texas**		SA	
149th OG	182d FS(FTU) 'Lone Star Gunfighters'		F-16C/D (Block 30)		
150th FW		**Kirtland AFB, New Mexico**		NM	
150th OG	188th FS 'Tacos'		C-26B, F-16C/D (Block 30/40)		
185th FW		**Sioux Gateway Airport, Sioux City, Iowa**		(HA)	
185th OG	174th FS 'Bats'		F-16C/D (Block 30)		

* Wing controls squadrons assigned to ACC and AMC

The New Mexico–based 'Tacos' of the 188th FS fly Block 30/40 F-16 "Vipers" out of Kirtland AFB. This F-16D was photographed at London Airport, Canada, in 1998.

The New Mexico ANG also flies a C-26B Metro. This example is fitted with a centerline surveillance pod and is with the Florida ANG's 125th FW.

AIR COMBAT COMMAND (Continued)

Component	Unit	Base	Aircraft	Tail Code	Color
AFRC Tenth Air Force - NAS Fort Worth JRB/Carswell Field, Texas					
ACC–gained AFRC units					
301st FW		NAS Fort Worth JRB/Carswell Field, Texas		TX	
301st OG	457th FS 'Spads'		F-16C/D (Block 30)		
419th FW		Hill AFB, Utah		HI	
419th OG	466th FS 'Diamondbacks'		F-16C/D (Block 30)		
442d FW		Whiteman AFB, Missouri		KC	
442d OG	303d FS 'KC Hawgs'		A-10A, OA-10A		
482d FW		Dade County Homestead RAP/ARS, Florida		FM	
482d OG	93d FS 'Makos'		F-16C/D (Block 32)		
513th ACG *		Tinker AFB, Oklahoma		OK	
	970th AACS		E-3B/C		
917th Wing		Barksdale AFB, Louisiana		BD	
917th OG	47th FS 'Termites'		A-10A, OA-10A		Green/Blue
	93d BS 'Indian Outlaws'		B-52H		Blue/Yellow
926th FW		NAS New Orleans JRB, Louisiana		NO	
926th OG	706th FS 'Cajuns'		A-10A, OA-10A		
939th RQW		Portland IAP/ANGB, Oregon			
939th OG	303d RQS	Portland IAP, Oregon	C-130E, HC-130P	PD	
	304th RQS	Portland IAP, Oregon	HH-60G	PD	
	305th RQS	Davis-Monthan AFB, Ariz.	HH-60G	DR	
920th RQG	39th RQS	Patrick AFB, Florida	C-130E, HC-130N/P	FL	
	301st RQS 'Guardian Wings'	Patrick AFB, Florida	HH-60G	FL	
944th FW		Luke AFB, Arizona		LR	
944th OG	302d FS 'Sun Devils'		F-16C/D (Block 32)		

* Associate unit shares aircraft with active-component wing

AFRC Tenth Air Force (10 AF)
Hqtrs: NAS Fort Worth JRB, Texas

The Tenth Air Force is responsible for tactical, training and Special Operations units gained by ACC, AETC and AFSOC.

ACC supports eight wings and one air control group (AWACS unit), and includes the reserve's only bomber unit. The 93d Bomb Squadron's (BS) 'Indian Outlaws' fly B-52H aircraft from Barksdale AFB, Louisiana. Upon activation, these units would be assigned geographically to one of three ACC numbered tactical air forces.

Tinker AFB, Oklahoma, is home to ACC's 552d Airborne Control Wing (ACW) and the AFRC's 513th Airborne Control Group (ACG), both operators of the Boeing E-3B/C Sentry AWACS.

AETC is composed of the Second Air Force at Keesler AFB, Missouri, and the Nineteenth Air Force, headquartered at Randolph AFB, Texas. The latter comprises four wings, of which the 56th FW is located at Luke AFB, Arizona. Its eight fighter squadrons fly F-16C/Ds.

AIR EDUCATION and TRAINING COMMAND (AETC)
Randolph AFB, Texas

Component	Unit	Base	Aircraft	Tail Code	Color
Second Air Force - Keesler AFB, Missouri					
17th TRW	IAAFA	Lackland AFB, Texas	Instructional Airframes	LD	
81st TRW	45th AS	Keesler AFB, Mississippi	C-21A	KS	Blue
82d TRW		Sheppard AFB, Texas	Instructional Airframes	ST	
Nineteenth Air Force - Randolph AFB, Texas					
12th FTW		**Randolph AFB, Texas**		RA	
12th OG	99th FTS 'Panthers'		T-1A		Yellow
	435th FTS 'Black Eagles'		AT-38B		
	559th FTS 'Billy Goats'		T-37B		Black/White
	560th FTS 'Chargin' Cheetahs'		T-38A		Blue
	562d FTS 'Gators'		T-43A		Blue
	3d FTS	Hondo MAP, Texas	T-3A		Blue
	557th FTS	US Air Force Academy, Colorado	T-3A		Blue
14th FTW		**Columbus AFB, Mississippi**		CB	
14th OG	37th FTS 'Bengal Tigers'		T-37B		White
	41st FTS 'Flying Buzzsaws'		T-37B		
	48th FTS 'Alley Cats'		T-1A		
	49th FTS 'Black Knights'		AT-38B		Red
	50th FTS 'Strikin' Snakes'		T-38A		Black
47th FTW		**Laughlin AFB, Texas**		XL	
47th OG	84th FTS 'Panthers'		T-37B		
	85th FTS 'Tigers'		T-37B		Yellow
	86th FTS 'Rio Lobos'		T-1A		Black/White
	87th FTS 'Red Bulls'		T-38A		Maroon
56th FW		**Luke AFB, Arizona**		LF	
56th OG	21st FS* 'Gamblers'		F-16A/B (Block 20)		White/Red
	61st FS 'Top Dogs'		F-16C/D (Block 25)		Yellow/Black
	62d FS 'Spikes'		F-16C/D (Block 25)		White/Blue
	63d FS 'Panthers'		F-16C/D (Block 42)		Red/Black
	308th FS 'Emerald Knights'		F-16C/D (Block 42)		Green/White
	309th FS 'Wild Ducks'		F-16C/D (Block 25)		Blue/White
	310th FS 'Top Hats'		F-16C/D (Block 42)		Green/Yellow
	425th FS** 'Black Widows'		F-16C/D (Block 42)		Red/Black

* Squadron trains Republic of China pilots
** Squadron trains Republic of Singapore pilots

AIR EDUCATION AND TRAINING COMMAND (AETC)
Headquarters: Randolph AFB, Texas

Established on 1 July 1993, AETC combined the assets of the former Air Training Command (ATC) and the Air University (AU) under a single entity to supply training for USAF officers and enlisted personnel. AETC provides basic military training, technical training, flight training, professional military and degree-level education, as well as readiness, medical service, security and joint training. Approximately 42,000 active-duty personnel are assigned, along with more than 1,100 ANG and nearly 3,000 AFRC personnel. In addition, 23,000 civilians and contractors are employed.

The command has two numbered air forces, the Second and Nineteenth Air Forces; the AU at Maxwell AFB, Alabama; and the Inter-American Air Forces Academy.

Three DRUs assigned to AETC include the Air Force Recruiting Service, Air Force Security Assistance Training Squadron and the 59th Medical Wing.

Second Air Force (2 AF)
Hqtrs: Keesler AFB, Mississippi

The Second Air Force is primarily responsible for technical training and has four such wings and a single training group assigned. All of its flight instruction is conducted at Keesler AFB.

Nineteenth Air Force (19 AF)
Hqtrs: Randolph AFB, Texas

In addition to providing basic and intermediate aircrew training for the USAF and a number of foreign air forces, Nineteenth Air Force units provide advanced transition training on the F-15, F-16, C-130, C-141, C-5, C-17 and Special Operations aircraft. They also support operations at the USAF Survival School and control 11 active-duty wings and groups, one AFRC associate training group and three ANG training wings.

Sheppard AFB is home to the Euro-NATO Joint Jet Pilot Training Program administered by the 80th TRW. Soon to be consolidated at Moody AFB is the introduction to fighter fundamentals (IFF) mission, and two squadrons will be assigned to a newly activated flying training group (FTG).

AIR EDUCATION and TRAINING COMMAND (Continued)

Component	Unit	Base	Aircraft	Tail Code	Color

Nineteenth Air Force - Randolph AFB, Texas (Continued)

58th SOW — **Kirtland AFB, New Mexico**
58th OG.........512th SOS...HH-60G, UH-1N
 550th SOS 'Wolf Pack' MC-130N/P, MC-130H
 551st SOS 'Black Knights' MH-53J, NCH-53A, TH-53A

71st FTW — **Vance AFB, Oklahoma** — **VN**
71st OG.........8th FTS '8-Ballers' ....T-37B ....Red/Green
 25th FTS ....T-38A, AT-38B ....Red
 32d FTS 'Mustangers' ....T-1A ....Red
 33d FTS ....T-37B ....Blue/Yellow

80th FTW — **Sheppard AFB, Texas** — **EN**
80th OG.........88th FTS 'Lucky Devils' ....T-37B, T-38A, AT-38B ....Blue
 89th FTS ....T-37B ....Blue
 90th FTS 'Boxing Bears' ....T-38A, AT-38B ....Black

97th AMW — **Altus AFB, Oklahoma**
97th OG.........54th ARS* ....(KC-135R)
 55th ARS 'Masters of the Art' KC-135R
 56th AS C-5A
 57th AS C-141B
 58th AS C-17A

314th AW — **Little Rock AFB, Arkansas**
314th OG.......53d AS 'Black Jacks' ....C-130E ....Black
 62d AS 'Blue Barons' ....C-130E ....Blue

325th FW — **Tyndall AFB, Florida** — **TY**
325th OG.......1st FS 'Fightin' Furies' ....F-15C/D ....Red
 2d FS ....F-15C/D ....Yellow
 95th FS 'Boneheads' ....F-15C/D ....Blue

336th TRG — **Fairchild AFB, Washington**
 36th RQF UH-1N

Nineteenth Air Force units gained from Air Force Reserve Command
Tenth Air Force - NAS Fort Worth JRB/Carswell Field, Texas

340th FTG** — **Randolph AFB, Texas**
 5th FTS 'Spitten Kittens' ....Vance AFB, Oklahoma ....T-1A, T-37B, T-38A ....VN
 43d FTS ....Columbus AFB, Miss..............T-1A, T-37B, T-38A ....CB
 96th FTS...........................Laughlin AFB, Texas ....T-1A, T-37B, T-38A XL
 97th FTS...........................Sheppard AFB, Texas ....T-37B, T-38A, AT-38B ....EN
 100th FTS.........................Randolph AFB, Texas ....T-1A, T-37B, T-38A ....RA

Nineteenth Air Force–gained ANG units

162d FW — **Tucson IAP, Arizona** — **AZ**
162d OG ....148th FS F-16A/B, C-26B
 152d FS 'Tigers' ....F-16C/D (Block 25/42)
 195th FS 'Warhawks' F-16A/B
 AATC ....F-16A/A(ADF), C (Block 25)

173d FW — **Klamath Falls IAP-Kingsley Field, Oregon**
173d OG ....114th FS 'Eager Beavers' F-15A/B

189th AW — **Little Rock AFB, Arkansas**
189th OG........154th TRS 'Razorbacks' C-130E

* Squadron provides KC-135 Central Flight Instructors course using aircraft borrowed from 55th ARS
** Associate squadrons share aircraft with active-component squadrons

US Air Force

AIR FORCE MATERIEL COMMAND (AFMC)
Headquarters: Wright-Patterson AFB, Ohio

AFMC was established on 1 July 1992, when the assets of Air Force Systems Command (AFSC) and Air Force Logistics Command (AFLC) were combined, and is responsible for the development, testing, acquisition and support of USAF weapons systems. In addition to controlling the Air Force Flight-Test Center (AFFTC) at Edwards AFB, California; Air Force School of Aerospace Medicine; Air Force Test Pilot School; Air Force Research Laboratory; and Air Armament Center, AFMC operates the USAF's air logistic centers (ALCs) or depots and the Aerospace Maintenance and Regeneration Center (AMARC) located at Davis-Monthan AFB, Arizona. It also looks after the Beech C-12C/Ds operated for the Defense Security Assistance Agency and US embassies around the world.

Flight-test squadrons (FLTSs) assigned to ALCs are responsible for performing functional check flights of aircraft after they have received major modifications or programmed depot maintenance (PDM), and these units also undertake test and evaluation flights related to engineering projects. The three ALCs comprise Warner Robins at Robins AFB, Georgia; Oklahoma City at Tinker AFB, Oklahoma; and Ogden at Hill AFB, Utah.

About 32,000 active-duty personnel, along with 5,000 reservists and 70,000 civilians are assigned to AFMC.

Currently undergoing testing at the 411th FLTS at Edwards AFB, California, are two F-22A Raptors. The unit is part of the 412th Test Wing.

AIR FORCE MATERIEL COMMAND (AFMC)
Wright-Patterson AFB, Ohio

Component	Unit	Base	Aircraft	Tail Code	Color
	645th MATS	Palmdale Airp., California	EC-130H, NC-130E		
	Det. 2	Majors Field/Greenville MAP, Texas			
			C-135B, WC-135W	MF	
Air Force Flight-Test Center (AFFTC) Edwards AFB, California				ED	
412th TW	USAF TPS*	Edwards AFB, Calif.	(T-38A, AT-38B, UH-1N)		
412th LG	410th FLTS	AF Plant 42, Palmdale, Calif.	YF-117A		
	411th FLTS	Edwards AFB, California	F-22A		
	412th FLTS	Edwards AFB, California	C-135C		
	416th FLTS	Edwards AFB, California	F-16A/B/C/D		
	418th FLTS	Edwards AFB, California	C-12C, C-17A, NT-39A/B		
	419th FLTS	Edwards AFB, California	B-1B, B-2A, B-52H		
	445th FLTS	Edwards AFB, California	F-15A/B/C/D/E, NOA-37B, T-38A, UH-1N		
	452d FLTS	Edwards AFB, California	EC-18B, EC-135E, KC-135R, NKC-135B/E		

*Test pilot school borrows aircraft, as needed, from other squadrons

Air Armament Center		**Eglin AFB, Florida**		ET	
46th TW					
46th OG	39th FLTS		A-10A, OA-10A, F-16A/B/C/D		White/Blue
	40th FLTS		F-15A/B/C/D/E, NC-130A, UH-1N		White/Red
46th TESTG					
	586th FLTS	Holloman AFB, N.M.	AT-38B, C-12J, YF-15A	HT	Black

AIR FORCE SPACE COMMAND (AFSPC)
Headquarters: Peterson AFB, Colorado

Established on 1 September 1982, AFSPC is responsible for placing high-value payloads in space and providing weather, communications, ballistic missile warning and space-based intelligence to the unified commands. Additionally, AFSPC operates the Minuteman III and Peacekeeper intercontinental ballistic missiles (ICBMs), Delta II, Titan II, Atlas II and Titan IV launch vehicles, being responsible for the land-based ICBMs that form part of America's nuclear triad. Its commander holds the positions of CinC in NORAD and the US Space Command (USSPACECOM).

Besides missiles and launch vehicles, AFSPC controls a number of systems that include the Air Force Satellite Controls Network, Defense Meteorological Satellite Program, Ballistic Missile Early Warning System, Global Positioning System and satellites of the Defense Support Program.

Assigned to AFSPC are almost 20,000 active-duty personnel plus 16,000 civilians and contractors. Its assets include the Space Warfare Center and two numbered air forces.

Fourteenth Air Force (14 AF)
Hqtrs: Vandenberg AFB, California

The Fourteenth Air Force is the USSPACECOM component responsible for space forces, and its duties encompass missile warning, space surveillance, space launch, shuttle support and space operations. One wing only is currently assigned.

Twentieth Air Force (20 AF)
Hqtrs: F.E. Warren AFB, Wyoming

The Twentieth Air Force is responsible for the US ICBM force, and three space wings that control the Minuteman III and Peacekeeper ICBMs from a series of underground silos located throughout the northern tier of the Midwest region of the United States. UH-1N helicopters operated by flights within each of its wings comprise the command's only aircraft.

AFSPC's sole aircraft type is the UH-1N Huey. This example serves with the 40th Helicopter Flight, belonging to the 341st Space Wing (SPW), located at Malmstrom AFB, Montana.

AIR FORCE SPACE COMMAND (AFSPC)
Peterson AFB, Colorado

Component	Unit	Base	Aircraft	Tail Code	Color
Fourteenth Air Force - Vandenberg AFB, California					
30th SPW		**Vandenberg AFB, California**			
30th OG	76th HF		UH-1N	HV	
Twentieth Air Force - F.E. Warren AFB, Wyoming					
90th SPW		**F.E. Warren AFB, Wyoming**			
90th OG	319th MS		LGM-30G		
	320th MS		LGM-30G		
	321st MS		LGM-30G		
	400th MS		LGM-118A		
	37th HF		UH-1N	FE	
91st SPW		**Minot AFB, North Dakota**			
91st OG	740th MS		LGM-30G		
	741st MS		LGM-30G		
	742d MS		LGM-30G		
	54th HF 'Nomads of the North'		UH-1N	MT	
341st SPW		**Malmstrom AFB, Montana**			
341st OG	10th MS		LGM-30G		
	12th MS		LGM-30G		
	490th MS		LGM-30G		
	564th MS		LGM-30G		
	40th HF		UH-1N	MM	

Serial 860144 is an MC-130H Combat Talon II in service with AFSOC's 16th SOW at Hurlburt Field, Florida. The enlarged nose radome houses an APQ-170 multimode radar, which is designed for ground mapping and weather detection and also provides terrain-following assistance to aircrews.

AIR FORCE SPECIAL OPERATIONS COMMAND (AFSOC)
Headquarters: Hurlburt Field, Florida

AFSOC is the USAF component of US Special Operations Command (USSOCOM), and was established on 22 May 1990. The command is responsible for providing support in the areas of unconventional warfare, special reconnaissance, direct action, foreign internal defense, psychological warfare and counterterrorism for the unified commands, and flies a number of specialized platforms in support of its missions. Usually, this means taking aircraft into hostile environments at night and at extremely low level to evade enemy radars, to deliver Special Operations teams and their supplies and to extract such forces on completion of their missions.

The command controls a single active-duty wing and two forward-deployed subordinate groups. In addition, both the ANG and AFRC each provide an additional wing to the command. AFSOC will replace its MH-53J fleet with CV-22B tilt-rotors in the coming years, and has transferred the assets of its sole MH-60G squadron to ACC.

In addition to the assets assigned directly to AFSOC, the command gains the 919th Special Operations Wing (SOW) from the AFRC's Tenth Air Force and the 193d SOW from the ANG.

Assigned to AFSOC are over 9,000 active-duty personnel and some 1,200 each from the AFRC and the ANG, in addition to 500 civilians.

AIR FORCE SPECIAL OPERATIONS COMMAND (AFSOC)
Hurlburt Field, Florida

Component	Unit	Base	Aircraft	Tail Code	Color
	2d SOF	Robins AFB, Georgia	EC-137D		
	427th SOS	Pope AFB, North Carolina	CASA 212-200		
16th SOW		**Hurlburt Field, Florida**			
16th OG	4th SOS 'Ghostriders'	Hurlburt Field, Florida	AC-130U		
	6th SOS 'Commandos'	Hurlburt Field, Florida	CASA 212-200, UH-1N		
	8th SOS 'Blackbirds'*	Hurlburt Field, Florida	C-130E, MC-130E		
	9th SOS 'Night Wings'	Eglin AFB, Florida	MC-130P		
	15th SOS	Hurlburt Field, Florida	MC-130H		
	16th SOS 'Spectre'	Hurlburt Field, Florida	AC-130H		
	20th SOS 'Green Hornets'	Hurlburt Field, Florida	MH-53J/M, NCH-53A		
352d SOG		**RAF Mildenhall, England**			
	7th SOS 'Air Commandos'		MC-130H		
	21st SOS 'Dust Devils'		MH-53J/M		
	67th SOS 'Night Owls'		C-130E, MC-130N/P		
353d SOG		**Kadena AB, Okinawa, Japan**			
	1st SOS		C-130E, MC-130H		
	17th SOS		MC-130P		
	31st SOS 'Black Knights'	Osan AB, Korea	MH-53J		

AFSOC–gained AFRC units
Tenth Air Force - NAS Fort Worth JRB/Carswell Field, Texas

919th SOW		**Eglin AFB (Duke Field), Florida**			
919th SOG					
	711th SOS	Duke Field, Florida	C-130E/H, MC-130E		
	5th SOS **	Duke Field, Florida	MC-130P		

*Unit to relocate to Eglin's main base

AFSOC–gained ANG units

193d SOW		**Harrisburg IAP, Pennsylvania**			
193d OG	193d SOS* 'Quiet Professionals'		C-130E, EC-130E		

* Unit to relocate to Duke Field (Both Duke Field and Hurlburt Field are located within the confines of Eglin AFB)
** Unit to transition to EC-130J

A Special Operations team with the 16th SOW uses the "fast rope" method to exit an MH-60G Pave Hawk during a practice covert insertion mission. The wing provides support for Air Force, Navy and Army special forces needing to infiltrate hostile areas at night, in all weathers and at extremely low level to avoid detection by radar.

Serial 660215, a C-141B Starlifter, climbs out from McChord AFB, Washington. It is home to the 62d Airlift Wing's (AW) three squadrons that operate the type. One unit, the 7th Airlift Squadron (AS), has also begun flying the C-17A Globemaster III.

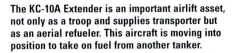

AIR MOBILITY COMMAND (AMC)
Headquarters: Scott AFB, Illinois

AMC is tasked with providing strategic and tactical airlift, aeromedical evacuation and tanker support for all branches of the US military, and is the USAF component of US Transportation Command (USTRANSCOM). During a war, AMC is responsible for supplying forces to theater commands. Since its activation on 1 June 1992, several elements have been restructured and it currently controls two numbered air forces; the AMC Tanker Airlift Control Center at Scott AFB, Illinois; and the Air Mobility Warfare Center at McGuire AFB, New Jersey. Supporting AMC's own numbered air forces are AFRC elements from the Fourth and Twenty-Second Air Forces.

AMC has nearly 53,000 active-duty personnel and more than 45,000 AFRC and 35,000 ANG members assigned, and employs 9,000 civilians.

The KC-10A Extender is an important airlift asset, not only as a troop and supplies transporter but as an aerial refueler. This aircraft is moving into position to take on fuel from another tanker.

Well into its takeoff roll, this KC-10A belonging to the 9th Air Refueling Squadron (ARS) departs Travis AFB, California. The aircraft is equipped with two underwing, hose-and-reel refueling units as well as a tail boom system. As a result of operational experience gained during Operation Desert Storm, the capability to refuel probe-equipped types was added.

Fifteenth Air Force (15 AF)
Hqtrs: Travis AFB, California

The Fifteenth Air Force's region of operations extends west of the Mississippi River to the east coast of Africa, and from pole to pole. However, it is often tasked with supporting AMC's operations worldwide. The primary mission of this air force is to provide airlift, aeromedical evacuation and air refueling for all DoD agencies in peace and war. It is headquartered at Travis AFB, California, and has seven wings and groups assigned. The Fifteenth Air Force received its first C-17As in June 1999 when the 62d AW began converting to the Globemaster III.

AIR MOBILITY COMMAND (AMC)
Scott AFB, Illinois

Component	Unit	Base	Aircraft	Tail Code	Color
Fifteenth Air Force - Travis AFB, California					
22d ARW		**McConnell AFB, Kansas**			
22d OG	344th ARS 'Ravens'		KC-135R/T		Black
	349th ARS 'Blue Knights'		KC-135R/R(RT)		Blue
	350th ARS 'Red Falcons'		KC-135R		Red
	384th ARS 'Square Patches'		KC-135R/R(RT)		Maroon
60th AMW		**Travis AFB, California**			
60th OG	6th ARS		KC-10A		Blue
	9th ARS 'Universal'		KC-10A		Red
	21st AS 'Beeliners'		C-5A/B/C		Blue
	22d AS		C-5A/B/C		Gold
62d AW		**McChord AFB, Washington**			
62d OG	4th AS 'Fighting Fourth'		C-141B		
	7th AS		C-17A, C-141B		
	8th AS 'Soaring Stallions'		C-141B		
92d ARW		**Fairchild AFB, Washington**			
92d OG	92d ARS		KC-135R/T		Black
	93d ARS		KC-135R/T		Blue
	96th ARS 'Screaming Eagles'		KC-135R/T		Green
	97th ARS		KC-135R/T		Gold
317th AG		**Dyess AFB, Texas**			
	39th AS 'Trail Blazers'		C-130H		Red
	40th AS 'Screaming Eagles'		C-130H		Blue
319th ARW		**Grand Forks AFB, North Dakota**			
319th OG	905th ARS		KC-135R/T		Blue
	906th ARS		KC-135R/T		Yellow
	911th ARS		KC-135R/T		Red
	912th ARS		KC-135R/T		White
375th AW		**Scott AFB, Illinois**			
375th OG	11th AS	Scott AFB, Illinois	C-9A		
	457th AS*	Andrews AFB, Maryland	C-21A		
	12th ALF	Langley AFB, Virginia	C-21A		
	47th ALF	Wright-Patterson AFB, Ohio	C-21A		
	54th ALF	Maxwell AFB, Alabama	C-21A		
	458th AS	Scott AFB, Illinois	C-21A		
	84th ALF	Peterson AFB, Colorado	C-21A		
	311th ALF	Offutt AFB, Nebraska	C-21A		
	332d ALF	Randolph AFB, Texas	C-21A		

* Unit operates two C-21As in support of the Air Force Flight Standards Agency (AFFSA)

US Air Force

AIR MOBILITY COMMAND (Continued)

Component	Unit	Base	Aircraft	Tail Code	Color
Fifteenth Air Force–gained ANG units					
126th ARW		Scott AFB-MidAmerica Airport, Illinois			
126th OG	108th ARS		KC-135E		
127th Wing		Selfridge ANGB, Mount Clemens, Michigan			
191st AG	171st AS 'Red Devils'		C-130E		Yellow/Black
133d AW		Minneapolis-St. Paul IAP/ARS, Minnesota		MN	Blue
133d OG	109th AS		C-130H		
136th AW		NAS Fort Worth JRB/Carswell Field, Texas			
136th OG	181st AS		C-130H		
137th AW		Will Rogers World Airport, Oklahoma		OK	Blue
137th OG	185th AS		C-130H		
139th AW		Rosecrans Mem. Airport, St Joseph, Missouri			
139th OG	180th AS		C-130H		
140th Wing*		Buckley ANGB, Denver, Colorado			
140th OG	200th AS		C-21A, C-26B		
141st ARW		Fairchild AFB, Washington			
141st OG	116th ARS		C-26B, KC-135E		
146th AW		NAS Point Mugu/ Channel Islands ANGS, California		CI	Green
146th OG	115th AS		C-130E		
151st ARW		Salt Lake City IAP, Utah			
151st OG	191st ARS 'Salty Guard'		KC-135E		
152d AW		Reno-Tahoe IAP/May ANGB, Nevada			
152d OG	192d AS 'High Rollers'		C-130E		
153d AW		Cheyenne Airport, Wyoming		WY	
153d OG	187th AS		C-130H		
155th ARW		Lincoln MAP/ANGB, Nebraska			
155th OG	173d ARS 'Huskers'		KC-135R		
161st ARW		Phoenix Sky Harbor IAP, Arizona			
161st OG	197th ARS 'Copperheads'		KC-135E		
163d ARW		March ARB, California			
163d OG	196th ARS		KC-135R		
182d AW		Greater Peoria RAP, Illinois			
182d OG	169th AS		C-130E		
190th ARW		Forbes Field, Topeka, Kansas			
190th OG	117th ARS 'Kansas Coyotes'		KC-135E/D		

* Wing controls squadrons gained by ACC and AMC.

A C-130H Hercules of the 185th AS. The unit belongs to the 137th AW at Will Rogers World Airport in Oklahoma City. Although AMC units do not normally carry tail codes, several C-130 squadrons have retained them since their assignment to ACC ended.

The old and the new. Whereas the C-5 Galaxy (background) has been in operational service since the late 1960s and still carries the largest cargoes for AMC, the C-17A Globemaster III recently entered service with four active-duty and four AFRC squadrons. Early reports suggest the USAF's latest strategic airlifter is showing excellent reliability and performance.

AIR MOBILITY COMMAND (Continued)

Component	Unit	Base	Aircraft	Tail Code	Color
Twenty-First Air Force - McGuire AFB, New Jersey					
6th ARW		**MacDill AFB, Florida**			
6th OG	91st ARS*		KC-135R, EC-135N, CT-43A		Blue

* The EC-135N and CT-43A are operated on behalf of USCENTCOM and USSOUTHCOM, respectively

Component	Unit	Base	Aircraft	Tail Code	Color
19th ARG		**Robins AFB, Georgia**			
	99th ARS		KC-135R		Blue
43d AW		**Pope AFB, North Carolina**			
43d OG	2d AS 'Lancers'		C-130E		Blue
	41st AS 'Black Cats'		C-130E		Green
89th AW		**Andrews AFB, Maryland**			
	PPO		VC-25A		
89th OG	1st HS		UH-1N		
	1st AS		VC-137C, C-12C/D, C-32A		
	99th AS		VC-9C, C-20B/C/H, C-37A		
305th AMW		**McGuire AFB, New Jersey**			
305th OG	2d ARS 'Second to None'		KC-10A		Red
	6th AS 'Bully Beef Express'		C-141B		Blue
	13th AS 'Black Cats'		C-141B		Red
	32d ARS 'Capt. Shreve Sqn.'		KC-10A		Blue
436th AW		**Dover AFB, Delaware**			
436th OG	3d AS		C-5A/B		
	9th AS 'Pelicans'		C-5A/B		
437th AW		**Charleston AFB, South Carolina**			
437th OG	14th AS 'Pelicans'		C-17A		
	15th AS 'Global Eagles'		C-17A		
	16th AS		C-141B		
	17th AS 'AAA Moving'		C-17A		
463d AG		**Little Rock AFB, Arkansas**			
	50th AS 'Red Devils'		C-130H		Red
	61st AS 'Green Hornets'		C-130E		Green

Twenty-First Air Force (21 AF)
Hqtrs: McGuire AFB, New Jersey

This command controls air mobility forces over the Atlantic region. Missions assigned include strategic and intratheater transport, plus aerial refueling and administrative airlift support for the president and other government officials. Eight wings and groups are assigned to the Twenty-First Air Force.

AIR MOBILITY COMMAND (Continued)

Component	Unit	Base	Aircraft	Tail Code	Color
Twenty-First Air Force–gained ANG units					
101st ARW		Bangor IAP, Maine			
101st OG	132d ARS 'Maineiacs'		KC-135E		
105th AW		Stewart IAP/ANGB, Newburgh, New York			
105th OG	137th AS 'Fearless Ones'		C-5A		
107th ARW		Niagara Falls IAP/ARS, New York			
107th OG	136th ARS 'New York's Finest'		KC-135R		
108th ARW		McGuire AFB, New Jersey			
108th OG	141st ARS 'Tigers'		C-135B, KC-135E		
	150th ARS		KC-135E		
109th AW		Schenectady CAP/Stratton ANGS, Scotia, New York			
109th OG	139th AS		C-26B, C-130H, LC-130H		
113th Wing		Andrews AFB, Maryland			
113th OG	201st AS		C-21A, C-22B, C-38A		
117th ARW		Birmingham IAP/Sumpter Smith ANGB, Alabama			
117th OG	106th ARS 'Rebels'		KC-135R		
118th AW		Nashville IAP, Tennessee			Red
118th OG	105th AS 'Old Hickory'		C-130H		
121st ARW		Rickenbacker IAP/ANGB, Columbus, Ohio			
121st OG	145th ARS 'Tazz'		KC-135R		
	166th ARS 'Sluff'		KC-135R		
123d AW		Louisville IAP-Standiford Field, Kentucky			
123d OG	165th AS		C-130H		
128th ARW		Gen. Mitchell IAP/ARS, Milwaukee, Wisconsin			
128th OG	126th ARS		KC-135R		
130th AW		Yeager Airport, Charleston, West Virginia			
130th OG	130th AS 'Mountaineers'		C-130H		
134th ARW		McGhee Tyson Airport/ANGB, Knoxville, Tennessee			
134th OG	151st ARS		KC-135E		

Based on the Boeing 727-100 airliner and operated by the ANG's 201st AS of the 113th Wing, Andrews AFB, Maryland, this C-22B (serial 86-34616) is one of three remaining in USAF operational service.

AIR MOBILITY COMMAND (Continued)

Component	Unit	Base	Aircraft	Tail Code	Color
Twenty-First Air Force–gained ANG units (Continued)					
143d AW		Quonset State Airport, Providence, Rhode Island		RI	Red
143d OG	143d AS		C-130E		
145th AW		Charlotte/Douglas IAP, North Carolina		NC	Blue
145th OG	156th AS		C-130H		
156th AW		Luiz Munoz Marin IAP/Muñiz ANGB, Puerto Rico			
156th OG	198th AS 'Buccaneros'		C-130E, UC-26C		
157th ARW		Pease International Tradeport/ANGB, Portsmouth, New Hampshire			
157th OG	133d ARS		KC-135R		
164th AW		Memphis IAP, Tennessee			
164th OG	155th AS		C-141B/C		
165th AW		Savannah IAP, Georgia			Black
165th OG	158th AS		C-130H		
166th AW		New Castle County Airport, Delaware			Gray
166th OG	142d AS		C-130H		
167th AW		Eastern West Virginia RAP-Shepherd Field, Martinsburg, West Virginia			Black
167th OG	167th AS		C-130H		
171st ARW		Greater Pittsburgh IAP, Pennsylvania			
171st OG	146th ARS		KC-135E		Black
	147th ARS		KC-135E		Yellow
172d AW		Jackson IAP-Allen C. Thompson Field/ANGR, Mississippi			
172d OG	183d AS		C-141B/C		
175th Wing		Martin State Airport/Warfield ANGB, Baltimore, Maryland			
135th AG	135th AS		C-130E/J		
179th AW		Mansfield Lahm Airport, Ohio			
179th OG	164th AS		C-130H		
186th ARW		Key Field/ANGB, Meridian, Mississippi			
186th OG	153d ARS 'Magnolia Militia'		C-26B, KC-135R		

In urgent need of replacement due to fatigue and high flight hours, all C-141s are scheduled to be gone from active-duty USAF service by 2003. The fleet currently comprises 158 Starlifters, of which 113 are with active-duty units and 45 serve with the AFRC and the ANG. As a short-term measure, 64 examples will be upgraded to C-141C standard during the next couple of years.

In addition to an upward-lifting visor nose, the C-5 Galaxy has rear "clamshell"-type doors that also provided generous access to the main cargo deck, which is more than 120 feet long.

US Air Force

Component	Unit	Base	Aircraft	Tail Code	Color

AIR MOBILITY COMMAND (Continued)

AMC-gained AFRC units
AFRC Fourth Air Force - March ARB, California

349th AMW* — Travis AFB, California
349th OG......70th ARS KC-10A
79th ARS KC-10A
301st AS C-5A/B/C
312th AS C-5A/B/C

433d AW — Kelly AFB, Texas
433d OG ......68th AS C-5A

434th ARW — Grissom ARB, Indiana
434th OG......72d ARS ......KC-135R ......Blue
74th ARS ......KC-135R ......Red

445th AW — Wright-Patterson AFB, Ohio
445th OG......89th AS 'Rhinos' C-141B/C
356th AS C-141B/C

446th AW* — McChord AFB, Washington
446th OG......97th AS C-141B
313th AS C-141B
728th AS C-17A, C-141B

452d AMW — March ARB, California
452d OG ......336th ARS 'Rats' ......KC-135R ......Yellow
729th AS 'Pegasus' C-141B/C
730th AS C-141B/C

507th ARW — Tinker AFB, Oklahoma
507th OG......465th ARS 'Okies'......KC-135R ......Blue
931st ARG 18th ARS ......McConnell AFB, Kansas KC-135R

916th ARW — Seymour Johnson AFB, North Carolina
916th OG......77th ARS KC-135R

927th ARW — Selfridge ANGB, Michigan
927th OG......63d ARS ......KC-135E ......Purple

932d AW — Scott AFB, Illinois
932d OG ......73d AS C-9A

940th ARW — Beale AFB, California
940th OG......314th ARS 'Warhawks'......KC-135E ......Red

AFRC Twenty-Second Air Force - Dobbins ARB, Georgia

94th AW — Dobbins ARB, Georgia ......Black
94th OG......700th AS C-130H

302d AW — Peterson AFB, Colorado ......Green
302d OG ......731st AS C-130H

315th AW* — Charleston AFB, South Carolina
315th OG......300th AS C-17A
317th AS 'First in Reserve' C-17A
701st AS 'Turtles' C-17A
707th AS C-141B

403d Wing — Keesler AFB, Mississippi
403d OG ......53d WRS 'Hurricane Hunters'** ......WC-130H ......Blue
815th AS 'Jennies' ......C-130E/J ......Red

439th AW — Westover ARB, Massachusetts
439th OG......337th AS C-5A

* Unit shares aircraft with active-component wing
** Unit to transition to WC-130J

AFRC Fourth Air Force (4 AF)
Hqtrs: March ARB, California

The Fourth Air Force controls 12 AFRC airlift and aerial refueling wings and groups gained by AMC, including three associate units. At this time, only two AFRC tanker squadrons still operate the KC-135E.

AIR MOBILITY COMMAND (Continued)

Component	Unit	Base	Aircraft	Tail Code	Color

AFRC Twenty-Second Air Force - Dobbins ARB, Georgia (Continued)

440th AW — General Mitchell IAP/ARS, Milwaukee, Wisconsin
440th OG........95th AS 'Flying Badgers' ....C-130H ....Yellow

459th AW — Andrews AFB, Maryland
459th OG........756th AS C-141B/C

512th AW* — Dover AFB, Delaware
512th OG........326th AS C-5A/B
709th AS C-5A/B

514th AMW* — McGuire AFB, New Jersey
514th OG........76th ARS 'Freedom's Spirit' KC-10A
78th ARS KC-10A
702d AS C-141B
732d AS 'Rams' C-141B

908th AW — Maxwell AFB, Alabama
908th OG........357th AS ....C-130H...............Blue

910th AW — Youngstown/Warren RAP/ARS, Ohio
910th OG........757th AS 'Blue Tigers' ....C-130H...............Blue
773d AS 'Quiet Professionals' ....C-130H...............Red

911th AW — Greater Pittsburgh IAP/ARS, Pennsylvania
911th OG........758th AS ....C-130H...............Black

913th AW — NAS Willow Grove JRB, Pennsylvania
913th OG........327th AS C-130E

914th AW — Niagara Falls IAP/ARS, New York
914th OG........328th AS ....C-130H...............Green

934th AW — Minneapolis-St Paul IAP/ARS, Minnesota
934th OG........96th AS 'Flying Vikings' ....C-130E ....Purple

AFRC Twenty-Second Air Force (22 AF)
Hqtrs: Dobbins ARB, Georgia

The Twenty-Second Air Force is responsible for strategic airlift and all AFRC tactical airlift assets. In all, 15 wings are assigned, including two associate wings and the Air Force's only weather reconnaissance squadron. 22 AF has now begun to receive Lockheed Martin C-130Js, which were assigned initially to Keesler AFB where training will be carried out. The base will also be home to the WC-130J Hurricane Hunters as soon as modifications to the aircraft have been completed.

With its tail boom extended, this 514th AMW KC-10A, based at McGuire AFB, New Jersey, prepares to begin refueling other aircraft. The wing comprises four squadrons gained by AMC from AFRC.

US Air Force

PACIFIC AIR FORCES (PACAF)
Headquarters: Hickam AFB, Hawaii

PACAF was established on 1 July 1957, with responsibility for planning and conducting offensive and defensive air operations in the Pacific and Asian theaters. It is the USAF component of USPACOM and besides having a headquarters-assigned wing, controls three numbered air forces that employ tactical fighters, intratheater airlift, aerial refueling and combat rescue assets. The command also retains operational control of two ANG wings based in Alaska, plus a third located in Hawaii. PACAF's Thirteenth Air Force, based in Guam, does not operate any aircraft at this time.

Today, PACAF has approximately 32,000 active-duty and 4,700 ANG personnel assigned, along with a small number of AFRC reservists and more than 8,000 civilians.

An 18th Wing KC-135R refuels a trio of F-15Cs also stationed at Kadena AB, Okinawa, Japan. PACAF maintains five wings on foreign soil, three in Japan and two in South Korea. In addition to Eagles and Stratotankers, the wing also flies HH-60G combat rescue helicopters.

PACIFIC AIR FORCES (PACAF)
Hickam AFB, Hawaii
Direct Reporting Units

Component	Unit	Base	Aircraft	Tail Code	Color
15th ABW		**Hickam AFB, Hawaii**			
15th OG	65th AS 'Special Missions Hawaii'		C-135C/E/K		
Fifth Air Force - Yokota AB, Japan					
18th Wing		**Kadena AB, Okinawa, Japan**		ZZ	
18th OG	12th FS 'Dirty Dozen'	Kadena AB, Japan	F-15C/D		Yellow
	33d RQS	Kadena AB, Okinawa	HH-60G		
	Det. 1	Osan AB, Korea	HH-60G		
	44th FS 'Vampires'	Kadena AB, Japan	F-15C/D		Blue
	67th FS 'Fighting Cocks'				
		Kadena AB, Japan	F-15C/D		Red
	909th ARS 'Young Tigers'				
		Kadena AB, Japan	KC-135R		White
	Det. 1	Andersen AFB, Guam	KC-135R		
	961st AACS	Kadena AB, Japan	E-3B/C		Orange
35th FW		**Misawa AB, Japan**		WW	
35th OG	13th FS 'Panthers'		F-16C/D (Block 50D)		Red
	14th FS 'Samurais'		F-16C/D (Block 50)		Yellow
374th AW		**Yokota AB, Japan**		YJ	
374th OG	30th AS		C-9A		
	36th AS 'Eagle Airlifters'		C-130E/H		Red
	459th AS 'Orient Express'		C-21A, UH-1N		

Fifth Air Force (5 AF)
Hqtrs: Yokota AB, Japan

The Fifth Air Force comprises three wings and is responsible for all units based on Japanese soil. PACAF's only airlift wing, the 374th AW, is located at Yokota AB. The Fifth Air Force's other two wings, the "composite" 18th Wing and the 35th FW are located at Kadena AB and Misawa AB, respectively.

Seventh Air Force (7 AF)
Hqtrs: Osan AB, South Korea

The Seventh Air Force's mission is to direct and conduct combined air operations in the Republic of Korea and throughout the northwest Pacific. In addition to USPACOM, this air force supports United Nations Command, US–South Korea Combined Forces Command and US Forces Korea. Currently, two fighter wings are assigned, the 8th FW and 51st FW, based at Kunsan AB and Osan AB, respectively.

Eleventh Air Force (11 AF)
Hqtrs: Elmendorf AFB, Alaska

Until 1990, the Eleventh Air Force was known as Alaskan Air Command. Today, its units maintain defense capabilities at remote operating sites throughout that state and are responsible for defense of the northern Pacific region. It is assigned one fighter wing and one composite wing.

Thirteenth Air Force (13 AF)
Hqtrs: Andersen AFB, Guam

The Thirteenth Air Force's primary mission is to preserve peace and foster relations within its area of operations (AO), which stretches from the east coast of Africa to the west coast of South America. Although it has the largest AO in the USAF, no aircraft are assigned to its single air base wing.

Hawaii ANG patch

PACIFIC AIR FORCES (Continued)

Component	Unit	Base	Aircraft	Tail Code	Color
Seventh Air Force - Osan AB, Korea					
8th FW		**Kunsan AB, Korea**		WP	
8th OG	35th FS 'Pantons'		F-16C/D (Block 30)		Blue
	80th FS 'Juvats'		F-16C/D (Block 30)		Yellow
51st FW		**Osan AB, Korea**		OS	
51st OG	25th FS 'Assam Dragons'		A-10A, OA-10A		Green
	36th FS 'Flying Fiends'		F-16C/D (Block 40)		Red/Black
	55th ALF		C-12J		
Eleventh Air Force - Elmendorf AFB, Alaska					
3d Wing		**Elmendorf AFB, Alaska**		AK	
3d OG	19th FS 'Gamecocks'		F-15C/D		Blue
	54th FS 'Fightin' 54th'		F-15C/D		Yellow
	90th FS 'Pair O' Dice'		F-15E		Red
	517th AS 'Firebirds'		C-130H		White
	Det. 1		C-12F/J		
	962d AACS 'Eye of the Eagle'		E-3B/C		Green
354th FW		**Eielson AFB, Alaska**		AK	
354th OG	18th FS 'Blue Foxes'		F-16C/D (Block 40)		Blue
	355th FS 'Fighting Falcons'		A-10A, OA-10A		Black
PACAF–gained ANG units					
154th Wing		**Hickam AFB, Hawaii**			
154th OG	199th FS		F-15A/B		
	203d ARS		KC-135R		
	204th AS		C-130H		
168th ARW		**Eielson AFB, Alaska**			
168th OG	168th ARS		KC-135R		
176th Wing		**Anchorage IAP/Kulis ANGB, Alaska**		AN	
176th OG	144th AS		C-130H		
	210th RQS		HC-130N, HH-60G		
	Det. 1	Eielson AFB, Alaska	HH-60G		
Thirteenth Air Force - Anderson AFB, Guam					
36th ABW			No aircraft assigned.		

The 90th FS is the sole PACAF operator of the F-15E Strike Eagle. Stationed at Elmendorf AFB, Alaska, the squadron is one of five units belonging to the composite 3d Wing. As this photograph clearly shows, the 90th FS trains over some of America's most spectacular scenery.

In the European theater, the F-15E serves with two USAFE units belonging to the 48th FW at RAF Lakenheath, England. With its dorsal air brake extended, this 'Madhatters' Strike Eagle makes its approach to the British base.

UNITED STATES AIR FORCES in EUROPE (USAFE)
Headquarters: Ramstein AB, Germany

Established on 15 August 1947, USAFE has seen its operations reduced significantly in recent years following the fall of the Soviet Union and the end of a divided Europe, despite increased tensions in the former Yugoslavia. As the USAF component of USEUCOM, the command is responsible for supporting US operations in Europe, the Mediterranean, Middle East and Africa. With just two air forces now assigned, its area of responsibility extends from the northern tip of Norway to the southern tip of Africa. Reporting to the USAFE are 27,000 active-duty and small numbers of AFRC and ANG personnel. In addition, 5,000 civilians work for the command.

Third Air Force (3 AF)
Hqtrs: RAF Mildenhall, England

The Third Air Force is responsible for all USAFE operations north of the Alps and is an integral part of America's commitment to NATO. It controls one fighter wing and one airlift wing based in Germany, along with another fighter wing and an air refueling wing based in England. The Third Air Force is also responsible for contingency planning and for supporting American security interests in Africa.

UNITED STATES AIR FORCES in EUROPE (USAFE)
Ramstein AB, Germany

Component	Unit	Base	Aircraft	Tail Code	Color
Third Air Force - RAF Mildenhall, England					
48th FW		**RAF Lakenheath, United Kingdom**		LN	
48th OG	492d FS 'Madhatters'		F-15E		Blue
	493d FS 'Grim Reapers'		F-15C/D		Black
	494th FS 'Panthers'		F-15E		Red
52d FW		**Spangdahlem AB, Germany**		SP	
52d OG	22d FS 'Stingers'		F-16C/D (Block 50)		Red
	23d FS 'Fighting Hawks'		F-16C/D (Block 50D)		Blue
	81st FS 'Panthers'		A-10A, OA-10A		Black
86th AW		**Ramstein AB, Germany**		RS	Yellow/Blue
86th OG	37th AS 'Bluetail Flies'		C-130E		
	75th AS		C-9A, C-20A		
	76th AS		C-21A, C-135B/C		
	HQ USEUCOM	Stuttgart AAF, Echterdingen, Germany	C-21A		
100th ARW		**RAF Mildenhall, United Kingdom**			
100th OG	351st ARS		KC-135R		
Sixteenth Air Force - Aviano AB, Italy					
31st FW		**Aviano AB, Italy**		AV	
31st OG	510th FS 'Buzzards'		F-16C/D (Block 40)		Purple
	555th FS 'Triple Nickle'		F-16C/D (Block 40)		Green
39th Wing		**Incirlik AB, Turkey**			
39th OG	Rotational Squadrons				

Sixteenth Air Force (16 AF)
Hqtrs: Aviano AB, Italy

The Sixteenth Air Force is responsible for supporting Commander Allied Forces Southern Europe (AFSOUTH) and expeditionary forces in Europe's southern region. In addition to a single fighter wing, the command controls a composite wing based in Turkey and supported two air expeditionary wings (AEWs) during the Kosovo crisis in 1999. As Aviano is extremely close to the Balkans, in recent years it has proved vital to the United States and its allies during operations conducted against warring factions in the former Yugoslavia.

Outside of Britain, USAFE's Third Air Force operates from bases at Spangdahlem and Ramstein in Germany, whereas the Sixteenth Air Force flies from Aviano, Italy and Incirlik, Turkey. These F-16Cs are with the Aviano-based 31st FW.

This Sixteenth Air Force F-16C was sporting special anniversary tail markings when photographed during a landing approach, in 1997. It is assigned to the 31st FW at Aviano AB.

The 86th AW's 37th AS flies C-130E Hercules aircraft from Ramstein AB, Germany. Other airlift assets at the base include the C-9A, C-20A, C-21A and C-135B/C, which serve with two sister units.

On final approach at Nellis AFB during the 1998 Green Flag exercise, this B-52H Stratofortress is from AFRC's 93d BS, based at Barksdale AFB, Louisiana. It is the only reserve unit flying the bomber.

AIR FORCE RESERVE COMMAND (AFRC)
Headquarters: Robins AFB, Georgia

The AFRC was established as the USAF's ninth major command on 17 February 1997. Prior to this it had been a field-operating agency since its establishment on 14 April 1948. Commanded by a major general, AFRC is assigned three numbered air forces and, in the event of mobilization, the command is responsible for providing trained personnel to each of the USAF's major commands from its "pool" of 174,000 reservists. It is regularly engaged in support of operational missions throughout the world and the overwhelming majority of its assets are gained by ACC or AMC.

In addition to its own fleet of combat and support aircraft, AFRC personnel fly and maintain aircraft shared with active-duty AMC units as part of the Reserve Associate Program. The latter trains reserve crews to fly and maintain about 300 active-duty aircraft as well as the command's own fleet of ground attack aircraft, bombers, transports, tankers and helicopters. AFRC's primary fields of operation and expertise comprise airlift and air refueling although, in nonflying capacities, its members also engage in civil engineering, security, intelligence, training, communications and combat logistics support.

Fourth Air Force (4 AF)
Hqtrs: March ARB, California

The Fourth Air Force controls 11 AFRC airlift and aerial refueling wings and a single air refueling group gained by AMC that include three associate units. At this time, just two AFRC tanker squadrons still operate the KC-135E.

Tenth Air Force (10 AF)
Hqtrs: NAS Ft. Worth JRB/Carswell Field, Texas

The Tenth Air Force is responsible for tactical, training and Special Operations units gained by ACC, AETC and AFSOC, and controls 11 AFRC wings and groups that include an associate Airborne Warning and Control System (AWACS) unit. Also included are five combat rescue squadrons, the command's only bomber squadron and a single associate training unit.

Twenty-Second Air Force (22 AF)
Hqtrs: Dobbins ARB, Georgia

The Twenty-Second Air Force is responsible for strategic airlift and all AFRC tactical airlift assets. In all, 15 wings are assigned including two associate wings and the USAF's only weather reconnaissance squadron. Its assets are gained operationally by ACC.

AIR FORCE RESERVE COMMAND (AFRC)
Robins AFB, Georgia
Summary of AFRC Wings by Air Force and Gaining Command
(Refer to Commands for Unit Details)

Fourth Air Force - March ARB, California

349th AMW	AMC
433d AW	AMC
434th ARW	AMC
445th AW	AMC
446th AW	AMC
452d AMW	AMC
507th ARW	AMC
916th ARW	AMC
927th ARW	AMC
932d AW	AMC
940th ARW	AMC

Tenth Air Force - NAS Ft. Worth JRB, Texas

301st FW	ACC
340th FTG	AETC
419th FW	ACC
442d FW	ACC
482d FW	ACC
513th ACG	ACC
917th Wing	ACC
919th SOW	AFSOC
926th FW	ACC
939th RQW	ACC
944th FW	ACC

Twenty-Second Air Force - Dobbins ARB, Georgia

94th AW	AMC
302d AW	AMC
315th AW	AMC
403d Wing	AMC
439th AW	AMC
440th AW	AMC
459th AW	AMC
512th AW	AMC
514th AMW	AMC
908th AW	AMC
910th AW	AMC
911th AW	AMC
913th AW	AMC
914th AW	AMC
934th AW	AMC

AIR NATIONAL GUARD (ANG)
Headquarters: The Pentagon

Established on 18 September 1947, units of the ANG augment the active-duty Air Force by participating in operations and exercises worldwide at the behest of the air staff, major commands or joint and unified commands.

Composed of civilian volunteers, much like the AFRC, its members are commanded in peacetime by the governors of the 50 states or territories and commanding general of the District of Columbia. Each governor is represented, in terms of state or territorial chain of command, by an adjutant general (TAG). Upon mobilization in times of national emergency, however, the units are assigned to their applicable direct gaining command as shown in the accompanying tables.

Currently, the ANG has more than 110,000 guardsmen on strength who play a vital role in US military air operations, supporting the USAF with a wide range of warfighting capabilities. At this time the ANG provides the total force with the following:

Manned interceptors	100%	B-1B bombers	10%
Tactical airlift	44%	Combat rescue	28%
Tactical fighters	33%	Aerial refueling	43%
Strategic airlift	8%	Special Operations	6%

Above their hometown, the 'Jersey Devils' of the 177th FW operate from Atlantic City IAP/ANGB, New Jersey. Despite being retasked as a general purpose fighter squadron, the unit remains assigned to the First Air Force.

The B-1B is the only bomber flown by guardsmen. This aircraft serves with the 116th BW at Robins AFB, Georgia, part of the Ninth Air Force. A second wing is assigned to the Eighth Air Force.

AIR NATIONAL GUARD (ANG)
Andrews AFB, Maryland
Summary of ANG Wings by Air Force and Gaining Command
(Refer to Commands for Unit Details)

First Air Force - Tyndall AFB, Florida

102d FW	ACC
119th FW	ACC
120th FW	ACC
125th FW	ACC
142d FW	ACC
144th FW	ACC
147th FW	ACC
148th FW	ACC
158th FW	ACC
177th FW	ACC

Eighth Air Force - Barksdale AFB, Louisiana

110th FW	ACC
115th FW	ACC
122d FW	ACC
127th Wing*	ACC
131st FW	ACC
159th FW	ACC
181st FW	ACC
183d FW	ACC
184th BW	ACC
187th FW	ACC
188th FW	ACC

Ninth Air Force - Shaw AFB, South Carolina

103d FW	ACC
104th FW	ACC
106th RQW	ACC
111th FW	ACC
113th Wing*	ACC
116th BW	ACC
169th FW	ACC
174th FW	ACC
175th Wing*	ACC
178th FW	ACC
180th FW	ACC
192d FW	ACC

Twelfth Air Force - Davis-Monthan AFB, Ariz.

114th FW	ACC
124th Wing*	ACC
129th RQW	ACC
132d FW	ACC
138th FW	ACC
140th Wing*	ACC
149th FW	ACC
150th FW	ACC
185th FW	ACC

Fifteenth Air Force - Travis AFB, California

126th ARW	AMC
127th Wing*	AMC
133d AW	AMC
136th AW	AMC
137th AW	AMC
139th AW	AMC
140th Wing*	AMC
141st ARW	AMC
151st ARW	AMC
152d AW	AMC
153d AW	AMC
155th ARW	AMC

* Wing controls squadrons assigned to ACC and AMC

US Air Force

Like the AFRC, the ANG plays an important role in aerial refueling operations. This KC-135E is supplying two F-16Cs from the 354th FW, stationed at Eielson AFB, Alaska.

Serial 87-0764 is a TG-7A serving as a trainer with the 94th Flight Training Squadron (FTS) at the US Air Force Academy. This is one of two instructional units belonging to the 34th TRW.

UNITED STATES AIR FORCE ACADEMY (USAFA)
Hqtrs: Colorado Springs, Colorado

Aside from the ANG, the USAF has five direct reporting units (DRUs) that comprise the Air Force Communications and Information Center, Air Force Operational Test and Evaluation Center, 11th Wing, HQ Air Force Doctrine Center and the USAFA. Of these, only the latter operates aircraft.

Established in 1954, the academy prepares cadets for careers as Air Force officers through a combination of academic and military training. Qualified students may enter flight training upon graduation. The 34th Operations Group administers the USAFA airmanship programs which, at any one time, involve 4,200 cadets at various stages of training. The unit ensures course standards are achieved for soaring, parachuting and powered flight, and conducts Undergraduate Flying Training (UFT) selection.

Overall, the USAFA logs some 75,000 sorties annually at what is the Air Force's busiest airfield.

US AIR FORCE ACADEMY (USAFA) - Colorado Springs, Colorado					
Component	Unit	Base	Aircraft	Tail Code	Color
34th TRW		**U.S. Air Force Academy, Colorado**			
34th OG	94th FTS	U.S. Air Force Academy, Colorado			
			TG-3A, TG-4A, TG-7A,	AF	
			TG-9A, TG-11A,		
			Cessna 150, T-41D		
	98th FTS	Peterson AFB, Colorado	UV-18B		

Lockheed Martin (formerly General Dynamics) F-16C Block 30B Fighting Falcon
Unit: 174th Fighter Squadron, 185th Fighter Wing, Air National Guard
Base: Sioux Gateway Airport, Sergeant Bluff, Iowa

Walter Wright

In February 1996, serial 85-1565 was painted in this clear coat finish, black and gold scheme to commemorate the squadron's golden anniversary. Following appearances at a number of air shows and events that year, the "Viper" was returned to its two-tone gray and black combat colors after eight months.

AIRCRAFT

ALEXANDER SCHLEICHER

TG-9A (ASK-21)

First flown in 1979, the German ASK-21 is designated the TG-9A in Air Force service and was delivered to the USAFA in 1984. Having a wooden main wing spar, this tandem-seat, medium-performance sailplane is constructed of fiberglass honeycomb and was modified to serve as the academy's primary spin trainer. Four examples are used to provide dual instruction to students before they graduate to solo cross-country flights in the single-seat TG-3A. The glider carries an oxygen system and communications for high-altitude flying, and is used regularly in national competitions.

Schleicher TG-9A Specifications

Maximum Takeoff Weight:	1,320 lb (599 kg)
Empty Weight:	794 lb (360 kg)
Overall Length:	27 ft 5 in (8.34 m)
Wingspan:	55 ft 9 in (16.99 m)
Height:	5 ft 0 in (1.52 m)
Maximum Speed:	130 kts (240 km/h)
Service Ceiling:	25,000 ft (7620 m)
Crew:	2
Missions:	Aerobatics, cross-country flights, spin training

BEECH AIRCRAFT (SEE RAYTHEON AIRCRAFT)

USAF UH-1Ns serve with PACAF in Japan as well as several other commands within the continental USA. Introduction of the Twin Pac power plant brought increased operational safety over earlier, single-engine models.

BELL HELICOPTER TEXTRON

Bell UH-1N/HH-1N Iroquois

The UH-1N is a twin-engine version of the original Iroquois based on the Bell Model 212 and fitted with a single main rotor. It entered Air Force service in October 1970 as a SAR helicopter but has taken on many other missions over the years. It is now used primarily for airlifting emergency and disaster forces, medical evacuation and general airlift support. With the AFSPC, the UH-1N serves in the security surveillance role at missile bases and range areas when missiles are tested and when nuclear weapons are moved off base. It now flies SAR missions only as a secondary role.

In service with six major commands, the Iroquois supports AMC and PACAF as a priority transport, and flies with AETC's 58th SOW at Kirtland AFB, New Mexico, as a trainer. Meanwhile, the Iroquois is used for aircrew survival training by the 336th TRG at Fairchild AFB, Washington.

Bell UH-1N Specifications

Maximum Takeoff Weight:	11,200 lb (5080 kg)
Empty Weight:	6,143 lb (2786 kg)
Fuselage Length:	42 ft 4.8 in (12.92 m)
Overall Length:	57 ft 3.25 in (17.46 m)
Main Rotor Diameter:	48 ft 2.25 in (14.69 m)
Height:	14 ft 10.25 in (4.53 m)
Power Plant:	Two Pratt & Whitney Canada T400-CP-400 turbines, rated at 1,290 shp (962 kW) at takeoff
Maximum Fuel Capacity:	1,451 lb (658 kg)
Maximum Speed:	123 kts (228 km/h)
Operating Range:	227 nm (420 km)
Service Ceiling:	14,200 ft (4328 m)
Crew:	1
Missions:	Security and surveillance, utility transport, SAR

BOEING COMPANY
(INCLUDING MCDONNELL DOUGLAS AND ROCKWELL INTERNATIONAL)

Rockwell B-1B Lancer

Originally conceived for the nuclear role and developed in response to the advanced manned strategic aircraft (AMSA) requirement, the first of four B-1A prototypes flew on 23 December 1974. In June 1977 the program was cancelled but was resurrected in a revised form in October 1981. A larger aircraft than the B-1A, the B-1B took to the air on 18 October 1984 and was first delivered to the USAF at Dyess AFB, Texas, in June 1985. It was officially declared operational on 1 October 1986 and the last example was accepted on 2 May 1988. Currently, there are 93 Lancers in the USAF's inventory, making it the most numerous bomber in service. Typically, 80 aircraft are available to theater commanders at any one time.

The B-1B's structure incorporates radar-absorbent materials that reduce its radar cross section significantly compared with the B-52. Fitted with variable-geometry wings, it is capable of high-speed, low-level bombing as well as high-altitude drops. However, the emphasis is now on the carriage of conventional weapons and the type is presently undergoing modification under the Conventional Mission Upgrade Program (CMUP), designed to allow the B-1B to carry an array of new guided and unguided ordnance. Although it will retain limited nuclear capabilities, the Lancer will have no such operational requirement in the future and crews no longer train for that mission.

Among the bomber's new weapons are the Joint Direct-Attack Munition (JDAM), added in 1999; and the Wind-Corrected Munitions Dispenser (WCMD), Joint Standoff Weapon (JSOW) and Joint Air-to-Surface Standoff Missile (JASSM), which will equip the bomber by 2002. However, the Lancer will continue to carry 500-lb (227-kg) Mk 82 and 2,000-lb (907-kg) Mk 84 bombs for use against non-precision targets, and can also drop sea mines. It can deliver up to 84 general purpose (GP) or cluster bombs for the purpose of halting an enemy's initial advance, and is capable of deploying on the first day of a conflict.

The program to enhance the lethality of the Lancer will be ongoing in the coming years, and planned improvements include a new avionics computer, defensive upgrades and additional weapons' development aimed at improving the bomber's operational effectiveness.

B-1Bs saw combat for the first time on 17 December 1998, when two aircraft hit separate targets at the Al Kut barracks complex in northwest Iraq flying six-hour, daylight missions. Two more were flown the following day. For these sorties, each Lancer carried 66 500-lb Mk 82 GP low-drag bombs in 28-carry bomb modules in the forward and intermediate bays, and in a 10-carry module in the aft

Rockwell B-1B Lancer Specifications

Maximum Takeoff Weight:	477,000 lb (216360 kg)
Empty Weight:	192,000 lb (87090 kg)
Overall Length:	147 ft 0 in (44.81 m)
Wingspan (at minimum sweep):	136 ft 8.5 in (41.67 m)
Wingspan (at maximum sweep):	78 ft 2.5 in (23.84 m)
Height:	34 ft 10 in (10.62 m)
Power Plant:	Four General Electric F101-GE-102 turbofans, each rated at 30,780 lb st (136.92 kN) with afterburner
Maximum Fuel Capacity:	195,000 lb (88451 kg)
Maximum Speed:	Mach 1.25/715 kts (1324 km/h)
Low-level Penetration Speed:	521 kts (965 km/h)
Operating Range:	6,475 nm (11992 km)
Crew:	4
Armament Options:	Nonnuclear – Mk 82 AIR1, Mk 82 LDGP2, Mk 62 QS3, CBU-87/B, CBU-89/B, CBU-97/B, Mk 82 Series, GBU-31/1/B (Mk 84 JDAM), GBU-31/3/B (BLU-109 JDAM), Mk 84 LDGP Nuclear – B61, B83 (gravity bombs)
Mission Equipment:	AN/APN-164 multimode strike radar, AN/ALQ-161 defensive electronic countermeasures system, chaff and flare systems, moving target indicator, terrain-following radar, Inertial Navigation System (INS), ALE-50 towed decoy
Missions:	Primary – Strategic and tactical conventional bombing Secondary – Strategic and tactical nuclear bombing

The most numerous bomber in USAF service, the B-1B is currently undergoing the Conventional Mission Upgrade Program (CMUP), designed to enhance its weapon delivery capabilities.

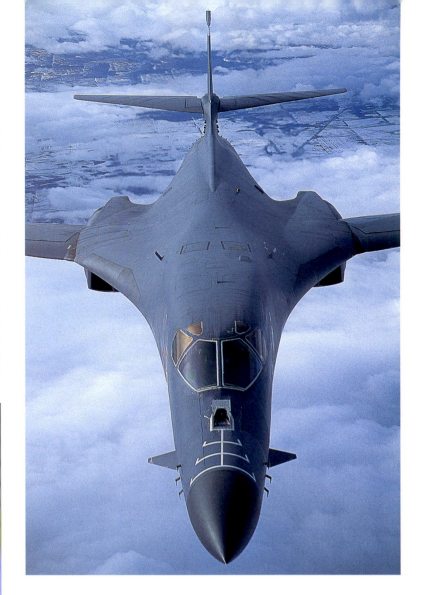

Since the end of the Cold War, the primary role of the Rockwell B-1B has changed from nuclear to conventional bomber. This Lancer serves with the 7th BW at Dyess AFB, Texas.

bay. The weapons were dropped from a height of approximately 20,000 feet (6100 m).

Currently, active-duty B-1Bs are assigned to the 9th and 28th BS with the 7th BW at Dyess AFB, Texas; the 37th and 77th BS with the 28th BW at Ellsworth AFB, South Dakota; and the 34th BS with the 366th Wing at Mountain Home AFB, Idaho. Meanwhile, ANG operators include the 128th BS of the 116th BW at Robins AFB, Georgia, and the 127th BS belonging to the 184th BW at McConnell AFB, Kansas.

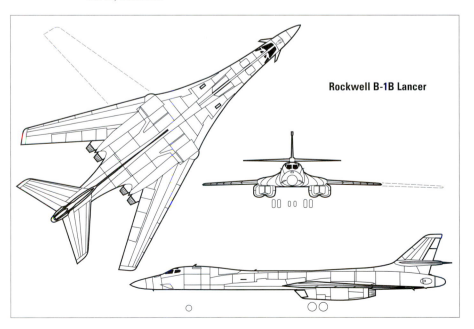

Rockwell B-1B Lancer

US Air Force

Boeing B-52H Stratofortress

The Boeing B-52A first flew in 1954 and the B-52B Stratofortress entered USAF service the following year. In frontline operation ever since, the bomber is already the longest-serving combat aircraft in history. Even more remarkable, it is scheduled to remain there for another two decades at least, despite the fact that production ended in 1962.

The B-52H first entered service in May 1961 and is the only variant left flying today. Along with the B-2A Spirit, it comprises the manned-bomber portion of the US nuclear triad. However, ongoing development of the Stratofortress focuses primarily on conventional missions. Not only have these capabilities been improved in recent years but "smart" tactics are being developed to integrate the roles of all bomber types more effectively. Due to the modest size of the B-2A fleet, ongoing modernization of B-52s was deemed essential to meet future defense needs, even though the number of airframes has been trimmed from the original 102 examples.

The B-52H is capable of delivering a wide array of munitions. The JDAM and WCMD were added to the B-52H's arsenal in 1998, and the JSOW will follow by 2000. Sometime in 2001, the bomber should be capable of delivering the JASSM. Like the B-1B, the Stratofortress will retain the ability to drop standard nonprecision ordnance like GP and cluster munitions, as well.

The B-52's bomb bay can accommodate two four-weapon cluster racks or three nine-weapon clip-in racks. The Common Strategic Rotary Launcher (CSRL), an eight-station dispenser, is also employed internally. In addition to an internal bomb bay, which occupies most of the center fuselage, the B-52 is fitted with underwing pylons that add to its delivery options. Besides being able to drop AGM-86C Conventional Air-Launched Cruise Missiles (CALCMs) with precision, the bomber can launch the optically guided AGM-142. The CALCM Block 2 missile is currently under development and will also enable the B-52H to make effective attacks on hardened shelters.

In support of Operation Desert Fox in late 1998, 15 B-52Hs were stationed on the small island of Diego Garcia in the Indian Ocean and began launching CALCMs against Iraqi targets on the second day of the campaign. In all, these aircraft fired 90 such munitions.

The Stratofortress is assigned to the 2d BW's 11th, 20th and 96th BS at Barksdale AFB, Louisiana; and the 5th BW's 23d BS at Minot AFB, North Dakota. In addition, the 917th Wing's 93d BS, a reserve unit, operates B-52Hs from Barksdale. After accounting for training needs and backup inventory, about 80 B-52s are available to theater commanders at any one time.

Belonging to the 5th BW at Minot AFB, North Dakota, this Boeing B-52H Stratofortress is returning home after a routine training mission.

A B-52H from the 93d BS (AFRC), Barksdale AFB, Louisiana.

Boeing B-52 Stratofortress Specifications

Maximum Takeoff Weight:	505,000 lb (229068 kg)
Empty Weight:	Approx. 170,000 lb (77111 kg)
Overall Length:	160 ft 11 in (49.05 m)
Wingspan:	185 ft 0 in (56.39 m)
Height:	40 ft 8 in (12.40 m)
Power Plant:	Eight Pratt & Whitney TF-33-P3 turbofans, each rated at 17,000 lb st (75.62 kN) dry
Maximum Fuel Capacity:	299,434 lb (135823 kg) internally plus 9,114 lb (4134 kg) in two 700-gal underwing tanks
Maximum Speed:	450 kts (833 km/h)
Cruise Speed:	422 kts (782 km/h)
Operating Range:	6,865 nm (12714 km)
Crew:	5
Armament Options:	Nonnuclear – AGM-84D Harpoon; AGM-86C CALCM; AGM-142 Have Nap; AGM-154 JSOW; AGM-158 JASSM; GBU-31 JDAM; GBU-10, GBU-12, SUU-64/B and SUU-65/B tactical munitions dispensers; CBU-103, CBU-104 and CBU-105 WCMD; Mk 82 500-lb, Mk 117 750-lb, Mk 83 1,000-ll and Mk 84 2,000-lb GP bombs Nuclear – AGM-86B ACALCM, AGM-129 ACM
Mission Equipment:	AN/ASQ-181 electro-optical weapon system, warning receivers, chaff/flare and countermeasures, communications jammers
Missions:	Strategic and tactical, conventional and nuclear bombing

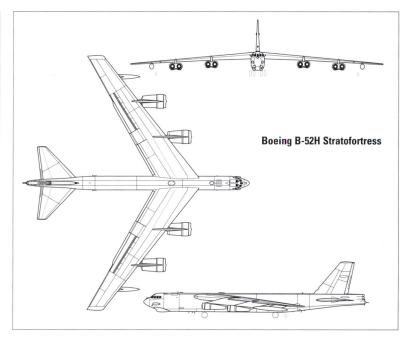

Boeing B-52H Stratofortress

McDonnell Douglas C-9A/VC-9C Nightingale

A modified version of the DC-9-32F airliner, which first flew on 25 February 1965, the Nightingale serves chiefly with the AMC in the aeromedical evacuation role, being the only aircraft in the USAF inventory specifically designed for this purpose. Equipped with a large cargo door and hydraulically actuated ramp, the aircraft can carry a maximum of 40 litter patients. The entire fleet is used for this mission except for one example assigned to USAFE, which serves as a transport for the commander of Supreme Headquarters Allied Powers Europe (SHAPE). The C-9A made its maiden flight on 8 August 1968 and currently serves with one AFRC unit and three active-duty units. Used as VIP transports, three VC-9Cs are configured for 42 passengers and a crew of eight. This variant is assigned only to the 89th AW at Andrews AFB, Maryland.

This McDonnell Douglas VC-9C Nightingale serves as a VIP transport with the 89th AW, at Andrews AFB, Maryland. Aside from internal differences, the aircraft is not equipped with the large cargo door fitted to the C-9A.

McDonnell Douglas C-9A Nightingale Specifications

Maximum Takeoff Weight:	121,000 lb (54885 kg)
Empty Weight:	57,190 lb (25941 kg)
Overall Length:	119 ft 3.5 in (36.36 m)
Wingspan:	93 ft 5 in (28.47 m)
Height:	27 ft 6 in (8.38 m)
Power Plant:	Two Pratt & Whitney JT8D-9 turbofans, each rated at 14,500 lb st (64.50 kN)
Maximum Fuel Capacity:	3,679 gal (13927 lit)
Maximum Cruise Speed:	490 kts (907 km/h)
Typical Cruise Speed:	443 kts (820 km/h)
Typical Operating Range:	1,290–1,670 nm (2389–3093 km)
Aircrew:	3
Missions:	Aeromedical evacuation, VIP transport

McDonnell Douglas KC-10A Extender

Winner of the 1977 Advanced Tanker/Cargo Aircraft (ATCA) competition, the KC-10A is based on the DC-10-30CF airliner, which first flew on 29 August 1970. Retaining 88 percent commonality in terms of systems, the type is additionally equipped with military avionics, satellite communications, an aerial refueling boom, hose-and-drogue systems and a station for the refueling operator, as well as its own refueling receptacle. The aircraft first entered service at March AFB, California, in October 1981 and, as currently configured, can service probe- or receptacle-equipped aircraft during the same mission. Its boom system can transfer fuel at the rate of 1,100 gal (4164 lit) per minute, whereas the hose-and-drogue system is limited to 470 gal (1779 lit) per minute.

The Extender's primary role is that of an air-to-air refueler but it is also an important strategic airlift asset. In fact, it can fulfill both duties during the same mission by tanking other aircraft while transporting personnel and equipment on overseas deployments. In the latter role, it is capable of carrying 75 people and almost 170,000 lb (77111 kg) of cargo over an unrefueled distance of about 3,800 nautical miles (7038 km). Besides three main fuel tanks in the wings, three more are located under the cargo floor. In all, the KC-10A can carry more than 356,000 lb (161480 kg) of fuel, twice that of the KC-135.

The type is in service with four active-duty and four AFRC squadrons.

Capable of being used as a transport and a refueler on the same mission, the dual-role Extender has brought added flexibility to AMC operations. As the Air Force is now committed to the concept of deploying expeditionary forces overseas, the KC-10A will have an important role to play well into the 21st century.

McDonnell Douglas KC-10A Extender Specifications

Maximum Takeoff Weight:	590,000 lb (267620 kg)
Empty Weight:	240,065–244,630 lb (108891–110962 kg)
Overall Length:	181 ft 7 in (55.35 m)
Wingspan:	155 ft 4 in (47.35 m)
Height:	58 ft 1 in (17.70 m)
Power Plant:	Three General Electric CF6-50C2 turbofans, each rated at 52,500 lb st (233.53 kN)
Maximum Fuel Capacity:	356,000 lb (161480 kg)
Cruise Speed:	490 kts (907 km/h)
Operating Range:	3,800 nm (7038 km)
Crew:	4
Mission Equipment:	Tail boom, hose-and-drogue refueling systems
Missions:	Aerial refueling, strategic airlift

US Air Force

Boeing C-17A Globemaster III

The Air Force's newest strategic airlifter was long in development but ultimately made its first flight on 15 September 1991. Chosen as the winner of the C-X competition in August 1981, and subsequently given the name Globemaster III, this four-engine, T-tail transport achieved IOC in 1995 and entered operational service with AMC's 437th AW, at Charleston AFB, South Carolina.

One of the most costly aircraft programs in US history (others being the E-3 Sentry, B-2 Stealth Bomber and F-22 Raptor), the C-17A has nevertheless given a much needed boost to USAF airlift capabilities and is proving to be a reliable and efficient platform. Representing a quantum leap in technology over previous transports, the Globemaster III has an ergonomically designed flight deck optimized for the comfort of its two pilots. Fitted with a control stick in place of the more traditional yoke, it is also the first transport to have a head-up display (HUD) and employ a quadruple-redundant, fly-by-wire control system.

The cargo interior was designed with the realities of modern freight handling in mind and includes a palletized load/unload system that can be operated by one loadmaster, as well as a ground-level roll-on/roll-off ramp at the rear of the aircraft and powered rollers. The main cargo deck measures more than 68 feet and can accommodate 18 standard pallets. The maximum payload exceeds 172,000 lb (78000 kg), which is some 34 percent less than that of the C-5 Galaxy.

The Boeing C-17A Globemaster III is the latest heavy airlifter to enter USAF service, having been chosen for development in 1981 after McDonnell Douglas proposed the aircraft to fill the service's C-X cargo aircraft requirement. Today, the type is rapidly replacing AMC's fleet of aging Lockheed C-141 StarLifters.

at Charleston AFB, C-17As have now been delivered to the 315th AW's 300th, 317th and 701st AS. These AFRC units are also located at Charleston. Additionally, the active-duty 58th AS of the 97th AMW at Altus AFB, Oklahoma, and the 7th AS belonging to the 62d AW at McChord AFB, Washington, are now flying the type. Most recently, the AFRC's McChord-based 728th AS of the 446th AW began Globemaster III operations.

Boeing EC-18B (See Boeing C-137)

Boeing C-22B/C (727-100/200)

First flown on 9 February 1963, the Boeing 727-100 did not enter USAF service until the mid-1980s when one example was purchased for the commander of USSOUTHCOM. Four more, previously with Pan Am and American Airlines were acquired for use by the ANG.

Although the C-22A is no longer in service, three of four C-22Bs still fly with the guard's 201st AS at Andrews AFB, Maryland. In addition, a single C-22C (based on the longer B727-200) is also flying with the USAF.

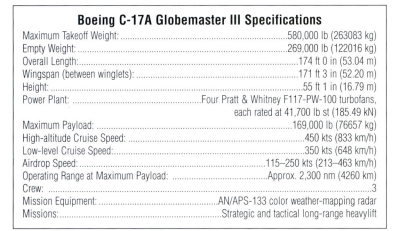

Boeing C-17A Globemaster III Specifications	
Maximum Takeoff Weight:	580,000 lb (263083 kg)
Empty Weight:	269,000 lb (122016 kg)
Overall Length:	174 ft 0 in (53.04 m)
Wingspan (between winglets):	171 ft 3 in (52.20 m)
Height:	55 ft 1 in (16.79 m)
Power Plant:	Four Pratt & Whitney F117-PW-100 turbofans, each rated at 41,700 lb st (185.49 kN)
Maximum Payload:	169,000 lb (76657 kg)
High-altitude Cruise Speed:	450 kts (833 km/h)
Low-level Cruise Speed:	350 kts (648 km/h)
Airdrop Speed:	115–250 kts (213–463 km/h)
Operating Range at Maximum Payload:	Approx. 2,300 nm (4260 km)
Crew:	3
Mission Equipment:	AN/APS-133 color weather-mapping radar
Missions:	Strategic and tactical long-range heavylift

Designed for strategic movement of troops and cargo to main operating bases, the C-17A is also able to serve in the tactical airlift and airdrop roles. In February 1985, the USAF determined it needed 210 C-17As and, in ensuing years, several expensive modifications were added to the program, like the ability to operate from unpaved airstrips in forward locations, although this is unlikely ever to be employed. In 1990, then Secretary of Defense Richard Cheney reduced the requirement to 120 airframes but the AMC has since been pressing for 134 aircraft. To date, Boeing has delivered almost half of the confirmed order.

Besides having joined the 14th, 15th and 17th AS of the 437th AW

Boeing C-22B Specifications	
Maximum Takeoff Weight:	170,000 lb (77111 kg)
Empty Weight:	81,920 lb (37158 kg)
Overall Length:	133 ft 2 in (40.59 m)
Wingspan:	108 ft 0 in (32.92 m)
Height:	34 ft 0 in (10.36 m)
Power Plant:	Three Pratt & Whitney JT8D-9A turbofans, each rated at 14,500 lb st (64.50 kN) dry
Cruise Speed:	470–520 kts (870–963 km/h)
Operating Range:	1,739 nm (3221 km)
Aircrew:	4
Missions:	Passenger transport

As one of the world's most successful airliners, it is surprising more Boeing 727s did not see military service with the USAF. In all, just six aircraft were acquired during the 1980s.

Serial 82-8000 is one of two Boeing VC-25As that serve as Air Force One with the 89th AW at Andrews AFB, Maryland.

Boeing VC-25A (747-200)

Best known as Air Force One, the VC-25A is based on the Boeing 747-200B airframe and is used to provide transport for the president of the United States. Besides reduced passenger seating and a substantially modified internal configuration, the two VC-25As in service are fitted with advanced electronics and communications plus a self-contained baggage loader, front and aft stairs, and an in-flight refueling receptacle. The interior features a stateroom and office for the president; a conference/dining room; and separate accommodations for senior staff, guests, the Secret Service, security personnel and the press. Although assigned to the AMC's 89th AW at Andrews AFB, Maryland, these aircraft are flown by dedicated presidential aircrews and maintained by the Presidential Maintenance Branch. The type flew its first mission on 6 September 1990.

Boeing C-32A (757-200)

In August 1996, the USAF announced it had selected the Boeing 757-200 airliner as the platform to replace its long-serving VC-137Cs (later redesignated C-137s) in the special air mission role. Designated the C-32A, the aircraft is similar in size and capacity to its predecessor, although it has a shorter range. Its primary purpose is to transport the vice president, cabinet members and members of congress traveling on government business. It is configured for 45 passengers and a crew of 16, and the first of four examples was delivered to the 89th AW on 19 June 1998. Boeing is contracted to maintain these aircraft through 2005.

C-32As are replacing Air Force Boeing 707s (designated C-137s) that have been used as VIP transports for many years. However, the new platform does not offer the range of its predecessor.

Boeing VC-25A Specifications

Maximum Takeoff Weight:	833,000 lb (377840 kg)
Empty Weight:	526,500 lb (238820 kg)
Overall Length:	231 ft 10 in (70.66 m)
Wingspan:	195 ft 8 in (59.64 m)
Height:	63 ft 5 in (19.33 m)
Power Plant:	Four General Electric CF6-80C2B1 turbofans, each rated at 56,700 lb st (252.21 kN) dry
Maximum Fuel Capacity	361,875 lb (164142)
Cruise Speed:	525 kts (972 km/h)
Service Ceiling	45,100 ft (13746 m)
Operating Range:	6,800 nm (12594 km)
Crew:	26
Mission:	Presidential transport (Air Force One)

Boeing C-32A Specifications

Maximum Takeoff Weight:	250,000 lb (113395 kg)
Empty Weight:	125,750 lb (57039 kg)
Overall Length:	154 ft 10 in (47.19 m)
Wingspan:	124 ft 10 in (38.05 m)
Height:	44 ft 6 in (13.56 m)
Power Plant:	Two Pratt & Whitney PW2040 turbofans, each rated at 41,700 lb st (185.49 kN)
Maximum Fuel Capacity	77,800 lb (35289 kg)
Cruise Speed:	490 kts (907 km/h)
Operating Range:	4,150 nm (7686 km)
Crew:	16
Mission:	Priority air transport

Boeing C-135B/C/E, EC-135E/K/N, KC-135D/E/R/T and NKC-135B/E Stratolifter/Stratotanker

Initially flown in August 1956, the first production KC-135 Stratotanker was received at Castle AFB, California, in June 1957 and deliveries to the Air Force continued for eight years thereafter. Since that time approximately 350 examples have been upgraded with significantly quieter, fuel-efficient F108-CF-100 (CFM-56) turbofans in place of the original J57 turbojets. Capable of offloading 50 percent more fuel, these modified KC-135As and KC-135Qs are designated KC-135Rs and KC-135Ts, respectively.

Until the mid-1990s, at which time fleet strengths were dramatically reduced, almost all tankers were assigned to active-duty forces. However, the KC-135R was subsequently introduced into service with the ANG and AFRC after 140 KC-135As were fitted with TF33-PW-102 engines taken from surplus Boeing 707s. These aircraft are designated KC-135Es and offer a 14 percent improvement in fuel efficiency over the A model, as well as the capability of offloading 20 percent more fuel. Four KC-135Ds also have been given TF33 power plants but retain the old designation. A number of AFRC and ANG platforms subsequently were upgraded to KC-135R standard under a program that continues today.

In the late 1990s, four KC-135Rs were fitted with multipoint refueling systems (MPRS). Already equipped with a steerable refueling boom under the tail, a hose-and-drogue system in a wingtip-mounted pod was added as part of the new program. After evaluation, the USAF decided to similarly equip another 45 aircraft, adding considerably to the type's flexibility. In addition to being able to refuel USAF aircraft via the boom, these aircraft will have the ability to service NATO and US Navy aircraft via the hose-and-drogue. The new system was expected to reach IOC in February 2000, at which point 12 examples will be flying.

US Air Force

Boeing KC-135E Stratotanker of the ANG's 191st ARS,
151st ARW, based at Salt Lake City IAP, Utah.

Boeing KC-135R Stratotanker Specifications

Maximum Takeoff Weight:	322,500 lb (146280 kg)
Overall Length:	136 ft 3 in (41.53 m)
Wingspan:	130 ft 10 in (39.88 m)
Height:	41 ft 8 in (12.70 m)
Power Plant:	Four CFM International F108-CF-100 turbofans each rated at 21,634 lb st (96.23 kN)
Maximum Fuel Capacity:	203,300 lb (92215 kg)
Cruise Speed:	461 kts (854 km/h)
Operating Range:	2,500 nm (4630 km)
Service Ceiling	50,000 ft (15240 m)
Crew:	3
Mission:	Aerial refueling

Under a program referred to as Pacer CRAG, the KC-135 fleet and other AMC assets are having their flight decks updated with new avionics. Once consequence is elimination of the navigator's position in these aircraft, thereby reducing the crew to three (pilot, copilot and boom operator).

Unlike the reconnaissance variants, not all Stratotankers can be refueled in the air. Eight aircraft are equipped with receptacles and designated KC-135R(RT)s. The suffix means "refuelable tanker."

The KC-135E is currently operational with 11 ANG and two AFRC squadrons, whereas the KC-135R serves with 18 active-duty, 11 ANG and six AFRC units. In addition, a test fleet exists at Edwards AFB, California, comprising a number of specially modified Stratolifter and Stratotanker platforms designated NKC-135B (formerly EC-135C), NKC-135E (formerly NKC-135A) and EC-135E (formerly EC-135N). In addition, aircraft designated C-135B, C-135C, C-135E, EC-135K and EC-135N serve as transports for unified commanders in chief (CinCs).

Boeing OC-135B, RC-135S/U/V/W, TC-135S/W and WC-135W Stratolifter

ACC's 55th Wing at Offutt AFB, Nebraska, operates a large fleet of C-135B transports that have been modified to perform specific reconnaissance duties.

Tasked with Open Skies treaty verification, the OC-135B was once a weather reconnaissance WC-135B and is now fitted with three KS-87 framing cameras and a single KA-91 pan camera. This equipment is used to conduct low- and medium-altitude surveillance of foreign military installations.

Intelligence variants of the C-135B include the RC-135S 'Cobra Ball,' RC-135U 'Combat Sent' and RC-135V/W 'Rivet Joint.' Initially developed to obtain signals intelligence (SIGINT), and measurements and signatures intelligence (MASINT) from Soviet missiles and re-entry vehicles, the RC-135S continues to be an important reconnaissance asset, particularly as other countries pursue development of intercontinental ballistic missiles (ICBMs). Previously equipped with an infrared optical-tracking system, the sole RC-135X 'Cobra Eye' has been modified to 'Cobra Ball' configuration in support of theater ballistic missile defense efforts. It is equipped with new systems that will be retrofitted to older 'Cobra Ball' platforms.

The missions of the 'Combat Sent' and 'Rivet Joint' aircraft comprise signals, electronic and telemetry intelligence gathering. The 'Rivet Joints' are the first intelligence variants to be fitted with F108-CF-100 turbofans, and a single RC-135V and one RC-135W have already received new engines. Two C-135Bs, one designated a TC-135S and the other a TC-135W, have been modified to serve as flight trainers for RC-135S and RC-135V/W crews.

Formerly a weather reconnaissance WC-135B, a single WC-135W remains in service for atmospheric sampling following nuclear weapons tests. A second aircraft, designated an NC-135W, is bailed to Raytheon as a test aircraft.

The first re-engined RC-135W 'Rivet Joint,' serial 62-4138, is seen here during a recent Boeing test flight. The aircraft is one of 16 that serve as a signals, electronic and telemetry intelligence platform, and all are set to receive the F108-CF-100 turbofans as part of an Air Force program to upgrade such assets. A newly installed JTIDS antenna is clearly visible at the top of the fin.

Boeing C-137C, EC-137D, VC-137D, EC-18B and TC-18E

Designated VC-137Cs and based at Andrews AFB, Maryland, a number of Boeing 707s were acquired as transports for the 89th AW. Two examples, utilizing B707-300 airframes, were obtained specifically as presidential transports but later assumed the role of general staff and VIP transports as C-137Cs, along with others that previously had entered service. They were still being acquired by the Air Force for various duties in the early 1990s.

The impending retirement of the last of these particular variants will leave a single EC-137D in service, which currently flies in support of the CinC of US Special Operations Command (USSOCOM). However, within a few years it could be replaced by a C-37A, which has only recently entered Air Force and Army service but is ideally suited for the CinC support mission. Meanwhile, the VC-137C also remains in service.

Beginning in the late 1970s, the Air Force also acquired a number of used Boeing 707 airliners. Many were simply stripped of their engines and used as a source of parts for the KC-135A re-engining program. However, a small number of the old airliners were kept intact, reconfigured for various test missions and returned to service. In theory, these platforms should also have been designated C-137s because that was the number assigned to the Boeing 707 program. Instead, they were given the military designation C-18A. With different roles assigned to these aircraft, some received designation modifiers as well. Today, only the EC-18B variant is still flying. Several of

the retired C-18 airframes will be remanufactured by Northrop Grumman and returned to service as E-8C Joint STARS.

Referred to as the advanced range instrumentation aircraft (ARIA), the EC-18B is easily recognized by its bulbous, drooping nose that houses a seven-foot (2.13 m), steerable tracking/telemetry antenna. Also fitted were wingtip-mounted high-frequency probe antennas and a high-frequency trailing-wire antenna under the fuselage. The ARIA systems came from EC-135N variants used to support space and missile programs since the mid-1960s. First flown in March 1985, EC-18Bs were initially assigned the mission at Wright-Patterson AFB, Ohio. However, the three aircraft still in service fly out of Edwards AFB, California.

The USAF also has two TC-18Es in its inventory although these are currently grounded because of metal fatigue. Previously, they served as "bang and bounce" trainers for E-3B/C Sentry crews assigned to the 552d ACW at Tinker AFB, Oklahoma. Reports suggest the Air Force is looking for two replacements.

Three Boeing EC-18Bs remain in service with AFMC at Edwards AFB, California. They are used as advanced range instrumentation aircraft (ARIA).

US Air Force

Boeing E-3B/C Sentry

Whereas the E-8 Joint STARS provides imaging of vehicles on the ground to facilitate control of the battlefield, the E-3 Sentry Airborne Warning and Control System (AWACS) provides similar analysis of combat zone airspace, and offers all-weather, command, control and communications capabilities. Equipped with an airborne warning radar, and built around a modified Boeing 707-320B airframe, the Sentry replaced the propeller-driven EC-121 in the late 1970s.

The platform was developed in response to an Air Force requirement for modification of two B707s to EC-137D configuration, to test competing radar systems. The first aircraft took to the air on 9 February 1972 and, after several months of flight tests, a Westinghouse-developed radar was selected in October over a rival Hughes system. Production aircraft were designated E-3As and the radar became known as the AN/APY-1.

The Air Force has taken delivery of 34 E-3As including two EC-137Ds upgraded to the standard. The final nine aircraft and first production example were equipped with the AN/APY-2 radar, which

Boeing E-3C Sentry Specifications	
Maximum Takeoff Weight:	325,000 lb (147420 kg)
Empty Weight:	171,950 lb (77995 kg)
Overall Length:	152 ft 11 in (46.61 m)
Wingspan:	145 ft 9 in (44.43 m)
Height:	41 ft 9 in (12.73 m)
Diameter of Rotodome:	30 ft (9.14 m)
Power Plant:	Four Pratt & Whitney TF33-P-100/100A turbofans, each rated at 21,000 lb st (93.41 kN)
Maximum Fuel Capacity:	161,912 lb (73442 kg)
Unrefueled Endurance:	11 hours
Maximum Speed:	460 kts (852 km/h)
Operating Radius and Ceiling:	870 nm (1611 km)/29,000 ft (8839 m)
Crew:	20
Mission Equipment:	AN/APY-1 or -2 long-range surveillance radar, AN/AYR-1 passive electronic support measures
Missions:	Command, control and communications relay near battle zone

The Boeing E-3B Sentry AWACS achieved IOC in April 1978. Today, the platform serves with five ACC units at Tinker AFB, Oklahoma, and one expeditionary squadron based at Prince Sultan AB, Saudi Arabia. Additionally, the Sentry flies with two PACAF squadrons.

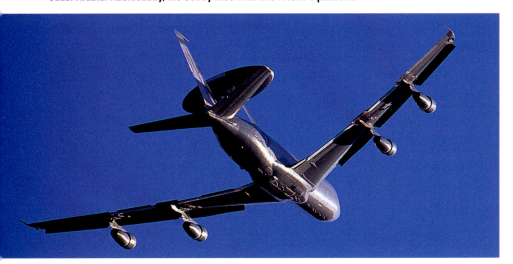

offered improved maritime capabilities. Subsequent upgrades standardized the fleet and original AN/APY-1 aircraft were redesignated E-3Bs, whereas later models became E-3Cs. With a range of about 174 nautical miles (322 km), the radar, combined with an identification friend or foe (IFF) subsystem, can identify and track enemy and friendly low-flying aircraft by eliminating ground clutter returns that confuse other systems.

The 552d Airborne Warning and Control Wing at Tinker AFB, Oklahoma, took delivery of the first E-3A on 24 March 1977. Today, there are 23 E-3Bs and nine E-3Cs in service plus the JE-3C avionics test bed operated by Boeing. Current upgrades to the E-3B and E-3C, under what is termed the Block 30/35 Upgrade Program, include an AN/AYR-1 electronic support measures system (ECM), improved secure datalink communications (Class 2H JTIDS) and central computer, and a GPS. IOC was achieved on 31 March 1998, at which point 10 Sentries had received the modifications. Separately, a radar system improvement project enables the AN/APY1-2 to deal more effectively with small targets and ECM. Both programs should be completed in 2001.

A large dorsal fairing on the E-4B houses the super-high-frequency communications system.

Boeing E-4B/C NAOC

The National Airborne Operations Center (NAOC), sometimes referred to as the "Doomsday Plane," is an aerial command station designed to facilitate execution of war orders in the event ground communication facilities are destroyed in a nuclear conflict. The system allows the president and key government officials to maintain a chain of leadership in such a situation.

The E-4 platform is based on the Boeing 747-200 airframe and four examples have been fitted with highly advanced communications and other specialized systems. First flown on 13 June 1973, the type began replacing the EC-135 in that role in December 1974. The first three aircraft were delivered as E-4As but were subsequently upgraded to E-4B standard. By 1985, a fleet of four Bs was in service. Another modification soon will bring them up to E-4C configuration.

The airborne command post can accommodate up to 114 people, including a joint-service operations team, maintenance and security staff, communications specialists and an ACC crew. One aircraft and a crew of 63 are generally on 24-hour ground alert at all times. The fleet is assigned to the 1st ACCS of the 55th Wing, at Offutt AFB, Nebraska. In addition to its "doomsday" role, the E-4 is also available to the Federal Emergency Management Agency (FEMA) to assist during a natural emergency.

Boeing E-4B Specifications	
Maximum Takeoff Weight:	800,000 lb (362874 kg)
Overall Length:	231 ft 4 in (70.51 m)
Wingspan:	195 ft 8 in (59.64 m)
Height:	63 ft 5 in (19.94 m)
Power Plant:	Four General Electric F103-GE-100 turbofans, each rated at 52,500 lb st (233.53 kN)
Maximum Fuel Capacity:	331,565 lb (150395 kg)
Cruise Speed:	Estimated at 500 kts (926 km/h)
Operating Endurance:	12 hours unrefueled
Crew:	63
Mission Equipment:	Advanced communications suites, including a super-high-frequency system enabling direct TV/radio broadcasts to the general public
Missions:	Nuclear war national command post, natural disaster assistance

Boeing T-43A, serial 71-1405, belongs to the 558th FTS of the 12th FTW at Randolph AFB, Texas. The aircraft is one of 10 assigned to the wing for navigator training.

Boeing T-43A/CT-43A (737-200)

Developed from the Boeing 737-200 airliner, the T-43A is flown as part of the Air Force's Undergraduate Navigator Training Program (UNTP), which provides instruction to students assigned to tactical and strategic platforms. Making its maiden flight in March 1973, the first aircraft was received at Mather AFB, California, in September of that year where it replaced propeller-driven T-29s. The military version differs from the commercial airliner by having fewer windows and several small-blade antennas, sextant ports and a wire antenna for high-frequency radio communications fitted.

Ten T-43As are currently assigned to the UNTP and are operated by the 12th FTW at Randolph AFB, Texas. In addition, five former USAF examples have been bailed to a civilian contractor supporting DoD programs in the southwest of the United States. These aircraft operate from McCarran IAP in Las Vegas, Nevada.

Several T-43As have been configured to carry passengers and provide operational support to assigned commands. The CT-43A designation was adopted for aircraft flying transport missions to distinguish them from those assigned to navigational training. One was lost in April 1996. It crashed in Croatia when its crew attempted a landing during bad weather.

McDonnell Douglas F-4F, QF-4E/G, QRF-4C Phantom II

Retired from the USAF's operational inventory in April 1996, the only Phantoms still wearing Air Force markings are F-4Fs at Holloman AFB, New Mexico, and QF-4E/G full-scale aerial targets (FSATs) flying at Holloman and Tyndall AFB, Florida. However, the F-4Fs are actually owned by the German *Luftwaffe* and are operated from the base as trainers.

In 1992, the USAF selected the platform as its FSAT and Tracor Flight Systems (now Marconi Flight Systems) undertook conversion of three RF-4Cs, five F-4Es and two F-4Gs to drone configuration. Although the initial production contract specified modification of all three versions, the second production lot and all subsequent contracts covered only the QF-4G.

As part of the conversion, several systems were installed to remotely control and also allow destruction of the aircraft should it become necessary. The first live shootdown took place on 1 April 1997 and, by January 1998, QF-4E/Gs had entirely replaced Convair QF-106A/Bs as target drones.

In addition to filling that mission, the Phantoms can be flown conventionally by pilots. As such, they are often used for weapons and electronic countermeasures (ECM) development work, and as manned targets.

Boeing T-43A Specifications

Maximum Takeoff Weight:	115,500 lb (52390 kg)
Empty Weight:	60,210 lb (27311 kg)
Overall Length:	100 ft 0 in (30.48 m)
Wingspan:	93 ft 0 in (28.35 m)
Height:	37 ft 0 in (11.28 m)
Power Plant:	Two Pratt & Whitney JT8D-9 turbofans, each rated at 14,500 lb st (64.50 kN)
Maximum Fuel Capacity:	34,769 lb (15771 kg)
Cruise Speed:	500 kts (926 km/h)
Operating Range:	2,600 nm (4815 km)
Crew:	2 pilots
Accommodations:	6 instructors and 12 students
Missions:	Navigation training, medium-distance transport

McDonnell Douglas QF-4G Specifications

Maximum Takeoff Weight:	62,390 lb (28300 kg)
Overall Length:	63 ft 0 in (19.20 m)
Wingspan:	38 ft 5 in (11.71 m)
Height:	16 ft 6 in (5.03 m)
Power Plant:	Two General Electric J79-GE-17A engines, each rated at 11,810 lb st (52.53 kN) dry/17,900 lb st (79.62 kN) in afterburner
Maximum Fuel Capacity:	12,290 lb (5575 kg)
Maximum Speed:	1,290 kts (2389 km/h)
Cruise Speed:	496 kts (919 km/h)
Missions:	Unmanned target drone, weapons/ECM development, manned target

QF-4G Phantom IIs fly as target drones with the 53d Weapon Evaluation Group at Holloman AFB, New Mexico, and Tyndall AFB, Florida, as part of the Air Warfare Center's 53d Wing.

McDonnell Douglas F-15A/B/C/D Eagle

In December 1969, it was announced that the F-15 was the winner of the USAF's F-X (Fighter Experimental) competition and a single-seat F-15A, the first of 12 full-scale development (FSD) aircraft, took to the air on 27 July 1972. The first production example to follow was a twin-seat TF-15A. It was delivered to Luke AFB, Arizona, on 14 November 1974 and the Eagle reached IOC eight months later. The type's first combat-coded operator, the 1st TFW, stood up in 1977 and the two-seater was redesignated the F-15B on 1 December of that same year. Production switched to more capable F-15C/D variants in 1979. Fitted with upgraded avionics, these Eagles can carry an additional 2,000 lb (907 kg) of fuel internally and can be fitted with conformal fuel tanks. At 68,000 lb (30844 kg), the F-15C has a maximum takeoff weight some 20 percent higher than the F-15A.

To ensure the platform remained an effective fighter, a multistage improvement program (MSIP) was begun in February 1983 and the first F-15C MSIP was delivered back to the Air Force two years later. The variant received an upgraded central computer and a program-

mable armament control set that allows advanced versions of AIM-7, AIM-9 and AIM-120 missiles to be carried. Additionally, an expanded tactical electronic warfare system was incorporated that included improvements to the ALR-56C radar warning receiver and the ALQ-135 countermeasures set. The modifications were later incorporated into F-15A/Bs so the fleet was able to field common avionics.

When Eagle production began, a total run of 729 aircraft was expected. However, by the time the Air Force accepted its last example this had swelled to 905. Today, all operational F-15A/Bs are assigned to six ANG squadrons, whereas the F-15C/D fleet is operated by 13 active-duty fighter units.

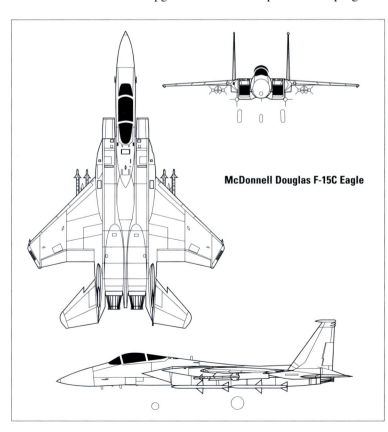

McDonnell Douglas F-15C Eagle

McDonnell Douglas F-15C Eagle Specifications	
Maximum Takeoff Weight:	68,000 lb (30844 kg)
Empty Weight:	28,600 lb (12973 kg)
Overall Length:	63 ft 9 in (19.43 m)
Wingspan:	42 ft 9.75 in (13.05 m)
Height:	18 ft 5.5 in (5.63 m)
Power Plant:	Two Pratt & Whitney F100-PW-220 turbofans, rated at 23,830 lb st (106.0 kN)
Maximum Fuel Capacity:	13,455 lb (6103 kg) internal, 11,462 lb (5199 kg) in two CFTs, 11,895 lb (5396 kg) in three external drop tanks
Maximum Speed:	1,450 kts (2685 km/h)
Cruise Speed:	495 kts (917 km/h)
Typical Combat Radius:	1,000 nm (1852 km)
Crew:	1
Armament:	M61A1 cannon, AIM-9 Sidewinder, AIM-120 AMRAAM, AIM-7 Sparrow
Mission Equipment:	AN/ALR-56C RWR, AN/ASN-109 INS, AN/ALQ-135 ICS, AN/APG-63/70 multimode radar, AN/ALQ-128 EWWS, AN/ALE-45 chaff/flare dispensers
Mission:	Air superiority fighter

Boeing (McDonnell Douglas) F-15E Strike Eagle

Although the McDonnell Douglas F-15 first was built specifically as an air-to-air fighter, the capability to field air-to-ground munitions was incorporated into its design. Following a series of air-to-ground tests, made initially with the second FSD F-15B (serial 71-0291) in July 1980, the F-15E proposal was accepted to fill the USAF's dual-role fighter (DRF) requirement. It was chosen in preference to a

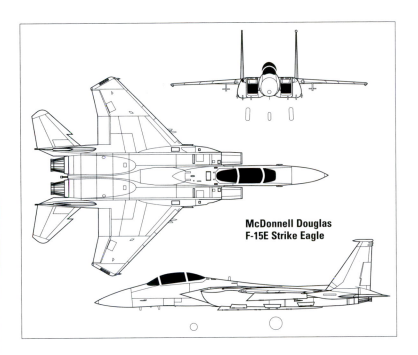

**McDonnell Douglas
F-15E Strike Eagle**

Boeing (McDonnell Douglas) F-15E Strike Eagle Specifications

Maximum Takeoff Weight:	81,000 lb (36741 kg)
Empty Weight:	31,700 lb (14379 kg)
Overall Length:	63 ft 9 in (19.43 m)
Wingspan:	42 ft 9.75 in (13.05 m)
Height:	18 ft 5.5 in (5.63 m)
Power Plant:	Two Pratt & Whitney F100-PW-220 turbofans, each rated at 14,670 lb st (65.26 kN) dry and 23,830 lb st (106.0 kN) with afterburning; or two Pratt & Whitney F100-PW-229 IPE turbofans, each rated at 17,800 lb st (79.18 kN) dry and 29,100 lb st (129.44 kN) with afterburning
Max. Fuel Capacity:	13,123 lb (5952 kg) internal, 11,462 lb (5199 kg) in two CFTs, and 11,895 lb (5396 kg) in three 600-gal (2271-lit) drop tanks
Maximum Speed:	1,433 kts (2654 km/h)
Cruise Speed:	495 kts (917 km/h)
Typical Combat Radius:	700 nm (1296 km)
Crew:	2
Armament:	M61A1 cannon; AIM-7 Sparrow; AIM-120 AMRAAM, AIM-9 Sidewinder; Mk 82 and Mk 84 GP bombs; GBU-10/12/15 guided munitions; CBU-52/58/71/87/89/90/92/93 cluster bombs; AGM-65 Maverick; AGM-88 HARM; AGM-130 EO-guided bomb
Mission Equipment:	LANTIRN AAQ-13 nav. pod and AAQ-14 targeting pod, APG-70 radar, AN/ALR-56 RWR, AN/ALQ-135 ICS, AN/ASN-109 INS, AN/ALQ-128 EWWS, AN/ALE-45 chaff/flare dispensers
Missions:	Deep-strike, interdiction and multirole fighter

proposed F-16E from General Dynamics.

Production was authorized in May 1984 and the first F-15E undertook its maiden flight on 11 December 1986. In April 1988, the 405th Tactical Training Wing (TTW) at Luke AFB, Arizona, began receiving Strike Eagles. By then it had become the replacement training unit (RTU) for the type. However, that role now belongs to the 4th FW's 333d and 334th FS at Seymour Johnson AFB, North Carolina. After the RTU received its F-15Es, deliveries began to the 3d Wing at Elmendorf AFB, Alaska; the 366th Wing at Mountain Home AFB, Idaho; and the 48th FW at RAF Lakenheath, England.

Although the Air Force had planned to operate a fleet of 392 Strike Eagles, that number was never authorized. Less than 200 examples have entered service to date, although Boeing is currently producing 17 more aircraft referred to internally as E210s. They comprise serials 96-0200 through -0205, 97-0217 through -0222, and 98-0131 through -0135. The first of these flew from Lambert – St. Louis IAP on 1 April 1999.

It seems unlikely that production of more F-15Es will be funded for the USAF as the service considers the acquisition of Lockheed Martin F-22A Raptors a higher priority. However, with that program thrown into some doubt and severe restrictions on funding imposed by the United States Congress in 1999, the situation could change.

Today, the F-15E is flown by four ACC squadrons at Seymour Johnson AFB and another at Mountain Home AFB. In addition, it is operated by one PACAF unit at Elmendorf AFB and two USAFE units flying from RAF Lakenheath.

While it retains formidable air-to-air capabilities, the F-15E can deliver up to 24,250 lb (11000 kg) of air-to-ground ordnance, including free-fall bombs, laser- and EO-guided munitions and cluster weapons.

Powered by two Pratt and Whitney F100-PW-229 IPEs (Improved Performance Engines), an F-15E Strike Eagle from the 90th FS lifts off with full afterburning from Elmendorf AFB, Alaska. A total of 81 F-15Es have been fitted with this engine, which offers 22 percent more thrust than the -220 power plant. Early on, however, the engine was prone to problems that caused reliability issues for the Air Force. Such difficulties have largely been resolved and the engine remains in service.

BOEING COMPANY/NORTHROP GRUMMAN

E-8C Joint STARS, TE-8A

In September 1985, Grumman Aerospace was contracted to produce two E-8A development aircraft as medium/long-range, battlefield surveillance platforms. Boeing refurbished three used 707-300 airliners for the purpose and the prime contractor installed the Joint STARS radar system and associated equipment. The first equipped E-8A made its maiden flight in December 1988 and, although still under development at the time, two aircraft were deployed to Saudi Arabia during Operation Desert Storm.

The current version of the platform is the E-8C, and both prototypes and production examples saw service over the Balkans in the mid- and late-1990s. Like its predecessors, each E-8C platform is based on a B707 airframe, although the refurbishing work is being undertaken by Northrop Grumman.

The E-8C's most prominent feature is a 40-foot (12.2-m) canoe-shaped radome that runs under the fuselage and houses a 24-foot (7.3-m) side-looking, phased-array antenna. It is capable of operating in wide-area-surveillance, moving-target-indicator and synthetic-aperture-radar modes, and can detect targets at ranges between 26 and 135 miles (42–217 km). As well as being able to detect, locate and track large numbers of ground vehicles, it can recognize helicopters, rotating antennas and slow-moving fixed-wing aircraft. In an eight-hour mission, one E-8C can survey almost 400,000 square miles (more than one million sq km) of surface terrain.

The first operational E-8C was delivered to the 93d Air Control Flight Wing at Warner Robins AFB, Georgia, on 11 June 1996, and the fifth example entered service in August 1999. The USAF plans to operate a fleet of between 14 and 19 Joint STARS. The two E-8A development aircraft have been redesignated TE-8A trainers.

E-8C Joint STARS, serial 90-0175, is seen here high over New Mexico undergoing testing by the AFMC. The aircraft is equipped with 17 operator consoles.

Boeing/Northrop Grumman E-8C Joint STARS Specifications

Maximum Takeoff Weight:	333,600 lb (151315 kg)
Empty Weight:	171,000 lb (77564 kg)
Overall Length:	152 ft 11 in (46.61 m)
Wingspan:	145 ft 9 in (44.43 m)
Height:	42 ft 5 in (12.93 m)
Power Plant:	Four Pratt & Whitney JT3D-3B turbofans, each rated at 18,000 lb st (80.07 kN)
Maximum Fuel Capacity:	159,560 lb (72375 kg)
Cruise Speed:	464 kts (859 km/h)
Operating Range:	5,000 nm (9260 km)
Crew:	Flight – 4, Mission – 15-18
Mission Equipment:	AN/APY-3 long-range surveillance radar, defensive electronics
Missions:	Battlefield surveillance and control

Clearly visible running along the lower fuselage of the E-9A is the radome housing surveillance and electronically steerable, phased-array radars.

de Havilland Canada E-9A Specifications

Maximum Takeoff Weight:	34,500 lb (15649 kg)
Empty Weight:	22,000 lb (9979 kg)
Overall Length:	73 ft 0 in (22.25 m)
Wingspan:	85 ft 0 in (25.91 m)
Height:	24 ft 7 in (7.49 m)
Power Plant:	Two Pratt & Whitney Canada PW120A turboprops, each rated at 2,000 shp (1491 kW)
Maximum Fuel Capacity:	5,678 lb (2576 kg)
Cruise Speed:	265 kts (491 km/h)
Operating Range:	550–1,190 nm (1019–2204 km) depending on load
Crew:	2
Mission Equipment:	AN/APS-128D surveillance and phased-array radars
Missions:	Long-range support, surveillance

BOMBARDIER AEROSPACE
(INCLUDING DE HAVILLAND CANADA AND LEARJET)

de Havilland Canada E-9A (Dash 8)

The ACC's 53d Weapon Evaluation Group at Eglin AFB, Florida, operates two highly modified de Havilland Canada DHC-8s as long-range support aircraft from Tyndall AFB, Florida. They are designated E-9As and have been modified by Sierra Research to carry an AN/APS-128D surveillance radar and an electronically steerable phased-array radar in a 30-foot (9.1-m) radome. The system is capable of simultaneously tracking five targets including missiles, target drones and aircraft.

de Havilland Canada UV-18A/B Twin Otter

First flown on 20 May 1965, the de Havilland Canada DHC-6 entered Air Force service in 1977 when two examples, designated UV-18Bs, were delivered to the USAFA. Based on the DHC-6-300 model, the aircraft are used for parachute training at Peterson AFB, Colorado. Although they carry civil registrations, each has also been assigned a military serial. During 1998, a single UV-18A was added to the Air Force fleet after it was retired from Army service in Alaska.

Learjet C-21A

Based on the Gates Learjet Model 35A business jet, the C-21A is used for priority passenger and cargo airlift and can also be adapted for medical evacuation of litter patients. In 1983, the type was selected along with the Beech C-12F to replace the CT-39A in those roles.

Built in Wichita, Kansas, the aircraft were outfitted in Tucson, Arizona, and the first of some 80 examples began reaching the USAF in April 1984. They were procured under a five-year, $175-million lease but subsequently were purchased by the Air Force. In 1986, four more were acquired for the ANG and the type now serves with five active-duty squadrons and two guard units.

de Havilland Canada UV-18A/B Twin Otter Specifications

Maximum Takeoff Weight:	12,500 lb (5670 kg)
Empty Weight:	7,415 lb (3363 kg)
Overall Length:	51 ft 9 in (15.77 m)
Wingspan:	65 ft 0 in (19.81 m)
Height:	19 ft 6 in (5.94 m)
Power Plant:	Two Pratt & Whitney Canada PT6A-27 turboprops, each rated at 620 shp (462 kW)
Maximum Fuel Capacity:	2,583 lb (1172 kg)
Cruise Speed:	175–182 kts (324–337 km/h)
Typical Operating Range:	700 nm (1296 km)
Crew:	2
Mission:	Parachute training

Operated from Peterson AFB, Colorado, the Twin Otter is used to provide parachute drop training at the USAFA.

When configured to carry passengers, the Learjet C-21A can accommodate eight. The USAF became an early operator of the type, taking delivery of at least 80 examples beginning in 1984.

Learjet C-21A Specifications

Maximum Takeoff Weight:	18,300 lb (8301 kg)
Empty Weight:	9,838 lb (4462 kg)
Overall Length:	48 ft 8 in (14.83 m)
Wingspan:	39 ft 6 in (12.04 m)
Height:	12 ft 3 in (3.73 m)
Power Plant:	Two Garrett TFE731-2-2B turbofans, each rated at 3,500 lb st (15.57 kN)
Maximum Fuel Capacity:	6,285 lb (2851 kg)
Cruise Speed:	418–460 kts (774–852 km/h)
Operating Range:	2,300 nm (4260 km)
Crew:	2
Missions:	Priority airlift, medical evacuation

CASA

CASA 212

Developed by Construcciones Aeronauticas S.A. as a short takeoff and landing (STOL) transport, the CASA 212C made its maiden flight on 26 March 1971. The 212-200 series was first flown on 30 April 1978 and the US Army is reported to have acquired several in the late 1980s. After serving as electronic test beds it is believed the surviving aircraft were transferred to the AFSOC, which currently operates at least four examples. However, these aircraft have never been assigned standard military designations.

Equipped with an air-operable hydraulic ramp and quick-change interior, the 212s operate from Pope AFB, North Carolina, and Hurlburt Field, part of the Eglin AFB complex in Florida. They are assigned to Special Operations test, training and support missions.

CASA 212 Specifications

Maximum Takeoff Weight:	16,425 lb (7450 kg)
Empty Weight:	8,333 lb (3780 kg)
Overall Length:	49 ft 11 in (15.22 m)
Wingspan:	62 ft 4 in (19.00 m)
Height:	20 ft 8 in (6.30 m)
Power Plant:	Two Allied Signal (Garrett AIResearch) TPE 331-10 501C turboprops, each rated at 900 shp (671 kW), driving four-blade propellers
Maximum Fuel Capacity:	3,527 lb (1600 kg)
Cruise Speed:	197 kts (365 km/h)
Service Ceiling:	26,000 ft (7925 m)
Maximum Operating Range:	950 nm (1759 km)
Crew:	2
Accommodations:	Up to 26 passengers/cargo
Mission:	Special Operations training and support

Operated amid some secrecy by the Air Force Special Operations Command (AFSOC), a number of CASA 212 aircraft are based at Pope AFB, North Carolina, and Hurlburt Field, Florida.

US Air Force

CESSNA AIRCRAFT

Cessna T-37B Tweet

Originating as the XT-37, which made its first flight on 12 October 1954, the T-37A entered service in 1956 as the USAF's first jet-powered trainer. It is used to instruct student pilots, navigators and tactical navigators in the fundamentals of jet handling, instrument and formation flying, as well as night sorties. It was scheduled for replacement in the late 1980s by the subsequently cancelled T-46A next-generation trainer (NGT). Instead, in 1989, it began undergoing a structural life-extension program to add a further decade of operational life. Retirement will begin as the Raytheon T-6A Texan II starts entering AETC service in 2000. At this time, the T-37B serves with nine AETC squadrons and five AFRC associate units.

The Cessna T-37 features side-by-side crew positions and was the USAF's first basic jet trainer. Uprated power plants, along with improved avionics and provision for tip tanks, gave rise to the T-37B designation in the late 1950s.

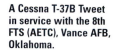

A Cessna T-37B Tweet in service with the 8th FTS (AETC), Vance AFB, Oklahoma.

Cessna T-41D Mescalero (Cessna 172)

The T-41D is a military version of the Cessna 172, equipped with modern avionics that include a GPS. It is used by the USAFA for orientation flights, flying team support and tactical navigation. The T-41A entered service with the USAF as a flight screening aircraft in 1964 and served in that role until it was replaced by the ill-fated Slingsby T-3A Firefly in 1994. The T-41C joined the academy's fleet in 1968 and was followed by the T-41D the following year. The aircraft was the subject of an upgrade in 1996 at which time new avionics and a constant-speed propeller were fitted.

Cessna 150

Three Cessna 150s have served with the USAFA since 1984 and are used for competition flying. The school competes against 130 colleges and universities in regional and national competitions, which test landing accuracy, message drops and advanced navigation. The all-metal, single-engine aircraft has a fixed-tricycle undercarriage and features side-by-side seating. All three examples are fitted with modern electronics and upgraded 150 hp engines.

The rugged little Cessna 150 continues to serve extensively as a basic trainer in both civilian and military sectors. In Air Force service, the type is still flown by the USAFA.

Cessna T-37B Tweet Specifications

Maximum Takeoff Weight:	6,600 lb (2994 kg)
Empty Weight:	3,870 lb (1755 kg)
Overall Length:	29 ft 3 in (8.92 m)
Wingspan:	33 ft 9.3 in (10.30 m)
Height:	9 ft 2.3 in (2.80 m)
Power Plant:	Two Teledyne Continental J69-T-25 engines, each rated at 1,025 lb st (4.56 kN) dry
Maximum Fuel Capacity:	2,086 lb (946 kg)
Maximum Speed:	369 kts (683 km/h)
Cruise Speed:	330 kts (611 km/h)
Operating Range:	809 nm (1498 km)
Crew:	2
Missions:	Jet-handling fundamentals; instrument, formation and night-flying

Cessna T-41D Mescalero Specifications

Maximum Takeoff Weight:	2,550 lb (1157 kg)
Empty Weight:	1,600 lb (726 kg)
Overall Length:	26 ft 6 in (8.11 m)
Wingspan:	36 ft 2 in (11.02 m)
Height:	8 ft 11 in (2.7 m)
Power Plant:	One Continental IO-360-DB piston engine rated at 210 hp (157 kW), driving a two-blade, constant-speed propeller
Maximum Speed:	158 kts (293 km/h)
Operating Range:	594 nm (1100 km)
Service Ceiling:	16,000 ft (4877 km)
Crew:	2
Missions:	USAFA flying team support, orientation flights

Cessna 150 Specifications

Maximum Takeoff Weight:	1,760 lb (798 kg)
Empty Weight:	985 lb (447 kg)
Overall Length:	23 ft 11 in (7.30 m)
Wingspan:	33 ft 4 in (10.16 m)
Height:	8 ft 6 in (2.59 m)
Power Plant:	One Textron Lycoming 0-320-E2D piston engine rated at 150 hp (112 kW), driving a two-blade propeller
Maximum Speed:	141 kts (261 km/h)
Service Ceiling:	14,000 ft (4267 m)
Operating Range:	351 nm (650 km)
Crew:	2
Mission:	Competition flying

This C-26B is operated by the ANG as a priority transport aircraft.

DE HAVILLAND CANADA (See Bombardier Aerospace)

FAIRCHILD REPUBLIC (See Lockheed Martin)

FAIRCHILD AIRCRAFT

Fairchild C-26B Metro 23 and UC-26C Merlin IVC

Obtained in 1986 as an operational support transport for the ANG, the C-26A was developed from the Fairchild Aircraft SA227AC Metro civil airliner. In all, 11 examples were purchased, followed by a number of C-26B models based on the SA227DC, which have replaced most "A" models in service. Operated exclusively by guardsmen, the Metro features quick-change passenger, medevac and cargo interiors, and is used for urgent transportation of passengers and cargo.

A single Merlin IVC was also acquired from a commercial source and modified for antidrug missions. For this purpose, an AN/APG-66 radar has been installed. In addition, at least 10 C-26Bs have been fitted with enhanced military/civil law enforcement communications, a removable reconnaissance pod with two framing cameras, a FLIR TV sensor and an operator station.

Fairchild C-26B Specifications	
Maximum Takeoff Weight:	14,500 lb (6577 kg)
Empty Weight:	9,180 lb (4164 kg)
Overall Length:	59 ft 4.25 in (18.09 m)
Wingspan:	57 ft 0 in (17.37 m)
Height:	16 ft 8 in (5.08 m)
Power Plant:	Two Garrett TPE331-121UAR turboprops, each rated at 1,119 shp (834 kW)
Maximum Fuel Capacity:	4,342 lb (1970 kg)
Cruise Speed:	250–280 kts (463–519 km/h)
Operating Range:	1600 nm (2963 km) at half payload
Crew:	2
Mission Equipment:	AN/APG-66 radar, reconnaissance pod with framing cameras and FLIR TV sensor for antidrug missions
Missions:	Priority airlift, antidrug surveillance

GENERAL ATOMICS AERONAUTICAL SYSTEMS

RQ-1A Predator

The RQ-1A Predator system comprises a medium-altitude, endurance (MAE) unmanned aerial vehicle (UAV), a ground control station and a satellite communications suite composed of two Humvees, one 20-foot satellite dish and additional equipment. Development from the earlier Gnat 750 began in January 1984 when the manufacturer

General Atomics RQ-1A Predator Specifications	
Maximum Takeoff Weight:	2,250 lb (1021 kg)
Empty Weight:	950 lb (431 kg)
Overall Length:	27 ft 0 in (8.23 m)
Wingspan:	48 ft 8 in (14.83 m)
Height:	6 ft 10.8 in (2.10 m)
Power Plant:	One Rotax four-cyl. piston engine rated at 81 hp (60.4 kW), driving a two-blade propeller
Maximum Fuel Capacity:	665 lb (302 kg)
Maximum Speed:	80 kts (148 km/h)
Service Ceiling:	25,000 ft (7620 m)
Operating Range:	400 nm (741 km)
Crew:	4 ground personnel
Mission Equipment:	Synthetic aperture radar, electro-optical and infrared sensors
Missions:	Airborne surveillance, reconnaissance, target acquisition

was given an order for 10 systems, and the first flight took place in July 1994. The Predator was deployed over Bosnia the following year even while development continued, and its highly satisfactory battlefield performance will lead to 12 systems being assigned to two reconnaissance squadrons at Indian Springs Air Force Auxiliary Airfield, Nevada. Experience gained with the RQ-1A is leading to some modifications in the craft's avionics and communications, and an ice-mitigation system is under development that will require an uprated turbocharged engine to be fitted.

GENERAL DYNAMICS
(Including Gulfstream Aerospace)

Gulfstream Aerospace C-20A/B/C Gulfstream III

In June 1983, the Gulfstream III was chosen as the replacement for the C-140B JetStar. Designated the C-20A, an initial order covered three leased aircraft, which were delivered in September of that year and purchased outright two years later. Seven C-20Bs then followed, at which time the C-20As were moved to Ramstein AB, Germany, to

With the exception of three C-20As based in Germany, the Gulfstream III fleet is located at Andrews AFB, Maryland, where it serves with the 89th AW.

replace C-140s stationed there. Differences between the two variants primarily relate to their electrical and avionics systems.

The USAF also operates three C-20Cs, termed "war order" aircraft, although little is known about them. They are thought to be equipped with hardened communications systems and will be used to transport high-ranking government officials in the event of a nuclear conflict.

Gulfstream Aerospace C-20H Gulfstream IV

In 1990, the Air Force purchased the first of two Gulfstream IVs, designated C-20Hs. They are fitted with Rolls-Royce Tay turbofans instead of Rolls-Royce Speys, which power Gulfstream IIIs, and their entry into service enabled the USAF to dispose of two C-20Bs. One went to the US Coast Guard and the other was sold to a foreign government. The type is used for special air missions by the 99th AS.

Gulfstream Aerospace C-37A Gulfstream V

After declaring the Gulfstream V the winner of its VC-X competition, the USAF ordered two of the long-range business jets in April 1997, under a $70 million contract that included options for up to four more. Significant differences between this model and earlier Gulfstreams led to assignment of a completely different designation (C-37A). In March 1999, an option for one aircraft was exercised and two more were exercised a month later.

Reports suggest the latest aircraft will be used for counterterrorism and disaster-response missions. Like the C-20 series, the C-37A fills

Gulfstream Aerospace C-20B Specifications	
Maximum Takeoff Weight:	68,200 lb (30935 kg)
Empty Weight:	38,000 lb (17237 kg)
Overall Length:	83 ft 1 in (25.32 m)
Wingspan:	77 ft 10 in (23.72 m)
Height:	24 ft 4.5 in (7.43 m)
Power Plant:	Two Rolls-Royce Spey RB.168 Mk 511-8 turbofans, each rated at 11,400 lb st (50.71 kN)
Maximum Fuel Capacity:	28,300 lb (12837 kg)
Cruise Speed:	450-500 kts (833-926 km/h)
Operating Range:	3,647 nm (6754 km)
Maximum Service Ceiling	45,000 ft (13716 m)
Crew:	Flight – 2, Mission – 3
Missions:	VIP transport, priority airlift

A pair of C-20H Gulfstream IVs serve with the 99th AS at Andrews AFB, Maryland.

the role of priority airlift for senior government and military officials but, unlike its predecessors, can be operated nonstop across the Atlantic. Both aircraft now in service are assigned to the 99th AS of the 89th AW, at Andrews AFB.

Gulfstream C-20H Specifications	
Maximum Takeoff Weight:	73,200 lb (33203 kg)
Empty Weight:	39,500 lb (17197 kg)
Overall Length:	88 ft 4 in (26.92 m)
Wingspan:	77 ft 10 in (23.72 m)
Height:	24 ft 10 in (7.57 m)
Power Plant:	Two Rolls-Royce Tay Mk 611-8 turbofans, each rated at 13,850 lb st (61.61 kN)
Maximum Fuel Capacity:	29,500 lb (13381 kg)
Cruise Speed:	454–509 kts (841–943 km/h)
Maximum Operating Range:	2,000 nm (3704 km)
Service Ceiling:	45,000 ft (13716 m)
Crew:	2
Missions:	VIP transport, priority airlift

Gulfstream C-37A Specifications	
Maximum Takeoff Weight:	90,500 lb (41050 kg)
Empty Weight:	48,000 lb (21772 kg)
Overall Length:	96 ft 5 in (29.39 m)
Wingspan:	93 ft 6 in (28.50 m)
Height:	25 ft 10 in (7.87 m)
Power Plant:	Two BMW/Rolls-Royce BR710 turbofans, each rated at 14,750 lb st (65.61 kN)
Maximum Fuel Capacity:	41,300 lb (18733 kg)
Cruise Speed:	499 kts (924 km/h)
Service Ceiling:	51,000 ft (15,545 m)
Operating Range:	6,500 nm (12038 km)
Crew:	Flight – 2, Mission – 2
Accommodations:	18 passengers
Missions:	Priority airlift, special missions

The Gulfstream V offers substantially better range than its predecessors. Two of the five examples ordered by the USAF are now in service.

IAI/GALAXY AIRCRAFT

C-38A Astra

Based on the Israeli Aircraft Industries/Galaxy Aircraft Astra SPX business jet, two military variants initially were created when Tracor Flight Systems modified and delivered two examples to the Air Force on 17 April 1998. Accommodating up to nine passengers, the C-38A features a quick-change interior that allows it to be reconfigured for aeromedical missions. The aircraft is fitted with a digital cockpit and advanced commercial systems that include a Collins ProLine 4 integrated avionics suite, UHF/VHF radios, IFF, traffic collision avoidance and global positioning systems. It also is equipped with a

terrain-aeronautical radiotelephone for passenger use.

Featuring a lower-mounted wing than that of the 1960s-era Jet Commander and IAI Westwind from which it was developed, the Astra was afforded a more spacious cabin. Its construction also made more extensive use of composite materials.

The Astra prototype flew for the first time in March 1984 and, on entering USAF service, the type replaced two Learjet C-21As previously with the District of Columbia ANG's 201st AS, located at Andrews AFB.

IAI/Galaxy Aircraft C-38A Astra, serial 94-1570, serves with
the ANG's 201st Airlift Squadron at Andrews AFB.

IAI/Galaxy Aircraft C-38A Astra Specifications

Maximum Takeoff Weight:	24,650 lb (11181 kg)
Empty Weight:	13,700 lb (6214 kg)
Overall Length:	55 ft 7 in (16.94 m)
Wingspan:	54 ft 7 in (16.64 m)
Height:	18 ft 2 in (5.54 m)
Power Plant:	Two Allied Signal TFE 731-40R-200G turbofans, each rated at 4,250 lb st (18.91 kN)
Maximum Fuel Capacity:	9,365 lb (4248 kg)
Cruise Speed:	470 kts (870 km/h)
Operating Range:	3,248 nm (6015 km)
Operating Ceiling:	45,000 ft (13716 m)
Crew:	2
Accommodations:	9 passengers
Missions:	Operational support airlift, aeromedical airlift

LOCKHEED MARTIN
(INCLUDING FAIRCHILD REPUBLIC AND GENERAL DYNAMICS)

Fairchild Republic A-10A/OA-10A Thunderbolt II

Beating out the Northrop YA-9, following the 1973
fly-off that was the culmination of the Air Force
C-X competition, the YA-10 was chosen to fill the
requirement for a close air support (CAS) platform.
The first A-10 entered service in March 1976. In all,
715 were built during the seven years that followed
and very few differences exist between the first and
last examples, something unusual for a combat aircraft. Although a number of upgrade programs were
proposed over the years, including the addition of
night-attack avionics and new engines, few came to
fruition. By 1980, the Air Force had decided to uti-
lize some aircraft for forward air control (FAC)
missions (designated OA-10As) and retire much of
the rest of the fleet. However, the less-than-
glamorous "Warthog," as it is better known, was
saved by events unfolding in the Middle East. Iraq's
invasion of Kuwait and the US and coalition
response saw the A-10 deployed for the Gulf War where it proved to
be a potent tank buster and formidable CAS asset. The platform flew
more than 8,500 missions during the conflict. Thunderbolt IIs were
subsequently called to service over Bosnia and a number remain

Although conceived for CAS missions, the "Warthog" scored its first air-to-air kills
in February 1991 against Iraqi helicopters during Operation Desert Storm.

forward deployed in Europe, in light of continuing commitments in
the Balkans.

Minor modifications have improved low-altitude safety and targeting and added NVG-compatible cockpit lighting. More significant
changes are planned. In 1998, Lockheed Martin's Federal Systems
Division became the prime contractor for future development, including the USAF's A/OA-10A Combat Upgrade Plan Integrated Details
(A-CUPID), which will mean new avionics and electronic warfare
systems for a number of Thunderbolt IIs. The project is designed to

**Fairchild Republic
A-10A Thunderbolt II**

Fairchild Republic A-10A Thunderbolt II Specifications

Maximum Takeoff Weight:	50,000 lb (22680 kg)
Empty Weight:	21,451 lb (9730 kg)
Overall Length:	53 ft 4 in (16.26 m)
Wingspan:	57 ft 6 in (17.53 m)
Height:	14 ft 8 in (4.47 m)
Power Plant:	Two General Electric TF34-GE-100 nonafterburning turbofans, each rated at 9,065 lb st (40.32 kN)
Max. Fuel Capacity:	11,110 lb (5039 kg), plus 12,150 lb (5511 kg) in three external tanks
Maximum Speed:	355 kts (657 km/h)
Cruise Speed:	274 kts (507 km/h)
Combat Radius::	250–540 nm (463–1000 km)
Crew:	1
Armament Options:	GAU-8/A Avenger seven-barrel, 30-mm Gatling gun; AIM-9L Sidewinders; AGM-65 Mavericks; 2.75-in folding-fin aircraft rockets (FFAR); Mk 82 and Mk 84 GP bombs in slick and retarded configurations; GBU-10, GBU-12 and GBU-24 laser-guided bombs; cluster munitions (CBU-52/58/71/87/89/97)
Mission Equipment:	AN/ALE-40 chaff/flare dispensers, AN/ALQ-119 and -131 jamming pods or AN/ALQ-184 ECM, AN/AAS-35 Pave Penny laser tracking pod, AN/ALR-69 radar warning receiver (RWR)
Missions:	Close air support (CAS), deep strike, forward air control (FAC)

59

US Air Force

keep the platform viable until 2028. The contractor has also teamed with Northrop Grumman to propose replacing the current engines with uprated CF-34 turbofans.

The type is currently operational with nine active-duty squadrons, six ANG and three AFRC units. Overseas, the ACC has deployed "Warthogs" to Ahmed Al Jaber AB in Kuwait, while PACAF has stationed them at Osan AB in Korea. Meanwhile, USAFE is flying the aircraft out of Spangdahlem AB, Germany.

Lockheed C-5A/B/C Galaxy

First flown on 30 June 1968, the C-5A Galaxy was the winner of the Air Force's 1964 Cargo Experimental-Heavy Logistic System (CX-HLS) competition. Capable of carrying extremely large cargoes over intercontinental distances, the strategic airlifter can take off within a distance of 8,300 feet (2530 m) when fully loaded and can come to a landing stop inside 4,900 feet (1494 m). Front and rear doors and full-width drive-on ramps facilitate loading and unloading, and the C-5's ability to "kneel" enables cargoes to be moved at truck-bed level. It is the largest transport in USAF service, having sufficient capacity to hold up to 36 standard 463L pallets. Furthermore, a troop compartment on the upper level can accommodate 73 passengers and, although it is rarely used solely as a troop transport, the cargo compartment can be reconfigured with 267 airline seats.

Stationed at Travis AFB, California, two C-5As have been modified for space/missile-related cargo carrying and are under the operational control of NASA. Designated C-5Cs, they have had their upper-deck troop compartments removed and one loading access is

Lockheed C-5B Galaxy Specifications

Maximum Takeoff Weight:	837,000 lb (379657 kg)
Empty Weight:	374,000 lb (169643 kg)
Overall Length:	247 ft 10 in (75.54 m)
Wingspan:	222 ft 8.5 in (67.88 m)
Height:	65 ft 1.5 in (19.85 m)
Power Plant:	Four General Electric TF39-GE-1C turbofans, each rated at 43,000 lb st (191.27 kN)
Maximum Fuel Capacity:	332,500 lb (150815 kg)
Maximum Payload:	261,000 lb (118387 kg)
Cruise Speed:	450–480 kts (833–889 km/h)
Operating Range at Maximum Payload:	2,982 nm (5523 km)
Crew:	6
Missions:	Strategic airlift, air drops

sealed shut, among other modifications. Deliveries of 50 slightly upgraded C-5Bs began in January 1985, after the production line was restarted. This was necessary because of a shortfall in airlift capacity. The new variant was fitted with strengthened wings and improved avionics.

In addition to six flight deck positions, a relief crew of seven can be carried on the upper forward deck, along with eight more passengers. The first Galaxy was delivered to the training unit at Altus AFB, Oklahoma, in December 1969, and the first operational aircraft went to the 437th AW at Charleston AFB, South Carolina, in June 1970. Today, the type is flying with five active-duty, one ANG and six AFRC squadrons.

Whereas the Galaxy has been the backbone of the USAF's strategic airlift fleet, aging avionics and engines have begun to plague reliability. However, tests show that 80 percent of the aircraft's structural life remains, which has prompted proposals from Lockheed Martin and General Electric to modernize the 126-airframe fleet. Under its C-5 Avionics Modernization Program (AMP), Lockheed Martin is proposing an updated digital avionics system, while GE's new power plant, based on the CF6-80C2 engine that powers the VC-25A, would increase the Galaxy's flight performance. Takeoff thrust would be enhanced some 22 percent, reducing the takeoff roll by 30 percent and improving the rate of climb substantially. New engines would also raise the initial cruise ceiling from 24,000 feet (7315 m) to 33,000 feet (10058 m). However, it is highly unlikely funds will be available to re-engine the Galaxy before 2003.

The Lockheed C-5's lack of reliability has become a problem for the Air Force, which relies heavily on its largest airlifter.

A C-5A of the ANG's 105th AW, based at Stewart IAP/ANGB, Newburgh, New York.

Fairchild Republic A-10A Thunderbolt II
Unit: USAF Weapons School (USAFWS), 57th Wing
Base: USAF Tactics and Weapons Center, Nellis AFB, Nevada

Walter Wright

One of 715 "Warthogs" built, serial 81-0958 is assigned to development work at the USAFWS and has accumulated several thousand flight hours as a test platform.

The 'Firebirds' of the 517th AS belong to PACAF's 3d Wing and fly the C-130H from Elmendorf AFB, Alaska.

Lockheed/Lockheed Martin C-130E/H/J, LC-130H Hercules

To meet the Air Force's 1951 requirement for a medium-size, tactical airlifter, Lockheed successfully proposed its Hercules design. The YC-130 made its maiden flight on 23 August 1954 and deliveries of the C-130A began in December 1956. Arguably the most successful military transport aircraft of all time, the rugged Hercules is capable of operating from dirt airstrips and making low-level drops.

Over the years, a range of airlift and specialized platform variants has evolved and more continue to be developed today. The oldest model still in service is the C-130E, which began production in 1962. Upgraded engines were subsequently fitted to a number of these aircraft, which led to the C-130H, the most numerous of the variants currently in service. This platform is also the basis for a number of other permanent and temporary models flown in a variety of roles. Besides air drops and ground resupply missions, cargo variants are called upon to provide aeromedical airlift and aerial spraying while others are used for firefighting. Designated LC-130Hs, a small number are equipped with skis for operations in the polar regions and two more H models will be similarly equipped when Raytheon completes modification of two LC-130Rs that once flew with the US Navy.

The latest Hercules variant is the C-130J, which has been developed as a follow-on to the C-130H. It flew for the first time on 5 April 1996 and a number of the world's air forces have placed orders for the advanced transport. The USAF received its first example on 28 January 1999 and the type has now entered service with both the AFRC and ANG. Features include new turboprop engines and propellers, and a completely redesigned cockpit.

Lockheed/Lockheed Martin HC-130H/N/P, MC-130P, WC-130H/J

Based on the C-130E, the HC-130H flew for the first time in 1964 and was developed to perform search and rescue (SAR) missions, to recover personnel and satellites using a ground recovery system known as Fulton STARS, and as a command and control platform. HC-130N and HC-130P variants followed, which were designed to extend the range of combat helicopters by acting as in-flight refuelers. The HC-130N was not equipped with Fulton STARS, however. In the late 1980s, all earlier HC-130Hs were upgraded to HC-130P configuration and the N designation was reused for a new variant more closely configured to the original HC-130N.

HC-130P/Ns serving with the AFSOC have undergone a number of modifications to improve their operational effectiveness. These have included installation of a FLIR system and NVG-compatible cockpit lighting, and the modified aircraft carry the designation MC-130P Combat Talon. The rest of the Air Force's HC-130 fleet is currently undergoing a series of upgrades to its navigation, communications, threat detection and countermeasures systems but the Air Force would like to replace these aircraft with a new variant of the C-130J in due course.

A number of early HC-130Hs were modified as weather reconnaissance platforms and are designated WC-130Hs. Universally known as "Hurricane Hunters," they are flown into tropical cyclones and hurricanes at altitudes between 500 and 10,000 feet (150-3033 m) to collect data inside storms. The information is relayed by satellite to the National Hurricane Center in Miami, Florida, and is used to help determine a storm's intensity and probable track. The first example was delivered to the AFRC in October 1999 and WC-130Js have now begun replacing WC-130Hs.

Lockheed Martin C-130J Hercules Specifications	
Maximum Takeoff Weight:	175,000 lb (79379 kg)
Empty Weight:	75,562 lb (34274 kg)
Overall Length:	97 ft 9 in (29.79 m)
Wingspan:	132 ft 7 in (40.41 m)
Height:	38 ft 9 in (11.81 m)
Power Plant:	Four Rolls-Royce Allison AE2100D3 turboprops, each rated at 4,591 shp (3424 kW)
Maximum Fuel Capacity:	45,900 lb (20820 kg)
Cruise Speed:	348 kts (645 km/h)
Operating Range:	2,833 nm (5247 km)
Service Ceiling:	30,600 ft (9327 m)
Crew:	3
Accommodations:	92 troops, 64 paratroops or 74 litters
Mission:	Intratheater airlift

PACAF's 374th AW operates C-130E/H models from Yokota AB, Japan. This aircraft was photographed during a visit to Singapore's Changi Airport.

Although seen here at Nellis AFB, Nevada, this MC-130E serves with the AFRC at Duke Field, Florida.

Lockheed MC-130E/H Combat Talon I/II

Tasked with transporting Special Operations personnel and equipment into hostile areas, day or night and in all weathers, Combat Talons are vital to AFSOC's activities. To support helicopters undertaking deep penetration missions, the MC-130E is also capable of carrying tanking pods. Additionally, both variants are equipped with in-flight refueling receptacles; terrain-following/avoidance radar; an INS, GPS and FLIR; and a high-speed, low-level, aerial delivery system. However, the Fulton STARS that once equipped a number of MC-130Es is no longer operational.

Whereas all MC-130Es are operated by one AFSOC active-duty squadron and one AFRC unit, the MC-130Hs fly with three active-duty AFSOC units. One is at Hurlburt Field in Florida, another is stationed at RAF Mildenhall, Great Britain, and the third is at Kadena AB in Japan.

Among electronic countermeasures carried by the AC-130U Spectre are AN/ALE-40 chaff/flare dispensers. The type saw service in Operations Just Cause and Desert Storm.

Lockheed/Lockheed Martin EC-130E/H/J

To support its electronic warfare missions, the Air Force flies a number of Hercules variants that are normally based at Davis-Monthan AFB, Arizona. They include the EC-130E airborne battlefield command and control center (ABCCC). During operations, the ABCCC provides a link between ground commanders, airborne reconnaissance and offensive air assets, headquarters units and the national command authority.

The EC-130E Commando Solo is equipped to conduct psychological operations and make civil affairs broadcasts over regular radio, television and military communications bands. Secondarily, it flies command and control communications countermeasures jamming missions and some limited intelligence gathering. These aircraft are operated by the Pennsylvania ANG's 193d SOW on behalf of the AFSOC, but will be augmented and subsequently replaced by EC-130Js modified for the Commando Solo mission.

The EC-130H version is known as the Compass Call and serves with two ACC units at Davis-Monthan AFB. Its primary purpose is jamming enemy command and control communications.

Each of the EC-130 variants is equipped with specialized avionics for its specific mission, and the first of three EC-130Js was accepted by the Air Force on 17 October 1999. These new aircraft will serve with the 193d SOW beginning in mid-2001, by which time installation and testing of the type's sophisticated electronics should be completed.

Lockheed AC-130H/U Spectre

AC-130 gunship platforms were developed for close air support during the Vietnam War when existing C-130s were fitted with side-firing weapons. The Hercules were designated AC-130As and AC-130Es. Today, eight AC-130H and 13 AC-130U models serve with the AFSOC's 16th and 4th SOS, respectively, at Hurlburt Field, Florida. These squadrons are part of the 16th SOW.

H models are re-engined AC-130Es fitted for in-flight refueling,

Lockheed MC-130P Hercules Specifications

Maximum Takeoff Weight:	155,000 lb (70307 kg)
Overall Length:	98 ft 9 in (30.10 m)
Wingspan:	132 ft 7 in (40.41 m)
Height:	38 ft 6 in (11.74 m)
Power Plant:	Four Allison T56-A-15 turboprops, each rated at 4,910 shp (3661 kW)
Cruise Speed:	250 kts (463 km/h)
Operating Range:	3,500+ nm (6482+ km)
Service Ceiling:	33,000 ft (10058 m)
Crew:	8
Missions:	Special Operations support, aerial refueling

Lockheed MC-130H Combat Talon II Specifications
(Largely per MC-130P except as shown below)

Overall Length:	99 ft 9 in (30.40 m)
Cruise Speed:	260 kts (482 km/h)
Operating Range:	2,616 nm (4845 km)
Crew:	9
Accommodations:	75 troops or 52 paratroops
Mission Equipment:	AN/APQ-170 ground-mapping, terrain-following radar
Missions:	Special Operations

Lockheed EC-130E Commando Solo Specifications
(Largely per MC-130P except as shown below)

Overall Length:	100 ft 6 in (30.63 m)
Cruise Speed:	260 kts (482 km/h)
Operating Range:	1,825+ nm (3380+ km)
Service Ceiling:	20,000 ft (6096 m)
Crew:	11
Mission Equipment:	Specialized electronic warfare suites
Missions:	Psychological warfare, electronic intelligence

and the type has seen service during the last 15 years in operations over Panama, Grenada, the Persian Gulf, Somalia and the Balkans. Development of the AC-130U began in 1988 and the first example flew on 20 December 1990, having been created from a newly built C-130H (serial 87-0128). It came on line in 1995 with a slightly different Rockwell-developed weapons configuration, although both variants pack impressive firepower. The cannon carried by the AC-130U is self-contained and fires beltless ammunition, obviating the need for someone to clear away spent casings that could cause it to jam. Consequently, one less crewman is required.

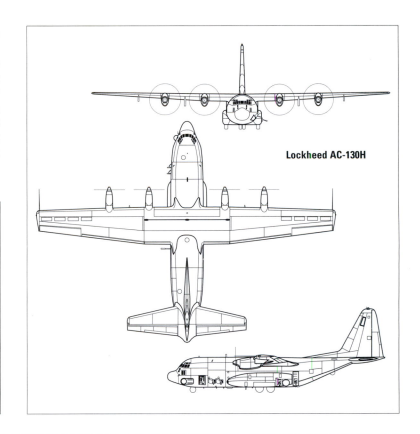

Lockheed AC-130H

Lockheed AC-130H/U Spectre Specifications
(Largely per C-130P except as shown below)

Maximum Takeoff Weight:	155,000-175,000 lb (70307-79379 kg)
Empty Weight:	72,892 lb (33063 kg)
Maximum Speed:	328 kts (607 km/h)
Maximum Cruise Speed:	307 kts (569 km/h)
Operating Range:	4,213 nm (7803 km)
Service Ceiling:	34,000 ft (10363 m)
Accommodation:	AC-130H – 14, AC-130U – 13
Armament:	AC-130H – Two M61A1 Vulcan cannons, One 40-mm L-60 Bofors cannon, One 105-mm M102 howitzer
	AC-130U – One 25-mm GE GAU-12 gatling gun, One 40-mm L-60 Bofors, One 105-mm M102 howitzer
Mission Equipment:	AN/AAQ-145 LLLTV, AN/APQ-180 radar (AC-130U),
Mission:	Close air support

Lockheed C-141B/C StarLifter

Making its first flight on 17 December 1963, the C-141A began squadron operations in April 1965 and soon became the Air Force's airlift "workhorse." Of slender design for a cargo carrier, the type's limitations were soon apparent and, often, loads were limited more by volume than by weight. Production of this model ended in 1967 but Lockheed began a program to stretch the aircraft by 23 feet in the mid-1970s. This had the effect of adding 30 percent to the type's cargo-carrying capacity. At the same time, an in-flight refueling receptacle was added.

The modified transport was designated the C-141B and the first example reached the USAF in December 1979. Conversion of 271 aircraft was completed by 1982. Separately, 13 StarLifters received equipment to enable them to perform the Special Operations Low Level (SOLL) mission. Included were upgraded navigation and communications systems, a FLIR turret, RWR, infrared and missile plume detectors. The role of these enhanced airlifters is covert insertion, resupply and extraction of Special Operations forces.

On 31 October 1998, the first of 64 C-141Cs was rolled out at Robins AFB, Georgia. This variant is the result of an upgrade that added a digital "glass" cockpit to the StarLifter, along with updated flight controls, a GPS and defensive countermeasures. The modifications were developed by Raytheon/E-Systems of Waco, Texas, in conjunction with WR-ALC. They were scheduled for completion during the latter half of 1999.

The initial operator of the C-141C is the 452d AMW at March ARB, California, and the variant is expected to remain in service through 2004 or 2005. At that point, the last examples should be replaced by C-17As. Currently, C-141B/Cs are flying with six active-duty, nine AFRC and two ANG squadrons, although two units are now transitioning to the Globemaster III.

The C-141B incorporates a 23-ft "plug" that added 30 percent more carrying capacity. Heavily tasked during the Gulf War, the Air Force's StarLifter fleet is being replaced by new C-17A Globemaster IIIs.

Lockheed C-141B StarLifter Specifications

Maximum Takeoff Weight:	343,000 lb (155580 kg)
Empty Weight:	144,500 lb (65544 kg)
Overall Length:	168 ft 3 in (51.31 m)
Wingspan:	159 ft 11 in (48.74 m)
Height:	39 ft 3 in (11.96 m)
Power Plant:	Four Pratt & Whitney TF33-P-7 turbofans, each rated at 21,000 lb st (93.41 kN)
Maximum Fuel Capacity:	23,592 US gal (89305 lit)
Maximum Payload:	90,880 lb (44851 kg)
Cruise Speed:	430-492 kts (796-911 km/h)
Operating Range (Depending on load):	2,550-5,550 nm (4723-10279 km)
Service Ceiling:	41,500 ft (12649 m)
Crew:	5
Missions:	Inter-theater airlift, Special Operations Low Level (SOLL) support

Lockheed AC-130H Spectre
Unit: 16th Special Operations Squadron (SOS), 16th Special Operations Wing (SOW)
Base: Hurlburt Field, Florida

Mark Styling

USAF.
96575

"Wicked Wanda" is one of eleven AC-130H gunships converted from AC-130E aircraft. Besides two M61A1 Vulcan cannons, it is fitted with a 40-mm L-60 Bofors cannon, capable of firing 100 rounds per minute, and a 105-mm M102 howitzer with a firing rate of six to 10 rounds per minute.

US Air Force

Lockheed Martin (General Dynamics) F-16A/B/C/D and F-16A/B(ADF) Fighting Falcon

Developed as part of the Lightweight Fighter (LWF) program, the General Dynamics model 401 took to the air as the YF-16 on 2 February 1974 and was selected over the Northrop YF-17 in a fly-off on 13 January 1975. The type was subsequently chosen as the basis for the USAF's air combat fighter (ACF) program, and the F-16A made its maiden flight on 8 December 1976. The 58th Tactical Training Wing at Luke AFB, Arizona, was the first unit to fly the fighter on 17 August 1978, whereas the first operational F-16A was received by the 388th Tactical Fighter Wing at Hill Air Force Base, Utah, on 6 January 1979. The Fighting Falcon is more commonly referred to as the "Viper" by its crews.

During FY83 production switched to the F-16C, equipped with the AN/APG-68 radar, modified cockpit controls and displays, and the first example was delivered on 19 July 1984. The Block 30 version and subsequent F-16C/Ds can be powered by the Pratt & Whitney F100 or General Electric F110 turbofans, although the two engines are not interchangeable.

In October 1986, General Dynamics was awarded a contract to modify 270 F-16As to Air Defense Fighter (ADF) configuration, which saw incorporation of new radios, an identification spotlight, two 600-gallon external fuel tanks and a modified identification friend or foe (IFF) system. In addition, design changes made to the AN/APG-66 radar allowed radar-guided AIM-7 and AIM-120 missiles to be carried. ADFs replaced F-106s and F-4s assigned to the continental air defense mission. The LANTIRN navigation and targeting system became operational on the "Viper" in December 1988.

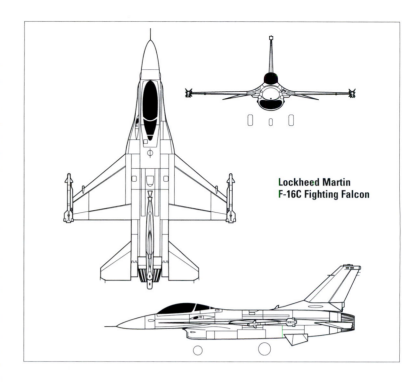

Lockheed Martin F-16C Fighting Falcon

F-16As remain assigned to three ANG units only, while the ADF variant is assigned to three additional ANG squadrons. However, a single USAF unit operates F-16As owned by the Republic of China Air Force, which are used to train Taiwanese crews. F-16C/Ds are currently operational with 30 active-duty, 22 ANG and four AFRC squadrons.

Lockheed Martin (General Dynamics) F-16C Specifications

Maximum Takeoff Weight (Block 50/52):	42,300 lb (19187 kg)
Empty Weight (Block 50/52):	18,600 lb (8437 kg)
Overall Length:	49 ft 4 in (15.04 m)
Wingspan (excl. missiles):	31 ft 0 in (9.45 m)
Height:	16 ft 8.5 in (5.09 m)
Power Plant:	One General Electric F100-GE-129 turbofan rated at 29,000 lb st (129.0 kN) with afterburning; or one Pratt & Whitney F100-PW-229 turbofan rated at 229,100 lb st (129.4 kN) with afterburning
Max. Fuel Capacity (Block 50/52):	Internal – 7,162 lb (3249 kg) External (3 drop tanks) – 6,760 lb (3066 kg)
Maximum Speed:	1,150 kts (2130 km/h)
Typical Combat Radius:	300 nm (556 km)
Crew:	1
Mission Equipment:	AN/APG-68 multimode radar, Depending on Block designation – AN/AAS-13 LANTIRN nav. pod, AN/AAS-14 LANTIRN targeting pod, AN/ASQ-213 HARM targeting pod
Armament:	M61A1 20-mm cannon, AIM-9 Sidewinder, AIM-7 Sparrow, AIM-120 AMRAAM, AFGM-88 HARM, GBU-series LG bombs (with LANTIRN)
Missions:	Multirole fighter, SEAD

An F-16A belonging to the 'Happy Hooligans' of the ANG's 178th FS.

An F-16C carrying a GBU-24/A Paveway III low-level, laser-guided bomb.

An F-16B from the 416th FLTS flying over Edwards AFB, California, on 5 February 1999, during a celebration to mark the 25th anniversary of the Fighting Falcon's first flight. To date, more than 3,900 F-16s have been built and delivered to the air forces of some 20 nations, making it the most popular jet fighter of all time.

Two Lockheed Martin F-22A Raptor EMD aircraft (91-4001 and 91-4002) are currently undergoing flight and systems testing at Edwards AFB, California. The 1999 decision of the US Congress to fund only a small number of additional development aircraft for the time being, means the future of the program is in some doubt. Viewed by the Air Force as the "backbone" of its planned fighter force by 2020, the government has signalled it believes there are other priorities.

Lockheed Martin F-22A Raptor

On 23 April 1991, the YF-22 was selected over the Northrop-McDonnell Douglas YF-23 as winner of the USAF's Advanced Tactical Fighter (ATF) competition. The first of nine engineering and manufacturing development (EMD) F-22As subsequently made its maiden flight from Marietta, Georgia, on 7 September 1997. The EMD batch will be followed by two production-representative test vehicles (PRTVs), which are scheduled to fly in November 2001 and January 2002, respectively.

The USAF wants to acquire 339 F-22As to replace its fleet of F-15A/B/C/D air superiority fighters, and had hoped to see low-rate initial production (LRIP) begin with a funding provision in the FY00 defense budget. However, in mid-1999 a number of US congressmen attempted to cut off future funding for the F-22 program on the basis the new jet was not meeting expectations and because they felt the Air Force should be pursuing other priorities. As adopted, the budget did include funding for six additional F-22As and long-lead funding for FY01 LRIP. Rather than LRIP Raptors, however, the six authorized aircraft will be development models.

Besides prohibiting LRIP aircraft in FY00, language in the defense bill also precludes any more examples until an F-22A equipped with Block 3.0 software completes a successful flight. This version of the software integrates the aircraft and its weapon, navigation, counter-measures and communications systems. In addition, use of the

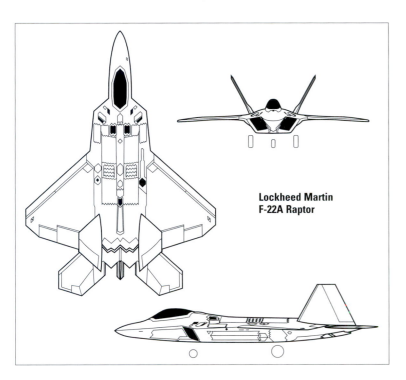

Lockheed Martin F-22A Raptor

Lockheed F-22A Raptor Specifications

Maximum Takeoff Weight:	Est. 60,000 lb (27,216 kg)
Empty Weight:	Est. 30,000 lb (13,608 kg)
Overall Length:	62 ft 1 in (18.92 m)
Wingspan:	44 ft 6 in (13.56 m)
Height:	16 ft 5 in (5.00 m)
Power Plant:	Two Pratt & Whitney F119-PW-100 turbofans with thrust vectoring, each rated at approximately 35,000 lb st (155.69 kN)
Maximum Fuel Capacity:	N/A
Maximum Speed:	Mach 2+
Cruise Speed:	668 kts (1237 km/h)
Operating Range:	N/A
Service Ceiling:	Est. 50,000 ft (15240 m)
Crew:	1
Mission Equipment:	AN/APG-77 multimode radar
Armament:	Internal – AIM-120C, AIM-9, GBU-32 JDAM; External – Provision for additional stores on four wing stations, M61A2 20-mm cannon
Mission:	Air dominance fighter

advance procurement funding is banned until the defense secretary is able to certify the F-22 has met all of the criteria specified by the 1999 Defense Acquisition Board. This means its avionics, stealth and weapon-delivery performance must match the aircraft's design requirements.

The six aircraft funded in FY00 bring the authorized total to 17, including the EMD and PRTV examples, and the US Congress has mandated that the USAF cannot build more than 17 flight-capable test vehicles. If all requirements are met, the type should enter production in 2001. Meanwhile, the test program being conducted by the 411th FLTS with serials 91-4001 and 91-4002 continues at Edwards AFB, California, and the two aircraft combined had accumulated 443 flight-test hours as of early November 1999. In the spring of 2000 they will be joined by 91-4003, which came off the Marietta production line on 22 May 1999. It is receiving structural instrumentation and undergoing a series of ground tests.

There is speculation that the combat loss of an F-117A over Serbia during Operation Allied Force might have been the result of it being banked too sharply. This could have resulted in the belly of the Stealth Fighter returning a "signature" that allowed the aircraft to be detected on radar.

Sheep' of the 8th FS and the 'Flying Knights' of the 9th FS. Both units saw action during the 1991 Gulf War and that conflict proved, without a doubt, the value of the Nighthawk's mission. Since that time, the fleet has been the subject of a number of important upgrades that have added considerably to the lethality of the platform. The only combat loss was over Serbia in 1999, during Operation Allied Force. The pilot ejected safely and was quickly rescued after his aircraft was hit by a surface-to-air missile (SAM).

Lockheed F-117A Nighthawk

Following evaluation of two proof-of-concept Have Blue demonstrators, which included initial taxi tests by HB 1001 in November 1977 at Groom Lake, Nevada, and an initial flight on 1 December, Lockheed Advanced Development Projects was awarded a contract to develop the F-117 Stealth Fighter. Amid strict secrecy, work progressed quickly at the "Skunk Works" in Burbank. Just 31 months after the November 1978 decision was taken to proceed with full-scale development, the Nighthawk flew for the first time on 18 June 1982. That aircraft was one of five full-scale development (FSD) examples that began reaching the USAF two months later. They were received by a new and top secret operating unit, the 4450th Tactical Group, located at the remote base at Tonopah, Nevada. IOC was achieved in October 1983.

Incredibly, the program remained secret for 10 years even though the stealthy new jet was in full service for most of that time. A cover was provided for operations at the base, the official response being that a team was flying A-7 Corsairs to conduct avionics tests. In all, 59 F-117As were built and the last example was delivered to the Air Force during the summer of 1990. This figure was predicated on two 18-aircraft frontline squadrons, a training unit, inventory backups and attrition replacements.

Today, all operational aircraft are at Holloman AFB, New Mexico, serving two squadrons with the 49th FW. They comprise the 'Black

Lockheed F-117A Nighthawk Specifications

Maximum Takeoff Weight:	52,500 lb (23814 kg)
Empty Weight:	29,500–30,000 lb (13381–13608 kg)
Overall Length:	65 ft 11 in (20.09 m)
Wingspan:	43 ft 4 in (13.21 m)
Height:	12 ft 5 in (3.78 m)
Power Plant:	Two General Electric F404-GE-F1D2 nonafterburning turbofans, each rated at 10,800 lb st (48.04 kN)
Maximum Fuel Capacity:	N/A
Maximum Speed:	600± kts (1111± km/h)
Cruise Speed:	500 kts (926 km/h)
Typical Combat Radius:	600+ nm (1111 km)
Crew:	1
Mission Equipment:	Infrared acquisition and targeting system (IRADS), laser designator
Armament:	GBU-10 Paveway II LGB, GBU-27 Paveway III LGB, GPS-guided weapons capabilities being added include JDAM and JSOW
Missions:	Deep strike (employing Low Observables)

The 410th FLTS, belonging to Air Force Materiel Command's Air Force Flight Test Center at Edwards AFB, California, operates the YF-117A from AF Plant 2 at Palmdale.

Lockheed Martin F-117A Nighthawk

Lockheed Martin F-117A Nighthawk
Unit: 'Black Sheep' of the 8th FS, 49th FW
Base: Holloman AFB, New Mexico

Stealth Fighter, serial 85-0819, flew 30 missions during Operation Desert Storm bearing the name "Raven Beauty."

Lockheed Martin F-117A Nighthawk
Unit: 'Nightstalkers' of the 37th FW
Base: Tonopah Test Range, Nevada

As '"Mad Max" serial 84-0825 was deployed to Saudi Arabia for Operation Desert Storm and amassed 33 strike missions.

Mark Styling

US Air Force

Lockheed U-2S/TU-2S Dragon Lady

A true product of the Cold War, the Lockheed U-2 was designed to penetrate enemy airspace and gather photographic and electronic intelligence by flying too high for Soviet fighters and surface-to-air missiles to be a threat. The first flight, which was undertaken by the CIA, took place on 19 June 1956 over what was then East Germany. Although 70,000 feet represented a safe height for very early operations, the Soviet Union was forced to develop a missile capable of bringing down the U-2. Followed by much publicity, Francis Gary Powers was shot down near Sverdlovsk, Russia, on 1 May 1960. The event caused significant embarrassment for President Dwight Eisenhower who had authorized the overflight.

In 1967, the larger U-2R variant entered Air Force service along

Serial 80-1096 is with the 9th Reconnaissance Wing at Beale AFB, California. Following a recent re-engining program, the Air Force now operates only U-2S and TU-2S models.

with a two-seat training version designated the TU-2R. The larger airframe was essential to enable more intelligence gathering equipment to be carried. In 1992, a program was begun to re-engine all aircraft with a General Electric F118-GE-F100 turbofan in place of the Pratt & Whitney J75-P-13B turbojet. The GE engine provides the aircraft with 15% greater endurance and allows it to operate at altitudes up to 80,000 feet (24400 m), which the earlier power plant could not support.

Redesignated the U-2S and TU-2S, the newly engined aircraft began re-entering ACC service in late 1994. Today, the type serves solely with the 9th Reconnaissance Wing at Beale AFB, California, which maintains a detachment at Akrotiri, Cyprus, and a squadron (the 5th RS) at Osan AB, Korea. In addition, the 363d ERS (a rotational unit) is attached to the 363d Aerospace Expeditionary Wing, which is operating from Prince Sultan AB, Saudi Arabia.

NORTHROP GRUMMAN (Including Teledyne Ryan)

Northrop B-2A Spirit

With the range and ability to penetrate defended airspace and strip away enemy air defenses, command-and-control nodes and other targets like storage and production facilities for weapons of mass destruction, the B-2A is critical to the USAF's warfighting strategy. Capable of precision drops of conventional munitions, the Stealth Bomber is also a key element of the nation's nuclear force.

Development of the B-2A began in strict secrecy in November 1981 when Northrop was awarded a $7.3-billion contract to develop the advanced technology bomber (ATB) intended as a replacement for the B-1B Lancer. It covered six engineering, manufacturing and development (EMD) aircraft and two static-test articles. At that time, 132 production aircraft were envisaged. The design drew from Jack Northrop's early work on the flying wing concept, pursued decades earlier, plus studies conducted on remote-piloted vehicles and on reducing radar cross sections. It represented a radical departure from earlier bombers.

As a subsonic aircraft possessing advanced stealth characteristics, the Spirit is capable of flying long-distance missions without being detected. With this in mind, it was conceived during the Cold War years as a weapon capable of destroying Soviet intercontinental ballistic missile sites before a missile attack against the United States could be mounted. However, even before the first example rolled off the production line, the Soviet Union had collapsed. With this event went many of the perceived threats the bomber was designed to counter. As a result, the USAF was forced to rethink the mission profiles of its entire fleet

All operational B-2A Stealth Bombers are assigned to the 509th BW at Whiteman AFB, Missouri. The wing will have 20 Block 30-configured aircraft in service by mid-2000.

of strategic bombers. Coupled with this, significant cost escalations helped drive a decision to reduce the number of aircraft from 132 to 75 and, ultimately, to just 15 examples. However, this number was later raised to 20 and then to 21 aircraft so that two full squadrons could be equipped. The type was displayed for the first time on 22 November 1988 at Air Force Plant 42, Palmdale, California. The first flight by a B-2A took place on 17 July 1989.

First entering service with the ACC on 17 December 1993, the B-2A became operational in 1997 when initial aircraft were delivered in Block 10 configuration with limited combat capabilities. At that time the Spirit was capable of carrying 2000-lb Mk 84 conventional bombs or gravity nuclear weapons. Subsequent Block 20 aircraft had the capability to launch GPS-aided nuclear and conventional munitions. The fleet is currently the subject of a Block 30 upgrade, which is adding more advanced systems to provide low-observable combat qualities and dramatically reduce its vulnerability to threats. Compared with the earlier Block configurations, the Stealth Bomber is now being equipped with almost double the number of radar modes. Initially fitted with first-generation terrain-following and global-positioning navigation systems, the aircraft is receiving better communications, situational awareness and advanced targeting systems. By mid-2000 the entire fleet will be Block 30 configured, which means all of the bombers will be fully combat-capable.

The type's deployment in operations over the Balkans during 1999, as part of Operation Allied Force, represented the Stealth Bomber's combat debut and quickly validated the concept of stealthy, long-distance precision strikes. During 35-hour, nonstop sorties that took the bomber from Whiteman AFB in Missouri to the skies over Serbia and then back home, B-2As made precision-drops on selected targets within cities and military facilities elsewhere. These missions were designed to damage Serbia's infrastructure severely and cripple the ability of its military forces to mount attacks against ethnic population groups in Kosovo. In all, such operations accounted for one percent of the aerial missions flown by NATO and 11 percent of the bomb load dropped during the conflict. Excluding low-observable maintenance, related primarily to the radar-absorbent materials used on the surface of the bomber, the Air Force reported a mission-capable rate of 75 percent during the 78-day conflict.

The Stealth Bomber has two side-by-side weapons bays, each capable of holding a single rotary launcher or two bomb racks. Like the Common Strategic Rotary Launcher (CSRL) employed on the B-52H and the Conventional Rotary Launcher (CRL) fitted to the B-1B, the B-2A's rotary launcher can hold up to eight weapons. Ejector racks can be installed in staggered positions, forward and aft, to allow weapon-fin clearance. Two types of bomb rack can carry 20 500-lb (227-kg) weapons in four rows of five, or nine 1,000-lb (454-kg) bombs in three rows of three. Two racks can equip each bay.

A fleet of 19 B-2As currently serves two squadrons with the 509th Bomb Wing at Whiteman AFB, Missouri: the 393d BS and 394th CTS. The wing is scheduled to receive its 20th aircraft in late 2000 but the last example will continue to be used for test work at Edwards AFB, California, for another two years.

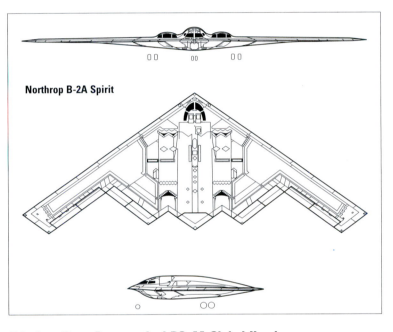

Northrop B-2A Spirit

Teledyne Ryan Aeronautical RQ-4A Global Hawk

Originally known as the Tier 2+ UAV, the RQ-4A was one of two high-altitude, high-endurance vehicles developed by the Defense Advanced Research Projects Agency (DARPA). It flew for the first time on 28 February 1998 and is undergoing flight tests at Edwards AFB, California. The UAV can carry a 2,000-lb (907-kg) payload in its large sensor bays for missions lasting as long as 42 hours. Sensors include a synthetic aperture radar (SAR), and infrared (IR) and electro-optical (EO) systems. Controllers on the ground will be able to operate two sensors simultaneously while viewing single or multiple targets, and coverage from any two can be transmitted to ground controllers at one time via satellite datalink or line-of-sight. Up to 40,000 square miles (103600 sq km) can be surveyed daily.

Teledyne Ryan Aeronautical RQ-4A Global Hawk Specifications

Maximum Takeoff Weight:	26,500 lb (12020 kg)
Empty Weight:	14,500 lb (6577 kg)
Overall Length:	44 ft 4.75 in (13.53 m)
Wingspan:	116 ft 2.5 in (35.42 m)
Height:	15 ft 2.5 in (4.64 m)
Power Plant:	One Rolls-Royce Allison AWE3007H turbofan, rated at 7,600 lb st (33.81 kN)
Maximum Fuel Capacity:	14,500 lb (6577 kg)
Maximum Speed:	350 kts (648 km/h)
Service Ceiling:	65,000 ft (19812 m)
Operating Range:	11,731 nm (21726 km)
Crew:	4 (ground)
Mission Equipment:	Synthetic aperture radar, moving target indicator, infrared sensors, AN/ALR-69 radar warning receiver (RWR), AN/ALE-50 towed decoys
Missions:	Airborne surveillance, target acquisition

US Air Force

Northrop T-38A/AT-38B Talon and Boeing/Northrop Grumman T-38C Talon

The YT-38 was developed from the Northrop model N-156 lightweight fighter and was first flown on 10 April 1959. Production of the T-38A began two years later and more than 1,100 examples were built during the ensuing 12 years. Some 300 remain in service today.

The Talon is one of three jet aircraft used in the USAF's Undergraduate Pilot Training (UTP) program that enables students to gain supersonic techniques, as well as practice aerobatics, formation, night and instrument flying. It also serves as a platform for instruction in cross-country navigation. Besides the standard T-38A, the USAF operates a number of AT-38Bs as lead-in fighter trainers under the Introduction to Fighter Fundamental (IFF) program. This aircraft is equipped with a gunsight and has the ability to carry a limited number of training weapons on the centerline station normally reserved for external fuel or travel pods.

The Talon is currently undergoing a structural life extension and avionics update under modernization programs called Pacer Classic and the Avionics Upgrade Program (AUP). They will bring T-38As and AT-38Bs up to a single configuration for the purpose of enabling the Talon to remain in useful service through 2010. After modification the type is redesignated the T-38C.

A small number of T-38As are assigned to ACC as companion trainers for the B-2A, F-117A and U-2S programs, and to AFMC for testing and training at Edwards AFB, California. The majority of T-38As and all of the AT-38Bs serve with the AETC and the AFRC, however, at five training bases.

Northrop T-38A/AT-38B Talon Specifications

Maximum Takeoff Weight:	12,050 lb (5466 kg)
Empty Weight:	7,174 lb (3254 kg)
Overall Length:	46 ft 4.5 in (14.14 m)
Wingspan:	25 ft 3 in (7.70 m)
Height:	12 ft 10.5 in (3.92 m)
Power Plant:	Two General Electric J85-GE-5 turbojets, each rated at 2,680 lb st (11.92 kN) dry and 3,850 lb st (17.13 kN) with afterburners
Maximum Fuel Capacity:	3,960 lb (1796 kg)
Maximum Speed:	745 kts (1380 km/h)
Cruise Speed:	500 kts (926 km/h)
Operating Range:	860 nm (1593 km)
Service Ceiling:	53,600 ft (16,337 m)
Crew:	2
Missions:	Advanced jet training, lead-in fighter training

Northrop T-38A Talon

Compared with the T-38A, the AT-38B variant is better equipped to simulate an attack fighter. It is used as a lead-in fighter trainer.

RAYTHEON AIRCRAFT (INCLUDING BEECH AIRCRAFT)

Beech C-12C/D/F/J Huron

In 1975, the Super King Air A200 was selected by the USAF as a platform to support US embassies and military attaches throughout the world, thereby filling the CX-X requirement. Some 30 C-12As were purchased, although the majority were redesignated C-12Cs when they were fitted with a more powerful version of the PT6A turboprop engine. Subsequently, six King Air B200s equipped with high-floatation landing gear and a cargo door were ordered. This variant was designated the C-12D.

Some 20 C-12Cs and C-12Ds are still operated by the Air Force overseas, primarily for the Defense Security Cooperation Agency (DSCA) and, whereas Air Force Materiel Command is responsible for the aircraft, aircrew

The Super King Air 200 is larger than its predecessors and introduced a T-tail configuration to the airframe's design. Designated C-12s, variants have already served the USAF for about 25 years.

Beech C-12J Huron Specifications

Maximum Takeoff Weight:	12,500 lb (5670 kg)
Empty Weight:	7,538 lb (3419 kg)
Overall Length:	43 ft 9 in (13.34 m)
Wingspan:	54 ft 6 in (16.61 m)
Height:	15 ft 0 in (4.57 m)
Power Plant:	Two Pratt & Whitney Canada PT6A-42 turboprop engines, each rated at 850 shp (634 kW), driving three-blade constant-speed propellers
Maximum Fuel Capacity:	2,606 lb (1182 kg)
Maximum Speed:	295 kts (546 km/h)
Cruise Speed:	282 kts (522 km/h)
Operating Range:	1,680 nm (3111 km)
Crew:	2
Missions:	Operational support airlift, theater airlift

training is undertaken by the US Army at Fort Rucker, Alabama. Furthermore, in September 1983, the USAF decided to use the King Air B200C for operational airlift support duties alongside the C-21A Learjet, whereby both aircraft took over the mission of the CT-39A Sabreliner.

The Air Force received the first of 40 leased C-12Fs in May 1984 and six more were acquired for the ANG, which also received six stretched C-12Js based on the B1900C commuter aircraft two years later. However, during 1996, most of the C-12Fs and two C-12Js were transferred to the Army. The two C-12Fs and four C-12Js left in USAF service are now flown by active-duty units.

T-1A Jayhawk, serial 92-0354, is operated by the 86th Flight Training Squadron, at Laughlin AFB, Texas.

Beech T-1A Jayhawk

Developed by Japan's Mitsubishi Heavy Industries, the predecessor to the T-1A was the MU-300 Diamond, which first flew on 29 August 1978. The design was sold to Beech Aircraft in 1985 and the platform was chosen in February 1990, as part of the Tanker/Transport Training System (TTTS), to serve as a trainer for student pilots destined to fly airlifters or refueling aircraft. Renamed the Beechjet 400T, it received the military designation T-1A Jayhawk and made its first flight on 5 July 1991.

The aircraft differs from its commercial counterpart by having a single-point refueling system and greater fuel capacity. It also has better protection against bird strikes incorporated into the windshield and leading edges. This was deemed necessary because the T-1A is subjected to sustained, low-level operations. Cockpit seating is provided for an instructor and two student pilots, plus four other passengers.

The first Jayhawk was delivered to Reese AFB, Texas, in January 1992 and student training in the type began the following year. Today, the T-1A serves with five of the AETC's training wings and groups. These include the 12th FTW and 340th FTG at Randolph AFB, Texas; the 14th FTW at Columbus AFB, Mississippi; the 47th FTW at Laughlin AFB, Texas; and the 71st FTW at Vance AFB, Oklahoma. In many cases, it operates alongside the T-37B Tweet and T-38A Talon.

Beech T-1A Jayhawk Specifications

Maximum Takeoff Weight:	15,780 lb (7158 kg)
Empty Weight:	10,115 lb (4588 kg)
Overall Length:	48 ft 6 in (14.78 m)
Wingspan:	43 ft 5 in (13.23 m)
Height:	13 ft 9 in (4.19 m)
Power Plant:	Two Pratt & Whitney Canada JT15D-58 turbofans, each rated at 2,900 lb st (12.90 kN)
Maximum Fuel Capacity:	4,904 lb (2224 kg)
Maximum Speed:	461 kts (854 km/h)
Cruise Speed:	388-447 kts (719-828 km/h)
Operating Range:	1,930 nm (3574 km)
Crew:	2
Mission:	Basic jet training

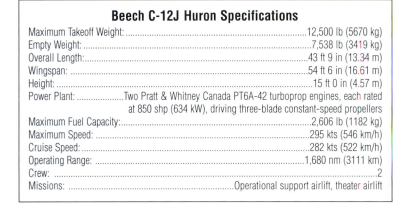

Raytheon T-6A Texan II

The Raytheon T-6A Texan II, formerly known as the Beech/Pilatus PC-9 Mk II, was the winner of the Joint Primary Aircraft Training System (JPATS) competition. A substantially different aircraft from the original PC-9, the Texan II has a strengthened fuselage and a pressurized cockpit, and has been fitted with a new digital avionics suite.

Rolled out on 29 June 1998, the first example made its maiden flight from Beech Field in Wichita, Kansas, on 15 July 1998. During the course of the initial test flight, which lasted one hour and 48 minutes, the aircraft climbed to 13,000 feet (3962 m) and performed idle-power stalls and various aerobatics, and functional checks were performed to test the electronic flight instrument system (EFIS), on-board oxygen-generating system and environmental controls.

Initial deliveries to the AETC at Randolph AFB, Texas, began during 1999 and are scheduled to continue through 2017. It is anticipated that some 700 examples will be built for the USAF and US Navy as replacements for the Cessna T-37B Tweet and Beech T-34C Mentor, respectively.

The Raytheon T-6A Texan II has begun replacing the T-37B as the USAF's primary training aircraft.

Raytheon T-6A Texan II Specifications

Maximum Takeoff Weight:	6,500 lb (2948 kg)
Empty Weight:	4,638 lb (2104 kg)
Overall Length:	33 ft 3 in (10.14 m)
Wingspan:	33 ft 4 in (10.16 m)
Height:	10 ft 8 in (3.25 m)
Power Plant:	One Pratt & Whitney Canada PT6A-68 turboprop rated at 1,100 shp (820 kW) driving a four-blade propeller
Fuel Load:	1,109 lb (503 kg)
Operating Range:	899 nm (1665+ km)
Speed:	270 kts (500 km/h)
Service Ceiling:	31,000 ft (9449 m)
Crew:	2
Mission:	Primary training

Serial 60-3478 is one of the few Sabreliners still in service. It is used for test purposes at Edwards AFB.

SABRELINER CORP. (INCL. NORTH AMERICAN)

North American NT-39A/B Sabreliner

Developed by North American Aviation in response to a USAF request for a Utility Trainer Experimental (UTX) aircraft in the mid-1950s, the prototype, designated N.A.246, flew for the first time on 16 September 1956 at Palmdale, California. None of the other contractors in the competition actually flew a UTX contender and North American was declared the winner. The first T-39A (Model N.A.265) took to the air on 30 June 1960. The initial order was for seven examples but USAF orders for T-39s (A, B and F variants) exceeded 140 aircraft altogether.

Only a handful of aircraft were actually employed for training because the majority were used as communications aircraft, a role now referred to as operational support airlift (OSA). However, six were fitted with F-105D navigation/bombing systems for radar training and were designated T-39Bs.

By 1985, most of the USAF's fleet had been replaced with C-12F Hurons and C-21A Gulfstream IIIs, although a few Sabreliners were retained. Designated NT-39A/Bs, they still serve as test platforms with AMC's 418th Flight Test Squadron, 412th Test Wing, located at Edwards AFB, California.

North American NT-39A/B Sabreliner Specifications

Maximum Takeoff Weight:	18,340 lb (8319 kg)
Empty Weight:	9,895 lb (4488 kg)
Overall Length:	43 ft 9 in (13.34 m)
Wingspan:	44 ft 5 in (13.54 m)
Height:	16 ft 0 in (4.88 m)
Power Plant:	Two Pratt & Whitney JT12A-8 turbojets, each rated at 3,300 lb st (14.68 kN)
Maximum Fuel Capacity:	4,024 gal (15232 lit)
Maximum Speed:	490 kts (907 km/h)
Maximum Operating Range:	1,900 nm (3519 km)
Service Ceiling:	45,000 ft (13716 m)
Crew:	2
Mission:	Test platform

SCHWEIZER AIRCRAFT

Schweizer TG-3A (SGS 1-26E)

As an intermediate-training and medium-performance aircraft, the TG-3A glider is operated by the USAFA for cross-country flights and spin training. The type first flew in 1954 and serves to provide students with basic flight maneuver training before they progress to the Schleicher TG-9A glider.

Of metal construction, the aircraft features a fabric-covered horizontal stabilizer and control surfaces, and is capable of high-altitude operation. Accordingly, each of the academy's three TG-3As is equipped with an oxygen system.

Students at the USAFA enjoy a spectacular setting for their flight training. Preliminary instruction begins in gliders like this Schweizer TG-4A.

Used for basic training, the TG-7A is one of two types of motorized glider in service with the USAFA. The other is the high-performance Stemme TG-11.

Schweizer TG-4A (SGS 2-33A)

One of the world's most popular primary soaring trainers, the TG-4A sailplane was first flown in 1968 and entered service with the USAFA in October 1984. It is a conventional two-place aircraft with a tandem configuration. The academy operates a fleet of 12, which it uses for its "Soar for All" program and general training. For the latter, students fly aerotows in the type and practice stall recovery, steep turns and slow-flight, and undergo traffic pattern training.

The glider's construction comprises a steel-tube airframe; aluminum fuselage skin, wings and vertical tail; and a fabric-covered horizontal stabilizer. Although the aircraft is fitted with dual flight controls, flight instruments and radios are present in the forward cockpit only.

Schweizer TG-7A (SGM 2-37)

Built specifically for use by the USAFA, the TG-7A is a motorized glider powered by a small engine driving a three-blade propeller. The type handles much like the TG-4A when the engine is at idle. First flown in 1987 as the SGM 2-37, the aircraft is of low-wing design and has a two-place cockpit with side-by-side seating.

Constructed primarily of aluminum alloy, the engine cowling and some non-structural elements are made of fiberglass and plastic. Although fairly conventional in terms of its construction, the TG-7A incorporates a number of components from other aircraft. For instance, the nose section is from the Piper Tomahawk and the wings and tail are modified elements from Schweizer's SGS 1-36 and SGS 2-32 models, respectively. In all, nine examples were built for the academy and they are used extensively for traffic pattern training and aerial maneuvering.

Schweizer TG-3A Specifications

Maximum Takeoff Weight:	700 lb (318 kg)
Empty Weight:	445 lb (202 kg)
Overall Length:	21 ft 6.5 in (6.57 m)
Wingspan:	40 ft 0 in (12.19 m)
Height:	7 ft 2.5 in (2.20 m)
Maximum Speed:	100 kts (185 km/h)
Service Ceiling:	25,000 ft (7620 m)
Crew:	1
Missions:	Cross-country flights, spin training

Schweizer TG-4A Specifications

Maximum Takeoff Weight:	1,040 lb (472 kg)
Empty Weight:	600 lb (272 kg)
Overall Length:	25 ft 9 in (7.85 m)
Wingspan:	51 ft 0 in (15.55 m)
Height:	9 ft 3.5 in (2.83 m)
Maximum Speed:	85 kts (157 km/h)
Service Ceiling:	14,000 ft (4267 m)
Crew:	2
Mission:	Basic soaring

Schweizer TG-7A Specifications

Maximum Takeoff Weight:	1,850 lb (833 kg)
Empty Weight:	1,200 lb (544 kg)
Overall Length:	27 ft 6 in (8.38 m)
Wingspan:	59 ft 6 in (18.14 m)
Height:	7 ft 2.5 in (2.20 m)
Power Plant:	One Teledyne (Lycoming) 0-235-L2C 4-cyl. engine rated at 112 hp (83.52 kW) driving a three-blade, fixed-pitch propeller
Maximum Speed:	118 kts (219 km/h)
Service Ceiling:	14,000 ft (4267 m)
Crew:	2
Mission:	Basic training

SIKORSKY AIRCRAFT

Sikorsky MH-53J/M, NCH-53A and TH-53A Pave Low

The MH-53J and MH-53M currently in Air Force service trace their history to the HH-53B combat rescue helicopter, which first flew on 15 March 1967. This early platform was followed by HH-53C and CH-53C models, more specifically equipped for rescue and transport roles, respectively.

To improve operational capabilities, a single HH-53 was fitted with a low-light-level television (LLLTV) system in 1969, as part of the Pave Low I program. Thereafter a terrain-following radar and other night-operation equipment was added to one of the HH-53B platforms and the aircraft was designated the YHH-53H Pave Low II. Upgrades to a number of HH-53Cs and CH-53Cs followed as part of Pave Low III, which included fitting a terrain-following radar, an INS, FLIR, improved navigation and moving-map display, as well as defensive countermeasures. Under the Pave Low III (Enhanced) program, nine MH-53H and 32 HH-53B/C airframes received the upgrades described, plus additional equipment for night and adverse-weather operation including NVG-compatible cockpits. Among enhancements were armor plating, a variety of additional counter-measures, positions for several guns to suppress enemy ground fire and external fuel tanks. The modification program lasted four years and was completed in 1990. Aircraft equipped to this standard are

Serial 68-8286 is an MH-53J, technologically one of the most advanced transport helicopters in the world.

A Sikorsky MH-53J with the 20th Special Operations Squadron at Hurlburt Field, Florida, deploys defensive flares during a night mission. The Pave Low is equipped with a number of self-defense electronic countermeasures and improved systems are being added under the Pave Low IV upgrade program.

Sikorsky MH-53J Pave Low Specifications

Maximum Takeoff Weight:	42,000 lb (19051 kg)
Empty Weight:	23,569 lb (10691 kg)
Fuselage Length:	67 ft 2 in (20.47m)
Overall Length (Rotors turning):	88 ft 3 in (26.90 m)
Main Rotor Diameter:	72 ft 3 in (22.02 m)
Height (To top of rotor head):	17 ft 1.5 in (5.22 m)
Power Plant:	Two General Electric T64-GE-7A turboshafts, each rated at 3,936 shp (2936 kW)
Maximum Fuel Capacity:	Internal – 630 gal (2385 lit) External – Up to 900 gal (3407 lit)
Maximum Speed:	170 kts (315 km/h)
Cruise Speed:	150 kts (278 km/h)
Operating Range:	468 nm (867 km)
Service Ceiling:	20,400 ft (6218 m)
Crew:	4-5
Armament:	Provision for 0.50-cal machine guns/7.62-mm miniguns
Mission Equipment:	AN/APQ-158 terrain-following radar, AN/AAQ-10 FLIR INS, GPS, NVG cockpit, AN/ALQ-162 radar missile jammers, AN/ALE-40 chaff/flare dispensers, ALR-69 missile warning receivers
Missions:	Long-range Special Operations

Sikorsky HH-60G, MH-60G Pave Hawk

Although the USAF had planned to obtain an advanced variant of the Army's UH-60A, designated the HH-60D, budgetary considerations ultimately forced cancellation of the program. Still needing a new combat rescue and Special Operations helicopter, however, the service looked to Sikorsky for a less-advanced alternative. This led to development of the MH/HH-60G from the UH-60A utility platform.

Among enhancements is an in-flight refueling boom and probe that allows the Pave Hawk to tank from Lockheed HC/KC/MC-130s. The helicopter is also equipped with a weather/search radar, FLIR, RWR, chaff/flare dispensers, infrared jamming and hover infrared suppression systems, and an electric rescue winch. The cockpit is compatible with night-vision goggles and is fitted with a low-altitude warning system as well as satellite communications. The Pave Hawk's tanks provide sufficient fuel for two hours of flight time but that duration can be doubled when an auxiliary tank is carried in the cargo compartment.

A series of planned enhancements include a service-life extension program designed to keep the type flying through 2027 and what is termed the Block 152 Upgrade (also known as UCN/IEW). The latter will field upgraded communications and navigation systems and an integrated electronic warfare suite that will automatically dispense countermeasures in the event the helicopter comes under threat from

designated MH-53Js and are among the most technologically advanced helicopters in the world. The type's primary mission is long-range, low-level penetration of hostile airspace in all weathers, in support of Special Operations forces.

To further improve the capabilities of this platform, the fleet is currently being upgraded to Pave Low IV standard by Lockheed Martin. Designated the MH-53M, the latest variant is equipped with a new, interactive defensive-avionics system and multimission advanced tactical terminal (DAS/MATT). The first "glass" cockpit example was delivered to the USAF on 17 April 1998.

Besides the MH-53J/M, the Air Force also operates a small number of ex-USMC CH-53As modified for training and test duties.

a missile, radar or laser. Plans call for 49 Pave Hawks to be modified to this standard.

MH-60Gs served with AFSOC until 1999, at which time all examples were withdrawn from the command and allocated to various ACC units.

Serial 88-26119 is an HH-60G in service with the 129th RQW of the California ANG. The type is used extensively throughout the Air Force by four commands: ACC, AETC, PACAF and AFRC, including the USAF Weapons School. Units flying the Pave Hawk outside the USA are deployed to Iceland, Kuwait, Japan and Korea.

Sikorsky HH-60G Pave Hawk Specifications

Maximum Takeoff Weight:	22,000 lb (9979 kg)
Empty Weight:	11,300 lb (5126 kg)
Fuselage Length:	57 ft 0.25 in (17.37 m)
Overall Length (Rotors turning):	64 ft 10 in (19.76 m)
Main Rotor Diameter:	53 ft 8 in (16.36 m)
Height (To top of rotor head):	12 ft 4 in (3.76 m)
Power Plant:	Two General Electric T700-GE-700 turboshafts, each rated at 1,622 shp (1210 kW)
Max. Fuel Capacity:	Internal – 360 gal (1363 lit), External – 1,017 gal (3850 lit)
Maximum Cruise Speed:	145 kts (269 km/h)
Operating Range (Internal fuel only):	325 nm (602 km)
Maximum Service Ceiling:	9,500 ft (2896 m)
Crew:	2 pilots plus 1 crew chief
Armament:	Door-mounted machine guns
Mission Equipment:	Weather/search radar, FLIR, RWR, chaff/flare dispensers, winch
Mission:	Combat search and rescue

SLINGSBY AVIATION

Slingsby T-3A Firefly

Temporarily grounded since July 1997, following three fatal training crashes, AETC announced a permanent grounding of the T-3A Firefly in October 1999. Options are being reviewed, pending disposal of the entire 110-aircraft fleet.

Chosen as the Enhanced Flight Screening (EFS) platform in April 1992, the prototype began flying in 1991 and AETC accepted the first aircraft in February 1994. It was supposed to allow screening of pilot candidates by exposing them to military-style traffic patterns,

aerobatics and spin recovery. Of composite structure and equipped with dual controls and integral fuel tanks in each wing, the type entered service with training squadrons at Hondo, Texas, as well as the USAFA in Colorado Springs, Colorado.

The decision to cease flying the type was taken after the 412th TW at Edwards AFB undertook special testing of the aircraft in an attempt to identify the cause of several engine failures. However, it failed to determine the nature of the problem. The Royal Air Force operates a version of the British-built trainer fitted with a different engine and has experienced none of the failures reported by the USAF.

Slingsby T-3A Firefly Specifications

Maximum Takeoff Weight:	2,565 lb (1164 kg)
Overall Length:	24 ft 10 in (7.57 m)
Wingspan	34 ft 9 in (10.59 m)
Height:	7 ft 9 in (2.36 m)
Power Plant:	One Textron (Lycoming) AEIO-540-D4A5 piston engine, rated at 260 hp (194 kW)
Maximum Fuel Capacity:	252 lb (114 kg)
Maximum Speed:	170 kts (315 km/h)
Operating Range:	306 nm (567 km)
Service Ceiling:	12,000 ft (3658 m)
Crew:	2
Mission:	Primary screener for specialized undergraduate pilot training

Acquired as a primary trainer, the ill-fated Slingsby T-3A has been permanently grounded and the Air Force is now seeking to dispose of its entire fleet.

STEMME

Stemme TG-11

This high-performance motor-glider is capable of self-launch and can transition from powered to unpowered flight within a few seconds. Its origins date back to 1981 when the Stemme S-10V made its first flight. The USAFA has used two TG-11As since 1985 for cross-country training. The aircraft features side-by-side seating and is constructed of fiberglass and composite materials, and has a Kevlar-reinforced cockpit and foldable wings for ease of storage. Fitted with a variable-pitch propeller that folds into the nose cone, the TG-11A's engine is located within the fuselage below the wing section and drives the propeller by means of a carbon shaft that passes beneath the cockpit. For powered flight, the nose cone moves forward and the propeller blades extend by centrifugal force. The TG-11A also has a fully retractable undercarriage.

Stemme TG-11A Specifications

Maximum Takeoff Weight:	1,874 lb (850 kg)
Empty Weight:	1,400 lb (635 kg)
Fuselage Length:	27 ft 7.25 in (8.41 m)
Wingspan:	75 ft 6 in (23.01 m)
Height:	5 ft 9 in (1.75 m)
Power Plant:	One Limbach L-2400 EB1.AD 4-cyl. engine rated at 93 hp (69.35 kW), driving a two-blade, variable-pitch propeller
Maximum Speed (powered):	120 kts (222 km/h)
Maximum Speed (unpowered):	145 kts (269 km/h)
Operating Range:	989 nm (1832 km)
Service Ceiling (powered):	17,450 ft (5319 m)
Service Ceiling (unpowered):	25,000 ft (7620 m)
Crew:	2
Mission:	Cross-country trainer

AIR BASES

Active runway locations and their assignments

UNITED STATES & PUERTO RICO

Anchorage IAP-Kulis ANGB, Alaska
Location: Anchorage IAP
Major Command: (ANG)
Unit: 176th Wing (PACAF, gained from ANG)
Aircraft: C-130H, HC-130N, HH-60G

Altus AFB, Oklahoma
Location: Altus
Major Command: AETC
Unit: 97th AMW
Aircraft: C-5A, C-17A, C-141B, KC-135R

Andrews AFB, Maryland
Named for Lt. Gen. Frank M. Andrews, killed in an aircraft accident on 3 May 1943.
Location: 11 miles southeast of Washington, D.C.
Major Command: AMC
Units: 89th AW, 113th Wing (ACC/AMC, gained from ANG), element of 375th AW, 459th AW (AMC, gained from AFRC)
Aircraft: C-12C/D, C-20B/C/H, C-21A, C-22B, C-32A, C-37A, C-38A, C-141B/C, F-16C/D, UH-1N, VC-9C, VC-25A, VC-137C

Atlantic City IAP/ANGB, New Jersey
Location: 10 miles west of Atlantic City
Major Command: (ANG)
Unit: 177th FW (ACC, gained from ANG)
Aircraft: F-16C/D

Bangor IAP, Maine
Location: 4 miles northwest of Bangor
Major Command: (ANG)
Unit: 101st ARW (AMC, gained from ANG)
Aircraft: KC-135E

Barksdale AFB, Louisiana
Named for Lt. Eugene H. Barksdale, a WWI airman killed near Wright Field, Ohio, in August 1926.
Location: Bossier City
Major Command: ACC
Units: 2d BW, elements of 53d Wing and 57th Wing, 917th Wing (ACC, gained from AFRC)
Aircraft: A-10A/OA-10A, B-52H

Barnes MAP/ANGB, Massachusetts
Location: 3 miles northwest of Westfield
Major Command: (ANG)
Unit: 104th FW (ACC, gained from ANG)
Aircraft: A-10A/OA-10A

Beale AFB, California
Named for Brig. Gen. E.F. Beale, an Indian agent in California prior to the Civil War.
Location: 13 miles east of Marysville

Major Command: ACC
Units: 9th RW, 940th ARW (AMC, gained from AFRC)
Aircraft: KC-135E, T-38A, U-2S/TU-2S

Birmingham IAP/Sumpter Smith ANGB, Alabama
Location: Birmingham
Major Command: (ANG)
Unit: 117th ARW (AMC, gained from ANG)
Aircraft: KC-135R

Boise Air Terminal-Gowen Field, Idaho
Location: 6 miles south of Boise at the air terminal
Major Command: (ANG)
Unit: 124th Wing (ACC, gained from ANG)
Aircraft: A-10A/OA-10A, C-130E

Bradley IAP/ANGB, Connecticut
Named after Lt. Eugene M. Bradley, killed in a P-40 crash in August 1941.
Location: Windsor Locks
Major Command: (ANG)
Unit: 103d FW (ACC, gained from ANG)
Aircraft: A-10A/OA-10A

Buckley ANGB, Colorado
Named after Lt. John H. Buckley, a National Guardsman killed in France on 27 September 1918.
Location: 8 miles east of Denver
Major Command: (ANG)
Unit: 140th Wing (ACC/AMC, from ANG)
Aircraft: C-21A, C-26B, F-16C/D

Burlington IAP, Vermont
Location: 3 miles east of Burlington
Major Command: (ANG)
Unit: 158th FW (ACC, gained from ANG)
Aircraft: F-16C/D

Cannon AFB, New Mexico
Named for Gen. John K. Cannon, the WWII commander of all allied air forces in the

Mediterranean and former commander of Tactical Air Command.
Location: 7 miles west of Clovis
Major Command: ACC
Unit: 27th FW
Aircraft: F-16C/D

Capital Airport, Illinois
Location: 2 miles northwest of Springfield.
Major Command: (ANG)
Unit: 183d FW (ACC, gained from ANG)
Aircraft: F-16C/D

Charleston AFB, South Carolina
Location: North Charleston
Major Command: AMC
Units: 437th AW, 315th AW (AMC, gained from AFRC)
Aircraft: C-17A, C-141B

Charlotte/Douglas IAP, North Carolina
Location: Charlotte
Major Command: (ANG)
Unit: 145th AW (AMC, gained from ANG)
Aircraft: C-130H

Barksdale AFB is home to the ACC's 2d Bomb Wing and the Reserve's 917th Wing, both of which fly the B-52H.

Cheyenne Airport, Wyoming
Location: Cheyenne
Major Command: (ANG)
Unit: 153d AW (AMC, gained from ANG)
Aircraft: C-130H

Columbia Metro. Airport/McEntire ANGS, South Carolina
Named for Brig. Gen. "Barnie" B. McEntire, the first commander of the South Carolina Air National Guard.
Location: 12 miles east of Columbia
Major Command: (ANG)
Unit: 169th FW (ACC, gained from ANG)
Aircraft: C-130H, F-16C/D

Active-duty USAF Bases

McChord AFB
WASHINGTON
Fairchild AFB
OREGON
Malmstrom AFB
MONTANA
Minot AFB
Grand Forks AFB
NORTH DAKOTA
MINNESOTA
MAINE
VERMONT
NEW HAMPSHIRE
MASSACHUSETTS
RHODE ISLAND
CONNECTICUT

IDAHO
SOUTH DAKOTA
WISCONSIN
NEW YORK
PENNSYLVANIA

Mountain Home AFB
WYOMING
Ellsworth AFB
IOWA
MICHIGAN

Beale AFB
McClellan AFB
Travis AFB
NEVADA
Francis E. Warren AFB
NEBRASKA
Hill AFB
UTAH
COLORADO
Offutt AFB
ILLINOIS
INDIANA
OHIO
Wright-Patterson AFB
WEST VIRGINIA
VIRGINIA
McGuire AFB
NEW JERSEY
Dover AFB
DELAWARE

CALIFORNIA
USAF Academy
Peterson AFB
KANSAS
MISSOURI
Scott AFB
KENTUCKY
Langley AFB
Andrews AFB
MARYLAND

Nellis AFB
Vandenberg AFB
Edwards AFB
ARIZONA
Kirtland AFB
McConnell AFB
Whiteman AFB
Seymour Johnson AFB
Luke AFB
Cannon AFB
NEW MEXICO
Vance AFB
Tinker AFB
ARKANSAS
TENNESSEE
NORTH CAROLINA
Shaw AFB
Pope AFB

Davis-Monthan AFB
Holloman AFB
OKLAHOMA
Altus AFB
Little Rock AFB
Columbus AFB
GEORGIA
SOUTH CAROLINA
Robins AFB
Charleston AFB

Dyess AFB
Sheppard AFB
MISSISSIPPI
ALABAMA
Maxwell AFB
Moody AFB

Barksdale AFB
Laughlin AFB
Randolph AFB
TEXAS
LOUISIANA
Keesler AFB
Eglin AFB
Patrick AFB

Kelly AFB
Lackland AFB
Hurlburt Field
Tyndall AFB
MacDill AFB
FLORIDA

ALASKA
Eielson AFB
Elmendorf AFB

Hickam AFB
HAWAII

Luiz Munoz Marin IAP/ Muñiz ANGB
PUERTO RICO

Air Force Reserve and Air National Guard Bases

Springfield-Beckley MAP
W.K. Kellogg Airport/ Battle Creek ANGB
Rickenbacker IAP/ANGB
Toledo Express Airport
Selfridge ANGB
Westover ARB
MAINE
Bangor IAP

Portland IAP/ANGB
WASHINGTON
Great Falls IAP
MONTANA
Schenectady CAP/ Stratton ANGS
Stewart IAP/ ANGB
VERMONT
NEW HAMPSHIRE

OREGON
Hector IAP
Duluth IAP/ ANGB
NORTH DAKOTA
MINNESOTA
Syracuse IAP/ Hancock Field
Burlington IAP

Klamath Falls IAP-Kingsley Field
IDAHO
Boise Air Terminal-Gowen Field
Minneapolis-St. Paul IAP/ARS
WISCONSIN
Niagara Falls IAP/ARS
Pease Intl. Tradeport/ANGS
Barnes MAP/ANGB
MASSACHUSETTS
Otis ANGB
Quonset State Airport

CALIFORNIA
SOUTH DAKOTA
Gen. Mitchell IAP/ARS
MICHIGAN
NEW YORK
Mansfield Lahm Airport
McGuire AFB
Bradley IAP/ANGB
RHODE ISLAND
Francis S. Gabreski Airport/ANGB

NEVADA
WYOMING
Joe Foss Field
Dane County RAP-Truax Field
IOWA
Greater Peoria RAP
Fort Wayne IAP
Greater Pittsburgh IAP/ARS
PENN.
Atlantic City IAP/ANGB
NEW JERSEY

Reno-Tahoe IAP/ May ANGB
Sioux Gateway Airport
NEBRASKA
Des Moines IAP
Grissom ARB
Harrisburg IAP
NAS Willow Grove JRB
DELAWARE
New Castle County Airport

Moffet Federal Airport/ANGS
Cheyenne Airport
Lincoln MAP/ANGB
Capital Airport
INDIANA
OHIO
Youngstown-Warren RAP/ARS
Martin State Airport/ Warfield ANGB
MARYLAND

Fresno-Yosemite IAP/ANGB
Salt Lake City IAP
UTAH
Buckley ANGB
Rosecrans MAP
MISSOURI
Terre Haute IAP-Hulman Field
W.V.
Yeager Airport
VIRGINIA
Richmond IAP Byrd Field
Eastern West Virginia RAP/ Shepherd Field

NAS Point Mugu/ Channel Islands ANGS
Indian Springs AFAF
COLORADO
Forbes Field
Lambert-St. Louis IAP
KANSAS
Louisville IAP-Standiford Field
KENTUCKY
McGhee Tyson Airport/ANGB
NORTH CAROLINA
Charlotte/Douglas IAP

Palmdale Airport/AF Plant 42
Nashville IAP
TENNESSEE

March ARB
ARIZONA
Sky Harbor IAP
NEW MEXICO
Tulsa IAP
OKLAHOMA
Will Rogers World Airport
Memphis IAP
ARKANSAS
Dobbins ARB
SOUTH CAROLINA
Columbia/McEntire ANGS

Tuscon IAP
Fort Smith RAP-Ebbing ANGB
Jackson IAP-Thompson Field/ANGB
Birmingham IAP/ Sumpter Smith ANGB
Savannah IAP

NAS Fort Worth JRB/Carswell Field
Key Field/ANGB
ALABAMA
GEORGIA
Jacksonville IAP

TEXAS
Montgomery RAP-Dannelly Field
MISSISSIPPI

LOUISIANA
Ellington Field/ANGB
NAS New Orleans JRB
FLORIDA
Dade County Homestead RAP/ARS

US Air Force

Columbus AFB, Mississippi
Location: 10 miles north-northwest of Columbus
Major Command: AETC
Unit: 14th FTW
Aircraft: T-1A, T-37B, T-38A/AT-38B

Dade County Homestead RAP/ARS, Florida
Location: Homestead
Major Command: AFRC
Units: 482d FW (ACC, gained from AFRC), 125th FW Det. (ACC, gained from ANG)
Aircraft: F-15C, F-16C/D

Dane County RAP-Truax Field, Wisconsin
Named for Lt. T.L. Truax, killed in 1941 during a P-40 training mission.
Location: Madison
Major Command: (ANG)
Unit: 115th FW (ACC, gained from ANG)
Aircraft: F-16C/D

Davis-Monthan AFB, Arizona
Named for lst Lt. Samuel H. Davis, killed 28 December 1921, and 2nd Lt. Oscar Monthan, killed 27 March 1924.
Location: Tucson
Major Command: ACC
Unit: 355th Wing
Aircraft: A-10A/OA-10A, EC-130E/H

Des Moines IAP, Iowa
Location: Des Moines
Major Command: (ANG)
Unit: 132d FW (ACC, gained from ANG)
Aircraft: F-16C/D

Dobbins ARB, Georgia
Named after Capt. Charles Dobbins, a WWII pilot killed in action near Sicily.
Location: 16 miles northwest of Atlanta
Major Command: AFRC
Unit: 94th AW (AMC, gained from AFRC)
Aircraft: C-130H

Dover AFB, Delaware
Location: 3 miles southeast of Dover
Major Command: AMC
Units: 436th AW, 512th AW (AMC, gained from AFRC)
Aircraft: C-5A/B

Duluth IAP/ANGB, Minnesota
Location: 5 miles northwest of Duluth
Major Command: (ANG)
Unit: 148th FW (ACC, gained from ANG)
Aircraft: F-16A/B(ADF)

Dyess AFB, Texas
Named for Lt. Col. William E. Dyess, a WWII fighter pilot who crashed and was killed in December 1943.
Location: Abilene
Major Command: ACC
Units: 7th BW, 317th AG (AMC)
Aircraft: B-1B, C-130H

Eastern West Virginia RAP-Shepherd Field, West Virginia
Location: 4 miles south of Martinsburg
Major Command: (ANG)
Unit: 167th AW (AMC, gained from ANG)
Aircraft: C-130H

Edwards AFB, California
Named for Capt. Glen W. Edwards, killed during the crash of a YB-49 "Flying Wing" on 5 June 1948.
Location: 20 miles east of Rosamond
Major Command: AFMC
Unit: 412th TW
Aircraft: B-1B, B-2A, B-52H, C-12C, C-17A, C-18B, C-135C, EC-18B, EC-135E, F-15A/B/C/D/E, F-16A/B/C/D, F-22A, NKC-135B/E, NOA-37B, NT-39A/B, T-38A/AT-38B, UH-1N

Eglin AFB, Florida (incl. Duke Field AS)
Named for Lt. Col. Frederick I. Eglin, a WWI flier killed in an aircraft accident on 1 January 1937.
Location: 7 miles northeast of Fort Walton Beach
Major Command: AFMC (Duke Field AS: AFRC)
Units: 33d FW (ACC), 46th TW (AFMC), element of 53d Wing (ACC), element of 16th SOW (AFSOC), 919th SOW (AFSOC, gained from AFRC)
Aircraft: A-10A/OA-10A, C-130E/H, F-15A/B/C/D/E, F-16A/B/C/D, MC-130E/P, NC-130A, UH-1N

Eielson AFB, Alaska
Named for Carl Ben Eielson, an arctic aviation pioneer who died in November 1929.
Location: 26 miles southeast of Fairbanks
Major Command: PACAF
Units: 55th Wing Det. (ACC), 168th ARW (PACAF, gained from ANG), 354th FW
Aircraft: A-10A/OA-10A, F-16C/D, KC-135R, RC-135S

Ellington Field/ ANGB, Texas
Named after Lt. Eric L. Ellington, a pilot killed in November 1913.
Location: 17 miles southeast of downtown Houston
Major Command: (ANG)
Unit: 147th FW (ACC, gained from ANG)
Aircraft: C-26B, F-16C/D

Ellsworth AFB, South Dakota
Named for Brig. Gen. Richard E. Ellsworth, killed 18 March 1953.
Location: 12 miles east-northeast of Rapid City
Major Command: ACC
Units: 28th BW, elements of 53d Wing and 57th Wing
Aircraft: B-1B

Elmendorf AFB, Alaska
Named for Capt. Hugh Elmendorf, killed during flight testing at Wright Field, Ohio, on 13 January 1933.
Location: Anchorage
Major Command: PACAF
Unit: 3d Wing
Aircraft: C-12F/J, C-130H, E-3B/C, F-15C/D/E

The 'Pair O' Dice' of the 90th FS fly F-15E Strike Eagles from Elmendorf AFB, while two fellow units in the 3d Wing, the 19th FS and 54th FS, operate F-15C/D Eagles from the Alaskan base.

Fairchild AFB, Washington
Named for Gen. Muir S. Fairchild, an Air Force vice-chief of staff.
Location: 12 miles west-southwest of Spokane
Major Command: AMC
Units: 92d ARW, 141st ARW (AMC, gained from ANG), 336th TRG (AETC)
Aircraft: C-26B, KC-135E/R/T, UH-1N

Forbes Field, Kansas
Location: 2 miles south of Topeka
Major Command: (ANG)
Unit: 190th ARW (AMC, gained from ANG)
Aircraft: KC-135E/D

Fort Smith RAP/Ebbing ANGB, Arkansas
Location: Fort Smith
Major Command: (ANG)
Unit: 188th FW (ACC, gained from ANG)
Aircraft: F-16A/B

Fort Wayne IAP, Indiana
Location: 5 miles south-southwest of Fort Wayne
Major Command: (ANG)
Unit: 122d FW (ACC, gained from ANG)
Aircraft: F-16C/D

Francis E. Warren AFB, Wyoming

Named for Francis Emory Warren, a Wyoming senator and the first state governor.
Location: Cheyenne
Major Command: AFSPC
Unit: 90th SPW
Aircraft: UH-1N

Francis S. Gabreski Airport/ANGB, New York

Named for Col. Francis S. Gabreski, the third leading USAAF/USAF ace of all time.
Location: Westhampton Beach
Major Command: (ANG)
Unit: 106th RQW (ACC, gained from ANG)
Aircraft: HC-130N/P, HH-60G

Fresno-Yosemite IAP/ANGB, California

Location: 5 miles northeast of Fresno
Major Command: (ANG)
Unit: 144th FW (ACC, gained from ANG)
Aircraft: C-26B, F-16C/D

General Mitchell IAP/ARS, Wisconsin

Named for Gen. Billy Mitchell, a vocal pioneer for a separate Air Force.
Location: 3 miles south of Milwaukee
Major Command: AFRC
Units: 128th ARW (AMC, gained from ANG), 440th AW (AMC, gained from AFRC)
Aircraft: C-130H, KC-135R

Grand Forks AFB, North Dakota

Location: 16 miles west of Grand Forks
Major Command: AMC
Unit: 319th ARW
Aircraft: KC-135R/T

Greater Peoria RAP, Illinois

Location: 7 miles southwest of Peoria
Major Command: (ANG)
Unit: 182d AW (AMC, gained from ANG)
Aircraft: C-130E

Greater Pittsburgh IAP/ARS, Pennsylvania

Location: 15 miles northwest of Pittsburgh
Major Command: AFRC/ANG
Units: 171st ARW (AMC, gained from ANG), 911th AW (AMC, gained from AFRC)
Aircraft: C-130H, KC-135E

Great Falls IAP, Montana

Location: 5 miles southwest of Great Falls
Major Command: (ANG)
Unit: 120th FW (ACC, gained from ANG)
Aircraft: F-16A/B(ADF)

Grissom ARB, Indiana

Named for Lt. Col. Virgil "Gus" Grissom, an astronaut killed in the Apollo capsule fire at Cape Kennedy, Florida, on 27 January 1967.
Location: 8 miles southwest of Peru
Major Command: AFRC
Unit: 434 ARW (AMC, gained from AFRC)
Aircraft: KC-135R

Harrisburg IAP, Pennsylvania

Location: 10 miles east of Harrisburg
Major Command: (ANG)
Unit: 193d SOW (AFSOC, gained from ANG)
Aircraft: C/EC-130E

Hector IAP, North Dakota

Location: Fargo
Major Command: (ANG)
Unit: 119th FW (ACC, gained from ANG)
Aircraft: F-16A/B(ADF)

Hickam AFB, Hawaii

Named for Lt. Col. Horace M. Hickam, an air pioneer killed on 5 November 1934.
Location: 9 miles west of Honolulu
Major Command: PACAF
Units: 15th ABW, 154th Wing (PACAF, gained from ANG)
Aircraft: C-130H, C-135C/E/K, F-15A/B, KC-135R

Hill AFB, Utah

Named for Maj. Ployer P. Hill, killed while test-flying the first B-17 on 30 October 1935.
Location: 8 miles south of Ogden
Major Command: AFMC
Units: 388th FW (ACC), 419th FW (ACC, gained from AFRC) Ogden Air Logistics Center
Aircraft: F-16C/D

Holloman AFB, New Mexico

Named for Col. George Holloman, killed in a B-17 crash on 19 March 1946.

Location: 8 miles southwest of Almagordo
Major Command: ACC
Units: 49th FW, Dets. of 53d Wing, element of 46th TW (AFMC)
Aircraft: C-12J, F-117A, F-4F, T-38A/AT-38B, YF-15A, QF-4E/G

Terre Haute IAP-Hulman Field, Indiana

Location: 5 miles east of Terre Haute
Major Command: (ANG)
Unit: 181st FW (ACC, gained from ANG)
Aircraft: F-16C/D

Hurlburt Field, Florida

Named for Lt. Donald W. Hurlburt, a WWII pilot killed on the Eglin AFB reservation on 1 October 1943.
Location: 5 miles west of Fort Walton Beach
Major Command: AFSOC
Unit: 16th SOW
Aircraft: AC-130H/U, C-130E, CASA 212-200, MC-130E/H, MH-53J/M, NCH-53A, UH-1N

Indian Springs AFAF, Nevada

Location: 2 miles north of Indian Springs
Major Command: ACC
Units: Elements of 57th Wing
Aircraft: RQ-1A

Jackson IAP-Allen C. Thompson Field/ANGB, Mississippi

Location: 7 miles east of Jackson
Major Command: (ANG)
Unit: 172d AW (AMC, gained from ANG)
Aircraft: C-141B/C

Jacksonville IAP, Florida

Location: 15 miles northwest of Jacksonville
Major Command: (ANG)
Unit: 125th FW (ACC, gained from ANG)
Aircraft: C-26B, F-15A/B

Joe Foss Field, South Dakota

Named for Brig. Gen. Joseph J. Foss, a WWII ace, a former governor of South Dakota and the founder of the state's ANG.
Location: North of Sioux Falls
Major Command: (ANG)
Unit: 114th FW (ACC, gained from ANG)
Aircraft: F-16C/D

Keesler AFB, Mississippi

Named for 2nd Lt. Samuel R. Keesler Jr., a WWI aerial observer killed in action near Verdun, France, on 9 October 1918.
Location: Biloxi
Major Command: AETC

The 'Griffins' of the ANG's 144th FW are stationed at Fresno-Yosemite IAP/ANGB in California, and fly Block 25 models of the Lockheed Martin F-16C/D. The Guard's contribution is essential to ACC fighter operations.

US Air Force

Units: 81st TRW, 403d Wing (AMC, gained from AFRC)
Aircraft: C-12C, C-21A, C-130E/J, WC-130H

Kelly AFB, Texas
Named for Lt. George Kelly, the first Army pilot to be killed in a military aircraft on 10 May 1911.
Location: 5 miles southwest of downtown San Antonio
Major Command: AFMC
Units: 149th FW (ACC), 433d AW (AMC, gained from AFRC)
Aircraft: C-5A, F-16C/D

Key Field/ANGB, Mississippi
Location: Meridian
Major Command: (ANG)
Unit: 186th ARW (AMC, gained from ANG)
Aircraft: C-26A/B, KC-135R

Klamath Falls IAP-Kingsley Field, Oregon
Location: 5 miles southeast of Klamath Falls
Major Command: (ANG)
Unit: 173d FW (AETC, gained from ANG)
Aircraft: F-15A/B

Kirtland AFB, New Mexico
Named for Col. Roy C. Kirtland, the commandant of Langley Field in the 1930s.
Location: Southeast of Albuquerque
Major Command: AFMC
Units: 150th FW (ACC), 58th SOW (AETC)

Aircraft: C-26B, F-16C/D, HH-60G, MC-130 H/N/P, MH-53J, NCH-53A, TH-53A, UH-1N

Lackland AFB, Texas
Named for Brig. Gen. Frank D. Lackland, an early commandant of Kelly Field flying school.
Location: 8 miles southwest of downtown San Antonio
Major Command: AETC
Unit: 17th TRW
Aircraft: Various training airframes

Lambert-St. Louis IAP, Missouri
Location: Bridgeton
Major Command: (ANG)
Unit: 131st FW (ACC, gained from ANG)
Aircraft: F-15A/B

Langley AFB, Virginia
Named for Samuel Pierpont Langley, an aviation pioneer and scientist.
Location: 3 miles north of Hampton
Major Command: ACC
Units: 1st FW, 119th FW Det., element of 375th AW (AMC)
Aircraft: C-21A, F-15C/D, F-16A(ADF)

Laughlin AFB, Texas
Named for 1st Lt. Jack Thomas Laughlin, a Del Rio native and B-17 pilot killed over Java on 29 January 1942.
Location: 6 miles east of Del Rio
Major Command: AETC
Unit: 47th FTW
Aircraft: T-1A, T-37B, T-38A

Lincoln MAP/ANGB, Nebraska
Location: 1 mile northwest of Lincoln
Major Command: (ANG)
Unit: 155th ARW (AMC, gained from ANG)
Aircraft: KC-135R

Little Rock AFB, Arkansas
Location: Jacksonville
Major Command: AETC
Units: 189th AW (AETC, gained from ANG), 314th AW, 463d AG (AMC)
Aircraft: C-130E/H

Louisville IAP-Standiford Field, Kentucky
Location: Louisville
Major Command: (ANG)
Unit: 123d AW (AMC, gained from ANG)
Aircraft: C-130H

Luiz Munoz Marin IAP/Muñiz ANGB, Puerto Rico
Location: San Juan
Major Command: (ANG)
Units: 156th AW (AMC, gained from ANG), Coronet Oak (AMC, gained from ANG and AFRC detachments)
Aircraft: C-130E, UC-26C

Both operational F-117A Stealth Fighter squadrons, the 8th FS and 9th FS, are located at Holloman AFB, Nevada. It is also home to the 'Screamin' Demons' of the 7th Combat Training Squadron (CTS) and the 'Silver Lobos' of the 20th FS, that fly the T-38A Talon and F-4F Phantom II, respectively. The 20th FS is the *Luftwaffe* training unit.

Headquarters of the AFRC's Fourth Air Force and an important facility for AMC operations, March Air Reserve Base is home to three units with the 452d AMW. The 336th Air Refueling Squadron flies the KC-135R Stratotanker, whereas the 729th and 730th Airlift Squadrons operate C-141B/C Starlifters (shown). The command also gains the ANG's 163d Air Refueling Wing, another KC-135R unit stationed there.

Luke AFB, Arizona
Named for 2nd Lt. Frank Luke Jr., the first American aviator to receive the Medal of Honor and who was killed in action in France on 29 September 1918.
Location: 20 miles west-northwest of downtown Phoenix
Major Command: AETC
Units: 56th FW, 944th FW (ACC, gained from AFRC)
Aircraft: F-16C/D

MacDill AFB, Florida
Named for Col. Leslie MacDill, killed in an aircraft accident on 8 November 1938.
Location: Tampa
Major Command: AMC
Unit: 6th ARW
Aircraft: CT-43A, EC-135N, KC-135R

Malmstrom AFB, Montana
Named for Col. Einar A. Malmstrom, a WWII fighter commander later killed in an aircraft accident on 21 August 1954.
Location: 2 miles east of Great Falls
Major Command: AFSPC
Unit: 341st SPW
Aircraft: UH-1N

Mansfield Lahm Airport, Ohio
Named for Brig. Gen. Frank P. Lahm, a local aviation pioneer.
Location: 3 miles north of Mansfield
Major Command: (ANG)
Unit: 179th AW (AMC, gained from ANG)
Aircraft: C-130H

March ARB, California
Named for 2nd Lt. Peyton C. March.
Location: 9 miles southeast of Riverside
Major Command: AFRC
Units: 452d AMW (AMC, gained from AFRC), 144th FW Det. (ACC, gained from ANG), 163d ARW (AMC, gained from ANG)
Aircraft: C-141B/C, F-16C, KC-135R

Martin State Airport/ Warfield ANGB, Maryland
Named for Glenn L. Martin.
Location: 8 miles east of Baltimore
Major Command: (ANG)
Unit: 175th Wing (ACC and AMC, gained from ANG)
Aircraft: A-10A/OA-10A, C-130E/J

Maxwell AFB, Alabama (incl. Gunter Annex)
Named for 2nd Lt. William C. Maxwell, killed in an air accident in the Philippines on 12 August 1920.
Location: Montgomery
Major Command: AETC
Units: 908th AW (AMC, gained from AFRC), element of 375th AW (AMC)
Aircraft: C-21A, C-130H

McChord AFB, Washington
Named for Col. William C. McChord, killed during a forced landing in Virginia on 18 August 1937.
Location: 8 miles south of Tacoma
Major Command: AMC
Units: 62d AW, 446th AW (AMC, gained from AFRC)
Aircraft: C-17A, C-141B

McConnell AFB, Kansas
Named for Capt. Fred J. McConnell, a WWII B-24 pilot who died in a private plane crash on 25 October 1945; also for his brother, 2d Lt. Thomas L. McConnell, a WWII B-24 pilot killed during a combat mission on 10 July, 1943.
Location: 5 miles southeast of Wichita
Major Command: AMC
Units: 22nd ARW, element of 507 ARW (AMC, gained from AFRC), 184th BW (ACC, gained from ANG)
Aircraft: B-1B, KC-135R/R(RT)/T

McGhee Tyson Airport/ANGB, Tennessee
Location: 10 miles southwest of Knoxville
Major Command: (ANG)
Unit: 134th ARW (AMC, gained from ANG)
Aircraft: KC-135E

McGuire AFB, New Jersey
Named for Maj. Thomas B. McGuire Jr., a P-38 pilot and Medal of Honor recipient who was killed in action on 7 January 1945.
Location: 18 miles southeast of Trenton
Major Command: AMC
Units: 108th ARW (AMC, gained from ANG), 305th AMW, 514th AMW (AMC, gained from AFRC)
Aircraft: C-135B, C-141B, KC-10A, KC-135E

Long a familiar sight at McChord AFB, Washington, C-141B/Cs are now beginning to be replaced by C-17A Globemaster IIIs, the USAF's newest airlifter.

US Air Force

Memphis IAP, Tennessee
Location: Memphis
Major Command: (ANG)
Unit: 164th AW (AMC, gained from ANG)
Aircraft: C-141B/C

Minneapolis-St. Paul IAP/ARS, Minnesota
Location: Minneapolis
Major Command: AFRC
Units: 133d AW (AMC, gained from ANG),
934th AW (AMC, gained from AFRC)
Aircraft: C-130E/H

Minot AFB, North Dakota
Location: 13 miles north of Minot
Major Command: ACC
Units: 5th BW, 91st SPW (AFSPC)
Aircraft: B-52H, UH-1N

Aircraft: B-1B, F-15C/D/E, F-16C/D,
KC-135R

NAS Fort Worth JRB/Carswell Field, Texas
Location: 7 miles west-northwest of
downtown Fort Worth
Major Command: (US Navy facility)
Units: 136th AW (AMC, gained from ANG),
301st FW (ACC, gained from AFRC)
Aircraft: C-130H, F-16C/D

NAS New Orleans JRB, Louisiana
Location: 15 miles south of New Orleans
Major Command: (US Navy facility)
Units: 159th FW (ACC, gained from ANG),
926th FW (ACC, gained from AFRC)
Aircraft: A-10A/OA-10A, C-130H, F-15A/B

Major Command: (ANG)
Unit: 166th AW (AMC, gained from ANG)
Aircraft: C-130H

Niagara Falls IAP/ARS, New York
Location: 6 miles east of Niagara Falls
Major Command: AFRC
Units: 914th AW (AMC, gained from AFRC),
107th ARW (AMC, gained from ANG)
Aircraft: C-130H, KC-135R

Well-known as the headquarters of the Air Warfare
Center, Nellis AFB is a site for advanced mission
testing of a number of aircraft types. The 57th Wing
detaches personnel to the 28th BW at Ellsworth AFB,
South Dakota, and the bomber unit provides a B-1B
Lancer for test purposes.

Moffett Federal Airport/ANGS, California
Location: 2 miles north of Mountain View
Major Command: (ANG)
Unit: 129th RQW (ACC, gained from ANG)
Aircraft: HH-60G, MC/HC-130P

Montgomery RAP-Dannelly Field, Alabama
Named after Ens. Clarence Dannelly, a
Navy pilot killed at Pensacola, Florida,
during WWII.
Location: 7 miles southwest of
Montgomery
Major Command: (ANG)
Unit: 187th FW (ACC, gained from ANG)
Aircraft: F-16C/D

Moody AFB, Georgia
Named for Maj. George P. Moody, killed
while testing a Beech AT-10 on 5 May 1941.
Location: 10 miles north-northeast of
Valdosta
Major Command: ACC
Unit: 347th Wing
Aircraft: A-10A/OA-10A, C-130E,
F-16C/D, HC-130P, HH-60G

Mountain Home AFB, Idaho
Location: 10 miles southwest of Mountain
Home
Major Command: ACC
Unit: 366th Wing

NAS Point Mugu/Channel Islands ANGS, California
Location: Port Hueneme
Major Command: (US Navy facility)
Unit: 146th AW (AMC, gained from ANG)
Aircraft: C-130E

NAS Willow Grove JRB, Pennsylvania
Location: 14 miles north of Philadelphia
Major Command: (US Navy facility)
Units: 913th AW (AMC, gained from
AFRC), 111th FW (ACC, gained from ANG)
Aircraft: A-10A/OA-10A, C-26A, C-130E

Nashville IAP, Tennessee
Location: 6 miles southeast of Nashville
Major Command: (ANG)
Unit: 118th AW (AMC, gained from ANG)
Aircraft: C-130H

Nellis AFB, Nevada
Named for 1st Lt. William H. Nellis, a WWII
P-47 pilot killed in Europe on 27 December
1944.
Location: 8 miles northeast of Las Vegas
Major Command: ACC
Units: 57th Wing, elements of 53d Wing
Aircraft: A-10A, F-15C/D/E, F-16C/D,
HH-60G

New Castle County Airport, Delaware
Location: 5 miles south of Wilmington

Offutt AFB, Nebraska
Named for 1st Lt. Jarvis J. Offutt, a WWI
pilot who died 13 August 1918.
Location: 8 miles south of Omaha
Major Command: ACC
Units: 55th Wing, element of 375th AW
(AMC)
Aircraft: C-21A, E-4B, OC-135B,
RC-135S/U/V/W, TC-135W, WC-135W

Otis ANGB, Massachusetts
Named after 1st Lt. Frank J. Otis, an ANG
flight surgeon and pilot, killed in 1937.
Location: 7 miles north-northeast of
Falmouth
Major Command: (ANG)
Unit: 102d FW (ACC, gained from ANG)
Aircraft: F-15A/B

Palmdale Airport/AF Plant 42, California
Location: Palmdale
Major Command: AFMC
Units: 645th MATS, element of 412th TW
Aircraft: EC-130H, NC-130E, YF-117A

Patrick AFB, Florida
Named for Maj. Gen. Mason M. Patrick,
chief of the AEF Air Service in WWI and the
Air Service/Air Corps from 1921-27.
Location: 2 miles south of Cocoa Beach
Major Command: AFSPC
Units: Elements of 939th RQW (ACC,

gained from AFRC)
Aircraft: C-130E, HC-130N/P, HH-60G

Pease Intl. Tradeport/ANGS, New Hampshire (formerly Pease AFB)
Location: Portsmouth
Major Command: (ANG)
Unit: 157th ARW (AMC, gained from ANG)
Aircraft: KC-135R

Peterson AFB, Colorado
Named for 1st Lt. Edward J. Peterson, killed in an aircraft crash at the base on 8 August 1942.
Location: East of Colorado Springs
Major Command: AFSPC
Units: 98th FTS (USAFA), element of 375th AW (AMC), 302d AW (AMC, gained from AFRC)
Aircraft: C-21A, C-130H, UV-18B

Pope AFB, North Carolina
Named for 1st Lt. Harley H. Pope, a WWI flier killed when his JN-4 "Jenny" crashed into Cape Fear River on 7 January 1917.
Location: 12 miles north-northwest of Fayetteville
Major Command: AMC
Units: 43d AW, elements of 347th Wing (ACC), 427th SOS (AFSOC)
Aircraft: A-10A/OA-10A, CASA 212-200, C-130E

Portland IAP/ANGB, Oregon
Location: Portland
Major Command: (ANG)
Units: 142d FW (ACC, gained from ANG), element of 939th RQW (ACC, gained from AFRC)
Aircraft: C-130E, F-15A/B, HC-130P, HH-60G

Quonset State Airport, Rhode Island (formerly NAS Quonset Point)
Location: 20 miles south of Providence
Major Command: (ANG)
Unit: 143d AW (AMC, gained from ANG)
Aircraft: C-130E

Randolph AFB, Texas
Named after Capt. William M. Randolph, killed when his AT-4 crashed on takeoff from Gorman Field, Texas, on 17 February 1928.
Location: San Antonio

ACC, AFSOC and AMC each have assets at Pope AFB. The 74th and 75th FS operate A-10A and OA-10A Thunderbolt IIs from the North Carolina base, whereas the 427th Special Operations Squadron (SOS) stations its CASA 212-200 there. In addition, Pope AFB is home to two C-130E Hercules units, the 2d and 41st AS of the 43d AW.

Major Command: AETC
Units: 12th FTW, 340th FTG (AETC, gained from AFRC), element of 375th AW (AMC)
Aircraft: C-21A, T-1A, T-37B, T-38A/AT-38B, T-43A

Reno-Tahoe IAP/May ANGB, Nevada
Location: 5 miles southeast of Reno
Major Command: (ANG)
Unit: 152d AW (AMC, gained from ANG)
Aircraft: C-130E

Richmond IAP-Byrd Field, Virginia
Named after Adm. Richard E. Byrd, an arctic explorer.
Location: Sandston
Major Command: (ANG)
Unit: 192d FW (ACC, gained from ANG)
Aircraft: F-16C/D

Rickenbacker IAP/ANGB, Ohio
Named for Capt. Edward V. Rickenbacker, a Medal of Honor recipient and top WWI ace.
Location: Columbus
Major Command: (ANG)
Unit: 121st ARW (AMC, gained from ANG)
Aircraft: KC-135R

Robins AFB, Georgia
Named after Brig. Gen. Augustine Warner Robins, a former chief of the Air Corps' Materiel Division.
Location: 15 miles southeast of Macon
Major Command: AFMC
Units: 93d ACW (ACC), 116th BW (ACC, gained from ANG), 2d SOF (AFSOC), 19th ARG (AMC), Warner Robins Air Logistics Center (AFMC)
Aircraft: B-1B, E-8C, EC-137D, KC-135R, TE-8A

Rosecrans MAP, Missouri
Location: 4 miles west of St. Joseph
Major Command: (ANG)

Unit: 139th AW (AMC, gained from ANG)
Aircraft: C-130H

Salt Lake City IAP, Utah
Location: 3 miles west of Salt Lake City
Major Command: (ANG)
Unit: 151st ARW (AMC, gained from ANG)
Aircraft: KC-135E

Savannah IAP, Georgia
Location: 4 miles northwest of Savannah
Major Command: (ANG)
Unit: 165th AW (AMC, gained from ANG)
Aircraft: C-130H

Schenectady CAP/Stratton ANGS, New York
Location: Scotia
Major Command: (ANG)
Unit: 109th AW (AMC, gained from ANG)
Aircraft: C-26B, C-130H, LC-130H

Scott AFB-MidAmerica Airport, Illinois
Named for Cpl. Frank S. Scott, the first enlisted man to die in an aircraft accident, killed September 1912.
Location: 6 miles east-northeast of Belleville
Major Command: AMC
Units: 126th ARW (AMC, gained from ANG), 375th AW, 932d AW (AMC, gained from AFRC)
Aircraft: C-9A, C-21A, KC-135E

Selfridge ANGB, Michigan
Named for 1st Lt. Thomas E. Selfridge, the first fatality of powered flight, who was killed on 17 September 1908 when a plane piloted by Orville Wright crashed.
Location: 3 miles northeast of Mount Clemens
Major Command: (ANG)
Units: 127th Wing (ACC/AMC, gained from ANG), 927th ARW (AMC, gained from AFRC)
Aircraft: C-130E, F-16C/D, KC-135E

US Air Force

Seymour Johnson AFB, North Carolina
Named for Navy Lt. Seymour A. Johnson, killed in an aircraft accident on 5 March 1941.
Location: Goldsboro
Major Command: ACC
Units: 4th FW, 916th ARW (AMC, gained from AFRC)
Aircraft: F-15E, KC-135R

Shaw AFB, South Carolina
Named for 2nd Lt. Ervin D. Shaw, killed in action during a reconnaissance mission over France on 9 July 1918.
Location: 10 miles west-northwest of Sumter
Major Command: ACC
Unit: 20th FW
Aircraft: F-16C/D

Sheppard AFB, Texas
Named for U.S. Sen. Morris E. Sheppard.
Location: 4 miles north of Wichita Falls
Major Command: AETC
Units: 80th FTW, 82nd TRW
Aircraft: T-37B, T-38A/AT-38B, various training airframes

Sioux Gateway Airport, Iowa
Location: 7 miles south of Sioux City
Major Command: (ANG)
Unit: 185th FW (ACC, gained from ANG)
Aircraft: F-16C/D

Sky Harbor IAP, Arizona
Location: Phoenix
Major Command: (ANG)
Unit: 161st ARW (AMC, gained from ANG)
Aircraft: KC-135E

Springfield-Beckley MAP, Ohio
Location: 5 miles south of Springfield
Major Command: (ANG)
Unit: 178th FW (ACC, gained from ANG)
Aircraft: F-16C/D

Stewart IAP/ANGB, New York
Location: Newburgh
Major Command: (ANG)
Unit: 105th AW (AMC, gained from ANG)
Aircraft: C-5A

Syracuse IAP/Hancock Field, New York
Location: 5 miles northeast of Syracuse
Major Command: (ANG)
Unit: 174th FW (ACC, gained from ANG)
Aircraft: F-16C/D

Tinker AFB, Oklahoma
Named after Maj. Gen. Clarence L. Tinker, who was lost at sea on 7 June 1942.
Location: 8 miles southeast of Oklahoma City
Major Command: AFMC
Units: 552d ACW (ACC), 513th ACG (ACC, gained from AFRC), 507th ARW (AMC, gained from AFRC), Oklahoma City Air Logistics Center (AFMC)
Aircraft: E-3B/C, KC-135R, TC-18E

Toledo Express Airport, Ohio
Location: 14 miles west of Toledo
Major Command: (ANG)
Unit: 180th FW (ACC, gained from ANG)
Aircraft: F-16C/D

Travis AFB, California
Named after Brig. Gen. Robert F. Travis, killed as a result of a Boeing B-29 accident on 5 August 1950.
Location: Fairfield
Major Command: AMC
Units: 60th AMW, 349th AMW (AMC, gained from AFRC)
Aircraft: C-5A/B/C, KC-10A

Tucson IAP, Arizona
Location: Tucson
Major Command: (ANG)
Unit: 162d FW (AETC, gained from ANG)
Aircraft: C-26B, F-16A/B/C/D and F-16A(ADF)

Tulsa IAP, Oklahoma
Location: Tulsa
Major Command: (ANG)
Unit: 138th FW (ACC, gained from ANG)
Aircraft: F-16C/D

Tyndall AFB, Florida
Named after 1st Lt. Frank B. Tyndall, a WWI fighter pilot killed in a P-1 crash on 15 July 1930.
Location: 12 miles east of Panama City
Major Command: AETC
Units: 325th FW (AETC), element of 53d Wing (ACC), 148th FW Det. (ACC, gained from ANG)
Aircraft: E-9A, F-15C/D, F-16A (ADF), QF-4E/G

US Air Force Academy, Colorado
Location: Colorado Springs
Major Command: (Direct Reporting Unit)
Units: 34th TRW, element of 12th FTW
Aircraft: Cessna 150, T-3A, T-41D, TG-3A, TG-4A, TG-7A, TG-9A, TG-11A

Vance AFB, Oklahoma
Named after Lt. Col. Leon R. Vance Jr., a Medal of Honor recipient killed 26 July 1944.
Location: 5 miles southwest of Enid
Major Command: AETC
Unit: 71st FTW
Aircraft: T-1A, T-37B, T-38A/AT-38B

Vandenberg AFB, California
Named after Gen. Hoyt S. Vandenberg, the Air Force's second chief of staff.
Location: 8 miles northwest of Lompoc
Major Command: AFSPC
Unit: 30th SPW
Aircraft: UH-1N

W.K. Kellogg Airport/Battle Creek ANGB, Michigan
Location: Battle Creek
Major Command: (ANG)
Unit: 110th FW (ACC, gained from ANG)
Aircraft: A-10A/OA-10A

Westover ARB, Massachusetts
Named for Maj. Gen. Oscar Westover, the chief of the Air Corps killed on 21 September 1938 in an aircraft accident near Burbank, California.
Location: 5 miles northeast of Chicopee
Major Command: AFRC
Unit: 439th AW (AMC, gained from AFRC)
Aircraft: C-5A

Not only does Stewart IAP/ ANGB support C-5A Galaxy operations of the ANG's 105th AW but also both the US Army and US Marine Corps base aviation elements at the facility.

Best known as home to the entire USAF B-2A Spirit fleet, Whiteman AFB supports both operational Stealth Bomber squadrons belonging to the 509th BW and the wing's training unit which is equipped with T-38A Talons. The B-2's first combat missions were conducted over the former Yugoslavia during the Kosovo crisis, which entailed the bombers flying nonstop directly from and back to Whiteman. The flights, which typically lasted 30 hours, were made possible with aerial refuelings.

Whiteman AFB, Missouri
Named after 2d Lt. George A. Whiteman, the first pilot to die during aerial combat in the Japanese attack on Pearl Harbor.
Location: 2 miles south of Knob Noster
Major Command: ACC
Units: 509th BW, element of 53d Wing, 442d FW (ACC, gained from AFRC)
Aircraft: A-10A/OA-10A, B-2A, T-38A

Will Rogers World Airport, Oklahoma
Location: 7 miles southwest of Oklahoma City
Major Command: (ANG)

Unit: 137th AW (AMC, gained from ANG)
Aircraft: C-130H

Wright-Patterson AFB, Ohio
Named after aviation pioneers, Wilbur and Orville Wright, and 1st Lt. Frank S. Patterson who was killed in an aircraft crash on 19 June 1918.
Location: 10 miles east-northeast of Dayton
Major Command: AFMC
Units: Element of 375th AW (AMC), 445th AW (AMC, gained from AFRC)
Aircraft: C-21A, C-141B/C

Yeager Airport, West Virginia
Named for Brig. Gen. Charles "Chuck" Yeager, the first person to break the sound barrier on 14 October 1947.
Location: 4 miles northeast of Charleston
Major Command: (ANG)
Unit: 130th AW (AMC, gained from ANG)
Aircraft: C-130H

Youngstown-Warren RAP/ARS, Ohio
Location: 16 miles north of Youngstown
Major Command: AFRC
Unit: 910th AW
Aircraft: C-130H

US Air Force

OVERSEAS

Ahmed Al Jaber AB, Kuwait
Units: Elements of 363d AEW (ACC)
Aircraft: A-10/OA-10A, F-16C/D, HH-60G

Akrotiri AB, Cyprus
Location: Akrotiri
Unit: 9th RW Det. (ACC)
Aircraft: U-2S

Al Dhafra AB, United Arab Emirates
Units: Elements of 363d AEW (ACC)
Aircraft: KC-135E/R

Al Seeb AB, Oman
Unit: Element of 363d AEW (ACC)
Aircraft: C-130E/H

Ali Al Salem AB, Kuwait
Units: Elements of 363d AEW (ACC)
Aircraft: C-130E/H, HC-130P

Andersen AFB, Guam
Named for Gen. James Roy Andersen, lost at sea on 26 February 1946.
Location: 2 miles north of Yigo
Major Command: PACAF
Unit: 36th ABW 18th Wing Det.
Aircraft: KC-135R

Aviano AB, Italy
Location: 50 miles north of Venice
Major Command: USAFE
Unit: 31st FW
Aircraft: F-16C/D

Incirlik AB, Turkey
Location: 10 miles east of Adana
Major Command: USAFE
Unit: 39th Wing
Aircraft: (Rotational)

Kadena AB, Japan
Location: 15 miles north of Naha, Okinawa
Major Command: PACAF
Units: 18th Wing, element of 55th Wing (ACC), 353d SOG (AFSOC)
Aircraft: C-130E, E-3B/C, F-15C/D, HH-60G, KC-135R, MC-130E/P, RC-135U/V/W

Kunsan AB, South Korea
Location: 8 miles from Kunsan City
Major Command: PACAF
Unit: 8th FW
Aircraft: F-16C/D

Misawa AB, Japan
Location: Misawa
Major Command: PACAF
Unit: 35th FW
Aircraft: F-16C/D

NAS Keflavik, Iceland
Location: Keflavik Airport, 22 miles southwest of Reykjavik
Major Command: (US Navy facility)

Unit: 85th Group (ACC)
Aircraft: F-15, F-16, HH-60G and TDY F-15/F-16, HC-130

Osan AB, South Korea
Named for nearby city of Osan, site of the first fighting between US and North Korean forces in July 1950.
Location: 38 miles south of Seoul
Major Command: PACAF
Units: 51st FW, element of 9th RW (ACC), 18th Wing Det., element of 353d SOG (AFSOC)
Aircraft: A-10A/OA-10A, C-12J, F-16C/D, HH-60G, MH-53J, U-2S

Prince Sultan AB, Saudi Arabia
Location: Al Kharj
Unit: 363d AEW (ACC)
Aircraft: C-130E/H, E-3B/C, KC-135E/R, RC-135V/W, U-2S

RAF Lakenheath, England (Royal Air Force base)
Location: 25 miles from Cambridge
Major Command: USAFE
Unit: 48th FW
Aircraft: F-15C/D/E

RAF Mildenhall, England (Royal Air Force base)
Location: 30 miles northeast of Cambridge
Major Command: USAFE
Units: Element of 55th Wing (ACC), 100th ARW (USAFE), 352d SOG (AFSOC)
Aircraft: C-130E, KC-135R, MC-130N/P, MH-53J/M, RC-135V/W

Ramstein AB, Germany
Location: 8 miles west of Kaiserslautern
Major Command: USAFE
Unit: 86th AW
Aircraft: C-9A, C-20A, C-21A, C-130E, C-135B/C

Spangdahlem AB, Germany
Location: 8 miles east of Bitburg
Major Command: USAFE
Unit: 52d FW
Aircraft: A-10A/OA-10A, F-16C/D

Yokota AB, Japan
Location: 30 miles west of Tokyo
Major Command: PACAF
Unit: 374th AW
Aircraft: C-9A, C-21A, C-130E/H, UH-1N

Other USAF Facilities

- Alpena ANG CRTC/Alpena County RAP, Michigan - Michigan National Guard
- Araxos AS, Greece - USAFE
- Arnold AFB, Tennessee - AFMC
- Avon Park AS, Florida - ACC
- Bolling AFB, DC - (Direct Reporting Unit)
- Brooks AFB, Texas - AFMC
- Cape Canaveral AS, Florida - AFSPC
- Cape Cod AS, Massachusetts - AFSPC
- Cavalier AS, North Dakota - AFSPC
- CFB North Bay, Canada - ACC
- Cheyenne Mountain AS, Colorado - AFSPC
- Eldorado AS, Texas - AFSPC
- Galena Airport, Alaska - PACAF
- Ghedi AB, Italy - USAFE
- Gila Bend Air Force Aux. Field, Ariz. - AETC
- Goodfellow AFB, Texas - AETC
- Greenfield MAP-Majors Field, Texas - AFMC
- Griffis Business and Technology Park (formerly Griffiss AFB), N.Y. - ANG, AFMC
- Gulfport ANG CRTC/Gulfport Biloxi RAP - Mississippi National Guard
- Hanscom AFB, Massachusetts - AFMC
- Hato IAP, Curacao, Neth. Ant. - ACC/ANG
- Hondo MAP, Texas - AETC
- Istres AB, France - USAFE
- Izmir AS, Turkey - USAFE
- King Salmon Airport, Alaska - PACAF
- Lajes Field, Azores, Portugal - ACC
- Los Angeles AFB, California - AFMC
- Moron AB, Spain - USAFE
- New Boston AS, New Hampshire - AFSPC
- Onizuka AS, California - AFSPC
- RAF Croughton, England - USAFE
- RAF Fairford, England - USAFE
- RAF Molesworth, England - USAFE
- Rhein-Main AB, Germany - USAFE
- San Vito dei Normanni AS, Italy - USAFE
- Schriever AFB, Colorado - AFSPC
- Souda Bay, Crete - USAFE
- Stuttgart AAF, Germany - USAFE
- Thule AB, Greenland - AFSPC
- Taszar AB, Hungary - USAFE
- Tuzla AB, Bosnia-Herzegovina - USAFE
- Volk Field CRTC/Camp Williams - Wisconsin National Guard
- Woomera AS, Australia - AFSPC

PACAF's 18th Wing has three F-15C/D Eagle squadrons stationed at Kadena AB, Okinawa, Japan.

NAS Keflavik
ICELAND

GREAT BRITAIN

RAF Lakenheath
RAF Mildenhall

GERMANY

Spangdalhem AB
Ramstein AB

Aviano AB

ITALY

TURKEY

Incirlik AB

Akrotiri AB

CYPRUS

KUWAIT

Ali Al Salem AB

Ahmed Al Jaber AB

Prince Sultan AB

Al Dhafra AB

Al Seeb AB

SAUDI ARABIA

OMAN

UNITED ARAB EMIRATES

Major USAF
Bases Overseas

NORTH KOREA

Osan AB

KunsanAB

SOUTH KOREA

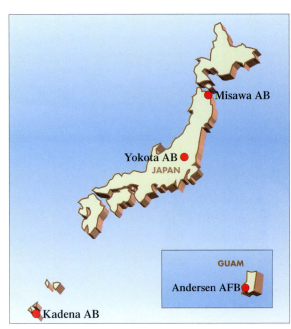

Misawa AB

Yokota AB

JAPAN

GUAM

Andersen AFB

Kadena AB

TAIL CODES

Tail Code	Unit	Location	Command
AC	177th FW	Atlantic City IAP/ANGB	ANG
AF	34th TRW	US Air Force Academy	USAFA
AK	3d Wing	Elmendorf AFB	PACAF
AK	354th FW	Eielson AFB	PACAF
AL	187th FW	Montgomery RAP	ANG
AN	176th Wing	Anchorage IAP/Kulis ANGB	PACAF
AV	31st FW	Aviano AB, Italy	USAFE
AZ	162d FW	Tucson IAP	AETC
BB	9th RW	Beale AFB	ACC
BC	110th FW	Battle Creek ANGB	ANG
BD	917th Wing	Barksdale AFB	AFRC
CA	129th RQW	Moffett Federal Airport ANGS	ANG
CB	14th FTW	Columbus AFB	AETC
CC	27th FW	Cannon AFB	ACC
CI*	146th AW	NAS Point Mugu/C.I. ANGS	ANG
CO	140th Wing	Buckley ANGB	ANG
CT	103d FW	Bradley IAP/ANGB	ANG
DC	113th Wing	Andrews AFB	ANG
DE*	166th AW	New Castle County Airport	ANG
DM	355th Wing	Davis Monthan AFB	ACC
DR	305th RQS	Davis Monthan AFB	AFRC
DY	7th BW	Dyess AFB	ACC
ED	412th TW	Edwards AFB	AFMC
EF	147th FW	Ellington Field/ANGB	ANG
EG	33d FW	Eglin AFB	ACC
EL	28th BW	Ellsworth AFB	ACC
EN	80th FTW	Sheppard AFB	AETC
ET	46th TW	Eglin AFB	AFMC
FE	90th SPW	F.E. Warren AFB	AFSPC
FF	1st FW	Langley AFB	ACC
FL	125th FW	Jacksonville IAP	ANG
FL	920th RQG	Patrick AFB	AFRC
FM	482d FW	Dade County Hmstd. RAP/ARS	AFRC
FS	188th FW	Fort Smith RAP/Ebbing ANGB	ANG
FT	23d FG	Pope AFB	ACC
FW	122d FW	Fort Wayne IAP	ANG
GA	116th BW	Robins AFB	ANG
(HA)	185th FW	Sioux Gateway Airport	ANG
HI	419th FW	Hill AFB	AFRC
HL	388th FW	Hill AFB	ACC
HO	49th FW	Holloman AFB	ACC

Tail Code	Unit	Location	Command
HT	46th TESTG	Holloman AFB	AFMC
HV	30th SPW	Vandenberg AFB	AFSPC
IA	132d FW	Des Moines IAP	ANG
ID	124th Wing	Boise Air Term.-Gowen Field	ANG
IS	85th Group	NAS Keflavik, Iceland	ACC
JZ	159th FW	NAS New Orleans JRB	ANG
KC	442d FW	Whiteman AFB	AFRC
KS	81st TRW, 45th AS	Keesler AFB	AETC
LA	2d BW	Barksdale AFB	ACC
LD	17th TRW	Lackland AFB	AETC
LF	56th FW	Luke AFB	AETC
LI	106th RQW	Gabreski Airport/ANGB	ANG
LN	48th FW	RAF Lakenheath, UK	USAFE
LR	944th FW	Luke AFB	AFRC
MA	102d FW	Otis ANGB	ANG
MA	104th FW	Barnes MAP/ANGB	ANG
MD	175th Wing	Martin St. Airport/Warfield ANGB	ANG
MF	645th MATS Det. 2	Greenville MAP	AFMC
MI	127th Wing	Selfridge ANGB	ANG
MM	341st SPW	Malmstrom AFB	AFSPC
MN*	133d AW	Minneapolis-St Paul IAP/ARS	ANG
MO	366th Wing	Mountain Home AFB	ACC
MT	5th BW	Minot AFB	ACC
MT	91st SPW	Minot AFB	AFSPC
MY	347th Wing	Moody AFB	ACC
NC*	145th AW	Charlotte/Douglas IAP	ANG
NM	150th FW	Kirtland AFB	ANG
NO	926th FW	NAS New Orleans JRB	AFRC
NY	174th FW	Syracuse Hancock IAP	ANG
OF	55th Wing	Offutt AFB	ACC
OH	178th FW	Springfield-Beckley MAP	ANG
OH	180th FW	Toledo Express Airport	ANG
OK	552d ACW/513th ACG*	Tinker AFB	ACC/AFRC
OK	138th FW	Tulsa IAP	ANG
OK*	137th AW	Will Rogers World Airport	ANG
OS	51st FW	Osan AB, Rep. of Korea	PACAF
OT	53d Wing, 85th TES	Eglin AFB	ACC
OT	53d Wing, 422d TES	Nellis AFB	ACC
PA	111th FW	NAS Willow Grove JRB	ANG
PD	939th RQW	Portland Intl. Airport	AFRC
RA	12th FTW	Randolph AFB	AETC
RI*	143d AW	Quonset State Airport	ANG
RS	86th AW	Ramstein AB, Germany	USAFE
SA	149th FW	Kelly AFB	ANG
(SC)	169th FW	McEntire ANGS	ANG
SI	183d FW	Capital Airport	ANG
SJ	4th FW	Seymour Johnson AFB	ACC
SL	131st FW	Lambert-St Louis IAP	ANG
SP	52d FW	Spangdahlem AB, Germany	USAFE
ST	82d TRW	Sheppard AFB	AETC
SW	20th FW	Shaw AFB	ACC
TH	181st FW	Terre Haute IAP-Hulman Field	ANG
TX	301st FW	NAS Fort Worth JRB-Carswell Field	AFRC
TY	325th FW	Tyndall AFB	AETC
VA	192d FW	Richmond IAP-Byrd Field	ANG
VN	71st FTW	Vance AFB	AETC
(VT)	158th FW	Burlington IAP/Ethan Allen ANGB	ANG
WA	57th Wing	Nellis AFB	ACC
WE	53d WEG	Tyndall AFB	ACC
WI	115th FW	Dane County RAP-Truax Field	ANG
WM	509th BW	Whiteman AFB	ACC
WP	8th FW	Kunsan AB, ROK	PACAF
WR	93d ACW	Robins AFB	ACC
WV*	167th AW	Eastern WV RAP-Shepherd Field	ANG
WW	35th FW	Misawa AB, Japan	PACAF
WY*	153d AW	Cheyenne Airport	ANG
XL	47th FTW	Laughlin AFB	AETC
YJ	374th AW	Yokota AB, Japan	PACAF
ZZ	18th Wing	Kadena AB, Japan	PACAF

Codes shown in parentheses have been assigned but are not carried currently.
* Although units are assigned to AMC, ACC-style codes are carried.

Holloman AFB, New Mexico, is home to the 'Black Sheep' of the 8th FS, one of two operational F-117A Stealth Fighter units.

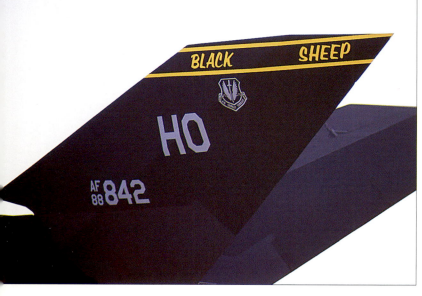

Lockheed Martin F-16C Block 40B Night Falcon (serial 88-0413)
Unit: 510th FS, 31st FW
Base: Aviano AB, Italy

Assigned to Lt. Col. Ed "EZ" Ryder in 1997, "Buzzard 01" is armed with an AGM-65 Maverick and is fitted with an AN/AAQ-14 LANTIRN targeting pod. Two LGB symbols below the cockpit indicate missions flown over the Balkans.

US NAVY

AVIATION OVERVIEW

Carrying two AIM-9s, two AIM-7s and a TARPS pod, the 'Black Aces' CAG F-14A is readied for a reconnaissance mission over Yugoslavia during Operation Allied Force in 1999. VF-41 was deployed aboard the USS *Theodore Roosevelt* (CVN 71) as part of CVW-8.

The US Navy demonstrated an interest in aviation as early as 1908 but did not officially test an airplane until 14 November 1910, when Eugene Ely flew a Curtiss biplane from the deck of the armored cruiser USS *Birmingham* (CL 2), in Hampton Roads, Virginia. However, the date recognized as marking the birth of naval aviation is 8 May 1911, when the Bureau of Navigation signed a contract for the purchase of two Curtiss biplanes. A flying school and naval aeronautical station were subsequently established at Pensacola, Florida, in January 1914. Three months later, on 14 April, the Office of Naval Aviation was created within the Bureau of Navigation. Formal recognition came on 1 July, when the Office of Naval Aeronautics was established as part of the Division of Operations reporting to the secretary of the Navy. In November 1914, the officer in charge of naval aviation was given the title Director of Naval Aeronautics.

The Navy had a single air station and owned just 54 aircraft when the United States entered World War I on 6 April 1917. By the time the war ended on 11 November 1918, however, its inventory had swelled to 2,107 aircraft and included 695 seaplanes, 1,170 flying boats and 242 land-based aircraft. During the war, naval aviators flew from 27 European bases, two bases in Canada, one in the Panama Canal Zone and 12 throughout the United States.

Benefiting from its wartime experience, the service began to concentrate on developing more capable platforms and basing more aircraft aboard ships. The 1920 Naval Appropriations Act included funding for the conversion of the collier USS *Jupiter* (AC 3) to an aircraft carrier, and two merchant ships as seaplane tenders. By July 1920, with more types entering service, it was necessary for the Navy to establish a designation system to distinguish between lighter-than-air craft and heavier-than-air craft, and identify their assigned missions. The system remained in effect for more than 40 years before it was replaced by a joint service system in 1962.

On 10 August 1921, after an act of congress authorized its creation, the Bureau of Aeronautics was established. This was quickly followed by entry into service of the first US Navy aviation support ship, the USS *Wright* (AZ 1), which was commissioned as a seaplane tender on 16 December. Three months later, the Navy's first aircraft carrier, the USS *Langley* (CV 1), was commissioned at Norfolk, Virginia. It served primarily as a prototype from which the Navy developed operational procedures to launch aircraft from the decks of ships. The first carrier takeoff from the vessel took place on 17 October 1922, when a Vought VE-7SF was launched while the carrier was at anchor on Virginia's York River. One month later, on 18 November 1922, an aircraft was catapulted from the carrier's deck for the first time. After two years of experimentation, CV 1 joined the battle fleet on 17 November 1924.

Although the first takeoff from a vessel was viewed as atrial, by 1 July 1922 the service had already authorized conversion of two unfinished battle cruisers. The resulting aircraft carriers, the USS *Lexington* (CV 2) and the USS *Saratoga* (CV 3), were much larger than the *Langley* and ultimately allowed the battle fleet to deploy a significant number of aircraft. CV 3 joined the fleet on 16 November 1927 and was followed by CV 2 on 14 December.

By the early 1930s, aircraft carriers had been integrated into naval exercises and planning, and a hydraulic arresting system was under development. Meanwhile, more

advanced aircraft continued to enter service. The Navy began looking at designs for a retractable landing gear and, in April 1931, placed an order with Grumman Aircraft for a two-seat biplane fighter designated the XFF-1, which was to be so equipped. That same year, construction of the Navy's first purpose-built carrier began. The keel of the USS *Ranger* (CV 4) was laid on 26 September 1931 at Newport News Shipbuilding in Virginia, and the ship was commissioned on 4 June 1934. Later that month, the Navy ordered its first monoplane when a contract was issued to Douglas Aircraft for the XTBD-1.

By late 1936, the USS *Langley* had outlived its usefulness as an aircraft carrier and was converted to a seaplane tender through removal of the forward portion of her flight deck. The fleet's fifth carrier, the USS *Yorktown* (CV 5), was commissioned on 30 September 1937, followed by the USS *Enterprise* (CV 6) on 12 May 1938. The title Commander Carrier Air Group was created on 1 July and squadrons became organized into groups named for their assigned carrier.

When the United States entered World War II on 7 December 1941, the Navy operated seven fleet carriers and had over 20 years of operational carrier experience. The Pacific Fleet's loss of its battleships at Pearl Harbor, coupled with experience gained from fighting many air battles during the ensuing months, caused a marked change in naval warfare thinking. The aircraft carrier was rapidly eclipsing the mighty dreadnought as the Navy's means of power projection. Throughout the Pacific campaign, few major battles were decided quickly without contribution from the Navy's fast carriers. Meanwhile, in the Atlantic, small escort carriers (designated CVEs) helped defeat Hitler's feared U-boats, long considered the bane of allied shipping. Built from the hulls of merchant ships, CVEs and their

dedicated composite squadrons paved the way for development of antisubmarine carriers (CVSs) during the Cold War. Adding to naval aviation's strength was a fleet of long-range patrol aircraft that served in both World War II theaters. When the Japanese surrendered on 2 September 1945, the US Navy had almost 100 aircraft carriers in service, including 20 fleet carriers (CVs), eight light carriers (CVLs) and 70 CVEs. US naval aviators, including marines, sank 564 Japanese vessels and claimed the destruction of more than 9,000 enemy aircraft, in the air and on the ground, during the course of the war.

New technologies advanced quickly during the postwar period and less than 11 months after the war's end, the Navy's first jet-powered fighter, a McDonnell FH-1 Phantom, made a conventional landing and takeoff from the deck of the USS *Franklin D. Roosevelt* (CVA 42) on 21 July 1946. Flight-testing continued and, on 5 May 1948, VF-17A was declared operational with the type. Within a year, the last floatplanes were replaced by helicopters in observation roles, and to ensure it could operate heavier jet-powered aircraft then on the drawing boards, the Navy began updating its veteran Essex-class carriers. Long-range, land-based bombers, flying boats and amphibious aircraft developed during World War II also set the stage for creation of a far more effective patrol force designed to combat submarines.

When North Korean troops crossed the 38th parallel on 25 June 1950, the US Navy had approximately 14,000 aircraft in service. Its jets entered combat for the first time on 3 July 1950 when strikes were launched from

the USS *Valley Forge* (CVA 45) and, on 9 November, a US Navy F9F Panther downed a Russian-made MiG-15 in the first air combat between two jet fighters. The Navy activated its first antisubmarine helicopter squadron on 3 October 1951 with the establishment of HS-1, and development of naval aviation progressed rapidly during the next decade.

The keel of the Navy's first super carrier, the USS *Forrestal* (CVA 59), was laid in July 1952 and trials using angled decks began in January 1953. That same year, the designation CVS was given to carriers dedicated to antisubmarine warfare (ASW). In 1955, the World War II escort carrier, the USS *Thetis*, became the Navy's first assault helicopter carrier (CVHA 1) paving the way for later purpose-built amphibious assault ships in the Guadalcanal (LPH), Tarawa (LHA) and Wasp (LHD) classes.

Other key events in naval aviation during this period include the commissioning of the USS *Forrestal* on 1 October 1955, and an end to the use of modified World War II bombers for ASW duties. New aircraft designed specifically for patrol missions emerged and the turboprop-powered Lockheed P3V-1 made its maiden flight on 29 August 1958. The keel for the USS *Enterprise* (CVAN 65) was laid on 4 February of that year, and the Navy commissioned its first nuclear-powered aircraft carrier on 25 November 1961. The Navy decommissioned its last airship units on 31 August 1962 and, just over a year later, on 20 December 1963, carrier air groups (CVGs) officially became carrier air wings (CVWs).

Naval aviation assets were first used in the war in Vietnam when missions against North Vietnamese torpedo boats were launched on 2 August 1964. By 26 March 1965, the period of "Rolling Thunder" had begun in the skies over North Vietnam and, on 17 June

An SH-60B assigned to HSL-44 approaches the deck of a Tarawa-class LHA in the Mediterranean Sea.

1965, a Navy pilot downed the first North Vietnamese MiG. Over the course of the eight-year conflict, the Navy lost 526 fixed-wing aircraft and 13 helicopters to hostile fire. After the cease-fire, 144 naval aviator POWs were returned home, and the Navy's last action in the conflict involved four attack carriers and a single assault ship, which were used to evacuate personnel from Saigon during Operation Frequent Wind.

The end of operations in Southeast Asia was followed by a reduction in force levels for all US military branches, although the fleet still had to meet a growing threat from the Soviet Union. The consolidation of shipboard ASW and tactical aviation assets aboard large multimission aircraft carriers enabled the Navy to phase out its Essex-class ASW carriers. The USS *Intrepid* (CVS 11) was retired on 15 March 1974, and when the USS *Oriskany* (CVA 34) was decommissioned on 30 September 1976, the Navy was left with a fleet of "super carriers" designed to fill almost all of its carrier-based mission needs.

Throughout the 1970s and 1980s, carriers were frequently called upon to project US air power around the world when American interests were at stake. By the late 1980s, the carrier battle group (CVBG) was firmly established as a foreign policy tool and carriers were called to action in Lebanon, Libya, Grenada, Panama and the Persian Gulf. Within three days of Iraq's 2 August 1990 invasion of Kuwait, an American carrier battle group arrived in the Gulf of Oman. When opening air strikes were launched as part of

Operation Desert Storm on 16 January 1991, the Navy had six of its carriers operating in the region, two of which were positioned in the Persian Gulf. In addition, a 13-ship amphibious task force was also in theater, the largest assembled since the Korean War, and 10 patrol squadrons equipped with Lockheed P-3s were deployed. By the time the short war ended on 27 February 1991, more than 100 Navy squadrons and eight carriers had served. Even now, they are regularly called to action in the region. Since 1993, US naval aircraft have also been operating in support of operations over the Balkans by conducting air strikes as well as humanitarian relief missions.

In 1980, then President Ronald Reagan reversed the drawdown in US military forces that had occurred under former President Jimmy Carter. A 600-ship fleet, including 15 aircraft carriers, was envisaged. Soon after the decade ended, however, the Soviet Union collapsed and another downsizing began. On 4 February 1992, the DoD announced the carrier fleet would be reduced to 12 ships. The decision included assignment of a single carrier to the Naval Reserve and the assumption that one vessel would always be undergoing a refueling and complex overhaul (RCOH). Later, as a result of the 1997 Bottom Up Review, the number of carrier air wings was reduced to 10 while land-based patrol squadrons were reduced from 24 active-duty and 12 reserve units to the current level of 12 active-duty and seven reserve squadrons.

Other developments brought a decrease in

each carrier's complement of F-14 Tomcats and an increase in the number of dual-mission F/A-18s deployed. A reduction in the number of potentially hostile submarines after the demise of the Soviet Union also meant there was little need to maintain such a large ASW force. The Navy has since assigned new missions to its S-3B fleet, provided its P-3Cs with additional surface and land attack capabilities, and has begun a program to create a single ASW variant of the SH-60 Seahawk. It is to be operated from escort vessels and carriers.

While the unified commanders in chief (CinCs) have expressed a view that the Navy needs 15 carriers to properly fulfill its mission, it is not surprising that individual fleet commanders find these assets are available to them for shorter periods. Keeping a carrier battle group in the Persian Gulf at all times, in support of USCENTCOM, often leaves USEUCOM and USPACOM without a vessel of their own. During 1999, USEUCOM's Sixth Fleet was without a carrier for 40 percent of the time, despite the volatile situation in the Balkans.

With the assignment of littoral missions to the Navy, the force now finds itself covering the same amount of territory with only half the number of ships it had before fleet downsizing began. This is forcing the Navy to operate with a thinly stretched force at a tempo that is taking a toll on its equipment and personnel. Unless the Navy receives a significant boost in funding, however, it is unlikely the situation will improve in the foreseeable future.

ORGANIZATION OF NAVAL AVIATION

Headquartered in Arlington, Virginia, the Department of the Navy is led by the Chief of Naval Operations (CNO) who is a four-star admiral serving as a member of the Joint Chiefs of Staff and as an advisor to the president. Reporting directly to the CNO are the Navy's major commands (MACOMs), which fall into two categories. Operating forces comprise units supporting the fleet directly, and include active-duty and reserve components, whereas all other elements are considered part of the shore establishment.

OPERATING FORCES
- Commander in Chief, US Atlantic Fleet (CINCLANTFLT)
- Commander in Chief, US Pacific Fleet (CINCPACFLT)
- Commander in Chief, US Naval Forces Europe (CINCUSNAVEUR)
- Commander, US Naval Forces Central Command (COMNAVFORCENT)
- Commander, Naval Reserve Force (COMNAVRESFOR)
- Commander, Operational Test and Evaluation Force (COMOPTEVFOR)

Although aviation units are assigned to nine MACOMs, deployable squadrons are primarily assigned to CINCLANTFLT and CINCPACFLT under the control of Commander, Naval Air Force, US Atlantic Fleet (COMNAVAIRLANT) and Commander, Naval Air Force, US Pacific Fleet (COMNAVAIRPAC), respectively. Both are three-star vice admirals. Separately, a small number of units report operationally to CINCUSNAVEUR and COMNAVFORCENT but they are administratively attached to COMNAVAIRLANT and COMNAVAIRPAC, and the Naval Air Reserve Force normally reports to COMNAVRESFOR, although its units also support the fleet commands.

In much the same way other branches of the US military report via a dual command system when deployed away from home, so do the US Navy's fleet commanders. While answering administratively to the CNO, they are required to provide naval forces and surface and air assets to all five CinCs. Accordingly, whenever naval forces enter an area of operations controlled by a particular commander in chief, they are assigned to the

numbered fleet under his control for operational purposes. A carrier battle group (CVBG) in the Mediterranean, for instance, comes under the US Sixth Fleet, which is part of US European Command (USEUCOM). While it is operating in the Atlantic Ocean, however, the CVBG reports directly to the US Second Fleet, which controls that geographical area as part of the US Joint Forces Command. This command procedure thus means that squadrons deployed aboard a carrier also have to report differently from the way they do when engaged in training or missions at their respective air stations.

Whereas the carrier and its air wing represents its nucleus, a battle group nominally consists also of two guided-missile cruisers (CGs), a destroyer (DD), a guided-missile destroyer (DDG), a guided-missile frigate (FFG), two attack submarines (SSNs) and a fast combat stores ship (AOE). The CVBG is also supported by additional aircraft including SH-60B and CH/HH/UH-46D helicopters, which are usually deployed as detachments aboard some of the surface ships listed.

Carrier Air Wings

Although the means of identifying carrier air groups in the 1930s and 1940s was quite specific and changed several times, on 1 September 1948 the carrier air group (CVG) designation was re-established. As indicated earlier, however, this was changed to carrier air wing (CVW) on 20 December 1963 when the term air group commander became air wing commander, although he is still referred to as the CAG, to this day. Operationally, he reports directly to the battle group commander.

By the mid-1970s, the Navy had transitioned to conventionally-powered and nuclear-powered multimission carriers (CVs and CVNs, respectively), and its carrier air wings had become true composite wings. This was some 20 years before the Air Force established similar organizations. Today, all air wings assigned to COMNAVAIRLANT are headquartered at NAS Oceana, Virginia, whereas four of those assigned to COM-NAVAIRPAC are based at NAS Lemoore, California, while the fifth (CVW-5) is forward deployed to NAF Atsugi, Japan. In addition, a single carrier air wing is assigned to the Naval Reserve Force at NAS Atlanta, Georgia.

The 1990s brought many changes to the assignment of aircraft and squadrons, the most significant of which was the demise of dedicated attack squadrons from air wings when the A-6E Intruder was retired. In the early 1980s carriers normally deployed with as many as 90 aircraft. Today, the figure is between 69 and 72 depending on how units are assigned. However, F/A-18s and strike capable F-14s ensure the number of strike platforms within each air wing is about the same as it was when dedicated attack aircraft were in service.

Nominal CVW Assignments

No. Sqns.	Sqn. Type	No. Aircraft	Type Aircraft
1	VF	10	F-14
3	VFA/VMFA	36	F/A-18
1	VAQ	4 or 5	EA-6B
1	VAW	4	E-2C
1	HS	4/3	SH-60F/HH-60H
1	VS	8	S-3B
1	VRC Det.	2	C-2A

(71 or 72 aircraft in total)

Alternate CVW Assignments

No. Sqns.	Sqn. Type	No. Aircraft	Type Aircraft
2	VF	20	F-14
2	VFA	24	F/A-18C
1	VAQ	4 or 5	EA-6B
1	VAW	4	E-2C
1	HS	4/3	SH-60F/HH-60H
1	VS	8	S-3B
1	VRC Det.	2	C-2A

(69 or 70 aircraft in total)

With an SH-60B flying overhead, the US Navy Spruance-class destroyer the USS *Paul Foster* (DD 964) sails alongside the USS *Ranger* (CV 61) in May 1991.

Deployments

Not only do carrier-based squadrons assigned to carrier air wings undertake six-month deployments, the majority of the Navy's other operational squadrons also undertake rotational tours, usually of six months duration as well. Twelve active-duty patrol squadrons, supported by seven reserve units, deploy from their home stations every 18 months to forward bases in Europe, Iceland, Japan, the Indian Ocean and the Persian Gulf. The purpose is to carry out maritime patrol and counternarcotics missions. As well as deploying aboard escort vessels within CVBGs, light antisubmarine squadron detachments are assigned to individual surface warships for periods lasting from three to six months, as well. Furthermore, detachments from helicopter combat support squadrons generally deploy for six-month periods aboard Navy replenishment and amphibious assault ships assigned to CVBGs and amphibious ready groups (ARGs), while Naval Reserve logistic support (VR) squadrons deploy to bases in the Pacific, Europe and Southwest Asia. Finally, while the Navy's four joint EA-6B Prowler squadrons have made regular deployments for Operations Northern Watch and Southern Watch in Southwest Asia, they are now included within USAF expeditionary air force rotations, each of which lasts for three months.

SHORE ESTABLISHMENT

The shore establishment is responsible for developing, testing and evaluating new equipment and weapons systems for the fleet, and repairing and servicing equipment already in use. It is also charged with recruit-

US Navy Aviation Command Structure

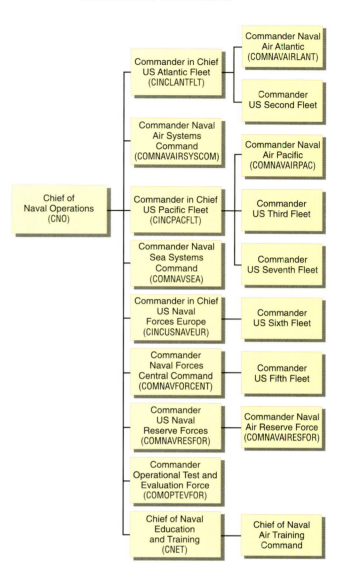

ing and training naval personnel and with developing naval doctrine. Aviation units are assigned to the following commands:
- Commander, Naval Air Systems Command (COMNAVAIRSYSCOM)
- Commander, Naval Sea Systems Command (COMNAVSEASYSCOM)
- Chief of Naval Education and Training (CNET)

COMMANDERS AND FLEET WINGS

COMMANDER IN CHIEF, US ATLANTIC FLEET (CINCLANTFLT)

The US Atlantic Fleet is the naval component of the US Joint Forces Command (USJFCOM), and is headed by a four-star admiral headquartered at NAVSTA Norfolk, Virginia. The command is responsible for providing forces to US Southern Command (USSOUTHCOM), US Central Command (USCENTCOM) and US European Command (USEUCOM).

CINCLANTFLT controls 122,000 personnel, six aircraft carriers and approximately 1,200 aircraft assigned to 64 squadrons. The fleet's operational area extends from pole to pole, and from the eastern half of the United States to the Indian Ocean. Deployed units are attached either to the Second, Fifth or Sixth Fleets, depending on their location.

Commander, Naval Air Force, US Atlantic Fleet (COMNAVAIRLANT)

Also headquartered at NAVSTA Norfolk, COMNAVAIRLANT was established on 1 January 1943, and is responsible for the administration of naval air forces assigned to the US Atlantic Fleet. The commander is a three-star vice admiral.

COMNAVAIRLANT controls eight functional and type wings. The former comprise multiple type wings at multiple locations and come under the control of a one-star rear admiral. A type wing, however, is comprised of multiple squadrons with similar missions and is generally commanded by a captain (O-6), known as a commodore.

The Atlantic fleet has five carrier air wings assigned that are composite in nature. They include fighter, strike, cargo, electronic warfare, antisubmarine and antiship assets.

Until the mid-1990s, each type and functional wing had its own Fleet Readiness Squadron (FRS), which is a training unit responsible for crew type conversion. Aircrews are assigned to one FRS (often referred to as the "RAG") prior to assignment or reassignment to an operational squadron. The term dates back some 40 years, when such squadrons came under a Replacement Air Group.

Fleet downsizing has resulted in fewer of these training squadrons but those that remain have been expanded to accommodate training for both Atlantic and Pacific fleet units. Today, only the F/A-18 Hornet and SH-60B Seahawk communities maintain more than one FRS. Separately, aircrew training for the Bell HH-1N and Sikorsky MH-53E helicopters is carried out by Marine Corps units.

Commander in Chief, US Atlantic Fleet (CINCLANTFLT)
NAVSTA Norfolk, Virginia
Commander, Naval Air Force, US Atlantic Fleet (COMNAVAIRLANT)
Chambers Field, NAVSTA Norfolk, Virginia

Command/Squadron	Location	Aircraft	Tail Code
Commander, Airborne Early Warning Wing Atlantic (COMAEWWINGLANT)			
Chambers Field/NAVSTA Norfolk, Virginia			
VAW-120 (FRS) 'Greyhawks'	Chambers Field, Norfolk	E-2C/C (Group II), C-2A	AD
VAW-121 'Bluetails'	Chambers Field, Norfolk	E-2C (Group II)	AG
VAW-123 'Screwtops'	Chambers Field, Norfolk	E-2C (Group II)	AB
VAW-124 'Bear Aces'*	Chambers Field, Norfolk	E-2C	AJ
VAW-125 'Tigertails'	Chambers Field, Norfolk	E-2C (Group II)	AA
VAW-126 'Seahawks'	Chambers Field, Norfolk	E-2C	AC
VRC-40 'Rawhides'	Chambers Field, Norfolk	C-2A	
Squadron will begin transition to Group II in April 2000.			
Commander, Helicopter Tactical Wing Atlantic (COMHELTACWINGLANT)			
Chambers Field/NAVSTA Norfolk, Virginia			
HC-2 (FRS) 'Fleet Angels'	Chambers Field, Norfolk	UH-3H, VH-3A	HU
HC-4 'Black Stallions'*	NAS Sigonella, Italy	MH-53E	HC
HC-6 'Chargers'	Chambers Field, Norfolk	HH-46D, UH-46D	HW
HC-8 'Dragon Whales'	Chambers Field, Norfolk	CH-46D, HH-46D, UH-46D	BR
HM-14 'Vanguard'	Chambers Field, Norfolk	MH-53E	BJ
HM-15 'Black Hawks'	NAS Corpus Christi, Texas	MH-53E	TB
VC-6 'Firebees'	Chambers Field, Norfolk		
Det. **	NAS Patuxent River, Maryland	RQ-2A	FB
Det.	FCTC Dam Neck, Virginia	BQM-74E	
Operationally tasked by Commander Fleet Air Mediterranean			
**Located at Webster Field*			
Commander, Helicopter Antisubmarine Light Wing Atlantic (COMHSLWINGLANT)			
NAVSTA Mayport, Florida			
HSL-40 (FRS) 'Airwolves'	NAVSTA Mayport	SH-60B	HK
HSL-42 'Proud Warriors'	NAVSTA Mayport	SH-60B	HN
HSL-44 'Swamp Fox'	NAVSTA Mayport	SH-60B	HP
HSL-46 'Grandmasters'	NAVSTA Mayport	SH-60B	HQ
HSL-48 'Vipers'	NAVSTA Mayport	SH-60B	HR
Commander, Helicopter Antisubmarine Wing Atlantic (COMHSWINGLANT)			
NAS Jacksonville, Florida			
HS-3 'Tridents'	NAS Jacksonville	SH-60F, HH-60H	AJ
HS-5 'Night Dippers'	NAS Jacksonville	SH-60F, HH-60H	AG
HS-7 'Shamrocks'	NAS Jacksonville	SH-60F, HH-60H	AC
HS-11 'Dragonslayers'	NAS Jacksonville	SH-60F, HH-60H	AB
HS-15 'Red Lions'	NAS Jacksonville	SH-60F, HH-60H	AA
Commander, Patrol and Reconnaissance Force Atlantic (COMPATRECONFORLANT)			
NAVSTA Norfolk, Virginia			
VP-30 (FRS) 'Pro's Nest'	NAS Jacksonville, Florida	P-3C, VP-3A	LL
VP-Det.	NAVSTA Roosevelt Roads, P.R.	P-3C	
Commander, Patrol and Reconnaissance Wing Five (COMPATRECONWING FIVE)			
NAS Brunswick, Maine			
VP-8 'Tigers'	NAS Brunswick	P-3C	LC
VP-10 'Red Lancers'	NAS Brunswick	P-3C	LD
VP-26 'Tridents'	NAS Brunswick	P-3C	LK
VPU-1 'Old Buzzards'	NAS Brunswick	P-3C, UP-3A	OB

All five of COMNAVAIRLANT's air wings are active duty and the majority comprise eight squadrons each, composed of three strike fighter (VFA) units along with one fighter (VF), one airborne early warning (VAW), one helicopter antisubmarine warfare (HS), one electronic combat (VAQ) and one sea control (VS) unit, plus a detachment of two C-2A Greyhound carrier onboard delivery (COD) aircraft. In some cases, one VFA squadron is replaced by another VF unit. Until May 1999, each deployed air wing was also assigned a detachment of two ES-3A electronic intelligence (ELINT) aircraft. These aircraft are no longer in service, however.

Commander in Chief, US Atlantic Fleet (CINCLANTFLT) (Continued)

Command/Squadron	Location	Aircraft	Tail Code
Commander, Patrol and Reconnaissance Wing Eleven (COMPATRECONWING ELEVEN) NAS Jacksonville, Florida			
VQ-2 'Batmen'*	NAVSTA Rota, Spain	EP-3E, P-3C	JQ
VP-5 'Mad Foxes'	NAS Jacksonville	P-3C	LA
VP-16 'War Eagles'	NAS Jacksonville	P-3C	LF
VP-45 'Pelicans'	NAS Jacksonville	P-3C	LN
* Operationally tasked by Commander Fleet Air Mediterranean.			
Commander, Sea Control Wing Atlantic (COMSEACONWINGLANT) - NAS Jacksonville, Florida			
VS-22 'Checkmates'	NAS Jacksonville	S-3B	AC
VS-24 'Scouts'	NAS Jacksonville	S-3B	AJ
VS-30 'Diamondcutters'	NAS Jacksonville	S-3B	AA
VS-31 'Topcats'	NAS Jacksonville	S-3B	AG
VS-32 'Maulers'	NAS Jacksonville	S-3B	AB
Commander, Strike Fighter Wing Atlantic (COMSTRIKFIGHTWINGLANT) - NAS Oceana, Virginia			
VFA-15 'Valions'	NAS Oceana	F/A-18C	AJ
VFA-34 'Blue Blasters'	NAS Oceana	F/A-18C	AA
VFA-37 'Bulls'	NAS Oceana	F/A-18C	AC
VFA-81 'Sunliners'	NAS Oceana	F/A-18C	AA
VFA-82 'Marauders'	MCAS Beaufort, South Carolina	F/A-18C	AB
VFA-83 'Rampagers'	NAS Oceana	F/A-18C	AA
VFA-86 'Sidewinders'	MCAS Beaufort, South Carolina	F/A-18C	AB
VFA-87 'Golden Warriors'	NAS Oceana	F/A-18C	AJ
VFA-105 'Gunslingers'	NAS Oceana	F/A-18C	AC
VFA-106 (FRS) 'Gladiators'	NAS Oceana	F/A-18A/B/C/D	AD
VFA-131 'Wildcats'	NAS Oceana	F/A-18C	AG
VFA-136 'Knighthawks'	NAS Oceana	F/A-18C	AG
SFWSL	NAS Oceana	T-34C	
Commander, Fleet Air Keflavik (COMFLEETAIRKEF) - NAS Keflavik, Iceland			
VP-Det.	NAS Keflavik	P-3C	
AOD	NAS Keflavik	UP-3A	
Commander, Fighter Wing Atlantic (COMFITWINGLANT) - NAS Oceana, Virginia			
VC-8 'Redtails'	NAVSTA Roosevelt Roads, P.R.	TA-4J, UH-3H	GF
VF-2 'Bounty Hunters'	NAS Oceana	F-14D	NE
VF-11 'Red Rippers'	NAS Oceana	F-14B	AG
VF-14 'Tophatters'	NAS Oceana	F-14A	AJ
VF-31 'Tomcatters'	NAS Oceana	F-14D	NK
VF-32 'Swordsmen'	NAS Oceana	F-14B	AC
VF-41 'Black Aces'	NAS Oceana	F-14A	AJ
VF-101 (FRS) 'Grim Reapers'	NAS Oceana	F-14A/B/D, T-34C	AD
VF-102 'Diamondbacks'	NAS Oceana	F-14B	AB
VF-103 'Jolly Rogers'	NAS Oceana	F-14B	AA
VF-143 'Pukin' Dogs'	NAS Oceana	F-14B	AG
VF-154 'Black Knights'	NAF Atsugi, Japan	F-14A	NF
VF-211 'Checkmates'	NAS Oceana	F-14A	NG
VF-213 'Black Lions'	NAS Oceana	F-14D	NH

Atlantic Fleet Wings

Commander, Airborne Early Warning Wing Atlantic (COMAEWWINGLANT)

Based at NAVSTA Norfolk, Virginia, COMAEWWINGLANT is responsible for five operational carrier airborne early warning squadrons (CARAEWRON), as well as the E-2C/C-2A FRS and a single fleet logistic support squadron (FLELOGSUPRON) that normally detaches two C-2As to each deployed carrier air wing.

NAVAIRLANT FLEET READINESS SQUADRONS

Unit	Location	Aircraft
HC-2	NAVSTA Norfolk	UH-3H
HSL-40	NAVSTA Mayport, Florida	SH-60B
VAW-120	NAVSTA Norfolk, Virginia	E-2C, C-2A
VF-101	NAS Oceana, Virginia	F-14A/B/D
VFA-106	NAS Oceana, Virginia	F/A-18A/B/C/D
VP-30	NAS Jacksonville, Florida	P-3C

BuNo 164767/BJ is one of 12 MH-53E Sea Dragons operated by the 'Vanguard' of HM-14.

Commander, Helicopter Tactical Wing Atlantic (COMHELTACWINGLANT)

Established on 1 September 1993, the wing is based at NAVSTA Norfolk and controls seven units conducting combat support missions. Detachments from its helicopter combat support squadrons (HELSUPRONs) regularly deploy aboard amphibious assault and combat support vessels for SAR and vertical replenishment (VERTREP) purposes.

Operationally tasked by Commander Mine Warfare Command (COMINEWARCOM) in Corpus Christi, Texas, aircraft operated by mine countermeasures squadrons (HEL-MINERONs) HM-14 and HM-15 are detached aboard the USS *Inchon* (MCS 12), a Guadalcanal–class amphibious assault ship converted to fulfill this mission. Another unit, VC-6, provides UAVs for reconnaissance purposes and as aerial and seaborne training targets.

Stationed at NAS Oceana, Virginia, the 'Bounty Hunters' of VF-2 operate F-14D Tomcats. The squadron deploys as part of CVW-2 aboard the USS *Constellation* (CV 64).

Commander, Helicopter Antisubmarine Light Wing Atlantic (COMHSLWINGLANT)

The five Light Airborne Multipurpose System (LAMPS Mark III) squadrons assigned to COMHSLWINGLANT, which include the FRS, are based at NAVSTA Mayport, Florida. The wing received its current designation on 1 September 1993. Its SH-60B Seahawks are normally deployed as one- or two-aircraft detachments aboard destroyers, guided-missile frigates or guided-missile cruisers for periods of between three and six months. Missions encompass antisurface and antisubmarine warfare; command, control and communications; electronic warfare; SAR; and logistics. Each operational squadron (HELANTISUBRON-LIGHT) has 10 aircraft and the wing also maintains a support detachment at NAS Sigonella, Italy.

Commander, Helicopter Antisubmarine Wing Atlantic (COMHSWINGLANT)

Given its current designation on 1 September 1993, this wing has five helicopter antisubmarine squadrons assigned and is based at NAS Jacksonville, Florida. Units are tasked with undersea warfare, SAR, airborne utility services and CSAR, and operate their SH-60F and HH-60H Seahawks from aircraft carriers rather than small vessels. All training is carried out at NAS North Island, California, and each squadron is usually assigned four SH-60F and three HH-60H helicopters.

Commander, Patrol and Reconnaissance Force Atlantic (COMPATRECONFORLANT)

Based at NAVSTA Norfolk, Virginia, this is the only functional wing within COM-NAVAIRLANT. Two patrol and reconnaissance wings (PATWINGs), the P-3 Orion FRS and a special projects squadron are assigned. The functional wing, led by a rear admiral (lower half) and its two PATWINGs were redesignated on 26 March 1999. Six patrol squadrons (PATRONs), each with 10 P-3Cs assigned, undertake six-month deployments at three different locations. Two units are normally deployed at the same time, with one on station in Sigonella, Italy, while the other splits its assets between Puerto Rico and Iceland.

Although administratively assigned to PATWINGs, VQ-2 and the PATRON detached to Italy are both tasked by Fleet Air Mediterranean, via Commander Maritime Surveillance and Reconnaissance Forces, US Sixth Fleet (CTF-67). Likewise, the unit detached to Iceland is tasked by Fleet Air Keflavik.

Commander, Sea Control Wing Atlantic (COMSEACONWINGLANT)

Established in 1970 as Commander Sea Strike Wing One, this command was redesignated COMSEACONWINGLANT on 1 September 1993. Until 1997, the operational squadrons assigned were based at NAS Cecil Field, Florida. Due to its closure, however, they have been relocated to NAS Jacksonville, Florida. Today, the wing is responsible for five sea control squadrons (SEACONRONs) and each unit operates eight S-3Bs. However, no FRS is assigned because S-3B Viking training is carried out by VS-41 at NAS North Island, California.

Commander, Strike Fighter Wing Atlantic (COMSTRIKFIGHTWINGLANT)

Established in 1970 as Light Attack Wing One, COMSTRIKFIGHTWINGLANT assumed its current name on 1 September 1993, and relocated to NAS Oceana, Virginia, in June 1999. Assigned is one FRS as well as 11 deployable strike fighter squadrons (STRIKFITRONs), each of which is equipped with 12 F/A-18C Hornets. All but two units are based at NAS Oceana and the remaining squadrons were due to move to MCAS Beaufort, South Carolina, early in 2000. The wing also controls the Strike Fighter Weapons School Atlantic (SFWSL).

COMMANDER IN CHIEF, US PACIFIC FLEET (CINCPACFLT)

Established on 1 September 1942, and headquartered at NAVSTA Pearl Harbor, Oahu, Hawaii, the US Pacific Fleet is the naval component of US Pacific Command (USPACOM) and is commanded by a four-star admiral. With 177,000 personnel assigned,

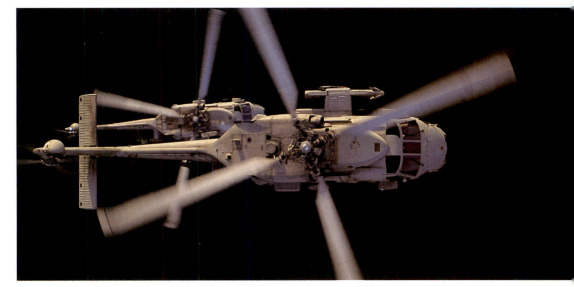

Two SH-60B Seahawks assigned to HSL-41 include BuNos 164461/TS-01 and 161560/TS-07. The former is armed with an AGM-119 Penguin antiship missile.

CINCPACFLT provides forces to USCENTCOM and USSOUTHCOM.

Commander, Naval Air Force, US Pacific Fleet (COMNAVAIRPAC)

Headquartered at NAS North Island, California, COMNAVAIRPAC is the primary advisor to the US Pacific Fleet for the operation and administration of naval aviation in the Pacific. The three-star vice admiral commanding is responsible for training all Pacific naval air units serving with the US Third, Fifth and Seventh Fleets.

Assets assigned to this commander include 1,400 aircraft operated by 68 squadrons, as well as six aircraft carriers. COMNAVAIRPAC is responsible for eight type and functional wings, and a territorial area that

Commander, Fleet Air Keflavik (COMFLEETAIRKEF)

Headquartered at NAS Keflavik, Iceland, COMFLEETAIRKEF is a rear admiral (lower half) responsible for coordinating the maritime operations of rotational NAVAIRLANT P-3C squadrons. These units are deployed to the air station for a period of six months in support of US Antisubmarine Reconnaissance Forces Eastern Atlantic. The deployed squadron normally maintains a detachment of four aircraft at Keflavik, with additional aircraft and crews assigned to NAVSTA Roosevelt Roads, Puerto Rico.

Commander, Fighter Wing Atlantic (COMFITWINGLANT)

COMFITWINGLANT came into being on 1 September 1993, with the redesignation of Commander Fighter Wing One. Following the disestablishment of Commander Fighter Wing Pacific (COMFITWINGPAC) in 1996, NAS Oceana, Virginia, became home to the Navy's entire fleet of F-14 Tomcats. In addition to being responsible for the FRS and 11 operational squadrons at the air station, the wing maintains administrative control of a single Tomcat unit forward deployed to Japan, as well as a fleet composite squadron (FLECOMPRON) in Puerto Rico. Each fighter squadron (FITRON) now comprises just 10 F-14s.

NAVAIRPAC FLEET READINESS SQUADRONS

Unit	Location	Aircraft
HC-3 *	NAS North Island, California	CH/HH/UH-46D
HSL-41	NAS North Island	SH-60B
VAQ-129	NAS Whidbey Island, Washington	EA-6B
VRC-30	NAS North Island	UC-12B
VS-41	NAS North Island	S-3B
VFA-125	NAS Lemoore, California	F/A-18A/B/C/D
VFA-122	NAS Lemoore	F/A-18E/F
HS-10	NAS North Island	SH-60F

* Will become the FRS for the CH-60S

BuNo 165169 was the fifth engineering and manufacturing development (EMD) F/A-18E Super Hornet, and one of two single-seaters used for weapons separation tests.

US Navy

Commander in Chief, US Pacific Fleet (CINCPACFLT) NAVSTA Pearl Harbor, Hawaii Commander, Naval Air Force, US Pacific Fleet (COMNAVAIRPAC) NAS North Island, California			
Command/Squadron	Location	Aircraft	Tail Code

Commander, Airborne Early Warning Wing Pacific (COMAEWWINGPAC) - NAS Point Mugu, Calif.

VAW-112 'Golden Hawks'	NAS Point Mugu	E-2C (Group II)	NG
VAW-113 'Black Hawks'	NAS Point Mugu	E-2C (Group II)	NK
VAW-115 'Liberty Bells'	NAF Atsugi, Japan	E-2C (Group II)	NF
VAW-116 'Sun Kings'	NAS Point Mugu	E-2C (Group II)	NE
VAW-117 'Wallbangers'	NAS Point Mugu	E-2C (Group II)	NH
VRC-30 'Providers'	NAS North Island	C-2A, UC-12B/F	RW

Commander, Electronic Attack Wing Pacific (COMVAQWINGPAC) - NAS Whidbey Island, Wash.

VAQ-128 'Fighting Phoenix'*	NAS Whidbey Island	EA-6B	NL
VAQ-129 (FRS) 'Vikings'	NAS Whidbey Island	EA-6B	NJ
VAQ-130 'Zappers'	NAS Whidbey Island	EA-6B	AC
VAQ-131 'Lancers'	NAS Whidbey Island	EA-6B	NE
VAQ-132 'Scorpions'	NAS Whidbey Island	EA-6B	AA
VAQ-133 'Wizards'*	NAS Whidbey Island	EA-6B	NL
VAQ-134 'Garudas'*	NAS Whidbey Island	EA-6B	NL
VAQ-135 'Black Ravens'	NAS Whidbey Island	EA-6B	NH
VAQ-136 'Gauntlets'	NAF Atsugi, Japan	EA-6B	NF
VAQ-137 'Rooks'	NAS Whidbey Island	EA-6B	AB
VAQ-138 'Yellowjackets'	NAS Whidbey Island	EA-6B	NG
VAQ-139 'Cougars'	NAS Whidbey Island	EA-6B	NK
VAQ-140 'Patriots'	NAS Whidbey Island	EA-6B	AG
VAQ-141 'Shadowhawks'	NAS Whidbey Island	EA-6B	AJ
VAQ-142 'Gray Wolves'*	NAS Whidbey Island	EA-6B	NL

* Joint USAF/USN unit

Commander, Helicopter Tactical Wing Pacific (COMHELTACWINGPAC) - NAS North Island

HC-3 (FRS) 'Packrats'*	NAS North Island	CH-46D, HH-46D	SA
HC-5 'Providers'**	Andersen AFB, Guam	HH-46D, UH-46D	RB
HC-11 'Gunbearers'***	NAS North Island	HH-46D, UH-46D, UH-3H	VR

* HC-3 will gain CH-60S FRS mission
** HC-5 is tasked by Commander, Fleet Air Western Pacific, and will transition to the CH-60S
*** HC-11 operates UH-3H in support of 3d Fleet

Commander, Helicopter Antisubmarine Light Wing Pacific (COMHSLWINGPAC) - NAS North Island

HSL-37 'Easyriders'	MCAF Kaneohe Bay, Hawaii	SH-60B	TH
HSL-41 (FRS) 'Seahawks'	NAS North Island	SH-60B	TS
HSL-43 'Battle Cats'	NAS North Island	SH-60B	TT
HSL-45 'Wolfpack'	NAS North Island	SH-60B	TZ
HSL-47 'Sabrehawks'	NAS North Island	SH-60B	TY
HSL-49 'Scorpions'	NAS North Island	SH-60B	TX
HSL-51 'Warlords'*	NAF Atsugi, Japan	SH-60B, UH-3H	TA

* HSL-51 Det. 11 operates UH-3H in support of 7th Fleet.

Commander, Helicopter Antisubmarine Wing Pacific (COMHSWINGPAC) - NAS North Island

HS-2 'Golden Falcons'	NAS North Island	SH-60F, HH-60H	NE
HS-4 'Black Knights'	NAS North Island	SH-60F, HH-60H	NK
HS-6 'Indians'	NAS North Island	SH-60F, HH-60H	NH
HS-8 'Eightballers'	NAS North Island	SH-60F, HH-60H	NG
HS-10 (FRS) 'Warhawks'	NAS North Island	SH-60F, HH-60H	RA
HS-14 'Chargers'	NAF Atsugi, Japan	SH-60F, HH-60H	NF

encompasses the Pacific and Indian Oceans. The geographical area falling under its command stretches from pole to pole, from the Mississippi River west to the Persian Gulf. Personnel strength totals 50,000.

Four of COMNAVAIRPAC's carriers are nuclear powered and four of its five carrier air wings are continental United States (CONUS) based, whereas the fifth is forward deployed in Japan. The basic structure of Pacific air wings is the same as for those under the Atlantic command, and eight FRS are assigned in all.

Pacific Fleet Wings

Commander, Airborne Early Warning Wing Pacific (COMAEWWINGPAC)

COMAEWWINGPAC was established when Commander Fighter Airborne Early Warning Wing Pacific was disestablished on 1 August 1993. Four of the wing's E-2C Hawkeye squadrons recently relocated from MCAS Miramar, California, to NAS Point Mugu, California, whereas the fifth unit is forward deployed to Japan. Other assets include three King Airs flown by a single fleet logistic support unit based at NAS North Island, which serves as the FRS for the UC-12B/F, and 16 C-2A Greyhounds, including two that permanently support CVW-5 in Japan.

Commander, Electronic Attack Wing Pacific (COMVAQWINGPAC)

COMVAQWINGPAC is based at NAS Whidbey Island in Washington and controls 15 electronic attack squadrons (VAQRONs), including the FRS plus 10 assigned to NAVAIRLANT and NAVAIRPAC carrier air wings. Led by a US Navy commander (O-5), four additional squadrons comprise joint US Air Force/US Navy expeditionary units and are made up of personnel from both services. Each squadron has four EA-6B Prowlers that can be deployed worldwide for electronic jamming missions.

Commander, Helicopter Tactical Wing Pacific (COMHELTACWINGPAC)

NAS North Island is home to COMHELTACWINGPAC and was established on 1 July 1993. The commander controls three combat support helicopter squadrons that provide VERTREP or SAR services when deployed with combat support or amphibious assault ships. HC-3 is the H-46 Sea Knight FRS and the squadron will also assume the CH-60S Knighthawk FRS mission during 2000, although it will continue to provide SAR training for the Navy. In addition to Sea Knight operations, HC-11 flies a single UH-3H from the deck of the USS *Coronado* (AGF 11), for Commander Third Fleet.

Commander, Helicopter Antisubmarine Light Wing Pacific (COMHSLWINGPAC)

Established on 5 May 1993, and based at NAS North Island, California, the wing has seven LAMPS Mark III squadrons assigned, including the SH-60B Seahawk FRS. Each of its operational squadrons is equipped with 10 Seahawks. One unit is based in Hawaii and another is forward deployed to Japan.

Commander, Helicopter Antisubmarine Wing Pacific (COMHSWINGPAC)

COMHSWINGPAC was established on 1 July 1993 and controls six helicopter anti-submarine squadrons. These comprise five operational units plus the SH-60F FRS, which undertakes training for both NAVAIR-LANT and NAVAIRPAC squadrons. The wing is based at NAS North Island, California, although a single unit is forward deployed to Japan.

Commander, Patrol and Reconnaissance Force Pacific (COMPATRECONFORPAC)

Headquartered at MCB Hawaii, COMPA-TRECONFORPAC is a functional wing with responsibility for a patrol and reconnaissance wing (COMPATRECONWING), a strategic communications wing (COM-STRATWING) and the Pacific Missile Range Facility (PMRF) in Hawaii. In addition, three PATRONs and a special projects patrol squadron (SPECPROJPATRON), now based at MCB Hawaii/MCAF Kaneohe Bay, are assigned directly. These units relocated from NAS Barbers Point in 1999 as a direct result of that station's closure. Separately, three PATRONs and a fleet air reconnaissance squadron (FAIRECONRON) are assigned to Commander Patrol and Reconnaissance Wing Ten, headquartered at NAS Whidbey Island, Washington.

PATRONs from both MCAF Kaneohe Bay and NAS Whidbey Island make six-month rotational deployments that normally require one unit to go to NAF Misawa, Japan, with aircraft and personnel detached to Kadena AB, Japan. A second squadron is deployed to the Naval Support Facility (NSF) at Diego Garcia, British Indian Ocean Territory (BIOT), but detaches aircraft and personnel to NAF Bahrain and Al Masirah AB, Oman. VQ-1 normally detaches EP-3Es from Whidbey Island to NAF Misawa and NAF Bahrain, as well. The units operating from Japan and BIOT are under the control of Commander Patrol and Reconnaissance Wing One (COMPATRECONWING ONE), located at Kamiseya, Japan, while those deployed to locations in Southwest Asia are attached to US Naval Forces Central Command (COMNAVFORCENT).

E-6A/B Mercury aircraft operated by FAIRECONRONs with COMSTRATWING ONE are detached to locations worldwide from the wing's headquarters at Tinker AFB, Oklahoma, to support the operations of US Strategic Command (USSCOM). Sites are also maintained at Travis AFB, California, and NAS Patuxent River, Maryland. In addition, the wing has maintained a detachment at Offutt AFB, Nebraska, since it assumed the "Looking Glass" mission from the USAF on 25 September 1998.

Command/Squadron	Location	Aircraft	Tail Code
Commander in Chief, US Pacific Fleet (CINCPACFLT) (Continued)			
Commander, Patrol and Reconnaissance Force Pacific (COMPATRECONFORPAC)			
MCB Hawaii/MCAF Kaneohe Bay, Hawaii			
VPU-2 'Wizards'	MCAF Kaneohe Bay	P-3C, UP-3A	(SP)
VP-4 'Skinny Dragons'	MCAF Kaneohe Bay	P-3C	YD
VP-9 'Golden Eagles'	MCAF Kaneohe Bay	P-3C	PD
VP-47 'Golden Swordsmen'	MCAF Kaneohe Bay	P-3C	RD
Commander, Strategic Communications Wing One (COMSTRATCOMWING ONE)			
Tinker AFB, Oklahoma			
Det. 1	Offutt AFB, Nebraska	E-6B	
VQ-3 'Ironmen'	Tinker AFB	E-6B	(TC)
Det	Travis AFB, California	E-6B	
VQ-4 'Shadows'	Tinker AFB	E-6A/B	(HL)
Det	NAS Patuxent River, Maryland	E-6A/B	
NTSU (FRS)	Tinker AFB	TC-18F	
Commander, Patrol and Reconnaissance Wing Ten (COMPATRECONWING TEN)			
NAS Whidbey Island, Washington			
VP-1 'Screaming Eagles'	NAS Whidbey Island	P-3C	YB
VP-40 'Marlins'	NAS Whidbey Island	P-3C	QE
VP-46 'Gray Knights'	NAS Whidbey Island	P-3C	RC
VQ-1 'World Watchers'	NAS Whidbey Island	P-3C, EP-3E, UP-3A	PR
Pacific Missile Range Facility (PMRF) - NAVSTA Barking Sands Kauai, Hawaii			
AOD	Barking Sands PMRF, Hawaii	RC-12F*, UH-3H	
*RC-12F aircraft will be replaced by RC-26D			
Commander, Sea Control Wing Pacific (COMSEACONWINGPAC) - NAS North Island, California			
VS-21 'Redtails'	NAF Atsugi, Japan	S-3B	NF
VS-29 'Dragonfires'	NAS North Island	S-3B	NH
VS-33 'Screwbirds'	NAS North Island	S-3B	NG
VS-35 'Blue Wolves'	NAS North Island	S-3B	NK
VS-38 'Red Griffins'	NAS North Island	S-3B	NE
VS-41 (FRS) 'Shamrocks'	NAS North Island	S-3B	NJ

BuNo 163935 is a Bell AH-1W Cobra assigned to the 'Vampires' of VX-9 at NAWS China Lake, California. The squadron is the operational evaluation unit for naval strike and attack platforms.

NAS Point Mugu, California, is home to the 'Evaluators,' a detachment from VX-9 that serves as the operational evaluation unit for the F-14 Tomcat. The unit is the sole operator of the type on the West Coast.

Commander, Sea Control Wing Pacific (COMSEACONWINGPAC)

Five operational SEACONRONs and the S-3B Viking FRS are assigned to COMSEA-CONWINGPAC, which was established on 22 April 1993. The wing's single FAIRE-CONRON was recently deactivated and, with the exception of one forward-deployed squadron, its remaining units are located at NAS North Island, California. The FRS conducts all S-3B training.

Commander, Strike Fighter Wing Pacific (COMSTRIKFIGHTWINGPAC)

Established on 15 April 1991, this wing is based at NAS Lemoore, California, and controls 13 deployable STRIKFITRONs as well as VFA-125, the F/A-18A/B/C/D FRS. Three of its units are forward deployed to NAF Atsugi, Japan. VFA-122, the new F/A-18E/F FRS, is also assigned to the wing. The Super Hornet will soon begin replacing the F-14 Tomcat in fleet service.

Commander, Fleet Air Western Pacific (COMFAIRWESTPAC)

Headquartered at NAF Atsugi, Japan, COM-FAIRWESTPAC provides logistic support to naval units deployed in Japan and the western Pacific area, and is also responsible for tasking HC-5 at Anderson AFB, Guam, as well as the patrol squadrons deployed with COMPATWING ONE. HC-5 will be the first operational squadron to fly the CH-60S in the VERTREP role. COMFAIRWESTPAC is a rear admiral (lower half).

Commander, Operational Test and Evaluation Force (COMOPTEVFOR)

Headquartered at NAVSTA Norfolk, COMOPTEVFOR is a rear admiral who reports directly to the Chief of Naval Operations (CNO). The force became the Navy's sole independent agency for operational test and evaluation in 1971. Missions include establishing operational suitability during R&D phases, fleet introduction of new weapons systems and development of tactics. In addition, the command exercises operational control over two air test and evaluation squadrons (AIRTEVRONs) and maintains close liaison with Marine Corps Squadron HMX-1 at Quantico, Virginia. It coordinates test and evaluation activities with test agencies within other branches of the military, as well as with the DoD's Director of Operational Test and Evaluation.

Commander in Chief, US Pacific Fleet (CINCPACFLT) (Continued)

Command/Squadron	Location	Aircraft	Tail Code
Commander, Strike Fighter Wing Pacific (COMSTRIKFIGHTWINGPAC) - NAS Lemoore, California			
VFA-22 'Fighting Redcocks'	NAS Lemoore	F/A-18C	NH
VFA-25 'Fist of the Fleet'	NAS Lemoore	F/A-18C	NK
VFA-27 'Chargers'	NAF Atsugi, Japan	F/A-18C	NF
VFA-94 'Mighty Shrikes'	NAS Lemoore	F/A-18C	NH
VFA-97 'Warhawks'	NAS Lemoore	F/A-18A	NH
VFA-113 'Stingers'	NAS Lemoore	F/A-18C	NK
VFA-115 'Eagles'	NAS Lemoore	F/A-18C	NK
VFA-122 (FRS) 'Flying Eagles'	NAS Lemoore	F/A-18E/F	NJ
VFA-125 (FRS) 'Rough Raiders'	NAS Lemoore	F/A-18A/B/C/D, T-34C	NJ
VFA-137 'Kestrels'	NAS Lemoore	F/A-18C	NE
VFA-146 'Blue Diamonds'	NAS Lemoore	F/A-18C	NG
VFA-147 'Argonauts'	NAS Lemoore	F/A-18C	NG
VFA-151 'Fighting Vigilantes'	NAS Lemoore	F/A-18C	NE
VFA-192 'Golden Dragons'	NAF Atsugi	F/A-18C	NF
VFA-195 'Dambusters'	NAF Atsugi	F/A-18C	NF
Commander, Fleet Air Western Pacific (COMFAIRWESTPAC) - NAF Atsugi, Japan			
AOD	NAF Atsugi	UC-12F	
AOD	Andersen AFB, Guam	HH-1N	8J
AOD	NAF Misawa, Japan	UC-12F	8M
AOD	NAF Kadena, Okinawa, Japan	UC-12F	8H
Commander, Patrol and Reconnaissance Wing One (COMPATRECONWING ONE) NRRF Kamiseya, Japan			
VP-Det.	NSF Diego Garcia, BIOT	P-3C	
VP-Det.	NAF Misawa, Japan	P-3C	
VP-Det.	NAF Kadena, Okinawa, Japan	P-3C	
VQ-1 Det.	NAF Misawa, Japan	EP-3E	

Commander, Operational Test & Evaluation Force (COMOPTEVFOR)
NAVSTA Norfolk, Virginia

Command/Squadron	Location	Aircraft	Tail Code
Aviation Warfare Division - NAVSTA Norfolk, Virginia			
VX-1 'Pioneers'	NAS Patuxent River, Maryland	SH-60B/F, P-3C, S-3B	JA
VX-9 'Vampires'	NAWS China Lake, California	F/A-18A/B/C/D/E/F, AV-8B	
		AH-1W, EA-6B	XE
VX-9 Det. 'Evaluators'	NAS Point Mugu, California	F-14A/B/D	XF

Commander Naval Sea Systems Command (COMNAVSEA) - Washington, D.C.

Command/Squadron	Location	Aircraft	Tail Code
Naval Undersea Warfare Center - Newport, Rhode Island			
AUTEC Aviation Services	Andros Island, Bahamas	S-61N, Beech 1900D	

* Aircraft operated under contract by Raytheon Range Systems Engineering Company.

Command/Squadron	Location	Aircraft	Tail Code
Naval Surface Warfare Center Dahlgren Division - Dahlgren, Virginia			
CSS Aviation Unit 'Dragon Masters'	Panama City, Florida	MH-53E, HH-1N	

Commander, Naval Sea Systems Command (COMNAVSEA)

Headquartered in Arlington, Virginia, NAVSEA is led by a vice admiral and is responsible for designing and building ships and shipboard weapons, and includes two warfare centers.

Naval Undersea Warfare Center (NUWC)

Located in Newport, Rhode Island, the NUWC was established on 2 January 1992, as the center for research, development, testing, engineering and fleet support of submarines, autonomous underwater systems and weapons systems related to undersea warfare. The Atlantic Underwater Test and Evaluation Center (AUTEC), a comprehensive undersea warfare test complex located on Andros Island in the Bahamas, provides support for such development.

Naval Surface Warfare Center Dahlgren Division (NSWCDD)

Headquartered in Dahlgren, Virginia, NSWCDD is responsible for research, development, testing, engineering and fleet support of surface warfare systems. The division's Coastal Systems Station (CSS), located at St. Andrew Bay in Panama City, Florida, is responsible for coastal missions like mine warfare, amphibious warfare, special warfare and diving systems. The Airborne Mine Countermeasures (MCM) Division handles the management and technical direction of relevant MCM combat systems deployed from airborne platforms.

Chief of Naval Education and Training (CNET) - NAS Pensacola, Florida

Command/Squadron	Location	Aircraft	Tail Code
Chief Naval Air Training Command (CNATRA) - NAS Corpus Christi, Texas			
NFDS 'Blue Angels'	NAS Pensacola, Florida	F/A-18A/B, TC-130G	
Training Air Wing One (TAW-1) - NAS Meridian, Mississippi			A
VT-7 'Strike Eagles'	NAS Meridian	T-45C	
VT-9 'Tigers'	NAS Meridian	T-2C	
Training Air Wing Two (TAW-2) - NAS Kingsville, Texas			B
VT-21 'Fighting Red Hawks'	NAS Kingsville	T-45A	
VT-22 'Golden Eagles'	NAS Kingsville	T-45A	
Training Air Wing Four (TAW-4) - NAS Corpus Christi, Texas			G
VT-27 'Boomers'	NAS Corpus Christi	T-34C	
VT-28 'Rangers'	NAS Corpus Christi	T-34C	
VT-31 'Wise Owls'	NAS Corpus Christi	T-44A	
VT-35 'Stingrays'	NAS Corpus Christi	TC-12B, UC-12B	
Training Air Wing Five (TAW-5) - NAS Whiting Field, Florida			E
VT-2 'Doer Birds'	NAS Whiting Field	T-34C	
VT-3 'Red Knights'	NAS Whiting Field	T-34C	
VT-6 'Shooters'	NAS Whiting Field	T-34C	
HT-8 'Eight Ballers'	NAS Whiting Field	TH-57B/C	
HT-18 'Vigilant Eagles'	NAS Whiting Field	TH-57B/C	
Training Air Wing Six (TAW-6) - NAS Pensacola, Florida			F
VT-4 'Mighty Warbucks'	NAS Pensacola	T-34C, T-1A	
VT-10 'Wildcats'	NAS Pensacola	T-34C, T-1A	
VT-86 'Sabrehawks'	NAS Pensacola	T-39G/N, T-2C	

Home stationed at NAS Pensacola, Florida, the 'Blue Angels' of the Naval Flight Demonstration Squadron have operated F/A-18As since transitioning from A-4F Skyhawks in 1987. BuNo 161932 is seen here during a visit to Republic Airport, New York, on 4 June 1998.

COMMANDER, US NAVAL FORCES CENTRAL COMMAND (COMNAVFORCENT)

COMNAVFORCENT is a two-star rear admiral (lower half) and the forces at his disposal make up the naval component of USCENTCOM. Headquartered at Manama, Bahrain, the command's Administrative Support Unit Southwest Asia handles logistics for units deployed with the US Fifth Fleet. These include forward-based detachments equipped with P-3C, EP-3E, UH-3H and MH-53E aircraft, and operational support airlift missions conducted by UC-12Ms based at Bahrain IAP.

Chief of Naval Education and Training (CNET)

Headquartered at NAS Pensacola, Florida, CNET is a vice admiral who reports directly to the CNO, and is responsible for the education and training of Navy and Marine Corps officers as well as enlisted personnel.

Chief, Naval Air Training Command (CNATRA)

Headquartered at NAS Corpus Christi, Texas, the CNATRA is a rear admiral (upper half) who is responsible for the Navy's aviation training resources. These include five training air wings, two helicopter training squadrons (HELATRA-RONs), 14 fixed-wing training squadrons (TRARONs) and the 'Blue Angels' Naval Flight Demonstration Squadron. Joint flight training is conducted with the Air Force both at Randolph AFB, Texas, and Vance AFB, Oklahoma.

Training Air Wing One (TAW-1) was commissioned in 1971 at NAS Meridian, Mississippi. It is responsible for intermediate and advanced strike jet instruction and has two squadrons assigned. Its T-2C-equipped unit will soon begin converting to the T-45C.

Training Air Wing Two (TAW-2) is located at NAS Kingsville, Texas, and provides intermediate and advanced training for pilots who will fly tactical aircraft. The syllabus includes advanced strike training and carrier qualification.

Training Air Wing Four (TAW-4) was established in June 1976 at NAS Corpus Christi, Texas, and provides primary and intermediate training in T-34Cs, plus advanced multiengine and instrument training in T-44A and TC-12B aircraft.

Training Air Wing Five (TAW-5) was activated in 1972 at NAS Whiting Field, Florida, and conducts primary and intermediate fixed- and rotary-wing flight training. Its five squadrons operate more than 200 T-34Cs and nearly 150 TH-57s.

Training Air Wing Six (TAW-6) is located at NAS Pensacola, Florida, and trains US Navy and Marine Corps flight officers and navigators. The wing is also responsible for training USAF navigators. On completion of their primary training with VT-4 or VT-10, students destined for large, multiengine aircraft transfer to Randolph AFB, Texas, while those selected for tactical multiengine platforms remain with the wing for intermediate training.

COMMANDER, NAVAL AIR SYSTEMS COMMAND (COMNAVAIRSYSCOM)

Headquartered at NAS Patuxent River, Maryland, COMNAVAIRSYSCOM was established on 7 May 1966, and the vice admiral is tasked with overseeing naval aviation research, development, procurement, testing and evaluation. Generally referred to as NAVAIR, the command controls six major facilities including two air warfare centers, and naval aviation depots at NAS North Island, California; NAS Jacksonville, Florida; and MCAS Cherry Point, North Carolina.

Naval Air Warfare Center Aircraft Division (NAWCAD)

NAWCAD, headquartered at NAS Patuxent River, Maryland, is responsible for systems development including propulsion systems, air vehicles, avionics, aviation support equipment and catapult-arresting systems. The Naval Test Pilot School is also assigned, and the division is led by a rear admiral (lower half).

Naval Air Warfare Center Weapon Division (NAWCWD)

Headquartered at Naval Air Weapons Station China Lake, California, the center conducts its operations both there and at NAS Point Mugu, California. The commanding rear admiral (lower half) is responsible for the development and testing of air-launched weapons and target systems.

Commander, Naval Air Systems Command (COMNAVAIRSYSCOM)
NAS Patuxent River, Maryland

Command/Squadron	Location	Aircraft	Tail Code
Naval Air Warfare Center Aircraft Division (NAWCAD) - NAS Patuxent River, Maryland			
Commander Naval Test Wing Atlantic			
NSATS	NAS Patuxent River, Maryland	EA-6B, AV-8B, F-14A/B/D, F/A-18A/B/C/D/E/F, T-45A	SD
NFATS	NAS Patuxent River	S-3B, C-2A, UP-3A, P-3C, NP-3B/C/D, NT-34C, KC-130F/T, NC-130H, E-2C	
NRWATS	NAS Patuxent River	UH-1N, AH-1W, SH-2G, NVH-3A, CH-46E, CH/MH-53E, TH-57C, HH-60H, SH-60B/F/R	
USNTPS	NAS Patuxent River	F/A-18B, T-2C, T-38A, NP-3D, NU-1B, U-6A, C-12C, TH-6B, OH-58C, UH-60A, NSH-60B, X-26A	
F/A-18E/F ITT	NAS Patuxent River	F/A-18E/F	
V-22 ITT	NAS Patuxent River	MV-22B	
Naval Air Warfare Center Weapon Division (NAWCWD) - NAWS China Lake, California			
Commander Naval Test Wing Pacific			
NWTS 'Dust Devils'	NAWS China Lake, California	F/A-18A/B/C/D, AV/TAV-8B, AH-1W, HH-1N, T-39D, SA227AC *	
NWTS 'Bloodhounds'	NAS Point Mugu, California	QF-4N/S, YF-4J, F-14A/B/D, NP-3D, SA227AC*	BH
Naval Aviation Depots (NADEPs)			
NADEP Jacksonville	NAS Jacksonville, Florida	(P-3C, EP-3E, NP-3D, UP-3A, F-14A/B/D, EA-6B)	
NADEP Cherry Point	MCAS Cherry Point, North Carolina	(QF-4N/S, CH-46D/E, UH/HH-46D)	
NADEP North Island	NAS North Island, California	(F/A-18A/B/C/D, S-3B, E-2C, C-2A)	

* Aircraft owned and maintained by Flight International Inc.

Chief of Naval Operations (CNO) - Washington, D.C.

Command/Squadron	Location	Aircraft	Tail Code
DIRECT REPORTING UNITS			
Naval Strike and Air Warfare Center (NSAWC) - NAS Fallon, Nevada			
NSAWC 'Strike'	NAS Fallon	F-14A, F/A-18A/B, SH-60F, E-2C	
Chief of Naval Research - Arlington, Virginia			
NRL FSD	NAS Patuxent River, Maryland	NP-3D, P-3C	
Commander in Chief US Naval Forces Europe (CINCUSNAVEUR) - London, UK			
AOD	NAF Mildenhall, UK	UC-12M	8G
Commander Fleet Air Mediterranean (COMFAIRMED) - NSA Naples, Italy			
AOD	NAVSTA Rota, Spain	UC-12M	
AOD	NAS Sigonella, Italy	C-26D	
AOD	NAF Naples/Capodichino AP, Italy	C-26D	
HC-2 Det. 1*	NAF Naples/Capodichino AP	UH-3H	HU
HC-4 Det.	Palese Macchie AP, Bari, Italy	MH-53E	HC
VP-30 Det.**	NAS Sigonella, Italy	VP-3A	
VP-Det.***	NAS Sigonella	P-3C	

* HC-2 Det. 1 operates UH-3H from USS *LaSalle* (AGF 3) in support of Commander U.S. Sixth Fleet
** Operates VP-3A in support of CINCAFSE
*** Operationally tasked by Commander Fleet Air Mediterranean

Commander US Naval Forces Central Command (COMNAVCENT) - ASU SWA Manama, Bahrain			
FSD	NAF Bahrain IAP, Bahrain	UC-12M	
VQ-1 Det.	NAF Bahrain IAP	EP-3E	PR
HC-2 Det. 2*	NAF Bahrain IAP	UH-3H	HU
HM-14 Det. 1	NAF Bahrain IAP	MH-53E	HC
VP-Det.	NAF Bahrain IAP	P-3C	
VP-Det.	Al Masirah AB, Oman	P-3C	

* HC-2 Det. 2 operates UH-3H in support of Commander U.S. Fifth Fleet

DIRECT REPORTING UNITS

Fleet Information Warfare Center (FIWC)

Responsible for the development of information warfare and command and control, the FIWC is located at Naval Amphibious Base Little Creek, Virginia. The command's training missions also are augmented by reserve squadron VAQ-209.

Warfare Center and the Carrier Airborne Early Warning Weapons School at a single location. Naval aircrews are provided with air-to-air and strike training at the center, which also serves as a training site for carrier air wings prior to deployment.

Naval Strike and Air Warfare Center (NSAWC)

Located at NAS Fallon, Nevada, NSAWC provides graduate-level training in tactics. The center is led by a rear admiral (lower half) and consolidated the former Navy Fighter Weapons School, the Naval Strike

Chief of Naval Research

The Naval Research Laboratory (NRL) in Washington, D.C., was commissioned in 1923 and is a field command conducting scientific research with maritime applications. Research areas include new materials, equipment and systems. The NRL also studies the ocean, atmosphere and space sciences and related technologies. Its Flight Support Detachment (FSD) is located at NAS Patuxent River, Maryland, and operates six uniquely modified NP-3Ds as airborne research platforms. When Oceanographic Development Squadron 8 (VXN-8) was disestablished in September 1993, the detachment acquired two aircraft and their associated missions. These included "Project Magnet," which measures and maps the earth's magnetic variations, and "Project Birdseye," which involves hydroacoustic research. Its aircraft are the only airborne platforms used for projects such as bathymetry, electronic countermeasures, gravity mapping and radar development research.

COMMANDER IN CHIEF, US NAVAL FORCES EUROPE (CINCUSNAVEUR)

CINCUSNAVEUR is the naval component of USEUCOM and is headquartered in London, England. US Atlantic Fleet units within the commander's area of operations are attached to the US Sixth Fleet.

Commander Fleet Air Mediterranean (COMFAIRMED)

Located at NSA Naples, Italy, COMFAIRMED provides operational logistics support, airlift and intermediate-level main-

The Naval Strike and Air Warfare Center at NAS Fallon, Nevada, operates a small number of Sikorsky SH-60Fs, including BuNo 164092.

tenance for all Sixth Fleet assets. Commander, Maritime Surveillance and Reconnaissance Forces, US Sixth Fleet, handles the maritime patrol P-3C squadrons as well as VQ-2, the fleet air reconnaissance squadron located in Spain.

Naval Air Stations

Although all of the services reduced the number of C-12 aircraft supporting operational support airlift, many are still assigned directly to air stations and flown by their air operations departments. Mission tasking for such aircraft is handled by the Joint Operational Support Airlift Center (JOSAC) at Scott AFB, Illinois. Most stations also operate UH-3Hs or HH-1Ns for SAR duties.

COMMANDER, NAVAL AIR RESERVE FORCES (COMNAVAIRRESFOR)

Three type wings and a single carrier air wing report to the Commander, Naval Air Reserve Forces. He is a rear admiral (lower half), headquartered at NSA New Orleans.

Stationed at NAS North Island, California, HC-85 operates UH-3Hs in a variety of roles, including training missions with Navy SEALs on San Clemente Island.

Naval Air Station Flights and Miscellaneous Units

Command/Squadron		Location	Aircraft	Tail Code
AOD	OMD	NAS Patuxent River, Maryland	UC-12B, UH-3H	7A
AOD	OMD	NAS Atlanta, Georgia	UC-12B	7B
AOD	OMD	Chambers Field, Norfolk, Virginia	UC-12B/M	7C
AOD	OMD	NAS Fort Worth JRB, Texas	UC-12B	7D
AOD	OMD	NAS Jacksonville, Florida	UC-12B, UH-3H	7E
AOD	OMD	NAS Brunswick, Maine	HH-1N	7F
AOD	OMD	NAS Whidbey Island, Washington	UC-12B, UH-3H	7G/FW
AOD	OMD	NAS Fallon, Nevada	UC-12B, HH-1N	7H
AOD	OMD	NAS North Island, California	NC/UC-12B	7M
AOD	OMD	NAF Washington, Maryland	UC-12B	7N
AOD	OMD	NAWS China Lake, California	HH-1N	7P
AOD	OMD	NAS Key West, Florida	UC-12B, UH-3H	7Q
AOD	OMD	NAS Oceana, Virginia	UH-3H	7R
AOD	OMD	NAS Lemoore, California	UC-12B, HH-1N	7S
AOD	OMD	NAS Willow Grove JRB, Pennsylvania	UC-12B	7W
AOD	OMD	NAS New Orleans JRB, Louisiana	UC-12B	7X
AOD	OMD	NAVSTA Roosevelt Roads, P.R.	UC-12M, RC-12M	8E
AOD	OMD	NAVSTA Guantanamo Bay, Cuba	UC-12B, HH-1N	8F
AOD	OMD	NAF El Centro, California	UC-12B	8N
AOD	ETD	MCAF Kaneohe Bay, Hawaii	VP-3A	
AOD	OMD	NAS Meridian, Mississippi	HH-1N	D
AOD	OMD	NAS Pensacola, Florida	UH-3H	F
AOD	OMD	NAS Corpus Christi, Texas	HH-1N	G

Carrier Air Wing Reserve Twenty (CVWR-20)

With the 1994 disestablishment of Carrier Air Wing Reserve Thirty at MCAS Miramar, California, CVWR-20 remained the last reserve air wing. It is headquartered at NAS Atlanta, Georgia, and although the wing operates equipment similar to its active-duty counterpart, it will never be an exact mirror of an active-duty carrier air wing. A single airborne early warning unit is tasked with counternarcotics missions and two composite fighter squadrons (FITCOMPRONs) provide dissimilar air combat training (DACT). They are considered fleet support units.

Commander, Reserve Patrol Wing (COMRESPATWING)

Headquartered at NAVSTA Norfolk, Virginia, this wing controls eight squadrons. The fleet's sole air reconnaissance unit is assigned, an electronic "adversary" squadron scheduled for deactivation in March 2000.

Commander, Helicopter Reserve Wing (COMHELRESWING)

Headquartered at NAS North Island, California, COMHELRESWING's structure will change significantly as new variants of the Sikorsky H-60 begin replacing almost all current aircraft flown by the wing. It is made up of a single helicopter antisubmarine warfare unit and two helicopter antisubmarine light squadrons. In addition it has one combat support helicopter squadron and two combat support (special) helicopter squadrons (HELSUPRONSPECs). The wing was established on 1 January 1976, when Carrier Antisubmarine Group Reserve Eighty (CVSGR-80) was redesignated.

A Lockheed P-3C on routine patrol over the Pacific Ocean on 13 March 1997. The Orion belongs to the 'Tridents' of Naval Reserve Squadron VP-65, based at NAS Point Mugu, California.

Commander, US Naval Reserve Forces (COMNAVAIRRESFOR)
NSA New Orleans, Louisiana

Command/Squadron	Location	Aircraft	Tail Code
Carrier Air Wing Reserve Twenty (CVWR-20) - NAS Atlanta, Georgia			
VFA-201 'Hunters'	NAS Fort Worth JRB, Texas	F/A-18A	AF
VFA-203 'Blue Dolphins'	NAS Atlanta, Georgia	F/A-18A	AF
VFA-204 'River Rattlers'	NAS New Orleans JRB, Louisiana	F/A-18A	AF
VAQ-209 'Star Warriors'	NAF Washington, Maryland	EA-6B	AF
VAW-77 'Night Wolves'	NAS Atlanta, Georgia	E-2C	AF
VAW-78 'Fighting Escargots'	Chambers Field, Norfolk, Virginia	E-2C	AF
VFC-12 'Fighting Omars'	NAS Oceana, Virginia	F/A-18A/B	AF
VFC-13 'Saints'	NAS Fallon, Nevada	F-5E/F	AF
Commander, Reserve Patrol Wing (COMRESPATWING) - NAVSTA Norfolk, Virginia			
VQ-11 'Bandits'*	NAS Brunswick, Maine	P-3C	LP
VP-62 'Broadarrows'	NAS Jacksonville, Florida	P-3C	LT
VP-64 'Condors'	NAS Willow Grove JRB, Pennsylvania	P-3C	LU
VP-65 'Tridents'	NAS Point Mugu, California	P-3C	PG
VP-66 'Liberty Bells'	NAS Willow Grove JRB, Pennsylvania	P-3C	LV
VP-69 'Totems'	NAS Whidbey Island, Washington	P-3C	PJ
VP-92 'Minutemen'	NAS Brunswick, Maine	P-3C	LY
VP-94 'Crawfishers'	NAS New Orleans JRB, Louisiana	P-3C	PZ

* VQ-11 to be inactivated March 2000.

Command/Squadron	Location	Aircraft	Tail Code
Commander, Helicopter Reserve Wing (COMHELRESWWING) - NAS North Island, California			
HCS-4 'Red Wolves'	Chambers Field, Norfolk, Virginia	HH-60H	NW
HCS-5 'Firehawks'	NAS Point Mugu, California	HH-60H	NW
HS-75 'Emerald Knights'*	NAS Jacksonville, Florida	SH-60F, HH-60H	NW
HSL-84 'Thunderbolts'**	NAS North Island, California	SH-2G	NW
HC-85 'Golden Gators'	NAS North Island	UH-3H	NW
HSL-94 'Titans'**	NAS Willow Grove JRB, Pennsylvania	SH-2G	NW

* Squadron began transition from SH-3H, UH-3H during FY00.
** Unit to inactivate 2001, HSL-60 to be established at NAVSTA Mayport with SH-60B.

Command/Squadron	Location	Aircraft	Tail Code
Commander, Fleet Logistic Support Wing (COMFLEETLOGSUPWING) - NAS Fort Worth JRB, Texas			
VR-1 'Star Lifters'	NAF Washington, Maryland	C-20D	JK
VR-46 'Peach Airlines'	NAS Atlanta, Georgia	C-9B, DC-9	JS
VR-48 'Capital Skyliners'	NAF Washington, Maryland	C-20G	JR
VR-51 'Wind Jammers'	MCAF Kaneohe Bay, Hawaii	C-20G	RW
VR-52 'Taskmasters'	NAS Willow Grove JRB, Pennsylvania	C-9B, DC-9	JT
VR-53 'Capital Express'	NAF Washington, Maryland	C-130T	WV
VR-54 'Revelers'	NAS New Orleans JRB, Louisiana	C-130T	CW
VR-55 'Minutemen'	NAS Point Mugu, California	C-130T	RU
VR-56 'Globemasters'	Chambers Field, Norfolk, Virginia	C-9B	JU
VR-57 'Conquistadors'	NAS North Island, California	C-9B, DC-9	RX
VR-58 'Sun Seekers'	NAS Jacksonville, Florida	C-9B, DC-9	JV
VR-59 'Lone Star Express'	NAS Fort Worth JRB, Texas	C-9B, DC-9	RY
VR-61 'Islanders'	NAS Whidbey Island, Washington	DC-9	RS
VR-62 'Nor' Easter	NAS Brunswick, Maine	C-130T	JW

Commander, Fleet Logistic Support Wing (COMFLEETLOGSUPWING)

Now headquartered at NAS Fort Worth JRB, Texas, COMFLEETLOGSUPWING handles Navy logistic missions. Those flown by C-9/C-130 logistic support squadrons (FLELOGSUPRONs) are scheduled by the Naval Aviation Logistics Office in New Orleans, Louisiana, whereas C-20G missions are under the control of JOSAC. VR-1's role is to provide airlift support for the CNO and the secretary of the Navy (SECNAV).

CARRIERS AND CARRIER AIR WINGS

The USS *John F. Kennedy* (CV 67) is one of the Navy's few non-nuclear-powered carriers and serves as a naval training as well as an operational vessel.

During 1999, the Navy provided initial funding for construction of its last Nimitz–class carrier. The as-yet-unnamed CVN 77 represents a stepping-stone to a new-generation vessel referred to as the CVNX. Based around the design of the *Nimitz*, the new carrier will be fitted with the improved flight deck and hull structure developed for CVN 76. However, it will operate with a smaller crew and feature a new "island" superstructure based around an integrated combat system and phased-array radar. Initial funding for research and development (R&D) was released in 1997, followed by a larger increment the following year and advanced production funding was set aside in the 1999 budget. A further $751.5 million was appropriated in Fiscal Year 2000 for advanced procurement plus $45.3 million for R&D. CVN 77 will be commissioned in 2008, at which time the USS *Kitty Hawk* (CV 63) will be retired.

Although the Navy has named its aircraft carriers in recent times for US presidents or other politicians, many hope that CVN 77 will honor the memory of America's first man in space, Rear Admiral Alan Sheppard, who retired from the Navy in 1974 and died in July 1998.

Despite the fact that plans for the revolutionary new CVNX carrier have been scaled back, the first vessel will be equipped with a new propulsion plant and several updated systems. The latter will include an electromagnetic aircraft launch system (EMALS) in place of standard steam catapults. In December 1999, General Atomics Corporation and Northrop Grumman were issued development contracts related to this new system. Construction of CVNX 1 is set to begin in 2006 and work on a second CVNX carrier is scheduled to start five years later. Besides new designs for the hull and flight deck, the second vessel in this class will have an electromagnetic aircraft recovery system (ERAS) in place of the traditional arresting wire system. Furthermore, it will need a crew complement numbering just 70 to 90 percent that for CVNX 1. This represents a significant crewing development given the fact that CVNX 1 will be manned by 20 percent fewer personnel than are needed for a current US carrier.

When each carrier deploys, embarked aboard is a carrier air wing (CVW). COMNAVAIRLANT has five such air wings assigned, most of which comprise eight squadrons. Typically included are three strike fighter (VFA) units plus one fighter (VF), one airborne early warning (VAW), one helicopter antisubmarine warfare (HS), one electronic combat (VAQ) and one sea control (VS) squadron. In some instances, a second fighter unit replaces a strike fighter squadron.

During the Kosovo crisis in the summer of 1999, these F/A-18Cs from VFA-15 and VFA-87 flew strike missions from the deck of the USS *Theodore Roosevelt* (CVN 71), as part of CVW-8. They were armed with AGM-65 Mavericks and LGBs.

The US Navy operates 12 aircraft carriers of which 11 are in service at any one time. Each forms the nucleus of a carrier battle group (CVBG) and all but three of the vessels are nuclear powered. Whereas six are assigned to CINCLANTFLT's US Second Fleet, one of them is usually deployed with the US Sixth Fleet in the Mediterranean or the US Fifth Fleet in the Persian Gulf.

Of the six carriers assigned to CINCPACFLT, it is usual for one to be on station at all times in the Pacific, under the command of the US Seventh Fleet, or deployed to the Persian Gulf with the US Fifth Fleet. Otherwise, vessels involved in training or local operations in the eastern Pacific come under the control of the US Third Fleet.

Recent changes in the composition of the carrier fleet include the commissioning of the USS *Harry S. Truman* (CVN 75) and the retirement of the USS *Independence* (CV 62) in 1998. Meanwhile, construction of the latest carrier, the USS *Ronald Reagan* (CVN 76), is progressing on schedule and the vessel is expected to enter service in 2002.

Each of these deployed air wings is commanded by a captain, referred to as the CAG, who operationally reports directly to the carrier battle group's commander. The term is a holdover from the days when carrier air wings were known as carrier air groups.

COMNAVAIRPAC is also assigned five carrier air wings, which are identical in composition to those deploying with Atlantic fleet carriers. However, just four are CONUS based, whereas the fifth is forward deployed to Japan.

ATLANTIC FLEET

USS *Enterprise* (CVN 65)

The world's first nuclear-powered aircraft carrier and the eighth ship to carry this name was commissioned on 24 November 1961. The carrier's home port is Norfolk, Virginia, to which she returned on 6 May 1999 from a six-month deployment to the Mediterranean Sea and Persian Gulf. While deployed, aircraft from CVW-3 and other CVBG assets were involved in strikes against Iraq that began on 16 December 1998, as part of Operation Desert Fox. The USS *Enterprise* entered the yards at Newport News Shipbuilding for a $12.7 million extended selected restricted availability (ESRA) period beginning on 13 August 1999, and the vessel returned to NAVSTA Norfolk on 18 December 1999. The carrier is set to remain in the fleet until she is replaced by the first CVNX–class vessel in FY13.

At this time, no carrier air wing is assigned to the vessel.

Specifications:
Builders: Newport News Shipbuilding Co., Newport News, Virginia
Power Plant: Eight Westinghouse A2W nuclear reactors, four shafts, 280,000 shp (208800 kW)
Dimensions: Length overall 1,101 ft (335.6 m), flight deck width 248 ft (75.6 m),
    beam 133 ft (40.5 m), draft 39 ft (11.9 m)
Displacement: Approx. 92,400 tons (83824 metric tons) full load
Performance: Maximum speed 30+ knots

USS *John F. Kennedy* (CV 67)

Named for the 35th president of the United States, the USS *John F. Kennedy* was commissioned on 7 September 1968. This followed the laying of her keel on 22 October 1964 and her launch on 27 May 1967. The "JFK's" home port is Mayport, Florida.

During July 1999 the carrier, with CVW-1 embarked, took part in Joint Task Force Exercise (JTFEX) 99-2 in preparation for a 22 September deployment to the Mediterranean Sea and Persian Gulf. She operated in the Mediterranean until late October and then passed through the Suez Canal and Red Sea before entering the gulf on 5 November 1999. Like all carrier deployments, this one was scheduled to last six months. Now assigned to the Naval Reserve and Carrier Group Six, the "JFK" will return to the operational fleet during 2000. Plans call for her to continue in service until FY18, when she is due to be replaced by the second CVNX–class vessel. By then she will be 50 years old and her retirement will mark the end of conventionally powered US carrier operations.

Carrier Air Wing One (CVW-1)		AB
Unit/Name	Aircraft	Modex
VF-102 'Diamondbacks'	F-14B	1xx
VMFA-251 'Thunderbolts'	F/A-18C(N)	2xx
VFA-82 'Marauders'	F/A-18C(N)	3xx
VFA-86 'Sidewinders'	F/A-18C	4xx
VAQ-137 'Rooks'	EA-6B	50x
VAW-123 'Screwtops'	E-2C (Group II)	60x
HS-11 'Dragonslayers'	SH-60F, HH-60H	61x
VS-32 'Maulers'	S-3B	7xx
VRC-40		
Det. 2 'Rawhides'	C-2A	xx

The USS *Enterprise* (CVN 65) takes on aviation fuel from the replenishment oiler USS *Kalamazoo* (AOR 6). This refueling cycle took place in the Virginia Capes operating area.

During her most recent deployment, the USS *John F. Kennedy* entered the Persian Gulf on 5 November 1999. The vessel is currently assigned to the Naval Reserve with CVW-1 embarked aboard.

Specifications:
Builders: Newport News Shipbuilding and Dry Dock Company, Newport News, Virginia
Power Plant: Eight boilers, four geared steam turbines, four shafts, 280,000 shp (208800 kW)
Dimensions: Length overall 1,073 ft (327.1 m), flight deck width 252 ft (76.8 m),
    beam 130 ft (39.6 m), draft 37 ft (11.3 m)
Displacement: Approx. 81,500 tons (73936 metric tons) full load
Performance: Maximum speed 30+ knots

US Navy

The "Ike" at anchor during the summer of 1998 in the Golfe de la Napoule off the south coast of France. From there, the carrier left for the Persian Gulf with CVW-17 embarked to relieve the USS *Abraham Lincoln* (CVN 72).

USS *Dwight D. Eisenhower* (CVN 69)

Named in honor of America's 34th president and one-time general of the Army, this carrier was commissioned on 18 October 1977. Her keel was laid some seven years before, on 15 August 1970, and she was launched on 11 October 1975.

With CVW-7 embarked, CVN 69 took part in a composite training unit exercise (COMPTUEX) in October 1999 and JTFEX 00-1, which began on 29 November. The latter represents the final phase of training before a CVBG deploys. The "Ike's" home port is Norfolk, Virginia. Upon completion of her next deployment with CVW-7, scheduled to last from February until August 2000, the carrier will enter the yards for a $17 million refueling and complex overhaul (RCOH).

Specifications:
Builders: Newport News Shipbuilding and Dry Dock Company, Newport News, Virginia
Power Plant: Two Westinghouse A4W nuclear reactors, four shafts, 280,000 shp (208800 kW)
Dimensions: Length overall 1,098 ft (334.7 m), flight deck width 257 ft (78.3 m), beam 134 ft (40.8 m), draft 37 ft (11.3 m)
Displacement: Approx. 95,400 tons (86545 metric tons) full load
Performance: Maximum speed 30+ knots

Carrier Air Wing Seven (CVW-7)		AB
Unit/Name	Aircraft	Modex
VF-143 'Pukin' Dogs'	F-14B	1xx
VF-11 'Red Rippers'	F-14B	2xx
VFA-136 'Knighthawks'	F/A-18C(N)	3xx
VFA-131 'Wildcats'	F/A-18C(N)	4xx
VAQ-140 'Patriots'	EA-6B	50x
VAW-121 'Bluetails'	E-2C	60x
HS-5 'Night Dippers'	SH-60F, HH-60H	61x
VS-31 'Top Cats'	S-3B	7xx
VRC-40		
Det. 3 'Rawhides'	C-2A	xx

Specifications:
Builders: Newport News Shipbuilding and Dry Dock Company, Newport News, Virginia
Power Plant: Two Westinghouse A4W nuclear reactors, four shafts, 280,000 shp (208800 kW)
Dimensions: Length overall 1,092 ft (332.8 m), flight deck width 252 ft (76.8 m), beam 134 ft (40.8 m), draft 37 ft (11.3 m)
Displacement: Approx. 98,200 tons (89086 metric tons) full load
Performance: Maximum speed 30+ knots

USS *Theodore Roosevelt* (CVN 71)

The fourth Nimitz–class carrier is named for the 26th president of the United States, who was also a former secretary of the Navy and leader of the "Rough Riders." The vessel's keel was laid on 31 October 1981, just eight months after a fleet ballistic missile submarine (SSBN 600) carrying the same name was decommissioned. CVN 71 was launched on 27 October 1984, and was placed in commission on 25 October 1986. The ship's home port is Norfolk, Virginia.

The *Roosevelt* took part in JTFEX 99-1 during March 1999 and deployed on 26 March when she sailed directly to the Mediterranean and then to the Adriatic Sea, arriving on 5 April. Embarked aboard was CVW-8, which flew combat sorties over the Balkans for a period of 10 weeks during the Kosovo crisis. The CVBG ended its support of Operation Allied Force when it left for the Persian Gulf, to relieve the USS *Kitty Hawk* on 15 July. Subsequently, the USS *Theodore Roosevelt* was relieved by the USS *Constellation* and CVW-2 on 28 August, whereupon she returned to Norfolk, arriving home on 20 September 1999.

Deck operations aboard the USS *Theodore Roosevelt* (CVN 71) during the Kosovo crisis in 1999. The F/A-18C Hornet in the foreground belongs to VFA-15.

Carrier Air Wing Eight (CVW-8)		AJ
Unit/Name	Aircraft	Modex
VF-41 'Black Aces'	F-14A	1xx
VF-14 'Tophatters'	F-14A	2xx
VFA-15 'Valions'	F/A-18C(N)	3xx
VFA-87 'Golden Warriors'	F/A-18C(N)	4xx
VAQ-141 'Shadowhawks'	EA-6B	50x
VAW-124 'Bear Aces'	E-2C	60x
HS-3 'Tridents'	SH-60F, HH-60H	61x
VS-24 'Scouts'	S-3B	7xx
VRC-40		
Det. 1* 'Rawhides'	C-2A	xx
* Last deployed with CVW-8 but will deploy next with CVW-3.		

USS *George Washington* (CVN 73)

Named in honor of America's first president, the USS *George Washington* had her keel laid on 25 August 1986. The name was previously borne by the Navy's first nuclear-powered fleet ballistic missile submarine (SSBN 598), which was decommissioned some 17 months earlier.

The USS *George Washington* (CVN 73) pulls into port at Jebel Ali, United Arab Emirates, in early 1998. The carrier was conducting operations in the Persian Gulf in support of Operation Southern Watch.

CVN 73 was launched on 21 July 1990, and was commissioned on 4 July 1992. Her home port is Norfolk, Virginia.

Following a deployment that lasted from October 1997 until March 1998, the carrier entered the yards for a 10-month planned incremental availability (PIA) period, from which she emerged in March 1999. The crew carried out flight deck certification in late March, followed by local operations in the Atlantic Ocean and Caribbean Sea from July through November 1999. CVW-17 has now been assigned to the vessel and will deploy aboard CVN 73 in August 2000.

Specifications:
Builders: Newport News Shipbuilding and Dry Dock Company, Newport News, Virginia
Power Plant: Two Westinghouse A4W nuclear reactors, four shafts, 280,000 shp (208800 kW)
Dimensions: Length overall 1,092 ft (332.8 m), flight deck width 257.5 ft (78.5 m), beam 134 ft (40.8 m), draft 37 ft (11.3 m)
Displacement: Approx. 98,200 tons (89086 metric tons) full load
Performance: Maximum speed 30+ knots

Carrier Air Wing Seventeen (CVW-17)		AA
Unit/Name	Aircraft	Modex
VF-103 'Sluggers'	F-14B	1xx
VFA-34 'Blue Blasters'	F/A-18C(N)	2xx
VFA-83 'Rampagers'	F/A-18C(N)	3xx
VFA-81 'Sunliners'	F/A-18C	4xx
VAQ-132 'Scorpions'	EA-6B	50x
VAW-125 'Tigertails'	E-2C	60x
HS-15 'Red Lions'	SH-60F, HH-60H	61x
VS-30 'Diamond Cutters'	S-3B	7xx
VRC-40		
Det. 4* 'Rawhides'	C-2A	xx
* Will deploy as part of CVW-17		

USS *Harry S. Truman* (CVN 75)

The keel for the Navy's newest carrier was laid on 30 June 1988, and the USS *Harry S. Truman* was launched at Newport News Shipbuilding and Dry Dock in Virginia on 7 September 1996. Following completion of the builder's sea trials on 12 June 1998, the vessel was commissioned at Naval Base Norfolk, Virginia, on 25 July 1998. Named in honor of America's 33rd president, CVN 75's home port is Norfolk and CVW-3 is assigned.

The carrier's flight deck was certified during the period 25 August through 2 September 1999, and the ship was involved in carrier qualifications from 22 September through 7 October in the western Atlantic. Prior to this, however, follow-on sea trials were conducted on board for the Boeing F/A-18E/F Super Hornet program. The first such landing was made on 3 March 1999.

Carrier Air Wing Three (CVW-3)		AC
Unit/Name	Aircraft	Modex
VF-32 'Swordsmen'	F-14B	1xx
VMFA-312 'Checkerboards'	F/A-18C(N)	2xx
VFA-37 'Bulls'	F/A-18C(N)	3xx
VFA-105 'Gunslingers'	F/A-18C(N)	4xx
VAW-126 'Seahawks'	E-2C	60x
HS-7 'Shamrocks'	SH-3H	61x
VAQ-130 'Zappers'	EA-6B	62x
VS-22 'Checkmates'	S-3B	7xx
VRC-40		
Det. 1* 'Rawhides'	C-2A	xx
* Last deployed with CVW-8 but will deploy next with CVW-3		

Specifications
Builders: Newport News Shipbuilding and Dry Dock Company, Newport News, Virginia
Power Plant: Two Westinghouse A4W nuclear reactors, four shafts, 280,000 shp (208800 kW)
Dimensions: Length overall 1,092 ft (332.8 m), flight deck width 257.5 ft, (78.5 m), beam 134 ft (40.8 m), draft 37 ft (11.3 m)
Displacement: Approx. 98,200 tons (89086 metric tons) full load
Performance: Maximum speed 30+ knots

The USS *Harry S. Truman* (CVN 75) pulls alongside the Military Sealift Command fleet oiler USS *Patuxent* (T-AO 201) for replenishment on 17 November 1998.

US Navy

PACIFIC FLEET

USS *Kitty Hawk* (CV 63)

The keel for the lead ship in her class was laid on 27 December 1956, and CV 63 was launched on 21 May 1960. She was placed in commission on 29 April 1961. Named for the location of the Wright brothers first flight, the *Kitty Hawk* has been based in Yokosuka, Japan, since 11 August 1998, and became the Navy's oldest commissioned ship on 30 September 1998 when the the USS *Independence* was decommissioned. Since then, she has been flying the First Navy Jack, also known as the "Don't Tread on Me" flag.

CV 63, with CVW-5 aboard, spent much of 1999 at sea. She was involved in exercises in the South China Sea and completed an extended deployment to the Persian Gulf and Indian Ocean that began on 2 March 1999. In early April, the CVBG was ordered to the Persian Gulf in place of the USS *Theodore Roosevelt* and, after relieving CVN 65, the *Kitty Hawk* and her battle group sailed through the Straits of Hormuz and entered the gulf on 20 April 1999. She was eventually replaced by CVN 71 on 15 July. While operating in support of Operation Southern Watch, CVW-5 flew 5,426 sorties and carried out five strikes in response to Iraqi aggression before returning to Japan on 25 August 1999. However, the vessel put to sea again late that year to participate in Operation Foal Eagle 99 and ANNUALEX 11G exercises with South Korea and Japan. The carrier returned to her home port on 10 November 1999 and entered the Yokosuka Ship Repair Facility (SRF) five days later. The vessel's PIA period was scheduled to end on 21 February 2000. Retirement is planned for FY08 when CVN 77 is to be delivered.

The carrier's crew spell out a greeting on the flight deck of the USS *Kitty Hawk's* (CV 63) as the vessel heads into her new home port of Yokosuka, Japan, in August 1998.

Carrier Air Wing Five (CVW-5)		NF
Unit/Name	Aircraft	Modex
VF-154 'Black Knights'	F-14A	1xx
VFA-27 'Chargers'	F/A-18C(N)	2xx
VFA-192 'Golden Dragons'	F/A-18C	3xx
VFA-195 'Dam Busters'	F/A-18C	4xx
VAQ-136 'Gauntlets'	EA-6B	50x
VAW-115 'Liberty Bells'	E-2C (Group II)	60x
HS-14 'Chargers'	SH-60F, HH-60H	61x
VS-21 'Fighting Redtails'	S-3B	7xx
VRC-30		
Det. 5 'Providers'	C-2A	43x

Specifications:
Builders: New York Ship Building Company., Camden, New Jersey
Power Plant: Eight boilers, four geared steam turbines, four shafts, 280,000 shp (208800 kW)
Dimensions: Length overall 1,069 ft (325.8 m), flight deck width 282 ft (86.0 m), beam 130 ft (39.6 m), draft 36 ft (11.0 m)
Displacement: Approx. 82,000 tons (74389 metric tons) full load
Performance: Maximum speed 30+ knots

The USS *Constellation* (CV 64) steams near the Hawaiian Islands during a Western Pacific (WESTPAC) deployment.

USS *Constellation* (CV 64)

The USS *Constellation* was named in honor of the US Navy frigate built in 1797, and her keel was laid on 14 September 1957. She was launched on 8 October 1960, and entered commission on 27 October 1961. Her home port is NAS North Island, California.

The "Connie" deployed to the western Pacific and Persian Gulf with CVW-2 embarked on 18 June 1999, and conducted operations in

areas of the Pacific until late July, whereas most of August was spent there or in the Indian Ocean. On 28 August, CV 64 entered the Persian Gulf to relieve the USS *Theodore Roosevelt* and help enforce Operation Southern Watch. In turn, she was relieved by the USS *John F. Kennedy* (CV 67) on 5 November 1999 and, after making several port calls, ended her 19th overseas deployment and returned to NAS North Island on 17 December 1999. The vessel will be retired in FY03 after the USS *Ronald Reagan* (CVN 76) enters service.

Specifications:
Builders: New York Naval Shipyard, Brooklyn, New York
Power Plant: Eight boilers, four geared steam turbines, four shafts, 280,000 shp (208800 kW)
Dimensions: Length overall 1,073 ft (327.1 m), flight deck width 282 ft (86.0 m), beam 130 ft (39.6 m), draft 37 ft (11.3 m)
Displacement: Approx. 82,167 tons (74541 metric tons) full load
Performance: Maximum speed 30+ knots

Carrier Air Wing Two (CVW-2)		NE
Unit/Name	Aircraft	Modex
VF-2 'Bounty Hunters'	F-14D	1xx
VMFA-323 'Death Rattlers'	F/A-18C(N)	2xx
VFA-151 'Fighting Vigilantes'	F/A-18C(N)	3xx
VFA-137 'Kestrels'	F/A-18C(N)	4xx
VAQ-131 'Lancers'	EA-6B	50x
VAW-116 'Sun Kings'	E-2C (Group II)	60x
HS-2 'Golden Falcons'	SH-60F, HH-60H	61x
VS-38 'Red Griffins'	S-3B	7xx
VRC-30		
Det. 3 'Providers'	C-2A	xx

USS *Nimitz* (CVN 68)

The lead ship in her class, the USS *Nimitz* is named for Fleet Admiral Chester W. Nimitz, and was the second nuclear-powered carrier to be built. Her keel was laid on 22 June 1968 and she was launched on 13 May 1972. CVN 68 was placed in commission on 3 May 1975.

For her most recent deployment, the *Nimitz* departed Bremerton, Washington, on 1 September 1997, and undertook a world cruise with CVW-9 aboard. At its conclusion on 1 March 1998, she sailed into Norfolk, Virginia.

The carrier began a $1.2 billion, 33-month RCOH at Newport News Shipbuilding on 26 May 1998, completing her dry-dock period on 8 November 1999. The overhaul is scheduled for completion in February 2001, at which time she will move to her new home port, which will be San Diego, California. Currently no carrier air wing is assigned to the vessel.

Specifications:

Builders: Newport News Shipbuilding and Dry Dock Company, Newport News, Virginia
Power Plant: Two Westinghouse A4W nuclear reactors, four shafts, 280,000 shp (208800 kW)
Dimensions: Length overall 1,092 ft (332.8 m), flight deck width 257 ft (78.3 m),
  beam 134 ft (40.8 m), draft 38 ft (11.6 m)
Displacement: Approx. 95,400 tons (86545 metric tons) full load
Performance: Maximum speed 30+ knots

USS *Carl Vinson* (CVN 70)

The Navy's fourth nuclear-powered carrier is named for the late Georgia congressman, and is often referred to as the "Starship Vinson." Her keel was laid on 11 October 1975 and she was launched on 15 March 1980. CVN 70's commissioning date was 13 March 1982.

The *Vinson*'s home port is the Puget Sound Naval Shipyard in Bremerton, Washington, from which she departed with CVW-11 to the western Pacific and Persian Gulf on 6 November 1998. After the carrier entered the gulf on 19 December, she launched a single strike in support of Operation Desert Fox. The CVBG was relieved by CVN 65 on 18 March and returned to Bremerton on 6 May 1999. Five months later the carrier began a 10-month overhaul and will remain in dry-dock until May 2000.

Specifications:

Builders: Newport News Shipbuilding and Dry Dock Company, Newport News, Virginia
Power Plant: Two Westinghouse A4W nuclear reactors, four shafts, 280,000 shp (208800 kW)
Dimensions: Length overall 1,098 ft (334.7 m), flight deck width 257 ft (78.3 m),
  beam 134 ft (40.8 m), draft 37 ft (11.3 m)
Displacement: Approx. 95,000 tons (86183 metric tons) full load
Performance: Maximum speed 30+ knots

Carrier Air Wing Eleven (CVW-11)		NH
Unit/Name	Aircraft	Modex
VF-213 'Black Lions'	F-14D	1xx
VFA-97 'Warhawks'	F/A-18A	2xx
VFA-22 'Fighting Redcocks'	F/A-18C(N)	3xx
VFA-94 'Mighty Shrikes'	F/A-18C(N)	4xx
VAQ-135 'Black Ravens'	EA-6B	50x
VAW-117 'Wallbangers'	E-2C (Group II)	60x
HS-6 'Indians'	SH-60F, HH-60H	61x
VS-29 'Dragonfires'	S-3B	7xx
VRC-30		
Det. 2 'Providers'	C-2A	xx

US Navy

USS *Abraham Lincoln* (CVN 72)

The keel for the namesake of America's 16th president was laid on 3 November 1984, and the vessel was launched on 13 February 1988. CVN 72 entered commission on 11 November 1989 and is based at Everett, Washington. The previous vessel with the same name was a fleet ballistic missile submarine (SSBN 602).

CVN 72, with CVW-11 embarked, deployed to the western Pacific and Persian Gulf in June 1998 and returned home in December. A little over three months later, the carrier entered the Puget Sound Naval Shipyard to begin its PIA period. This was completed on 16 June 1999, and postoverhaul sea trials were conducted from 15 to 20 September 1999. The air wing now assigned is CVW-14.

Specifications:
Builders: Newport News Shipbuilding and Dry Dock Company, Newport News, Virginia
Power Plant: Two Westinghouse A4W nuclear reactors, four shafts, 280,000 shp (208800 kW)
Dimensions: Length overall 1,092 ft (332.8 m), flight deck width 257.5 ft (78.5 m), beam 134 ft (40.8 m), draft 37 ft (11.3 m)
Displacement: Approx. 98,200 tons (89086 metric tons) full load
Performance: Maximum speed 30+ knots

The USS *Abraham Lincoln* (CVN 72) departs San Diego, California, for a cruise to the western Pacific Ocean. CVW-14 is currently assigned to the carrier.

Carrier Air Wing Fourteen (CVW-14)		NK
Unit/Name	Aircraft	Modex
VF-31 'Tomcatters'	F-14D	1xx
VFA-115 'Eagles'	F/A-18C	2xx
VFA-113 'Stingers'	F/A-18C(N)	3xx
VFA-25 'Fist of the Fleet'	F/A-18C(N)	4xx
VAQ-139 'Cougars'	EA-6B	50x
VAW-113 'Black Eagles'	E-2C (Group II)	60x
HS-4 'Black Knights'	SH-60F, HH-60H	61x
VS-35 'Blue Wolves'	S-3B	7xx
VRC-30		
Det. 1 'Providers'	C-2A	xx

USS *John C. Stennis* (CVN 74)

The keel for the ship honoring "the father of America's modern Navy," an eight-term senator from Mississippi, was laid on 13 March 1991. The hull of the *Stennis* was launched 32 months later on 13 November 1993, and the vessel entered commission on 11 November 1995.

The USS *John C. Stennis* (CVN 74) is seen here supporting the UN-sponsored Operation Southern Watch, in the Persian Gulf, during April 1998. In January 2000 she was deployed with CVW-9 aboard.

The carrier departed Norfolk, Virginia, on her inaugural deployment in February 1998 with CVW-7 aboard. Completing a world cruise, she arrived at her assigned home port of San Diego, California, on 26 August 1998. Along with her assigned carrier air wing, CVW-9, the vessel participated in a COMPTUEX in August 1999. Following local operations in October and November, she deployed as part of Carrier Group Seven on 7 January 2000.

Specifications:
Builders: Newport News Shipbuilding and Dry Dock Company, Newport News, Virginia
Power Plant: Two Westinghouse A4W nuclear reactors, four shafts, 280,000 shp (208800 kW)
Dimensions: Length overall 1,092 ft (332.8 m), flight deck width 257.5 ft (78.5 m), beam 134 ft (40.8 m), draft 37 ft (11.3 m)
Displacement: Approx. 98,200 tons (89086 metric tons) full load
Performance: Maximum speed 30+ knots

Carrier Air Wing Nine (CVW-9)		NG
Unit/Name	Aircraft	Modex
VF-211 'Checkmates'	F-14A	1xx
VMFA-314 'Black Knights'	F/A-18C(N)	2xx
VFA-146 'Blue Diamonds'	F/A-18C(N)	3xx
VFA-147 'Argonauts'	F/A-18C(N)	4xx
VAQ-138 'Yellowjackets'	EA-6B	50x
VAW-112 'Golden Hawks'	E-2C (Group II)	60x
HS-8 'Eightballers'	SH-60F, HH-60H	61x
VS-33 'Screwbirds'	S-3B	7xx
VRC-30		
Det. 4 'Providers'	C-2A	xx

The F/A-18 is the most numerous asset within a carrier air wing, with three squadrons most commonly assigned. However, the 'River Rattlers' of VFA-204 fly with Carrier Air Wing Reserve Twenty (CVWR-20), which would deploy with four Hornet units.

USS *Ronald Reagan* (CVN 76)

Construction of the new vessel began at the Newport News Shipbuilding yard when CVN 76's keel was laid on 9 February 1996. The carrier is named for America's 40th president and will be commissioned in 2002. She will replace the USS *Constellation* (CV 64) in fleet service in 2003.

Specifications:
Builders: Newport News Shipbuilding and Dry Dock Company, Newport News, Virginia
Power Plant: Two Westinghouse A4W nuclear reactors, four shafts, 280,000 shp (208800 kW)
Dimensions: Length overall 1,092 ft (332.85 m), flight deck width 257.5 ft (78.5 m),
    beam 134 ft (40.8 m), draft 37 ft (11.3 m)
Displacement: Approx. 98,200 tons (89086 metric tons) full load
Performance: Maximum speed 30+ knots

MINE COUNTERMEASURES SUPPORT SHIP

USS *Inchon* (MCS 12)

In 1996, Ingalls Shipbuilding completed conversion of this former amphibious assault ship to the role of mine countermeasures support vessel. The ship's keel was originally laid on 8 April 1968 and the hull was launched on 24 May 1969. She originally entered service on 20 June 1970. Substantial modifications to her command, control, communications, computers and intelligence (C^4I) system were carried out as part of the conversion program and included upgrades to the Phalanx close-in weapon and radar systems. Eight CH-53Es and two SAR/spotter helicopters are carried aboard the *Inchon* and she deployed on 1 March 1999, as the flagship for Mine Countermeasures Squadron Two. Elements of HM-14, HM-15 and HC-8 were embarked aboard.

Carrier Air Wing Reserve Twenty (CVWR-20)
AIR WING IS NOT ASSIGNED TO A SPECIFIC CARRIER

Unit/Name	Aircraft	Modex
VFA-201 'Hunters'	F/A-18A	1xx
VMFA-142 'Flyin' Gators'	F/A-18A	2xx
VFA-203 'Blue Dolphins'	F/A-18A	3xx
VFA-204 'River Rattlers'	F/A-18A	4xx
VAW-78 'Escargots'	E-2C	60x
HS-75 'Emerald Knights'	SH-3H	61x
VAQ-209 'Star Warriors'	EA-6B	62x
CVWR-20 also controls three other units:		
VAW-77 'Night Wolves' *	E-2C	xx
VFC-12 'Fighting Omars' *	F/A-18A/B	xx
VFC-13 'Saints' *	F-5E/F	xx
* Fleet support units would not normally deploy with CVWR-20		

That same year, her aviation units were tasked with providing humanitarian assistance in Kosovo and, as a consequence, she spent several months operating in the Adriatic.

Specifications:
Builders: Ingalls Shipbuilding Inc., Ingalls, Mississippi
Power Plant: One steam plant, one shaft, 22,000 shp (16405 kW)
Dimensions: Length overall 602 ft (183.5 m), beam 84 ft (25.6 m), draft 30 ft (9.1 m)
Displacement: Approx. 19.468 tons (17661 metric tons) full load
Performance: Maximum speed 21 knots

The USS *Inchon* (MCS 12) is a modified Iwo Jima–class amphibious assault ship. Operations during the 1991 Gulf War highlighted the need for a dedicated vessel to adequately support joint mine warfare duties by providing C^4I (command, control, communications, computers and intelligence) capabilities. Conversion of the ship was completed during the summer of 1996.

AIRCRAFT

BEECH AIRCRAFT (SEE RAYTHEON AIRCRAFT)

BELL HELICOPTER TEXTRON

Bell HH-1N Iroquois ("Huey")

The Bell HH-1N remains in limited US Navy service, primarily as a SAR asset assigned to air operations divisions at naval air stations. However, a few are also used for testing purposes. The helicopters were originally delivered as UH-1N models and given the newer designation in 1991. A major upgrade program to be undertaken for the Marine Corps will bring UH/HH-1N variants up to UH-1Y standard, but it is unlikely Navy "Hueys" will be included. It is more probable they will be replaced by Sikorsky CH-60S Knighthawks, instead.

(See USMC Aircraft section for more details)

Bell UH-1N Iroquois Specifications

Maximum Takeoff Weight:	11,200 lb (5080 kg)
Empty Weight:	6,196 lb (2811 kg)
Fuselage Length:	57 ft 3.5 in (17.46 m)
Overall Length:	42 ft 4.75 in (12.92 m)
Main Rotor Diameter:	48 ft 0 in (14.63 m)
Height:	14 ft 10.75 in (4.54 m)
Power Plant:	Two Pratt & Whitney T400-CP-400 turboshaft engines, rated at 1,290 shp (962 kW), driving two-blade main and tail rotor
Maximum Fuel Capacity:	1,451 lb (659 kg)
Maximum Speed:	149 kts (276 km/h) at sea level
Operating Range:	172 nm (319 km)
Crew:	3–4
Accommodations:	8–10 troops or six litters and a single attendant, or 5,000 lb (2268 kg) of cargo
Armament:	None normally carried
Mission:	Search and rescue (SAR)

BuNo 158770 is one of the Bell HH-1Ns "Hueys" used for SAR missions at NAWS China Lake, California. The helicopters are flown by the Naval Weapons Test Squadron operating from Armitage Field. Today, only 35 examples remain in service with the US Navy.

Aside from two helicopters based at NAS Patuxent River, Maryland, the Navy's entire fleet of TH-57s is assigned to TAW-5 at NAS Pensacola, Florida, including BuNo 162015/E-15. Some 44 TH-57Bs provide primary flight instruction and 83 TH-57Cs are used for advanced instrument training.

Bell TH-57B/C Sea Ranger

Developed from the Bell Jet Ranger 206A, the TH-57A entered service with the US Navy in 1968 as a primary training helicopter. It is fitted with dual controls. In 1982, the Navy also obtained 124 variants built around the Model 206B, of which 47 examples are TH-57Bs used to provide visual flight (VFR) training, whereas the other 77 aircraft are TH-57Cs and serve as instrument flight (IFR) trainers. The entire fleet is located at NAS Whiting Field, Florida, with the exception of two helicopters assigned to the Naval Air Warfare Center at NAS Patuxent River, Maryland.

Bell TH-57C Sea Ranger Specifications

Maximum Takeoff Weight:	3,200 lb (1452 kg)
Empty Weight:	1,595 lb (723 kg)
Fuselage Length:	31 ft 0 in (9.45 m)
Overall Length:	38 ft 9.5 in (11.82 m)
Main Rotor Diameter:	33 ft 4 in (10.16 m)
Height:	9 ft 6.5 in (2.91 m)
Power Plant:	One Rolls-Royce Allison 250-C20BJ turboshaft engine, rated at 317 shp (236 kW), driving two-blade main and tail rotors
Maximum Fuel Capacity:	513 lb (233 kg)
Maximum Speed:	120 kts (222 km/h)
Operating Range:	330 nm (611 km) with maximum payload
Crew:	2
Accommodations:	Up to 3 students
Armament:	None
Missions:	Primary and advanced rotary-wing trainer

Bell OH-58C Kiowa

Although the US Army retains ownership, four OH-58Cs have replaced OH-58As in service with the US Naval Test Pilot School at NAS Patuxent River, Maryland. The aircraft are used to train student test pilots as well as engineers, as part of the school's rotary-wing curriculum. They are also used to introduce fixed-wing-flight students to rotary-wing operations.

(See US Army Aircraft section for more details)

When the last TA-4Js were retired by VT-7 in October 1999, VC-8 was left as the last Navy squadron operating the Skyhawk. Assigned to the unit is BuNo 153525/GF-02, seen here during a visit to NAS Oceana, Virginia. Its home base is NAVSTA Roosevelt Roads, Puerto Rico.

BOEING COMPANY (INCL. McDONNELL DOUGLAS, HUGHES HELICOPTERS AND ROCKWELL INTERNATIONAL)

McDonnell Douglas TA-4J Skyhawk

Designed as a light attack platform, the first single-seat Douglas A4D-1 Skyhawk (A-4A after 1962) entered service with the US Navy in September 1956. Production continued until February 1979, at which time McDonnell Douglas delivered the last of 162 A-4M variants. After the Marine Corps retired its remaining A-4Ms in August 1994, two-seat TA-4Js were the only Skyhawk trainers left in service. TAW-1 was the final operator and used them for intermediate and advanced instruction until they were retired in October 1999. However, nine Skyhawks still fly with VC-8 at NAVSTA Roosevelt Roads, Puerto Rico, in fleet support roles as "aggressors" and target tugs.

McDonnell Douglas TA-4J Skyhawk Specifications

Maximum Takeoff Weight:	24,500 lb (11113 kg)
Empty Weight:	10,602 lb (4809 kg)
Fuselage Length:	42 ft 7.25 in (12.99 m) excluding refueling probe
Wing Span:	27 ft 6 in (8.41 m)
Height:	15 ft 3 in (4.65 m)
Power Plant:	One Pratt & Whitney J52-P-8A turbojet engine, rated at 9,300 lb st (41.4 kN)
Maximum Fuel Capacity:	Internal – 4,455 lb (2021 kg) External – 2,228 lb (1011 kg)
Maximum Speed:	587 kts (1087 km/h) at sea level
Service Ceiling:	38,700 ft (11796 m)
Operating Range:	1176 nm (2178 km)
Crew:	2
Armament:	One 20-mm cannon
Missions:	Intermediate and advanced strike training, fleet support

McDonnell Douglas C-9B, DC-9-30 Skytrain II

The C-9B is the military variant of the commercial DC-9-30 series airliner manufactured by McDonnell Douglas Corporation, which is now part of the Boeing Company. Designed to transport passengers and cargo, the aircraft first flew in February 1973 and is powered by two turbofan engines mounted on the rear fuselage below a T-tail. The Skytrain II's primary mission is to provide intra-theater logistic support to naval forces and, besides the 15 C-9Bs that began entering service in 1976, the Navy flies 12 standard DC-9-30 series aircraft. Unlike the C-9B, the DC-9-30 is not equipped with a cargo door and so cannot carry palletized freight. Planned upgrades to the fleet will allow

both variants to comply with reduced vertical separation requirements (RVSR) during transoceanic flights, and the cockpits in 19 aircraft are being upgraded with new radios, navigation aids and electronic flight instrumentation. Serving aircraft are currently assigned to seven Naval Reserve fleet support squadrons within the Fleet Logistic Support Wing. CONUS missions are scheduled by the Joint Operational Support Airlift Center (JOSAC) at Scott AFB, Illinois, whereas OCONUS flights are controlled by the Naval Air Logistics Office (NALO) at NAS New Orleans, Louisiana.

McDonnell Douglas C-9B Skytrain II Specifications

Maximum Takeoff Weight:	108,000 lb (48988 kg)
Empty Weight:	Cargo configuration – 59,706 lb (27082 kg) Passenger configuration – 65,283 lb (29612 kg)
Fuselage Length:	119 ft 3 in (36.35 m)
Wing Span:	93 ft 3 in (28.42 m)
Height:	27 ft 6 in (8.38 m)
Power Plant:	Two Pratt & Whitney JT8D-9 low-bypass tubofan engines, each rated at 14,500 lb st (64.5 kN)
Maximum Fuel Capacity:	24,833 lb (11264 kg)
Maximum Speed:	491 kts at 25,000 ft (909 km/h at 7620 m)
Service Ceiling:	37,000 ft (11278 m)
Operating Range:	899 nm with 30,140 lb (1665 km with 13671 kg) of payload
Crew:	4
Accommodations:	Up to 90 passengers or 30,140 lb (13671 kg) of cargo or a combination of both [Up to eight standard 88 x 108 in (2.24 x 2.74 m) pallets can be carried]
Armament:	None
Missions:	Operational support airlift (OSA), fleet logistic support

The Navy's Skytrain II fleet includes 15 C-9Bs and 12 DC-9-30 series airliners. BuNo 159120/JU-120, a C-9B, is one of four examples operated by VR-56 from Chambers Field, NAVSTA Norfolk, Virginia. In 2001, the Boeing C-40A will begin replacing these aircraft in the OSA and fleet logistic support roles.

US Navy

Boeing TC-18F

The Navy operates two Boeing 707-382Cs at Tinker AFB, Oklahoma, as in-flight trainers (IFTs) for crews that will fly the Boeing E-6A/B Mercury. Initially leased from Chrysler Technologies, the aircraft flew with civil registrations until purchased by the service in August 1995. The Naval Training Support Unit (NTSU) was established in December 1988 and serves as the FRS for the type. Pilots, navigators and flight engineers are assigned to the NTSU for periods of between four and 12 weeks. Initially, they receive simulator training on the E-6A/B Contract Flight Crew Training System (CFCTS), provided by Raytheon Technical Services Company, and pilots subsequently undergo in-flight training conducted by NTSU instructors in TC-18F and E-6A/B aircraft.

Specifications: See USAF section for details

Missions: In-flight trainer for E-6A/B Mercury

Boeing E-6A/B Mercury

In 1977, the Naval Air Development Center initiated a replacement study for the Navy's EC-130Q communications aircraft, and it established the ECX program in 1979. After considering variants of the DC-8 airliner and C-130 Hercules, the Boeing 707-320B was selected and the company was awarded a development contract in April 1983. The E-6A first flew in February 1987 and began to replace the EC-130Q in the strategic communications role in August 1989. When it entered service, its primary purpose was to provide a survivable communications link between the National Command Authority (NCA) and the Navy's fleet ballistic missile (FBM) submarine force. For the TACAMO (TAke Charge And Move Out) mission, the E-6A deploys 4,000-foot (1220-m) and 26,000-foot (7925-m) trailing wire antennas that enable communication with submerged submarines to be conducted using a very low frequency (VLF) radio. With the trailing wires deployed, the crew flies a wide banked turn that allows the longer wire to hang in an almost vertical position, which enhances the strength of the signal.

The E-6A fleet is currently being modified to E-6B configuration through an avionics block update (ABU) developed by Raytheon E-Systems (formerly Chrysler Technology Airborne Systems). Separately, a DoD replacement study for the Air Force's EC-135C command post resulted in the transfer of that particular mission to the E-6A. In January 1985, the airborne command post (ABNCP) modification program was initiated and a contract was subsequently awarded to Raytheon E-Systems. The first E-6B was delivered in October 1997 and the

The Navy's TC-18Fs flew as civilian aircraft until they were ultimately assigned bureau numbers. One of two such aircraft operated by the Naval Training Support Unit (NTSU) at Tinker AFB, Oklahoma, carried the registration N46RT but has now been assigned BuNo 165343.

BuNo 164406 is a Boeing E-6B fitted with equipment previously carried by an Air Force EC-135 for the Looking Glass mission. In service with VQ-3, the aircraft provides command and control for the Navy's fleet ballistic submarine missile force and Air Force land-based ICBM force.

upgraded aircraft assumed the Looking Glass mission in September 1998, which had previously been flown by the Air Force.

Like TACAMO, Looking Glass provides a command and control link between authorities and US strategic forces including ballistic missile submarines, manned bombers and ICBM silos. Modifications made to the platform under the ABU and command post programs include installation of a new radome containing a MILSTAR

Boeing E-6A Mercury Specifications

Maximum Takeoff Weight:	342,000 lb (155129 kg)
Empty Weight:	172,795 lb (78378 kg)
Fuselage Length:	152 ft 11 in (46.61 m)
Wing Span:	145 ft 2 in (44.25 m)
Height:	42 ft 5 in (12.93 m)
Power Plant:	Four CFM International F108-CF-100 high-bypass turbofan engines, each rated at 24,000 lb st (106.8 kN)
Maximum Fuel Capacity:	155,000 lb (70307 kg)
Maximum Speed:	530 kts at 35,000 ft (982 km/h at 10668 m)
Service Ceiling:	42,000 feet (12802 m)
Range:	10.5 hours on station at 1000 nm (1852 km), Unrefueled – 6,350 nm (11760 km)
Crew:	22
Armament:	None
Mission Equipment:	Classified communication systems, AN/ALR-66 electronic support measures (ESM)
Missions:	Strategic communications, airborne command post

McDonnell Douglas QF-4N/S, YF-4J Phantom II

The McDonnell F4H-1 first took to the air in May 1958, and Phantom II variants served as the Navy's primary fleet defense for nearly 20 years. Some 10 years after leaving active-duty operational service, the Naval Reserve's last Phantom was retired in 1987. However, the type continues to serve at NAS Point Mugu, California, where the Naval Weapon Test Squadron uses former F-4N and F-4S aircraft as aerial targets. QF-4S models began replacing QF-4Ns as the Navy's principal full-scale aerial target (FSAT) in 1998 but, unlike the Air Force FSAT program, which uses a civilian contractor to manufacture its drones, the Naval Aviation Depot (NADEP) is responsible for modifying former Navy and Marine Corps F-4S fighters to QF-4S configuration. This is carried out at MCAS Cherry Point, North Carolina. The NADEP delivered its first QF-4S in 1997 and will modify as many as 50 examples, which will be capable of operating within all F-4S flight envelopes for manned or NOLO (no live operator) flight. Completion of the program is expected during 2001. Manned missions typically include research, development, test and evaluation (RDTE); chase duties; functional check flights; and remote training for drone pilots. In contrast, when operated as a NOLO aircraft, the Phantom is "flown" via radio signals from a pilot in a remote ground station. The aircraft can carry the Navy Standard Tow Target System (NSTTS), electronic countermeasures pods and threat simulators. In addition to the QF-4N/S drones, a single YF-4J is based at Point Mugu and is used for ejection seat testing.

communications antenna on the fuselage spine, a GPS and upgrades to the flight deck and mission avionics. The command post modification also added a battle staff compartment housing the airborne launch control center (ALCC), upgraded UHF radios and a Digital Airborne Intercommunications Switching System (DAISS) taken from Pacer Link EC-135Cs. The ALCC provides the E-6B with the capability to check the status of the ICBMs, launch the missiles and change their target assignments. Furthermore, Boeing recently received a contract to develop a multifunction display system that will replace analog instruments with six flat-panel displays and dual flight management systems based on those used in the Boeing 737-700 cockpit. A proposed E-6C enhancement will also provide a terminal collision avoidance system, an updated GPS, an altitude alert system, a dual satellite communications system (SATCOM) and new communications equipment that will include a modified miniature receiver terminal (MMRT).

The E-6A/B fleet operates from Tinker AFB, Oklahoma, and maintains alert aircraft there as well as at NAS Patuxent River, Maryland, and Travis AFB, California. Command post E-6Bs are detached to Offutt AFB, Nebraska, which is home to USSTRATCOM.

Besides acting as full-scale aerial targets (FSATs), QF-4N Phantoms with the Naval Weapons Test Squadron at NAS Point Mugu, California, serve as launch platforms for the Raytheon AQM-37C missile target. In this case, BuNo 150465 is supporting development of the Electronic Warfare Advanced Technology (EWAT) program.

McDonnell Douglas Phantom II QF-4S Specifications

Maximum Takeoff Weight:	62,390 lb (28300 kg)
Empty Weight:	28,000 lb (12701 kg)
Fuselage Length:	58 ft 4 in (17.78 m)
Wing Span:	38 ft 7.5 in (11.77 m), Folded – 27 ft 7 in (8.41 m)
Height:	16 ft 5 5 in (5.02 m)
Power Plant:	Two General Electric J79-GE-10B turbojet engines, each rated at 17,900 lb st (79.62 kN)
Maximum Fuel Capacity:	Internal – 13,500 lb (6124 kg) External – 9,045 lb (4103 kg)
Maximum Speed:	1,277 kts (2365 km/h) at 40,000 ft (12192 m)
Operating Range:	2,000 nm (3704 km) ferry range
Service Ceiling:	61,000 ft (18593 m)
Crew:	2 (0 if operated as a drone)
Armament:	None normally carried
Missions:	Target drone, test support

This F/A-18C Hornet flies with the 'Kestrels' of VFA-137 and is seen here in formation with an S-3B Viking from the 'Red Griffins' of VS-38. Both squadrons are with CVW-2, deployed aboard the USS *Constellation* (CV 64). Home base for the Kestrels is NAS Lemoore, California.

McDonnell Douglas F/A-18A/B/C/D Hornet

Built in response to a requirement for a fighter/attack aircraft (VFAX), the McDonnell Douglas F/A-18A Hornet flew for the first time in November 1978 and entered the Navy's inventory in February 1981. It became operational in 1983 and was first deployed at sea aboard the USS Constellation (CV 64) in February 1985. Intended to replace Navy A-7E Corsairs and Marine Corps F-4N/S Phantoms, the Hornet is fitted with a multimode AN/APG-65 radar and has the capacity to carry offensive and defensive weapons simultaneously, thereby allowing it to supplement the role of the F-14 Tomcat as a fleet defender.

Following delivery of more than 600 A models and two-seat F/A-18Bs (originally designated TF-18As), US production for the Navy and Marine Corps switched to newer F/A-18C/D variants in September 1987. However, earlier models continued to come off the production lines to meet foreign orders. The newer aircraft incorporated updated avionics, better weapon capabilities and improved ejection seats. Furthermore, night-attack capabilities were introduced effective with the 137th aircraft, which was delivered in October 1989, and the two-seat D model ultimately took over the all-weather strike mission from the Grumman A-6 Intruder. Developed for the F/A-18E/F, the AN/APG-73 radar has also equipped all Hornets procured since FY94, and a program is underway to incorporate the system into earlier F/A-18C/Ds.

The Hornet currently serves with 26 active-duty squadrons, including the FRS and four reserve units.

McDonnell Douglas F/A-18C Hornet Specifications

Maximum Takeoff Weight:	51,900 lb (23541 kg)
Empty Weight:	29,619 lb (13435 kg)
Fuselage Length:	56 ft 0 in (17.07 m)
Wing Span:	37 ft 6 in (11.43 m), Folded – 27 ft 6 in (8.38 m)
Height:	15 ft 3.5 in (4.66 m)
Power Plant:	Two General Electric F404-GE-402 low-bypass turbofan engines, rated at 11,875 lb st (52.82 kN) and at 17,775 lb st (79.07 kN) in max. afterburner
Maximum Fuel Capacity:	Internal – 10,860 lb (4926 kg) External – 6,732 lb (3054 kg)
Maximum Speed:	1,034 kts (1915 km/h)
Service Ceiling:	50,000+ ft (15240 m)
Typical Range:	574 nm (1063 km) for "hi-lo-hi" air-to-ground mission
Crew:	1
Armament:	One 20-mm M61A1 gatling gun with 570 rounds, Nine weapon stations capable of carrying 17,000 lb (7711 kg) of stores including: AIM-7 Sparrow, AIM-9 Sidewinder, AIM-120 AMRAAM air-to-air missiles; AGM-65 Maverick, AGM-84 Harpoon, AGM-88 HARM air-to-surface missiles; AGM-154 joint stand-off weapon (JSOW); GBU-31 joint direct-attack munition (JDAM); Mk82/83/84 general-purpose (GP) bombs; laser-guided (LGBs) bombs; cluster munitions
Mission Equipment:	AN/APG-65 or AN/APG-73 radar, AN/AAS-38A NITE Hawk targeting FLIR-LTD (laser target-designator-ranger) pod, or AN/AAS-38 FLIR and AN/ASQ-173 laser spot tracker
Missions:	All-weather strike fighter, "aggressor" trainer

The Naval Strike Air Warfare Center (NSAWC) at NAS Fallon, Nevada, flies a number of early-model Hornets including BuNo 161733. The F/A-18B is seen carrying a pair of laser-guided training rounds (LTGRs) on a multiple ejector rack (MER). The inert training rounds are equipped with a laser seeker head and simulate the characteristics of operational laser-guided bombs.

McDonnell Douglas F/A-18A Hornet, BuNo 162894

When operated by the Navy Fighter Weapons School (Topgun) at NAS Miramar, California, this "aggressor" was painted in a blue/gray splinter camouflage scheme to represent a Sukhoi Su-35.

McDonnell Douglas F/A-18A Hornet, BuNo 162832

To depict an adversary in mid-eastern colors, a three-tone desert camouflage scheme has been applied to this "aggressor" aircraft currently operated by NSAWC at NAS Fallon, Nevada. Like the Hornet above, it is shown carrying inert AIM-7s, AIM-9s and a centerline fuel tank.

US Navy

Boeing F/A-18E/F Super Hornet

Development by McDonnell Douglas (now Boeing) of the single-seat F/A-18E and two-seat F/A-18F began in 1987 under the Hornet 2000 program. This followed a Naval Air Systems Command study for potential evolutionary upgrades to the platform. The Super Hornet was subsequently proposed as an alternative to the cancelled McDonnell Douglas A-12A Avenger in 1991, and will now replace earlier F/A-18 variants as well as the F-14 Tomcat in fleet service. In June 1992, McDonnell Douglas was awarded an EMD contract and the first E model took to the air in November 1995. Initial carrier landings were conducted in January 1997, and LRIP was approved that same fiscal year when Boeing received a contract for 12 aircraft. Deliveries commenced in 1999, the year the EMD program was completed and OPEVAL began. Contracts were also placed in FY98 for 20 LRIP aircraft and in FY99 for 30 more examples. Full production was authorized in FY00 with an initial order for 36 aircraft and deliveries to VFA-122, the FRS, began during September 1999.

In addition to the F/A-18E assuming the Navy's strike fighter role, Boeing has proposed production of a modified F/A-18F variant to replace the EA-6B in the electronic combat role. This aircraft has been dubbed the F/A-18G.

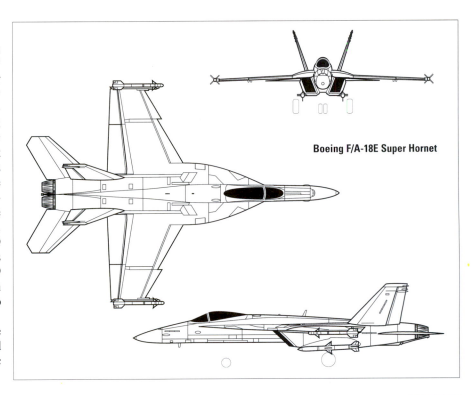

Boeing F/A-18E Super Hornet

Boeing F/A-18E Super Hornet Specifications:

Maximum Takeoff Weight:	66,000 lb (29937 kg)
Empty Weight:	30,500 lb (13835 kg)
Fuselage Length:	60 ft 2.5 in (18.35 m)
Wing Span:	44 ft 10.75 in (13.68 m), Folded – 30 ft 7.25 in (9.32 m)
Height:	16 ft 0 in (4.88 m)
Power Plant:	Two General Electric F414-GE-400 low-bypass turbofan engines, rated at 22,000 lb st (97.86 kN)
Maximum Fuel Capacity:	Internal – 14,400 lb (6532 kg) External – 9,780 lb (4436 kg) in three tanks
Maximum Speed:	1,034 kts (1915 km/h)
Service Ceiling:	50,000 ft (15240 m)
Operating Range:	780 nm (1445 km) for "hi-lo-hi" attack mission
Crew:	1
Armament:	One 20-mm M61A1 gatling gun with 570 rounds; Eleven weapon stations capable of carrying 17,750 pounds (8051 kg) of stores including: AIM-7 Sparrow, AIM-9 Sidewinder, AIM-120 AMRAAM air-to-air missiles; AGM-65 Maverick, AGM-84 Harpoon, SLAM, AGM-88 HARM air-to-surface missiles; AGM-154 joint stand-off weapon (JSOW); GBU-31 joint direct-attack munition (JDAM); Mk82/83/84 general-purpose (GP) bombs; laser-guided bombs (LGBs); cluster munitions
Mission Equipment:	AN/APG-73 radar, AN/AAS-50 Nav/FLIR pod, AN/AAS-38A NITE Hawk targeting FLIR-LTD (laser target-designator-ranger) pod
Mission:	All-weather strike fighter

The larger size of the Super Hornet compared with its forbears is readily apparent in this view of an F/A-18E in formation with an F/A-18C flying below it. The larger wings and prominent leading-edge root extension (LERX) clearly distinguish the newer variant.

The fourth EMD F/A-18E served as the program's spin-test aircraft. BuNo 165168 was one of seven Super Hornets to be painted in this high-visibility color scheme.

Six former US Army OH-6As, including serial 65-12967, have been modified to TH-6B configuration, and are operated by the Naval Test Pilot School at NAS Patuxent River, Maryland.

Hughes TH-6B Cayuse Specifications

Maximum Takeoff Weight:	2,400 lb (1089 kg)
Empty Weight:	1,229 lb (557 kg)
Fuselage Length:	23 ft 0 in (7.01 m)
Overall Length:	30 ft 3.75 in (9.24 m)
Main Rotor Diameter:	26 ft 4 in (8.03 m)
Height:	8 ft 1.5 in (2.48 m)
Power Plant:	One Rolls-Royce Allison T63-A-720 turboshaft engine, rated at 420 shp (313 kW), driving four-blade main rotor and two-blade tail rotor
Maximum Fuel Capacity:	415 lb (188 kg)
Maximum Speed:	130 kts (241 km/h) at sea level
Range:	Operating – 330 nm (611 km), Ferry – 1,335 nm (2472 km) ferry
Crew:	2
Armament:	None
Mission:	Test pilot flight training

Hughes TH-6B Cayuse

The Hughes Helicopter OH-6A was initially delivered to the US Army for use as an observation and target-spotting platform. Although the type no longer flies that mission, the US Navy Test Pilot School operates six former US Army OH-6As, modified by McDonnell Douglas Helicopter Systems to MD-369H configuration, for in-flight instruction and demonstration of flying qualities, performance and mission systems. The program upgraded the OH-6As as part of a conversion-in-lieu-of-procurement (CILOP) arrangement, and involved installing components to increase the power rating of the helicopter's T63 turboshaft. The aircraft were subsequently redesignated TH-6Bs and have been in US Navy service since 1991.

Boeing CH/HH/UH-46D Sea Knight

The Boeing Sea Knight initially came about through a US Army contract, and first flew in April 1958 as the YHC-1A. The helicopter was based on the Vertol Model 107 but was not ordered in quantity by the Army because it selected the larger Model 114 instead. Development continued, however, and the type ultimately entered Navy and Marine Corps service as the HRB-1. Redesignated the CH-46A in 1962, the Sea Knight continues to serve the Navy as a vertical replenishment (VERTREP) asset and as a SAR aircraft at naval air stations. Currently assigned to five combat support squadrons and the air operations departments at several air stations, those providing combat support will be among the first replaced by CH-60S Seahawks starting in 2000.

Specifications: See the USMC section for details

Missions: Vertical replenishment (VERTREP) and search and rescue (SAR)

Stationed at NAS North Island, California, HC-3 serves as the FRS for the Sea Knight. In addition to flying CH-46D and UH-46D variants, the squadron operates HH-46Ds including BuNo 151910/SA-07.

The Rockwell T-2 Buckeye celebrated its 40th anniversary in naval service during 1999 but only the C model is still flying today. It is flown by one training squadron at NAS Meridian, Mississippi, plus the Naval Test Pilot School at NAS Patuxent River, Maryland.

After producing 79 T-45A Goshawks for the Navy, Boeing switched production to the T-45C model, which is equipped with a digital cockpit. BuNo 165080/A-101 was the first such aircraft delivered to TAW-1 at NAS Meridian, Mississippi.

North American/Rockwell International T-2C Buckeye

In addition to providing student aviators with intermediate training at NAS Meridian, Mississippi, the North American T-2C is used by student naval flight officers (NFOs) for advanced strike and strike-fighter training. The twin-engine aircraft was developed from the single-engine T2J-1, which first flew in January 1958. The Buckeye entered service in 1959 and is currently flown by two training squadrons, although a few aircraft are assigned to the US Naval Test Pilot School at NAS Patuxent River, Maryland. They are used there as part of the school's fixed-wing curriculum or as chase aircraft. The T-2C will be replaced in service by the T-45C Goshawk starting in 2003.

Rockwell International T-2C Buckeye Specifications

Maximum Takeoff Weight:	13,180 lb (5978 kg)
Empty Weight:	8,115 lb (3681 kg)
Fuselage Length:	38 ft 3.5 in (11.67 m)
Wingspan:	38 ft 1.5 in (11.62 m)
Height:	14 ft 9.5 in (4.51 m)
Power Plant:	Two General Electric J85-GE-4 turbojet engines, each rated at 2,950 lb st (13.1 kN)
Maximum Fuel Capacity:	4,664 lb (2116 kg)
Maximum Speed:	454 kts (840 km/h) at 25,000 ft (7620 m)
Service Ceiling:	44,400 ft (13533 m)
Operating Range:	791 nm (1465 km)
Crew:	2
Armament:	Up to 3,500 lb (1588 kg) of stores can be carried on four hard points
Mission:	Intermediate trainer

McDonnell Douglas T-45A/C Goshawk

Developed from the British Aerospace Hawk trainer, the McDonnell Douglas (now Boeing) T-45A was selected as the winner of the US Navy's VTXTS program in November 1981. The aircraft is one element of the T-45 Training System that includes academics, simulators and logistic support. Although it physically resembles the RAF Hawk variant, significant structural redesign was undertaken to ensure the T-45A is capable of withstanding the stress of carrier landings and takeoffs. During development, the aircraft experienced a number of stability problems that delayed its deployment but the first of two prototypes flew in April 1988. The first production aircraft reached the Navy in October 1990 and deliveries of the T-45A ended in 1998, by which time production had switched to the T-45C variant. Equipped with a "glass" cockpit, the C model first flew in October 1997 and was delivered the following month. The Navy's original requirement for 302 aircraft was scaled back to just 187 aircraft and 153 have been funded through FY00. Conversion of T-45As to T-45C configuration is scheduled to begin in 2001 and should be completed by 2007.

The T-45A fleet is operated by two squadrons located at NAS Kingsville, Texas, whereas new production Goshawks are being accepted at NAS Meridian, Mississippi.

McDonnell Douglas T-45A Goshawk Specifications

Maximum Takeoff Weight:	13,500 lb (6123 kg)
Empty Weight:	9,394 lb (4261 kg)
Fuselage Length:	39 ft 4 in (11.99 m)
Wingspan:	30 ft 10 in (9.40 m)
Height:	13 ft 6 in (4.11 m)
Power Plant:	One Rolls-Royce Allison F405-RR-401 turbofan engine (Adour 871) rated at 5,527 lb st (24.6 kN)
Maximum Fuel Capacity:	2,893 lb (1312 kg)
Maximum Speed:	560 kts (1037 km/h)
Service Ceiling:	18,800 ft (5730 m)
Operating Range:	700 nm (1296 km)
Crew:	2
Armament:	None
Missions:	Intermediate and advanced trainer

DE HAVILLAND CANADA

de Havilland Canada NU-1B Otter

First flown in December 1951, the DHC-3 Otter was designated the UC-1 when ordered by the Navy but was subsequently redesignated the U-1 in 1962. In all, the service received 14 examples from de Havilland Canada and several were delivered to VXE-6 to support the Antarctic development squadron. Today a single NU-1B serves the Naval Test Pilot School at NAS Patuxent River, Maryland. The Otter's antiquated systems and unique flying characteristics present special challenges for student pilots.

de Havilland Canada NU-1B Otter Specifications

Maximum Takeoff Weight:	8,000 lb (3629 kg)
Empty Weight:	4,431 lb (2010 kg)
Fuselage Length:	41 ft 10 in (12.75 m)
Wingspan:	58 ft 0 in (17.68 m)
Height:	12 ft 7 in (3.84 m)
Power Plant:	One Pratt & Whitney R1340 Wasp radial engine rated at 660 hp (492 kW), driving a three-blade propeller
Maximum Fuel Capacity:	1,391 lb (631 kg)
Maximum Speed:	140 kts (259 km/h) at 5,000 ft (1524 m)
Service Ceiling:	18,800 ft (5730 m)
Operating Range:	835 nm (1546 km)
Crew:	2
Accommodations:	Up to 10 passengers or a 3,000-lb (1361-kg) payload
Armament:	None
Missions:	Training, utility

BuNo 144670 is the sole DHC-3 Otter left from a fleet of 14 that once served with the Navy. Designated the NU-1B, it is operated by the US Naval Test Pilot School.

de Havilland Canada U-6A Beaver

Beginning in 1951, the US Army ordered more than 650 L-19 Beavers for liaison duties. Built by de Havilland Canada, the Model DHC-2 flew for the first time in August 1947 and the Navy acquired several from the Army in 1962, which it redesignated U-6As. Today, the Naval Test Pilot School at NAS Patuxent River, Maryland, operates two examples. Their short takeoff and landing (STOL) characteristics make them ideal for the role of pilot assessment aircraft.

The US Naval Test Pilot School operates two de Havilland U-6A Beavers at NAS Patuxent River, Maryland, including BuNo 164525.

de Havilland Canada U-6A Beaver Specifications

Maximum Takeoff Weight:	5,100 lb (2313 kg)
Empty Weight:	2,850 lb (1293 kg)
Fuselage Length:	30 ft 3 in (9.22 m)
Wingspan:	48 ft 0 in (14.63 m)
Height:	9 ft 0 in (2.74 m)
Power Plant:	One Pratt & Whitney R985 Wasp Jr radial engine rated at 450 hp (336 kW), driving a two-blade propeller
Maximum Fuel Capacity:	618 lb (280 kg)
Maximum Speed:	133 kts (246 km/h) at 5,000 ft (1524 m)
Service Ceiling:	18,500 ft (5639 m)
Operating Range:	408 nm (756 km) with a 1,350-lb (612-kg) load
Crew:	2
Accommodations:	Up to seven passengers or a 1,500-lb (680-kg) payload
Armament:	None
Missions:	Training, utility

FAIRCHILD AEROSPACE

Fairchild C-26D, RC-26D, SA227AC Metro

Flight International operates a large number of aircraft under contract to the US Navy including N766C, an SA227AC Metroliner. This example is one of four stationed at NAWS China Lake or NAS Point Mugu, California. Others are flown by Berry Aviation, also under contract to the Navy.

During FY97, the Navy acquired seven ex-Air Force C-26Bs previously operated by the Air National Guard. Fairchild Aerospace and its subsidiary, Merlin Express in San Antonio, Texas, reworked the aircraft that now carry the designation C-26D. Initial deliveries of the upgraded platform began in July 1999, and four aircraft are now based in Italy where they serve in the operational support airlift (OSA) role. The other three are being modified for range support duties, with the designation RC-26D, and will be based in Hawaii. Maintenance and support are the responsibility of Lear Siegler Services.

The Navy also flies four civil-registered SA227AC Metros between its weapons test facilities at NAS Point Mugu and NAWS China Lake, California. Although operated by naval crews, these aircraft are nonetheless owned and maintained by a private contractor. Contractor-operated SA227ACs also provide a shuttle between NAS North Island and NAAS San Clemente, California.

Specifications: See the US Army section for details

Missions: Operational support airlift (OSA), range support

GENERAL DYNAMICS (Including Gulfstream Aerospace)

Gulfstream Aerospace C-20D/G Gulfstream III/IV

The Navy operates Gulfstream III and IV variants built by Gulfstream Aerospace Corporation, a company that is now part of General Dynamics. The III model is designated the C-20D and is powered by two Rolls-Royce Spey Mk511-8 turbofan engines. It has an executive compartment that can accommodate five passengers and a staff compartment with room for eight passengers. The Gulfstream IV is designated the C-20G and is powered by two Rolls-Royce Tay Mk611-8 turbofans. It can be configured to carry cargo, passengers or a combination of both. The aircraft is capable of accommodating up to 26 passengers and a crew of four but, with all passenger seats removed, it can be used to carry three freight pallets instead. An hydraulically operated cargo door on the starboard side of the aircraft and a ball-roller cargo floor facilitate loading and unloading of freight. Although the fleet is relatively new and is equipped with

Gulfstream Aerospace C-20G Gulfstream IV Specifications

Maximum Takeoff Weight:	74,600 lb (33838 kg)
Empty Weight:	42,400 lb (19232 kg)
Fuselage Length:	88 ft 3.5 in (26.91 m)
Wingspan:	77 ft 10.75 in (23.74 m)
Height:	24 ft 3.5 in (7.40 m)
Power Plant:	Two Rolls-Royce Tay Mk 611-8 turbofan engines, each rated at 13,850 lb st (61.6 kN)
Maximum Fuel Capacity:	29,500 lb (13381 kg)
Maximum Speed:	509 kts (943 km/h) at 30,000 ft (9144 m)
Service Ceiling:	45,000 ft (13716 m)
Operating Range:	3,983 nm (7377 km)
Crew:	3
Accommodations:	Up to 26 passengers or 6,500 lb (2948 kg) of cargo or a combination of both
Armament:	None
Missions:	Operational support airlift (OSA), fleet logistic support

The 'Capital Skyliners' of VR-48 operate two C-20G Gulfstream IVs, including BuNo 165093 based at NAF Washington, Andrews AFB, Maryland.

modern avionics, modifications are underway to add TCAS equipment and a wind shear detection system. Whereas the C-20Ds are normally reserved to support high-ranking Navy officials, the Navy's four C-20Gs are divided between two reserve fleet logistic squadrons. They fly CONUS missions scheduled by the Joint Operational Support Airlift Center (JOSAC) at Scott AFB, Illinois, and OCONUS missions handled by the Naval Air Logistics Office (NALO) at NAS New Orleans, Louisiana.

Seahawk, and was given a composite main rotor. Dubbed the Super Seasprite, the new variant was also equipped with a forward-looking infrared (FLIR), updated electronic support measures (ESM) and an onboard acoustic processor never carried by the SH-2F. It was also given limited capabilities to handle airborne mine countermeasures (AMCM) through the addition of the Magic Lantern mine detection pod. The Naval Air Reserve currently operates 12 Super Seasprites shared between two squadrons. However, the type is scheduled for retirement from Navy service by March 2001 and the SH-60B will be its replacement.

HUGHES HELICOPTERS (See Boeing Company)

KAMAN AEROSPACE

Kaman SH-2G Seasprite

First flown in 1959 as the HU2K-1, the first Seasprite was a single-engine helicopter used as a utility platform. Subsequently equipped with two engines, and redesignated the UH-2C, the type was modified to meet the Navy's requirement for a light airborne, multipurpose system (LAMPS I). An interim SH-2D entered operational service in 1972 and was followed by the SH-2F in 1973. The type mainly served from Navy surface vessels in antisubmarine warfare, antiship surveillance and targeting roles but was also used for SAR and VERTREP. Although largely replaced in the years that followed by SH-60B LAMPS III Seahawk helicopters, the Seasprite continued to operate from ships unable to accommodate the Seahawk. A more capable variant was also developed. First flown in December 1989, the SH-2G was fitted with the same T700 engine that powers the

Kaman SH-2G Seasprite Specifications

Maximum Takeoff Weight:	13,500 lb (6123 kg)
Empty Weight:	7,600 lb (3447 kg)
Fuselage Length:	40 ft 6 in (12.34 m)
Overall Length:	52 ft 9 in (16.08 m)
Main Rotor Diameter:	44 ft 4 in (13.51 m)
Height:	15 ft 0.5 in (4.58 m)
Power Plant:	Two General Electric T700-GE-401C turboshaft engines, each rated at 1,723 shp (1285 kW), driving four-blade main and tail rotors
Maximum Fuel Capacity:	Internal – 1,863 lb (845 kg) External (two tanks) – 1,350 lb (612 kg)
Maximum Speed:	138 kts (256 km/h) at sea level
Operating Range:	434 nm (804 km) with two external fuel tanks
Crew:	3
Accommodations:	Four passengers or two litters with mission equipment removed or 4,000 lb (1814 kg) of external cargo
Armament:	Mk 46/50 torpedoes, crew-operated 7.62mm M60 machine guns
Mission Equipment:	LN-66 surveillance radar, AN/ALR-66 electronic support measures, AN/ASQ-81 magnetic anomaly detector (MAD), AN/ARR-84 sonobuoy receiver and AN/UYS-503 acoustic processor, Magic Lantern mine detection system.
Missions:	Surface warfare (SUW), undersea warfare (USW), mine countermeasures

Kaman SH-2G Seasprites are currently operated by Naval Reserve squadrons at NAS Willow Grove, Pennsylvania, and NAS North Island, California. However, both units will be deactivated in March 2001 and the type is expected to end its naval service at that time. BuNo 161647 is one of 18 SH-2Fs modified to SH-2G configuration.

This Kaman SH-2G is fitted with the Magic Lantern mine system, seen here on the starboard side aft of the main wheel. The helicopter is currently flying with two reserve squadrons.

BuNo 164997 is one of four Lockheed Hercules operated by Naval Reserve Squadron VR-53 from NAF Washington at Andrews AFB, Maryland. This example is a C-130T.

Three ex-Air Force DC-130A Hercules are flown from Mojave Airport, California, to support naval operations at NAS Point Mugu, California. The aircraft, including serial 57-0497 shown here, serve as airborne launchers for BQM-34S subscale aerial target drones.

LOCKHEED MARTIN (INCLUDING FAIRCHILD REPUBLIC AND GENERAL DYNAMICS)

Lockheed DC-130A, KC-130F/T, TC-130G, NC-130H, C-130T Hercules

Transferred to the Navy from the Air Force three DC-130As are modified C-130As used to support the Naval Air Warfare Center Weapon Division (NAWC-WD) and US Navy fleet readiness exercises. Three examples, operated and maintained by Avtel Services, Mojave, California, fly from NAS Point Mugu.

The C-130T, first delivered in 1992, gives the Navy the capability to transport heavy or oversized cargoes like aircraft engines, helicopter rotor blades, large ship parts and missiles but can also transport a mix of cargo and passengers. For long-range missions, wing-mounted aerial refueling pods can be fitted. The cockpits of the entire fleet are being updated with a traffic collision avoidance system (TCAS), a GPS, a ground-proximity warning system (GPWS), night-vision lighting, AN/ARC-210 radios, a flight data recorder and an emergency locator transmitter. The fleet currently consists of 20 aircraft shared between four Naval Air Reserve fleet logistic support squadrons, and all mission scheduling is handled by the Naval Air Logistics Office (NALO) at NAS New Orleans, Louisiana.

Although listed within the Marine Corps inventory, a single KC-130F and one KC-130T are assigned to the Naval Air Warfare Center Aircraft Division (NAWC-AD) at NAS Patuxent River, Maryland. In addition, a Marine Corps crew operates a single TC-130G as a support aircraft for the 'Blue Angels' aerobatic team, and a former US Coast Guard EC-130V (now designated NC-130H) is assigned to the NAWC-AD. It is used in conjunction with tests of new airborne early warning radar equipment.

Specifications: See USMC section for details

Missions: UAV/RPV support, transport, inflight refueling

Lockheed P-3B/C, EP-3E/J, NP-3D, UP-3A, VP-3A Orion

Developed from the Lockheed Model L-188 Electra airliner, the Orion has been in US Navy service since July 1962, when the first P3V-1 (P-3A after September 1962) was delivered. In 1964, production switched to the P-3B, which was equipped with updated sensors and improved engines. Although a variety of earlier variants developed from these models remain in service, only the P-3C, first delivered in 1969, is currently tasked with operational patrol missions. Over the years, the P-3C has undergone a number of changes to enhance its capabilities including Updates I, II and III. Orions were first flown in these configurations in 1975, 1977 and 1981, respectively, and a number of the earlier models have also been upgraded to Update III standard. Most Update I aircraft still in service are now assigned to the FRS.

The Orion was developed primarily to counter the threat posed by Soviet attack and ballistic missile submarines during the Cold War years. Following the collapse of the Soviet Union, that threat dimin-

Retired to the Aerospace Maintenance and Regeneration Center (AMARC) at Davis Monthan AFB, Arizona, in December 1999, BuNo 153433 is a UP-3B Orion. It most recently supported VQ-1 at NAS Whidbey Island, Washington.

The Naval Weapons Test Squadron at NAS Point Mugu, California, operates five NP-3D Orions. BuNo 150521 is one of three equipped with a phased-array telemetry antenna capable of tracking five independent information sources simultaneously, such as those for HARPOON, SLAM or Tomahawk missiles.

been authorized and the first aircraft modified to this standard was scheduled for delivery in January 2000. In addition, a sustained readiness program will extend the operational service lives of some 221 Orions to approximately 38 years, and a follow-on service life extension plan is currently in development. This could extend the type's useful life to at least 2020. Ongoing upgrades to the P-3 have been necessary because development of a replacement, designated the P-7A long-range air antisubmarine warfare capable aircraft (LRAACA), was cancelled in 1990. Two years later, a proposed systems upgrade dubbed Update IV was also dropped, although some of the modifications now taking place would have been included under that program.

Today, P-3Cs are flown by 13 active-duty patrol squadrons including a single FRS. Eight Naval Reserve squadrons also operate

ished significantly and it was determined that some littoral warfare missions could be handled by the Orion. Maritime surveillance has now taken on a greater importance and the aircraft's surface warfare capabilities are being upgraded. Incorporation of the anti-surface warfare improvement plan (AIP) is providing P-3Cs with enhanced radar, countermeasures, electronic support measures, sensors and better communications. Furthermore, new weapons configurations include carriage of AGM-65F Maverick and AGM-84E SLAM air-to-surface missiles. The first AIP Orions were deployed in September 1998 and current plans call for 146 examples in all to be modified. By mid-1999, 18 aircraft had received the modifications and 24 additional kits had been funded. Meanwhile, remaining Update II and II.5 Orions are being upgraded to Update III configuration via a block modification update program (BMUP). By the end of 1999, 25 BMUP kits had

Lockheed VP-3As used as executive transports are the oldest Orion variants still in service. The aircraft are not equipped with antisubmarine equipment and thus do not possess a long tail "stinger" used to house the magnetic anomaly detection (MAD) equipment. BuNo 149675 is a VP-3A operated by the executive transport detachment at MCAF Kaneohe Bay, Hawaii, in support of the Commander in Chief, US Pacific Fleet (CINCPACFLT).

Lockheed P-3C Orion Specifications

Maximum Takeoff Weight:	142,000 lb (64410 kg)
Empty Weight:	61,490 lb (27891 kg)
Fuselage Length:	116 ft 10 in (35.61 m)
Wingspan:	99 ft 8 in (30.38 m)
Height:	33 ft 8.5 in (10.27 m)
Power Plant:	Four Rolls-Royce Allison T56-A-14 turboprop engines, each rated at 4,910 shp (3661 kW), driving four-blade constant-speed propellers
Maximum Fuel Capacity:	62,500 lb (28350 kg)
Maximum Speed:	411 kts (761 km/h) at 15,000 ft (4572 m)
Operating Range:	3 hours on station at 1,336 nm (2474 km)
Crew:	11
Armament:	Internal weapons bay and 10 external stations can accommodate up to 20,000 lb (9072 kg) of stores, including Mk 46/50 torpedoes; Mk 54/57/101 depth bombs; Mk 25/36/39/52/55/56 mines; AGM-65 Maverick, AGM-84 Harpoon and SLAM air-to-surface missiles
Mission Equipment:	AN/APS-137 inverse synthetic aperture radar (ISAR), AN/AAS-36 infrared detection set (IRDS), AN/ASQ-81 magnetic anomaly detector (MAD), AN/ALQ-78 electronic support measures (ESM)
Missions:	Maritime patrol/surveillance, surface warfare (SUW), undersea warfare (USW), electronic intelligence (ELINT), staff transport, utility, weapons development

the variant and two special projects patrol squadrons (VPUs) fly specialized models. Transport variants of the Orion include the VP-3A, equipped as a staff/VIP transport, and the UP-3A, which have been stripped of mission equipment and configured to carry passengers or cargo. The designation NP-3D is assigned to 11 aircraft permanently modified to various configurations. Additionally, 11 EP-3Es operate in the signals intelligence (SIGINT) role with two fleet air reconnaissance squadrons. Based on the P-3C, airborne reconnaissance integrated intelligence system (ARIES) II platforms have replaced earlier EP-3B "Bat Rack" and EP-3E ARIES I aircraft, based on P-3B and P-3A airframes, respectively. Another P-3C is being modified to ARIES II configuration to replace a twelfth aircraft damaged beyond repair in an accident.

An upgrade to the EP-3E communication and data automation system is undergoing tests at NAS Patuxent River as part of what is called the sensor system improvement program (SSIP), for incorporation into the entire EP-3E fleet. The EP-3E will also be used to develop a prototype of the Joint SIGINT avionics family (JSAF), to be carried by Navy EP-3Es by 2003. A single EP-3J, was in service with the Naval Reserve and served as an electronic "aggressor" but was retired to AMARC in September 1999, as was the last UP-3B.

Lockheed S-3B Viking

The Lockheed S-3A was declared the winner of the Navy's VSX competition in 1969, and the prototype first flew in January 1972. Production deliveries began in 1974 and the Viking became the first antisubmarine warfare (ASW) aircraft to be integrated into an all-purpose carrier air wing. However, it has assumed many new missions over the years making it an important asset beyond antisubmarine warfare. Today it is tasked primarily with armed surface reconnaissance (ASR) and surface warfare (SUW). The first of 119 S-3As modified to S-3B configuration took to the air in September 1984. The new variant was equipped with an inverse synthetic aperture radar (ISAR), better electronic support measures, an improved FLIR and updated ASW equipment. Separately, 16 S-3As were modified to ES-3A configuration to fill the signals intelligence (SIGINT) role but were retired at the end of FY99.

Lockheed Martin is currently developing additional upgrades for the Viking that will keep the aircraft viable until the planned deployment of a common support aircraft (CSA) after 2015. A critical avionics update will replace the automatic flight control system (AFCS), inertial navigation system (INS), flight instruments, displays and armament controls. Furthermore, a service life extension program will increase the longevity of the airframe from the current 13,000

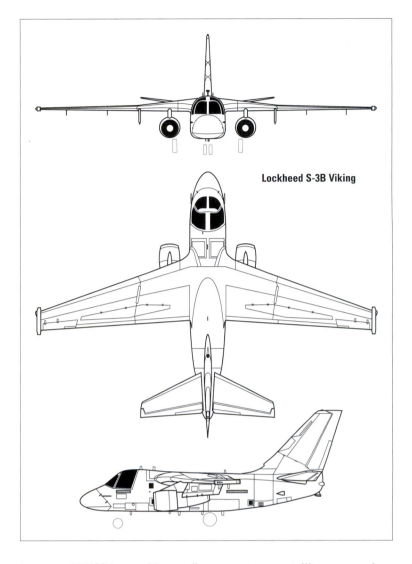

Lockheed S-3B Viking

Lockheed S-3B Viking Specifications

Maximum Takeoff Weight:	52,540 lb (23832 kg)
Empty Weight:	26,650 lb (12088 kg)
Fuselage Length:	49 ft 5 in (15.06 m), MAD boom extended – 67 ft 4 in (20.52 m)
Wingspan:	Extended – 68 ft 8 in (20.93 m), Folded – 29 ft 6 in (8.99 m)
Height:	Tail extended – 22 ft 9 in (6.93 m), Tail folded – 15 ft 3 in (4.65 m)
Power Plant:	Two General Electric TF34-GE-400B high-bypass turbofan engines, each rated at 9,275 lb st (41.3 kN)
Maximum Fuel Capacity:	Internal – 12,863 lb (5835 kg) External – 2,025 lb (919 kg)
Maximum Speed:	450 kts (833 km/h)
Operating Range:	350 nm (648 km)
Crew:	4
Armament:	Internal weapons bay and two external hardpoints can accomodate up to 7,000 lb (3175 kg) of stores, including Mk 46/50 torpedoes; Mk 52/55/56/60 mines; AGM-65 Maverick, AGM-84 Harpoon and SLAM air-to-surface missiles; Mk 7/20 cluster munitions; LAU-10/68/69 rocket pods
Mission Equipment:	AN/APS-137 inverse synthetic aperture radar (ISAR), AN/OR-263 forward-looking infrared (FLIR), AN/ALR-76 electronic support measures (ESM), AN/ARR-78 sonobuoy receiving system, AN/UYS-1 spectrum analyzer unit, AN/ASQ-81 magnetic anomaly detector (MAD), A/A42R-1 refueling pod
Missions:	Surface warfare (SUW), armed surface reconnaissance (ASR), undersea warfare (USW), surface search and clarification (SSC), aerial refueling

hours to 17,500 hours. New radios, computers, satellite communications (SATCOM) and navigation equipment will also follow. Proposed upgrades thereafter include adding a moving target indicator to the radar system, improving the surveillance systems and adding a long-range electro-optical system. NAWCAD is also developing a precision surveillance and targeting system for the Viking.

S-3Bs are currently assigned to 11 active-duty squadrons including a single FRS. Although sea control units will continue to deploy with eight Vikings each, reports suggest four of those aircraft will be dedicated as tankers and their mission equipment will be removed. Furthermore, the four aircraft flying sea control missions will lose their acoustic undersea warfare (USW) systems.

With retirement of the last of the Grumman KA-6D refuelers in the mid-1990s, the S-3B Viking became the fleet's primary tanker asset. Although the S-3 has already been in service for more than 25 years, the Navy and Lockheed Martin are currently developing a life-extension program for the type. Today, 116 Vikings are flying, including this example operated by the 'Blue Wolves' of VS-35.

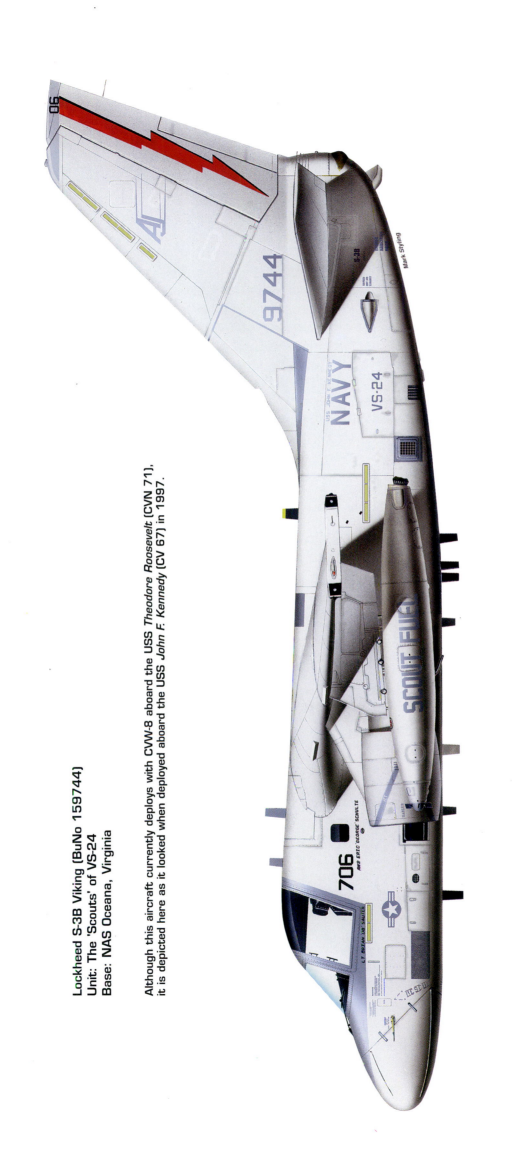

Lockheed S-3B Viking (BuNo 159744)
Unit: The 'Scouts' of VS-24
Base: NAS Oceana, Virginia

Although this aircraft currently deploys with CVW-8 aboard the USS *Theodore Roosevelt* (CVN 71), it is depicted here as it looked when deployed aboard the USS *John F. Kennedy* (CV 67) in 1997.

Vital assets aboard each carrier, Grumman EA-6Bs are also assigned to USAF Air Expeditionary Forces. BuNo 164402 flies with the 'Black Ravens' of VAQ-135 from the deck of the USS *Carl Vinson* (CVN 70) as part of CVW-11.

NORTHROP GRUMMAN CORPORATION
(INCLUDING GRUMMAN AND NORTHROP)

Grumman EA-6B Prowler

The EA-6B Prowler first flew in May 1968 and production aircraft entered naval service in 1971. Over the 20 years that followed, 170 examples were delivered to the Navy and Marine Corps in four distinct versions for the purpose of jamming and/or destroying enemy radar and communications sites and providing escort for strike aircraft. In fact, since the Air Force retired the last of its General Dynamics F-111s in 1998, the Prowler has been the only tactical jamming platform available to US forces. Operating from the deck of a carrier, the four-seat, all-weather, subsonic platform is equipped with an AN/ALQ-99 tactical jamming system and can be armed with an AGM-88A high-speed, antiradiation missile (HARM).

The Navy has begun a program to modify 69 Block 82 and 56 Block 89 Prowlers to a common baseline configuration known as Block 89A. Thereafter they will be updated to Improved Capability III (ICAP III) standard. Block 89A provides a common avionics package including an AN/AYK-14 computer, AN/ARC-210 radios, a GPS, a new instrument landing system (ILS), a commercial off-the-shelf (COTS) electronic flight instrumentation system (EFIS), a very high speed integrated circuit (VHSIC) and a control display unit (CDU). Improved high- and low-band jamming pods are also being developed and should reach IOC in 2003. Meanwhile, upgraded universal exciters are now entering service along with the AN/USQ-113 communications jammer. A Block 89A validation aircraft flew for the first time at Northrop Grumman's St. Augustine, Florida facility on 8 June 1997.

ICAP III will further update the fleet with new electronic support measures (ESM) capable of determining hostile radar characteristics more quickly and precisely, thereby enabling Prowler crews to use their HARMs more effectively. The program will also integrate the stand-alone AN/USQ-113 into the AN/ALQ-99 tactical jammer via the multifunction information distribution system (MIDS). In addition, new controls and a display suite, including flat panel and solid-state tactical situation displays, are part of a multimission advanced tactical terminal (MATT) being installed in the positions occupied by electronic countermeasures officers (ECMOs). Northrop Grumman is currently modifying two Block 89A EA-6Bs to ICAP III configuration, and operational test and evaluation (OT&E) is scheduled to begin in 2002. A production decision is expected in 2003 and IOC should be achieved in 2004. The new system will provide a reactive jamming capability against frequency-agile radars and allow rapid retargeting for the HARM.

The Navy's 15 Prowler units include four joint service squadrons nominally tasked to support the Air Force and the FRS. EA-6Bs are also assigned to a reserve squadron and several test units.

Grumman EA-6B Prowler Specifications	
Maximum Takeoff Weight:	61,500 lb (27895 kg)
Empty Weight:	33,600 lb (15241 kg)
Fuselage Length:	59 ft 10 in (18.24 m)
Wingspan:	Extended – 53 ft 0 in (16.15 m), Folded – 25 ft 10 in (7.87 m)
Height:	16 ft 3 in (4.95 m)
Power Plant:	Two Pratt & Whitney J52-P-408 turbojet engines, each rated at 11,200 lb st (49.8 kN)
Maximum Fuel Capacity:	Internal – 15,422 lb (6995 kg) External – 10,025 lb (4547 kg)
Maximum Speed:	566 kts (1048 km/h) at sea level
Service Ceiling:	37,600 ft (11460 m)
Operating Range:	849 nm (1572 km) unrefueled
Crew:	4
Armament:	Five external stores stations are capable of carrying electronic jamming pods, external fuel tanks or a maximum of two AGM-88 HARM air-surface missiles
Mission Equipment:	AN/ALQ-99 tactical jamming system (TJS)
Mission:	Electronic attack

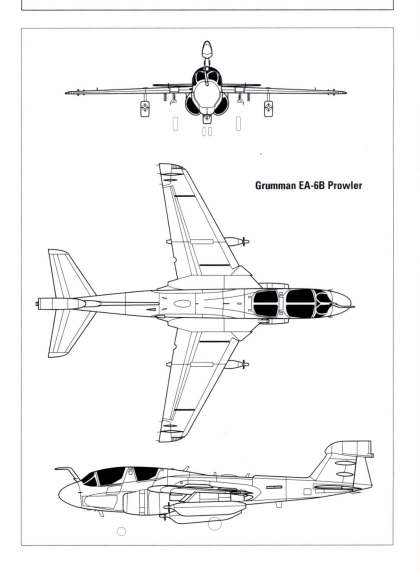

Grumman EA-6B Prowler

Grumman C-2A Greyhound

Designed to transport personnel and cargo between land bases and deployed aircraft carriers, the C-2A was developed from the airframe of the E-2A Hawkeye. The first of 19 C-2As was delivered to the Navy in 1966 and a service life extension program (SLEP) was implemented in the mid-1970s. However, the high utilization rate of the small C-2A fleet, combined with the need to replace earlier generation C-1As, forced the Navy to reopen the production line in 1984. Delivery of the first of 39 new Greyhounds was made in 1985 and the last of the original aircraft was retired in 1987. Equipped with updated avionics and having a longer fatigue life, the new-build C-2A is capable of air dropping supplies via its aft cargo ramp. Northrop Grumman is currently conducting a full-scale fatigue test program to determine the feasibility of undertaking a structural life extension modification on the type that would increase its service life from 10,000 hours to 15,000 hours. This would allow it to remain in the inventory until at least 2015. By that time, the service hopes to have deployed a common support aircraft (CSA).

The fleet is operated by a single E-2C/C-2A training squadron and two fleet logistic support squadrons that detach aircraft and personnel to each deployed carrier air wing. During a typical six-month peacetime deployment, a detachment of two Greyhounds will accumulate approximately 1,000 flight hours, transport 5,000 passengers and haul about 500 tons of cargo.

Grumman C-2A Greyhound Specifications

Maximum Takeoff Weight:	57,000 lb (25855 kg)
Empty Weight:	36,346 lb (16486 kg)
Fuselage Length:	57 ft 7 in (17.50 m)
Wingspan:	Extended – 80 ft 7 in (24.56 m), Folded – 29 ft 4 in (8.94 m)
Height:	16 ft 10.5 in (5.14 m)
Power Plant:	Two Rolls-Royce Allison T56-A-425 turboprop engines, each rated at 4,910 shp (3661 kW)
Maximum Fuel Capacity:	12,400 lb (5625 kg)
Maximum Speed:	310 kts (574 km/h) at 25,000 ft (7620 m)
Service Ceiling:	30,000 ft (9144 m)
Operating Range:	1,043 nm (1932 km) with a 10,000-lb (4536-kg) load
Crew:	3
Accommodations:	39 passengers or 10,000 lb (4536 kg) or a combination of both
Armament:	None
Missions:	Carrier on-board delivery (COD), transport, medical evacuation, Special Operations

BuNo 162161/NK-24 and BuNo 162163/NG-25 are C-2A Greyhounds assigned to VRC-30 Detachments 1 and 4 with CVW-14 and CVW-9, respectively. The squadron normally provides two aircraft to each deployed carrier.

The Navy is still acquiring new E-2C Hawkeyes and 21 are currently being built under a multi-year contract. The service hopes to upgrade as many as 75 examples to Hawkeye 2000 standard.

Grumman E-2C Hawkeye

First flown in 1961 as the W2F-1, the current Northrop Grumman E-2C bears only a basic resemblance to the earliest Hawkeyes that entered service in 1964. Like most naval aircraft, the E-2C has undergone numerous modifications since becoming operational in 1973. The type's radar system has seen four designations and the aircraft is now equipped with a powerful AN/APS-145 early warning system, which was developed as part of the Group II radar modernization program. This Hawkeye has improved performance over land and is equipped with a joint tactical information distribution system (JTIDS) and a global positioning system (GPS). The E-2C can detect and track 2,000 targets within its large surveillance envelope while simultaneously directing up to 20 intercepts.

E-2C production was to have ended with the delivery of four E-2T aircraft to Taiwan but additional orders were received in FY95, and Northrop Grumman relocated its production line to St. Augustine, Florida. Development of an advanced variant dubbed Hawkeye 2000 is under way there, and the manufacturer was recently awarded a multi-year contract covering 21 new aircraft. This configuration incorporates a mission computer upgrade (MCU), advanced control indicator sets (ACIS), advanced satellite communications (SATCOM) equipment and the AN/USG-3 cooperative engagement capability (CEC) system that allows multiple air- and sea-based platforms to share sensor data. CEC will make it possible for the E-2C to share its radar data with Aegis-equipped surface ships and will provide long-range targeting for the vessel's air defense systems. Five Group II E-2Cs were initially fitted with the MCU/ACIS, an updated

Grumman E-2C Hawkeye Specifications

Maximum Takeoff Weight:	51,933 lb (23556 kg)
Empty Weight:	38,200 lb (17327 kg)
Fuselage Length:	57 ft 6.75 in (17.55 m)
Wingspan:	Extended – 80 ft 7 in (24.56 m), Folded – 29 ft 4 in (8.94 m)
Height:	Rotodome up – 18 ft 3.75 in (5.58 m), Rotodome down – 16 ft 5.5 in (5.02 m)
Power Plant:	Two Rolls-Royce Allison T56-A-627 turboprop engines, each rated at 4,910 shp (3661 kW), driving four-blade constant-speed propellers
Maximum Fuel Capacity:	12,400 lb (5625 kg)
Maximum Speed:	326 kts at (604 km/h)
Service Ceiling:	31,000 feet (9449 m)
Typical Operating Range:	On station – 5.6 hours at 200 nm (370 km), Ferry – 1,395 nm (2584 km)
Crew:	5
Armament	None
Mission Equipment:	AN/APS-145 radar, AN/ALR-73 passive detection system (PDS)
Mission:	Airborne early warning (AEW) command and control (C2)

inertial navigation system and an automatic flight control system (AFCS). Assigned to VAW-113, the new aircraft will reach IOC in 2002. Besides 21 new production Hawkeye 2000s ordered in 1999, as many as 75 Group II E-2Cs may be modified to the standard.

Hawkeyes currently serve with 10 active-duty squadrons, a single FRS and two reserve units.

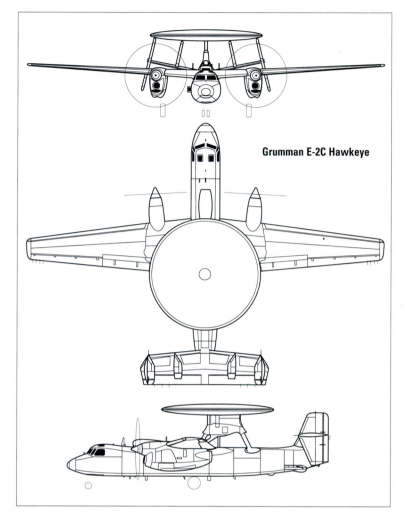

Grumman E-2C Hawkeye

Northrop F-5E/F Tiger II

Developed from the Northrop F-5A Freedom Fighter, the F-5E flew for the first time in August 1972 and has since served US forces primarily in the dissimilar air combat training (DACT) or "aggressor" role. The US Navy has operated the type for this mission since the mid-1970s, when it received several examples initially destined for South Vietnam. The first F-5Es replaced T-38As assigned to the Navy Fighter Weapons School at NAS Miramar, California, in 1975.

Before being transferred to the US Navy, this Northrop F-5F (serial 84-0456/AF-30) served with the Air Force at Williams AFB and flew with the 425th Tactical Fighter Training Squadron. The aircraft is now assigned to the 'Saints' of VFC-13 at NAS Fallon, Nevada.

Although the Tiger II saw service with a small number of active-duty "aggressor" squadrons, by the mid-1980s it had largely been replaced by the F-16N Fighting Falcon. However, fatigue problems soon ended the F-16's role as a DACT platform. As a result, the Navy was forced to reintroduce the Tiger II for this purpose and the type is still flown by one reserve squadron today. As well as those aircraft originally delivered to the Navy, the service has acquired additional ex-Air Force examples that are now flown by a single Marine Reserve Forces squadron. Although the Navy has considered implementing a service life extension on the F-5E/F fleet, recent reports suggest it will consider using F-16s again instead.

Northrop F-5E Tiger II Specifications

Maximum Takeoff Weight:	24,676 lb (11193 kg)
Empty Weight:	9,683 lb (4392 kg)
Fuselage Length:	48 ft 2.5 in (14.69 m)
Wingspan:	26 ft 8.5 in (8.14 m)
Height:	13 ft 2.5 in (4.03 m)
Power Plant:	Two General Electric J85-GE-21B turbojet engines, each rated at 3,500 lb st (15.6 kN) dry or 5,000 lb st (22.2 kN) with maximum afterburner
Maximum Fuel Capacity:	4,502 lb (2042 kg)
Maximum Speed:	918 kts (1700 km/h) at 36,000 ft (10973 m)
Service Ceiling:	51,800 ft (15789 m)
Operating Range:	760 nm (1408 km) with 2 AIM-9 missiles, Ferry – 1,715 nm (3176 km)
Crew:	1
Armament:	Two 20-mm M39A2 cannon with 280 rounds per gun
Mission Equipment:	AN/APQ-159 fire control radar
Mission:	Dissimilar air combat training (DACT)

Grumman F-14A/B/D Tomcat

The Grumman F-14A was chosen to undertake the VFX mission as a replacement for the ill-fated F-111B and its predecessor, the F-4 Phantom. First flown in December 1970, the Tomcat was initially deployed in September 1974 aboard the USS Enterprise (CVN 65) and made its combat debut flying combat air patrol (CAP) missions in support of the United States' evacuation of Saigon. Equipped with a powerful radar and extended range missiles, the F-14 was primarily intended to defend the fleet against manned bombers and cruise missiles. However, the Tomcat also assumed a reconnaissance role when the tactical air reconnaissance pod system (TARPS) was later added to a number of examples.

Grumman delivered 557 F-14As to the Navy before production switched to the F-14A(PLUS), which was first flown in November 1987 and entered service in 1988. Three years later, its designation was changed to F-14B. Although the new variant retained most of the

Grumman F-14D Tomcat Specifications

Maximum Takeoff Weight:	74,500 lb (33793 kg)
Empty Weight:	40,150 lb (18212 kg)
Fuselage Length:	62 ft 8 in (19.10 m)
Wingspan (Min. sweep 20°):	64 ft 1.5 in (19.55 m)
Wingspan (Max. sweep 68°):	38 ft 2.5 in (11.65 m)
Wingspan (Oversweep/storage):	33 ft 3.5 in (10.15 m)
Height:	16 ft 0 in (4.88 m)
Power Plant:	Two General Electric F100-GE-400 low-bypass turbofan engines, each rated at 16,333 lb st (72.7 kN) dry or 26,950 lb st (119.9 kN) with full afterburner
Maximum Fuel Capacity:	Internal – 16,200 lb (7348 kg) External – 3,800 lb (1724 kg) in tanks on two stations
Maximum Speed:	1,341 kts (2483 km/h)
Service Ceiling:	50,000+ ft (15240+ m)
Operating Range:	1,734 nm (3211 km)
Crew:	2
Armament:	One 20-mm M61A1 gatling gun with 675 rounds; eight weapons stations capable of accommodating 13,000 lb (5897 kg) of stores, including AIM-7 Sparrow, AIM-9 Sidewinder or AIM-54 Phoenix air-to-air missiles; AGM-88 HARM air-to-ground missile; Mk 82/83/84 general purpose and laser-guided bombs and cluster munitions
Mission Equipment:	AN/APG-71 radar, AN/AAS-42 infrared search and track system (IRST), AN/AVX-1 television camera set, AN/AAQ-14 LANTIRN, tactical air reconnaissance pod system (TARPS)
Missions:	All-weather strike fighter, reconnaissance

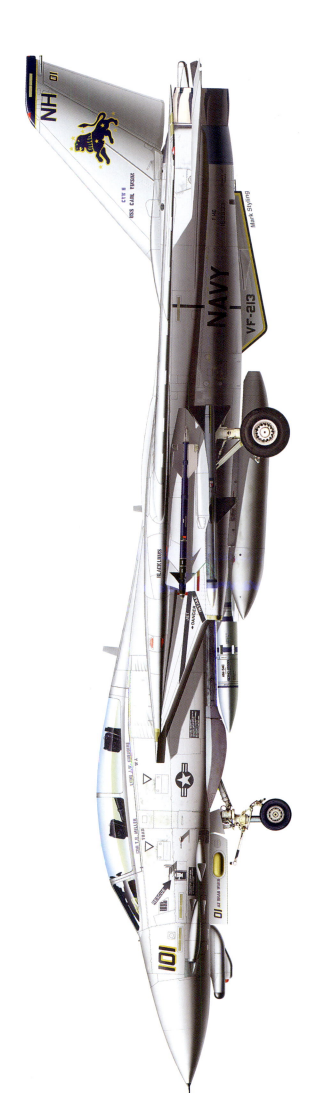

Grumman F-14D Tomcat BuNo 163893
Unit: VF-213 'Black Lions'
Base: NAS Oceana, Virginia

This Super Tomcat deploys aboard the USS *Carl Vinson* as part of Carrier Air Wing Eleven (CVW-11)

"Vandy One" (BuNo 164604/XF-1) was the last of 37 F-14Ds built by Grumman for the US Navy, and the last of 712 Tomcats delivered in total. The aircraft has been based at NAS Point Mugu, California since entering service and is currently assigned to the VX-9 detachment at the air station.

F-14A's avionics systems, General Electric F110-GE-400 power plants and associated systems developed for the F-14D replaced the Pratt & Whitney TF30 engines. Only 38 new F-14Bs were built but 47 low-time F-14As were converted to the standard. Development of the advanced F-14D Super Tomcat began in 1983 and the first flight was made in 1990. The aircraft incorporated not only the new engines already in use with the F-14A(PLUS) but also a digital avionics suite and a series of other modifications. Other major improvements included a new radar which, although developed from the AN/AWG-9, utilizes components common to the F-15E's radar, and new cockpit displays also used in the F/A-18 Hornet. Total production was limited to just 37 new F-14Ds but 18 older F-14As were completely remanufactured to this advanced configuration and given the designation F-14D(R) (R for Remanufacture). As well as serving as the fleet's primary interceptor and reconnaissance platform, the Tomcat has been able to perform precision strike missions since being equipped with the LANTIRN system in 1997. Meanwhile, in addition to more avionics and weapons system modifications, the Tomcat fleet is undergoing structural improvements to increase the type's service life from 6,000 to 9,000 flight hours. These changes should allow the Navy to maintain the F-14 until 2010.

Thus far, the avionics and weapons system modifications have added both multimission and precision strike capabilities, a BOL chaff system, night vision goggle-compatible lighting and instruments, a new head-up display (HUD) and a digital flight control system. Furthermore, the TARPS has been updated to digital configuration and now has the capacity to transmit images directly to a carrier via a real time data link.

Thirteen fighter squadrons, including the FRS for the type, currently fly the Tomcat. The Navy has all three variants in service and is scheduled to complete both the F-14B (Upgrade) and strike upgrade programs during FY00. Current plans call for the new F/A-18E/F Super Hornet to begin replacing the F-14A in FY01.

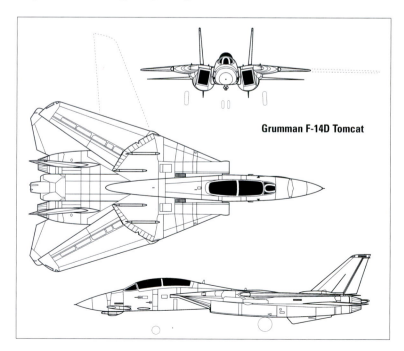

Grumman F-14D Tomcat

Northrop T-38A Talon

The Naval Test Pilot School at NAS Patuxent River, Maryland is home to the Navy's entire fleet of Northrop T-38A Talons. Whereas the type once served the fleet as an "aggressor" and drone aircraft, it is now used only as a supersonic trainer. Although five T-38As were transferred to the Navy directly from Air Force stocks, most of the 11 now assigned to the NTPS are bailed from the service.

Specifications: See the USAF section for details

Although several Navy squadrons have operated T-38A Talons over the years, the type is currently assigned only to the US Naval Test Pilot School at NAS Patuxent River, Maryland. Serial 70-1575 is one of several on loan from the Air Force.

PIONEER UAV

Pioneer UAV RQ-2A Pioneer

Manufactured under a joint venture between AAI Corporation and Israeli Aircraft Industries (IAI) Malav Division, the Pioneer was first deployed as a land-based system in 1986. Equipped with electro-optical and infrared (EO/IR) sensors, autopilot, navigation and communication equipment, the RQ-2A can operate in preprogrammed or manual control modes. The Pioneer is tasked with providing naval gunfire support; reconnaissance, surveillance and target acquisition (RSTA); and battle damage assessment (BDA). It is normally used as part of a system consisting of up to five air vehicles, a ground control station, a tracking communication unit, a portable control station, four remote-receiving stations, pneumatic- or rocket-assisted launchers and a net- or runway-arrestment recovery system.

The Navy has operated the Pioneer since 1988, first deploying the UAV aboard New Jersey-class battleships. Except for a single system assigned to the Naval Air Maintenance Training Group Detachment at Fort Huachuca, Arizona, all of the Navy's RQ-2As are operated by VC-6, which is based at NAS Patuxent River, Maryland. However, the UAVs are actually located at Webster Field, an auxiliary field for the air station. The squadron operates six Pioneer systems that are normally deployed by small detachments aboard dock landing ships (LPDs) assigned to amphibious ready groups (ARGs).

The manufacturer recently began delivering 15 new RQ-2A air vehicles funded by the FY98 defense bill. They will continue operating until they are replaced by tactical UAVs (TUAVs).

BuNo 161203, a Beech UC-12B, is one of three versions of the Super King Air operated by the Navy for operational support airlift (OSA) missions. Two additional variants, equipped with sea search radar, support test range activities.

Pioneer UAV RQ-2A Specifications	
Maximum Takeoff Weight:	463 lb (210 kg)
Empty Weight:	276 lb (125 kg)
Fuselage Length:	14 ft 0 in (4.27 m)
Wingspan:	16 ft 10.75 in (5.15 m)
Height:	3 ft 3.5 in (1.0 m)
Power Plant:	One rear-mounted Sachs SF2-350 two-cylinder, two-cycle engine, rated at 26 hp (19.4 kW)
Maximum Fuel Capacity:	85 lb (39 kg)
Maximum Speed:	96 kts (177 km/h)
Service Ceiling:	15,000 ft (4572 m)
Operating Endurance:	6.5 hours at 87 nm (161 km)
Crew:	None
Armament:	None
Mission Equipment:	Taman MKD-200 and MKD-400 electro-optical and infrared sensors
Missions:	Target location, naval gunfire support, bomb damage assessment

RAYTHEON AIRCRAFT (INCLUDING BEECH AIRCRAFT)

Beech 1900D Airliner

Raytheon Corporation's Range Systems Engineering Company operates a shuttle between the Navy's Atlantic Underwater Test and Evaluation Center (AUTEC) at Andros Island in the Bahamas, and AUTEC's facilities in West Palm Beach, Florida. For this purpose, it utilizes two Beech Model 1900D Airliners developed from the Model 1900C. The aircraft are operated under contract to the US Navy and carry civil registrations.

Specifications: See the US Army section for more details

N45AR is one of two Beech B1900Ds operated by AUTEC Aviation Services between West Palm Beach, Florida and Andros Island in the Bahamas, in support of the Atlantic Underwater Test and Evaluation Center (AUTEC). The company is the flight department of Raytheon Range Systems Engineering.

Beech C-12C, RC-12F/M, TC-12B, UC-12B/F/M Super King Air (Huron)

Naval units currently operate at least seven different versions of the Beech Super King Air. The first of 66 UC-12Bs (Model 200Cs) was delivered in 1979, and the service later procured 12 UC-12Fs and 12 UC-12Ms (Model B200Cs). The majority of these aircraft were assigned to utility and support roles at Navy and Marine Corps air stations. Whereas most of the UC-12Bs are based within the continental United States, many UC-12Fs are stationed at bases in the Pacific and the majority of UC-12Ms are assigned to European facilities.

During the mid-1990s, a major joint service reorganization of operational support airlift (OSA) that impacted fleet size and mission scheduling was undertaken. Although the Hurons remain assigned to air station operations departments, most OSA missions within CONUS are now scheduled by the Joint Operational Support Airlift Center (JOSAC) at Scott AFB, Illinois. OCONUS missions, however, are the responsibility of the Naval Aviation Logistics Office (NALO) at NAS New Orleans, Louisiana. One consequence of this consolidation was that it provided the Navy with enough surplus airframes to convert 20 UC-12Bs into trainers. Now designated TC-12Bs, these aircraft supplement T-44As as multi-engine trainers and fill the void created in 1997 when the Air Force shifted its turboprop training to the Navy.

In addition to the utility and trainer variants, two RC-12Fs and two RC-12Ms, which are equipped with the AN/APS-140 sea search radar, operate as range support aircraft. Furthermore, a small number of C-12Cs recently replaced four U-21Fs assigned to the US Naval Test Pilot School at NAS Patuxent River, Maryland. Although the US Army retains ownership of them, these aircraft are used to train student test pilots and engineers as part of the school's fixed-wing curriculum.

Modifications under way for the UC-12 fleet include installation of a GPS, a traffic collision avoidance system (TCAS), upgraded weather radar, wind shear detection equipment, an upgraded radar altimeter and a cockpit voice recorder.

Beech UC-12B Huron Specifications	
Maximum Takeoff Weight:	12,500 lb (5670 kg)
Empty Weight:	7,315 lb (3318 kg)
Fuselage Length:	43 ft 9 in (13.34 m)
Wingspan:	54 ft 6 in (16.61 m)
Height:	18 ft 5 in (5.61 m)
Power Plant:	Two Pratt & Whitney Canada PT6A-41 turboprop engines, each rated at 850 shp (634 kW), driving three-blade constant-speed propellers
Maximum Fuel Capacity:	3,645 lb (1653 kg)
Maximum Speed:	289 kts (535 km/h) at 15,000 feet (4572 m)
Service Ceiling:	31,000 ft (9449 m)
Operating Range:	1,887 nm (3495 km) with maximum fuel
Crew:	2
Accommodations:	Up to 13 passengers or 2,000 lb (907 kg) of cargo, or a combination of both
Armament:	None
Mission Equipment:	AN/APS-130 sea search radar (RC-12F/M)
Missions:	Operational support airlift (OSA), fleet logistic support, utility, missile/weapons range support, multi-engine training

Beech T-1A Jayhawk

A small number of Air Force T-1A Jayhawks support naval training requirements with TAW-6 at NAS Pensacola, Florida. These aircraft are on loan to the Navy and retain their USAF markings.

Specifications: See the USAF section for details

US Navy

Raytheon Aircraft T-6A Texan II

Developed from the Pilatus PC-9 trainer, the Raytheon Aircraft T-6A was selected as the winner of the Joint Primary Aircraft Training System (JPATS) competition. The platform was designed to replace both the Air Force T-37B and Navy T-34C for primary training and, in late 1999, the T-6A began entering the Air Force's inventory. The type will reach IOC in 2001, and the first 12 examples funded by the Navy will be delivered that same year.

Specifications: See the USAF section for details

Beech T-34C Turbo Mentor

First flown on 21 September 1973, the T-34C was manufactured by Beech Aircraft, a company that is now part of Raytheon Aircraft. The unpressurized airplane was developed from the T-34A/B (Beech Model 45) and serves both as a basic and intermediate trainer. Student naval aviators receive 23 weeks of initial training on the type with TAW-4 or TAW-5, followed by 14 weeks of intermediate level instruction provided by TAW-6.

Besides serving the training air wings, the T-34C is operated in a variety of support roles including range clearance, target spotting and proficiency checks. Additionally, a single NT-34C is dedicated to testing and chase duties with the Naval Force Warfare Test Squadron at NAS Patuxent River, Maryland. Today, more than 300 Turbo Mentors serve with the Navy but they will be replaced by T-6A Texan IIs beginning in 2003.

NAS Whiting Field, Pensacola, Florida is home to three squadrons equipped with T-34C Turbo Mentors. BuNo 160479 is assigned to Training Air Wing Five (TAW-5), as indicated by its tail code.

Beech T-34C Turbo Mentor Specifications

Maximum Takeoff Weight:	4,300 lb (1950 kg)
Empty Weight:	2,960 lb (1343 kg)
Fuselage Length:	28 ft 8.5 in (8.75 m)
Wingspan:	33 ft 5 in (10.19 m)
Height:	9 ft 11 in (3.02 m)
Power Plant:	One Pratt & Whitney Canada PT6A-25 turboprop engine, rated at 400 shp (298 kW), driving a three-blade constant-speed propeller
Maximum Fuel Capacity:	879 lb (399 kg)
Service Ceiling:	30,000 ft (9144 m)
Maximum Speed:	223 kts (413 km/h) at 5,335 ft (1626 m)
Operating Range:	652 nm (1207 km)
Crew:	2
Armament:	None
Missions:	Primary and intermediate training

BuNo 160849 is a T-44A Pegasus assigned to Training Air Wing Four (TAW-4) at NAS Corpus Christi, Texas. The Navy's entire fleet of such aircraft is operated by the 'Wise Owls' of VT-31.

Beech T-44A Pegasus

Based on the Beech King Air 100 turboprop executive aircraft, the T-44A entered service in 1977 as a replacement for the Grumman TS/US-2A Tracker. It is used primarily to provide advanced maritime multi-engine flight training to Navy students who will fly the P-3 or C-130, and Marine Corps and Air Force pilots slated to fly the C-130. In all, 61 T-44As were procured as commercial-derivative aircraft and 55 examples are still operated by one training squadron. The Pegasus can carry a crew of two as well as three passengers.

Beech T-44A Pegasus Specifications

Maximum Takeoff Weight:	9,650 lb (4377 kg)
Empty Weight:	6,326 lb (2869 kg)
Fuselage Length:	35 ft 6 in (10.82 m)
Wingspan:	50 ft 3 in (15.32 m)
Height:	14 ft 2.5 in (4.33 m)
Power Plant:	Two Pratt & Whitney Canada PT6A-34B turboprop engines, each rated at 680 shp (507 kW) and flat rated at 550 shp (410 kW), driving three-blade constant-speed propellers
Maximum Fuel Capacity:	3,200 lb (1451 kg)
Maximum Speed:	249 kts (461 km/h) at 12,000 ft (3658 m)
Service Ceiling:	27,620 ft (8419 m)
Operating Range:	1,266 nm (2345 km)
Crew:	2
Accommodations:	2 students
Armament:	None
Missions:	Intermediate and advanced training

SABRELINER CORPORATION (INCLUDING NORTH AMERICAN)

North American T-39D, CT-39G, T-39N Sabreliner

Manufactured by North American Aviation (later Rockwell International), the T-39D was developed from the NA.265/277 Sabreliner Series 40 airframe. In all, 42 of these aircraft were delivered as T3J-1 radar training platforms and served until they were replaced by contractor-operated T-47As in 1984. However, a single example remains operational and is used for test purposes at NAWS China Lake, California.

The second variant, the CT-39G, was developed from the eight-passenger NA.306 Sabreliner Series 60 executive jet and served primarily as a VIP transport until replaced by C-20D/G aircraft. Currently, a single example is operated by the Marine Corps in this role.

The Navy recently reclaimed two CT-39Gs from that service and removed several others from storage at the Aircraft Maintenance and Regeneration Center (AMARC) at Davis-Monthan AFB, Arizona for use as trainers at NAS Pensacola, Florida. Now designated T-39Gs, the first of eight aircraft was reassigned to the role in October 1999. In May 1997, the Navy also purchased 17 T-39Ns that were operated by Sabreliner Corporation on its behalf since they replaced T-47As in 1991. Equipped with an AN/APG-66NT radar and thrust-reversers, these aircraft are currently used for advanced strike/radar training by student naval flight officers destined to fly carrier-based tactical aircraft. The T-39N is based on the commercial Model NA.282 Sabreliner Series 40.

North American T-39N Sabreliner Specifications

Maximum Takeoff Weight:	18,340 lb (8319 kg)
Empty Weight:	9,895 lb (4488 kg)
Fuselage Length:	43 ft 9 in (13.34 m)
Wingspan:	44 ft 5.25 in (13.54 m)
Height:	16 ft 0 in (4.88 m)
Power Plant:	Two Pratt & Whitney JT12A-8 turbojet engines, each rated at 3,300 lb st (14.7 kN)
Maximum Fuel Capacity:	1,913 lb (868 kg)
Maximum Speed:	489 kts at 21,500 ft (906 km/h at 6553 m)
Service Ceiling:	45,000 ft (13716 m)
Maximum Operating Range:	1,903 nm (3524 km)
Crew:	3
Accommodations:	3 students
Mission Equipment:	AN/APG-66 radar
Armament:	None
Mission:	Radar systems training

The Navy initially leased 19 T-39Ns including N311NT/F-11 from Sabreliner Corporation but later purchased the aircraft outright. Although this Sabreliner still carries a civil registration it has been assigned the bureau number 165519.

The only glider in the US Navy's inventory is a Schweizer X-26A assigned the bureau number 159260. It is one of many types operated by the US Naval Test Pilot School at NAS Patuxent River, Maryland.

SCHWEIZER AIRCRAFT

Schweizer X-26A

The US Naval Test Pilot School operates a single Schweizer Model SGS 2-32 sailplane for its training programs at NAS Patuxent River, Maryland. Designated the X-26A, the glider is the last of four delivered to the school.

Schweizer X-26A Specifications

Maximum Takeoff Weight:	1,430 lb (649 kg)
Empty Weight:	857 lb (389 kg)
Fuselage Length:	26 ft 9 in (8.15 m)
Wingspan:	57 ft 1 in (17.40 m)
Height:	9 ft 3 in (2.82 m)
Power Plant:	None
Maximum Glide Speed:	137 kts (254 km/h)
Maximum Tow Speed:	96 kts (177 km/h)
Crew:	2
Armament:	None
Mission:	Training

SIKORSKY AIRCRAFT

Sikorsky UH-3H, NVH-3A, VH-3A/D Sea King

Designated the HSS-2, the Sikorsky Sea King was first flown in March 1959 and was once the Navy's premier carrier-based antisubmarine helicopter. However, its missions have since been assumed by the Sikorsky SH-60F and by SAR-configured HH-60Hs. A few Naval Reserve aircraft have also operated in this role in recent years but they were replaced by Seahawks beginning in FY00. Today, most of the Sea Kings in service are UH-3Hs that have had their antisubmarine equipment removed and are operated primarily for utility and fleet support missions or as SAR aircraft at naval air stations. However, a small number of those supporting fleet commanders are VH-3As. Although both the UH-3H and VH-3A variants are to be replaced by the CH-60S, four UH-3Hs are being modified to serve in the interim as executive transports.

In addition to the Sea King models now in naval service, two Sikorsky Model S-61N helicopters operate from West Palm Beach, Florida in support of the US Navy's Atlantic Underwater Test and Evaluation Center (AUTEC), based at Andros Island in the Bahamas. The S-61Ns both carry civil registrations and are operated under contract by the Raytheon Range Systems Engineering Company to transport personnel and support the center's missions.

Sikorsky UH-3H Sea King Specifications

Maximum Takeoff Weight:	21,000 lb (9525 kg)
Empty Weight:	12,350 lb (5602 kg)
Fuselage Length:	54 ft 9 in (16.7 m)
Overall Length:	Extended – 72 ft 8 in (22.15 m), Folded – 47 ft 3 in (14.40 m)
Main Rotor Diameter:	62 ft 0 in (18.90 m)
Height:	16 ft 10 in (5.13 m)
Power Plant:	Two General Electric T58-GE-402 turboshaft engines, each rated at 1,500 shp (1119 kW), driving five-blade main and tail rotors
Maximum Fuel Capacity:	5,670 lb (2572 kg)
Maximum Speed:	144 kts (267 km/h)
Service Ceiling:	14,700 ft (4480 m)
Operating Range:	541 nm (1002 km)
Crew:	4
Armament:	None
Mission Equipment:	None
Missions:	Utility, fleet support

seaborne mines using its mine-hunting sonar in conjunction with mechanical, acoustic and magnetic mine sweeping equipment, the Sea Dragon is secondarily tasked with utility and VERTREP missions. A more advanced mine-hunting sonar is currently under development and Sikorsky is also building kits to enable the type to be powered by the 4,750-shp (3544-kW) T64-GE-419 engine.

The Navy's two mine countermeasures squadrons that fly the Sea Dragon are staffed by active-duty and reserve personnel, and each unit operates 12 of the helicopters. One combat support squadron also flies the type, as does the Marine Corps' CH/MH-53E FRS.

Sikorsky MH-53E Sea Dragon

Developed from the CH-53E and first flown in 1983, the Sikorsky MH-53E was built as a replacement for the Sikorsky RH-53D airborne mine countermeasures (AMCM) helicopter. It entered service in 1988. Capable of detecting and destroying a wide variety of

Designed as an airborne mine countermeasures platform, the Sikorsky MH-53E is among the largest of the world's military helicopters. BuNo 164862/BJ-553 is one of 12 Sea Dragons operated by HM-14 at NAVSTA Norfolk, Virginia.

Sikorsky MH-53E Sea Dragon Specifications

Maximum Takeoff Weight:	73,500 lb (33339 kg)
Empty Weight:	36,627 lb (16614 kg)
Fuselage Length:	73 ft 4 in (22.35 m)
Overall Length:	Boom extended – 99 ft .5 in (30.30 m), Boom folded – 60 ft 6 in (18.44 m)
Main Rotor Diameter:	72 ft 3 in (22.00 m)
Height:	Boom extended – 28 ft 4 in (8.64 m), Boom folded – 18 ft 7 in (5.66 m)
Power Plant:	Three General Electric T64-GE-416 or 416A turboshaft engines, each rated at 4,380 shp (3266 kW), driving seven-blade main rotor and four-blade tail rotor
Maximum Fuel Capacity:	21,600 lb (9798 kg)
Maximum Speed:	170 kts (315 km/h)
Operating Range:	973 nm (1802 km) or six-hour endurance
Crew:	3-8
Accommodations:	Up to 55 passengers or 24 litters when operating in the utility role
Armament:	Crew-operated .50-cal. (12.7mm) machine gun
Mission Equipment:	AN/ASQ-14/20 towed sonar; Mk 103/104/105 mechanical, acoustic and magnetic mine sweeping equipment
Missions:	Mine warfare, utility, vertical replenishment (VERTREP)

Sikorsky SH-60B/F/R, HH-60H Seahawk

In September 1977, Sikorsky Aircraft was awarded a contract to develop what was dubbed the Light Airborne Multipurpose System III (LAMPS III) for operation from naval frigates, destroyers and cruisers. The prototype platform, the YSH-60B, flew for the first time in December 1979. Although the Seahawk retained significant commonality with the Army's UH-60A, it is powered by a navalized version of the T700 engine and has folding main and tail rotors, a folding tail boom and different landing gear. Internally, the most notable difference is the LAMPS equipment, for which IBM Federal Systems (now part of Lockheed Martin) acted as prime contractor.

Included are a search radar, a magnetic anomaly detector (MAD), electronic support measures (ESM), sonobuoy launchers and the computer systems associated with antisubmarine warfare missions. An AN/AAS-44 FLIR provides passive detec-

Sikorsky SH-60B Seahawk Specifications

Maximum Takeoff Weight:	21,884 lb (9926 kg)
Empty Weight:	13,648 lb (6191 kg)
Fuselage Length:	50 ft .75 in (15.26 m)
Overall Length:	Boom extended – 64 ft 10 in (19.76 m)
	Boom folded – 40 ft 11 in (12.47 m)
Main Rotor Diameter:	53 ft 8 in (16.36 m)
Height:	12 ft 5 in (3.78 m)
Power Plant:	Two General Electric T700-GE-401C turboshaft engines, each rated at 1,900 shp (1417 kW), driving four-blade main and tail rotors
Maximum Fuel Capacity:	3,983 lb (1807 kg)
Maximum Speed:	126 kts (233 km/h) at sea level
Operating Range:	150 nm (278 km) with one-hour loiter time
Crew:	3
Armament:	Mk 46/50 torpedoes, AGM-114 Hellfire and AGM-119 Penguin air-to-surface missiles, crew-operated 7.62mm M60 machine guns
Mission Equipment:	AN/ASQ-81 magnetic anomaly detector (MAD), AN/ARR-75 sonobuoy receiving set and AN/UYS-1 acoustic processor, AN/APS-124 search radar, AN/ALQ-142 electronic support measures
Mission:	Light airborne multipurpose system (LAMPS)

tion for the AGM-119B Penguin missile as well as laser designation for the AGM-114 Hellfire missile. A Block I program has since added a GPS, updated radios, defensive countermeasures and the ability to field the Mk 50 torpedo and the Penguin. These systems are not carried by all SH-60Bs, however.

Intended to replace the SH-3H and provide carrier battle groups with the foremost inner-zone antisubmarine capabilities, the SH-60F was developed from the SH-60B and first flew in March 1987. Externally, the aircraft is similar in appearance but internal differences are significant. In lieu of a MAD system and search radar, the aircraft is equipped with a dipping sonar and an additional weapons station. Designed to operate at a heavier weight than the LAMPS version, it began replacing the SH-3H in fleet service in 1991.

The HH-60H is the most recent naval variant and was designed to replace the Bell HH-1K in combat search and rescue (CSAR) and Special Operations support roles. Development began in September 1986, and the aircraft first flew in August 1988. The type was eventually added to the inventory of each of the Navy's antisubmarine helicopter squadrons and was first deployed in 1991. The SH-60B's FLIR/AGM-114 combination, along with defensive countermeasures, was also incorporated into 24 HH-60Hs.

Ultimately, the Navy plans to upgrade as many as 273 SH-60B/F and HH-60H platforms to a common configuration known as the SH-60R. This variant is specially adapted for littoral warfare. Planned modifications, under development by Lockheed Martin Federal Systems, will allow the new version to operate in a complex environment from vessels in shallow waters. The type's equipment includes new passive detection, active detection and countermeasures systems; and a new multimode AN/APS-147 inverse synthetic aperture radar (ISAR) capable of detecting extremely small targets. This system will replace the SH-60B's current radar. Also to be fitted into the SH-60R is a new airborne low-frequency sonar (ALFS) capable of processing active sonar and sonobuoy data simultaneously. Furthermore, a modified sonobuoy launcher will replace the one currently carried in the SH-60B/F, and AN/ALQ-210 electronic support measures (ESM) will include an integrated self-defense system (ISD). The latter comprises laser detectors, radar warning detector/jammers, infrared and missile plume detectors and chaff/flare dispensers. Avionics updates include a new flight control computer, an auxiliary power unit (APU) and an

upgraded mission computer. In addition, a voice satellite communications (SATCOM) capability will be added. Sikorsky modified two SH-60Bs to fly as SH-60R prototypes and, after the new avionics were installed, the SH-60R made its maiden flight at Owego, New York, on 22 December 1999.

Remanufacturing of SH-60Bs began in 1999 and Navy plans call for the first of the SH-60Fs to be modified in 2000. The HH-60Hs are set to follow in 2004. The new variant will replace SH-60Bs serving with 12 light antisubmarine (HSL) squadrons, and SH-60Fs and HH-60Hs flying with 11 carrier-based antisubmarine (HS) squadrons. IOC should be achieved in 2002. The FY00 budget includes funding for the modification of seven SH-60Bs. Separately, the contractor is developing an H-60 Common Cockpit under a $61 million contract issued in August 1998. This is designed to give the SH-60R and CH-60S a common "glass" cockpit along with the same updated communications and computer equipment.

Sikorsky CH-60S Knighthawk

The Sikorsky CH-60S is a Blackhawk hybrid that combines the fuselage of the UH-60L with components from the SH-60B/F, including the aft bulkhead, folding tail pylon, folding main rotor, tail rotors, crew doors, hover in-flight refueling system, automatic flight control systems and a rescue hoist. Installation of an external stores suspension system (ESSS) will allow two 230-gallon (776-liter) and two 450-gallon (1519-liter) external fuel tanks to be carried, whereas the external tank suspension (ETS) system will provide for just two 230-gallon external tanks. The cabin floor includes rollers and guides to facilitate the movement of cargo, and large sliding cabin doors allow 40 x 48 inch (1.02 m x 1.22 m) pallets to be accommodated.

The YCH-60 prototype was first flown in October 1997 and the production variant, having made its maiden flight on 27 January 2000, is expected to reach IOC in 2001. Initial deliveries will include the six aircraft funded in FY98 and FY99, and a further 17 examples provided for in the FY00 budget.

HC-3 will serve as the Knighthawk FRS and will be the type's first operator. The squadron is based at NAS North Island, California. Initially the CH-60S will fly vertical replenishment (VERTREP) and utility missions but it will be tasked sometime later with SAR and CSAR duties.

CH-60S Knighthawk Specifications

Maximum Takeoff Weight:	23,500 lb (10659 kg)
Empty Weight:	12,580 lb (5706 kg)
Fuselage Length:	50 ft 0.75 in (15.26 m)
Overall Length:	Boom extended – 64 ft 10 in (19.76 m),
	Boom folded – 40 ft 11 in (12.47 m)
Main Rotor Diameter:	53 ft 8 in (16.36 m)
Height:	12 ft 5 in (3.78 m)
Power Plant:	Two General Electric T700-GE-401C turboshaft engines, each rated at 1,900 shp (1417 kW), driving four-blade main and tail rotors
Maximum Fuel Capacity:	2,430 lb (1102 kg)
Operating Range:	Estimated – 300-995 nm (555-1842 km)
Crew:	4
Accommodations:	Internal – Up to 13 passengers or 4,800 lb (2177 kg) of cargo External – Up to 9,000 lb (4082 kg) of cargo
Armament:	AGM-114 Hellfire air-to-ground missiles, various crew-operated weapons
Missions:	Search and rescue (SAR), combat search and rescue (CSAR), fleet combat support

NAVAL AIR STATIONS & FACILITIES

MAJOR ESTABLISHMENTS

NAS Atlanta, Georgia

Opened in 1959, NAS Atlanta is situated at Dobbins Air Reserve Base in Marietta, Georgia, and is home to reserve units of both the Navy and Marine Corps. The base also supports units of the AFRC (USAF), USARC (Army) and the Georgia ARNG (Army), and is where Lockheed Martin Aeronautical Systems Division is located.

NAS Brunswick, Maine

Built primarily as a training site for Canadian and British air force pilots with the British Naval Command, NAS Brunswick was commissioned on 15 April 1943 and deactivated in 1947. It was reactivated in 1951 primarily to support antisubmarine warfare missions and is currently home to Commander Patrol Wing Five. Four active-duty and three naval reserve squadrons operate from the air station.

NAWS China Lake, California

Located near Inyokern, China Lake was established as the Naval Ordnance Test Station (NOTS) on 8 November 1943. NOTS China Lake was renamed the Naval Weapons Center (NWC) in July 1967 but became a naval air weapons station in 1992. At that time NOTS and the Pacific Missile Test Center (PMTC) were merged at NAS Point Mugu, California. NAWS China Lake is operated by the Naval Air Warfare Center Weapons Division (NAWCWPNS), and its Armitage Field is used by the Naval Weapons Test Squadron and one Air Test and Evaluation unit. On 30 May 1945, the airfield was dedicated to Lt. John Armitage, USNR, who was killed on 21 August 1944 while conducting air firing tests of the Tiny Tim rocket.

NAS Corpus Christi, Texas

During World War II, NAS Corpus Christi was the only facility available within the United States for primary, intermediate and advanced training. Commissioned on 12 March 1941, it was once the largest pilot training facility in the world. Naval Air Training Command Headquarters moved to the air station in 1972, having previously been at NAS Pensacola, Florida, and Training Air Wing Four was established at that

time. NAS Corpus Christi's Truax Field is also home to the US Army's main aviation depot, a Coast Guard air station and the US Customs Service.

NAF El Centro, California

Located in the high desert of California's Imperial Valley, NAF El Centro serves as winter home to the US Navy Flight Demonstration Squadron, better known as the 'Blue Angels.' The facility also serves as a forward base for naval training squadrons that deploy to NAS Fallon for instruction in strike tactics. Furthermore, it is utilized by both Pacific and Atlantic fleet replacement squadrons, which deploy to NAF El Centro 235 days a year for air-to-ground weapons training, and by Marine Corps, Army, NATO and allied air and ground units. The latter use the facility as a staging base for Joint Task Force Six counternarcotics operations.

NAS Fallon, Nevada

Built by the US Army during World War II, NAS Fallon was subsequently designated a naval auxiliary air station before being deactivated and then reactivated during the Korean War. During the 1950s and 1960s the facility and its bombing ranges were expanded and, in 1972, it received its current designation. The air station now serves as the primary aircraft familiarization and weapons training site for Navy carrier air wings prior to carrier deployments. It is also the base of operations for the Naval Strike and Air Warfare Center (NSAWC), which provides advanced tactical air-to-ground and air-to-air combat instruction. Named Van Voorhis Field on 1 November 1959, the station's airfield was dedicated to the memory of Cdr. Bruce A. Van Voorhis. He was posthumously awarded the Congressional Medal of Honor after being killed during an attack on enemy positions in the Solomon Islands in 1944.

NAS Fort Worth Joint Reserve Base, Texas

This facility was once known as Carswell AFB but, with the departure of the Air Force in 1993, the Navy assumed control of the facility for the purpose of relocating its reserve activities from NAS Dallas. The airfield is named in honor of Major Horace S. Carswell who was killed in the crash of a B-24 in 1944. The JRB is now home to reserve units from the Navy, Marine Corps and Air Force, as well as the Texas ANG. Lockheed Martin Tactical Aircraft Systems Division is also located at the facility.

NAVSTA Guantanamo Bay, Cuba

A naval air station was officially established on the eastern end of the island of Cuba on 1 February 1941. At that time McCalla Field officially opened but a second airfield at

Leeward Point was expanded to accommodate jet aircraft operations and remains in service today. Leeward Point Field supports transient traffic as well as an air operations division.

NAS Jacksonville, Florida

Commissioned on 15 October 1940, NAS Jacksonville is home to Commander Sea Control Wing, US Atlantic Fleet; Commander Helicopter Antisubmarine Wing, US Atlantic Fleet; and Commander Patrol Wing Eleven. In all, 18 active-duty and reserve squadrons operate from the station's John Tower Field, which was dedicated to Adm. John H. Tower (Naval Aviator No. 3) on 14 October 1960. The air station is also the location of Naval Aviation Depot (NADEP) Jacksonville and supports a US Customs Service air interdiction unit.

NAS Keflavik, Iceland

The US built Keflavik Airport during the early months of World War II during which it served as a refueling point for aircraft ferried to Europe as well as for cargo flights going to and from the continent. The US has maintained a presence at this NATO facility ever since and the air station is the key element. The Navy is responsible for its operation and has a rotational patrol squadron assigned to Fleet Air Keflavik. This is part of the Icelandic Defense Force assigned to US Atlantic Command (USACOM).

NAS Key West, Florida

Established during World War II as an advanced training base, NAS Key West is located north of the city on Boca Chica Key. The only aircraft permanently based at the air station are those of the Air Operations Division. However, the facility serves as a major training base and AIRLANT Hornets and Tomcats regularly deploy to the station for air combat maneuvering (ACM) over its instrumented ranges. Present are the US Customs Service, Florida ANG and the Joint Interagency Task Force East (JIATF-E).

NAS Kingsville, Texas

Kingsville is located southwest of Corpus Christi and is home to Training Air Wing Two. As a component of Naval Air Training Command, the wing provides intermediate and advanced strike training.

NAES Lakehurst, New Jersey

Lakehurst's naval history dates to back 1917, at which time the Naval Aircraft Factory was established there. However, the facility may best be remembered for the loss of the German air ship *Hindenburg*, which exploded during a landing attempt on 6 May 1937. The station was also the site of naval aircraft

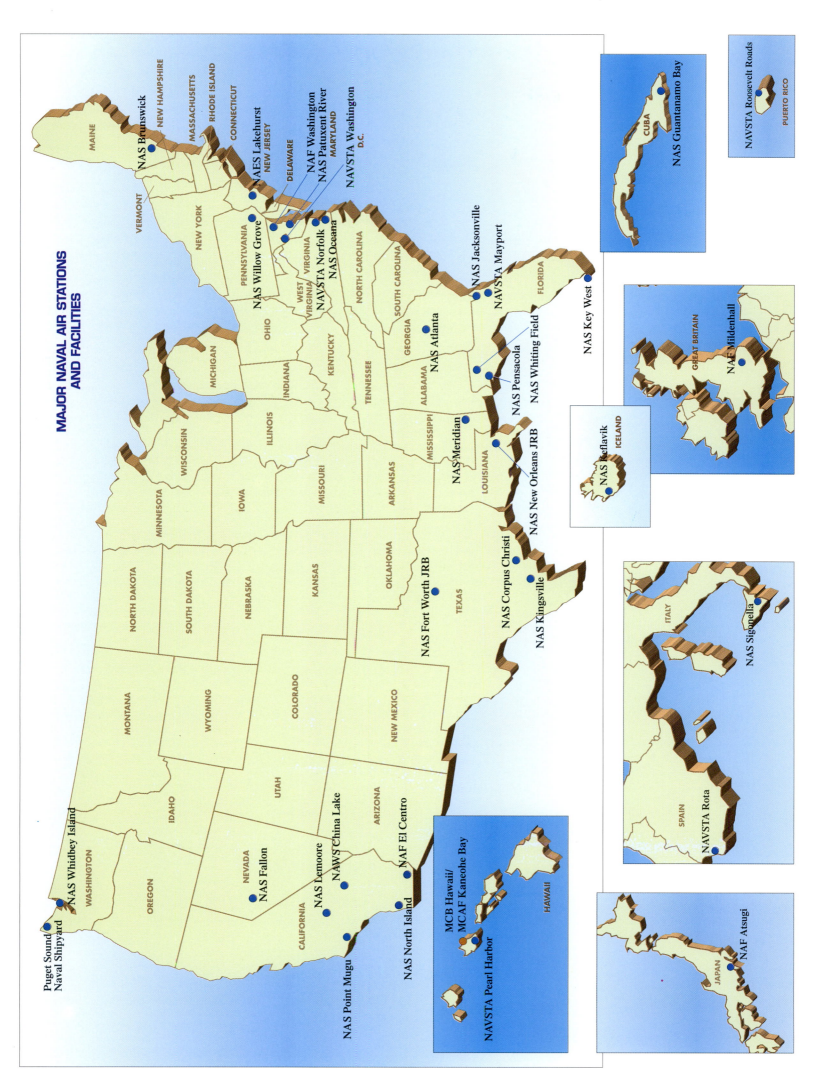

MAJOR NAVAL AIR STATIONS
AND FACILITIES

NAS Brunswick

NAES Lakehurst
NAF Washington
NAS Patuxent River
NAVSTA Washington D.C.

NAS Willow Grove
NAVSTA Norfolk
NAS Oceana

NAS Jacksonville
NAVSTA Mayport

NAS Atlanta

NAS Pensacola
NAS Whiting Field

NAS Key West

NAS Meridian

NAS New Orleans JRB

NAS Fort Worth JRB

NAS Corpus Christi
NAS Kingsville

NAS Fallon
NAS Lemoore
NAWS China Lake
NAF El Centro

NAS Whidbey Island
Puget Sound Naval Shipyard

NAS Point Mugu
NAS North Island

MCB Hawaii/
MCAF Kaneohe Bay

NAVSTA Pearl Harbor

NAS Guantanamo Bay

NAVSTA Roosevelt Roads

NAF Mildenhall

NAS Keflavik

NAS Sigonella

NAVSTA Rota

NAF Atsugi

MAINE
NEW HAMPSHIRE
MASSACHUSETTS
RHODE ISLAND
CONNECTICUT
NEW JERSEY
DELAWARE
MARYLAND
VERMONT
NEW YORK
PENNSYLVANIA
WEST VIRGINIA
VIRGINIA
NORTH CAROLINA
SOUTH CAROLINA
OHIO
KENTUCKY
TENNESSEE
GEORGIA
ALABAMA
FLORIDA
MICHIGAN
INDIANA
ILLINOIS
WISCONSIN
MINNESOTA
IOWA
MISSOURI
ARKANSAS
MISSISSIPPI
LOUISIANA
NORTH DAKOTA
SOUTH DAKOTA
NEBRASKA
KANSAS
OKLAHOMA
TEXAS
MONTANA
WYOMING
COLORADO
NEW MEXICO
UTAH
ARIZONA
NEVADA
CALIFORNIA
IDAHO
OREGON
WASHINGTON
HAWAII
CUBA
PUERTO RICO
GREAT BRITAIN
ICELAND
ITALY
SPAIN
JAPAN

143

US Navy

manufacturing throughout World War II but became a research facility soon thereafter. From April 1973 onwards it was known as the Naval Air Engineering Center and gained its current designation on 1 January 1992. NAES Lakehurst continues to serve as a research center supporting both Navy and Army development programs. Lakehurst's airfield was dedicated to the memory of Cdr. Louis H. Maxfield on 6 January 1944. He was killed in the crash of the R-38 dirigible on 24 August 1921.

NAS Lemoore, California

Located in the San Joaquin Valley, NAS Lemoore was commissioned on 8 July 1961, and serves as the headquarters of Commander, Strike Fighter Wing, US Pacific Fleet. Twelve strike fighter squadrons are assigned to the functional wing and operate from the station's Joseph Mason Reeves Field. The field was so designated on 20 November 1961, in honor of the rear admiral.

NAVSTA Mayport, Florida

What is now NAVSTA Mayport was commissioned in December 1942 and a landing field and taxiway were completed in 1943. An auxiliary air station was also commissioned at Mayport on 1 April 1944. The base was deactivated after World War II but, in June of 1948, was reactivated as a Naval Outlying Landing Field (NOLF). A master jet runway was added in 1955 and Mayport again was designated a naval auxiliary air station. Four years later it was renamed Naval Station Mayport and a naval air facility was also established in 1982. Ten years later, these were combined under the name NAVSTA Mayport. The air facility is home to Commander Helicopter Antisubmarine Light Wing, US Atlantic Fleet, and five squadrons operate from its airfield, which is named Adm. David L. McDonald Field.

NAS Meridian, Mississippi

Commissioned as NAAS Meridian on 14 July 1961, the station's airfield was named in honor of Adm. John S. McCain, a former deputy chief of Naval Operations. It is referred to as McCain Field. The facility was redesignated NAS Meridian in July 1968 and has been the home of Training Wing One since 1971.

NAS New Orleans JRB, Louisiana

The JRB is home to both Navy and Marine Corps reserve units and is also used by the Louisiana ANG and AFRC (USAF), as well as the US Coast Guard. The base's Alvin Callender Field was dedicated on 26 April 1958, in honor of a New Orleans native who was killed in combat during World War I. At the time he was serving as a captain with the Royal Flying Corps of Canada.

NAS Norfolk/Chambers Field, Virginia

Commissioned on 7 August 1918, NAS Norfolk initially supported operational and experimental flights but subsequently became a major seaplane base. The station is now home to Commander US Naval Air Force Atlantic Fleet; Commander Airborne Early Warning Wing, US Atlantic Fleet; Commander Helicopter Tactical Wing, US Atlantic Fleet; and Commander Patrol Wings, US Atlantic Fleet. A major reorganization of naval units in the Norfolk and Hampton Roads areas resulted in disestablished of the air station in February 1999. At that time the airfield was placed under the administrative control of NAS Oceana, which maintains a detachment at the facility. The airfield took its name from Capt. Washington I. Chambers on 1 June 1938.

NAS North Island, California

Originally commissioned as NAS San Diego on 8 November 1917, what is now NAS North island is officially recognized as the birthplace of naval aviation. Located in Coronado, it is the largest aviation industrial complex on the west coast and its airfield, Halsey Field, is home to 21 active-duty and reserve air squadrons. The air station also operates NALF San Clemente Island, 70 miles northwest of San Diego in the California Channel Islands, and OLF Imperial Beach/Ream Field, which is situat-

ed 10 miles south of the base. Functional wings at NAS North Island include Commander, Sea Control Wing, US Pacific Fleet; Commander, Antisubmarine Light Wing, US Pacific Fleet; Commander, Antisubmarine Wing, US Pacific Fleet; Commander, Helicopter Tactical Wing, US Pacific Fleet; and Commander, Helicopter Wing Reserve. NADEP North Island is also located at the facility and the US Customs Service maintains an air interdiction unit at the site.

NAS Oceana, Virginia

NAS Oceana was first commissioned as a naval auxiliary airfield in 1940 and was designated a naval auxiliary air station in 1943. It received its current designation on 1 April 1952. The airfield was named Apollo Souchek Field on 4 June 1957, to honor the vice admiral and former chief of the Bureau of Aeronautics. The air station is currently home to Commander Fighter Wing, US Atlantic Fleet, as well as Commander Strike Fighter Wing, US Atlantic Fleet. Following the 1999 closure of NAS Cecil Field in Florida, NAS Oceana became home to 23 fighter and strike fighter units, including two complete fleet readiness squadrons. It is also responsible for NALF Fentres, situated a few miles to the west.

NAS Patuxent River, Maryland

NAS Patuxent River was established before World War II to centralize widely dispersed air testing facilities. Although it has served as the base for a number of active-duty and reserve units since then, it has always remained naval aviation's primary flight test facility. The air station is currently home to the Naval Air Warfare Center Aircraft Division (NAWCAD) as well as Naval Air Systems Command (COMNAVAIRSYS-COM), which recently relocated from the District of Columbia. On 1 April 1976 the airfield was dedicated to honor Vice Admiral Frederick M. Trapnell.

NAS Fallon, Nevada, is home to the Naval Strike and Air Warfare Center (NSAWC), which was created when the activities of the former 'Topgun' and Naval Strike Warfare Center were merged in July 1996. The station fills a number of other important roles for the US Navy, not least of which is providing training facility for carrier air wing squadrons immediately prior to their deployments.

Serving with VFA-37, this F/A-18C Hornet (serial 164252) is based at NAS Oceana, Virginia. However, it is seen here during a visit to NAF Washington, Maryland.

NAS Pensacola, Florida
In 1914, the Navy established the US Naval Aeronautical Station in Pensacola. Three years later it was designated a naval air station and is currently home to Training Air Wing Six and the Naval Aviation Museum. The former Fort Barrancas Airfield at the site was renamed on 2 November 1951 to honor Adm. Forrest P. Sherman, who held the title Chief of Naval Operations from 1949 through 1951.

NAS Point Mugu, California
Point Mugu was named the US Naval Air Missile Test Center when it was commissioned on 1 October 1946. Subsequent designations included Pacific Missile Range, Naval Missile Center and Pacific Missile Test Center. In 1992, the latter was merged with the Naval Weapons Center at China Lake, which led to formation of the Naval Air Warfare Center Weapons Division (NAWCWD). From 1992 until 1999, Point Mugu was a naval air weapons station but the relocation from MCAS Miramar of Commander, Airborne Early Warning Wing, US Pacific Fleet, caused control of Point Mugu to be assumed by Commander Naval Air Force, US Pacific Fleet (COMNAVAIR-PAC). Accordingly, the facility was redesignated a naval air station. NAWCWD remains the primary organization at the air station.

NAVSTA Roosevelt Roads, Puerto Rico
Ofstie Field was so named on 21 May 1959, to honor Vice Adm. Ralph A. Ofstie, a former deputy chief of Naval Operations. Today, the airfield provides a forward operating area for fleet squadrons during carrier workups in the Caribbean area and fills the same function for patrol squadrons tasked with counternarcotics missions.

NAF Washington, Maryland
NAF Washington occupies ramp space opposite the 89th Airlift Wing at Andrews AFB. The facility supports four Naval Reserve and two Marine Forces Reserve units, and is particularly busy with transient traffic because of its proximity to the United States capital.

NAS Whidbey Island, Washington
Although commissioned as a base for seaplane patrol operations on 21 September 1942, plans were begun seven years later to make NAS Whidbey Island the Navy's primary airfield in the Pacific Northwest. Today, the station is home to Commander Electronic Attack Wing, US Pacific Fleet; Commander Patrol Wing Ten and units of the Naval Reserve. The airfield was designated Ault Field on 25 February 1943, to honor Commodore William B. Ault who was killed during the Battle of the Coral Sea.

NAS Willow Grove JRB, Pennsylvania
Located northeast of Philadelphia and officially commissioned in January 1943, NAS Willow Grove became a training station for the Naval Air Reserve immediately after World War II. Since then it has served primarily as a reserve facility and currently supports units belonging to the Navy, Marine Corps, Army and Air Force, plus the Pennsylvania ANG. In 1994, the station was designated a Joint Reserve Base.

NAS Whiting Field, Florida
NAAS Whiting Field was commissioned on 16 July 1943, and its airfield honors Capt. Kenneth Whiting, Naval Aviator No. 16 and first acting commander of the USS *Langley* (CV 1). Since 1956, it has served the Navy as a primary training base and is home to Training Air Wing Six. In addition to the main facility, the air station operates 11 auxiliary fields that include Barin, Brewton, Evergreen and Summerdale outlying fields in Alabama; and Harold, Pace, Santa Rosa, Saufley, Spencer, Choctaw and Holley Fields in Florida. All are located within a 60-mile (100-km) radius of the base.

NAF Atsugi, Japan
NAF Atsugi is home to Commander Fleet Air Western Pacific and Carrier Air Wing Five (CVW-5), assigned to the USS *Kitty Hawk* (CV-63).

NAF Mildenhall, United Kingdom
Located at RAF Mildenhall in England, this facility is home to a few UC-12Ms operated by the air operations division in support of Commander in Chief, US Naval Forces Europe (CINCUSNAVEUR).

NAF Misawa, Japan
As well as serving the Air Force's 35th Fighter Wing, Misawa AB is an operating base for maritime patrol P-3Cs and reconnaissance EP-3s. Its air operations division also flies several UC-12Fs from the facility.

NAVSTA Rota, Spain
Located on Spain's Atlantic Coast, NAVSTA Rota is a tenant command at Spain's largest naval installation, Base Naval de Rota. The air station's air operations division flies UC-12Ms from the facility.

NAS Sigonella, Italy
Located on Sicily's east coast, near the city of Catania, NAS Sigonella provides consolidated operational, command and control, administrative and logistical support to United States and other NATO forces. The station is a key element in US Sixth Fleet Mediterranean operations and supports Commander Fleet Air Mediterranean as well as a rotational patrol and reconnaissance squadron, a helicopter combat support squadron, plus C-2A, C-9B and C-130T detachments. In addition, NAS Sigonella serves shore-based fleet aircraft and transient USAF and NATO aircraft.

Tail Codes

US NAVY			
Tail Code	Unit	Location	Aircraft
(8A)	AOD	NAF Atsugi, Japan	UC-12F
(8C)	AOD	NAS Sigonella, Italy	C-26D
(8D)	AOD	NAVSTA Rota, Spain	UC-12M
(8K)	FSD	NAF Bahrain IAP, Bahrain	UC-12M
(HL)	VQ-4	Tinker AFB, Oklahoma	E-6A/B
(OB)	VPU-1	NAS Brunswick, Maine	P-3C, UP-3A
(SP)	VPU-2	MCAF Kaneohe Bay, Hawaii	P-3C, UP-3A
(TC)	VQ-3	Tinker AFB, Oklahoma	E-6B
7A	AOD	NAS Patuxent River, Maryland	UC-12B, UH-3H
7B	AOD	NAS Atlanta, Georgia	UC-12B
7C	AOD	Chambers Field, Norfolk, Virginia	UC-12B/M
7D	AOD	NAS Fort Worth JRB, Texas	UC-12B
7E	AOD	NAS Jacksonville, Florida	UC-12B, UH-3H
7F	AOD	NAS Brunswick, Maine	HH-1N
7G/FW	AOD	NAS Whidbey Island, Washington	UC-12B, UH-3H
7H	AOD	NAS Fallon, Nevada	UC-12B, HH-1N
7M	AOD	NAS North Island, California	NC/UC-12B, UC-12F
7N	AOD	NAF Washington, Maryland	UC-12B
7P	AOD	NAWS China Lake, California	HH-1N
7Q	AOD	NAS Key West, Florida	UC-12B, UH-3H
7R	AOD	NAS Oceana, Virginia	UH-3H
7S	AOD	NAS Lemoore, California	UC-12B, HH-1N
7W	AOD	NAS Willow Grove JRB, Pennsylvania	UC-12B
7X	AOD	NAS New Orleans JRB, Louisiana	UC-12B
8E	AOD	NAVSTA Roosevelt Roads, P.R.	UC-12M, RC-12M
8F	AOD	NAVSTA Guantanamo Bay, Cuba	UC-12B, HH-1N
8H	AOD	NAF Kadena, Okinawa, Japan	UC-12F
8J	AOD	Andersen AFB, Guam	HH-1N
8M	AOD	NAF Misawa, Japan	UC-12F
8N	AOD	NAF El Centro, California	UC-12B
A	VT-7	NAS Meridian, Mississippi	T-45C
A	VT-9	NAS Meridian	T-2C
AA	HS-15	NAS Jacksonville, Florida	SH-60F, HH-60H
AA	VAQ-132	NAS Whidbey Island, Washington	EA-6B
AA	VAW-125	Chambers Field, Norfolk, Virginia	E-2C
AA	VF-103	NAS Oceana, Virginia	F-14B
AA	VFA-34	NAS Oceana	F/A-18C
AA	VFA-81	NAS Oceana	F/A-18C
AA	VFA-83	NAS Oceana	F/A-18C
AA	VS-30	NAS Jacksonville, Florida	S-3B
AB	HS-11	NAS Jacksonville	SH-60F, HH-60H
AB	VAQ-137	NAS Whidbey Island, Washington	EA-6B
AB	VAW-123	Chambers Field, Norfolk, Virginia	E-2C
AB	VF-102	NAS Oceana, Virginia	F-14B
AB	VFA-82	MCAS Beaufort, South Carolina	F/A-18C
AB	VFA-86	MCAS Beaufort	F/A-18C
AB	VS-32	NAS Jacksonville, Florida	S-3B
AC	HS-7	NAS Jacksonville	SH-60F, HH-60H
AC	VAQ-130	NAS Whidbey Island, Washington	EA-6B
AC	VAW-126	Chambers Field, Norfolk, Virginia	E-2C
AC	VF-32	NAS Oceana, Virginia	F-14B
AC	VFA-105	NAS Oceana	F/A-18C
AC	VFA-37	NAS Oceana	F/A-18C
AC	VS-22	NAS Jacksonville, Florida	S-3B
AD	VAW-120	Chambers Field, Norfolk, Virginia	E-2C, C-2A
AD	VF-101	NAS Oceana, Virginia	F-14A/B/D, T-34C
AD	VFA-106	NAS Oceana	F/A-18A/B/C/D
AF	VAQ-209	NAF Washington, Maryland	EA-6B
AF	VAW-77	NAS Atlanta, Georgia	E-2C
AF	VAW-78	Chambers Field, Norfolk, Virginia	E-2C
AF	VFA-201	NAS Fort Worth JRB, Texas	F/A-18A
AF	VFA-203	NAS Atlanta, Georgia	F/A-18A
AF	VFA-204	NAS New Orleans JRB, Louisiana	F/A-18A
AF	VFC-12	NAS Oceana, Virginia	F/A-18A/B
AF	VFC-13	NAS Fallon, Nevada	F-5E/F
AG	HS-5	NAS Jacksonville, Florida	SH-60F, HH-60H
AG	VAQ-140	NAS Whidbey Island, Washington	EA-6B
AG	VAW-121	Chambers Field, Norfolk, Virginia	E-2C
AG	VF-143	NAS Oceana, Virginia	F-14B
AG	VFA-131	NAS Oceana	F/A-18C
AG	VFA-136	NAS Oceana	F/A-18C
AG	VS-31	NAS Jacksonville, Florida	S-3B
AG	VF-11	NAS Oceana, Virginia	F-14B
AJ	HS-3	NAS Jacksonville, Florida	SH-60F, HH-60H
AJ	VAQ-141	NAS Whidbey Island, Washington	EA-6B
AJ	VAW-124	Chambers Field, Norfolk, Virginia	E-2C
AJ	VF-14	NAS Oceana, Virginia	F-14A
AJ	VF-41	NAS Oceana	F-14A

US NAVY (Continued)			
Tail Code	Unit	Location	Aircraft
AJ	VFA-15	NAS Oceana, Virginia	F/A-18C
AJ	VFA-87	NAS Oceana	F/A-18C
AJ	VS-24	NAS Jacksonville, Florida	S-3B
B	VT-21	NAS Kingsville, Texas	T-45A
B	VT-22	NAS Kingsville, Texas	T-45A
BH	NWTS	NAS Point Mugu, Calif.	F-14A/B/D, NP-3D, QF-4N/S
BJ	HM-14	Chambers Field, Norfolk, Virginia	MH-53E
BR	HC-8	Chambers Field, Norfolk	CH-46D, HH-46D, UH-46D
CW	VR-54	NAS New Orleans JRB, Louisiana	C-130T
D	AOD	NAS Meridian, Mississippi	HH-1N
E	HT-18	NAS Whiting Field, Florida	TH-57B/C
E	HT-8	NAS Whiting Field	TH-57B/C
E	VT-2	NAS Whiting Field	T-34C
E	VT-3	NAS Whiting Field	T-34C
E	VT-6	NAS Whiting Field	T-34C
F	AOD	NAS Pensacola, Florida	UH-3H
F	VT-10	NAS Pensacola	T-34C, T-1A
F	VT-4	NAS Pensacola	T-34C, T-1A
F	VT-86	NAS Pensacola	T-39G/N, T-2C
FB	VC-6 Det.	NAS Patuxent River, Maryland	RQ-2A
G	AOD	NAS Corpus Christi, Texas	HH-1N
G	VT-27	NAS Corpus Christi	T-34C
G	VT-28	NAS Corpus Christi	T-34C
G	VT-31	NAS Corpus Christi	T-44A
G	VT-35	NAS Corpus Christi	TC-12B, UC-12B
GF	VC-8	NAVSTA Roosevelt Roads, P.R.	TA-4J, UH-3H
HC	HC-4	NAS Sigonella, Italy	MH-53E
HC	HC-4 Det.	Palese Macchie AP, Bari, Italy	MH-53E
HK	HSL-40	NAVSTA Mayport, Florida	SH-60B
HN	HSL-42	NAVSTA Mayport	SH-60B
HP	HSL-44	NAVSTA Mayport	SH-60B
HQ	HSL-46	NAVSTA Mayport	SH-60B
HR	HSL-48	NAVSTA Mayport	SH-60B
HU	HC-2	Chambers Field, Norfolk, Virginia	UH-3H, VH-3A
HW	HC-6	Chambers Field	HH-46D, UH-46D
JA	VX-1	NAS Patuxent River, Maryland	SH-60B/F, P-3C, S-3B
JK	VR-1	NAF Washington, Maryland	C-20D
JQ	VQ-2	NAVSTA Rota, Spain	EP-3E, P-3C
JR	VR-48	NAF Washington, Maryland	C-20G
JS	VR-46	NAS Atlanta, Georgia	C-9B, DC-9
JT	VR-52	NAS Willow Grove JRB, Pennsylvania	C-9B, DC-9
JU	VR-56	Chambers Field, Norfolk, Virginia	C-9B
JV	VR-58	NAS Jacksonville, Florida	C-9B, DC-9
JW	VR-62	NAS Brunswick, Maine	C-130T
LA	VP-5	NAS Jacksonville, Florida	P-3C
LC	VP-8	NAS Brunswick, Maine	P-3C
LD	VP-10	NAS Brunswick	P-3C
LF	VP-16	NAS Jacksonville, Florida	P-3C
LK	VP-26	NAS Brunswick, Maine	P-3C
LL	VP-30	NAS Jacksonville, Florida	P-3C, VP-3A
LN	VP-45	NAS Jacksonville	P-3C
LP	VQ-11	NAS Brunswick, Maine	P-3C
LT	VP-62	NAS Jacksonville, Florida	P-3C
LU	VP-64	NAS Willow Grove JRB, Pennsylvania	P-3C
LV	VP-66	NAS Willow Grove JRB	P-3C
LY	VP-92	NAS Brunswick, Maine	P-3C
NE	HS-2	NAS North Island, California	SH-60F, HH-60H
NE	VAQ-131	NAS Whidbey Island, Washington	EA-6B
NE	VAW-116	NAS Point Mugu, California	E-2C
NE	VF-2	NAS Oceana, Virginia	F-14D
NE	VFA-137	NAS Lemoore, California	F/A-18C
NE	VFA-151	NAS Lemoore	F/A-18C
NE	VS-38	NAS North Island, California	S-3B
NF	HS-14	NAF Atsugi, Japan	SH-60F, HH-60H
NF	VAQ-136	NAF Atsugi	EA-6B
NF	VAW-115	NAF Atsugi	E-2C
NF	VF-154	NAF Atsugi	F-14A
NF	VFA-192	NAF Atsugi	F/A-18C
NF	VFA-195	NAF Atsugi	F/A-18C
NF	VFA-27	NAF Atsugi	F/A-18C
NF	VS-21	NAF Atsugi	S-3B
NG	HS-8	NAS North Island, California	SH-60F, HH-60H
NG	VAQ-138	NAS Whidbey Island, Washington	EA-6B
NG	VAW-112	NAS Point Mugu, California	E-2C
NG	VF-211	NAS Oceana, Virginia	F-14A
NG	VFA-146	NAS Lemoore, California	F/A-18C
RA	HS-10	NAS North Island, California	SH-60F, HH-60H
RB	HC-5	Andersen AFB, Guam	HH-46D, UH-46D

US NAVY (Continued)

Tail Code	Unit	Location	Aircraft
RC	VP-46	NAS Whidbey Island, Washington	P-3C
RD	VP-47	MCAF Kaneohe Bay, Hawaii	P-3C
RS	VR-61	NAS Whidbey Island, Washington	DC-9
RU	VR-55	NAS Point Mugu, California	C-130T
RW	VR-51	MCAF Kaneohe Bay, Hawaii	C-20G
RW	VRC-30	NAS North Island, California	C-2A, UC-12B/F
RX	VR-57	NAS North Island	C-9B, DC-9
RY	VR-59	NAS Fort Worth JRB, Texas	C-9B, DC-9
SA	HC-3	NAS North Island, California	CH-46D, HH-46D
SD	NSATS	NAS Patuxent River, Maryland	Multiple types
TA	HSL-51	NAF Atsugi, Japan	SH-60B, UH-3H
TB	HM-15	NAS Corpus Christi, Texas	MH-53E
TH	HSL-37	MCAF Kaneohe Bay, Hawaii	SH-60B
TS	HSL-41	NAS North Island, California	SH-60B
TT	HSL-43	NAS North Island	SH-60B
TX	HSL-49	NAS North Island	SH-60B
TY	HSL-47	NAS North Island	SH-60B
TZ	HSL-45	NAS North Island	SH-60B
VR	HC-11	NAS North Island	HH-46D, UH-46D, UH-3H
WV	VR-53	NAF Washington, Maryland	C-130T
XE	VX-9	NAWS China Lake, California	Multiple types
XF	VX-9 Det.	NAS Point Mugu, California	F-14A/B/D
YB	VP-1	NAS Whidbey Island, Washington	P-3C
YD	VP-4	MCAF Kaneohe Bay, Hawaii	P-3C
NG	VFA-147	NAS Lemoore, California	F/A-18C
NG	VS-33	NAS North Island, California	S-3B
NH	HS-6	NAS North Island	SH-60F, HH-60H
NH	VAQ-135	NAS Whidbey Island, Washington	EA-6B
NH	VAW-117	NAS Point Mugu, California	E-2C
NH	VF-213	NAS Oceana, Virginia	F-14D
NH	VFA-22	NAS Lemoore, California	F/A-18C
NH	VFA-94	NAS Lemoore	F/A-18C
NH	VFA-97	NAS Lemoore	F/A-18A
NH	VS-29	NAS North Island, California	S-3B
NJ	VAQ-129	NAS Whidbey Island, Washington	EA-6B
NJ	VFA-122	NAS Lemoore, California	F/A-18E/F
NJ	VFA-125	NAS Lemoore	F/A-18A/B/C/D, T-34C
NJ	VS-41	NAS North Island, California	S-3B
NK	HS-4	NAS North Island	SH-60F, HH-60H
NK	VAQ-139	NAS Whidbey Island, Washington	EA-6B
NK	VAW-113	NAS Point Mugu, California	E-2C
NK	VF-31	NAS Oceana, Virginia	F-14D
NK	VFA-113	NAS Lemoore, California	F/A-18C
NK	VFA-115	NAS Lemoore	F/A-18C
NK	VFA-25	NAS Lemoore	F/A-18C
NK	VS-35	NAS North Island, California	S-3B
NL	VAQ-128	NAS Whidbey Island, Washington	EA-6B
NL	VAQ-133	NAS Whidbey Island	EA-6B
NL	VAQ-134	NAS Whidbey Island	EA-6B
NL	VAQ-142	NAS Whidbey Island	EA-6B
NW	HC-85	NAS North Island, California	UH-3H
NW	HCS-4	Chambers Field, Norfolk, Virginia	HH-60H
NW	HCS-5	NAS Point Mugu, California	HH-60H
NW	HS-75	NAS Jacksonville, Florida	SH-3H, UH-3H
NW	HSL-84	NAS North Island, California	SH-2G
NW	HSL-94	NAS Willow Grove JRB, Pennsylvania	SH-2G
PD	VP-9	MCAF Kaneohe Bay, Hawaii	P-3C
PG	VP-65	NAS Point Mugu, California	P-3C
PJ	VP-69	NAS Whidbey Island, Washington	P-3C
PR	VQ-1	NAS Whidbey Island	P-3C, EP-3E, UP-3A/B
PR	VQ-1 Det.	NAF Bahrain IAP, Bahrain	EP-3E
PZ	VP-94	NAS New Orleans JRB, Louisiana	P-3C
QE	VP-40	NAS Whidbey Island, Washington	P-3C

US MARINE CORPS

Tail Code	Unit	Location	Aircraft
5B	H&HS	MCAS Beaufort, South Carolina	UC-12B, HH-46D
(5C)	VMR-1	MCAS Cherry Point, North Carolina	C-9B, UC-12B, HH-46D
5D	H&HS	MCAS New River, North Carolina	UC-12B
5F	H&HS	MCAS Futenma, Japan	CT-39G, UC-12F
5G	H&HS	MCAS Iwakuni, Japan	UC-12F
(5T)	VMR-2	MCAS Miramar, California	UC-12B, HH-1N
5W	H&HS	MCAF Kaneohe Bay, Hawaii	UC-12B
5Y	H&HS	MCAS Yuma, Arizona	UC-12B, HH-1N
BH	VMGR-252	MCAS Cherry Point, North Carolina	KC-130F/R/T
BM(DC)	VMFA-122	MCAS Beaufort, South Carolina	F/A-18A
BM(DR)	VMFA-312	MCAS Beaufort	F/A-18C
BM(DW)	VMFA-251	MCAS Beaufort	F/A-18D
BM(EA)	VMFA(AW)-332	MCAS Beaufort	F/A-18D
BM(ED)	VMFA(AW)-533	MCAS Beaufort	F/A-18D

US MARINE CORPS (Continued)

Tail Code	Unit	Location	Aircraft
BM(VE)	VMFA-115	MCAS Beaufort, South Carolina	F/A-18A
BM(WK)	VMFA(AW)-224	MCAS Beaufort	F/A-18D
CB	VMAQ-1	MCAS Cherry Point, North Carolina	EA-6B
CE	VMFA(AW)-225	MCAS Miramar, California	F/A-18D
CF	VMA-211	MCAS Yuma, Arizona	AV-8B/B(NA)
CG	VMA-231	MCAS Cherry Point, North Carolina	AV-8B
CJ	HMH-461	MCAS New River, North Carolina	CH-53E
CY	VMAQ-2	MCAS Cherry Point, North Carolina	EA-6B
DT	VMFA(AW)-242	MCAS Miramar, California	F/A-18D
EG	HMM-263	MCAS New River, North Carolina	CH-46E
EH	HMM-264	MCAS New River	CH-46E
EM	HMM-261	MCAS New River	CH-46E
EN	HMH-464	MCAS New River	CH-53E
EP	HMM-265	MCAS Futenma, Japan	CH-46E
ES	HMM-266	MCAS New River, North Carolina	CH-46E
ET	HMM-262	MCAS Futenma, Japan	CH-46E
EZ	MASD	NAS New Orleans JRB, Louisiana	UC-12B, UC-35C
FF	VMU-2	MCAS Cherry Point, North Carolina	RQ-2A
FZ	VMU-1	MCAGCC Twentynine Palms	RQ-2A
GR	VMGRT-253	MCAS Cherry Point, North Carolina	KC-130F
GX	VMMT-204	MCAS New River, North Carolina	(MV-22B)
HF	HMLA-269	MCAS New River	UH-1N, AH-1W
HH	HMH-366	MCAF Kaneohe Bay, Hawaii	CH-53E
KD	VMAT-203	MCAS Cherry Point, North Carolina	AV-8B, TAV-8B
MA	VMFA-112	NAS Fort Worth JRB, Texas	F/A-18A
MB	VMFA-142	NAS Atlanta, Georgia	F/A-18A
MD	VMAQ-3	MCAS Cherry Point, North Carolina	EA-6B
MF	VMFA-134	MCAS Miramar, California	F/A-18A
MG	VMFA-321	NAF Washington, Maryland	F/A-18A
ML	HMM-764	Edwards AFB, California	CH-46E
MM	HMLA-775		
	Det. A	NAS New Orleans JRB, Louisiana	AH-1W, UH-1N
MP	HMLA-773(-)	NAS Atlanta, Georgia	AH-1W, UH-1N
MQ	HMM-774	Chambers Field, Norfolk, Virginia	CH-46E
MS	HMH-769	Edwards AFB, California	CH-53E
MT	HMH-772	NAS Willow Grove JRB, Pennsylvania	CH-53E
(MX)	HMX-1	MCAF Quantico, Virginia	CH-46E, VH-60N, CH-53E, VH-3D
NY	VMGR-452	Stewart ANGB, New York	KC-130T, KC-130T-30
PF	HMM-364	MCAS Camp Pendleton, California	CH-46E
QB	VMGR-352	MCAS Miramar, California	KC-130F/R
QD	VMGR-152	MCAS Futenma, Japan	KC-130F
QH	VMGR-234	NAS Fort Worth JRB, Texas	KC-130F/T, KC-130T-30
QT	HMT-303	MCAS Camp Pendleton, California	UH-1N, HH-1N, AH-1W
RM	VMAQ-4	MCAS Cherry Point, North Carolina	EA-6B
SH	VMFAT-101	MCAS Miramar, California	F/A-18A/B/C/D, T-34C
SM	HMLA-369	MCAS Camp Pendleton, California	UH-1N, AH-1W
SN	HMLA-169	MCAS Camp Pendleton	UH-1N, AH-1W
SU	HMT-301	MCAF Kaneohe Bay, Hawaii	CH-53D
TV	HMLA-167	MCAS New River, North Carolina	UH-1N, AH-1W
UT	HMT-302	MCAS New River	CH-53E, MH-53E
UV	HMLA-267	MCAS Camp Pendleton, California	UH-1N, AH-1W
VK	VMFA(AW)-121	MCAS Miramar, California	F/A-18D
VM	MASD	NAF Washington, Maryland	C-20G, UC-12B
VT	HMLA-367	MCAS Camp Pendleton, California	UH-1N, AH-1W
VW(NG)	VMFA-314	MCAS Miramar, California	F/A-18C
(WB)	VMFT-401	MCAS Yuma, Arizona	F-5E/F
WD	VMFA-212	MCAS Iwakuni, Japan	F/A-18C
WE	VMA-214	MCAS Yuma, Arizona	AV-8B/B(NA)/AV-8B+
WF	VMA-513	MCAS Yuma	AV-8B/B(NA)
WG	HMLA-773		
	Det. A	NAS Willow Grove JRB, Penn	AH-1W, UH-1N
WH	VMA-542	MCAS Cherry Point, North Carolina	AV-8B
WL	VMA-311	MCAS Yuma, Arizona	AV-8B/B(NA)
WP	VMA-223	MCAS Cherry Point, North Carolina	AV-8B
WR	HMLA-775(-)	MCAS Camp Pendleton, California	AH-1W, UH-1N
WS	VMFA-323	MCAS Miramar, California	F/A-18C
WT	VMFA-232	MCAS Miramar	F/A-18C
YF	HMH-462	MCAS Miramar	CH-53E
YH	HMH-463	MCAF Kaneohe Bay, Hawaii	CH-53D
YJ	HMH-465	MCAS Miramar, California	CH-53E
YK	HMH-466	MCAS Miramar	CH-53E
YL	HMH-362	MCAF Kaneohe Bay, Hawaii	CH-53D
YM	HMM-365	MCAS New River, North Carolina	CH-46E
YN	HMH-361	MCAS Miramar, California	CH-53E
YP	HMM-163	MCAS Miramar	CH-46E
YQ	HMM-268	MCAS Camp Pendleton, California	CH-46E
YR	HMM-161	MCAS Miramar, California	CH-46E
YS	HMM-162	MCAS New River, North Carolina	CH-46E
YT	HMM(T)-164	MCAS Camp Pendleton, California	CH-46E
YW	HMM-165	MCAS Miramar, California	CH-46E
YX	HMM-166	MCAS Miramar	CH-46E
YZ	HMH-363	MCAF Kaneohe Bay, Hawaii	CH-53D

US MARINE CORPS

AVIATION OVERVIEW

When the Wright brothers first flew at Kitty Hawk in 1903, ushering in an era that would forever change the face of warfare, there were those in the Marine Corps ready to seize the idea of flight and exploit its combat potential. That year, a young Alfred A. Cunningham, who would become "the Father of Marine Aviation," took his first balloon ride. Ultimately, he was the first from the Corps to be ordered to the Navy's new aviation camp at Annapolis on 22 May 1912, a date now considered the birth of Marine Corps aviation. Cunningham was dually designated as Naval Aviator Number Five, and Marine Aviator Number One. After a scant two hours and forty min-

utes of flight instruction at the Burgess Company in Massachusetts, he took off and successfully soloed in a Wright hydroplane. Marine aviation was thus born in the cradle of naval aviation, and remains in its imposed, dependent relationship with the Navy today.

Early Marine aviators were little more than poorly equipped volunteers who dared to learn by trial and error. However, from the successes and failures of those early years has evolved a highly respected and responsive air force, and one pivotal in developing air doctrine. In Vietnam, the Corps perfected vertical assault by helicopter, and close air support (CAS) from such aircraft as the A-4 Skyhawk, F-4 Phantom and A-6 Intruder. When the Gulf War began, Marine Corps AV-8B Harriers were forward deployed at primitive airstrips.

Developing an idea known as the Marine Expeditionary Unit (MEU), a task-sized amphibious force that combines a composite squadron of helicopters and Harriers with a ground combat element, the Marine Corps has effectively given the United States a first-response force. Today, the Corps has a fleet of modern warplanes at its disposal, capable of operating from carrier decks and shore bases, and fulfilling a host of missions.

Marine aviation was established to support Marine Corps forces on the ground and its aviators share a distinct bond with ground troops. "Every marine a rifleman" is more than a slogan. It is a Marine Corps philosophy that mandates everyone must train first to fight on the ground. Only after completing the grueling

ground school training can an officer begin flight training. This concept is at the very heart of the CAS doctrine that has defined Marine Corps aviation, and means the "grunt" on the ground and the aviator overhead ultimately share a common perspective of the battlefield.

In the early years of naval aviation, the Navy and Marine Corps tried to organize an advance base force of Marine infantry and artillery to support the Navy's battleship fleet from foreign shores. In 1911, a school was established for this purpose. Marine leaders had anticipated the military advantage of attaching aviators to an advanced base and, when they participated in maneuvers with the Naval fleet off the coast of Guantánamo, Cuba, in 1913, it proved the theory. That exercise confirmed that aircraft could be used to spot submarines and enemy surface vessels without being detected themselves, and attack such targets effectively with explosives. It marked the beginning of modern aerial reconnaissance and air-to-surface attack, and officers from both services were taken aloft for indoctrination flights. Among them was Marine Lt. Col. John Lejeune who quickly became one of Marine Corps aviation's influential supporters. Subsequently, he rose to become commandant.

Hesitantly, the Navy Department and Congress began to formally recognize military aviation. Legislation in 1913 limited the number of naval and marine aviator officers to 30, and authorized a pay increase of 35 percent for officers flying heavier-than-air machines. The Marine Corps adroitly circumvented the limit by teaching specially qualified enlisted troops to fly as well, designating them naval aviation pilots (NAPs). Meanwhile, the Office of Naval Aeronautics was created. However, almost as an afterthought, one marine officer was included on its staff.

Marine Aviator Number Two was Lt. "Banney" Smith, who is credited with an

Alfred A. Cunningham at Pensacola, Florida, in 1914, standing in front of a Curtiss JN.

early exercise that presaged the air-ground team concept marines use today. In early 1914, he led a two-airplane detachment to Culebra, Puerto Rico, to participate in the annual Atlantic Fleet exercise. This marked a seminal point in Marine Corps aviation because it successfully tested the service's ability to occupy and fortify an advance base while under attack. Marines repelled a night amphibious assault and a simulated bombardment by the Navy. At Culebra, the forces had also been expeditionary, clearing vegetation to provide a base for a C-3 flying boat used for reconnaissance missions. Smith sought a radio for the aircraft and transportable canvas shelters, but met with no success. Even so, the Corps proved his idea could work.

In the two years that followed, all aviation programs suffered as Congress took note of poor technological advances and doubted

marine aviators were admitted to the Army Signal Corps Aviation School in San Diego where a new training program was emerging. After basic flight instruction in Navy seaplanes at Pensacola, they went to San Diego for land-based flight training with the Army. It was just what the Marine Corps needed.

In 1916 the United States grew more concerned about the possibility of war with Mexico as well as the continuing menace of rogue German U-boat attacks. President Woodrow Wilson began to expand all of the nation's armed services although, while the Army and Navy were to define their own aviation roles, the Marine Corps could only hope to be included. The arrangement was far from ideal because it had the Army defending the Navy's advanced land bases. This was something neither service wanted and, with Marine aviators having received both land-based and sea-based training,

fight. The Marine Corps was the first to have a fully trained aviation unit to deploy in World War I, which was sent to the Azores in the Atlantic, some 900 miles from the Portuguese coast. From this location the Corps flew antisubmarine patrols. Still desperate to strengthen this small aviation force, Cunningham managed to recruit 78 aviators by having them resign from the Navy to join the Marine Corps in a similar capacity.

By the time the World War I armistice was signed, the attitude of the government and Navy towards aviation did not bode well for the Corps. Cunningham lobbied hard to extol the benefits of aerial reconnaissance, bombing in support of amphibious operations and the value of machine-gun fire and fragmentation bombs, and emphasized the importance of radio communications. His efforts paid off. Congress eventually established the Marine Corps at one-fifth the manpower strength of the Navy, making it just over 2,600 strong, and authorized 1,020 marine personnel for aviation. By the late 1920s, the Corps was building its own air bases in Quantico, Virginia, and Parris Island, South Carolina. Yet another was scheduled for San Diego, California.

Between the two world wars, the Marine Corps was the only US air arm to see air combat. Ordered to fight in the so-called Banana Wars in Latin America, the Corps was able to take the lead in defining missions that would prove invaluable when it came time to fight the Japanese in the Pacific, following the attack on Pearl Harbor, Hawaii. Away from interservice jealousies and politically motivated restrictions, the Marine Corps developed effective ways to deploy its

The Corps evacuates a wounded marine with the Second Battalion, Fifth Marines, during operations in Korea in the early 1950s.

aviation's value. New funding ceased. However, the new naval flight school at Pensacola struggled on and, in late 1915, Cunningham experimented with a primitive catapult launch system for aircraft. The Corps had a single member enrolled at the beginning of that year although, by its end, the situation had improved. Some naval and

Marine Corps aviation thus remained viable.

By early 1917, there were 59 commissioned officers and 431 enlisted men in naval aviation. Of those, only five were Marine aviators and 18 were enlisted Marine personnel. However, America's entry into World War I brought immediate expansion of the armed services and Marine Corps aviation grew. Now promoted, Capt. Cunningham campaigned aggressively for manpower and machines, so that aviation could join the

Engineering and Manufacturing Aircraft One (serial 163911) was the first Bell Boeing V-22 Osprey tilt-rotor prototype and made its maiden flight on 19 March 1989. When testing with this particular aircraft was concluded it was transferred to MCAS New River, North Carolina, to be used for training purposes.

163911

V-22

MARINES NAVY AIR FORCE ARMY

Zaur Eylanbekov

A pair of night-attack AV-8B Harrier IIs belonging to the 'Black Sheep' of VMA-214, based at MCAS Yuma, Arizona.

aviation assets. CAS became a reality in Nicaragua when ground troops under attack used makeshift canvas panels to indicate enemy positions nearby, and directed aerial firepower. CAS also became the Marine Corps' defining mission. Dive-bombing techniques were sharpened, medical evacuation in a two-seat aircraft was accomplished, re-supply from the air was practiced and aerial reconnaissance was improved. Rough landing strips were carved from the jungle and Marine Corps aviators, under the command of Maj. Ross Rowell, strafed and bombed enemy positions and made the first organized low-level, dive-bombing attacks.

As history ultimately showed, its seasoned pilots became the Marine Corps' senior aviators when hostilities began in the Pacific in late 1941, in what was to prove naval aviation's greatest test. It was some eight years before, however, that it was decided the Marine Corps would have the amphibious warfare role and that its aviation element would support it. The Fleet Marine Force (FMF) was created, which gave the marines a primary wartime mission: amphibious assault. Marine aviation's primary responsibilities were to include reconnaissance, CAS, artillery spotting, fighter escort and protection of the landing force. In 1939, a secondary mission was added when it was determined the service would also provide backup squadrons for naval carrier duty.

The Pacific Theater expanded the scope of aerial warfare. From the attack on Pearl Harbor to the long and bloody battles to retake the Pacific island groups, to the war-ending atomic bomb drops on the Japanese cities of Hiroshima and Nagasaki, the airplane brought new tactical advantages. The battle against Japan was waged heavily from the air, using aircraft carriers operating at great distances from their home ports. Marine aviators soon found themselves dogfighting, having to develop new air warfare skills and pioneering night-flying tactics in radar-equipped PV-1 Venturas. After the war, Marine aviation returned to its primary CAS mission but the Corps now had to consider the vulnerability of its amphibious landing forces, given the threat posed by a single atomic bomb. Amphibious assault doctrine

was modified to take advantage of a new class of aircraft, the helicopter.

Even before war erupted on the Korean Peninsula in 1950, marine aviators had been experimenting with rotary-winged platforms. Since 1947, HMX-1 at MCAS Quantico had worked on helicopter battlefield applications because the helicopter had matured sufficiently for use not only as an observation asset but also for medical evacuation, re-supply, rescue and troop insertion. Marines were the first to take the helicopter into combat and its use, on a large scale, represented one of two key developments that shaped Marine Corps aviation during that conflict. The other was introduction of the F9F Panther jet. By then, vertical assault tactics were close to becoming a reality, while high-speed jets ushered in a new era for CAS.

Not unexpectedly, American forces went through a drawdown after the Korean War ended in July 1953, but the Corps' leadership was convinced helicopters would be critical to the FMF.

The early 1960s brought considerable improvement to the service's transport capabilities, as the KC-130 Hercules joined the fleet. A transport of this size and versatility was key to supporting the Corps' expeditionary missions, and the type's contribution to the war effort in Vietnam cannot be overstated. The re-supplying of marines at Khe San is a shining example. The capabilities of the Hercules also brought additional self-sufficiency. Now the Corps could refuel and extend the mission ranges of its own aircraft.

Over the jungles and mountains of Vietnam, the service used helicopters as never before, expanding the range of their operations to include night-assault missions. Armed escort was needed for troop-carrying helicopters and, by the late summer of 1962, the Marine Corps could provide it. Door-mounted M-60 machine guns were fitted to some UH-34s and, eventually, the UH-1N gunship was acquired. It was followed by the more lethal AH-1G Cobra, in 1969. The helicopter came of age in Vietnam and those in marine aviation became fully committed to "verticality" as a concept, and CAS as its mission.

The widening conflict caused marine

aviation to grow rapidly and its missions to increase. Over time, North Vietnam's air defenses grew much more sophisticated and surface-to-air missiles began to take their toll. In response, the Corps was the first to operate the Grumman EA-6A Prowler tactical jamming aircraft, flying electronic warfare (EW) missions for the other military services, as it still does today.

While the war still raged in Asia, the Corps pressed hard in Washington to acquire the British-developed Hawker AV-8 Harrier. Representing a leap in technology, there were many operational problems associated with the "jump jet" but it represented a logical choice. Years later, in the aftermath of Operation Desert Storm in 1991, then Secretary of Defense Richard Cheney listed the Harrier as one of three weapon systems that significantly contributed to the victory by coalition forces.

Today, the Marine Corps has more than 100 aviation squadrons including active-duty and reserve units, operating an air fleet composed of some 1,200 aircraft. Like its sister services, it has experienced significant budget cuts but, with the closures in 1999 of MCAS El Toro and MCAS Tustin, both located in California, rationalization of its current aviation assets and stations is considered complete. Despite downsizing, however, the service has been able to acquire new and modernized weapon systems in recent years. Tactical aviation assets include the latest variants of the F/A-18 Hornet, while the Marine Corps' AV-8 Harriers, AH-1 Cobras and UH-1 Hueys are gaining new systems. The helicopters are being fitted with advanced power trains and other key upgrades.

Marine aviation continues to develop doctrine and push for improved technologies, and the service started receiving the revolutionary Bell Boeing MV-22 Osprey tilt-rotor in late 1999, thus beginning the replacement process for the Sikorsky CH-46 Sea Knight helicopter, which has served the Corps for 30 years. Early in the 21st century, the vertical and short takeoff and landing (VSTOL) variant of the multiservice Joint Strike Fighter (JSF) is supposed to begin replacing the Corps' current tactical platforms, as well. Meanwhile, as part of its planning for future threats, the service is developing advanced tactics to support ground forces in urban environments.

Technology, which initially lagged behind, is now bringing more flexibility. This is important because doctrine, tactics and platforms remain sound only for as long as they support Marine troops on the ground.

ORGANIZATION OF USMC AVIATION

Although it operates as an independent service, the Marine Corps is a component of the US Navy and functions as a combined air-ground force. It is headquartered in Arlington, Virginia, and is led by the commandant of the Marine Corps.

The active-duty element of the service is structured around two "MARFORs," Marine Forces Pacific (MARFORPAC) and Marine Forces Atlantic (MARFORLANT). Two-thirds of the Corps' personnel are organized, trained and equipped by the combat and combat support units that make up these two regional commands. Headquartered in Hawaii and Norfolk, Virginia, respectively, and reporting directly to the service's commandant, the commanders of MARFORPAC and MARFORLANT are responsible for providing regional commanders in chief (CinCs) with deployable forces and advice on how best to employ them. During combat operations, the MARFORs also serve as operational headquarters and the two commanders also serve as commanding generals of the FMF assigned to the commanders of the Navy's Atlantic and Pacific fleets.

Separate is the Marine Forces Reserve (MARFORRES), headquartered in Louisiana, with some 36,000 personnel under its command. MARFORRES also reports directly to the commandant.

US Marine Corps Aviation Command Structure

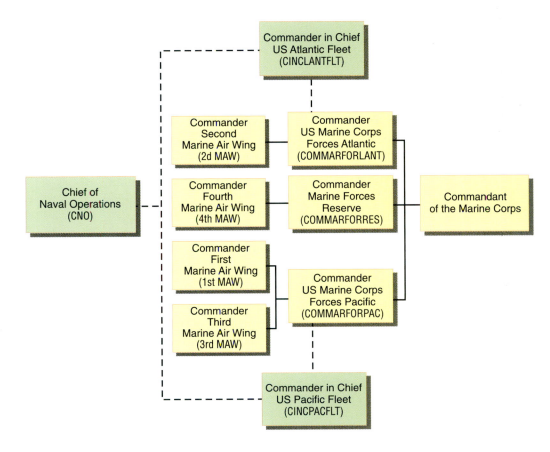

Sending in the Marines

When the Marine Corps is called to action, it responds by fielding its personnel in one or more marine air-ground task forces (MAGTFs). The size of a particular force depends on the situation it is called to address and the nature of its mission but, regardless, each MAGTF is always composed of four common organizational components that are scalable to meet precise needs. These comprise the Command Element, Ground Combat Element, Combat Service Support Element and the Aviation Combat Element, commonly referred to by its acronym, ACE. The latter is composed of helicopter and fixed-wing squadrons, surface-to-air missile and air control units, plus combat service support that is aviation specific.

Expeditionary in nature, and responding as an integrated unit, the MAGTF represents a flexible force that can deploy independently or as part of a

Today, the F/A-18 Hornet is the Marine Corps' most numerous strike asset. Plans call for it to be replaced early in the 21st century by the JSF, which is due to begin entering service in 2008.

US Marine Corps

joint operation. It might be called upon to go into combat, undertake peacekeeping duties, provide humanitarian assistance or tackle a range of other missions. In any event, it trains and is organized as a combined-arms force that is capable of operating on land, at sea and in the air.

Three MAGTFs are permanent, in that they exist in peacetime as well as wartime. They are known as Marine Expeditionary Forces (MEFs). It is from these organizations that smaller MAGTFs are created and tailored in times of conflict. I MEF is based in southern California, while III MEF is forward positioned in Hawaii, mainland Japan and on the Japanese island of Okinawa. They report to MARFORPAC. Similarly, II MEF, which is stationed at bases in North Carolina and South Carolina, falls under the command of MARFORLANT.

First on the Scene: The Marine Expeditionary Unit

Deploying its amphibious vessels in much the same way as its carrier battle groups, the Navy generally organizes such assets into a three- or four-ship Amphibious Ready Group (ARG). Typically, this comprises one of two types of amphibious assault ship, classified either as General Purpose (LHA) or Multipurpose (LHD); one amphibious transport dock (LPD) and one or two dock landing ships (LSD).

Embarked aboard each ARG is a unique unit within the MEF that represents the Corps' "first-on-the-scene" force. It is known as a Marine Expeditionary Unit

(Special Operations Capable), or MEU(SOC). In all, there are seven such forces · operating in the Mediterranean, Persian Gulf, Indian Ocean and Pacific Ocean. Three of the seven are based at Camp Lejeune, South Carolina, and three more are based at Camp Pendleton, California. The remaining unit is forward deployed in Japan. Essentially, the MEU(SOC) is an intervention or Special Operations unit capable of deploying quickly and fighting its way

ashore. Like the MAGTF to which it belongs, it is composed of four elements that include a composite squadron of helicopters and fixed-wing VSTOL aircraft as its ACE. A Medium Helicopter Squadron (HMM), equipped with 12 CH-46E Sea Knights, forms its nucleus and, when deployed, the

HMM is reinforced by aircraft detached or "chopped" from other squadrons. In addition to the CH-46Es, the ACE is normally assigned four CH-53E Super Stallions, four AH-1W SuperCobras, two or three UH-1N Hueys and four or six AV-8B Harriers. Two KC-130 Hercules are also kept on standby. Aircraft detached from other units normally fly from the LHA or LHD.

Like the Navy's carrier battle group and carrier air wing, the makeup of the MEU/ACE varies between deployments, and attached aircraft typically carry the markings and tail codes associated with the core helicopter squadron. Also, it is usual for two CH-46Ds to be detached from a US Navy Helicopter Composite Squadron (HC) and for these to be embarked separately from the ACE.

The long-serving Boeing CH-46 Sea Knight troop transport and medium-lift helicopter, nicknamed the "Phrog" by crews, will soon be replaced by the revolutionary Bell Boeing V-22 Osprey tilt-rotor. These CH-46Es are with HMM-261 at MCAS New River, North Carolina.

MARINE FORCES, AIR WINGS AND UNITS

F/A-18B, BuNo 162842, belongs to VMFAT-101 based at MCAS Miramar, California. The unit is the Marine Corps' Hornet FRS, attached to MAG-11 with the 3d MAW.

Assigned to four commands that include the three MARFORs and the Capital Support Wing (CSW), the Marine Corps' fleet is largely organized around four marine air wings (MAWs). The 1st MAW and 3d MAW are assigned to MARFORPAC, whereas the 2d MAW is assigned to MARFORLANT. The 4th MAW is made up of reserve units attached to MAR-FORRES. Aside from having a small number of units flying utility-type platforms, an air wing is composed of three or four marine air groups (MAGs) made up of between two and 11 squadrons each.

Among its missions, the Corps undertakes type and conversion training for its own personnel in all but a handful of instances. For this purpose, eight fleet readiness squadrons (FRS) are maintained, of which HMT-204 has been redesignated VMMT-204 in preparation for arrival of the first operational MV-22 Osprey tilt-rotor aircraft.

CAPITAL SUPPORT WING (CSW)

Headquartered at Marine Corps Air Facility (MCAF) Quantico, Virginia, the CSW is responsible for providing VIP transportation and also controls HMX-1, which is best known as the Presidential Squadron. The unit also serves as an evaluation squadron in support of Marine Corps rotary-wing development programs.

Besides an air facility at Quantico, HMX-1 maintains a small facility on the grounds of the former NAS Anacostia, now named NAVSTA Washington, in the District of Columbia.

BuNo 164540 is a twin-seat TAV-8B Harrier serving with VMAT-203 at MCAS Cherry Point, North Carolina. The unit belongs to MAG-14 with the 2d MAW.

Marine Corps Fleet Readiness Squadrons (FRS)

Unit	Location	Aircraft
HMM(T)-164	MCAS Camp Pendleton, California	CH-46E
HMT-301	MCAF Kaneohe Bay, Hawaii	CH-53D
HMT-302*	MCAS New River, North Carolina	CH/MH-53E
HMT-303**	MCAS Camp Pendleton, California	UH/HH-1N, AH-1W
VMFAT-101	MCAS Miramar, California	F/A-18A/B/C/D
VMAT-203	MCAS Cherry Point, North Carolina	TAV-8B, AV-8B
VMGRT-253	MCAS Cherry Point, North Carolina	KC-130F
VMMT-204	MCAS New River, North Carolina	MV-22B

* Also conducts Navy MH-53E training
** Also conducts Navy HH-1N training

Capital Support Wing (CSW)

Unit	Location	Aircraft
HMX-1	MCAF Quantico, Virginia	CH-46E, VH-60N, CH-53E, VH-3D
Det.	NAVSTA Washington, District of Columbia	

US Marine Corps

MARINE FORCES ATLANTIC (MARFORLANT)

Headquartered at Naval Station Norfolk, Virginia, MARFORLANT is the US Marine Corps component of US Joint Forces Command (USJFCOM). Its commander is a lieutenant general responsible for training, equipping and deploying Marine Corps forces at USJFCOM's direction and advising its CinC. Comprising some 45,000 personnel, the II MEF represents its warfighting arm and is made up of the 2d Marine Division; 2d Force Service Support Group; 2d Marine Aircraft Wing; and 2d Surveillance, Reconnaissance and Intelligence Group. COMMARFORLANT also serves as the commanding general, Fleet Marine Forces Atlantic; commander, US Marine Corps Forces Europe; and commander, US Marine Corps Forces Southern Command.

2d Marine Aircraft Wing (2d MAW)			
Unit	Location	Aircraft	Tail Code
VMR-1 'Roadrunners'	MCAS Cherry Point, North Carolina	C-9B, UC-12B, HH-46D	(5C)
H&HS	MCAS New River, North Carolina	UC-12B	5D
H&HS 'Swamp Foxes'	MCAS Beaufort, South Carolina	UC-12B, HH-46D	5B
MAG-14	**MCAS Cherry Point, North Carolina**		
VMAQ-1 'Banshees'	MCAS Cherry Point	EA-6B	CB
VMAQ-2 'Panthers'	MCAS Cherry Point	EA-6B	CY
VMAQ-3 'Moon Dogs'	MCAS Cherry Point	EA-6B	MD
VMAQ-4 'Seahawks'	MCAS Cherry Point	EA-6B	RM
VMAT-203 'Hawks'	MCAS Cherry Point	AV-8B, TAV-8B	KD
VMA-223 'Bulldogs'	MCAS Cherry Point	AV-8B	WP
VMA-231 'Ace of Spades'	MCAS Cherry Point	AV-8B	CG
VMA-542 'Flying Tigers'	MCAS Cherry Point	AV-8B	WH
VMGR-252 'Heavy Haulers'	MCAS Cherry Point	KC-130F/R/T	BH
VMGRT-253 'Titans'	MCAS Cherry Point	KC-130F	GR
VMU-2 'Night Owls'	MCAS Cherry Point	RQ-2A	FF
MAG-26	**MCAS New River, North Carolina**		
HMLA-167 'Warriors'	MCAS New River	UH-1N, AH-1W	TV
VMMT-204 (FRS) 'White Knights'	MCAS New River	MV-22B	GX
HMM-261 'Bulls'	MCAS New River	CH-46E	EM
HMM-264 'Black Bulls'	MCAS New River	CH-46E	EH
HMM-266 'Fighting Griffins'	MCAS New River	CH-46E	ES
HMH-461 'Iron Horse'	MCAS New River	CH-53E	CJ
MAG-29	**MCAS New River, North Carolina**		
HMM-162 'Golden Eagles'	MCAS New River	CH-46E	YS
HMM-263 'Red Lions'	MCAS New River	CH-46E	EG
HMLA-269 'Gunrunners'	MCAS New River	UH-1N, AH-1W	HF
HMT-302 (FRS) 'Phoenix'	MCAS New River	CH-53E, MH-53E	UT
HMM-365 'Sky Knights'	MCAS New River	CH-46E	YM
HMH-464 'Condors'	MCAS New River	CH-53E	EN
MAG-31*	**MCAS Beaufort, South Carolina**		
VMFA-115 'Silver Eagles'	MCAS Beaufort	F/A-18A	BM (VE)
VMFA-122 'Crusaders'	MCAS Beaufort	F/A-18A	BM (DC)
VMFA(AW)-224 'Bengals'	MCAS Beaufort	F/A-18D	BM (WK)
VMFA-251 'Thunderbolts'	MCAS Beaufort	F/A-18C	BM (DW)(AB)
VMFA-312 'Checkerboards'	MCAS Beaufort	F/A-18C	BM (DR)(AC)
VMFA(AW)-332 'Moonlighters'	MCAS Beaufort	F/A-18D	BM (EA)
VMFA(AW)-533 'Hawks'	MCAS Beaufort	F/A-18D	BM (ED)

* Although assigned individual tail codes, all aircraft belonging to MAG-31 squadrons carry the "BM" code on their tails

The 'Bengals' of VMFA(AW)-224 fly F/A-18Ds out of MCAS Beaufort, South Carolina. These Hornets are returning from a training mission over the Atlantic Ocean.

2d Marine Aircraft Wing (2d MAW)

The 2d MAW, headquartered at MCAS Cherry Point, North Carolina, is the aviation component of the II MEF and has four MAGs assigned. It provides aircraft and personnel for the 22d, 24th and 26th MEUs, and also supplies units for NATO operations in Bosnia and to support the 1st MAW in Japan. Specific Hornet squadrons also deploy aboard Atlantic Fleet aircraft carriers as part of the vessel's embarked carrier air wing. The wing controls the FRS for the AV-8B, KC-130, MV-22B and CH-53E based at MCAS Cherry Point, North Carolina, or MCAS New River, North Carolina.

As previously indicated, HMT-204 was redesignated VMMT-204 and has assumed the role of FRS for the MV-22B Osprey. Support aircraft at MCAS Cherry Point are operated by the air station's own transport squadron, whereas those at MCAS New River and at MCAS Beaufort, South Carolina, are operated by station headquarters and headquarters' squadrons.

Its fleet of CH-46Es enables the Marine Corps to build troop strength quickly during an amphibious assault. These Sea Knights are with the 'Red Lions' of HMM-263, based at MCAS New River, North Carolina.

MCAS Cherry Point, North Carolina, is home to all four EW squadrons flying the Grumman EA-6B Prowler. BuNo 161245 serves with the 'Moon Dogs' of VMAQ-3.

This Hawaii-based, heavy-lift Sikorsky CH-53D Sea Stallion flies with HMH-362's 'Ugly Angels' from MCAF Kaneohe Bay. The Marine Corps' entire fleet of CH-53Ds is located at the facility, shared between five squadrons.

MARINE FORCES PACIFIC (MARFORPAC)

Headquartered at Marine Corps Base (MCB) Camp H. M. Smith, Hawaii, MARFORPAC is the US Marine Corps component of US Pacific Command (USPACOM) and, like its East Coast counterpart, provides operating forces to unified or joint task force commanders and CinCs.

The I MEF and III MEF are the combat arms of MARFORPAC and each is composed of a marine division; a force service support group; a MAW; and a surveillance, reconnaissance and intelligence group.

Commander, US Marine Corps Forces Pacific (COMMARFORPAC) is a lieutenant general and also serves as commanding general, Fleet Marine Forces Pacific; commander, US Marine Forces Pacific; commander, US Marine Corps Forces Korea (Designate); commander, US Marines Central Command (Designate); and commander, Combined Marine Forces Command (Designate).

1st Marine Aircraft Wing (1st MAW)

Unit	Location	Aircraft	Tail Code
H&HS	MCAS Iwakuni, Japan	UC-12F	5G
H&HS	MCAF Kaneohe Bay, Hawaii	UC-12F	KB/5W
H&HS	MCAS Futemma, Japan	CT-39G, UC-12F	5F
MAG-12	**MCAS Iwakuni, Japan**		
VMFA(AW)-*	MCAS Iwakuni	F/A-18D	
VMAQ-*	MCAS Iwakuni	EA-6B	
VMFA-*	MCAS Iwakuni	F/A-18C	
VMFA-212 'Lancers'	MCAS Iwakuni	F/A-18C	WD
MAG-36	**MCAS Futemma, Japan**		
HMM-262 'Flying Tigers'	MCAS Futemma	CH-46E	ET
HMM-265 'Dragons'	MCAS Futemma	CH-46E	EP
HMH-*	MCAS Futemma	CH-53E	
HMLA-*	MCAS Futemma	AH-1W, UH-1N	
VMGR-152 'The Sumos'	MCAS Futemma	KC-130F	QD
1st MAW ASE	**MCB Hawaii**		
HMT-301 (FRS) 'Wind Walkers'	MCAF Kaneohe Bay	CH-53D	SU
HMH-362 'Ugly Angels'	MCAF Kaneohe Bay	CH-53D	YL
HMH-363 'Red Lions'	MCAF Kaneohe Bay	CH-53D	YZ
HMH-366 'Hammerheads'	MCAF Kaneohe Bay	CH-53D	HH
HMH-463 'Pegasus'	MCAF Kaneohe Bay	CH-53D	YH

* Unit Deployment Program (UDP) units

1st Marine Aircraft Wing (1st MAW)

Based at MCB Camp Smedley D. Butler, Okinawa, Japan, the 1st MAW is the air component of the III MEF and has two MAGs and an Aviation Support Element (ASE) assigned. Many of the units that make up the MAGs are based in the United States and deploy for six-month periods under the Unit Deployment Program (UDP). Consequently, only four of nine squadrons are permanently assigned. The 1st MAW ASE now operates the Corps' entire fleet of CH-53Ds, including the FRS for the type, although these helicopters will ultimately be replaced by the MV-22B Osprey. Search and rescue (SAR) and operational support aircraft are assigned directly to the individual air stations.

The "Huey" has filled many different roles during close to 40 years of service with the Marine Corps. BuNo 160177 is a UH-1N serving with HMLA-169 at MCAS Camp Pendleton, California.

3d Marine Aircraft Wing (3d MAW)

Having recently relocated from MCAS El Toro, California, to MCAS Miramar, California, the 3d MAW is the aviation component of the I MEF. It is the largest of the three active-duty wings with five MAGs assigned, and provides aircraft and personnel to the 11th, 13th, 15th and 31st MEUs. The MAGs also provide units to support the 1st MAW in Japan. A single marine transport squadron is directly assigned, as are the F/A-18, AH-1W and UH-1N FRS, whereas the air wing's operational support aircraft and search and rescue assets are assigned directly to an individual station's headquarters squadron or to a marine transport unit. Individual Hornet squadrons also deploy with specific US Navy carrier air wings.

3d Marine Aircraft Wing (3d MAW)			
Unit	Location	Aircraft	Tail Code
VMR-2	MCAS Miramar, California	UC-12B, HH-1N	5T
H&HS	MCAS Yuma, Arizona	UC-12B, HH-1N	5Y
MAG-11	**MCAS Miramar, California**		
VMFAT-101 (FRS) 'Sharpshooters'	MCAS Miramar	F/A-18A/B/C/D, T-34C	SH
VMFA(AW)-121 'Green Knights'	MCAS Miramar	F/A-18D	VK
VMFA(AW)-225 'Vikings'	MCAS Miramar	F/A-18D	CE
VMFA-232 'Red Devils'	MCAS Miramar	F/A-18C	WT
VMFA(AW)-242 'Bats'	MCAS Miramar	F/A-18D	DT
VMFA-314 'Black Knights'	MCAS Miramar	F/A-18C	VW(NG)
VMFA-323 'Death Rattlers'	MCAS Miramar	F/A-18C	WS(NE)
VMGR-352 'Raiders'	MCAS Miramar	KC-130F/R	QB
MAG-13	**MCAS Yuma, Arizona**		
VMA-211 'Avengers'	MCAS Yuma	AV-8B/B(NA)	CF
VMA-214 'Black Sheep'	MCAS Yuma	AV-8B/B(NA)	WE
VMA-311 'Tomcats'	MCAS Yuma	AV-8B/B(NA)	WL
VMA-513 'Nightmares'	MCAS Yuma	AV-8B/B(NA)	WF
VMU-1 'Watchdogs'	MCAGCC Twentynine Palms, Calif.	RQ-2A	FZ
MAG-16	**MCAS Miramar, California**		
HMM-161 'Greyhawks'	MCAS Miramar	CH-46E	YR
HMM-163 'Ridgerunners'	MCAS Miramar	CH-46E	YP
HMM-165 'White Knights'	MCAS Miramar	CH-46E	YW
HMM-166 'Sea Elk'	MCAS Miramar	CH-46E	YX
HMH-361 'Flying Tigers'	MCAS Miramar	CH-53E	YN
HMH-462 'Heavy Haulers'	MCAS Miramar	CH-53E	YF
HMH-465 'Warhorses'	MCAS Miramar	CH-53E	YJ
HMH-466 'Wolfpack'	MCAS Miramar	CH-53E	YK
MAG-39	**MCAS Camp Pendleton, California**		
HMM(T)-164 (FRS) 'Knightriders'	MCAS Camp Pendleton	CH-46E	YT
HMLA-169 'Vipers'	MCAS Camp Pendleton	UH-1N, AH-1W	SN
HMLA-267 'Stingers'	MCAS Camp Pendleton	UH-1N, AH-1W	UV
HMM-268 'Red Dragons'	MCAS Camp Pendleton	CH-46E	YQ
HMT-303 (FRS) 'Atlas'	MCAS Camp Pendleton	UH/HH-1N, AH-1W	QT
HMM-364 'Purple Foxes'	MCAS Camp Pendleton	CH-46E	PF
HMLA-367 'Scarface'	MCAS Camp Pendleton	UH-1N, AH-1W	VT
HMLA-369 'Gunfighters'	MCAS Camp Pendleton	UH-1N, AH-1W	SM

US Marine Corps

MARINE FORCES RESERVE (MARFORRES)

Headquartered at Naval Support Activity (NSA) New Orleans, Louisiana, the Commander Marine Forces Reserve (COM-MARFORRES), a major general, controls the 4th MAW, 4th Force Service Support Group, 4th Marine Division and the Marine Corps Reserve Support Command.

4th Marine Aircraft Wing (4th MAW)

The structure of the 4th MAW, also head-quartered at NSA New Orleans, differs significantly from that of the active-duty wings. Within the 4th MAW, the squadrons are geographically aligned under their respective MAGs, and the wing is unique in controlling two full KC-130 squadrons and two HMLA squadrons with separate detachments. During 1999, two reserve squadrons previously based at MCAS El Toro moved to Edwards AFB, following closure of the air station.

Unit	Location	Aircraft	Tail Code
4th Marine Aircraft Wing (4th MAW)			
MASD	NAS New Orleans JRB, Louisiana	UC-35C, UC-12B	EZ
MAG-41	**NAS Fort Worth JRB, Texas**		
VMFA-112 'Cowboys'	NAS Fort Worth JRB	F/A-18A	MA
VMGR-234 'Rangers'	NAS Fort Worth JRB	KC-130T, KC-130T-30	QH
MAG-42	**NAS Atlanta, Georgia**		
VMFA-142 'Flying Gators'	NAS Atlanta	F/A-18A	MB
HMLA-773(-) 'Red Dog' *	NAS Atlanta	AH-1W, UH-1N	MP
HMM-774 'Honkers'	NAVSTA Norfolk, Virginia	CH-46E	MQ
HMLA-775 Det. A 'Coyotes' **	NAS New Orleans JRB, Louisiana	AH-1W, UH-1N	MM
MAG-46	**MCAS Miramar, California**		
VMFA-134 'Smoke'	MCAS Miramar	F/A-18A	MF
VMFT-401 'Snipers'	MCAS Yuma, Arizona	F-5E/F	(WB)
HMM-764 'Moonlight'	Edwards AFB, California	CH-46E	ML
HMH-769 'Road Hogs'	Edwards AFB	CH-53E	MS
HMLA-775(-) 'Coyotes' **	MCAS Camp Pendleton, California	AH-1W, UH-1N	WR
MAG-49	**NAS Willow Grove JRB, Pennsylvania**		
VMFA-321 'Hell's Angels'	NAF Washington, Maryland	F/A-18A	MG
VMGR-452 'Yankees'	Stewart ANGB, New York	KC-130T, KC-130T-30	NY
HMH-772 'Flying Armadillos'	NAS Willow Grove JRB	CH-53E	MT
HMLA-773 Det. A 'Red Dog' *	NAS Willow Grove JRB	AH-1W, UH-1N	WG
MASD	NAF Washington, Maryland	C-20G, UC-12B	(VM)5A

* Headquarters is located at NAS Atlanta. Det A is located at NAS Willow Grove but geographically aligned under MAG-49

** Headquarters is located at MCAS Pendleton. Det A is located at NAS New Orleans but geographically aligned under MAG-42

Seen here over Hawaii's Kona coast, while participating in the 1999 "Pacific Impact" exercise, are F/A-18A Hornets from VMFA-134. The squadron is based at MCAS Miramar, California.

Flying Northrop F-5E/F Tiger IIs, the 'Snipers' of the reserve unit VMFT-401 are tasked with adversary training for the Marine Corps. The squadron is based at MCAS Yuma, Arizona.

AMPHIBIOUS ASSAULT SHIPS

The US Navy currently has five LHA (general purpose) and six LHD (multipurpose) amphibious assault ships in service. The first of the Tarawa-class LHAs will reach the end of its service life in 2011 and the Navy had hoped to fund the first of five $1.2 billion upgrades for these vessels in 1999. Under its Service Life-Extension Plan (SLEP) each ship's life was to be extended by up to 20 years. Instead, $50 million in advance procurement for an eighth Wasp-class LHD was included in the 1999 budget. This type of vessel serves as the lead ship for each ARG.

USS *Tarawa* (LHA 1)

Named for the bloody Pacific battle of World War II, LHA 1 is the second vessel to carry the name. The first ship was CV 40, an Essex-class aircraft carrier.
Home Port: San Diego, California
Keel Laid: 15 November 1971
Launched: 1 December 1973
Commissioned: 29 May 1976

Builders: Ingalls Shipbuilding Inc., Ingalls, Mississippi
Power Plant: Two boilers, two geared steam turbines, two shafts. Rated at 70,000 shp (52199 kW)
Dimensions: LOA 820 ft (249.9 m), flight deck width 106 ft (32.3 m), beam 106 ft (32.3 m), draft 26 ft (7.9 m)
Displacement: Approx. 39,250 tons (35607 tonnes) with full load
Performance: Maximum speed 24 knots

As yet unnamed, LHD 8 is to be funded in 2005 as the replacement for the USS *Tarawa*. The new vessel is scheduled to be commissioned in 2010.

USS *Saipan* (LHA 2)

LHA 2 is the second ship named for the Pacific Island battle of World War II. The first USS *Saipan* (CVL 48) was a light aircraft carrier.
Home Port: Norfolk, Virginia
Keel Laid: 21 July 1972
Launched: 18 July 1974
Commissioned: 15 October 1977

The USS *Saipan* (LHA 2) is one of five general purpose amphibious assault ships in current service.

USS *Belleau Wood* (LHA 3)

Named for the historic World War 1 battle, LHA 3 is the second USS *Belleau Wood*. The first ship to carry the name (CVL 24) was a light aircraft carrier.
Home Port: Sasebo, Japan
Keel Laid: 5 March 1973
Launched: 11 April 1977
Commissioned: 23 September 1978

Builders: Ingalls Shipbuilding Inc., Ingalls, Mississippi
Power Plant: Two boilers, two geared steam turbines, two shafts. Rated at 70,000 shp (52199 kW)
Dimensions: LOA 820 ft (249.9 m), flight deck width 106 ft (32.3 m), beam 106 ft (32.3 m), draft 27 ft (8.2 m)
Displacement: Approx. 39,945 tons (36237 tonnes) with full load
Performance: Maximum speed 24 knots

USS *Nassau* (LHA 4)

LHA 4 is the second ship named for the site of the first amphibious landing by the US Marines in 1776. CVE 16, an escort carrier, previously bore the name.
Home Port: Norfolk, Virginia
Keel Laid: 16 August 1973
Launched: 21 January 1978
Commissioned: 28 July 1979

Builders: Ingalls Shipbuilding Inc., Ingalls, Mississippi
Power Plant: Two boilers, two geared steam turbines, two shafts. Rated at 70,000 shp (52199 kW)
Dimensions: LOA 820 ft (249.9 m), flight deck width 106 ft (32.3m), beam 106 ft (32.3m), draft 27 ft (8.2m)
Displacement: Approx. 38,957 tons (35341 tonnes) with full load
Performance: Maximum speed 24 knots

USS *Peleliu* (LHA 5)

Named for the World War II battle on the Pacific Island where, for their heroic efforts, eight US Marines were awarded the Congressional Medal of Honor.

The USS *Wasp* (LHD 1) is the oldest of the multipurpose amphibious assault ships, having entered service in the late 1980s. Its home port is Norfolk, Virginia.

Home Port: San Diego, California
Keel Laid: 12 November 1976
Launched: 25 November 1978
Commissioned: 30 May 1980

Builders: Ingalls Shipbuilding Inc., Ingalls, Mississippi
Power Plant: Two boilers, two geared steam turbines, two shafts. Rated at 70,000 shp (52199 kW)
Dimensions: LOA 820 ft (249.9 m), flight deck width 106 ft (32.3m), beam 106 ft (32.3m), draft 27 ft (8.2m)
Displacement: Approx. 38,976 tons (35358 tonnes) with full load
Performance: Maximum speed 24 knots

USS *Wasp* (LHD 1)

LHD 1 is the 10th ship to bear the name *Wasp*. During World War II, aircraft carriers CV 7 and CV 18 were so named.
Home Port: Norfolk, Virginia
Keel Laid: 28 February 1984
Launched: 30 April 1985
Commissioned: 6 July 1989

Builders: Ingalls Shipbuilding Inc., Ingalls, Mississippi
Power Plant: Two boilers, two geared steam turbines, two shafts. Rated at 70,000 shp (52199 kW)
Dimensions: LOA 844 ft (257.3 m), flight deck width 110 ft (33.5 m), beam 106 ft (32.3 m), draft 28 ft (8.5 m)
Displacement: Approx. 40,530 tons (36768 tonnes) with full load
Performance: Maximum speed 20+ knots

US Marine Corps

USS *Essex* (LHD 2)
Named for the lead ship of the Navy's largest class of aircraft carrier, LHD 2 is the fifth ship to bear this name.
Home Port: San Diego, California
Keel Laid: 20 March 1989
Launched: 23 February 1991
Commissioned: 17 October 1992

Builders: Ingalls Shipbuilding Inc., Ingalls, Mississippi
Power Plant: Two boilers, two geared steam turbines, two shafts. Rated at 70,000 shp (52199 kW)
Dimensions: LOA 844 ft (257.3 m), flight deck width 110 ft (33.5 m), beam 106 ft (32.3 m), draft 30 ft (9.1 m)
Displacement: Approx. 40,530 tons (36768 tonnes) with full load
Performance: Maximum speed 20+ knots

USS *Kearsarge* (LHD 3)
LHD 3 is the fourth USS *Kearsarge*. The previous ship was an Essex-class aircraft carrier (CV 33) named for the New Hampshire mountain.
Home Port: Norfolk, Virginia
Keel Laid: 6 February 1990
Launched: 26 March 1992
Commissioned: 16 October 1993

Builders: Ingalls Shipbuilding Inc., Ingalls, Mississippi
Power Plant: Two boilers, two geared steam turbines, two shafts. Rated at 70,000 shp (52199 kW)
Dimensions: LOA 844 ft (257.3 m), flight deck width 110 ft (33.5 m), beam 106 ft (32.3 m), draft 30 ft (9.1 m)
Displacement: Approx. 40,530 tons (36768 tonnes) with full load
Performance: Maximum speed 20+ knots

USS *Boxer* (LHD 4)
LHD 4 is the fifth USS *Boxer*. The previous vessel to bear the name, CV 21, was an Essex-class aircraft carrier.
Home Port: San Diego, California
Keel Laid: 18 April 1991
Launched: 7 August 1993
Commissioned: 11 February 1995

Builders: Ingalls Shipbuilding Inc., Ingalls, Mississippi
Power Plant: Two boilers, two geared steam turbines, two shafts. Rated at 70,000 shp (52199 kW)
Dimensions: LOA 844 ft (257.3 m), flight deck width 110 ft (33.5 m), beam 106 ft (32.3 m), draft 30 ft (9.1 m)
Displacement: Approx. 40,530 tons (36768 tonnes) with full load
Performance: Maximum speed 20+ knots

USS *Bataan* (LHD 5)
LHD 5 is the second vessel to bear the name USS *Bataan*. The original ship (CVL 29) was an Independence-class light aircraft carrier.
Home Port: Norfolk, Virginia
Keel Laid: 22 June 1994
Launched: 15 March 1996
Commissioned: 20 September 1997

Builders: Ingalls Shipbuilding Inc., Ingalls, Mississippi
Power Plant: Two boilers, two geared steam turbines, two shafts. Rated at 70,000 shp (52199 kW)
Dimensions: LOA 844 ft (257.3 m), flight deck width 110 ft (33.5 m), beam 106 ft (32.3 m), draft 30 ft (9.1 m)
Displacement: Approx. 40,530 tons (36768 tonnes) with full load
Performance: Maximum speed 20+ knots

USS *Bon Homme Richard* (LHD 6)
LHD 6 is the newest Wasp-class ship and the second vessel to be named for the flagship of John Paul Jones. The original, CV 31, was an Essex-class aircraft carrier.
Home Port: San Diego, California
Keel Laid: 18 April 1995
Launched: 14 March 1997
Commissioned: 15 August 1998

Builders: Ingalls Shipbuilding Inc., Ingalls, Mississippi
Power Plant: Two boilers, two geared steam turbines, two shafts. Rated at 70,000 shp (52199 kW)
Dimensions: LOA 844 ft (257.3 m), flight deck width 110 ft (33.5 m), beam 106 ft (32.3 m), draft 30 ft (9.1 m)
Displacement: Approx. 40,530 tons (36768 tonnes) with full load
Performance: Maximum speed 20+ knots

USS *Iwo Jima* (LHD 7)
The seventh Wasp-class ship was named for the World War II island battle and also honors the amphibious assault ship (LPH 2), which was the lead vessel in its class.
Keel Laid: 12 December 1997
Commissioning: In 2001

Builders: Ingalls Shipbuilding Inc., Ingalls, Mississippi
Power Plant: Two boilers, two geared steam turbines, two shafts. Rated at 70,000 shp (52199 kW)
Dimensions: LOA 844 ft (257.3 m), flight deck width 110 ft (33.5 m), beam 106 ft (32.3 m), draft 30 ft (9.1 m)
Displacement: Approx. 40,530 tons (36768 tonnes) with full load
Performance: Maximum speed 20+ knots

With a number of CH-46E "Phrogs" on its deck, the USS *Kearsarge* (LHD 3) is seen here during a deployment. The vessel is one of six multipurpose amphibious assault ships currently in naval service.

An AV-8B Harrier belonging to the 'Flying Tigers' of VMA-542, based at MCAS Cherry Point, North Carolina. The squadron is part of MAG-14 with the 2d MAW.

AIRCRAFT

BEECH AIRCRAFT (SEE RAYTHEON AIRCRAFT)

BELL HELICOPTER TEXTRON

Besides HMT-303, the AH-1W FRS, the SuperCobra is flying with a dozen Marine Corps squadrons across all four marine air wings. Included is one UDP unit deployed to MCAS Futemma, Japan. The program to remanufacture 180 "Whiskey" models to "Zulu" configuration is aimed at extending the life of the platform until 2025. By that time it is assumed a joint-service aircraft will be ready to replace the AH-1Z.

Bell AH-1W/Z SuperCobra

The Marine Corps initially had to borrow 38 AH-1Gs from the Army before its own AH-1Js began arriving in September 1970. Unlike the Army variant, which started to enter service five years before, the AH-1J was equipped with a twin-engine Pratt & Whitney Canada T400 power plant, navalized avionics, a rotor brake and a three-barrel 20-mm cannon.

After the AH-1J came the stretched AH-1T, which was fitted with an uprated engine and transmission, and an improved rotor system as well as the longer fuselage. First flown in May 1976, the "Tango" entered service the following year and later production models were equipped to carry AGM-71 TOW missiles. Earlier examples were subsequently retrofitted with the same weapon system.

As a proposed upgrade, a single AH-1T was equipped with General Electric T700 engines and flew for the first time in April 1980. However, funding

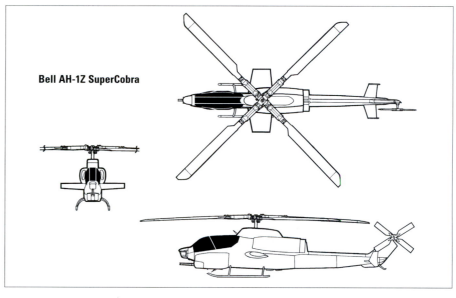

Bell AH-1Z SuperCobra

Bell AH-1Z SuperCobra Specifications

Maximum Takeoff Weight:	14,750 lb (6691 kg)
Empty Weight:	10,200 lb (4627 kg)
Fuselage Length:	45 ft 6 in (13.87 m)
Overall Length:	58 ft 0 in (17.68 m)
Main Rotor Diameter:	48 ft 0 in (14.63 m)
Height:	14 ft 2 in (4.32 m)
Power Plant:	Two General Electric T700-GE-401 turboshaft engines, each rated at 1,625 shp (1,212 kW), driving two-blade main and tail rotors
Maximum Fuel Capacity:	4,552 lb (2065 kg)
Maximum Speed (at sea level):	152 kts (282 km/h)
Service Ceiling:	14,000+ ft (4267+ m)
Operating Range:	317 nm (587 km)
Crew:	2
Armament:	One 20-mm M197 three-barrel gatling gun with 750 rounds; GPU-2/A 20-mm gatling gun pods; AGM-71 TOW, AGM-114 Hellfire, AGM-122A Sidearm missiles; AIM-9 Sidewinders, AIM-92 Stinger missiles; 2.75-in (70-mm) Hydra and 5-in Zuni rockets
Mission Equipment:	Night-targeting system (NTS) equipped with television and infrared sensors, and a laser range finder
Missions:	Close air support (CAS)

limitations delayed delivery of a production variant AH-1T Plus until November 1983. By that time, however, many more systems had been modified and the aircraft was redesignated the AH-1W when it entered service in October 1986. The "Whiskey" is flying today armed with AGM-114 Hellfires and AIM-9 Sidewinders.

The Corps is proceeding to reengine and remanufacture up to 180 AH-1Ws to AH-1Z configuration. The aircraft are receiving new four-blade composite main and tail rotors (first flown on the AH-1W in January 1989), new gearboxes and a transmission rated at 2,625 shp (1958 kW). The "Zulu's" power train, hydraulics and electrical system will have 85 percent commonality with the UH-1Y, and its main rotors will feature semiautomatic folding. A lengthened tail boom, incorporating a new end-plated elevator, will be added as will a fully integrated advanced targeting system and new sensors that include a laser range finder/designator, high-resolution FLIR, GPS with integrated INS and digital map display. The attack helicopter's internal fuel capacity will be increased and the new rotor, gearbox and transmission will provide the AH-1Z with 30 percent more power and a higher cruise speed. Additionally, the SuperCobra's useful load will almost double while its maximum range will improve by 25 percent.

Bell HH/UH-1N, UH-1Y Iroquois ("Huey")

Although the Marine Corps began receiving Bell UH-1Es in 1964, the twin-engine UH-1N variant flying today did not start to enter the inventory until 1971. These helicopters are assigned to a single FRS, six deployable active-duty units and two reserve squadrons, whereas the sub-variant HH-1Ns that remain in service are assigned to air stations for SAR. In addition to serving in traditional assault and utility roles, the "Huey" flies as a command and control (C²) platform as well as in reconnaissance, medical evacuation and combat search and rescue (CSAR) roles. The UH-1N is also used to a limited degree as a gunship to support assault forces.

The Marine Corps is proceeding with plans to reengine and remanufacture up to 100 UH-1Ns to UH-1Y configuration. This includes installing the T700-GE-401 turboshaft engine, new four-blade composite main and tail rotors, new gearboxes and a transmission rated at 2,625 shp (1958 kW) that will also result in a high degree of commonality with the AH-1Z, as described on the previous page. The old UH-1N's fuselage will be lengthened by 20 inches (0.51 m), thereby allowing avionics to be relocated and the internal fuel load to be increased. The avionics are being developed under the Huey 2000 program and include the AN/AAQ-22 FLIR, a "glass" cockpit compatible with night-vision goggles (NVG), a head-up display (HUD), a GPS and satellite communications (SATCOM).

Under the program, the helicopter's fuel load and endurance will nearly double, the latter increasing to 3.2 hours. In addition, its range will improve by almost one-third and the "Huey's" useful load will increase from 3,155 lb (1431 kg) to 7,100 lb (3221 kg). The upgrades are designed to allow the UH-1 to remain an effective Marine Corps platform through 2020.

Finished in tactical gray, BuNo 159208/QT-416 is a UH-1N serving with HMT-303, the "Huey" FRS at MCAS Pendleton, California.

Bell UH-1Y Iroquois Specifications

Maximum Takeoff Weight:	18,500 lb (8392 kg)
Empty Weight:	11,400 lb (5171 kg)
Fuselage Length:	43 ft 11.5 in (13.40 m)
Overall Length:	58 ft 2.75 in (17.74 m)
Main Rotor Diameter:	48 ft 0 in (14.63 m)
Height:	13 ft 10.5 in (4.23 m)
Power Plant:	Two General Electric T700-GE-401 turboshaft engines, each rated at 1,723 shp (1285 kW), driving four-blade main and tail rotors
Maximum Fuel Capacity:	2,584 lb (1172 kg)
Maximum Speed (at sea level):	159 kts (294 km/h)
Operating Range:	349 nm (646 km)
Crew:	3-4
Accommodations:	8/10 troops or six litters and a single attendant
Armament:	Crew-fired 7.62-mm M60 machine gun or 7.62-mm GAU-2B minigun or GAU-16 .50-cal (12.7-mm) machine gun. Aircraft also can carry forward-firing weapons including 2.75-in (70-mm) rockets.
Mission Equipment:	AN/AAQ-22 FLIR
Missions:	Command and control (C²), amphibious assault, air ambulance, search and rescue (SAR), combat search and rescue (CSAR), gunship

Painted in "hi-viz" red and yellow, this HH-1N, BuNo 158288/QT-420, serves as a search and rescue (SAR) and training ship with HMT-303, the "Huey" FRS at MCAS Pendleton.

BELL HELICOPTER TEXTRON/ BOEING COMPANY

Bell Boeing MV-22B Osprey

First flown in March 1989, the Bell Boeing MV-22B formally entered the Marine Corps inventory in May 1999 when the first production aircraft was delivered to the Multiservice Operational Test Team (MOTT) at NAS Patuxent River, Maryland. Low-rate initial production (LRIP) began in April 1997, and funding has been released for a total of 29 aircraft. The tilt-rotor initially will replace CH-46E Sea Knights in the medium-lift role, and later take over the missions of the remaining CH-53Ds as well as those performed by some CH-53Es. Twenty-two squadrons are scheduled to transition to the MV-22B, including 18 active-duty and 4 reserve units.

During February 1999, the MV-22B underwent initial sea trials aboard the USS *Saipan* (LHA 2) during which it logged 347 landings. Additional sea trials commenced in August 1999 and operational evaluation (OPEVAL) was begun during the fall. This test phase is expected to last six months.

Current plans call for a total of 360 MV-22Bs to be delivered to the Marine Corps by 2014, and the tilt-rotor is expected to reach IOC in 2001. The first operational squadron will deploy as part of an MEU in July 2003.

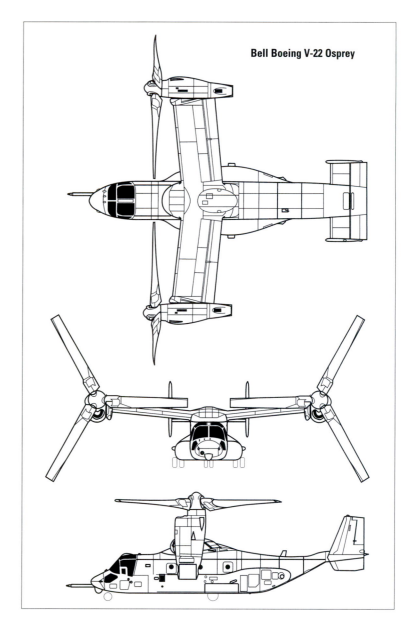

Bell Boeing V-22 Osprey

Bell Boeing MV-22B Osprey Specifications

Maximum Takeoff Weight:	Vertical takeoff – 52,870 lb (23981 kg)
	Short takeoff – 57,000 lb (25855 kg)
Empty Weight:	33,140 lb (15032 kg)
Fuselage Length:	Operational – 57 ft 4 in (17.48 m), Folded – 62 ft 7 in (19.08 m)
Overall Width:	83 ft 9.5 in (25.54 m)
Rotor Diameter:	38 ft 0 in (11.58 m)
Height:	21 ft 9 in (6.63 m)
Power Plant:	Two Rolls-Royce Allison T406-AD-400 turboshaft engines, each rated at 6,150 shp (4586 kW), driving tandem rotors
Maximum Fuel Capacity:	13,601 lb (6169 kg)
Maximum Speed (at sea level):	275 kts (509 km/h)
Service Ceiling:	26,000 ft (7925 m)
Operating Range:	514 nm (952 km)
Crew:	3
Accommodations:	24 troops or 12 litters or 10,000 lb (4536 kg) of cargo or a combination of both
Armament:	Crew-operated .50-cal (12.7-mm) machine guns
Mission Equipment:	AN/AAQ-15 FLIR
Missions:	Medium-lift amphibious assault

MV-22B, BuNo 165433, is the first of 12 Lot 1 low-rate initial production (LRIP) Ospreys being built for the Marine Corps.

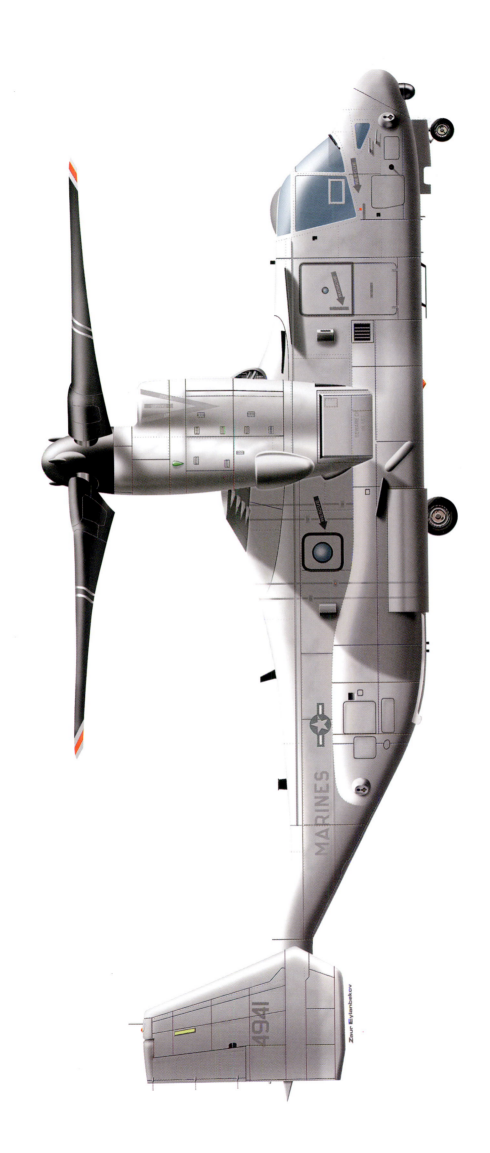

BuNo 164941, is the third Engineering and Manufacturing Development (EMD) Bell Boeing MV-22B Osprey. It was delivered to NAS Patuxent River, Maryland, on 3 October 1997.

MARINES

4941

Zaur Eylanbekov

BOEING COMPANY (INCL. McDONNELL DOUGLAS)

McDonnell Douglas AV-8B, TAV-8B Harrier II/Harrier II(Plus)

With the need to develop a follow-on aircraft to the AV-8A Harrier, the AV-8B flight-test program got underway in November 1978 when the first of two YAV-8B prototypes took to the air. McDonnell Douglas was issued a full-scale development contract for the new Harrier in April 1979, and the first example flew in November 1981. Whereas the prototypes were AV-8As fitted with a new composite wing, production AV-8Bs incorporated a redesigned fuselage with a raised cockpit and larger intakes, and were 18 inches (0.46 m) longer aft of the wing. In reality, this was a new airplane.

On completion of the flight-test program, the first production AV-8B flew in August 1983 and the type entered service in January 1984. Development of a night-attack variant began the following year. Equipped with a forward-looking infrared (FLIR) navigation system, a wide-angle head-up display (HUD), color head-down displays and a color digital moving-map display, it made its initial test flight in June 1987 fitted with an F402-RR-408 Pegasus engine in place of the earlier version. Four additional chaff/flare dispensers were also installed and a larger leading-edge root extension (LERX) was added as part of the aerodynamic modifications. The first production night-attack AV-8B was delivered on 15 September 1989.

McDonnell Douglas AV-8B Harrier II(Plus) Specifications

Maximum Takeoff Weight:	Short takeoff – 32,000 lb (14515 kg)
	Vertical takeoff – 18,950 lb (8596 kg)
Empty Weight:	14,867 lb (6744 kg)
Fuselage Length:	47 ft 9 in (14.55 m)
Wingspan:	30 ft 4 in (9.25 m)
Height:	11 ft 8 in (3.56 m)
Power Plant:	One Rolls-Royce Pegasus F402-RR-408A turbofan engine, rated at 23,400 lb st (104.09 kN)
Maximum Fuel Capacity:	Internal – 7,759 lb (3519 kg)
	External – Up to four 300-gal (1136 lit) fuel tanks
Maximum Speed (at sea level):	574 kts (1063 km/h)
Service Ceiling:	50,000+ ft (15240+ m)
Operating Range:	CAS – 90 nm (167 km) with 60 minutes time on station with short takeoff run; Ferry range – 1,751 nm (3243 km)
Crew:	1
Armament:	One GAU-12 25-mm five-barrel cannon with 300 rounds carried in two fuselage-mounted pods; 10 weapon stations capable of carrying 12,000 lb (5443 kg) of ordnance including Mk 82/83/84 GP bombs, cluster munitions or 2.75-in (70-mm) rockets; AGM-65 Maverick missiles; AIM-9 Sidewinder missiles
Mission Equipment:	AN/APG-65 radar, AN/AAR-51 navigation FLIR
Missions:	CAS, deep strike, interdiction

Meanwhile, development of a stretched, radar-equipped variant of the Harrier had begun the previous year and a prototype made its first flight in September 1992, followed by the first of 27 new-production aircraft in March 1993. Delivery to the Marine Corps began the following month. In addition to the radar system, the new variant retained the FLIR and night-attack capabilities.

The AV-8B is currently in service with seven squadrons assigned to the 2d and 3d MAWs, including the FRS, and each of the operational units is nominally assigned 16 aircraft. The FRS also flies twin-seat TAV-8Bs. The 3d MAW operates the AV-8B and its night-attack variant, and has begun receiving the radar-equipped AV-8B, whereas squadrons belonging to the 2d MAW fly a mix of standard AV-8Bs and radar-equipped models. Plans call for 72 day-attack AV-8Bs to be remanufactured to Harrier II(Plus) configuration but the service is considering modifying a further 16 examples as well. Despite having been built in three distinct versions, all single-seat Harriers are designated AV-8Bs.

Marine Corps Harrier squadrons are regularly tasked to provide MEU/ACE detachments for deployment aboard naval amphibious vessels.

The revised nose contour of the rocket-equipped AV-8B Harrier II(Plus) is clearly evident in this view of two MAG-14 aircraft in trail formation.

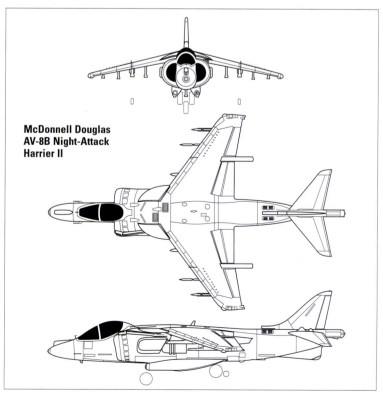

McDonnell Douglas AV-8B Night-Attack Harrier II

Boeing (McDonnell Douglas) AV-8B Harrier II(Plus), BuNo 164566/WP 04
Unit: VMA-223 'Bulldogs,' 2d MAW
Base: MCAS Cherry Point, North Carolina

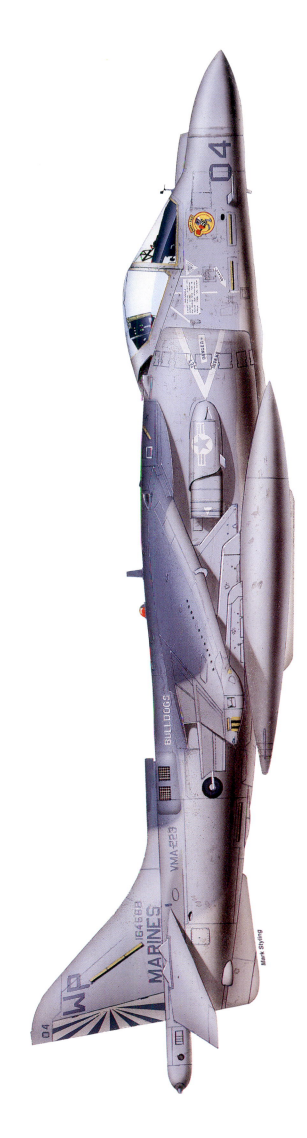

The radar-equipped Harrier II(Plus) has enhanced air-to-air potential and better day-attack capabilities.
This example carries on its nose the full-color insignia of 'the Great American Bulldogs.'

US Marine Corps

McDonnell Douglas C-9B Skytrain II

The Marine Corps operates a pair of C-9Bs from MCAS Cherry Point, North Carolina. Like those assigned to naval squadrons, they receive mission tasking from the Joint Operational Support Command (JOSAC) and Naval Aviation Logistic Office (NALO).

Specifications: See US Navy section for details.

Missions: Operational support airlift (OSA), fleet logistic support.

The McDonnell Douglas C-9B Skytrain II is a variant of the DC-9 airliner and is used to transport Marine Corps personnel and equipment. It is operated by the 'Roadrunners' of VMR-1.

Boeing CH-46E Sea Knight

The Boeing CH-46 is the primary assault helicopter of the Marine Corps and was first delivered in October 1964. It replaced the piston-engine Sikorsky CH-34, and more than 230 Sea Knights (or "Phrogs" as they are known to their crews) are serving today with 15 active-duty and two reserve, medium-lift helicopter squadrons. Each is assigned 12 aircraft. These units form the core of the ACE for an MEU and airlift troops, weapons and supplies during an amphibious assault. In addition to the fleet units, HMX-1 also operates the CH-46E for its presidential support mission.

Although MV-22B Ospreys will soon begin replacing Sea Knights in service, it will be some time before the type is retired completely. To ensure the aging helicopter continues to be an effective platform for the remainder of its planned life, Boeing is undertaking what is referred to as the Dynamic Component Update (DCU). Under this program, many of the parts that make up the power train are being replaced. The first modified aircraft was delivered back to the service in September 1995, and the program is scheduled for completion during 2000.

In service with the Marine Corps for more than 35 years, the CH-46E "Phrog" is a vital medium-lift assault asset. Over the course of the next decade it will be replaced by the Bell Boeing MV-22B Osprey.

Boeing CH-46E Sea Knight Specifications

Maximum Takeoff Weight:	24,300 lb (11022 kg)
Empty Weight:	15,537 lb (7048 kg)
Fuselage Length:	45 ft 8 in (13.92 m)
Overall Length:	Operational – 84 ft 4 in (25.71 m), Folded – 45 ft 8 in (13.92 m)
Rotor Diameter:	51 ft 0 in (15.55 m)
Height:	16 ft 8 in (5.08 m)
Power Plant:	Two General Electric T58-GE-16 turboshaft engines, each rated at 1,870 shp (1395 kW) driving tandem three-blade main rotors
Maximum Fuel Capacity:	2,362 lb (1071 kg)
Maximum Speed (at sea level):	143 kts (265 km/h)
Operating Range:	550 nm (1019 km) with a 2,400-lb (1089-kg) payload
Crew:	3
Accommodations:	Up to 24 passengers or 17 troops or 6,000 lb (2722 kg) of cargo, although operationally the normal load is 12 troops or 4,000 lb (1814 kg) of cargo. Alternatively, 15 litters and two attendants can be accommodated.
Armament:	Crew-operated .50-cal. (12.7-mm) machine gun
Missions:	Medium-lift assault

McDonnell Douglas F/A-18A/B/C/D Hornet

The Marine Corps began replacing its F-4N/S Phantoms when the service received its first F/A-18As in January 1983. Thereafter, F/A-18Cs replaced early Hornet variants in all but two active-duty squadrons. However, reserve squadrons continued to fly the F-4S until the last unit transitioned to the F/A-18A in 1992.

Beginning in 1990, night-attack variants of the two-seat F/A-18D replaced the A-6E in the all-weather strike role and later assumed the forward air controller (airborne) (FAC[A]) and tactical air controller (airborne) (TAC[A]) missions upon retirement of the OA-4M and OV-10A/D aircraft. With the introduction of the advanced tactical air reconnaissance system (ATARS) in 1999, these units are now being tasked with tactical reconnaissance, something they have been without since the last RF-4B Phantom was retired in August 1990. ATARS allows the aircraft to collect digital imagery to transmit in real time.

Although a reconnaissance variant of the Hornet was

McDonnell Douglas F/A-18D Hornet Specifications

Maximum Takeoff Weight:	51,900 lb (23541 kg)
Empty Weight:	25,319 lb (11485 kg)
Fuselage Length:	56 ft 0 in (17.07 m)
Wingspan:	Operational – 37 ft 6 in (11.43 m), Folded – 27 ft 6 in (8.38 m)
Height:	15 ft 31/2 in (4.66 m)
Power Plant:	Two General Electric F404-GE-402 low-bypass turbofan engines, each rated at 11,875 lb st (52.8 kN) and 17,775 lb st (79.1 kN) with maximum afterburning
Maximum Fuel Capacity:	10,166 lb (4611 kg)
Maximum Speed:	1,034 kts (1915 km/h)
Service Ceiling:	50,000+ ft (15240+ m)
Typical Combat Radius:	550 nm (1018 km)
Crew:	2
Armament:	20-mm M61A1 gatling gun with 570 rounds; nine weapon stations capable of carrying 17,000 lb (7711 kg) of stores including AIM-7/9/120 air-to-air missiles, AGM-65/84/88 air-to-surface missiles, AGM-154 JSOW, GBU-31 JDAM, Mk 82/83/84 GP bombs, laser-guided bombs and cluster munitions
Mission Equipment:	AN/APG-73 radar, AN/AAS-38 FLIR pod, AN/ASQ-173 laser designator, ATARS
Missions:	All-weather strike fighter, FAC, aerial reconnaissance

A pair of F/A-18A Hornets (BuNos 162455 and 162407) during a training sortie over southern California on 7 July 1998. They serve with the 'Smoke' of VMFA-134, a reserve unit with MAG-46, 4th MAW, based at MCAS Miramar.

proposed as early as 1981, ATARS development did not begin until 1988, and test flights commenced only in 1995. The system made its operational debut in combat conditions over the Balkans in 1999, and will be deployed ultimately with each of the six all-weather F/A-18D squadrons. A third LRIP lot of ATARSs was recently approved by the US Navy. Although similar to standard F/A-18Ds, the ATARS-equipped aircraft do not have dual controls, and the rear cockpit contains a pair of multifunction displays along with two side-stick weapon controllers.

Remaining F/A-18As, which are assigned to two active-duty and four reserve squadrons, will soon receive an avionics update that is still under development. It will include radar, communications and computer upgrades to make the variant operationally and logistically compatible with the F/A-18C. Although it is likely that the upgraded

aircraft will be known as the F/A-18A(Plus), the additional avionics and radar modifications will more accurately result in an F/A-18C(Minus). The upgrades will also allow the older Hornet to carry the AIM-120, and the AN/AAS-38B attack FLIR will enable it to deliver precision-guided munitions.

F/A-18s currently are assigned to 15 active-duty units, including the FRS, as well as four reserve units. Each of the attack (VMFA) and all-weather-attack (VMFA[AW]) squadrons are assigned 12 Hornets. The Corps has no plans to field the F/A-18E/F. Instead, it intends to fly the F/A-18C/D until the Joint Strike Fighter (JSF) enters operational service.

Another F/A-18A reserve operator is VMFA-321. The 'Hells Angels' are based at NAF Washington, Maryland. Sporting special red, white and blue tail markings this Hornet is seen making an approach to the field on 25 June 1998.

CESSNA AIRCRAFT

Cessna UC-35C Citation Ultra, UC-35D Citation Encore

The first of two UC-35Cs was delivered to the 4th MAW at NAS New Orleans, Louisiana, on 22 November 1999. The second aircraft will operate from NAS Miramar, California, and both will replace a pair of CT-39G Sabreliners that were transferred in mid-1999 to NAS Pensacola, Florida. They will be used there for training purposes.

The Citation Ultra is similar to the US Army's UC-35A, and the Marine Corps plans to purchase another variant, built to Citation Encore standard, that will be similar to the UC-35B in Army service.

Specifications: See US Army section for details.

Missions: Operational support airlift (OSA).

The Corps is adding two UC-35C Citation Ultras to its fleet to replace aging CT-39G Sabreliners.

US Marine Corps

The Gulfstream IV, designated the C-20G in Marine Corps service, is powered by two Rolls-Royce Tay Mk 611-8 turbofans, each rated at 13,850 lb st (61.61 kN). Fitted with drag-reducing winglets, the C-20G cruises at between 454 and 509 kts (841–943 km/h) and has a range of 2,000 nm (3704 km).

GENERAL DYNAMICS (INCL. GULFSTREAM AEROSPACE)

C-20G Gulfstream IV

A single C-20G, delivered in December 1994 to the Marine Aviation Support Detachment (MASD) at NAF Washington, Maryland, was acquired to transport the commandant of the Marine Corps. However, it has been out of service since 2 February 1998, when it was heavily damaged by a tornado at Miami International Airport. Although some minor work has been undertaken the cost of fully repairing the aircraft has been estimated at $15 million. In the meantime, it remains in storage at Midcoast Aviation's facility in Cahogia, Illinois.

Specifications: See the US Navy section for details.

Missions: Operational support airlift (OSA), fleet logistic support.

LOCKHEED MARTIN

Lockheed KC-130F/J/R/T

The Marine Corps ordered the Hercules in 1960 and the first of 46 examples, initially designated GV-1s, entered service in 1961. The aircraft was redesignated the KC-130F in 1962 and was based on a standard C-130B airframe powered by four 4,050-shp (3020-kW) Allison T56-A-7 turboprops. To serve as an in-flight refueler, it was equipped with a removable 3,600-gallon (13627-liter) fuel tank in the cargo compartment and removable refueling pods under each wing.

Beginning in 1976, the service accepted 14 KC-130Rs, which are based on the C-130H airframe and fitted with more powerful T56-A-15 engines. This variant can carry more fuel in two 1,360-gallon (5148-liter) external tanks. Seven years later, the first of 28 KC-130Ts was delivered to the Corps. Also based on the C-130H, all examples of this variant were delivered to the Marine Corps Reserve. They feature updated avionics, improved navigation systems and a color weather radar. Some examples have also received defensive countermeasures. Yet another variant, incorporating a 15-foot (4.57-m) fuselage "stretch," has recently entered service. The two KC-130T-30s are capable of carrying more cargo and accommodating up to 128 troops or 97 litters.

In Marine Corps service the primary role of the Hercules is to refuel fixed-wing aircraft and helicopters during deployments and tactical operations.

Lockheed KC-130R Hercules Specifications	
Maximum Takeoff Weight:	175,000 lb (79379 kg)
Empty Weight:	79,981 lb (36279 kg)
Fuselage Length:	97 ft 9 in (29.79 m)
Wingspan:	132 ft 7 in (40.41 m)
Height:	38 ft 3 in (11.66 m)
Power Plant:	Four Allison T56-A-15 turboprop engines, each rated at 4,591 shp (3424 kW), driving four-blade propellers.
Maximum Fuel Capacity:	Internal – 46,980 lb (21310 kg) Removable, internal – 18,360 lb (8328 kg) External – 24,300 lb (11022 kg)
Maximum Speed:	302 kts at 19,000 ft (559 km/h at 5791 m)
Service Ceiling:	25,000 ft (7620 m)
Operating Range:	2,564 nm (4749 km) with maximum payload
Crew:	5
Accommodations:	92 troops or 64 paratroops or 74 litters or 26,913 lb (12208 kg) of cargo; when operating in the tanker role, the KC-130R can off-load almost 50,000 lb (22680 kg) of fuel
Armament:	None
Missions:	Aerial refueling, aeromedical evacuation, fleet logistic support

The current KC-130R can carry more fuel in its two underwing tanks than its predecessor.

A KC-130F from VMGR-252 refuels two AV-8B Harriers from the 'Black Sheep' of VMA-214, based at MCAS Yuma, Arizona. The tanker is flown by a 'Heavy Haulers' crew from MCAS Cherry Point, North Carolina.

BuNo 162308 is a KC-130T Hercules assigned to VMGR-234, one of two 4th MAW units that fly the type.

However, it is also tasked with air assault and logistic support, and two KC-130s are nominally assigned to each deployed MEU.

Although a number of older KC-130F/Rs were included in an avionics system improvement program (ASIP) undertaken in the mid-1990s, the Navy intends to equip the entire Marine Corps Hercules fleet with "glass" cockpits. In the meantime, the Corps has already begun acquiring next-generation C-130s. The first of seven KC-130Js on order has been received by VMGR-252 at MCAS Cherry Point, North Carolina. That unit will operate all of the new airlifters, which are equipped with Mk32B-901E refueling pods made by Flight Refueling Ltd. Driven by ram-air boost pumps, the pods are capable of delivering fuel at nearly twice the rate of earlier KC-130 systems.

The Hercules platform has now served the Marine Corps for almost 40 years and, in addition to a single FRS, the tanker currently flies with three active-duty and two reserve squadrons.

The KC-130J's improved propulsion system means it can refuel other aircraft while flying some 30 knots faster than earlier Hercules tankers.

NORTHROP GRUMMAN

Grumman EA-6B Prowler

Since June 1998, the EA-6B Prowler has been the only tactical jamming platform available to US forces. A fixture aboard US Navy carriers since 1971, the type is flown today by four Marine Corps electronic jamming (VMAQ) squadrons, each of which is assigned five EA-6Bs. In addition to normal operations, and as part of the Unit Deployment Program (UDP), the units are also attached on a rotational basis to the 1st MAW at MCAS Iwakuni, Japan.

The first operational Prowlers were delivered on 1 December 1965 to Marine Composite Reconnaissance Squadron Two (VMCJ-2) at MCAS Cherry Point, North Carolina, and deployed to Southeast Asia the following year. The first 12 aircraft, all of which were built from Intruder airframes, were fitted with the AN/ALQ-53 electronic countermeasures (ECM) reconnaissance system, AN/ALR-15 radar warning receiver (RWR), and AN/ALQ-41, -51 and -55 jammers. Fifteen purpose-built EA-6As were also delivered to three units over 10 years, beginning in the mid-1960s.

The EA-6B was created by adding a 54-inch (1.37-m) "plug" forward of the wing. This was to accommodate an additional cockpit designed to house two more electronic countermeasures officers (ECMOs). [New systems fitted to the aircraft are described in the US Navy section of this book] VAQ-132 was the first unit to fly the new Prowler operationally and chalked up the first combat missions in July 1966, when deployed aboard the USS *America*.

Recently, the VMAQ units began supporting Operation Northern Watch from Incirlik AB in Turkey, and were heavily tasked during Operation Allied Force flying missions from Aviano AB in Northern Italy.

The 'Moondogs' of VMAQ-3 are based at MCAS Cherry Point, North Carolina, which is also home to the other three Marine Corps Prowler squadrons. This EA-6B is carrying a AN/ALQ-99 Tactical Jamming System (TJS) pod and external fuel tank under its port wing, and an air-to-ground AGM-88 HARM and another tank on the starboard side.

Specifications: See the US Navy section for details.

Missions: Electronic warfare (EW), suppression of enemy air defenses (SEAD).

US Marine Corps

Northrop F-5E/F Tiger II

As the only Marine Reserve fighter training or "aggressor" squadron, VMFT-401 has operated F-5E/Fs since 1989 when leased F-21A Kfirs it had been using for the same mission were returned to Israel. The Tiger IIs equipping the 'Snipers' are ex-Air Force and ex-Navy examples that are now used to instruct active-duty and reserve Marine Corps pilots in air combat tactics and doctrine. Fast and agile, the type is quite effective in the "threat" simulation role but does not possess the "high-alpha" and sustained-turn characteristics of advanced fighter jets like the MiG-29 'Fulcrum.' The Tiger II does not normally carry external fuel tanks and therefore has an endurance of about 40 minutes only.

The type is flown from MCAS Yuma in the Arizona desert, located close to 10,000 square miles (25900 sq km) of airspace and 2,000 square miles (5180 sq km) of land reserved for air combat maneuvering (ACM), aerial bombing and gunnery practice.

Specifications: See the US Navy section for details.

Missions: Dissimilar air combat training (DACT).

In addition to carrying AIM-9L Sidewinders on its wing rails for self-defense, the F-5E Tiger II is equipped with a pair of nose-mounted Colt Browning M39A2 20-mm cannon.

PIONEER UAV

RQ-2A Pioneer

The Pioneer is currently employed by two unmanned aerial vehicle (UAV) squadrons assigned to the 2d and 3d MAWs. Each unit operates a single system composed of six RQ-2As, a ground control station, a tracking unit, a portable control station, four remote receiving stations, pneumatic or rocket-assisted launchers and a net arrestment system for recovery. The UAVs are operated from land bases and from US Navy LPD vessels when deployed as part of an MEU.

Specifications: See the US Navy section for details.

Missions: Reconnaissance, surveillance and target acquisition (RSTA); bomb damage assessment.

An RQ-2A being sent aloft from a pneumatic launcher.

RAYTHEON AIRCRAFT (INCL. BEECH AIRCRAFT)

Beech T-34C Turbo Mentor

Developed from its earlier basic Model 45 trainer, Beech created the turbo-powered T-34C to serve the Navy as a more versatile initial training aircraft. It flies with just one Marine Corps unit, the 3d MAW's VMFAT-101, which is the F/A-18A/B/C/D FRS.

Specifications: See the US Navy section for details.

Mission: Range clearance.

The T-34C Mentor is flown by the 'Sharpshooters' of VMFAT-101 at MCAS Miramar, California.

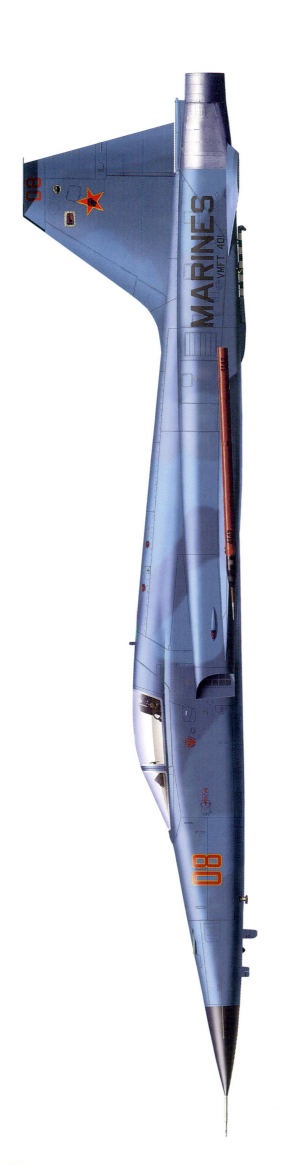

Northrop F-5E Tiger II
Unit: VMFT-401 'Snipers,' 4th MAW
Base: MCAS Yuma, Arizona

"Aggressor" aircraft serving with VMFT-401 are painted in a variety of camouflage schemes. They include the blue/gray combination (above) associated with the Su-27 'Flanker,' and earth colors that depict the MiG-23/27 'Flogger.'

US Marine Corps

BuNo 161320/5T is a UC-12A and one of three King Airs operated by VMR-2 at MCAS Miramar, California.

Beech UC-12B/F King Air (Huron)

Marine Corps UC-12Bs are assigned to most air stations within the United States while UC-12Fs are located at bases in Japan. The aircraft are assigned to air station headquarters and headquarters squadrons (H&HS) or marine transport squadrons (VMR), and operate in the OSA role. Their missions are scheduled by the Joint Operational Support Airlift Center or the Naval Air Logistics Office.

Specifications: See the US Navy section for details.

Missions: Operational support airlift (OSA), fleet logistic support.

Making an approach to the former MCAS El Toro, California, BuNo 159365 is a CT-39G Sabreliner, one of three operated by the Corps until 1999. Two have now been returned to the Navy.

SABRELINER CORPORATION (INCL. NORTH AMERICAN)

North American CT-39G Sabreliner

A single CT-39G remains assigned to MCAS Futemma, Japan, after two others that previously operated from MCAS Miramar, California, and NAS New Orleans JRB, Louisiana, were returned to the Navy. They will be replaced in Fiscal Year 2000 (FY00) by two Cessna UC-35C Citation Ultras.

Specifications: See the US Navy section for details.

Missions: Operational support airlift (OSA), fleet logistic support.

SIKORSKY AIRCRAFT

Sikorsky CH-53D/E Sea Stallion/Super Stallion

The Sikorsky CH-53D Sea Stallion entered service in 1968, replacing CH-53As in the heavy-lift role. Beginning in 1981, however, the more powerful CH-53E began to take over many of the CH-53D's missions and less than 50 remain in service today. All are located in Hawaii with eight examples assigned to each of four operational squadrons, while the remainder serve with the training unit. Plans call for the helicopter to be replaced by the MV-22B after 2006.

A CH-53D, operated by HMH-362, makes its approach to MCAF Kaneohe Bay, Hawaii. The Oahu base is home to the entire fleet of twin-engine Sea Stallions.

Sikorsky CH-53E Super Stallion, BuNo 162002 [Modex YJ-22]
Unit: HMH-465 'Warhorses,' MAG-16, 3d MAW
Base: MCAS Miramar, California

Sikorsky CH-53E Super Stallion, BuNo 161995 [Modex EN-16]
Unit: HMH-464 'Condors,' MAG-29, 2d MAW
Base: MCAS New River, North Carolina

Mark Styling

US Marine Corps

Sikorsky CH-53D Sea Stallion Specifications

Maximum Takeoff Weight:	42,000 lb (19051 kg)
Empty Weight:	24,606 lb (11161 kg)
Fuselage Length:	67 ft 2 in (20.47 m)
Overall Length:	88 ft 3in (26.90 m)
Main Rotor Diameter:	72 ft 3 in (22.02 m)
Height:	24 ft 11 in (7.59 m)
Power Plant:	Two General Electric T64-GE-413 turboshaft engines, each rated at 3,925 shp (2927 kW), driving a six-blade main rotor and four-blade tail rotor
Maximum Fuel Capacity:	Internal – 4,253 lb (1929 kg) External – 6750 lb (3062 kg)
Maximum Speed:	170 kts (315 km/h)
Service Ceiling:	21,000 ft (6401 m)
Operating Range (unrefueled):	886 nm (1641 km)
Crew:	3
Accommodations:	38 troops or 24 litters with four attendants, or 8,000 lb (3600 kg) of cargo carried internally or 20,000 lb (9072 kg) carried externally
Armament:	Crew-operated .50-cal. (12.7-mm) machine gun
Missions:	Heavy-lift assault helicopter

Capable of carrying 8,000 pounds of cargo internally or externally, the CH-53D can transport 38 troops or 24 litters and four attendants in place of cargo. Two reserve units transitioned to the CH-53E during 1998 and retired the last of the ex-Navy RH-53Ds. Fitted with three engines the Super Stallion, which first flew in March 1974, is capable of moving 16 tons of cargo or 55 troops, and six squadrons are operational with the type. Each has 16 aircraft. In addition, the CH-53E is assigned to HMX-1 and a single FRS operates a small number of MH-53Es in support of Navy training requirements.

Not all of the Sea Kings flown by HMX-1 are used as presidential transports. The "Green Tops" serve as priority airlift helicopters for other passengers.

Sikorsky VH-3D Sea King

The VH-3D entered service in 1976 as a replacement for the VH-3A, and 11 examples are in Marine Corps service with HMX-1 at MCAF Quantico, Virginia. Primarily the aircraft are used to transport the president on short trips, along with his staff and key government officials. Several examples are forward based at the former NAS Anacostia in Washington, DC, and those dedicated to presidential support duties are identified by a two-tone, white-over-green paint scheme, while those tasked with normal VIP transport are finished in overall gloss green.

Current initiatives to extend the Sea King's service life involve the addition of a GPS and Traffic Collision Avoidance System (TCAS), plus updates to its survivability system. The latter includes the AN/APR-39 missile-plume detection system, AN/AAR-47 RWR, AN/AVR-2 laser-detection system, AN/ALQ-144 infrared counter-measures system and AN/ALE-47 chaff/flare dispensers. A service-life extension program (SLEP) is currently under way to raise the VH-3D's flight-hour ceiling from 8,500 to 14,000 and thereby enable the aircraft to remain in the inventory through 2017. An upgrade to provide a secure communications link is also in progress.

Specifications: See the US Navy section for details.

Missions: Presidential airlift support, VIP transport.

Sikorsky VH-60N Seahawk

Based on the UH-60A Blackhawk variant, the VH-60N replaced the VH-1N as a Marine Corps executive transport in November 1988. The aircraft is equipped with the SH-60B's gearbox and flight control systems, advanced avionics, soundproofing and a cabin radio operator's station in the executive cabin. Furthermore, it is "hardened" against electromagnetic pulse. Nine examples are assigned to HMX-1 at Quantico, Virginia.

Sikorsky is currently performing a midlife upgrade (MUG) to the

Nine VH-60N Seahawks are operated by HMX-1 from its base at Quantico, Virginia, and represent the only Sikorsky Blackhawk variants in Marine Corps service.

VH-60N that is providing it with a rotor brake, an improved auxiliary power unit (APU) and a stronger landing gear to support higher gross weights. The first Seahawk entered the modification program in June 1998 and the last aircraft is expected to be completed in early 2002. A separate program will equip the VH-60N with a GPS and a TCAS, and the aircraft's survivability equipment, which includes the AN/APR-39 missile plume detection system, AN/AAR-47 RWR, AN/AVR-2 laser-detection system, AN/ALQ-144 infrared countermeasures and AN/ALE-47 chaff/flare dispensers, also is being updated. In addition, a communications system upgrade (CSU) will provide a secure communications link between the helicopter and other platforms like the VH-3D Sea King, Air Force One (VC-25A) and E-4B "Doomsday Plane," and the White House Communications Agency (WHCA).

Sikorsky VH-60N Seahawk Specifications

Maximum Takeoff Weight:	Approx. 24,000 lb (10433 kg)
Empty Weight:	11,284 lb (5118 kg)
Fuselage Length:	50 ft 0.75 in (15.26 m)
Overall Length:	64 ft 10 in (19.76 m)
Main Rotor Diameter:	53 ft 8 in (16.36 m)
Height:	16 ft 10 in (5.13 m)
Power Plant:	Two General Electric T700-GE-700 engines, each rated at 1,560 shp (1163 kW)
Maximum Fuel Capacity:	2,420 lb (1098 kg)
Maximum Speed:	160 kts (296 km/h)
Service Ceiling:	19,000 ft (5791 m)
Operating Range (UH-60L):	326 nm (604 km)
Crew:	4
Accommodations:	Equipped with a nonstandard executive cabin layout
Armament:	None
Mission Equipment:	Weather radar
Missions:	Executive transport helicopter

The Sikorsky CH-53E is flown by 11 Marine Corps units. Among them are the 'Condors' of HMH-464, seen here operating a Super Stallion during an exercise at Twentynine Palms, California, in February 1996.

AIR STATIONS AND FACILITIES

MCAS New River in North Carolina is home to the UH-1N "Hueys," CH-46E Sea Knights and AH-1W SuperCobras operated by MAG-26. Seen here is a pair of "Whiskeys" flying low over the station's McCutcheon Field. The facility has served the Corps since 1944, aside from a six-year spell immediately following World War II.

MCAS Beaufort, South Carolina

Commissioned as a naval air station in 1943, Beaufort served as a training center and supported antisubmarine squadrons during the Second World War. It was deactivated in 1946 but was reactivated as a Marine Corps Auxiliary Air Station (MCAAS) 10 years later, and received its current designation on 1 March 1960. To honor Maj. Gen. Lewis G. Merritt, the airfield was named Merritt Field on 19 September 1975. The facility is currently home to MAG-31 and six strike fighter squadrons.

MCB/MCAS Camp Joseph H. Pendleton, California

Purchased by the Department of the Navy in 1942, Camp Pendleton is located midway between San Diego and Los Angeles, and was declared a "permanent" installation in October 1944. Two years later it became the home of the 1st Marine Division and is now the Corps' largest expeditionary training facility. The camp is named for Maj. Gen. Joseph Henry Pendleton, whereas the airfield is named in honor of Lt. Gen. John C. Munn, the first marine aviator to command the air station, which is home to MAG-39 and eight medium and light-attack helicopter squadrons.

MCAS Cherry Point, North Carolina

Located in Havelock, Cherry Point is home to Commander Marine Corps Air Bases East, the 2d MAW and MAG-14. It was the Marine Corps' largest air station until MCAS Miramar was reestablished in California, in 1997. Naval Aviation Depot Cherry Point is located at the air station, which is also responsible for Marine Corps Auxiliary Landing Field Bogue Field. On 4 September 1941, the airfield was named Cunningham Field for Lt. Col. Alfred A. Cunningham, the first marine aviator.

Edwards AFB, California

On 13 May 1999, the Air Force's premier test facility also became the new home of two Marine Corps Reserve helicopter squadrons. The units belong to MAG-46 at MCAS Miramar and were relocated due to the closure of MCAS El Toro in 1999.

MCB Hawaii

Established on 15 April 1994, when MCAS Kaneohe Bay, Camp H. M. Smith and other Hawaii-based Marine Corps facilities were combined, MCB Hawaii is headquartered at the former MCAS Kaneohe Bay, which was subsequently redesignated a Marine Corps Air Facility.

Built as a small seaplane base in 1939, the facility was later commissioned as NAS Kaneohe Bay. However, naval aviation elements moved to Barbers Point in 1952 and the site was then used by a Marine Corps combined air-ground team. That same year it became a Marine Corps Air Station.

With the closure of NAS Barbers Point in 1999, the Navy returned to Kaneohe Bay. By July, three Navy patrol squadrons, a special projects patrol squadron and a helicopter antisubmarine light squadron had moved there. The Marine Corps currently operates five heavy-helicopter squadrons from the base, assigned to the 1st MAW Aviation Support Element (ASE).

MCAS Miramar, California

Acquired for Army infantry training in 1914, MCAS Miramar was then known as Camp Kearny. Following World War I the facility became an auxiliary field for the Navy and a major air base for the Marine Corps. With the United States' entry into World War II, the base quickly expanded and was named Marine Corps Aviation Base Kearny Mesa in March 1943. It was redesignated Marine Corps Air Depot Miramar the following September, and given the name MCAS Miramar in 1946. Later that same year, however, the Corps moved to MCAS El Toro and the facility was reduced to that of a naval auxiliary air station in June 1947. The Navy later developed Miramar as one of its master jet stations and it subsequently became the busiest field on the West Coast.

In 1993, the BRAC Commission recommended MCAS El Toro and MCAS Tustin be closed and that its Marine Corps units be relocated to Miramar. It was also decided the Navy's units should be moved to other facilities, including NAS Fallon, Nevada; NAS Oceana, Virginia; and NAS Point Mugu, California. As a consequence, NAS Miramar was redesignated MCAS Miramar on 1 October 1997. Today it is the headquarters of the 3d MAW and home to MAG-11 and -16.

Miramar's airfield, Mitscher Field, was given its name on 14 June 1955, in honor of Adm. Marc A. Mitscher, Naval Aviator Number 33. It supports a transport element, nine fixed-wing and eight rotary-wing units.

MCAS New River, North Carolina

Located in Jacksonville, MCAS New River was commissioned as Peterfield Point in

Marine Corps Air Stations and Facilities

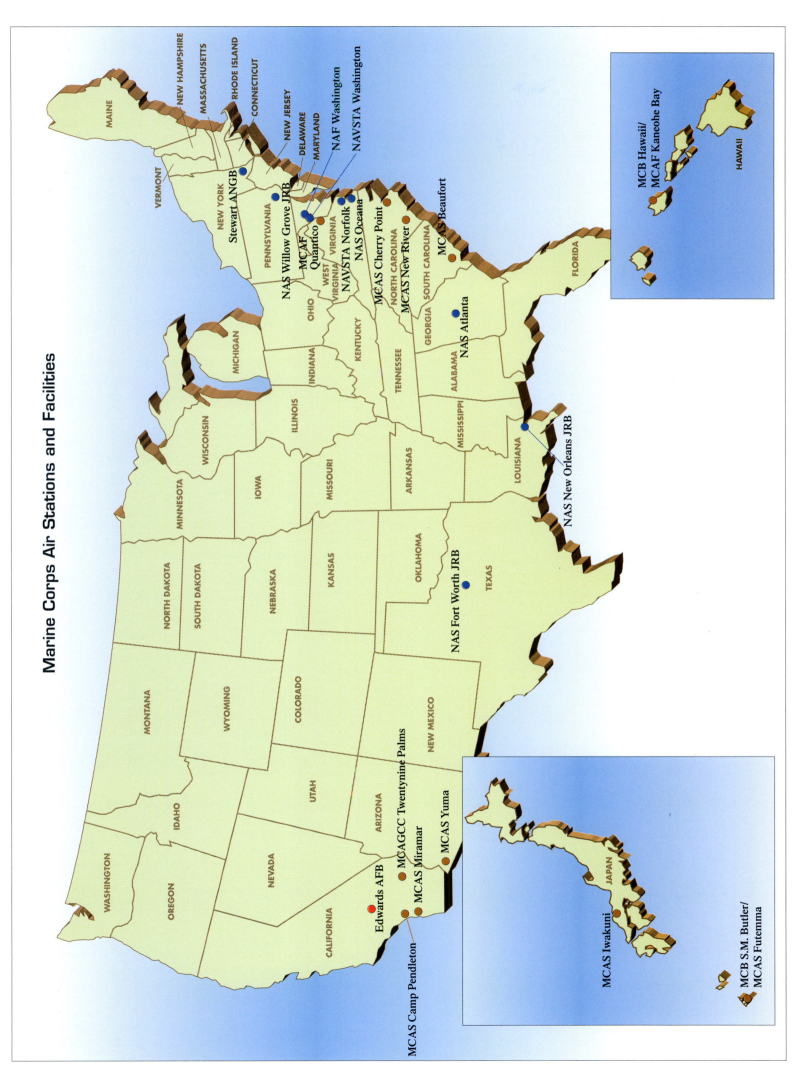

US Marine Corps

April 1944. At the end of World War II, however, it was closed and placed in caretaker status until reactivated as MCAF Peterfield Point, Camp Lejeune, in October 1951. One year later, it was renamed MCAF New River. The facility was given the prefix "MCAS (Helicopter)" on 1 September 1968, but that was changed to simply "MCAS" in 1984. The station is now home to 12 helicopter units assigned to MAG-26 and MAG-29.

In 1972, the airfield was given the name McCutcheon Field in honor of Gen. Keith B. McCutcheon, who was a pioneer in helicopter assault tactics.

MCAF Quantico, Virginia
On 1 July 1936, MCAF Quantico's airfield was named for Col. Thomas C. Turner, a former director of marine aviation. The facility serves as the base of operations for the Corps' VIP transport unit, HMX-1.

of San Bernardino County and, in 1952, the Marine Corps took it over. The site became Headquarters, Marine Corps Training Center, and was commissioned as a Marine Corps base five years later. It subsequently became the Marine Corps Air Ground Combat Center in 1979.

Twentynine Palms was briefly considered as a stationing point for the helicopter squadrons at MCAS Tustin, which was closed in 1999. The idea was subsequently abandoned, however.

MCAS Yuma, Arizona
Adjacent to Yuma International Airport, MCAS Yuma is home to Marine Aviation Weapons and Tactics Squadron One (MAWTS-1), the 3d MAW's MAG-13 and its three AV-8B-equipped attack squadrons, and VMFT-401. The latter is the Corps' adversary training unit.

MCAS Futemma, Japan
Located on the Japanese island of Okinawa, this air station was opened as a US bomber base in 1945. It was commissioned as a Marine Corps Air Facility 15 years later and became MCAS Futemma in 1976. The air station is now the headquarters for MAG-36, and supports the III Marine Expeditionary Force and MCB Camp Butler.

MCAS Iwakuni, Japan
Commissioned as a Japanese naval air station on 8 July 1940, Iwakuni served as a training and defense base throughout World War II. Thereafter it was occupied by various military forces from the United States, Britain, Australia and New Zealand, and was designated a Royal Australian Air Force Base in 1948. The US Air Force took over responsibility for the facility on 1 April 1952, and handed it to the US Navy 30

Stewart ANGB, New York
Located in Newburgh and formerly known as Stewart AFB, this new facility was built in the late 1980s to support a New York ANG unit equipped with C-5A Galaxies. Subsequently, the site was also chosen as the base for a new Marine Corps KC-130T Hercules squadron assigned to MAG-49.

MCAGCC Twentynine Palms, California
From a military standpoint, the history of this facility dates back to 1940 when the US Army used it to train glider crews and fighter pilots. In addition, the Navy had a bombing range at Twentynine Palms until 1945. As a result of changes made to local geographical boundaries at that time, the territory occupied by the facility became part

Opened in 1943, Yuma Army Air Base (AAB) was one of the busiest flying schools in the nation during World War II. At war's end, however, it was closed. In July 1951, the Air Force reactivated the facility as Yuma AB, and renamed it five years later Vincent AFB in memory of Brig. Gen. Clinton D. Vincent, a pioneer of bombing techniques who died in 1955. In January 1959, Yuma was turned over to the Navy and designated a Marine Corps Auxiliary Air Station. It received its current designation in July 1962.

The facility has access to substantial areas set aside nearby as bombing and aviation training ranges, and is the site for 80 percent of the Corps' air-to-ground aviation training. Takeoffs and landings at the station number approximately 300,000 each year.

MCAS Yuma in the Arizona desert is home to the 'Snipers' of VMFT-401 and their 'adversary' F-5E/F Tiger IIs as well as AV-8B night-attack Harrier squadrons VMA-211, -214, -311 and -513. It also serves as the base of operations for Marine Aviation Weapons and Tactics Squadron One. The air station is situated near to the Corps' largest tactical aviation range. Since World War II Yuma has also served variously as a Navy and Air Force facility.

months later. The 1st MAW moved its headquarters from Korea to Iwakuni in July 1956 and, six years later, it was designated an air station. Today, it serves elements of the 1st MAW (which is now headquartered on Okinawa), Japan's Fleet Air Wing 31 and other units of the Japan Maritime Self-Defense Force (JMSDF).

F/A-18A Hornets belonging to the 'Smoke' of Reserve Squadron VMFA-134 stand on the flight line at MCAS Miramar, California.

US COAST GUARD

AVIATION OVERVIEW

Headquartered on the Potomac River at Buzzard Point, in Washington, DC, the United States Coast Guard is a full-time military organization tasked with peacetime missions. It is the world's largest coast guard service, employing 43,000 active-duty, reserve and civilian personnel, and deploys more than 200 aircraft. Its commandant, an admiral, reports directly to the Secretary of Transportation although, for many years, the service came under the Department of the Treasury. In times of national emergency, however, it is attached to the Department of the Navy.

Whether at peace or war, the Coast Guard is at all times one of America's armed forces, as provided under Title 14 of the United States Code, and thus enjoys equal status with the Air Force, Army, Navy and Marine Corps. Officers graduate from the Coast Guard Academy in New London, Connecticut, having received their training and having earned their commissions like their fellow service officers who attended the US Military Academy in West Point, New York; the Naval Academy in Annapolis, Maryland; or the Air Force Academy in Colorado Springs, Colorado.

Coast Guard units regularly operate with those of sister services, which report instead to the Department of Defense, and its assets are regularly tasked to support US Atlantic Command (USACOM), US Pacific Command (USPACOM) and US Southern Command (USSOUTHCOM) via Joint Interagency Task Force East, West and South. During the Gulf War in 1991, for instance, its vessels and aircraft came under US Central Command (USCENTCOM) and HU-25B Guardians (commonly referred to as Falcons) were dispatched to chart oil spills in the Persian Gulf deliberately created by retreating Iraqi forces.

Possibly the least understood of all the services, the public's common perception of the Coast Guard is of an organization responsible for rescuing those stranded at sea. Indeed, many tens of thousands owe their lives to the Coast Guard and its fleet of brightly painted helicopters. However, the service's work extends far beyond.

The Coast Guard's five primary mission categories encompass maritime security, maritime safety, marine environmental protection, mobility and national security, and entail defense operations, pollution prevention, ice operations, maritime law enforcement and maintaining aids to navigation, as well as search and rescue (SAR).

Although it flies a relatively small number of aircraft, this aerial fleet is vital to US maritime interests.

The Coast Guard is the only military service with law enforcement authority and is charged with enforcing all federal maritime laws and international treaties. These include protecting fisheries and marine resources, combating narcotics trafficking, interdicting illegal immigrants at sea and enforcing environmental protection regulations. Other responsibilities include marine inspection, port safety and security.

Unlike other military arms, Coast Guard aviation is not organized into wings or squadrons, and its capabilities have typically been associated with air stations rather than military formations. In fact, throughout its history the service has only operated a squadron on a couple of occasions; the first being during World War II when VP-6 (later VPB-6) flew PBY-5A Catalinas out of Narsarssuak, Greenland. The Coast Guard was so tasked because it had more Arctic experience than any other of America's armed forces.

The origins of Coast Guard aviation go back as early as 1915 when service personnel began flying a borrowed Curtiss F flying boat after approaching the Curtiss Flying School

Normally based at Coast Guard Air Station (CGAS) San Diego and belonging to the 11th District, serial 6008, a Sikorsky HH-60J Jayhawk, is seen here over Camp Pendleton in southern California.

at Newport News, Virginia. Following a series of test flights, six Coast Guard personnel were were assigned to the Naval Aviation School in Pensacola, Florida, to begin flight training in April 1916.

Today, there are seven types of aircraft in the fleet, of which the most numerous is the French-built Dolphin that has overcome technical and fiscal problems to become a "guardian angel" in the SAR role. Other platforms, besides the fellow French-designed Dassault Falcon, include the Sikorsky HH-60J Jayhawk, Lockheed HC-130 Hercules, Grumman Aerospace VC-4A Gulfstream I, Gulfstream Aerospace C-20B Gulfstream III and Schweizer RU-38A Twin Condor.

A key player in combating the flow of illegal drugs into the United States, Coast Guard aviation shares with the US Customs Service responsibility for air interdiction. Working in conjunction with other federal agencies and regional foreign governments, its area of operations extends six million square miles, and encompasses the Caribbean, Gulf of Mexico and eastern Pacific. Of cocaine and marijuana shipments intercepted by US authorities each year, the Coast Guard accounts for nearly 25 percent of such seizures.

internationally recognized inland and maritime regions. The service's assets are required to be ready to proceed within 30 minutes of a distress notification, and be on scene within 90 minutes thereafter. To meet this obligation, it maintains facilities along the Atlantic, Pacific and Gulf coasts, and in Alaska, Hawaii, Guam and Puerto Rico, as well as on the Great Lakes and other inland waterways.

The Aérospatiale HH-65A *Dauphin* (Dolphin) is the most numerous type in Coast Guard service and its short-range SAR asset. It can hoist five people aboard during a rescue mission.

which serve as seaborne lighthouses to mark offshore reefs and channels.

Despite the modern nature of many of the missions, Coast Guard aviation elements now operate an aging fleet of aircraft. The service is caught in the same budgetary constraints and pressures to downsize that have been felt throughout the US armed forces. Today, it cannot afford the luxury of flying any "single-mission" aircraft, even though the size and shape of its aerial fleet have changed little over the years. Instead, familiar platforms like the Hercules, Dolphin and Jayhawk are expected to take on many more tasks not foreseen when these aircraft entered service.

The important issue of which aircraft the service will operate after 2010 is to be addressed as part of the Deepwater Initiative, a series of pending decisions that ultimately will provide the Coast Guard with new vessels and aircraft. These decisions are likely to focus on "packages" offered as integrated solutions by shipbuilders and aircraft manufacturers. At the same time, the Coast Guard is keen to rationalize the number of platforms it flies and most observers believe the Bell 609 tiltrotor, proposed as a development of the V-22 Osprey, will enter Coast Guard service. This would resolve the pressing problem of a replacement for the Dolphin, which is underpowered and has limited range. However, money for the tilt-rotor is not there yet and discussions to replace aging HC-130Hs with a variant of the S-3B Viking never progressed beyond the talking stage.

One of 30 Lockheed HC-130H Hercules currently in Coast Guard service, this aircraft is based at CGAS Kodiak, in Alaska, and is seen here undergoing deicing prior to a mission.

Using both cutters and aircraft, the Coast Guard is tasked with upholding international fishing laws and treaties, and enforcing laws protecting marine mammals and endangered species throughout what is called the US Exclusive Economic Zone (EEZ). This area extends 200 miles from the US coastline and includes 2.25 million square miles of water.

SAR is one of the oldest and, along with drug interdiction, most publicized missions of the Coast Guard, which is the maritime coordinator of the national search and rescue plan. This divides the continental US (CONUS) area of SAR responsibility into

Another vital mission of the Coast Guard is supporting the International Ice Patrol by helping search for icebergs in the North Atlantic shipping lanes. Each year, a reconnaissance detachment (RECDET) is deployed from CGAS Elizabeth City, North Carolina, to St. John's, Newfoundland, Canada. The RECDET flies regular missions throughout the ice season, usually from February through July, using a radar-equipped HC-130H aircraft. These sorties are flown over the Grand Banks, south of Newfoundland.

Although maintenance of offshore navigational aids is generally undertaken by seagoing buoy tenders and other vessels, Coast Guard helicopters are also used regularly to service large offshore navigational aids like the "Texas Towers" located in coastal waters,

ORGANIZATION AND UNITS

Coast Guard aviation is organized into Atlantic Area (LANTAREA) and Pacific Area (PACAREA) commands, plus two units that report directly to headquarters. The latter comprise the Aviation Training Center (ATC) and the Aircraft Repair and Supply Center (ARSC). Reporting to area commands are nine districts responsible for the operation of groups, air stations and other support units.

DIRECT-REPORTING UNITS
Coast Guard Aviation Training Center, Mobile, Alabama

The Coast Guard initiated fixed- and rotary-wing training at Bates Field, Mobile, Alabama, following the commissioning of this air station on 17 December 1966. The facility, located on former Air Force Reserve property, became the ATC in 1969 and has eight divisions that comprise Operations, Training, Aviation Engineering, Health and Human Services, Comptroller, Services, Polar Operations and Facilities Engineering.

HU-25A and HH-65A aircraft assigned to the Operations Division stand alert duty in support of the 8th Coast Guard District and fly SAR and maritime enforcement missions.

The Training Division is responsible for providing Coast Guard aviators with initial and recurrent training on HU-25A, HH-65A and HH-60J aircraft, that includes annual week-long refresher training in one of the ATC's three flight simulators.

The Polar Operations Division was created in 1969 as the Helicopter Icebreaker Support Unit (IBSU) and its HH-65As deploy on Coast Guard icebreakers in support of scientific, logistic and SAR missions.

In all, the ATC employs more than 500 personnel and is the largest air unit in the Coast Guard. It is also one of Mobile's larger nonindustrial employers.

US Coast Guard Aviation Command Structure

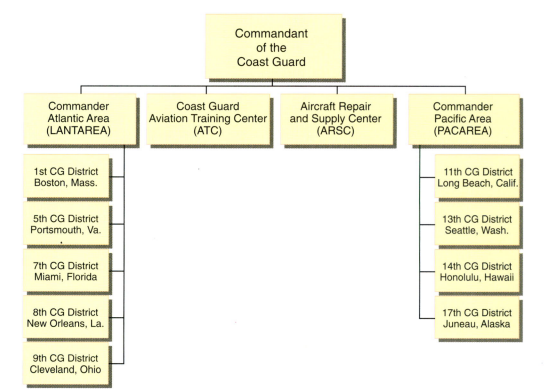

```
                    Commandant
                    of the
                    Coast Guard
    ┌───────────────┬──────────────┬───────────────┐
Commander        Coast Guard    Aircraft Repair   Commander
Atlantic Area    Aviation       and Supply        Pacific Area
(LANTAREA)       Training       Center            (PACAREA)
                 Center (ATC)   (ARSC)

1st CG District                                11th CG District
Boston, Mass.                                  Long Beach, Calif.

5th CG District                                13th CG District
Portsmouth, Va.                                Seattle, Wash.

7th CG District                                14th CG District
Miami, Florida                                 Honolulu, Hawaii

8th CG District                                17th CG District
New Orleans, La.                               Juneau, Alaska

9th CG District
Cleveland, Ohio
```

Aircraft Repair and Supply Center (ARSC) Air Station Elizabeth City, North Carolina

Though located at Air Station Elizabeth City, the ARSC is also assigned directly to Coast Guard headquarters and was established in 1947 at a former Consolidated Vultee Aircraft Company plant. The ARSC is composed of five divisions: Administration, Aircraft Engineering, Aviation Repair, Aviation Supply and Management Information Services, and provides the Coast Guard's aviation force with complete logistic support. It handles maintenance, repair, modification and periodic depot maintenance (PDM).

COMMANDER ATLANTIC AREA (LANTAREA)/ Maritime Defense Zone Atlantic (MDZA)

Headquartered at the Coast Guard Support Center (CGSC) in Portsmouth, Virginia, the LANTAREA commander, a vice admiral, is responsible for five Coast Guard districts that cover 40 states and border on 29 foreign countries. The operational area encompasses more than five million square miles of ocean and inland waterways.

This command center coordinates law enforcement and rescue missions on the high seas and manages international exercises, international maritime law enforcement and multinational maritime interception operations in the northern Red Sea and northern sector of the Persian Gulf. Its resources include 14 air stations, three air facilities and two air-interdiction facilities.

The LANTAREA commander is also directly responsible for the International Ice Patrol, the MDZA and the 5th Coast Guard District, whereas rear admirals each command the remaining four districts. Individual air stations within each district fall under the control of a captain or full commander.

Lockheed HC-130H Hercules, serial 1790, operates from Air Station Sacramento, located at McClellan Technology Center, California. This aircraft was assigned an out-of-sequence serial number to honor the Coast Guard's 200th anniversary.

Although a vital asset to Coast Guard operations, the HH-65A Dolphin was not the service's first choice for SAR duties. Instead, the Sikorsky S-76 would have been preferred. A replacement will be needed in the near future and many observers feel the proposed Bell 609 tiltrotor will be well suited to the role.

The Dolphin's construction includes a high percentage of composite materials, which has given rise to its "Plastic Puppy" nickname. Photographed in 1991, this example is shown in the Coast Guard's old color scheme.

1st Coast Guard District

Headquartered in Boston, Massachusetts, the 1st Coast Guard District is responsible for the Northeast United States from the Canadian border as far south as Sandy Hook, New Jersey. It includes a single air station.

5th Coast Guard District

Headquartered in Portsmouth, Virginia, this district extends over the states of Delaware, Maryland, Virginia, North Carolina and parts of New Jersey and Pennsylvania. The 5th Coast Guard District controls three air stations and also detaches aircraft to a facility under the control of the 1st Coast Guard District.

7th Coast Guard District

Headquartered in Miami, Florida, the 7th Coast Guard District's area of control extends from South Carolina down the Georgia coast, and to all of Florida except for the Panhandle. The entire Caribbean is also included. It operates four air stations and a single air facility, and detaches aircraft to a pair of remote operating locations in the Bahamas.

8th Coast Guard District

Headquartered in New Orleans, Louisiana, the 8th Coast Guard District is responsible for all or parts of 26 states along the Gulf Coast and much of the Midwest. It became the Coast Guard's largest district in 1996 when the 2nd Coast Guard District was merged. It covers some 1,200 miles of coastline and 10,300 miles of navigable inland waterways (with the exception of those along the Great Lakes, which come under the 9th Coast Guard District) that include the Illinois, Mississippi, Missouri and Ohio Rivers. The three air stations operated by the 8th Coast Guard District are located along the Gulf Coast, and the district is also supported by the Operations Division of the ATC.

9th Coast Guard District

Headquartered in Cleveland, Ohio, the boundaries of the 9th Coast Guard District extend across the shores of the Great Lakes states of Illinois, Indiana, Michigan, Minnesota, New York, Ohio, Pennsylvania and Wisconsin, from Alexandria, New York, to Duluth, Minnesota. In all, the district is responsible for some 6,700 miles of coastline and controls two air stations and a single air facility, all of which are located within the state of Michigan.

US COAST GUARD AVIATION ORGANIZATION

Headquarters US Coast Guard - Washington, D.C.

Coast Guard Aviation Training Center (CGATC) - Bates Field, Mobile, Alabama

Operations Division	Bates Field, Mobile, Alabama	HU-25A
Polar Operations Division	Bates Field, Mobile, Alabama	HH-65A
Training Division	Bates Field, Mobile, Alabama	HH-65A, HH-60J, HU-25A/B

Commander Atlantic Area (LANTAREA)
Maritime Defense Zone Atlantic (MDZA) - CGSC Portsmouth, Virginia

1st Coast Guard District - CGSC Boston, Massachusetts

CGAS Cape Cod	Otis ANGB, Falmouth, Massachusetts	HU-25A/B, HH-60J
CGAF Long Island	Gabreski Airport, Westhampton Beach, New York	HH-65A

5th Coast Guard District - CGSC Portsmouth, Virginia

CGAS Atlantic City	Atlantic City IAP, New Jersey	HH-65A
CGAS Washington	Ronald Reagan National Airport, Virginia	C-20B
CGAS Elizabeth City	ATTC Elizabeth City MAP, North Carolina	HC-130H, HH-60J

7th Coast Guard District - CGSC Miami, Florida

CGAS Miami	Opa Locka Airport, Florida	HU-25C, RU-38A, HH-65A, VC-4A
CGAS Clearwater	St. Petersburg - Clearwater IAP, Florida	HC-130H, HH-60J
CGAS Savannah	Hunter AAF, Georgia	HH-65A
CGAF Charleston	Charleston AFB/IAP, South Carolina	HH-65A
CGAS Borinquen	Rafael Hernandez Airport, Puerto Rico	HU-25A, HH-65A

8th Coast Guard District - CGSC New Orleans, Louisiana

CGAS New Orleans	NAS New Orleans JRB, Louisiana	HH-65A
CGAS Corpus Christi	NAS Corpus Christi, Texas	HH-65A, HU-25B
CGAS Houston	Ellington Field, Houston, Texas	HH-65A

9th Coast Guard District - CGSC Cleveland, Ohio

CGAS Traverse City	Cherry Capital Airport, Michigan	HH-65A
CGAS Detroit	Selfridge ANGB, Michigan	HH-65A
CGAF Muskegon	Northside Airport, Michigan	HH-65A

Commander Pacific Area (PACAREA)/
Maritime Defense Zone Pacific (MDZP) - CGSC Coast Guard Island, Alameda, California

11th Coast Guard District - CGSC Alameda, California

CGAS Los Angeles	Los Angeles IAP, California	HH-65A
CGAS San Diego	San Diego IAP/Lindbergh Field, California	HH-60J
CGAS San Francisco	San Francisco IAP, California	HH-65A
CGAS Sacramento	McClellan Technology Center, California	HC-130H
CGAS Humbolt Bay	Arcata Airport, California	HH-65A

13th Coast Guard District - CGSC Seattle, Washington

CGAS Astoria	Astoria Regional Airport, Oregon	HH-60J
CGAS North Bend	North Bend Municipal Airport, Oregon	HH-65A
CGAF Newport	Newport Municipal Airport, Oregon	HH-65A
CGAS Port Angeles	Port Angeles Airport, Washington	HH-65A

14th Coast Guard District - CGSC Honolulu, Hawaii

CGAS Barbers Point	NAS Barbers Point, Hawaii	HC-130H, HH-65A

17th Coast Guard District - CGSC Juneau, Alaska

CGAS Sitka	Sitka Rocky Guttierrez Airport, Alaska	HH-60J
CGAS Kodiak	USCG Support Ctr. Kodiak Airport, Alaska	HC-130H, HH-60J, HH-65A

Coast Guard Districts, Air Stations and Facilities

COMMANDER PACIFIC AREA (PACAREA)/Maritime Defense Zone Pacific (MDZP)

Headquartered at the Coast Guard Support Center, Coast Guard Island, Alameda, California, the PACAREA commander is a vice admiral who is responsible for four districts that cover 10 states and 73 million square miles of territory stretching across the Pacific Rim. Eleven air stations and a single air facility are assigned to him and he also commands the Maritime Defense Zone Pacific (MDZP) and the 11th Coast Guard District. The structure of the remaining districts and air stations under his control is similar to that for LANTAREA.

11th Coast Guard District

Headquartered in Alameda, the 11th Coast Guard District controls three air stations and a single, full-time air facility, all of which are located within the state of California. Other states under the district's control include Arizona, California, Nevada and Utah.

13th Coast Guard District

Headquartered in Seattle, Washington, the district's three air stations and single air facility are responsible for the entire northwestern area of the US, including Idaho, Montana and Oregon, as well as Washington.

14th Coast Guard District

Although the 14th Coast Guard District, headquartered in Honolulu, Hawaii, is assigned only a single air station, it covers almost the entire central and western areas of the Pacific, including Guam and American Samoa.

17th Coast Guard District

Headquartered in Juneau, Alaska, the 17th Coast Guard District's two air stations are both located in the southern part of the state. As well as covering the largest state in the union, the district is also responsible for the northern section of the Pacific Ocean, as well as the Bering Strait that separates Alaska and Russia.

Operated for medium-range missions, 41 Dassault HU-25 Guardians (Falcons) began service with the Coast Guard in 1981.

AIRCRAFT

DASSAULT AVIATION

Dassault HU-25A/B/C Guardian (Falcon Jet)

The Coast Guard purchased a total of 41 HU-25As in the late 1970s to fill its requirement for a medium-range surveillance (MRS) aircraft. Developed from the Falcon/Mystere 20G, the aircraft were outfitted by Falcon Jet Corporation (the manufacturer's subsidiary in Little Rock, Arkansas), although structural modifications were undertaken by Grumman Aerospace in St. Augustine, Florida. The aircraft received acrylic search windows, a drop hatch in the floor and an AN/APS-127 radar.

The HU-25A is used over medium-range distances for SAR, narcotics interdiction, regulation enforcement and marine environmental protection. Since reaching initial operational capability (IOC) in 1982, a number have been modified to meet specific mission requirements.

Eight aircraft were converted to HU-25B standard, fitted with equipment to locate and assess oil spills and other pollution at sea. The variant's Aireye surveillance system consists of a Motorola AN/APS-131 SLAR carried in a pod beneath the fuselage, a Texas Instruments RS-18C infrared/ultraviolet (IR/UV) line scanner mounted under the right wing and a Chicago Industries KS-87B reconnaissance camera. The SLAR detects pollution and the UV sensor helps identify the type and density of the matter. Meanwhile, the camera documents time and movement data.

The third Guardian variant is an interceptor, designated the HU-25C and also known as the "Night Stalker." Nine were converted from HU-25A airframes specifically for narcotics interdiction missions. These aircraft are designed to identify and track sea and airborne targets, and vector law enforcement personnel to the appropriate location. They carry no weapons and thus do not have the capability to attack or shoot down targets. The HU-25A's standard AN/APS-

Three variants of the HU-25 Guardian are operated by the Coast Guard. The HU-25C is an interceptor, most readily identified by its longer, tapered nose. Clearly visible beneath the fuselage is a WF-360 FLIR turret.

127 radar was replaced with an AN/APG-66 radar system developed from the unit used in USAF F-16As, which necessitated a longer, tapered nose cone and makes the aircraft readily identifiable. In addition, a Texas Instruments WF-360 FLIR was installed in a stabilized turret under the fuselage, and cockpit lighting was optimized for the use of night-vision goggles (NVGs). Finally, a SATCOM suite was also added.

The HU-25A may not have been the best choice of aircraft for the service. Although the type offers flexibility, it is expensive to operate and serviceability of the Garrett ATF3-6-2C turbofan engines has been a problem. These were developed specifically for the Falcon 20G. The HU-25A's high-utilization rate has caused the Coast Guard to remove 60 percent of them from service and, it is said, the possibility of retiring the whole fleet was considered. However, two HU-25As were recently removed from the Aerospace Maintenance and Regeneration Center (AMARC) and, following maintenance work at Elizabeth City, will be returned to service. Plans now call for the type to remain in service until 2010 at least, and there is the possibility the Guardian will receive a new powerplant.

At the present time, the HU-25A station allowance is eight aircraft and, of the 25 examples so configured, six are now in service. One aircraft fills a support role, two are in maintenance and 16 more are in storage. For the HU-25B, the station allowance is four aircraft. At this time, six are in service, one is in maintenance and the balance are serving as if they are HU-25As. The station allowance is eight aircraft for the HU-25C. Presently, eight are in service and one is in maintenance.

Dassault HU-25A Guardian Specifications

Maximum Takeoff Weight:	33,510 lb (15200 kg)
Empty Weight:	20,888 lb (9475 kg)
Length:	56 ft 3 in (17.15 m)
Wingspan:	53 ft 6 in (16.31 m)
Height:	17 ft 5 in (5.31 m)
Power Plant:	Two Allied Signal ATF3-6 turbofans, each rated at 5,440 lb thrust (24.20 kN)
Maximum Fuel Capacity:	10,626 lb (4820 kg)
Maximum Speed:	461 kts (854 km/h)
Operating Range:	2,252 nm (4171 km)
Crew:	5
Mission Equipment:	AN/APS-127 radar (HU-25A/B), AN/APS-131 SLAR, RS-18C line scanner/ultraviolet sensory system, KS-87B reconnaissance camera (HU-25B), AN/APG-66 radar, WF-360 FLIR system (HU-25C)

The Guardian is in service with the Coast Guard ATC's Operations Division, as well as three districts.

EUROCOPTER (AÉROSPATIALE)

Aérospatiale HH-65A Dauphin (Dolphin)

The Coast Guard purchased 96 HH-65A Dolphins from the French manufacturer Aérospatiale Helicopter (now Eurocopter), a type based on the model SA366G. The helicopters were delivered "green" to the manufacturer's subsidiary in Grand Prairie, Texas. Following outfitting, the Dolphin reached IOC in 1985. It is primarily tasked with short-range recovery (SRR) SAR operations but is also employed in narcotics interdiction, environmental protection, airlift and support of polar ice-breaking operations.

Making extensive use of new materials, the Dolphin is fitted with a composite rotor head, fiberglass rotor blades and a shrouded, 11-blade tail. Equipped with a Rockwell-Collins HFCS-8000 automated flight management system and Bendix RDR-1500 radar, the Dolphin is capable of flying search patterns automatically, freeing the pilot and copilot to assist in visual searches. The system can place the helicopter in a hover at an altitude of 50 feet. The aircraft is also equipped with an EFIS and Northrop Sea Hawk FLIR. Most of the early problems associated with the LTS-101 engine have now been eliminated but resulted in several design changes to the main gearbox.

The Coast Guard has 93 HH-65As and an authorized operational strength (station

A distinctive feature of the Dolphin is the shrouded, 11-blade tail rotor and, for a helicopter, the HH-65A is relatively quiet in flight. Wearing colors from the early 1990s, this example is seen over the coast of southern New Jersey.

Aérospatiale HH-65A Dolphin Specifications

Maximum Takeoff Weight:	9,200 lb (4173 kg)
Empty Weight:	6,092 lb (2763 kg)
Overall Length:	45 ft 6 in (13.87 m)
Fuselage Length:	38 ft 2 in (11.63 m)
Rotor Diameter:	39 ft 2 in (11.94 m)
Height:	13 ft 0 in (3.96 m)
Power Plant:	Two Allied Signal (Lycoming) LTS-101-750B-2 turboshaft engines, each rated at 690 shp (515 kW)
Maximum Fuel Capacity:	291 gals (1102 lit)
Maximum Speed:	165 kts (306 km/h)
Operating Range:	Standard – 150 nm (320 km), Maximum – 400 miles maximum (741 km) with auxiliary fuel tanks
Crew:	3
Mission Equipment:	Bendix RDR-1500 radar, Northrop Sea Hawk FLIR

allowance) of 80 aircraft. The balance is in maintenance.

With an operating range of about 152 nautical miles (282 km), the type can remain on station for about 30 minutes. Recovery missions are usually conducted from shore bases but the helicopter is sometimes carried aboard vessels.

The Dolphin's small "footprint" makes it suitable for shipboard operations and it is often deployed aboard icebreakers for polar missions. The type serves with all nine districts as well as two Coast Guard ATC divisions.

GENERAL DYNAMICS (GULFSTREAM AEROSPACE, GRUMMAN)

Grumman VC-4A Gulfstream I

A single VC-4A has served the Coast Guard for a number of assignments throughout its 36-year career and, until the US Army acquired a secondhand Gulfstream I, it was the only VIP variant of Grumman's Model G-159 in military service.

Purchased originally as a VIP transport, this aircraft was replaced in that role in 1969 by a VC-11A Gulfstream II and, in 1994, the VC-4A was transferred to CGAS Miami. In Florida it currently serves in VIP, training and logistic support roles with the 7th Coast Guard District.

Long in service, the single Grumman VC-4A Gulfstream I operated by the Coast Guard is based at CGAS Miami, at Opa Locka Airport, Florida. It flies with the 7th Coast Guard District. Retirement of the Navy's TC-4C and the Army's G-159 left serial -02 as the last Gulfstream I in US military service.

Grumman VC-4A Gulfstream I Specifications

Maximum Takeoff Weight:	36,000 lb (16329 kg)
Empty Weight:	24,575 lb (11147 kg)
Length:	63 ft 9 in (19.43 m)
Wingspan:	78 ft 4 in (23.87 m)
Height:	23 ft 4 in (7.11 m)
Power Plant:	Two Rolls-Royce Dart 529-8E turboprop engines, each rated at 2,210 shp (1648 kW)
Maximum Fuel Capacity:	9,393 lb (4261 kg)
Maximum Speed:	374 kts (693 km/h)
Maximum Range:	1,719 nm (3184 km)
Crew:	2
Accommodations:	10 passengers
Mission Equipment:	Standard commercial avionics

A sole Gulfstream Aerospace C-20B Gulfstream III is operated by the 5th Coast Guard District as a VIP transport. The USCG acquired this aircraft when the Gulfstream was excessed by the Air Force after being assigned to the 89th Air Wing at Andrews AFB, Maryland.

C-20B Gulfstream III

Formerly operated by the USAF's 89th Military Airlift Wing at Andrews AFB, Maryland, the Coast Guard's sole C-20B serves as a VIP transport. Essentially a Gulfstream III business jet, it replaced the Coast Guard's VC-11A Gulfstream II in 1995, which was sold on the commercial market.

In addition to supporting the commandant of the Coast Guard and senior service officials, this aircraft is also used by the Department of Transportation and is based at CGAS Washington, at Ronald Reagan National Airport.

The type's suitability for its assigned role is the reason it also serves with all four other services in a similar capacity.

Gulfstream Aerospace C-20B Gulfstream III Specifications

Maximum Takeoff Weight:	69,200 lb (31389 kg)
Empty Weight:	33,300 lb (15105 kg)
Length:	83 ft 1 in (25.32 m)
Wingspan:	77 ft 10 in (23.72 m)
Height:	24 ft 4 in (7.42 m)
Power Plant:	Two Rolls-Royce Spey MK511-8 turbofan engines, each rated at 11,400 lb thrust (50.71 kN)
Maximum Fuel Capacity:	28,800 lb (13063 kg)
Maximum Speed:	500 kts (926 km/h)
Maximum Range:	4,102 nm (7597 km)
Crew:	5
Accommodations:	14 passengers
Mission Equipment:	Standard commercial avionics

A number of the Coast Guard's HC-130H Hercules aircraft are currently being upgraded with more capable communications, radar and imaging systems.

LOCKHEED MARTIN

Lockheed HC-130H Hercules

Tasked with a wide range of missions including SAR, law enforcement, fisheries and environmental protection, narcotics interdiction, maritime surveillance, transport and support of the International Ice Patrol, the HC-130H is the Coast Guard's primary long-range aircraft. Typically, 26 examples are in service, while four more undergo maintenance. With an endurance of more than 14 hours, the variant's low-altitude range exceeds

Lockheed HC-130H Hercules Specifications

Maximum Takeoff Weight:	155,000 lb (70307 kg)
Empty Weight:	76,500 lb (34700 kg)
Overall Length:	98 ft 9 in (30.10 m)
Wingspan:	132 ft 7 in (40.41 m)
Height:	38 ft 6 in (11.74 m)
Power Plant:	Four Rolls-Royce/Allison T56-A-15 turboprop engines, each rated at 4,910 shp (3661 kW)
Maximum Fuel Capacity:	62,500 lb (28350 kg)
Maximum Speed:	325 kts (602 km/h)
Operating Range:	3,000 – 4,500 nm (5556 – 8334 km)
Crew:	5
Mission Equipment:	AN/APS-137 radar, AN/APS-135 or AN/APS-131 SLAR

3,000 miles (5556 km), with a crew of seven. In the SAR role, it is able to drop life rafts, food, medicine and other supplies.

The aircraft is equipped with advanced navigation equipment that includes an INS, Omega and Loran-C receivers and a GPS. Its AN/APS-137 inverse synthetic-aperture radar (ISAR) is capable of providing radar images of objects more than 50 miles (80 km) away, and a number of aircraft are additionally equipped with an AN/APS-135 side-looking airborne radar (SLAR) pod. The latter is used specifically for North Atlantic ice patrol missions.

The Coast Guard received the first of seven upgraded HC-130Hs in 1999 that came equipped with a forward-looking infrared (FLIR) imaging system, an airborne tactical workstation, satellite communications (SATCOM) and AN/APS-131 SLAR. The service plans to modify all 30 Hercules to accommodate this equipment. In addition, 10 aircraft will be equipped with kits that upgrade the T56A-7B engines to T56A-15 standard.

Supporting the International Ice Patrol, by searching for icebergs in North Atlantic shipping lanes, is an important mission for the HC-130H. Aircraft are typically deployed on such searches for six months each year.

Initial development of the MDX project began in 1988 at the same time testing of the NOTAR concept was initiated. Designated the MD 900 Explorer, the prototype first flew on 18 December 1992. The combat version, which has been in Coast Guard for more than a year, is referred to as the MH-90 Enforcer.

MD HELICOPTERS

MD Helicopters MH-90 Enforcer (MD 900)

Since late 1998, the Coast Guard has been operating two leased MD 900 Explorers as part of its previously classified program called Operation New Frontier that aims to counter the smuggling of narcotics by high-speed powerboat. Equipped with a FLIR system and 7.62-mm machine gun, the primary mission of the helicopter is to disable smugglers' boats in the event their operators ignore warnings to stop. One .50-cal sniper rifle is also carried aboard during such missions. Designated the MH-90 Enforcer in Coast Guard service, reports indicate that within the first few months of operation, its deployment led directly to the apprehension of a number of smugglers and the seizure of many tons of narcotics.

To date, the Coast Guard has not disclosed where the helicopters are based. However, it is most likely they are being flown from one or more locations in the Bahamas.

MD Helicopters MH-90 Enforcer Specifications

Maximum Takeoff Weight:	6,250 lb (2835 kg)
Empty Weight:	3,402 lb (1543 kg)
Overall Length:	38 ft 10 in (11.84 m)
Rotor Diameter:	33 ft 10 in (10.31 m)
Height:	12 ft 0 in (3.66 m)
Power Plant:	Two Pratt & Whitney PW206E turboshaft engines, each rated at 640 shp (477 kW) 5-blade main rotor / Engine bleed air supplied to a NOTAR (no tail rotor) antitorque system
Maximum Fuel Capacity:	1,073 lb (487 kg)
Maximum Speed:	136 kts (252 km/h)
Operating Range:	Standard – 302 nm (559 km), Maximum – 700 nm (1296 km) with two 120-gal (454-lit) and one 80-gal (303-lit) auxiliary tanks
Crew/ Accommodations:	2 crew/ 6 passengers or 3,000-lb (1361-kg) external load
Mission Equipment:	FLIR, rescue hoist
Armament:	M240G 7.62-mm machine gun

The RU-38A Twin Condor was to have conducted stealthy, low-altitude surveillance of coastal areas. However, a decision was taken in early 1999 not to add it to the Coast Guard's fleet.

SCHWEIZER AIRCRAFT

Schweizer RU-38A Twin Condor

Developed from the single-seat RG-8A powered glider, the RU-38A is a twin-engine, two-seat aircraft the Coast Guard had planned to use for narcotics interdiction, fishery patrols, pollution control and surveillance of illegal aliens.

Two RG-8As, converted by Schweizer, were to have entered service in 1996 but this did not occur. The aircraft were not even delivered to the 445th Test Squadron at Edwards AFB, California, for flight-envelope testing until some two years later. In early 1999, plans to deploy the type were dropped altogether.

Although powered by two engines, the RU-38A's operating procedure would have involved using only one engine as the aircraft cruised slowly along a coastline at an altitude of between 1,500 and 2,000 feet. The mission equipment proposed, which would have been carried within the forward sections of the twin booms, included an AN/APN-215(V) color radar with search and mapping capabilities housed in the port side, and an AN/AAQ-15 FLIR and low-light television (LLTV) in the starboard pod.

Schweizer RU-38A Twin Condor Specifications

Maximum Takeoff Weight:	5,300 lb (2404 kg)
Empty Weight:	3,360 lb (1524 kg)
Overall Length:	30 ft 2 in (9.19 m)
Wingspan:	64 ft 0 in (19.51 m)
Power Plant:	Two Teledyne Continental GIO-550A 6-cyl., reciprocating engines, each rated at 350 hp (261kW)
Maximum Fuel Capacity:	600 lb (272 kg)
Maximum Speed:	165 kts (306 km/h)
Operating Range:	773 nm (1432 km), equating to 6 – 10 hours endurance
Crew:	2
Mission Equipment:	AN/APN-215(V) color search and weather radar, AN/AAQ-15 FLIR and LLTV

SIKORSKY AIRCRAFT

Sikorsky HH-60J Jayhawk

The Coast Guard's fleet of 42 Sikorsky HH-60Js replaced aging Sikorsky HH-3F Pelicans in the medium-range recovery (MRR) role, beginning in 1991, when the Jayhawk reached IOC. The aircraft is very similar to the US Navy's HH-60H combat rescue helicopter and is tasked with most of the Coast Guard's missions, foremost of which is SAR. The Jayhawk's electronics suite includes an electronic flight instrumentation system (EFIS) cockpit, AN/APN-217 Doppler search and weather radar, AN/AAQ-15 FLIR, secure communications equipment and GPS receivers. Its cockpit is also compatible with NVGs. Smaller and lighter than its predecessor, the HH-60J is able to operate up to 260 nautical miles (482 km) from its base and remain airborne for as long as seven hours.

Normally stationed ashore, the Jayhawk can be carried aboard *Bear-* and *Hamilton-* class cutters. However, due to the Jayhawk's larger "footprint" the Dolphin is preferred for flight-deck operations. The HH-60J cruises at 135 knots and can hoist six people aboard during a rescue mission.

The Coast Guard's station allowance for the Jayhawk is 35 aircraft, with seven in maintenance.

Equipped with sophisticated electronics and avionics, the Jayhawk's cockpit allows the use of NVGs for full nighttime operation.

Although equipped with folding rotors and tail boom, and capable of operating aboard Coast Guard cutters, the Jayhawk is not the preferred choice because of its relatively large size. The smaller Dolphin is better suited for deck operations.

Sikorsky HH-60J Jayhawk Specifications

Maximum Takeoff Weight:	21,884 lb (9926 kg)
Empty Weight:	14,500 lb (6577 kg)
Overall Length:	64 ft 10 in (19.76 m)
Fuselage Length:	50 ft 0 in (15.24 m)
Rotor Diameter:	53 ft 8 in (16.36 m)
Height:	17 ft 0 in (5.18 m)
Power Plant:	Two General Electric T700-GE-401C turboshaft engines, each rated at 1,980 shp (2653 kW)
Maximum Fuel Capacity:	6,460 lb (2930 kg)
Maximum Speed:	160 kts (296 km/h)
Operating Range:	Standard – 300 nm (639 km), Maximum – 700 nm (1491 km) with two 120-gal (454-lit) and one 80-gal (303-lit) auxiliary tanks
Crew:	4
Mission Equipment:	AN/APN-217 Doppler search and weather radar, AN/AAQ-15 FLIR system

Offering seven-hour endurance, the HH-60J Jayhawk is the service's medium-range recovery helicopter and is capable of conducting rescue missions up to 300 miles out to sea. The Jayhawk is similar in configuration to the Navy's HH-60H, a CSAR variant.

AIR STATIONS AND FACILITIES

CGAS Astoria, Oregon

Located at Astoria Regional Airport in Warrenton, this Pacific Northwest air station was established in 1964. It is assigned to the 13th Coast Guard District and operates three Sikorsky HH-60J Jayhawks.

CGAS Atlantic City, New Jersey

Opened in May 1998 at Atlantic City International Airport, the Coast Guard's newest air station replaced operations at two former air stations: Brooklyn, New York, and Cape May, New Jersey. It is assigned to the 5th Coast Guard District and maintains seven HH-65A Dolphins.

CGAS Barbers Point, Hawaii

Air Station Barbers Point opened as an air detachment at the naval air station in 1949, and was subsequently commissioned as an air station in 1965. It is the only aviation unit under the operational command of the 14th Coast Guard District and operates four HC-130Hs and four HH-65As.

CGAS Borinquen, Puerto Rico

Assigned to the 7th Coast Guard District, Air Station Borinquen is located at Rafael Hernandez Airport, the former Ramey AFB, near Aquadilla. Four HH-65As are assigned and HU-25A operations will begin soon.

CGAS Cape Cod, Massachusetts

Located at Otis ANGB in Falmouth, on Cape Cod, this air station became the sole example assigned to the 1st Coast Guard District when Air Station Brooklyn, New York, was closed. Established in 1970, CGAS Cape Cod operates three HU-25As, a single HU-25B and four HH-60Js.

CGAS Clearwater, Florida

Assigned to the 7th Coast Guard District, and located at St. Petersburg - Clearwater International Airport, CGAS Clearwater operates seven HC-130Hs and 12 HH-60Js, and was activated in 1976. The high number of aircraft stationed there reflects the requirement to support Operation Bahamas Turks and Caicos (OPBAT), flying antinarcotics missions from Great Inaugua and Freeport, Bahamas.

CGAS Corpus Christi, Texas

Four HH-65As and three HU-25Bs operate from NAS Corpus Christi, which was activated in 1950. It is one of three stations assigned to the 8th Coast Guard District.

CGAS Detroit, Michigan

Assigned to the 9th Coast Guard District, this station is located at Selfridge ANGB and was opened in 1966. Three HH-65As are located there.

CGAS Elizabeth City, North Carolina

Located at Elizabeth City Municipal Airport, this air station is also home to the ARSC and the Aviation Technical Training Center (ATTC). The ATTC trains all of the service's maintenance personnel and its rescue swimmers (survivalmen) at the station, which opened in 1940 and is assigned to the 5th Coast Guard District. Three HH-60Js and five HC-130Hs operate from Elizabeth City.

CGAF Charleston, South Carolina

Air Station Savannah detaches a single HH-65A to this facility, located at Charleston AFB/ International Airport. It is assigned to the 7th Coast Guard District.

CGAS Houston, Texas

Opened in 1963 at Ellington Field, CGAS Houston operates four HH-65As in support of the 8th Coast Guard District. A new purpose-built facility at the air station was opened in 1987.

CGAS Humbolt Bay, California
Three HH-65As are assigned to this air station located at Arcata Airport in McKinleyville, California. It opened in 1977 and is assigned to the 11th Coast Guard District.

CGAS Kodiak, Alaska
Located at the US Coast Guard Support Center at Kodiak Airport (formerly NAS Kodiak), 250 miles southwest of Anchorage, this air station is one of two assigned to the 17th Coast Guard District. Kodiak was activated in 1947 as an air detachment and the air station was established in 1964.

In all, six HC-130Hs, four HH-60Js and five HH-65As operate from this location. The Dolphins are regularly deployed aboard *Hamilton*-class high-endurance cutters as part of the Alaska Patrol (ALPAT).

CGAF Long Island, New York
CGAS Atlantic City, New Jersey, detaches a single HH-65A to Francis S. Gabreski Airport in Westhampton Beach, New York, from April through November each year.

CGAS Los Angeles, California
Three HH-65As are assigned to this air station, which opened in 1962. Located at Los Angeles International Airport, it belongs to the 11th Coast Guard District.

CGAS Miami, Florida
Miami's Opa Locka Airport, originally a naval air station, has been home to this 7th Coast Guard District air station since 1965. The facility has the greatest diversity of aircraft assigned to any Coast Guard air station, with four types located there. They include a single Gulfstream 1, eight HU-25C interceptors, nine HH-65As and a pair of RU-38As.

Aviation Training Center (ATC) Mobile, Alabama
Located at Bates Field in Mobile, the ATC is assigned directly to Coast Guard headquarters but supports the 8th Coast Guard District as well. Aircraft assigned include three HH-60Js, nine HH-65As, four HU-25As and a single HU-25B. In addition, the ATC's Polar Operations Division often deploys HH-65As aboard two *Polar*-class icebreakers.

CGAF Muskegon, Michigan
This facility is operational from April through November each year at Northside Airport in Muskegon. During those months a single HH-65A is detached from CGAS Traverse City.

CGAS New Orleans, Louisiana
Assigned to the 8th Coast Guard District, the air station has been located at NAS New Orleans Joint Reserve Base (JRB) since 1957 and operates four HH-65As.

CGAF Newport, Oregon
This air facility at Newport Municipal Airport is operated by Air Station North Bend, which detaches a single HH-65A on 24-hour alert.

CGAS North Bend, Oregon
One of three air stations assigned to the 13th Coast Guard District, CGAS North Bend was commissioned in 1935, making it one of the Coast Guard's oldest air stations. It operates five HH-65As from the municipal airport and, as indicated above, maintains a single aircraft at CGAF Newport.

CGAS Port Angeles, Washington
Three HH-65As are located at Port Angeles Airport. The station is assigned to the 13th Coast Guard District.

CGAS Sacramento, California
Located at the former McClellan AFB in Sacramento, this station operates four HC-130Hs in support of the 11th Coast Guard District. The station opened in 1978 when the Hercules aircraft were relocated from CGAS San Francisco.

CGAS Savannah, Georgia
Located at Hunter Army Airfield, this air station operates five HH-65As in support of the 7th Coast Guard District. The station has been located here since 1963 when it was a United States Air Force facility.

CGAS Sitka, Alaska
Situated at Sitka Rocky Guttierez Airport, Sitka is one of two air stations operated by the 17th Coast Guard District. Opened in 1977, the air station has three HH-60Js assigned.

CGAS Traverse City, Michigan
Part of the 9th Coast Guard District, and located at Cherry Capital Airport, this station operates five HH-65As and detaches a single aircraft to Air Facility Muskegon from April through November. The air station has been in full-time operation since 1946.

The Coast Guard operates 42 HH-60J helicopters assigned to six of the Coast Guard's nine districts. The mission radius of the medium-range Jayhawk can be extended with three auxiliary fuel tanks that are carried externally, as shown below.

CGAS San Diego, California
Assigned to the 11th Coast Guard District, this air station is located adjacent to San Diego International Airport and operates three HH-60Js.

CGAS San Francisco, California
Opened in 1941, this air station has maintained four HH-65As since sending its HH-60Js to San Diego in 1996. It comes under the 11th Coast Guard District and is located at San Francisco International Airport.

CGAS Washington, Virginia
The Coast Guard has been active at what is now Ronald Reagan National Airport in Arlington since 1952 when Air Detachment Arlington was formed. The facility became an air station in 1964 and received its current name 10 years later. Today, it operates a single C-20B support aircraft for the commandant of the Coast Guard and reports to the 5th Coast Guard District. Hangar space is shared with the Federal Aviation Administration (FAA), which also has air assets based at the airport.

US ARMY

AVIATION OVERVIEW

Developed during the Vietnam War, the Bell AH-1 Cobra gunship continues to fly with the Army National Guard (ARNG). More than 300 examples remain in service.

The history of US Army aviation dates to 1908 when the Army Signal Corps began testing its first aircraft. Having used balloons for observation and artillery spotting since the American Civil War, the corps created a small aeronautics division in August 1907 and was responsible for the development of aviation within the service until 1926. That year, the Army Air Corps (AAC) was activated as a separate combat arm and the Army's aviation assets were assigned to its area commanders. In 1935, however, the establishment of a General Headquarters Air Force brought a change to the way these aircraft were managed. The new organization took control of all tactical aviation assets, leaving only observation units assigned as before. When the Army Air Forces and Army Ground Forces were established as distinct entities on 20 June 1941, the stage was set for the emergence of a separate military branch. The US Air Force was created six years later.

In June 1942, the secretary of war authorized the Army to develop its own air observation organization for its field artillery units. Accordingly, the Department of Air Training was activated within the Field Artillery School at Camp Sill, Oklahoma, and began acquiring light aircraft. It was tasked with artillery spotting, observation, communications and liaison duties, and with developing mission tactics. Experimentation with the use of light aircraft as airborne spotters for artillery units had begun during the 1930s, when they were frequently integrated into exercises. However, the role of these aircraft, nicknamed "grasshoppers," was greatly expanded during the 1940s and air combat experience was first gained when three Piper L-4s took off from the deck of the USS *Ranger* (CV 4) on 9 November 1942, for Operation Torch, which marked the invasion of North Africa.

By war's end, Army "grasshoppers" were active in every theater and on every front. Their crews not only directed artillery fire but assumed responsibility for naval gunfire spotting, casualty evacuation, wire laying, aerial photography and reconnaissance.

The Army's aviation element continued flying missions in these light aircraft after the war, but in December 1946 the service began evaluating helicopters after taking delivery of a Bell YR-13A (designated the H-13 after 1948). The following year, the National Security Act of 1947 authorized the Department of the Air Force to be created as a separate service. With its activation on 18 September 1947, the USAF assumed responsibility for providing the Army with close air support (CAS), airlift and reconnaissance needs. Although the Army retained an aviation element, its own missions were limited to such activities as liaison, artillery spotting and light transport.

When North Korea invaded its southern neighbor in June 1950, the US Army had a little over 700 aircraft in its inventory, most of which were World War II-era liaison types but included some 50 helicopters. During the conflict, Army pilots flew battlefield surveillance and transportation missions and Army Aeromedical Service helicopter detachments undertook the first casualty evacuations using H-13s. In 1951, the first Sikorsky H-19C transports entered service, and while the Army operated smaller helicopter fleets than the Air Force or the Marine Corps, it was effective in supporting deployed troops with these assets. By the time fighting ended in July 1953, it had demonstrated the value of the helicopter in combat. The Army had also evacuated more than 21,000 casualties during the conflict, thereby establishing the helicopter's role as an air ambulance.

After Korea, Army aviation was expanded with the establishment of 12 battalions of medium- and heavy-lift transport helicopters, as well as more scout observation platforms. In addition, newer fixed-wing liaison aircraft were introduced but these were largely off-the-shelf aircraft adapted from civil designs. In 1954, the relocation of Army aviation training from Camp Sill to Camp (later Fort) Rucker, Alabama, was begun. This resulted in significant improvement in the service's air capabilities. More powerful helicopters were acquired that could carry large numbers of troops, supplies and weapons across battlefields, at greater speed and with increased efficiency. By the time the Bell HU-1A and Grumman AO-1 (redesignated the UH-1A and OV-1A, respectively, in October 1962) entered Army service in 1960, there were more than 5,000 fixed- and rotary-wing types in the inventory.

The advent of these modern designs came at the height of the Cold War when the United States was trying to counter communist expansionism around the globe. The service also evaluated a variety of other fixed- and rotary-wing platforms during this period, including a number of small jets for the CAS role. However, Air Force objections to the Army operating new assets for this purpose put an end to such plans.

In January 1962, when the first sorties flown by Vertol H-21Cs began, US Army aviation assets started supporting special forces personnel serving as advisors to South Vietnam. Later that year, the service deployed turbine-powered UH-1A "Hueys" to Southeast Asia, and the type ultimately became synonymous with the war. Direct US involvement in Southeast Asia increased and the Army began to deploy more helicopters, replacing older types with more capable platforms, which could fill observation and transport roles in particular. By October 1964, the service was flying more than 250 helicopters and 150 fixed-wing aircraft in support of the US advisory team. Soon thereafter, American troops were deployed for direct combat operations and, by March 1966, 70 companies were operating some 1,500 aircraft across the country.

The Army began evaluating armed aircraft early in the conflict and eventually fielded

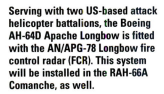
Serving with two US-based attack helicopter battalions, the Boeing AH-64D Apache Longbow is fitted with the AN/APG-78 Longbow fire control radar (FCR). This system will be installed in the RAH-66A Comanche, as well.

combat variants of the JOV-1A Mohawk, which proved valuable during operations. However, Air Force objections to the unauthorized use of these aircraft brought an end to the program. Meanwhile, the Army had also adapted the UH-1B to serve as a flying gunship, equipped with automatic weapons, rockets and missiles. It was so impressive in the limited-strike role that a dedicated, purpose-built attack helicopter was developed. The first Bell AH-1G Cobra flew in combat in 1967 and, by the end of 1970, the Army had 9,918 helicopters in service. Effective in conventional and unconventional operations, helicopters in Southeast Asia soon changed the nature of land warfare.

In addition to helicopters, fixed-wing types were used for missions that included forward air control (FAC) and electronic intelligence (ELINT). By the early 1970s, however, the Army was no longer using them for FAC sorties but had begun developing new types for ELINT missions.

US Army ground forces left Vietnam in August 1972 and, after the war, began to focus on Europe as did the other military services. With the benefit of lessons learned in Vietnam, development of advanced versions of existing aircraft, as well as more capable replacements, proceeded at a fast pace. Proposed were next-generation aircraft like the Lockheed AH-56 Cheyenne attack helicopter, fitted with advanced sensors. Although that program was terminated, it led

to production of the advanced attack helicopter (AAH) concept, which subsequently evolved into the AH-64 Apache. In addition, the contest for a utility tactical transport aircraft system (UTTAS), which began in the late 1960s, resulted in a competitive fly-off between the Sikorsky YUH-60 and the Boeing Vertol YUH-61. In turn, this led to development of the UH-60 Blackhawk and its derivatives, several of which are still in production today.

The oldest types still in service are "Hueys" and Cobras, which must be considered the backbone of the Army's strategic reserve, the Army National Guard (ARNG). Within general support units, assault companies and medical (air ambulance) companies, UH-1s progressively are being replaced by UH-60A/L/Q Blackhawks. However, the type will continue to serve for the foreseeable future in the light-utility role. Similarly, the Cobra has been partially replaced by the Apache, although at least 300 Cobras remain in ARNG service. Furthermore, it is assumed that many will remain until the RAH-66A Comanche comes on-line after 2006. Recently announced plans to restructure the AH-64D program may provide the ARNG with sufficient AH-64As to allow retirement of its last Cobras before then, however. Meanwhile, a life-extension program for the Chinook will result in 300 examples being upgraded to CH-47F configuration, enabling the heavy-lift helicopter to stay in service through 2033. The fielding of a Joint Transport Rotary Aircraft (JTRA) should be complete by then.

In terms of older fixed-wing aircraft, the Army already has retired most of its Beech C-12Cs and continues to reduce the size of its overall fleet. While taking delivery of new Cessna UC-35As, it needs to retain C-12F/R/Ts for operational support and theater airlift duties, however. The service plans to replace its two main intelligence types with a single aerial common sensor (ACS) platform, and hopes the same airframe can also be used for the theater airlift role. That will enable the Army to phase out the C-23B Sherpa.

Serial 99-0100 is a new UC-35A that has been assigned to C Company, 2d Battalion, 228th Aviation Regiment (TA) at Simmons AAF, North Carolina. However, it is seen here at NAS Willow Grove JRB, Pennsylvania, during January 2000. At that time, the Citation had accumulated a little over 30 hours of flight time.

US Army

ORGANIZATION OF ARMY AVIATION

On 12 April 1983, nearly 76 years after creating its first aeronautics division, the Army established aviation as a separate branch. Like aviation elements within the other services, its components normally operate from established facilities. However, as the primary mission of this force is to support Army troops in the field, in times of war it moves to forward locations or goes directly into the field to operate alongside infantry, armored and support units.

In 1985, the Army completed a major restructuring designed to bring about what was termed the "Army of Excellence" (AOE) and, today, the service is organized around 15 major commands (MACOMs) that report directly to the Army chief of staff. Operationally, however, several of these branches also answer to the unified commander in chief (CinC) for the geographical area in which they are deployed. This occurs in much the same way other military branches

- US Army Pacific (USARPAC)
- Eighth US Army (EUSA)
- US Army South (USARSO)
- US Army Space and Missile Defense Command (SMDC)
- US Army Special Operations Command (USASOC)
- US Army Training and Doctrine Command (TRADOC)

Typically, a MACOM is commanded by a three- or four-star general, and the majority of combat forces are assigned to five of these organizations: USAREUR, FORSCOM, INSCOM, USARPAC, USARSO and USASOC. Unlike commands with the other military services, however, MACOMs are fluid and possess unit structures based on their particular needs. Each is made up of some or all of the following elements, which are listed in descending order of size:

- Theater or Army – Referred to as an echelon above corps (EAC), a theater or numbered army is usually a headquarters

corps normally comprises an aviation brigade, a military intelligence brigade (MIBDE), an armored cavalry regiment (ACR), a number of armored and/or infantry divisions and a corps support command (COSCOM).

- Division (DIV) – Composed of multiple brigades, this organization represents the largest tactical formation having a fixed structure. The Army maintains 10 active, eight reserve and two active/reserve divisions. With the exception of the latter, each is assigned an integral aviation brigade designed around the mission performed. Mechanized infantry, cavalry and armored examples are considered heavy divisions and the aviation brigade within each has a common structure. The same is also true for light and medium infantry divisions, of which the latter are assigned only to the ARNG. The aviation brigades assigned to airborne and air assault divisions are designed specifically for those two missions.
- Regiment (REGT) – This independent organization is smaller than a division but larger than a brigade.
- Brigade or Group (BDE or GRP) – These self-contained maneuver formations have separate compositions. A brigade comprises between three and five battalions, whereas a group is made up of between one and three battalions. Both can be considered the equivalent of an Air Force wing.
- Battalion, Squadron or Task Force (Bn, Sqn or TF) – Comprising multiple companies under any one of the above names, this organization is the Army's primary command element and is equivalent to an Air Force squadron. This element is discussed in more detail in the *Aviation Commands and Units* section in the pages that follow.
- Company or Troop (CO or TRP) – Made up of several platoons, a company is assigned to its host for a specific mission and it is fair to say that both the battalion and company represent the common threads within theater, corps and divisional aviation brigades as well as ACRs.
- Platoon or Detachment (PLTN or DET) – Within Army aviation, the PLTN and DET represent the smallest of its organizational elements.

As part of the process of continued force restructuring, the Army Aviation Modernization Plan (AAMP) was approved in 1988 and the service began reducing the size of its aircraft fleet. Although the plan called for a decrease in the number of operational aircraft from 7,793 in 1992 to 6,150 by 1999, down to 5,900 aircraft by 2010, it was subsequently revised.

While it is true that Operation Desert

RC-12Ds comprise the airborne elements of the Improved Guardrail V (IGRV) system, and are currently operated by military intelligence battalions in Texas, Arizona and Korea. However, those assigned to IIICORPS' 15th MI Bn at Fort Hood, Texas, will soon be replaced by RC-12P/Q models.

report via a dual chain of command for administrative and operational purposes.

The MACOMs having aviation assets assigned comprise:
- US Army Europe (USAREUR)
- US Army Forces Command (FORSCOM)
- US Army Intelligence and Security Command (INSCOM)
- US Army Materiel Command (AMC)
- US Army Medical Command (MEDCOM)
- Military District of Washington (MDW)

element organized to control units supporting a unified command. Three of these organizations exist and each is assigned a single theater aviation brigade. The structure of the latter is tailored to meet the specific requirements of the theater to which it belongs.

- Corps (CORPS) – The Army's largest maneuver formation is composed of multiple independent units and all four of these formations share a common basic structure. A

Storm validated the AOE concept, the conflict revealed the need for some adjustments to the Army's proposed warfighting strategy. In 1993, the Army chief of staff approved the Aviation Restructure Initiative (ARI), which also addressed deficiencies in AOE aviation unit structures and tailored them for specific missions. Implementation of the ARI began in 1994 and largely will be completed during 2000, at which point the last ARNG aviation maintenance units will be reorganized. The initiative has brought about full integration of the ARNG and the US Army Reserve Command (USARC) into the total Army force. The contribution each element makes to overall missions is shown below.

Mission Area	Active Duty	ARNG	USARC
Combat	36%	58%	6%
Combat Support	45%	36%	19%
Combat Services Support	33%	31%	36%

Under ARI, the aviation assets assigned to a basic division nominally include 24 attack, 24 general support or assault, 11 or 12 command and control (C^2), and 16 cavalry helicopters. Recent changes mean the requirement to equip heavy divisions with a second attack helicopter battalion have been dropped, but a fourth general support company was added to each active-component heavy division. A third assault company also joined each of the light and airborne divisions. These additional units come from the ARNG and are dual tasked, being responsible to their primary division within the strategic reserve. Specialized maintenance units are assigned to the Division Support Command (DISCOM).

Although the structure of aviation brigades differs within specialized divisions, such as airborne and light infantry as well as regimental aviation squadrons of ACRs, the basic battalion structure remains the same.

Besides divisional aviation brigades, each Army theater and corps is assigned its own aviation brigade as well. The structure differs, however, depending on the primary mission of that organization. The same is also true for military intelligence and medical brigades.

Battalions assigned to a corps aviation brigade include assault, combat support, command, heavy helicopter, light-utility helicopter and attack units but they are frequently "chopped" from traditional division or corps activities and reassigned to specific deployments.

In 2000, the basics of ARI will be in place but its full objectives will not be met until the Boeing Sikorsky RAH-66A Comanche enters service in 2006. Modernization is being hampered because remaining Bell UH-1H and Bell AH-1F platforms need to be replaced within ARNG general support, assault and attack units. In the near future, the ARNG will continue to receive Sikorsky UH-60s, but a sufficient number of Boeing (McDonnell Douglas) AH-64s will not be available to this branch until Boeing Sikorsky Comanches come on-line within active-duty units and free up enough Apaches.

Assigned Aviation Assets

Beginning in 1975, the Army assigned each of its divisions 168 aircraft, split between a cavalry and a combat aviation battalion. By 1980, however, division aviation assets had been reduced to just 130 aircraft and were being operated by a separate aviation brigade. It is now closer to 100.

As previously indicated, the Army's rotary-wing fleet was reduced substantially between 1989 and 1999, and now comprises about 5,000 aircraft. Despite procurement of new types and the retirement of large numbers of older aircraft, the average age of the helicopter fleet still exceeds 17 years. In fact, even though the oldest examples are operated by reserve elements, active-duty units are still flying Boeing CH-47D Chinooks delivered as long ago as the early 1980s.

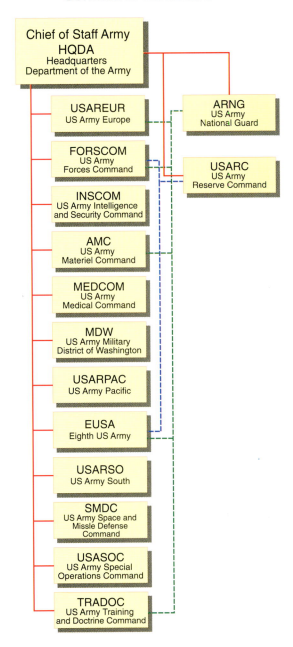

US Army Aviation Command Structure

- Chief of Staff Army HQDA — Headquarters Department of the Army
- USAREUR — US Army Europe
- ARNG — US Army National Guard
- FORSCOM — US Army Forces Command
- USARC — US Army Reserve Command
- INSCOM — US Army Intelligence and Security Command
- AMC — US Army Materiel Command
- MEDCOM — US Army Medical Command
- MDW — US Army Military District of Washington
- USARPAC — US Army Pacific
- EUSA — Eighth US Army
- USARSO — US Army South
- SMDC — US Army Space and Missile Defense Command
- USASOC — US Army Special Operations Command
- TRADOC — US Army Training and Doctrine Command

Although most OH-58A/C helicopters still in service are assigned to ARNG units, a small number continue to fly in support roles with active-duty Army elements.

AVIATION COMMANDS AND UNITS

The Army's aviation assets are assigned to a small number of direct reporting units in addition to the 12 MACOMs previously discussed. In the tables that follow, the commands and their units have been listed so the tables show the total force structure of combat and support units. Units belonging to guard and reserve elements have been integrated within the active-component command structure and are identified in parentheses.

The structure is illustrated down to company level. However, whenever it has become necessary to split them to platoon level, the headquarters unit is identified by a parenthetical minus symbol following the designation, and the platoons are shown as detachments to the company.

US ARMY EUROPE/SEVENTH ARMY (USAREUR/7A)
Headquarters: Campbell Barracks, Heidelberg, Germany

USAREUR was activated in 1945 and is the Army component of US European Command (USEUCOM). This MACOM currently has 91,000 personnel assigned, including 62,000 active-duty troops, and is the Army's largest forward-deployed command. It supports US, NATO and multinational objectives. One ARNG aviation battalion and an active-component provisional battalion are directly assigned.

The CH-47D Chinook continues to serve as the Army's heavy-lift "workhorse." Through Boeing's Improved Cargo Helicopter (ICH) program, which is currently in progress, the service hopes to upgrade as many as 300 of these helicopters to CH-47F standard.

US ARMY EUROPE/SEVENTH ARMY (USAREUR/7A)
Campbell Barracks, Heidelberg, Germany

Unit	Location	Aircraft
EACTAB(P)	Heidelberg AAF, Germany	
A(-)/214th AVN (TA)	Wiesbaden AAF, Germany	C-12F
Det. 1 A/214th AVN (TA)	Vicenza AB Italy	C-12F
HQ USEUCOM FLT DET	Stuttgart AAF, Echterdingen, Germany	C-12F/J
C/214th AVN (TA)	Heidelberg AAF, Germany	C-12F, UC-35A
D/214th AVN (CMD)	Heidelberg AAF	UH-60A
1-168th AVN (TAB) (ARNG)	Gray AAF, Fort Lewis, Washington	
A(-)/249th AVN (TA) (ARNG)	Eastern Oregon Regional Airport, Pendleton, Oregon	C-23B/B+
Det. 1 A/249th AVN (TA) (ARNG)	Will Rogers World Airport, Oklahoma City, Oklahoma	C-23B+
Det. 2 A/249th AVN (TA) (ARNG)	Gray AAF, Fort Lewis, Washington	C-23B+
Det. 3 A/249th AVN (TA) (ARNG)	Rapid City Regional Airport, South Dakota	C-23B+
I(-)/185th AVN (TA) (ARNG)	Gulfport-Biloxi Regional Airport, Mississippi	C-23B
Det. 1 I/185th AVN (TA) (ARNG)	Fresno-Yosemite International Airport, California	C-23B
Det. 2 I/185th AVN (TA) (ARNG)	Groton-New London Airport, Connecticut	C-23B
Det. 3 I/185th AVN (TA) (ARNG)	Springfield-Branson Regional Airport, Missouri	C-23B

* Unit to be activated as 1-214th AVN (TAB) on 1 October 2000.

7th Army Training Command	Grafenwoehr, Germany	
AVN DET	Grafenwoehr AAF, Germany	UH-1H, C-12F
CMTC AVN DET	Hohenfels AAF, Germany	UH-1H

V Corps - Campbell Barracks, Heidelberg, Germany

12th Aviation Brigade	Darmstadt AHP, Wiesbaden, Germany	
6-158th AVN (HHB) (USARC)	Hood AAF, Fort Hood, Texas	
F/159th AVN (HH)	Giebelstadt AAF, Mannheim, Germany	CH-47D
A/6-158th AVN (HH) (USARC)	Hood AAF, Fort Hood, Texas	CH-47D
B/4-123d AVN (HH)*	Wainwright AAF, Fort Wainwright, Alaska	CH-47D
5-158th AVN (CAB)	Giebelstadt AAF, Manheim, Germany	UH-60A
A/5-158th AVN (CMD)	Wiesbaden AAF, Germany	UH-60L
B/5-158th AVN (CMD)	Aviano AB, Italy	UH-60A
C/5-158th AVN (GS)	Wiesbaden AAF, Germany	UH-60L
C/158th AVN (ASLT)	Giebelstadt AAF, Germany	UH-60L
D/158th AVN (ASLT)	Giebelstadt AAF	UH-60L
1-207th AVN (CSAB)(ARNG)**	Bryant AHP, Fort Richardson, Alaska	
A/1-207th AVN (GS) (ARNG)**	Bryant AHP	UH-60L
B/1-207th AVN (GS) (ARNG)**	Bryant AHP	UH-60L
C/1-207th AVN (GS) (ARNG)**	Wainwright AAF, Fort Wainwright	UH-60L
3-126th AVN (LUHB) (ARNG)	Otis ANGB, Massachusetts	
A/3-126th AVN (LUH) (ARNG)	New Castle County Airport, Delaware	UH-1H/V
B/3-126th AVN (LUH) (ARNG)	Akron Canton Regional Airport, Ohio	UH-1H/V
11th AVN GP (ATK)	Storck Barracks, Illesheim, Germany	
2-6th CAV (ATK)	Storck Barracks	
A/2-6th CAV (ATK)	Storck Barracks	AH-64A
B/2-6th CAV (ATK)	Storck Barracks	AH-64A
C/2-6th CAV (ATK)	Storck Barracks	AH-64A

* Unit is dual tasked to US Army Alaska/4-123d AVN (TAB)
** Unit is dual tasked to US Army Alaska/207th Infantry Group

7th Army Training Command (ATC)
Hqtrs: Grafenwoehr, Germany

The 7th ATC is responsible for all training activities for the USAREUR, including the Combat Maneuver Training Center (CMTC). A single aviation detachment and the CMTC aviation detachment are assigned to this sub-command (SUBCOM).

The Army has acquired two Beech C-12Js from the USAF, including serial 86-0079, based at Stuttgart IAP, Germany. The aircraft serves Headquarters United States European Command.

US ARMY EUROPE/SEVENTH ARMY (Continued)
V Corps - Campbell Barracks, Heidelberg, Germany

Unit	Location	Aircraft
6-6th CAV (ATK)	Storck Barracks, Illesheim, Germany	
A/6-6th CAV (ATK)	Storck Barracks	AH-64A
B/6-6th CAV (ATK)	Storck Barracks	AH-64A
C/6-6th CAV (ATK)	Storck Barracks	AH-64A
205th MIBDE (CEWI)	**Wiesbaden, Germany**	
1st MI Bn (AE)	Wiesbaden AAF, Germany	
B/1st MI Bn (AE)	Wiesbaden AAF	RC-12D/K
3d COSCOM	**Wiesbaden, Germany**	
30th Medical Brigade	Heidelberg, Germany	
421st Medical Evacuation Battalion	Wiesbaden AAF, Germany	
45th MED CO (AA)	Katterbach AHP, Ansbach, Germany	UH-60A
159th MED CO (AA)	Darmstadt AHP, Germany	UH-60A
236th MED CO (AA)	Landstuhl AHP, Germany	UH-60A
1st Armored Division	**Bad Kreuznach, Germany**	
1AD AVNBDE	Fliegerhorst Barracks, Erlensee, Germany	
1-501st AVN (ATKHB)	Fliegerhorst AAF, Erlensee	
A/1-501st AVN (ATK)	Fliegerhorst AAF	AH-64A
B/1-501st AVN (ATK)	Fliegerhorst AAF	AH-64A
C/1-501st AVN (ATK)	Fliegerhorst AAF	AH-64A
2-501st AVN (GSAB)	Fliegerhorst AAF	
A/2-501st AVN (GS)	Fliegerhorst AAF	UH-60L
B/2-501st AVN (GS)	Fliegerhorst AAF	UH-60L
C/2-501st AVN (CMD)	Fliegerhorst AAF	UH-60A, EH-60A
A/2-104th AVN (GS) (ARNG)*	Muir AAF, Fort Indiantown Gap, Pennsylvania	UH-1H
1-1st CAV	Armstrong Barracks, Büdingen, Germany	
D/1-1st CAV	Armstrong AHP, Büdingen	OH-58D
E/1-1st CAV	Armstrong AHP	OH-58D

* Unit is dual tasked to 28ID(M)/2-104th AVN (GSAB)

1st Infantry Division (Mechanized)	**Leighton Barracks, Würzburg, Germany**	
1ID(M) AVNBDE	Katterbach AHP, Ansbach, Germany	
1-1st AVN (ATKHB)	Katterbach AHP	
A/1-1st AVN (ATK)	Katterbach AHP	AH-64A
B/1-1st AVN (ATK)	Katterbach AHP	AH-64A
C/1-1st AVN (ATK)	Katterbach AHP	AH-64A
2-1st AVN (GSAB)	Katterbach AHP	
A/2-1st AVN (GS)	Katterbach AHP	UH-60L
B/2-1st AVN (GS)	Katterbach AHP	UH-60L
C/2-1st AVN (CMD)	Katterbach AHP	UH-60L, EH-60A
B/1-140th AVN (GS) (ARNG)*	Los Alamitos AAF, California	UH-60A
1-4th CAV	Conn Barracks, Schweinfurt, Germany	
D/1-4th CAV	Schweinfurt AAF	OH-58D
E/1-4th CAV	Schweinfurt AAF	OH-58D

* Unit is dual tasked to 40ID(M)/1-140th AVN (GSAB)

Supreme Headquarters Allied Powers Europe (SHAPE) Mons, Belgium

US Army Element SHAPE FLT DET	Chiévres AB, Belgium	UH-60A
LSE FLT DET	Cigli AB, Izmir, Turkey	C-12F, UH-1H
SETAF AVN DET	Vicenza AB, Italy	UH-1H

V Corps

V Corps (VCORPS)
Hqtrs: Campbell Barracks, Heidelberg, Germany

VCORPS is assigned a corps aviation brigade and a military intelligence brigade; one armored and one infantry division; and a corps support command. In recent years its units have participated in United Nations operations in northern Iraq, Turkey, Rwanda, Somalia and the Balkans. Although it is forward deployed, active-duty units represent only 64 percent of its strength. Thirty percent comprises ARNG elements and six percent comes from the USARC.

1st Infantry Division (Mechanized)

Supreme Headquarters Allied Powers Europe (SHAPE)
Hqtrs: Mons, Belgium

SHAPE controls US Army assets that comprise three aviation detachments supporting four major NATO commands: Allied Forces Southern Europe (AFSOUTH), Allied Forces Central Europe (AFCENT), Allied Forces Northwest Europe (AFNORTHWEST) and Allied Forces Land Southeast (AFLANDSOUTHEAST).

US Army

US ARMY FORCES COMMAND (FORSCOM)
Headquarters: Fort McPherson, Georgia

FORSCOM is the Army component of US Joint Forces Command. Established on 1 October 1993, it is the Army's largest single MACOM and is composed of active-duty, ARNG and USARC units.

FORSCOM is tasked with the defense of the continental United States (CONUS) and Canada, and is also responsible for providing units and troops for deployment to trouble spots around the world. In addition to a pair of combat training centers, three deployable corps are assigned to FORSCOM, each consisting of active-duty and reserve divisions, brigades and regiments. In addition, the Army's Joint Readiness Training Center (JRTC) at Fort Polk, Louisiana, and the National Training Center (NTC), in California, are directly assigned. Besides 202,000 full-time troops and civilians assigned during peacetime, 360,000 ARNG and over 200,000 USARC troops are available for mobilization.

Aviation assets assigned to the JRTC and NTC include small numbers of helicopters (UH-1H, JUH-1H, UH-1V, OH-58C and UH-60A models) used primarily for operational support and medical evacuation (MEDEVAC) missions on the training ranges. Two additional infantry divisions were recently activated under FORSCOM. Whereas each is structured around three ARNG infantry brigades, it has an active-duty command element as well. The 24th and 7th Infantry Divisions are headquartered at Fort Riley, Kansas, and Fort Carson, Colorado, respectively. However, neither division has an "organic" aviation brigade currently assigned.

Assigned to FORSCOM are the First, Third and Fifth US Armies, abbreviated as ONEUSA, THREEUSA and FIVEUSA, respectively. Administratively, CONUS-based units report to ONEUSA and FIVEUSA, with the Mississippi River forming the east-west divide. THREEUSA is a component of US Army Forces Central Command (ARCENT) and is discussed later.

Joint Readiness Training Center (JRTC)
Hqtrs: Fort Polk, Louisiana

Provisionally activated at Fort Chafee, Arkansas, in 1987, as a training center for light infantry and Special Operations personnel, the JRTC relocated to Fort Polk following the BRAC recommendations. It was officially activated there on 20 August 1993.

The center integrates Army and joint-service wartime and contingency training for light forces, including infantry, paratroopers, air-assault soldiers, special forces and rangers. It is supported by a small flight

The AH-1F model is the only Cobra variant still in Army service. This example is assigned to Pennsylvania's 1-104th Cavalry Squadron,

US ARMY FORCES COMMAND (FORSCOM)
Fort McPherson, Georgia

Unit	Location	Aircraft
First US Army (ONEUSA) - Fort Gillem, Atlanta, Georgia		
Fifth US Army (FIVEUSA) - Fort Sam Houston, San Antonio, Texas		
Joint Readiness Training Center (JRTC)	**Fort Polk, Louisiana**	
JRTC FLT DET	Polk AAF, Fort Polk	OH-58C, UH-1H
JRTC OPS GRP	Polk AAF	RQ-5A
National Training Center (NTC)	**Fort Irwin, California**	
11th Armored Cavalry Regiment (OPFOR)	Fort Irwin	
NTC Corps Support Battalion	Fort Irwin	
NTC AVN CO (ASLT)	Barstow Daggett Airport, California	UH/JUH-1H, UH-60A
USAAAD	Barstow Daggett Airport	UH-60A
NTC FLT DET	Barstow Daggett Airport	OH-58C
I Corps - Fort Lewis, Washington		
USAG FLT DET	Gray AAF, Fort Lewis	UH-1H
103d COSCOM (ARNG)	**State Armory, Des Moines, Iowa**	
62d Medical Group	Fort Lewis, Washington	
85th Medical Evacuation Battalion	Fort Lewis	
54th MED CO (AA)	Gray AAF, Fort Lewis	UH-60A
126th MED CO (AA) (ARNG)	Sacramento Mather Airport, California	UH-60A
717th MED CO (AA) (ARNG)	Santa Fe County Municipal Airport, New Mexico	UH-60A
Det. 1 717th MED CO (ARNG)	Reno Stead Airport, Nevada	UH-60A
1022d MED CO (AA) (ARNG)	Cheyenne Municipal Airport, Wyoming	UH-60A
Det. 1 1022d MED CO (ARNG)	Buckley ANGB, Colorado	UH-60A
641st Medical Evacuation Battalion (ARNG)	McNary Field, Salem, Oregon	
1042d MED CO (AA)(ARNG)	McNary Field	UH-60L
1085th MED CO (AA) (ARNG)	Rapid City Regional Airport, South Dakota	UH-60A
Det. 1 1085th MED CO (ARNG)	Helena Regional County Airport, Montana	UH-1H/V
1133d MED CO (AA) (ARNG)	Mobile Downtown Airport, Alabama	UH-1H/V
278th Armored Cavalry Regiment	**State Armory, Knoxville, Tennessee**	
4-278th Regimental Aviation Sqn (ARNG)	Smyrna Airport, Tennessee	
Det. 1 HHT/4-278th ACR (CEWI) (ARNG)	Smyrna Airport	EH-60A
N/4-278th ACR (ATK) (ARNG)	McGhee Tyson Airport, Knoxville, Tennessee	AH-1F
O/4-278th ACR (ATK) (ARNG)	McGhee Tyson Airport	AH-1F
P/4-278th ACR (ATK) (ARNG)	McGhee Tyson Airport	AH-1F
Q/4-278th ACR (CAV) (ARNG)	Smyrna Airport, Tennessee	AH-1F
R/4-278th ACR (CAV) (ARNG)	Smyrna Airport	AH-1F
S/4-278th ACR (ASLT) (ARNG)	Smyrna Airport	UH-60A

detachment that operates RQ-5A unmanned aerial vehicles (UAVs) for training scenarios, as well as the OPTEC Threat Support Activity (OTSA). OPTEC is the abbreviation for the Operational Test and Evaluation Command.

National Training Center (NTC)
Hqtrs: Fort Irwin, California

Activated on 16 October 1980, the NTC is the Army's premier training center for mechanized armored units. It provides troops with training in harsh environments and against formidable opposing-force strengths. A permanently assigned assault aviation company flies UH-1Hs to simulate enemy aircraft, while UH-60A Blackhawks assigned to the 11th ACR fly in support of the opposing force. OH-58Cs are flown by observers.

28th Infantry Division

I Corps (ICORPS)
Hqtrs: Fort Lewis, Washington

ICORPS is known as the 'America's Corps' but is generally referred to as 'Eye Corps,' and is composed almost exclusively of ARNG units. It is the primary backup force for US Army Pacific in times of hostility, and the eight ARNG divisions assigned include single light infantry and armored divisions, two mechanized infantry and four medium infantry divisions. However, the military intelligence brigade assigned to ICORPS is the only one at corps level without an assigned aviation battalion.

As a result of the Army's Force XXI Heavy Division Redesign, five of the general support aviation companies belonging to four heavy divisions within ICORPS also report to active-component heavy divisions. Of the dual-tasked companies, two are still flying the UH-1H and, to meet their new mission requirements, probably will receive UH-60s in the near future. Similarly, six assault companies from four ARNG medium and light divisions have been dual tasked, reporting also to active-duty airborne and light divisions. Four of these units are also flying UH-1Hs. In all likelihood, funding for Blackhawks is imminent.

US ARMY FORCES COMMAND (Continued)
I Corps - Fort Lewis, Washington

Unit	Location	Aircraft
66th Aviation Brigade	**Camp Murray/Fort Lewis, Washington**	
185th AVN GP (LIFT) (ARNG)	Hawkins Field, Jackson, Mississippi	
1-108th AVN (AHB) (ARNG)	Forbes Field, Topeka, Kansas	
A(-)/1-108th AVN (ASLT) (ARNG)	Forbes Field	UH-60A
Det. A/1-108th AVN (ASLT)	Salina Municipal Airport, Kansas	UH-60A
B/1-108th AVN (ASLT) (ARNG)	Tulsa International Airport, Oklahoma	UH-60A
1-112th AVN (LUHB) (ARNG)	Bismarck Municipal Airport, North Dakota	
A/1-112th AVN (LUH) (ARNG)	Bismark Municipal Airport	UH-1H/V
B/1-112th AVN (LUH) (ARNG)	Helena Regional County Airport, Montana	UH-1H
C/1-112th AVN (LUH) (ARNG)	Helena Regional County Airport	UH-1H
D/1-112th AVN (LUH) (ARNG)	Los Alamitos AFRC, California	UH-1H
1-185th AVN (CAB) (ARNG)	Hawkins Field, Jackson, Mississippi	
A/1-185th AVN (TAR) (ARNG)	Gray AAF, Fort Lewis, Washington	OH-58C
B/1-185th AVN (CMD) (ARNG)	Gray AAF	UH-60A
C/1-185th AVN (CMD) (ARNG)	Hawkins Field, Jackson, Mississippi	MH-60A
D/1-185th AVN (CMD) (ARNG)	Hawkins Field	MH-60A
1-189th AVN (CSAB) (ARNG)	Helena Regional County Airport, Montana	
A/1-189th AVN (GS) (ARNG)	Helena Regional County Airport	UH-60A
B/1-189th AVN (GS) (ARNG)	Boise Air Terminal-Gowen Field, Idaho	UH-60A
C/1-189th AVN (GS) (ARNG)	Papago AAF, Phoenix, Arizona	UH-60A
D/1-189th AVN (GS) (ARNG)	Salt Lake City Municipal Airport, Utah	UH-60A
3-140th AVN (HHB) (ARNG)	Stockton Municipal Airport, California	
G(-)/140th AVN (HH) (ARNG)	Stockton Municipal Airport	CH-47D
Det. 1 G/140th AVN (HH)(ARNG)	Reno-Stead Municipal Airport, Nevada	CH-47D
E(-)/168th AVN (HH) (ARNG)	Gray AAF, Fort Lewis, Washington	CH-47D
Det. 1 E/168th AVN (HH) (ARNG)	Eastern Oregon Regional Airport, Pendleton, Oregon	CH-47D
C/193d AVN (HH) (ARNG)	Wheeler AAF, Schofield Barracks, Hawaii	CH-47D
B/214th AVN (HH)*	Wheeler AAF	CH-47D
211th AVN GRP (ATK)(ARNG)	Salt Lake City Municipal Airport, Utah	
1-151st AVN (ATKHB) (ARNG)	McEntire ANGS, Eastover, South Carolina	
A/1-151st AVN (ATK) (ARNG)	McEntire ANGS	AH-64A
B/1-151st AVN (ATK) (ARNG)	McEntire ANGS	AH-64A
C/1-151st AVN(ATK) (ARNG)	McEntire ANGS	AH-64A
1-183d AVN (ATKHB) (ARNG)	Boise Air Terminal-Gowen Field, Idaho	
A/1-183d AVN (ATK) (ARNG)	Boise Air Terminal-Gowen Field	AH-64A
B/1-183d AVN (ATK) (ARNG)	Boise Air Terminal-Gowen Field	AH-64A
C/1-183d AVN (ATK) (ARNG)	Boise Air Terminal-Gowen Field	AH-64A
1-285th AVN (ATKHB) (ARNG)	Silver Bell AHP, Marana, Arizona	
A/1-285th AVN (ATK) (ARNG)	Silver Bell AHP	AH-64A
B/1-285th AVN (ATK) (ARNG)	Silver Bell AHP	AH-64A
C/1-285th AVN (ATK) (ARNG)	Silver Bell AHP	AH-64A

* Unit is dual tasked to US Army Pacific

Unit	Location	Aircraft
28th Infantry Division (Mechanized)	**Fort Indiantown Gap, Anneville, Pennsylvania**	
28ID (M) AVNBDE (ARNG)	Muir AAF, Fort Indiantown Gap, Pennsylvania	
1-104th AVN (ATKHB) (ARNG)	Johnstown-Cambria County Airport, Pennsylvania	
A/1-104th AVN (ATK) (ARNG)	Johnstown-Cambria County Airport	AH-1F
B/1-104th AVN (ATK) (ARNG)	Johnstown-Cambria County Airport	AH-1F
C/1-104th AVN (ATK) (ARNG)	Johnstown-Cambria County Airport	AH-1F
2-104th AVN (GSAB) (ARNG)	Muir AAF, Fort Indiantown Gap, Pennsylvania	
A/2-104th AVN (GS) (ARNG)*	Muir AAF	UH-1H
B/2-104th AVN (GS) (ARNG)	Stockton Metropolitan Airport, California	UH-1H
C/2-104th AVN (CMD) (ARNG)	Ohio CAP/Stifel Field, Wheeling, West Virginia	UH-1H, OH-58C
1-104th CAV (ARNG)	State Armory Philadelphia, Pennsylvania	
D/1-104th CAV (ARNG)	Muir AAF, Fort Indiantown Gap, Pennsylvania	AH-1F
E/1-104th CAV (ARNG)	Muir AAF	AH-1F

* Unit is dual tasked to 1AD/2-501st AVN (GSAB)

US Army

Serial 93-26930, a UH-60L, was with HHC-1-149 AVN when photographed at its home base at Ellington Field, Houston, Texas. The unit is part of the Texas ARNG, assigned to the 49th Armored Division.

US ARMY FORCES COMMAND (Continued)
I Corps - Fort Lewis, Washington

Unit	Location	Aircraft
29th Infantry Division (Light)	**Fort Belvoir, Virginia**	
29ID(L) AVNBDE (ARNG)	State Armory, Edgewood, Maryland	
1-150th AVN (ATKHB) (ARNG)	Mercer County Airport, Trenton, New Jersey	
A/1-150th AVN (ATK) (ARNG)	Mercer County Airport	AH-1F
B/1-150th AVN (ATK) (ARNG)	Mercer County Airport	AH-1F
C/1-150th AVN (ATK) (ARNG)	Mercer County Airport	AH-1F
2-224th AVN (AHB) (ARNG)	Richmond International Airport/Byrd Field, Virginia	
A/2-224th AVN (ASLT) (ARNG)*	Richmond International Airport/Byrd Field	UH-1H
B/2-224th AVN (ASLT) (ARNG)	Richmond International Airport/Byrd Field	UH-60A
C/2-224th AVN (CMD) (ARNG)	Weide AHP, Aberdeen Proving Ground, Maryland	UH-1H
1-158th CAV (RECON) (ARNG)	State Armory, Edgewood, Maryland	
B/1-158th CAV (RECON) (ARNG)	Weide AHP, Aberdeen Proving Ground, Maryland	AH-1F
C/1-158th CAV (RECON) (ARNG)	Weide AHP	AH-1F

* Unit is dual tasked to 82d ABN DIV (AASLT)/2-82d AVN (AHB)

Unit	Location	Aircraft
34th Infantry Division	**State Armory, St. Paul, Minnesota**	
34ID AVNBDE (ARNG)	St. Paul Downtown Airport, Minnesota	
2-147th AVN (AHB) (ARNG)	St. Paul Downtown Airport	
A/2-147th AVN (ASLT) (ARNG)*	St Paul Downtown Airport	UH-1H
B/2-147th AVN (ASLT) (ARNG)	Eagle County Regional Airport, Gypsum, Colorado	UH-1H
C/2-147th AVN (ASLT) (ARNG)**	Abrams Municipal Airport, Grand Ledge, Michigan	UH-1H
D/2-147th AVN (CMD) (ARNG)	Abrams Municipal Airport	UH-1H, OH-58C
3-147th AVN (ATKHB) (ARNG)	St. Paul Downtown Airport, Minnesota	
A/3-147th AVN (ATK) (ARNG)	St. Paul Downtown Airport	AH-1F
B/3-147th AVN (ATK) (ARNG)	St. Paul Downtown Airport	AH-1F
C/3-147th AVN (ATK) (ARNG)	St. Paul Downtown Airport	AH-1F
1-113th CAV (ARNG)	Camp Dodge, Johnston, Iowa	
D/1-113th CAV (ARNG)	Waterloo Municipal Airport, Iowa	AH-1F
E/1-113th CAV (ARNG)	Waterloo Municipal Airport	AH-1F

* Unit is dual tasked to 101st AD (AASLT)/6-101st AVN (AHB)

** Unit is dual tasked to 25ID(L)/2-25th AVN (AHB)

I Corps

29th Infantry Division

40th Infantry Division (Mechanized)

US ARMY FORCES COMMAND (Continued)
I Corps - Fort Lewis, Washington

Unit	Location	Aircraft
35th Infantry Division (Mechanized)	**Fort Leavenworth, Kansas**	
35ID AVNBDE (ARNG)	State Armory, Warrensburg, Missouri	
1-135th AVN (ATKHB) (ARNG)	Whiteman AFB, Missouri	
A/1-135th AVN (ATK) (ARNG)	Whiteman AFB	AH-1F
B/1-135th AVN (ATK) (ARNG)	Whiteman AFB	AH-1F
C/1-135th AVN (ATK) (ARNG)	Whiteman AFB	AH-1F
1-114th AVN (AHB) (ARNG)	Camp Robinson, N. Little Rock, Arkansas	
A/1-114th AVN (ASLT) (ARNG)	Camp Robinson	UH-60A
B/1-114th AVN (ASLT) (ARNG)*	Capital City Airport, Frankfort, Kentucky	UH-60A
C/1-114th AVN (ASLT) (ARNG)**	Memorial Airport, Jefferson City, Missouri	UH-1H
D/1-114th AVN (CMD) (ARNG)	Salina Municipal Airport, Kansas	UH-1H, OH-58C
1-167th CAV (ARNG)	Lincoln Municipal Airport, Nebraska	
D/1-167th CAV (ARNG)	Lincoln Municipal Airport	AH-1F
E/1-167th CAV (ARNG)	Lincoln Municipal Airport	AH-1F

* Unit is dual tasked to 101AD (AASLT)/5-101st AVN (AHB)

** Unit is dual tasked to 10ID(L)/2-10th AVN (AHB)

38th Infantry Division

US Army
Corps and Division Names

I Corps
'Eye Corps'

III Corps
'Phantom Corps'

V Corps
'Victory Corps'

XVIII Airborne Corps
'Dragon Corps'

1st Armored Division
'Old Ironsides'

1st Cavalry Division
'First Team'

1st Infantry Division (Mechanized)
'Big Red One'

2d Infantry Division (Mechanized)
'Indianhead Division'

3d Infantry Division (Mechanized)
'Marne Division'

4th Infantry Division (Mechanized)
'Ivy Division'

7th Infantry Division (Light)
'Bayonet'

10th Infantry Division (Light)
'Mountain Division'

24th Infantry Division (Mechanized)
'Ivy'

25th Infantry Division (Light)
'Tropic Lightning'

82d Airborne Division
'All Americans'

101st Airborne Division (Air Assault)
'Screaming Eagles'

28th Infantry Division (Mechanized)
'Keystone'

29th Infantry Division (Light)
'Blue and Gray'

34th Infantry Division
'Red Bull'

35th Infantry Division
'Santa Fe'

38th Infantry Division
'Cyclone'

40th Infantry Division (Mechanized)
'Sunburst'

42d Infantry Division (Mechanized)
'Rainbow'

49th Armored Division
'Lone Star'

US ARMY FORCES COMMAND (Continued)
I Corps - Fort Lewis, Washington

Unit	Location	Aircraft
38th Infantry Division	**State Armory Indianapolis, Indiana**	
38ID AVNBDE (ARNG)	Shelbyville Municipal Airport, Indiana	
1-238th AVN (ATKHB) (ARNG)	Abrams Municipal Airport, Grand Ledge, Michigan	
A/1-238th AVN (ATK) (ARNG)	Abrams Municipal Airport	AH-1F
B/1-238th AVN (ATK) (ARNG)	Abrams Municipal Airport	AH-1F
C/1-238th AVN (ATK) (ARNG)	Abrams Municipal Airport	AH-1F
1-137th AVN (AHB) (ARNG)	Akron-Canton Regional Airport, Ohio	
A/1-137th AVN (ASLT) (ARNG)*	Rickenbacker ANGB, Ohio	UH-1H
B/1-137th AVN (ASLT) (ARNG)	Shelbyville Municipal Airport, Indiana	UH-1H
C/1-137th AVN (ASLT) (ARNG)	Bangor International Airport, Maine	UH-1H
D(-)/1-137th AVN (CMD) (ARNG)	Rickenbacker ANGB, Ohio	UH-1H, OH-58A
Det. 1 D/1-137th AVN (CMD)	Akron-Canton Airport, Ohio	UH-1H, OH-58A
2-107th CAV (ARNG)	State Armory, Kettering, Ohio	
D/2-107th CAV (ARNG)	Rickenbacker ANGB, Ohio	AH-1F
E/2-107th CAV (ARNG)	Rickenbacker ANGB	AH-1F

* Unit is dual tasked to 101AD (AASLT)/4-101st AVN (AHB)

Unit	Location	Aircraft
40th Infantry Division (Mechanized)	**AFRC Los Alamitos, California**	
40ID(M) AVNBDE (ARNG)	Fresno Air Terminal, California	
1-211th AVN (ATKHB) (ARNG)	Salt Lake City Municipal Airport, Utah	
A/1-211th AVN (ATK) (ARNG)	Salt Lake City Municipal Airport	AH-64A
B/1-211th AVN (ATK) (ARNG)	Salt Lake City Municipal Airport	AH-64A
C/1-211th AVN (ATK) (ARNG)	Salt Lake City Municipal Airport	AH-64A
1-140th AVN (GSAB) (ARNG)	Los Alamitos AAF, California	
A/1-140th AVN (GS) (ARNG)	Sacramento Mather Airport, California	UH-1H
B/1-140th AVN (GS) (ARNG)*	Los Alamitos AAF, California	UH-60A
C/1-140th AVN (CMD) (ARNG)	Los Alamitos AAF	UH-1H, OH-58C, EH-60A
1-18th CAV (ARNG)	State Armory, Ontario, California	
D/1-18th CAV (ARNG)	Los Alamitos AAF, California	AH-1F
E/1-18th CAV (ARNG)	Los Alamitos AAF	AH-1F

* Unit is dual tasked to 1ID(M)/2-1st AVN (GSAB)

Unit	Location	Aircraft
42d Infantry Division (Mechanized)	**State Armory, Troy, New York**	
42ID(M) AVNBDE (ARNG)	State Armory, Patchogue, New York	
1-142d AVN (ATKHB) (ARNG)	Rochester International Airport, New York	
A/1-142d AVN (ATK) (ARNG)	Rochester International Airport	AH-1F
B/1-142d AVN (ATK) (ARNG)	Rochester International Airport	AH-1F
C/1-142d AVN (ATK) (ARNG)	Rochester International Airport	AH-1F
2-126th AVN (GSAB) (ARNG)	Bradley IAP, Windsor Locks, Connecticut	
A/2-126th AVN (GS) (ARNG)	Long Island MacArthur Airport, New York	UH-1H
B/2-126th AVN (GS) (ARNG)*	Bradley IAP, Windsor Locks, Connecticut	UH-1H
C/2-126th AVN (CMD) (ARNG)	New Castle County Airport, Delaware	UH-1H, OH-58C
5-117th CAV (ARNG)	State Armory Vineland, New Jersey	
D/5-117th CAV (ARNG)	Quonset State Airport, N. Kingston, Rhode Island	AH-1F
E/5-117th CAV (ARNG)	Quonset State Airport	AH-1F

* Unit is dual tasked to 3ID(M)/2-3d AVN (GSAB)

Unit	Location	Aircraft
49th Armored Division	**Camp Mabry, Austin, Texas**	
49AD AVNBDE (ARNG)	Austin-Bergstrom International Airport, Texas	
1-149th AVN (ATKHB) (ARNG)	Ellington Field, Houston, Texas	
A/1-149th AVN (ATK) (ARNG)	Ellington Field	AH-64A
B/1-149th AVN (ATK) (ARNG)	Ellington Field	AH-64A
C/1-149th AVN (ATK) (ARNG)	Ellington Field	AH-64A
2-149th AVN (GSAB) (ARNG)	Martindale AAF, San Antonio, Texas	
A/2-149th AVN (GS) (ARNG)*	Austin-Bergstrom International Airport, Texas	UH-60L
B/2-149th AVN (GS) (ARNG)**	Grand Prairie AAF, Texas	UH-60L
C(-)/2-149th AVN (CMD) (ARNG)	Martindale AAF, San Antonio, Texas	UH-1H, OH-58C
Det. 1 C/2-149th AVN (CMD)	Austin-Bergstrom International Airport, Texas	EH-60A
D/2-149th AVN (GS) (ARNG)	Martindale AAF, San Antonio, Texas	UH-60L
1-124th CAV (ARNG)	State Armory Waco, Texas	
D/1-124th CAV (ARNG)	Austin-Bergstrom International Airport, Texas	AH-1F
E/1-124th CAV (ARNG)	Austin-Bergstrom International Airport	AH-1F

* Unit is dual tasked to 1CD/2-227th AVN (GSAB)
** Unit is dual tasked to 4ID(M)/2-4th AVN (GSAB)

US Army

III Corps (IIICORPS)
Hqtrs: Fort Hood, Texas

Often referred to as III Armored Corps, IIICORPS is also known as the 'Phantom Corps.' It is structured around an armored and mechanized force and is responsible for providing a deployable armored force in the event of conflicts in Europe or the Pacific region. The corps' combat element is composed of two active-component divisions, a military intelligence brigade and an ACR, but much of its support structure, including the support command and much of its aviation brigade come from reserve forces. Exceptions include two cavalry squadrons based in Korea, and a single cavalry brigade tasked with preparing units for the AH-64D Apache Longbow. Nineteen percent of IIICORPS units are active duty and account for most of the combat assets assigned, whereas 64 percent of its strength comes from the ARNG and 17 percent comes from the USARC. Reserve elements provide most of the support functions.

US ARMY FORCES COMMAND (Continued)
III Corps - Fort Hood, Texas

Unit	Location	Aircraft
21st Cavalry Brigade (Air Combat)	**Hood AAF, Fort Hood, Texas**	
HHT/21st CAV	Hood AAF	AH-64A/D, OH-58D
B/1-158th AVN (CMD)	Hood AAF	UH-60A
13th COSCOM	**Fort Hood, Texas**	
1st Medical Group	Fort Hood	
36th Medical Evacuation Battalion	Fort Hood	
36th MED DET (AA)	Polk AAF, Fort Polk, Louisiana.	UH-60A
82d MED CO (AA)	Marshall AAF, Fort Riley, Kansas	UH-60A
Det. 1 82d MED CO (AA)	Henry Post, AAF, Fort Sill, Oklahoma	UH-60A
507th MED CO (AA)	Hood AAF, Fort Hood, Texas	UH-60A
Det. 1 507th MED CO (AA)	Kelly AAF, Fort Sam Houston, Texas	UH-60A
571st MED CO (AA)	Butts AAF, Fort Carson, Colorado	UH-60A
Det. 1 571st MED CO (AA)	Biggs AAF, Fort Bliss, Texas	UH-60A
110th Medical Evacuation Battalion	Lincoln Municipal Airport, Nebraska	
24th MED CO (AA) (ARNG)	Lincoln Municipal Airport	UH-60A
Det. 1 24th MED CO (ARNG)	Forbes Field, Topeka, Kansas	UH-60A
172d MED CO (AA) (ARNG)	Robinson AAF, N. Little Rock, Arkansas	UH-60A
812th MED CO (AA) (ARNG)	Lakefront Airport, New Orleans, Louisiana	UH-1H/V
Det.1 812th MED CO (AA) (ARNG)	Muldrow AHP, Lexington, Oklahoma	UH-1H/V
832d MED CO (AA) (ARNG)	West Bend Municipal Airport, Wisconsin	UH-1H/V
3d Armored Cavalry Regiment	**Fort Carson, Colorado**	
4-3d Regimental Aviation Squadron	Butts AAF, Fort Carson	
HHT/4-3d ACR (CEWI)	Butts AAF	EH-60A
N/4-3d ACR (CAV)	Butts AAF	OH-58D
O/4-3d ACR (CAV)	Butts AAF	OH-58D
P/4-3d ACR (CAV)	Butts AAF	OH-58D
Q/4-3d ACR (ATK)	Butts AAF	AH-64A
R/4-3d ACR (ATK)	Butts AAF	AH-64A
S/4-3d ACR (ASLT)	Butts AAF	UH-60L
504th MIBDE (CEWI)	**Fort Hood, Texas**	
15th MI Bn (AE)	Robert Gray AAF, Fort Hood	
A/15th MI Bn (AE)	Robert Gray AAF	RQ-5A
B/15th MI Bn (AE)*	Robert Gray AAF	RC-12D

* Unit will transition to RC-12P/Q in FY00

This RC-12D Guardrail serves with the 15th MI Bn at Fort Hood, Texas. As part of the Improved Guardrail V (IGRV) program, the larger Beech platform replaced the RU-21H in the ELINT role.

Army UH-60A/L Blackhawks are assigned to general support, command aviation and assault companies with active-duty and guard units. Plans call for both variants to receive improved engines and avionics in the near future.

One of 48 Boeing CH-47D Chinooks with the 6th Cavalry Brigade's 63d Aviation Group. Serial 90-0226 is assigned to the ARNG's 3-149 AVN (HHB). The battalion is composed of guard and reserve units.

US ARMY FORCES COMMAND (Continued)
III Corps - Fort Hood, Texas

Unit	Location	Aircraft
6th Cavalry Brigade	**Desiderio AAF/Camp Humphreys, Seoul, Rep. of Korea**	
63d AVN GRP (LIFT) (ARNG)	Boone ARNG Center, Frankfort, Kentucky	
1-106th AVN (AHB) (ARNG)	Greater Peoria Regional Airport, Illinois	
A(-)/1-106th AVN (ASLT) (ARNG)	Decatur Airport, Illinois	UH-60A
Det. 1 A/1-106th AVN (ASLT) (ARNG)	Greater Peoria Regional Airport, Illinois	UH-60A
B/1-106th AVN (ASLT) (ARNG)	Midway Airport, Chicago, Illinois	UH-60A
C/1-106th AVN (ASLT) (ARNG)	Greater Peoria Regional Airport, Illinois	UH-60A
1-244th AVN (CAB) (ARNG)	Lakefront Airport, New Orleans, Louisiana	
A/1-244th AVN (TAR) (ARNG)	Alexandria-Esler Regional Airport, Louisiana	OH-58C
B/1-244th AVN (CMD) (ARNG)	Lakefront Airport, New Orleans, Louisiana	UH-60A
C/1-244th AVN (CMD) (ARNG)	Alexandria-Esler Regional Airport, Louisiana	UH-60A
B/158th AVN (CMD)	Hood AAF, Fort Hood, Texas	UH-60A
2-135th AVN (LUHB) (ARNG)	Buckley ANGB, Aurora, Colorado	
A/2-135th AVN (LUH) (ARNG)	Buckley ANGB	UH-1H
B/2-135th AVN (LUH) (ARNG)	Buckley ANGB	UH-1H
C/2-135th AVN (LUH) (ARNG)	Boone Municipal Airport, Iowa	UH-1H
D/2-135th AVN (LUH) (ARNG)	Camp Robinson, N. Little Rock, Arkansas	UH-1H
3-142nd AVN (CSAB) (ARNG)	Albany County Airport, Latham, New York	
A/3-142d AVN (GS) (ARNG)	Albany County Airport	UH-60A
B/3-142d AVN (GS) (ARNG)	Long Island MacArthur Airport, New York	UH-60A
C/3-142d AVN (GS) (ARNG)	Albany County Airport, Latham, New York	UH-60A
D/3-142d AVN (GS) (ARNG)	Isla Grande Airport, San Juan, Puerto Rico	UH-60A
3-149th AVN (HHB) (ARNG)	Grand Prairie AAF, Texas	
F(-)/106th AVN (HH) (ARNG)	Greater Peoria Regional Airport, Illinois	CH-47D
Det. 1 F/106th AVN (HH) (ARNG)	Boone Municipal Airport, Iowa	CH-47D
G(-)/149th AVN (HH) (ARNG)	Grand Prairie AAF, Texas	CH-47D
Det. 1 G/149th AVN (HH) (ARNG)	Mudrow AHP, Lexington, Oklahoma	CH-47D
F/158th AVN (HH) (USARC)	Johnson County Airport, Olathe, Kansas	CH-47D
G/185th AVN (HH) (ARNG)	Key Field, Meridian, Mississippi	CH-47D
385th AVN GRP (ATK) (ARNG)	Papago AAF, Phoenix, Arizona	
1-6th CAV (AC)	Camp Eagle, Pyongteak, Rep. of Korea	
A/1-6th CAV (AC)	Camp Eagle	AH-64A
B/1-6th CAV (AC)	Camp Eagle	AH-64A
C/1-6th CAV (AC)	Camp Eagle	AH-64A
3-6th CAV (AC)	Desiderio AAF/Camp Humphreys, Seoul, Republic of Korea	
A/3-6th CAV (AC)	Desiderio AAF/Camp Humphreys	AH-64A
B/3-6th CAV (AC)	Desiderio AAF/Camp Humphreys	AH-64A
C/3-6th CAV (AC)	Desiderio AAF/Camp Humphreys	AH-64A
8-229th AVN (ATKHB) (USARC)	Godman AAF, Fort Knox, Kentucky	
A/8-229th AVN (ATK) (USARC)	Godman AAF	AH-64A
B/8-229th AVN (ATK) (USARC)	Godman AAF	AH-64A
C/8-229th AVN (ATK) (USARC)	Godman AAF	AH-64A

Organization of the corps dates back to 16 May 1918, soon after which it saw action in World War I French campaigns at Aise-Marne and Meuse-Argone. However, it was inactivated on 9 August 1919 and then reactivated in 1940, assuming responsibility at that time for training combat divisions. Heavily involved in the European Theater of Operations (ETO) in World War II, IIICORPS established the bridgehead at Remagen, enabling the Allies to secure a foothold inside Germany. Since the end of that war, the corps has been inactivated and reactivated twice. Undertaking numerous overseas deployments, it made important contributions to the Vietnam War and, in more recent years, participated in operations in the Caribbean and Central America. It took part in the Gulf War and deployed for the conflict in Bosnia.

US Army
Brigade and Regiment Names

6th Cavalry Brigade
'Black Horse Brigade'

12th Aviation Brigade
'Wings of Victory'

17th Aviation Brigade
'Freedom's Eagles'

18th Aviation Brigade
'Black Barons'/'Wings of the Dragon'

21st Cavalry Brigade (Air Combat)
'Attack Warriors'

2d Armored Cavalry Regiment
'Regiment of Dragoons'

3d Armored Cavalry Regiment
'Brave Rifles'

11th Armored Cavalry Regiment
'Blackhorse Regiment'

278th Armored Cavalry Regiment
'Three Rivers Regiment'

160th Special Operations Aviation Regiment
'Nightstalkers'

501st Military Intelligence Brigade
'Red Dragon Brigade'

513th Military Intelligence Brigade
'Vigilant Knights'

US Army

US ARMY FORCES COMMAND (Continued)
III Corps - Fort Hood, Texas

Unit	Location	Aircraft
1st Cavalry Division	**Fort Hood, Texas**	
1CD AVNBDE	Robert Gray AAF, Fort Hood	
1-227th AVN (ATKHB)	Robert Gray AAF	
A/1-227th AVN (ATK)	Robert Gray AAF	AH-64D
B/1-227th AVN (ATK)	Robert Gray AAF	AH-64D
C/1-227th AVN (ATK)	Robert Gray AAF	AH-64D
2-227th AVN (GSAB)	Robert Gray AAF	
A/2-227th AVN (GS)	Robert Gray AAF	UH-60L
B/2-227th AVN (GS)	Robert Gray AAF	UH-60L
C/2-227th AVN (CMD)	Robert Gray AAF	UH-60A, EH-60A
A/2-149th AVN (GS) (ARNG)*	Austin-Bergstrom International Airport, Texas	UH-60L
4-7th CAV	Robert Gray AAF, Fort Hood, Texas	
D/4-7th CAV	Robert Gray AAF	OH-58D
E/4-7th CAV	Robert Gray AAF	OH-58D
7-6th CAV (AC) (USARC)	Montgomery County Airport, Conroe, Texas	
A/7-6th CAV (AC) (USARC)	Montgomery County Airport	AH-64A
B/7-6th CAV (AC) (USARC)	Montgomery County Airport	AH-64A
C/7-6th CAV (AC) (USARC)	Montgomery County Airport	AH-64A

* Unit is dual tasked to 49AD/2-149th AVN (GSAB)

Unit	Location	Aircraft
4th Infantry Division (Mechanized)	**Fort Hood, Texas**	
4ID(M) AVNBDE	Hood AAF, Fort Hood	
1-4th AVN (ATKHB)	Hood AAF	
A/1-4th AVN (ATK)	Hood AAF	AH-64A
B/1-4th AVN (ATK)	Hood AAF	AH-64A
C/1-4th AVN (ATK)	Hood AAF	AH-64A
2-4th AVN (GSAB)	Hood AAF	
A/2-4th AVN (GS)	Hood AAF	UH-60L
B/2-4th AVN (GS)	Hood AAF	UH-60L
C/2-4th AVN (GS)	Hood AAF	UH-60A, EH-60A
B/2-149th AVN (GS) (ARNG)*	Grand Prairie AAF, Texas	UH-60L
1-10th CAV	Hood AAF, Fort Hood, Texas	
D/1-10th CAV	Hood AAF	OH-58D
E/1-10th CAV	Hood AAF	OH-58D

* Unit is dual tasked to 49AD/2-149th AVN (GSAB)

III Corps

1st Cavalry Division

4th Infantry Division (Mechanized)

By the end of FY99, two attack helicopter battalions had been declared operational with the AH-64D Apache Longbow. Units being equipped with the upgraded Apache receive training from the 21st Cavalry Brigade at Fort Hood, Texas.

Unlike most weapon systems, Guardrail aircraft serve only to carry sensors controlled from a ground station. Ultimately, the Army wants to replace its Guardrail Common Sensor (GR/CS) and Airborne Reconnaissance Low (ARL) assets with a single Aerial Common Sensor (ACS) platform.

XVIII Airborne Corps (XVIIIABNCORPS)
Hqtrs: Fort Bragg, North Carolina

Although it is primarily responsible for supporting Central Command (CENTCOM) and Southern Command (SOUTHCOM), this corps, also known as 'Dragon Corps,' serves as a quick reaction force. It is composed of four divisions that comprise light and mechanized infantry divisions, and airborne and airmobile divisions. Also assigned is a light ACR, a military intelligence brigade, a corps aviation brigade and the corps support command. Active-duty units account for only about 48 percent of the strength of XVIII Airborne Corps and the balance comes from the ARNG. As is often the case, however, the vast majority of combat units come from the Army's active component, whereas the support force is made up largely of ARNG units.

First organized as the 11th Armored Corps at Camp Polk, Louisiana, on 17 January 1942, it became the XVIII Corps little more than one year later. "Airborne" was added to its designation on 25 August 1944 and some five weeks later the corps participated in the Allied invasion of the Netherlands. After returning to the United States in June 1945, it was deactivated on 15 October. Reactivation came almost six years later at Fort Bragg, its current home, on 21 May 1951.

In April 1965, XVIII Airborne Corps deployed to the Dominican Republic as part of Operation Power Pack, launched to guard against a communist takeover of that country. Returning to the region in October 1983, the corps played a significant role in Operation Urgent Fury following an attempted coup on the island of Grenada. It assisted with humanitarian efforts in the US Virgin Islands in 1989, after Hurricane Hugo wrought havoc to the area, and took part in Operation Just Cause in Panama only two months later. During the 1990s, the force deployed to 30 countries around the world.

US ARMY FORCES COMMAND (Continued)
XVIII Airborne Corps - Fort Bragg, North Carolina

Unit	Location	Aircraft
2d Armored Cavalry Regiment	**Fort Polk, Louisiana**	
4-2d Regimental Aviation Sqn (Light)	Polk AAF, Fort Polk	
HHT/4-2d ACR (CEWI)	Polk AAF	EH-60A
N/4-2d ACR (CAV)	Polk AAF	OH-58D
O/4-2d ACR (CAV)	Polk AAF	OH-58D
P/4-2d ACR (CAV)	Polk AAF	OH-58D
Q/4-2d ACR (CAV)	Polk AAF	OH-58D
R/4-2d ACR (ASLT)	Polk AAF	UH-60L
525th MIBDE (CEWI)	**Fort Bragg, North Carolina**	
224th MI Bn (AE)	Hunter AAF, Savannah, Georgia	
B/224th MI Bn (AE)	Hunter AAF	RC-12N
1st COSCOM	**Fort Bragg, North Carolina**	
1st USASB AVN CO	Opira Airfield, El Gorah, Egypt	UH-60A
Det.	Sharm El Shiekh Airport, Egypt	UH-60A
44th Medical Brigade	Fort Bragg, North Carolina	
56th Medical Evacuation Battalion	Fort Bragg	
USAAAD	Wheeler Sack AAF, Fort Drum, New York	UH-1H/V
57th MED CO (AA)	Simmons AAF, Fort Bragg, North Carolina	UH-60A
498th MED CO (AA)	Lawson AAF, Fort Benning, Georgia	UH-60A
Medical CECAT (ARNG)	Lovell Field, Chattanooga, Tennessee	UH-60A/Q
151st Medical Evacuation Battalion (ARNG)	Dobbins ARB, Georgia	
104th MED CO (AA) (ARNG)	Weide AHP, Aberdeen Proving Ground, Maryland	UH-60A
112th MED CO (AA) (ARNG)	Bangor International Airport, Maine	UH-60A
121st MED CO (AA) (ARNG)	Davison AAF, Fort Belvoir, Virginia	UH-1H/V
Det. 1 121st MED CO (ARNG)	Ohio County Airport, Wheeling, West Virginia	UH-1H/V
148th MED CO (AA) (ARNG)	Winder-Barrow Airport, Georgia	UH-1H/V
681st MED CO (AA) (ARNG)	Shelbyville Municipal Airport, Indiana	UH-1H/V
86th MED CO (AA) (ARNG)	Burlington International Airport, Vermont	UH-60A
Det. 1 86th MED CO (AA) (ARNG)	Otis ANGB Falmouth, Massachusetts	UH-60A
1159th MED CO (AA) (ARNG)	Concord Municipal Airport, New Hampshire	UH-60A
Det. 1 1159th MED CO (ARNG)	Mercer County Airport, West Trenton, New Jersey	UH-60A
18th Aviation Brigade	**Simmons AAF, Fort Bragg, North Carolina**	
449th AVN GRP (LIFT)	State Armory, Kinston, North Carolina	
1-126th AVN (LUHB) (ARNG)	Quonset State Airport, Kingston, Rhode Island	
A/1-126th AVN (LUH) (ARNG)	Quonset State Airport	UH-1H
B/1-126th AVN (LUH) (ARNG)	Picatinny Arsenal, New Jersey	UH-1H
C/1-126th AVN (LUH) (ARNG)	Otis ANGB, Massachusetts	UH-1H
D/1-126th AVN (LUH) (ARNG)	Westover ARB, Massachusetts	UH-1H
1-131st AVN (AHB) (ARNG)	Birmingham International Airport, Alabama	
A/1-131st AVN (ASLT) (ARNG)	Montgomery Regional Airport, Alabama	UH-60A
B/1-131st AVN (ASLT) (ARNG)	Birmingham International Airport, Alabama	UH-60A

US Army

US ARMY FORCES COMMAND (Continued)
XVIII Airborne Corps - Fort Bragg, North Carolina

Unit	Location	Aircraft
18th Aviation Brigade	**Simmons AAF, Fort Bragg, North Carolina (Continued)**	
1-159th AVN (CAB)	Simmons AAF, Fort Bragg, North Carolina	
A/1-159th AVN (CMD)	Simmons AAF	UH-60L, EH-60A
B/1-159th AVN (CMD) (ARNG)	Rowan County Airport, Salisbury, North Carolina	UH-60L
C/1-159th AVN (CMD) (ARNG)	McEntire ANGS, Eastover, South Carolina	UH-60L
D/1-159th AVN (TAR) (ARNG)	Tupelo Municipal Airport, Mississippi	OH-58D
1-169th AVN (HHB) (ARNG)	State Armory, Enfield, Connecticut	
G(-)/104th AVN (HH) (ARNG)	Muir AAF, Fort Indiantown Gap, Pennsylvania	CH-47D
Det. 1 G/104th AVN (HH) (ARNG)	Bradley IAP, Windsor Locks, Connecticut	CH-47D
B/159th AVN (HH)	Hunter AAF, Savannah, Georgia	CH-47D
C/159th AVN (HH)	Simmons AAF, Fort Bragg, North Carolina	CH-47D
F(-)/131st AVN (HH) (ARNG)	Birmingham International Airport, Alabama	CH-47D
Det. 1 F/131st AVN (HH) (ARNG)	Hunter AAF, Savannah, Georgia	CH-47D
1-171th AVN (CSAB) (ARNG)	Dobbins ARB, Georgia	
A/1-171st AVN (GS)	Simmons AAF, Fort Bragg, North Carolina	UH-60L
B/1-171st AVN (GS)	Simmons AAF	UH-60L
C/1-171st AVN (GS) (ARNG)	Dobbins ARB, Georgia	UH-60L
D/1-171st AVN (GS) (ARNG)	Lakeland-Linder Municipal Airport, Florida	UH-60L
229th AVN GRP (ATK)	Simmons AAF, Fort Bragg, North Carolina	
1-229th AVN (ATKHB)	Simmons AAF	
A/1-229th AVN (ATK)	Simmons AAF	AH-64A
B/1-229th AVN (ATK)	Simmons AAF	AH-64A
C/1-229th AVN (ATK)	Simmons AAF	AH-64A
3-229th AVN (ATKHB)	Simmons AAF	
A/3-229th AVN (ATK)	Simmons AAF	AH-64A
B/3-229th AVN (ATK)	Simmons AAF	AH-64A
C/3-229th AVN (ATK)	Simmons AAF	AH-64A
1-130th AVN (ATKHB) (ARNG)	Raleigh-Durham International Airport, North Carolina	
A/1-130th AVN (ATK) (ARNG)	Raleigh-Durham International Airport	AH-64A
B/1-130th AVN (ATK) (ARNG)	Raleigh-Durham International Airport	AH-64A
C/1-130th AVN (ATK) (ARNG)	Raleigh-Durham International Airport	AH-64A

**XVIII Airborne Corps
(Distinctive Unit Insignia)**

3d Infantry Division

The 3d Infantry Division (Mechanized), based at Fort Stewart, Georgia, will become an AH-64D Apache Longbow operator in 2001.

US ARMY FORCES COMMAND (Continued)
XVIII Airborne Corps - Fort Bragg, North Carolina

Unit	Location	Aircraft
3d Infantry Division (Mechanized)	**Fort Stewart, Georgia**	
3ID(M) AVNBDE	Hunter AAF, Savannah, Georgia	
1-3d AVN (ATKHB)	Hunter AAF	
A/1-3d AVN (ATK)	Hunter AAF	AH-64A
B/1-3d AVN (ATK)	Hunter AAF	AH-64A
C/1-3d AVN (ATK)	Hunter AAF	AH-64A
2-3d AVN (GSAB)	Hunter AAF	
A/2-3d AVN (GS)	Hunter AAF	UH-60L
B/2-3d AVN (GS)	Hunter AAF	UH-60L
C/2-3d AVN (CMD)	Hunter AAF	UH-60A, EH-60A
B/2-126th AVN (GS) (ARNG)*	Bradley IAP, Windsor Locks, Connecticut	UH-1H
3-7th CAV	Fort Stewart, Georgia	
D/3-7th CAV	Hunter AAF, Savannah, Georgia	OH-58D
E/3-7th CAV	Hunter AAF	OH-58D
1-111th AVN (ATKHB) (ARNG)	Craig Municipal Airport, Jacksonville, Florida	
A/1-111th AVN (ATK) (ARNG)	Craig Municipal Airport	AH-64A
B/1-111th AVN (ATK) (ARNG)	Craig Municipal Airport	AH-64A
C/1-111th AVN (ATK) (ARNG)	Craig Municipal Airport	AH-64A

* Unit is dual tasked to 42ID(M)/2-126th AVN (GSAB)

Inert AGM-114 Hellfires have been loaded onto this AH-64A Apache, flown by the 229th AVN (GP), located at Simmons AAF, Fort Bragg, North Carolina. The unit is assigned to the 18th Aviation Brigade, which controls two active-duty Apache battalions plus a third with the Florida ARNG.

Under current plans, 748 of the 827 AH-64As received by the Army will be upgraded to AH-64D Apache Longbow standard. However, the fire control radar will be fitted to 227 examples only.

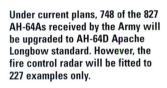

10th Infantry Division

82d Airborne Division

US ARMY FORCES COMMAND (Continued)

XVIII Airborne Corps - Fort Bragg, North Carolina

Unit	Location	Aircraft
10th Infantry Division (Light)	**Fort Drum, New York**	
10ID(L) AVNBDE	Wheeler Sack AAF, Fort Drum	
1-10th AVN (ATKHB)	Wheeler Sack AAF	
A/1-10th AVN (ATK)	Wheeler Sack AAF	OH-58D
B/1-10th AVN (ATK)	Wheeler Sack AAF	OH-58D
C/1-10th AVN (ATK)	Wheeler Sack AAF	OH-58D
2-10th AVN (AHB)	Wheeler Sack AAF	
A/2-10th AVN (ASLT)	Wheeler Sack AAF	UH-60L
B/2-10th AVN (ASLT)	Wheeler Sack AAF	UH-60L
C/2-10th AVN (CMD)	Wheeler Sack AAF	UH-60A, EH-60A
B/1-114th AVN (ASLT) (ARNG)*	Capital City Airport, Frankfort, Kentucky	UH-1H
3-17th CAV (RECON)	Wheeler Sack AAF, Fort Drum	
B/3-17th CAV (RECON)	Wheeler Sack AAF	OH-58D
C/3-17th CAV (RECON)	Wheeler Sack AAF	OH-58D

* Unit is dual tasked to 35ID/1-114th AVN (AHB)

Unit	Location	Aircraft
82d Airborne Division	**Fort Bragg, North Carolina**	
82ABD AVNBDE	Simmons AAF, Fort Bragg	
1-82d AVN (ATKHB)	Simmons AAF	
A/1-82d AVN (ATK)	Simmons AAF	OH-58D
B/1-82d AVN (ATK)	Simmons AAF	OH-58D
C/1-82d AVN (ATK)	Simmons AAF	OH-58D
2-82d AVN (AHB)	Simmons AAF	
A/2-82d AVN (ASLT)	Simmons AAF	UH-60L
B/2-82d AVN (ASLT)	Simmons AAF	UH-60L
C/2-82d AVN (CMD)	Simmons AAF	UH-60L, EH-60A/L
A/2-224th AVN (ASLT) (ARNG)*	Richmond International Airport/Byrd Field, Virginia	UH-1H
1-17th CAV (RECON)	Simmons AAF, Fort Bragg	
B/1-17th CAV (RECON)	Simmons AAF	OH-58D
C/1-17th CAV (RECON)	Simmons AAF	OH-58D
D/1-17th CAV (RECON)	Simmons AAF	OH-58D

* Unit is dual tasked to 29ID(L)/2-224th AVN (AHB)

US Army

101st Airborne Division

US ARMY FORCES COMMAND (Continued)
XVIII Airborne Corps - Fort Bragg, North Carolina

Unit	Location	Aircraft
101st Airborne Division (Air Assault)	**Fort Campbell, Kentucky**	
101AD (AASLT) AVNBDE	Campbell AAF, Fort Campbell	
1-101st AVN (ATKHB)	Campbell AAF	
A/1-101st AVN (ATK)	Campbell AAF	AH-64A
B/1-101st AVN (ATK)	Campbell AAF	AH-64A
C/1-101st AVN (ATK)	Campbell AAF	AH-64A
2-101st AVN (ATKHB)	Campbell AAF	
A/2-101st AVN (ATK)	Campbell AAF	AH-64D
B/2-101st AVN (ATK)	Campbell AAF	AH-64D
C/2-101st AVN (ATK)	Campbell AAF	AH-64D
3-101st AVN (ATKHB)	Campbell AAF	
A/3-101st AVN (ATK)	Campbell AAF	AH-64A
B/3-101st AVN (ATK)	Campbell AAF	AH-64A
C/3-101st AVN (ATK)	Campbell AAF	AH-64A
6-101st AVN (CAB)	Sabre AHP, Fort Campbell	
A/6-101st AVN (CMD)	Sabre AHP	UH-60L, EH-60A
B/6-101st AVN (CMD)	Sabre AHP	UH-60L
C/6-101st AVN (GS)	Sabre AHP	UH-60L
2-17th CAV (RECON)	Sabre AHP	
A/2-17th CAV (RECON)	Sabre AHP	OH-58D
B/2-17th CAV (RECON)	Sabre AHP	OH-58D
C/2-17th CAV (RECON)	Sabre AHP	OH-58D
D/2-17th CAV (RECON)	Sabre AHP	OH-58D
159th AVN BDE (ASLT)	Campbell AAF, Fort Campbell	
4-101st AVN (AHB)	Sabre AHP	
A/4-101st AVN (ASLT)	Sabre AHP	UH-60L
B/4-101st AVN (ASLT)	Sabre AHP	UH-60L
A/1-137th AVN (ASLT) (ARNG)*	Rickenbacker ANGB, Ohio	UH-1H
5-101st AVN (AHB)	Sabre AHP, Fort Campbell, Kentucky	
A/5-101st AVN (ASLT)	Sabre AHP	UH-60L
B/5-101st AVN (ASLT)	Sabre AHP	UH-60L
B/1-114th AVN (ASLT) (ARNG)**	Capital City Airport, Frankfort, Kentucky	UH-60A
7-101st AVN (HHB)	Campbell AAF, Fort Campbell	
A/7-101st AVN (HH)	Campbell AAF	CH-47D
B/7-101st AVN (HH)	Campbell AAF	CH-47D
C/7-101st AVN (HH)	Campbell AAF	CH-47D
9-101st AVN (AHB)	Sabre AHP, Fort Campbell	
A/9-101st AVN (ASLT)	Sabre AHP	UH-60L
B/9-101st AVN (ASLT)	Sabre AHP	UH-60L
A/2-147th AVN (ASLT) (ARNG)***	St. Paul Downtown Airport, Minnesota	UH-1H
101AD (AASLT) DISCOM	Fort Campbell	
326th Medical Evacuation Battalion	Fort Campbell	
50th MED CO (AA)	Campbell AAF	UH-60A

* Unit is dual tasked to 38ID/1-137th AVN (AHB)
** Unit is dual tasked to 35ID/1-114th AVN (AHB)
*** Unit is dual tasked to 34ID/2-147th AVN (AHB)

Defensive M130 chaff/flare dispenser systems are fitted to both sides of the AH-64's tail boom.

Now equipping all four of the armed services, as well as the US Coast Guard, the Sikorsky UH-60 Blackhawk first joined the Army's inventory in 1979. It remains in limited production for the service.

US ARMY FORCES COMMAND (Continued)
US Army Forces Central Command (ARCENT) /Third US Army (THREEUSA)
Fort McPherson, Georgia

Unit	Location	Aircraft
USARCENT AVN DET	Camp Doha, Kuwait	C-12D
167th Support Command (ARNG)	**State Armory Montgomery, Alabama**	
244th Aviation Brigade (USARC)	Fort Sheridan, Illinois	
1-147th AVN (CAB) (ARNG)	Dane County RAP/Truax Field, Madison, Wisconsin	
A/1-147th AVN (CMD) (ARNG)	Dane County RAP/Truax Field	UH-60A
B/1-147th AVN (GS) (ARNG)	Shelbyville Municipal Airport, Indiana	UH-60A
C/1-147th AVN (GS) (ARNG)	Dane County RAP/Truax Field, Madison, Wisconsin	UH-60A
5-159th AVN (HHB) (USARC)	Felker AAF, Fort Eustis, Virginia	
A/5-159th AVN (HH) (USARC)	Lewis AAF, Fort Lewis, Washington	CH-47D
B/5-159th AVN (HH)(USARC)	Felker AAF, Fort Eustis, Virginia	CH-47D
2-228th AVN (TAB) (USARC)	NAS Willow Grove JRB, Pennsylvania	
F(-)/192d AVN (TA) (ARNG)	Isla Grande Airport, San Juan, Puerto Rico	C-23B
Det. 1 F/192d AVN (TA) (ARNG)	Muir AAF, Fort Indiantown Gap, Pennsylvania	C-23B/B+
Det. 2 F/192d AVN (TA) (ARNG)	Quonset State Airport, N. Kingston, Rhode Island	C-23B/B+
Det. 3 F/192d AVN (TA) (ARNG)	Indianapolis International Airport, Indiana	C-23B/B+
Det. 4 F/192d AVN (TA) (ARNG)	Henry Rohlsen Airport, St. Croix, USVI	C-23B+
A(-)/2-228th AVN (TA) (USARC)	NAS Willow Grove JRB, Pennsylvania	C-12R
Det. 1 A/2-228th AVN(TA) (USARC)	Johnstown-Cambria County Airport, Pennsylvania	C-12R
B(-)/2-228th AVN (TA) (USARC)	McCoy AAF, Fort McCoy, Wisconsin	C-12R
Det. 1 B/2-228th AVN (TA) (USARC)	Godman AAF, Fort Knox, Kentucky	C-12R
C/2-228th AVN (TA) (USARC)	Simmons AAF, Fort Bragg, North Carolina	C-12D, UC-35A

Third US Army

Serving with the US Army Intelligence and Security Command (INSCOM), de Havilland RC-7Bs represent multimission variants of the Airborne Reconnaissance Low (ARL) system. The type serves with 3d MI Bn in the Republic of Korea, whereas the EO-5B COMINT version, known as ARL-C, is operated by the the 204th MI Bn at Fort Bliss, Texas. All will be modified to ARL-M standard.

US Army Forces Central Command (ARCENT)/Third US Army (THREEUSA)
Hqtrs: Fort McPherson, Georgia

The Third US Army was activated at Fort McPherson, Georgia, on 3 December 1982, as the US Army component of US Central Command (USCENTCOM). It provides command and control over US Army and designated allied forces operating in Southwest Asia and CENTCOM's area of operations. When required, THREEUSA draws on a pool of Army units and is responsible for planning, exercising and rapidly deploying them in crisis situations. The small number assigned to the command includes an aviation brigade composed mainly of USARC and ARNG elements. Aviation assets permanently assigned to ARCENT are composed entirely of nonactive-duty forces, with USARC providing 58 percent of the strength and the ARNG supplying the rest.

US ARMY INTELLIGENCE AND SECURITY COMMAND (INSCOM)
Headquarters: Fort Belvoir, Virginia

INSCOM was established on 1 January 1977 and is responsible for gathering and providing military intelligence to EACs. Its 11,000 personnel include almost 9,000 active-duty troops. Military intelligence brigades that support USPACOM and USARSO are assigned to INSCOM.

US ARMY INTELLIGENCE & SECURITY COMMAND (INSCOM)
Fort Belvoir, Virginia

Unit	Location	Aircraft
501st MIBDE (CEWI)	**Camp Humphreys, Seoul, Republic of Korea**	
3d MI Bn (AE)	Desiderio AAF/Camp Humphreys, Seoul	
A/3d MI Bn (AE)	Desiderio AAF/Camp Humphreys	RC-7B
B/3d MI Bn (AE)	Desiderio AAF/Camp Humphreys	RC-12D/H
513th MIBDE (CEWI)	Fort Gordon, Georgia	
204th MI Bn (AE)	Biggs AAF, Fort Bliss, Texas	
B/204th MI Bn (ARL)*	Biggs AAF	C-12F, EO-5B

* Aircraft are normally forward deployed to USSOUTHCOM AOR

US ARMY MATERIEL COMMAND (AMC)

Headquarters: Alexandria, Virginia

Established on 1 August 1962, AMC is responsible for the development of weapon systems, conducting advanced research on future technologies and with providing logistical support for deployed weapon systems. Although more than 62,000 personnel are assigned to the command, fewer than 4,000 actually serve with the command. Installations are maintained in 42 states and more than a dozen countries.

US Army Aviation and Missile Command (AMCOM)

Hqtrs: Redstone Arsenal, Huntsville, Alabama

Activated on 1 October 1997, following the consolidation of Aviation and Troop Command (ATCOM) in St. Louis, and the Army Missile Command (MICOM) at Redstone Arsenal, AMCOM is responsible for developing and maintaining Army aviation and missile programs. The command equates to a Naval Air Systems Command (NAVAIRSYSCOM) and the Air Force Materiel Command (AFMC).

In October 1998, it assumed responsibility for its own aviation depots, which were previously operated by US Army Industrial Operations Command (IOC), at Rock Island Arsenal, Illinois. Four ARNG Aviation Classification and Repair Activity Depots (AVCRADs) were similarly transferred to AMCOM's control in October 1999. Activated in 1979, these units are charged with performing limited depot-level aviation maintenance on guard aircraft. The area of responsibility for each AVCRAD is determined by geographic boundaries, with CONUS being broken into Western Central, Southeastern and Northeastern sectors. Staffed by active-duty personnel, active guard and reserve (AGR), traditional guardsmen and contract employees, each facility is responsible for approximately 500 ARNG aircraft. When mobilized, AVCRADs support AMCOM depots, and the Mobilization AVCRAD Control Element (MACE) is tasked with coordination of premobilization planning and with acting as headquarters for the four RADs. Based at the Aberdeen Proving Ground, the MACE is assigned to the Maryland ARNG. AMCOM is also responsible for all Army aircraft loaned or bailed to other government or civilian agencies.

Most C-23B/B+ Sherpas are flown by ARNG theater aviation battalions, divided into multistate detachments that each operate two aircraft.

US ARMY MATERIEL COMMAND (AMC)		
Alexandria, Virginia		
Unit	Location	Aircraft

US Army Aviation and Missile Command (AMCOM) - Redstone Arsenal, Huntsville, Alabama

Unit	Location	Aircraft
AATD	Felker AAF, Fort Eustis, Virginia	UH-1H, AH-1F, UH-60A, AH-64A, C-23B, King Air 100
Corpus Christi Army Depot	NAS Corpus Christi, Texas	UH-1H, UH-60A
MACE (ARNG)	Aberdeen Proving Ground, Maryland	UH-1H, UH-60A
1106th AVCRAD (ARNG)	Fresno-Yosemite International Airport, California	UH-1H
1107th AVCRAD (ARNG)	Springfield-Branson Regional Airport, Missouri	UH-1H
1108th AVCRAD (ARNG)	Gulfport-Biloxi Regional Airport, Mississippi	UH-1H
1109th AVCRAD (ARNG)	Groton-New London Airport, Connecticut	UH-1H

US Army Soldier and Biological Chemical Command (SBCCOM)
Aberdeen Proving Ground, Maryland

Unit	Location	Aircraft
SBCCOM AVN DET	Phillips AAF, Aberdeen Proving Ground	B1900D, UH-1H/N

US Army Communications Electronics Command (CECOM) - Fort Monmouth, New Jersey

Unit	Location	Aircraft
AEESB	NAES Lakehurst, New Jersey	NUH-1H, C-12C, RC-12D, C-23A, AH-1F, JAH-64A, NUH-60A
NVDAAB	Davison AAF, Fort Belvoir, Virginia	UH-1H, YEH-60B, BN.2T, UV-18A

US Army Industrial Operations Command (IOC) - Rock Island Arsenal, Illinois

Unit	Location	Aircraft
USAG AVN DET	Armedee AAF, Sierra Army Depot, California	UH-1H, OH-58A

US Army Tank Automotive and Armaments Command (USATACOM) - Warren, Michigan

Unit	Location	Aircraft
USAG AVN DET	Anniston Army Depot, Alabama	UH-1H

US Army Developmental Test Command (DTC) - Aberdeen Proving Ground, Maryland

Unit	Location	Aircraft
ATTC	Cairns AAF, Fort Rucker, Alabama	C-12C/D/F, JC-23A, JU-21H, T-34C, UH-1H, AH-1F, CH-47D, OH-58A/C/D, JUH-60A/L, EH-60A/L
USNTPS	NAS Patuxent River, Maryland	C-12C, OH-58A/C, UH-60A
AFDD	NASA Ames, Moffett Federal Airport, Calif.	UH/JUH/YEH-60A, NAH-1S, UH-1H, JAH-64A

Redstone Technical Test Center (RTTC) - Redstone Arsenal, Huntsville, Alabama

Unit	Location	Aircraft
RTTC AOD	Redstone AAF, Huntsville, Alabama	C-23A, UH-1H
DPG AVN DET	Michael AAF, Dugway Proving Ground, Utah	UH-1H

White Sands Missile Range (WSMR) - White Sands Missile Range, Arizona

Unit	Location	Aircraft
WSMR AOD	Holloman AFB, New Mexico	C-12D, UH-1H, OH-58A/C
EPG AVN DET	Libby AAF, Fort Huachuca, Arizona	UH-1H, EH-60A/L, C-12C

Yuma Proving Ground (YPG) - Yuma Proving Ground, Arizona

Unit	Location	Aircraft
YPG AOD	Laguna AAF, Yuma, Arizona	NUH-1H, OH-58C, JOH-58D, O-2A
CRTC AVN DET	Allen AAF, Fort Greely, Alaska	UH-1H

US Army Soldier and Biological Chemical Command (SBCCOM)
Hqtrs: Aberdeen Proving Ground, Edgewater, Maryland

Activated on 1 October 1997, SBCCOM is tasked with developing and maintaining nuclear, biological and chemical defense technologies, systems and services for US forces. It is also charged with providing safe storage and destruction of chemical materials and with such matters as chemical treaties and demilitarization issues.

BuNo 161800 is one of six T-34C Turbo Mentors loaned to the US Army by the US Navy. It is seen here at Edwards AFB, California, prior to relocation of the Army Aviation Technical Test Center (ATTC) to Fort Rucker, Alabama. Three of these aircraft remain in Army service today.

US Army Communications Electronics Command (CECOM)
Hqtrs: Fort Monmouth, New Jersey

CECOM is the command responsible for developing, deploying and supporting Army electronic systems. Accordingly, electronic intelligence programs like Guardrail and ARL are the responsibility of the command. Under its control is the Airborne Engineering Evaluation Support Branch at NAES Lakehurst, New Jersey, and the Night Vision Directorate Airborne Applications Branch (NVDAAB) at Fort Belvoir, Virginia.

US Army Industrial Operations Command (IOC)
Hqtrs: Rock Island Arsenal, Illinois

The IOC is responsible for maintaining, repairing and rebuilding Army weapon systems and maintaining the service's war reserve and munitions stocks. Operating a number of Army depots and ammunition plants, aviation assets assigned are limited to detachments supporting depot operations.

US Army Developmental Test Command (DTC)
Hqtrs: Aberdeen Proving Ground, Maryland

Activated on 1 October 1999, DTC facilities and units undertake environmental testing and simulations related to acquisition of aviation, missile, armored and electronics equipment. Under the command's control are the Aviation Technical Test Center (ATTC), the Dugway Proving Ground, the Electronic Proving Ground, White Sands Missile Range and Yuma Proving Ground.

US ARMY MEDICAL COMMAND (MEDCOM)
Headquarters: Fort Sam Houston, San Antonio, Texas

MEDCOM was established on 2 October 1994, and units assigned include the US Army Aeromedical Center (USAAMC) and the Aeromedical Research Laboratory (USAARL). The command is responsible for the development of aeromedical patient treatment and evacuation, and aviation units assigned include a handful of fixed- and rotary-wing aircraft at Fort Rucker, Alabama, and at Fort Sam, Houston. MEDCOM's personnel strength numbers 53,000, of which 26,000 are civilians.

MILITARY DISTRICT OF WASHINGTON (MDW)
Headquarters: Fort Lesley J. McNair, District of Columbia

Established on 1 July 1971, the MDW is headquartered at Fort Lesley J. McNair, in Washington, DC. With a total of 5,500 personnel assigned, about one-half are active-duty Army troops and the command supports Department of Defense (DoD) activities that encompass security and disaster-relief operations throughout the National Capital Region (NCR). MDW also conducts official and public events on behalf of the government. Its 12th Aviation Battalion provides diverse aerial support to the Army's 3d Infantry Regiment, also known as the 'Old Guard.'

US ARMY MEDICAL COMMAND (MEDCOM)
Fort Sam Houston, Texas

Unit	Location	Aircraft
USAG AVN DET	Fort Sam Houston AHP, Texas	UH-1H

US Army Aeromedical Center (USAAMC) - Fort Rucker, Alabama

Unit	Location	Aircraft
USAAMC-AAD (Flatiron)	Cairns AAF, Fort Rucker	UH-1H/V, C-12D
USAARL	Cairns AAF	OH-58C, UH-60A

MILITARY DISTRICT OF WASHINGTON (MDW)
Fort Lesley J. McNair, District of Columbia

Unit	Location	Aircraft
12th AVN BN (CAB)	Davison AAF, Fort Belvoir, Virginia	
A/12th AVN (GS)	Davison AAF	UH-1H
B/12th AVN (GS)	Davison AAF	UH-1H
C/12th AVN (CMD)	Davison AAF	UH-1H, UH-60L

25th Infantry Division (Light)

Alaskan CH-47Ds are operated by B/4-123 AVN, a heavy helicopter company based at Wainwright AAF, Fort Wainwright. The unit is part of 4-123d AVN (TAB) and is responsible for moving troops and equipment of the Arctic Support Brigade with US Army Alaska.

US ARMY PACIFIC (USARPAC)
Headquarters: Fort Shafter, Oahu, Hawaii

Established on 30 August 1990, USARPAC is headquartered at Fort Shafter, Oahu, Hawaii. The MACOM is the US Army component of US Pacific Command (USPACOM) and is composed of approximately 20,000 active-duty, 6,000 ARNG and 3,100 USARC troops based in Hawaii, Japan and Alaska. In addition to a light infantry division on Oahu, USARPAC is responsible for US Army Japan and US Army Alaska.

US Army Japan (USAJ)
Hqtrs: Camp Zama, Tokyo, Japan

The USAJ represents the Army command component of US Forces Japan (USFJ) and is also a major subordinate command of US Army Pacific (USARPAC). A single provisional aviation battalion is assigned.

US Army Alaska (USARAK)
Hqtrs: Fort Richardson, Alaska

USARAK is a major component of US Army Pacific (USARPAC) and the aviation units assigned include active-duty support elements of the Arctic Support Brigade, as well as ARNG companies.

US ARMY PACIFIC (USARPAC) - Fort Shafter, Oahu, Hawaii

Unit	Location	Aircraft
45th Corps Support Group (Forward)	**Wheeler AAF, Schofield Barracks, Hawaii**	
524th Combat Support Battalion	Wheeler AAF, Schofield Barracks	
68th MED CO(-) (AA)	Wheeler AAF	UH-60A
B/214th AVN (HH)*	Wheeler AAF	CH-47D

* Unit is dual tasked to I Corps/185th AVN GP

Unit	Location	Aircraft
25th Infantry Division (Light)	**Schofield Barracks, Oahu, Hawaii**	
25ID(L) AVNBDE	Wheeler AAF, Schofield Barracks	
1-25th AVN (ATKHB)	Wheeler AAF	
A/1-25th AVN (ATK)	Wheeler AAF	OH-58D
B/1-25th AVN (ATK)	Wheeler AAF	OH-58D
C/1-25th AVN (ATK)	Wheeler AAF	OH-58D
2-25th AVN (AHB)	Wheeler AAF	
A/2-25th AVN (ASLT)	Wheeler AAF	UH-60L
B/2-25th AVN (ASLT)	Wheeler AAF	UH-60L
C/2-25th AVN (CMD)	Wheeler AAF	UH-60A, EH-60A
C/2-147th AVN (ASLT) (ARNG)*	St Paul Downtown Airport, Minnesota	UH-1H
3-4 CAV (RECON)	Wheeler AAF, Schofield Barracks	
B/3-4 CAV (RECON)	Wheeler AAF	OH-58D
C/3-4 CAV (RECON)	Wheeler AAF	OH-58D

* Unit is dual tasked to 34ID/2-147th AVN (AHB)

US Army Japan (USAJ) - Camp Zama, Tokyo, Japan

Unit	Location	Aircraft
78th AVN (P) (CAB)	Kastner AAF, Camp Zama, Tokyo	
A/78th AVN (CMD)	Kastner AAF,	UH-60A, UH-1H
Det. A/6-52d AVN (TA)	NAF Atsugi, Japan	C-12J, UC-35A

US Army Alaska (USARAK) - Fort Richardson, Alaska

Unit	Location	Aircraft
Arctic Support Brigade	**Fort Richardson, Alaska**	
Det. 68th MED CO (AA)	Wainwright AAF, Fort Wainwright, Alaska	UH-60A
4-123d AVN (TAB)	Wainwright AAF	
B/4-123d AVN (HH)*	Wainwright AAF	CH-47D
D/4-123d AVN (ASLT)	Wainwright AAF	UH-60A
207th Infantry Group (Scout) (ARNG)	State Armory, Anchorage, Alaska	
1-207th AVN (CSAB) (ARNG)*	Bryant AHP, Fort Richardson	
A/1-207th AVN (GS) (ARNG)**	Bryant AHP	UH-60L
B/1-207th AVN (GS) (ARNG)**	Bryant AHP	UH-60L
C/1-207th AVN (GS) (ARNG)**	Bryant AHP	UH-60L
D/1-207th AVN (SCT) (ARNG)	Bryant AHP	C-23B+

* Unit is dual tasked to USARAK and V Corps in Germany
** Companies maintain detachments at Nome, Bethel and Juneau Airports

EIGHTH US ARMY (EUSA)
Headquarters:
Yongsan, Seoul, Korea

Activated on 10 June 1944, and headquartered at Yongsan, Seoul, Republic of Korea, EUSA provides forces to the CinC for United Nations Command; US Forces, Korea; and for Republic of Korea/US Combined Forces Command. EUSA is considered both an EAC and a MACOM, and units assigned include a mechanized infantry division and a theater aviation brigade. In addition, two cavalry squadrons are forward deployed to Korea, although these now are recorded within IIICORPS.

With almost 27,000 active-duty troops on strength, EUSA is largely composed of active-component Army commands that account for 89 percent of its units. Three percent come from the ARNG and eight percent is made up of USARC personnel. Although not assigned to USARPAC, Eighth US Army both supports and is supported by it.

Eighth Army

US ARMY SOUTH (USARSO)
Headquarters:
Fort Buchanan, Puerto Rico

Established in December 1986, USARSO moved from Fort Clayton, Panama, to Fort Buchanan in August 1999. It controls Army forces deployed throughout the US Southern Command (USSOUTHCOM) and currently has a single aviation brigade and 4,500 personnel assigned. The latter include approximately 2,200 civilians, 2,250 active-duty personnel and a handful of guardsmen and reservists.

The 1977 Panama Canal Treaty called for the withdrawal of all US forces from the Canal Zone prior to 31 December 1999. Most facilities were vacated long before the deadline, however. Fort Clayton was actually closed on 30 July 1999 and USARSO troops are now stationed in Honduras as well as Puerto Rico.

EIGHTH US ARMY (EUSA) - Yongsan Barracks, Seoul, Republic of Korea

Unit	Location	Aircraft
2d Infantry Division (Mechanized)	**Camp Red Cloud, Tongduchon, Republic of Korea**	
2ID(M) AVN BDE	Camp Stanley AHP, Uijongbu, Republic of Korea	
1-2d AVN (ATKHB)	Camp Page AAF, Chunchon, Republic of Korea	
A/1-2d AVN (ATK)	Camp Page AAF	AH-64A
B/1-2d AVN (ATK)	Camp Page AAF	AH-64A
C/1-2d AVN (ATK)	Camp Page AAF	AH-64A
2-2d AVN (AHB)	Camp Stanley AHP, Uijongbu, Republic of Korea	
A/2-2d AVN (ASLT)	Camp Stanley AHP	UH-60L
B/2-2d AVN (ASLT)	Camp Stanley AHP	UH-60L
C/2-2d AVN (CMD)	Camp Stanley AHP	UH-60A, EH-60A
4-7th CAV	Camp Gary Owen, Munsan, Republic of Korea	
D/4-7th CAV	Camp Stanton, Tonggo-ri, Republic of Korea	OH-58D
E/4-7th CAV	Camp Stanton	OH-58D
17th Theater Aviation Brigade	**Yongsan Barracks, Seoul, Republic of Korea**	
1-52d AVN (CAB)	Seoul K-16 AB, Sung Nam, Republic of Korea	
A/1-52d AVN (CMD)	Seoul K-16 AB	UH-60A
B/1-52d AVN (CMD)	Seoul K-16 AB	UH-60A
C/1-52d AVN (ASLT)	Seoul K-16 AB	UH-60A, UH-60A(C)
2-52d AVN (HHB)	Camp Humphreys, Yongsan, Republic of Korea	
A/2-52d AVN (HH)	Desederio AAF/Camp Humphreys	CH-47D
B/2-52d AVN (HH)	Desederio AAF/Camp Humphreys	CH-47D
6-52d AVN (TAB) (USARC)	Los Alamitos AAF, California	
A(-)/6-52d AVN (TA)	Seoul K-16 AB, Sung Nam, Republic of Korea	C-12F
Det. 1 A/6-52d AVN (TA)*	NAF Atsugi, Japan	C-12J, UC-35A
B(-)/6-52d AVN (TA) (USARC)	Dobbins ARB, Georgia	UC-35A
Det. 1 B/6-52d AVN (TA) (USARC)	Cairns AAF, Fort Rucker, Alabama	C-12R
C(-)/6-52d AVN (TA) (USARC)	Los Alamitos AAF, California	C-12R
Det. 1 C/6-52d AVN (TA) (USARC)	Robert Gray AAF, Fort Hood, Texas	C-12F, UC-35A
H(-)/171st AVN (TA) (ARNG)	Dobbins ARB, Georgia	C-23B
Det. 1 H/171st AVN (TA) (ARNG)	Lakeland Linder Regional Airport, Florida	C-23B+
Det. 2 H/171st AVN (TA) (ARNG)	Austin-Bergstrom International Airport, Texas	C-23B+
Det. 3 H/171st AVN (TA) (ARNG)	Capital City Airport, Frankfort, Kentucky	C-23B
18th Medical Command	**Yongsan Barracks, Seoul, Republic of Korea**	
52d Medical Evacuation Battalion	Yongsan Barracks, Seoul	
377th MED CO (AA)	Desederio AAF/Camp Humphreys, Rep. of Korea	UH-60A
Det. 1 377th MED CO (AA)	Camp Walker AAF, Taegu	UH-60A
542d MED CO (AA)	Camp Page AAF, Chunchon	UH-60A
Det. 1 542d MED CO (AA)	Camp Casey, Tongduchon	UH-60A

* Unit is under the operational control of US Army Japan (USAJ)

US ARMY SOUTH (USARSO) - Fort Buchanan, Puerto Rico

Unit	Location	Aircraft
1-228th AVN (CAB)	Soto Cano AB, Honduras	
A(-)/1-228th AVN (CMD)	Soto Cano AB	UH-60A
Det. 1 A/1-228th AVN (CMD)	NAVSTA Roosevelt Roads, Puerto Rico	UH-60A
Det. C/1-228th AVN (HH)	Soto Cano AB, Honduras	CH-47D
USAAAD	Soto Cano AB	UH-60A

Two full companies of UH-60A air ambulances are operated by the 52d Medical Evacuation Battalion of the 18th Medical Command, based in Korea.

US ARMY SPACE AND MISSILE DEFENSE COMMAND (SMDC)

Headquarters: Arlington, Virginia

Established on 1 October 1997, the SMDC is headquartered in Arlington, Virginia, and comprises the US Army component of the Joint US Space Command. It is the MACOM responsible for developing and deploying space and missile defense systems, and is charged with integrating theater missile defense. Of 1,700 personnel assigned to the command, 1,100 are civilians and less than 600 are active-duty military staff. Although the command is composed of five primary components, only the Space and Missile Defense Acquisition Center (SMDAC) and the Space and Missile Defense Technical Center (SMTDC) have aircraft at their disposal. Furthermore, with the exception of an aviation detachment on Kwajalein Atoll, the aircraft supporting these elements are operated exclusively by outside contractors.

US ARMY SPACE AND MISSILE DEFENSE COMMAND (SMDC) - Arlington, Virginia		
Unit	Location	Aircraft
Space and Missile Defense Acquisition Center (SMDAC) - Huntsville, Alabama		
US Army Kwajalein Atoll/Kwajalein Missile Range (USAKA/KMR) - Republic of the Marshall Islands		
AVN DET	Bucholz AAF, Kwajalein Atoll	UH-1H
(Private contractor)	Dyess AAF, Kwajalein Atoll	DHC-7
Space and Missile Defense Technical Center (SMDTC) - Huntsville, Alabama		
SMDTC Sensors Directorate - Kirtland AFB, New Mexico		
(Private contractor)	Holloman AFB, New Mexico	G-1159
(Private contractor)	King County IAP/Boeing Field, Seattle, Washington	B767-200

Based on a Boeing 767 airframe, the Airborne Surveillance Testbed (AST) is a technology demonstrator currently flown by the Army in connection with the development and evaluation of defensive antiballistic missile systems.

160th Aviation (Special Operations) (Airborne)

US ARMY SPECIAL OPERATIONS COMMAND (USASOC)

Headquarters: Fort Bragg, North Carolina

USASOC was activated on 1 October 1989, and personnel assigned to this MACOM include 13,000 active-duty members, 3,500 guardsmen and nearly 7,700 reservists. The command is responsible for a variety of missions that include counterterrorism (CT), counterinsurgency (COIN), low-intensity conflict (LIC) and operations other than war (OOTW). To support its missions, the command operates some of the most technologically advanced helicopters in the world and has a single aviation regiment. USASOC is assigned directly to the US Special Operations Command (USSOCOM), which is a joint-service command headquartered at MacDill AFB, Florida.

US ARMY SPECIAL OPERATIONS COMMAND (USASOC) Fort Bragg, North Carolina		
Unit	Location	Aircraft
160th Aviation (Special Ops) (Airborne)	**Fort Campbell, Kentucky**	
D/160th AVN (ASLT)	NAVSTA Roosevelt Roads, Puerto Rico	MH-60L
SOA Training Co	Campbell AAF, Fort Campbell	MH-6C, MH-47D/E, MH-60K/L
1-160th AVN (AHB)	Campbell AAF	
A/1-160th AVN (ASLT L)	Campbell AAF	MH-6J
B/1-160th AVN (ATK L)	Campbell AAF	AH-6J
C/1-160th AVN (ASLT)	Campbell AAF	MH-60K/L
D/1-160th AVN (ASLT)	Campbell AAF	MH-60K/L
2-160th AVN (HHB)	Campbell AAF	
A/2-160th AVN (HH)	Campbell AAF	MH-47E
B/2-160th AVN (HH)	Campbell AAF	MH-47E
3-160th AVN (AHB)	Hunter AAF, Savannah, Georgia	
A/3-160th AVN (ASLT)	Hunter AAF	MH-60L
B/3-160th AVN (HH)	Hunter AAF	MH-47D

Equipped for missions with Special Operations forces, the Boeing MH-47E carries advanced radars and electronic countermeasures. A prominent feature of this particular variant is the refueling probe, which enables the helicopter to stay aloft for extended periods when supported by an airborne tanker.

US ARMY TRAINING AND DOCTRINE COMMAND (TRADOC)
Headquarters: Fort Monroe, Virginia

Activated on 1 July 1973, TRADOC operates 16 different training facilities. It is responsible for developing the concepts and tactics the service employs during times of war and in operations other than war (OOTW), and also provides flight training for Army aviators. Of the 56,000 personnel at its disposal, more than 34,000 are active-duty members and major aviation units assigned to TRADOC include the US Army Aviation Center (USAAVNC) at Fort Rucker, Alabama, and the US Army Intelligence Center and School (USAICS) at Fort Huachuca, Arizona. ARNG facilities include the eastern, western and high-altitude aviation training sites (EAATS, WAATS and HATS).

US Army Aviation Center (USAAVNC)
Hqtrs: Fort Rucker, Alabama

As one of several combat arms training centers that fall under TRADOC, the USAAVNC is responsible for training Army and foreign aviators to fly fixed-wing and rotary-wing aircraft. USAF helicopter pilots also receive their training from the center, which is equipped to conduct basic, intermediate and advanced instruction at or near Fort Rucker provided by the Aviation Training Brigade (ATB).

In addition to flight training, the center is responsible for simulators and survival training, and instructs infantrymen in assault techniques. It also establishes doctrine and force levels and manages Army aviation medicine and safety programs. Three battalions assigned to the ATB provide flight training while a fourth instructs air traffic controllers.

The primary portion of the Initial Entry Rotary Wing (IERW) training course is

US ARMY TRAINING AND DOCTRINE COMMAND (TRADOC)
Fort Monroe, Virginia

Unit	Location	Aircraft
US Army Infantry Center and School (ASAINFCS) - Fort Benning, Georgia		
145th MED CO (AA)	Lawson AAF, Fort Benning	UH-1H/V, UH-60A
US Army Engineer Center and School (USAENGCS) - Fort Leonard Wood, Missouri		
USAG AVN DET	Waynesville RAP/Forney AAF, Fort Leonard Wood	UH-1H
US Army Intelligence Center and School (USAICS) - Fort Huachuca, Arizona		
111th MIBDE (Training)	**Fort Huachuca, Arizona**	
304th MI Bn (Training)	Libby AAF, Fort Huachuca, Arizona	
A/304th MI Bn (Training)	Libby AAF	RQ-5A
B/304th MI Bn (Training)	Libby AAF	RC-12D/N, EH-60A, UH-1H
US Army Aviation Center (USAAVNC) - Fort Rucker, Alabama		
USAG AVN DET	Cairns AAF, Fort Rucker	UH-1H
Aviation Training Brigade	Fort Rucker	
1-14th AVN (Training)	Hanchey AHP, Fort Rucker	
A/1-14th AVN	Hanchey AHP	AH-64D
Det. 1 A/1-14th AVN	Falcon Field, Mesa, Arizona	AH-64D
C/1-14th AVN	Hanchey AHP, Fort Rucker	OH-58D
D/1-14th AVN	Hanchey AHP	AH-64A
E/1-14th AVN	Hanchey AHP	OH-58A/C
F/1-14th AVN	Hanchey AHP	UH-60A
1-212th AVN (Training)	Lowe AHP, Fort Rucker	
A/1-212th AVN	Lowe AHP	UH-1H, OH-58A/C
B/1-212th AVN	Lowe AHP	UH-1H, OH-58A/C
C/1-212th AVN	Lowe AHP	UH-1H, OH-58A/C
E/1-212th AVN	Lowe AHP	UH-1H, OH-58A/C
1-223d AVN (Training)	Cairns AAF, Fort Rucker	
HHC/1-223d AVN*	Cairns AAF	TH-67A, C-12C/D
A/1-223d AVN	Cairns AAF	UH-1H, OH-58A/B/C, UH-60A, AH-64A/D
B/1-223d AVN	Knox AHP, Fort Rucker	CH-47D
IERW Contractor Training	Cairns AAF, Fort Rucker	TH-67A
Fixed-Wing Contractor Training	Dothan Municipal Airport, Alabama	C-12C/D

* HHC is responsible for surveillance of contractor-operated training and C-12 transition training

Helicopter School Battalion (HSB)*	Cairns AAF, Fort Rucker	
A/HSB	Cairns AAF, Fort Rucker	UH-1H
B/HSB	Cairns AAF, Fort Rucker	UH-60A

* HSB provides flight training in Spanish for Latin American and Caribbean countries

TRAINING AND DOCTRINE COMMAND (Continued)
US Army Aviation Center (USAAVNC) - Fort Rucker, Alabama

Unit	Location	Aircraft
EAATS (ARNG)	Weide AAF, Ft. Indiantown Gap, Pennsylvania	UH-1H, CH-47D, UH-60A
WAATS (ARNG)	Silver Bell AHP, Marana, Arizona	AH-1F, UH-60A, OH-58A
HATS (ARNG)	Eagle County Regional Airport, Gypsum, Colorado	UH-1H
USAALS	Felker AAF, Fort Eustis, Virginia	Ground instruction airframes

US Army Recruiting Command (USAREC) - Fort Knox, Kentucky

Unit	Location	Aircraft
USAPT AVN DET	Simmons AAF, Fort Bragg, North Carolina	C-31A, UV-18A, UV-20A

**Operational Support
Airlift Command
OSACOM**

currently administered by Lear Siegler Services under contract to the Army. The 20-week course provides students with pre-flight, primary and instrument training on the TH-67A Cayuse helicopter, and is monitored by personnel from the 1st Battalion, 223d Aviation Regiment. Twelve-week advanced phases cover transition and combat skills, and night-vision-goggle (NVG) training is conducted by the 1st Battalion, 212th Aviation Regiment, using OH-58A/C and UH-1H platforms. On completion of the course, newly rated pilots then receive qualification and combat skill instruction on the aircraft they will fly with the 1st Battalion, 14th Aviation Regiment.

The fixed-wing, multi-engine qualification course is provided by Flight Safety Inc. at Dothan Municipal Airport, Alabama. As with the contractor-operated IERW course, Army personnel (from the 1-223d AVN) monitor progress. The C-12 qualification course and transition/refresher training for previously rated fixed-wing pilots is conducted by 1-223d AVN, which is also responsible for carrying out maintenance test pilot courses for each of the primary aircraft. The battalion also handles all training related to the CH-47D Chinook. After graduating, most aviators are immediately assigned to their units, but those assigned to aeromedical evacuation or intelligence companies receive additional specialized training at Fort Benning, Georgia, or at Fort Huachuca, Arizona, respectively. The helicopter school battalion is responsible for training Spanish-speaking students from Central and South America.

Among the command's facilities, the US Army Aviation Logistics School at Fort Eustis, Virginia, is a brigade-size unit utilizing grounded airframes to provide maintenance personnel with hands-on training. In addition, the ARNG maintains three training sites that report to the USAAVNC. The EAATS trains aviators in medium-lift, assault and fixed-wing aircraft, whereas the WAATS concentrates on attack and aeroscout types, and the HATS looks after high-altitude training.

US Army Recruiting Command (USAREC)
Hqtrs: Fort Knox, Kentucky

With responsibility for all US Army recruiting activities and the Reserve Officer Training Corps (ROTC) program, USAREC is also the gaining command for the US Army Parachute Team, known as the 'Golden Knights.'

US ARMY NATIONAL GUARD (ARNG)
Headquarters: Arlington, Virginia

More than 367,000 part-time troops are assigned to the ARNG, whose units are responsible for federal assignments during wartime via a state area command (STARC). However, unless mobilized, they are controlled by the adjutant general (TAG) of their respective state, district or territory.

In addition, the ARNG controls the assets of OSACOM at Fort Belvoir, Virginia, and is responsible for the Army's entire CONUS-based operational support airlift (OSA) fleet.

The National Guard Counter Drug Directorate supports local and federal law enforcement agencies and is responsible for ARNG reconnaissance and interdiction detachments (RAIDs). The latter each operate between three and six OH-58A Kiowas and many have been fitted with longer skids, FLIR and night-vision systems, spotlights and enhanced communications.

Serial 84-0488 is a Beech C-12F operated by the Alaska ARNG's OSACOM Det. 54, normally stationed at Elmendorf AFB. In 1999, the aircraft was still wearing its old color scheme.

US ARMY RESERVE COMMAND (USARC)
Headquarters: Fort McPherson, Georgia

Many of USARC's aviation units were deactivated in recent years and, as part of the Army's overall restructuring, remaining USARC units (along with their aviation units) largely have been assigned to support roles. With the exception of a single attack helicopter battalion and a single cavalry squadron, USARC aviation is made up of fixed-wing support aircraft and heavy-lift helicopters. All USARC aviation assets are attached to active-duty Army divisions, corps or EACs and, in peacetime, all assets are assigned to a single aviation brigade. However, none of the units report outside of the normal structure.

California ARNG

Displaying the ARNG insignia on its cockpit is a Blackhawk with the Illinois National Guard.

US ARMY NATIONAL GUARD (ARNG) - National Guard Bureau, Arlington, Virginia

Unit	Location	Aircraft

Operational Support Airlift Agency (OSAA) - Davison AAF, Fort Belvoir, Virginia

Unit	Location	Aircraft
FWATS (ARNG)	Benedum Airport, Bridgeport, West Virginia	C-12D/T, C-23B+, C-26B

Operational Support Airlift Command (OSACOM) - Davison AAF, Fort Belvoir, Virginia

Unit	Location	Aircraft
US Army PATD	Andrews AFB, Maryland	C-20E/F, UC-35A, C-37A
Fort Belvoir RFC	Davison AAF, Fort Belvoir, Virginia	C-12T
Fort Hood RFC	Robert Gray AAF, Fort Hood, Texas	C-12F
Fort Lewis RFC	Gray AAF, Fort Lewis, Washington	C-12F
Puerto Rico RFC	Isla Grande Airport, Puerto Rico	C-12T
Alaska RFC	Elmendorf AFB, Alaska	C-12F, UC-35A
Hawaii RFC	Hickam AFB, Hawaii	C-12D, C-20E

National Guard State Area Command State Flight Detachments (SFDs)

Unit	Location	Aircraft
Alabama SFD (OSACOM Det. 5)	Montgomery Regional Airport, Alabama	C-12T
Alaska SFD (OSACOM Det. 54)	Elmendorf AFB, Alaska	C-12F
Arizona SFD (OSACOM Det. 31)	Papago AAF, Phoenix, Arizona	C-12R
Arkansas SFD (OSACOM Det. 30)	Robinson AAF, N. Little Rock, Arkansas	C-26B
California SFD (OSACOM Det. 32)	Sacramento Mather Airport, California	C-12T
Colorado SFD (OSACOM Det. 33)	Buckley ANGB, Aurora, Colorado	C-26B
Connecticut SFD (OSACOM Det. 6)	Bradley IAP, Windsor Locks, Connecticut	C-12D
Delaware SFD (OSACOM Det. 7)	New Castle County Airport, Delaware	C-12D
District of Columbia (OSACOM Det. 4)	Davison AAF, Fort Belvoir, Virginia	C-26B
Florida SFD (OSACOM Det. 8)	St. Augustine Airport, Florida	C-12T
Georgia SFD (OSACOM Det. 9)	Dobbins ARB, Marietta, Georgia	C-26B
Hawaii SFD (OSACOM Det. 55)	Wheeler AAF, Schofield Barracks, Hawaii	C-26B
Idaho SFD (OSACOM Det. 35)	Boise Air Terminal-Gowen Field, Idaho	C-12T
Illinois SFD (OSACOM Det. 36)	Decatur Airport, Illinois	C-12T
Indiana SFD (OSACOM Det. 10)	Indianapolis International Airport, Indiana	C-12T
Iowa SFD (OSACOM Det. 34)	Boone Municipal Airport, Des Moines, Iowa	C-12T
Kansas SFD (OSACOM Det. 37)	Forbes Field ANGB, Topeka, Kansas	C-12T
Kentucky SFD (OSACOM Det. 11)	Capital City Airport, Frankfort, Kentucky	C-12T
Louisiana SFD (OSACOM Det. 38)	Lakefront Airport, New Orleans, Louisiana	C-12T
Maine SFD (OSACOM Det. 14)	Bangor International Airport, Maine	C-12D
Maryland SFD (OSACOM Det. 13)	Phillips AHP, Aberdeen Proving Ground, Maryland	C-12F
Massachusetts SFD (OSACOM Det. 12)	Otis ANGB, Falmouth, Massachusetts	C-26B
Michigan SFD (OSACOM Det. 15)	Capital City Airport, Lansing, Michigan	C-12D
Minnesota SFD (OSACOM Det. 39)	St. Paul Downtown Airport, Minnesota	C-12F
Mississippi SFD (OSACOM Det. 16)	Hawkins Field, Jackson, Mississippi	C-12R
Missouri SFD (OSACOM Det. 40)	Memorial Airport, Jefferson City, Missouri	C-12T
Montana SFD (OSACOM Det. 41)	Helena County Regional Airport, Montana	C-12R
Nebraska SFD (OSACOM Det. 43)	Lincoln Municipal Airport, Nebraska	C-12T
Nevada SFD (OSACOM Det. 45)	Reno-Stead Municipal Airport, Nevada	C-12T
New Hampshire SFD (OSACOM Det. 18)	Concord Municipal Airport, New Hampshire	C-12F
New Jersey SFD (OSACOM Det. 19)	Mercer County Airport, W. Trenton, New Jersey	C-12D
New Mexico SFD (OSACOM Det. 44)	Santa Fe County Municipal Airport, New Mexico	C-12R
New York SFD (OSACOM Det. 20)	Albany County Airport, Latham, New York	C-12T
No. Carolina SFD (OSACOM Det. 17)	Raleigh-Durham Airport, Morrisville, North Carolina	C-26B
North Dakota SFD (OSACOM Det. 42)	Bismark Municipal Airport, North Dakota	C-12T
Ohio SFD (OSACOM Det. 21)	Rickenbacker International Airport, Columbus, Ohio	C-26B
Oklahoma SFD (OSACOM Det. 46)	Westheimer Airport, Norman, Oklahoma	C-12F
Oregon SFD (OSACOM Det. 47)	McNary Field, Salem, Oregon	C-12T
Pennsylvania SFD (OSACOM Det. 22)	Muir AAF, Fort Indiantown Gap, Pennsylvania	C-12T
Puerto Rico SFD (OSACOM Det. 56)	Isla Grande Airport, San Juan, Puerto Rico	C-12T
Rhode Island SFD (OSACOM Det. 23)	Quonset State Airport, Rhode Island	C-12D
So. Carolina SFD (OSACOM Det. 24)	McEntire ANGS, Eastover, South Carolina	C-26B
South Dakota SFD (OSACOM Det. 48)	Rapid City Regional Airport, South Dakota	C-12T
Tennessee SFD (OSACOM Det. 25)	Smyrna Airport, Tennessee	C-12T
Texas SFD (OSACOM Det. 49)	Austin-Bergstrom International Airport, Texas	C-12T
Utah SFD (OSACOM Det. 50)	Salt Lake City Municipal Airport, Utah	C-12T
Vermont SFD (OSACOM Det. 27)	Burlington International Airport, Vermont	C-12D
Virginia SFD (OSACOM Det. 26)	Richmond International Airport/Byrd Field, Virginia	C-12T
Washington SFD (OSACOM Det. 51)	Gray AAF, Fort Lewis, Washington	C-12R
West Virginia SFD (OSACOM Det. 28)	Wood County Airport, Parkersburg, West Virginia	C-12D
Wisconsin SFD (OSACOM Det. 52)	Dane County RAP/Truax Field, Madison, Wisconsin	C-26B
Wyoming SFD (OSACOM Det. 53)	Cheyenne Airport, Wyoming	C-12T

US Army

US ARMY NATIONAL GUARD (Continued)

Unit	Location	Aircraft

National Guard Bureau Counter Drug Directorate - Arlington, Virginia

Unit	Location	Aircraft
Alabama RAID	Dannelly Field, Montgomery, Alabama	OH-58A
Arizona RAID	Papago AAF, Phoenix, Arizona	OH-58A
Arkansas RAID	Robinson AAF, North Little Rock, Arkansas	OH-58A
California RAID	Sacramento Mather Airport, California	OH-58A
District of Columbia RAID	Davison AAF, Fort Belvoir, Virginia	OH-58A
Florida RAID	Craig Municipal Airport, Jacksonville, Florida	OH-58A
Georgia RAID	Dobbins ARB, Georgia	OH-58A
Hawaii RAID	Gen. Lyman Field, Hilo, Hawaii	OH-58A
Indiana RAID	Shelbyville Municipal Airport, Indiana	OH-58A
Kentucky RAID	Capital City Airport, Frankfort, Kentucky	OH-58A
Louisiana RAID	Alexandria-Esler Regional Airport, Louisiana	OH-58A
Maine RAID	Bangor International Airport, Maine	OH-58A
Maryland RAID	Weide AHP, Aberdeen Proving Ground, Maryland	OH-58A
Massachusetts RAID	Westover ARB, Massachusetts	OH-58A
Michigan RAID	Abrams Municipal Airport, Grand Ledge, Michigan	OH-58A
Minnesota RAID	St. Paul Downtown Airport, Minnesota	OH-58A
Mississippi RAID	Key Field, Meridian, Mississippi	OH-58A
Missouri RAID	Memorial Airport, Jefferson City, Missouri	OH-58A
North Carolina RAID	Raleigh-Durham International Airport, North Carolina	OH-58A
North Dakota RAID	Bismark Municipal Airport, North Dakota	OH-58A
Nevada RAID	Reno-Stead Municipal Airport, Nevada	OH-58A
New Jersey RAID	Mercer County Airport, West Trenton, New Jersey	OH-58A
New Mexico RAID	Las Cruces International Airport, New Mexico	OH-58A
Ohio RAID	Rickenbacker ANGB, Ohio	OH-58A
Oklahoma RAID	Muldrow AHP, Lexington, Oklahoma	OH-58A
Oregon RAID	McNary Field, Salem, Oregon	OH-58A
Pennsylvania RAID	Johnstown Cambria County Airport, Pennsylvania	OH-58A
South Carolina RAID	Columbia MAP/McEntire ANGS, South Carolina	OH-58A
Tennessee RAID	Smyrna Airport, Tennessee	OH-58A
Virginia RAID	Richmond International Airport/Byrd Field, Virginia	OH-58A
Washington RAID	Camp Murray, Tacoma, Washington	OH-58A
West Virginia RAID	Wood County Airport, Parkersburg, West Virginia	OH-58A
Wisconsin RAID	Dane County RAP/Truax Field, Madison, Wisconsin	OH-58A

HQDA DIRECT REPORTING UNITS

US Military Academy (USMA)
Headquarters: West Point, New York

Opened in 1802, the US Military Academy is located on the Hudson River in West Point, New York. It provides four-year, college degree courses and, on graduating, students receive their commissions as 2d lieutenants. The US Army garrison stationed there is supported by the 2d Aviation Detachment based at nearby Stewart International Airport. In addition to providing priority transport, the detachment supports the USMA Parachute Team as well as school aviators.

Operational Test and Evaluation Command (OPTEC)
Headquarters: Alexandria, Virginia

OPTEC was established on 16 November 1990, and is the US Army equivalent of the Navy's Operational Test and Evaluation Force. This staff field operating agency conducts tests and assessments of Army equipment, and reports on its effectiveness and suitability for operational use. The command is also responsible for the OPTEC Threat Support Activity (OTSA) and the Test and Experimentation Command (TEXCOM). Individual units assigned to TEXCOM include the Aviation Test Directorate (ATD), the Airborne Special Operations Test Directorate (ASOTD) and the Intelligence and Electronic Warfare (IEW) Directorate. OTSA operates a small number of Russian fixed-wing and rotary-wing aircraft.

DIRECT REPORTING UNITS

Unit	Location	Aircraft
US Military Academy (USMA) - West Point, New York		
2d AVN DET	Stewart IAP, Newburgh, New York	UH-1H, Cessna 182Q
Operational Test & Evaluation Command (OPTEC) - Alexandria, Virginia		
OTSA	Biggs AAF, Fort Bliss, Texas	An-2, Ka-32, Mi-2, Mi-8, Mi-14, Mi-17, Mi-24, Mi-25, misc. types
OTSA DET	Polk AAF, Fort Polk, Louisiana	An-2, Mi-2, Mi-24
Test and Experimentation Command (TEXCOM) - Fort Hood, Texas		
AVTD	Robert Gray AAF, Fort Hood, Texas	TDY aircraft
ABNSOTD	Simmons AAF, Fort Bragg, North Carolina	UH-1H, T-34C

OPTEC's fleet of ex-Soviet helicopters serves in a variety of test and evaluation roles, but the aircraft are frequently flown as adversary "ships" during combat exercises.

Boeing AH-64D Apache Longbow serial 97-5038

The upgraded AH-64D Apache platform is currently being fielded to active-duty Army units. In all, 748 examples are expected to be converted, although less than one-third are to be fitted with the Longbow fire control radar (FCR) under current plans.

AIRCRAFT

BEECH AIRCRAFT (SEE RAYTHEON AIRCRAFT)

BELL HELICOPTER TEXTRON

Bell AH-1F Cobra

In April 1966, Bell's Model 209 was chosen as the Army's Interim Advanced Aerial Fire Support System (Interim AAFSS), and initial-production AH-1G Cobras followed in May 1967. Although the type's structure was entirely new, early examples were fitted with the same engine, transmission and rotor system found in the UH-1 Iroquois series. A subsequent variant, the AH-1Q, fielded TOW anti-tank missiles and was first delivered in 1973. This was followed by

The ARNG's 1-142 AVN (ATKHB) operates 24 AH-1F Cobras from Greater Rochester IAP, New York. A number of these helicopters are fitted with the C-NITE targeting system and have been involved in operations in Haiti. The unit is assigned to the Aviation Brigade of the 42d Infantry Division (Mechanized).

the AH-1S, a designation that was applied to new-production aircraft first delivered in 1976 as well as to older aircraft retrofitted with the new systems, and referred to as AH-1S (Modified) models. The program also resulted in two other subvariants: the AH-1S (Production) and the Enhanced Cobra Armament System (ECAS). The Army later assigned standard designations to all three and they became known as the AH-1P, AH-1E and AH-1F, respectively. However, AH-1Gs and AH-1Qs modified to AH-1S (Modified) configuration were simply referred to as AH-1S variants, after that point.

Only the AH-1F is flying today, although service with active-duty units came to an end when the 25th Infantry Division (Light), based in Hawaii, retired the last of its Cobras on 15 March 1999. Today, the type is flown only by ARNG attack helicopter battalions and cavalry squadrons within corps and division aviation brigades, and by the regimental aviation squadron assigned to a single armored cavalry regiment. Despite a recent suggestion that the ARNG ultimately will be equipped with more AH-64A Apache attack helicopters, it is likely the AH-1F will continue to serve for the foreseeable future.

Bell UH-1H/V/N Iroquois ("Huey")

The XH-40 initial-development helicopter first flew on 20 October 1956. It became the Model 204, designated the HU-1 by the Army in 1959 and redesignated the UH-1 three years later. What were subsequently referred to as UH-1As first entered Army service in 1958, followed by UH-1Bs in 1961 and UH-1Cs in 1965.

Work on the Model 205, a larger platform, began in 1961 and led to the UH-1D variant, of which more than 2,000 examples ultimately entered Army service, beginning in 1963. Further development of the airframe led to the Model 205A during the mid-1960s and, in 1968, deliveries of the uprated helicopter began. Designated the UH-1H, the Army took delivery of some 5,000 examples over the years

Bell AH-1F Cobra Specifications:	
Maximum Takeoff Weight:	10,000 lb (4536 kg)
Empty Weight:	6,479 lb (2939 kg)
Fuselage Length:	45 ft 2 in (13.77 m)
Overall Length:	53 ft 1 in (16.18 m)
Main Rotor Diameter:	44 ft 0 in (13.41 m)
Height:	13 ft 6 in (4.11 m)
Power Plant:	One Allied Signal (Lycoming) T53-L-703 turboshaft engine, rated at 1,800 shp (1342 kW), driving two-blade main and tail rotors
Maximum Fuel Capacity:	1,748 lb (793 kg)
Maximum Speed:	149 kts (276 km/h)
Service Ceiling:	12,200 ft (3719 m)
Operating Range:	310 nm (574 km)
Crew:	2
Armament:	M97A4 aircraft armament subsystem (turret-mounted M197 three-barrel, 20-mm cannon) with 750 rounds; four underwing weapon stations capable of carrying 2.75-in rockets and BGM-71 TOW antiarmor missiles
Mission Equipment:	M65 TOW/C-NITE system or night targeting system (NTS) equipped with television and infrared sensors and a laser range finder
Missions:	Close air support (CAS), antiarmor, reconnaissance

that followed, including a number of reconfigured UH-1Ds. The UH-1V air ambulance was derived from the UH-1H and some 200 aircraft were adapted for the role.

In all, the Army received and operated more than 9,000 "Hueys" in various roles. The type flew as a gunship, ELINT platform and air assault transport, in addition to air ambulance. Today, only 900 UH-1H/Vs remain in service and the average age of the "Huey" fleet is 28 years. Most UH-1Hs serve ARNG general support, assault and light-utility helicopter (LUH) battalions assigned to division, corps and theater aviation brigades. However, examples assigned to active-duty units largely serve as support, training and test aircraft. The UH-1V still flies as an air ambulance with guard medical companies and a handful of active-component units, but is no longer considered a go-to-war asset. Progressively, both variants are being replaced by UH-60A/L/Qs and, although all H models built prior to 1968 are thought to have been retired, the newest "Hueys" are still almost 25 years old. During 1999, the entire fleet had to be grounded twice.

The Army's intention was to have the UH-1Hs assigned to LUH battalions replaced by an off-the-shelf aircraft. However, it now

Unofficially, this subvariant is referred to as the OH-58A+.

Today, only a handful of Kiowas remain in service with active-duty units but the helicopter is still used for training at Fort Rucker and also equips many guard units in observation and scout roles. Meanwhile, the OH-58A+ variant is assigned largely to ARNG reconnaissance and interdiction detachments (RAIDs), to assist law enforcement authorities with narcotics interdiction. Generally, they can be identified by their extended bush skids, which have been fitted to allow sufficient clearance for the large spotlights or FLIR turrets carried under the fuselage.

Bell UH-1H Iroquois Specifications

Maximum Takeoff Weight:	9,500 lb (4309 kg)
Empty Weight:	4,717 lb (2140 kg)
Fuselage Length:	44 ft 6 in (13.56 m)
Overall Length:	57 ft 1 in (17.40 m)
Main Rotor Diameter:	48 ft 0 in (14.63 m)
Height:	14 ft 7 in (4.45 m)
Power Plant:	One Allied Signal (Lycoming) T53-L-13B turboshaft engine, rated at 1,400 shp (1044 kW), driving two-blade main and tail rotors
Maximum Fuel Capacity:	1,485 lb (674 kg)
Maximum Speed:	126 kts (233 km/h)
Service Ceiling:	18,500 ft (5639 m)
Operating Range:	300 nm (556 km)
Crew:	3–4
Armament:	Although capable of carrying a variety of external weapons, the UH-1H normally only carries the M23 armament subsystem, which consists of a pair of pintle-mounted 7.62-mm M60D machine guns
Accommodations:	12 passengers or 6 litters or up to 3,880 lb (1760 kg) of cargo internally, or 5,000 lb (2268 kg) externally
Missions:	General support, air assault, utility, air ambulance

seems likely that some 160 aircraft will be modernized instead and will receive a new power plant, improved survivability features and new cockpit avionics. Most likely the Light Helicopter Turbine Engine Company (LHTEC) T800-LHT-800 engine will be chosen as it has been well tested in recent years in US Border Patrol UH-1Hs.

Besides the standard single-engine UH-1H/Vs now in service, a twin-engine UH-1N has been bailed from the USAF to Army Materiel Command (AMC). It supports the SBCCOM.

Bell OH-58C Kiowa Specifications

Maximum Takeoff Weight:	3,200 lb (1452 kg)
Empty Weight:	1,600 lb (726 kg)
Fuselage Length:	34 ft 4.5 in (10.48 m)
Overall Length:	40 ft 11.75 in (12.49 m)
Main Rotor Diameter:	35 ft 4 in (10.77 m)
Height:	9 ft 5 in (2.87 m)
Power Plant:	One Allison T63-A-720 turboshaft engine, rated at 420 shp (313 kW), driving two-blade main and tail rotors
Maximum Fuel Capacity:	493 lb (224 kg)
Maximum Speed:	122 kts (226 km/h)
Service Ceiling:	18,900 ft (5761 m)
Operating Range:	309 nm (572 km)
Crew:	2
Armament:	Provision for XM-27 7.62-mm minigun
Accommodations:	3–4 passengers
Missions:	Observation, reconnaissance

The extended bush skids on this OH-58A+ Kiowa indicate it is assigned to a Reconnaissance and Interdiction Detachment (RAID), in this instance with the Virginia ARNG at Richmond IAP. Whereas many examples still serve with the Guard, very few are flying with active-duty Army units today.

Bell OH-58A/C Kiowa

Initially losing the Army's Light Observation Helicopter (LOH) competition to the Hughes OH-6 in 1963, nevertheless the Bell Model 206A was ordered by the Army in May 1968, having flown for the first time in January 1966. Designated the OH-58A, the service ultimately accepted more than 2,000 examples before production ended.

Beginning in 1975, nearly 600 OH-58As were upgraded to OH-58C configuration and were fitted with new instruments and cockpit avionics, a radar warning system and more powerful engines that incorporated an infrared suppression system. In addition, an undisclosed number of standard OH-58As were equipped with the uprated engine, although the OH-58C's suite of updated avionics was not installed.

Bell OH-58D Kiowa Warrior

The first OH-58D entered service in 1989 but, unlike the OH-58A/C model from which it was developed, the Kiowa Warrior can carry a variety of weapons and is regularly tasked with both scout and attack missions. Equipped with a newer power plant and rotor system, as well as advanced avionics, the OH-58D is flown by cavalry troops within most Army divisions, and attack helicopter battalions within light infantry divisions and armored cavalry regiments. The helicopter is also assigned to theater aviation brigades.

Bell has begun to update the OH-58D fleet under what is referred to as the Safety/System Enhancement Program (S/SEP), which is equipping each Kiowa Warrior with a Rolls-Royce Allison C30R/3 engine with full-authority digital control (FADEC), which provides greater lift capability. In addition, the program means the helicopter receives a more advanced target identification and tracking system, upgraded communications, an improved master control processor unit with a digital map and video system, an improved data modem, as well as a SINCGARS radio and safety enhanced energy-attenuating seats. Except for improved seats, all Kiowa Warriors delivered since March 1997 are already equipped with S/SEP features and 311 more OH-58Ds will receive the modifications through 2006.

Bell OH-58D Kiowa Warrior Specifications

Maximum Takeoff Weight:	5,500 lb (2495 kg)
Empty Weight:	3,829 lb (1737 kg)
Fuselage Length:	34 ft 4.5 in (10.48 m)
Overall Length:	42 ft 2 in (12.85 m)
Main Rotor Diameter:	35 ft 0 in (10.67 m)
Height:	12 ft 9.5 in (3.90 m)
Power Plant:	One Rolls-Royce Allison 250-C30R turboshaft engine, rated at 650 shp (485 kW), driving four-blade main and two-blade tail rotors
Maximum Fuel Capacity:	709 lb (322 kg)
Maximum Speed:	129 kts (239 km/h)
Service Ceiling:	12,000 ft (3,658 m)
Operating Range:	300 nm (556 km)
Crew:	2
Armament:	7.62-mm minigun pods; 2.75-inch (70-mm) rockets; M296 .50-cal (12.7-mm) machine guns or Mk19 40-mm grenade launcher pods; AGM-114 antitank or AIM-92 air-to-air missiles
Accommodations:	Two external litters or 2,000 lb (907 kg) of cargo carried externally
Mission Equipment:	Mast-mounted site (MMS) equipped with television sensor (TVS), thermal imaging sensor (TIS) and laser range finder/designator (LRF/D)
Missions:	Observation, reconnaissance and attack

This OH-58D Kiowa Warrior is assigned to 4-2 RAS, 2 ACR(L), at Polk AAF, Fort Polk, Louisiana, and is equipped with AGM-118s and 0.5-in machine guns.

Bell TH-67A Creek

In March 1993, the Bell Model 206B-3 Jetranger III, a commercial off-the-shelf (COTS) aircraft, was named winner of the Army's New Training Helicopter (NTH) competition. It entered service to become the initial-entry rotary-wing (IERW) trainer. Designated the TH-67A Creek, 137 examples purchased by the Army began to enter opera-

Bell TH-67A Creek Specifications

Maximum Takeoff Weight:	3,200 lb (1452 kg)
Empty Weight:	1,630 lb (739 kg)
Fuselage Length:	31 ft 2 in (9.50 m)
Overall Length:	38 ft 9.5 in (11.82 m)
Main Rotor Diameter:	33 ft 4 in (10.16 m)
Height:	9 ft 6.5 in (2.91 m)
Power Plant:	One Rolls-Royce Allison 250-C20JN turboshaft engine, rated at 420 shp (313 kW), driving two-blade main and tail rotors
Maximum Fuel Capacity:	513 lb (233 kg)
Maximum Speed:	122 kts (226 km/h)
Service Ceiling:	13,500 ft (4115 m)
Operating Range:	364 nm (674 km)
Crew:	2–3
Armament:	None
Missions:	Training

The United States Army banner on the tail boom of this TH-67 Creek is the only marking to indicate it is actually a military helicopter. The Army's entire fleet carries civil registrations and the three-digit code on the aft cabin is common on those aircraft assigned to Fort Rucker, Alabama.

tional service in October 1993 at Fort Rucker, Alabama. Whereas some aircraft are equipped only for visual-flight-rules missions, others have been fitted for instrument flight rules (IFR) operations. However, both versions carry the same designation. In Army service, the Creek is similar to the US Navy's TH-57 aside from the fact that it has no stability augmentation system (SAS), no rotor brake nor air-conditioning. All examples are based at Fort Rucker, where civilian instructors administer the IERW course to student pilots under an Army contract.

BOEING COMPANY (Including McDonnell Douglas Helicopter)

Boeing 767-200

Under contract to the Army's Space and Missile Defense Command (SMDC), the Boeing Company flies the first 767-200 series airliner built. It is used to support the command's Sensors Directorate and Boeing crews operate the test platform from King County IAP - Boeing Field in Seattle, Washington.

In addition to its role supporting defensive antiballistic missile systems development, the Airborne Surveillance Testbed (AST) is used to test sensor and communications systems.

Boeing CH-47D/F/MH-47D/E Chinook

Developed from the Vertol (later Boeing Vertol) Model 114, initial-production CH-47As were fielded by the Army in 1962, followed by CH-47B and CH-47C variants in 1967 and 1969, respectively. Continuing development led to introduction of the CH-47D in 1982. This version has more powerful engines, upgraded transmissions, fiberglass rotor blades, an improved hydraulic flight control and new electrics. Since it entered service, more than 430 earlier variants have been remanufactured to 'Delta' standard.

Optimized for service with the USASOC, the MH-47D variant is equipped with a chin-mounted FLIR turret, advanced avionics and an in-fight refueling probe, and has provision for more fuel to be carried internally. Development of an advanced, longer-range, all-weather Chinook, designated the MH-47E, began in 1987 and the first new-production aircraft began entering service in January 1994. Designed

Boeing CH-47D Chinook Specifications

Maximum Takeoff Weight:	53,500 lb (24267 kg)
Empty Weight:	23,401 lb (10615 kg)
Fuselage Length:	51 ft 0 in (15.55 m)
Overall Length:	99 ft 0 in (30.18 m)
Main Rotor Diameter:	60 ft 0 in (18.29 m)
Height:	18 ft 11.5 in (5.78 m)
Power Plant:	Two Allied Signal (Lycoming) T55-L-712 turboshaft engines, each rated at 4,500 shp (3356 kW), driving tandem three-blade main rotors
Maximum Fuel Capacity:	6,953 lb (3,154 kg)
Maximum Speed:	161 kts (298 km/h)
Service Ceiling:	19,000 ft (5791 m)
Operating Range:	213 nm (394 km)
Crew:	3
Armament:	M24 and M41 armament subsystems, comprising door- and ramp-mounted 7.62-mm M60D machine guns
Accommodations:	Up to 55 troops or 24 litters or 15,500 lb (7031 kg) of cargo carried internally, or 26,000 lb (11793 kg) carried externally
Missions:	Heavy-lift transport, assault

to facilitate clandestine penetration missions, improved avionics carried by the MH-47E include an EFIS, a multimode radar and advanced defensive countermeasures. The new helicopter is also fitted with uprated T55-GA-714 engines and all examples are assigned to Special Operations units at Fort Campbell, Kentucky.

Despite the remanufacturing program, the average age of the fleet is now 11 years and the earliest CH-47Ds will reach the end of their service lives in 2002. Boeing is currently developing a new Chinook upgrade known as the Improved Cargo Helicopter (ICH) and designated the CH-47F. It is designed to extend the service life of the helicopter by another 20 years and the Army plans to remanufacture 302 of its 433 CH-47Ds to this configuration. The total cost will be close to $3.2 billion.

Under the program, T55-GA-712 engines currently used to power the CH-47Ds to be modified will be replaced by T55-GA-714 engines developed for the MH-47E. Equipped with a FADEC, the power plant

offers 20 percent more horsepower and slightly better fuel consumption over its predecessor. The CH-47F also features a new, low-maintenance rotor hub; vibration reduction; and an improved cargo handling system. Options include extended-range, internal fuel tanks that will double the 1,034-gallon (3914-lit) usable fuel load, and increased gross weight and cargo hook capacities. In addition, a digital cockpit may be added. It would incorporate four new multifunction displays, electronic horizontal situation and electronic attitude direction indicators, and associated controllers. The cost of the upgrade is estimated to be $10.3 million per aircraft.

Boeing began modifying two CH-47Ds to CH-47F configuration in January 1999, and expects to roll out the first aircraft in May 2001. Low-rate initial production (LRIP) is expected to commence in December of the same year. Delivery of the first production aircraft is scheduled to follow in March 2003, and entry into service is expected to happen in September 2004.

Chinooks currently are operated by the ARNG, USARC and active-component, heavy helicopter companies assigned primarily to theater and corps aviation brigades. Most commonly they are used to transport weapons, ammunition, cargo, equipment or troops and are expected to remain in service until replaced by a Joint Transport Rotary Aircraft (JTRA).

The MH-47E Chinook is the Army's most advanced helicopter. Assigned to 2-160th SOAR (ABN), this example is equipped with a rescue hoist and refueling boom on the starboard side and a podded terrain-following/terrain-avoidance radar on its port side.

McDonnell Douglas Helicopter AH-6J and MH-6C/J Cayuse "Little Bird"

The Hughes OH-6A (Model 500) entered US Army service in 1967 in observation and scout roles, and served until retired from the ARNG's inventory in 1997. AH/MH-6 variants currently flying with USASOC are based on the Hughes/McDonnell Douglas Helicopter Model 500/530 and are operated by a single active-duty Special Operations aviation regiment. Known to their crews as "Little Birds," they are used as transport and attack platforms, equipped with advanced navigation and communication systems and night-vision-compatible cockpits. A few MH-6Cs are used for training.

Under a new mission enhancement program, the AH/MH-6 fleet will be equipped with an improved drivetrain, incorporating a new transmission, a six-blade main rotor and a four-blade tail rotor similar to the AH-64A/D's unit. Additional modifications will include external conformal fuel tanks, lightweight planks, a lightweight

Hellfire system and an integrated weapon management system. The combination of structural modifications and new rotors will allow the Cayuse to operate at an increased gross weight of 4,700 lb (2132 kg).

McDonnell Douglas Helicopter AH/MH-6J Cayuse Specifications

Maximum Takeoff Weight:	3,950 lb (1792 kg)
Empty Weight:	1,564 lb (709 kg)
Fuselage Length:	24 ft 7 in (7.49 m)
Main Rotor Diameter:	26 ft 5 in (8.05 m)
Height:	8 ft 11 in (2.72 m)
Power Plant:	One Rolls-Royce Allison 250-C30 turboshaft engine, rated at 650 shp (485 kW), driving a five-blade main rotor and two-blade tail rotor
Maximum Fuel Capacity:	439 lb (199 kg)
Maximum Speed:	152 kts (282 km/h)
Service Ceiling:	17,500 ft (5334 m)
Operating Range:	Approximately 260 nm (482 km)
Crew:	2
Armament Options:	AH-6 – 7.62-mm minigun pods, 2.75-in (70-mm) rockets, M296 .50-cal (12.7-mm) machine guns, Mk 19 40-mm grenade launcher pods, AGM-114 antitank missiles, AIM-92 air-to-air missiles
Accommodations:	MH-6 – Up to 6 passengers on external planks
Mission Equipment:	FLIR
Missions:	Special Operations

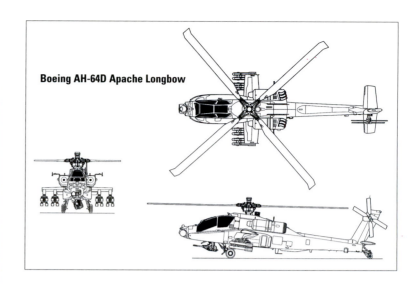

Boeing AH-64D Apache Longbow

Serial 81-23631, an MH-6J "Little Bird" assigned to A Company/1-160th SOAR(ABN), is seen here fitted with external planks, each capable of carrying three or four troops.

McDonnell Douglas AH-64A Apache

A contender for the Army's Advanced Attack Helicopter (AAH) competition, the YAH-64 (Hughes Helicopters Model 77) first flew on 30 September 1975, and was named the winner on 10 December 1976. The first production AH-64A was rolled out at Mesa, Arizona, on 30 September 1983, and made its maiden flight on 9 January 1984. That same year, Hughes Helicopters was purchased and renamed the McDonnell Douglas Helicopter Company.

The Apache made its combat debut in Operation Just Cause during the 1989 invasion of Panama but established its reputation during Operation Desert Storm in 1991. It was employed to good effect in that conflict and fired the opening salvoes against Iraqi positions.

When production ended in 1997, 827 examples had been delivered to the Army and are serving today with attack helicopter battalions and cavalry squadrons with the active-duty, ARNG and USARC branches.

Boeing AH-64D Apache Longbow

Plans for a more advanced Apache began in 1984. It was determined the new attack helicopter derivative would be equipped with an airborne adverse-weather weapons system (AAWWS), to comprise a millimeter-wave (MMW) fire control radar (FCR), a radio frequency (RF)–guided version of the Hellfire missile plus the M299 Longbow Hellfire Launcher (LBHL). Formal development began in August 1988 and the program was renamed Apache Longbow in April 1989. At that time, the AAWWS became known as the Longbow Fire Control Radar.

The first of six prototypes made its initial flight on 11 March 1991 and the service accepted its first AH-64D in 1997.

McDonnell Douglas AH-64A Apache Specifications

Maximum Takeoff Weight:	17,650 lb (8006 kg)
Empty Weight:	11,368 lb (5156 kg)
Fuselage Length:	49 ft 5 in (15.06 m)
Overall Length:	58 ft 2 in (17.73 m)
Main Rotor Diameter:	48 ft 0 in (14.63 m)
Height:	15 ft 2.88 in (4.65 m)
Power Plant:	Two General Electric T700-GE-701 turboshaft engines, each rated at 1,695 shp (1264 kW) or T700-GE-701C turboshaft engines, each rated at 1,940 shp (1447 kW), driving four-blade main and tail rotors
Maximum Speed:	162 kts (300 km/h)
Service Ceiling:	20,500 ft (6248 m)
Operating Range:	324 nm (600 km)
Crew:	2
Armament:	M230, 30-mm chain gun with 1,200 rounds; four underwing weapon stations for: 2.75-in (70-mm) rockets or AGM-114 antitank missiles; two wingtip stations for AIM-92 air-to-air missiles
Mission Equipment:	AN/AAQ-11 Pilots Night-Vision System (PNVS), AN/ASQ-170 Target Acquisition Designation Sight (TADS)
Missions:	Close air support (CAS), antiarmor, reconnaissance

Boeing AH-64D Apache Longbow Specifications
(Largely per AH-64A except as shown below)

Maximum Takeoff Weight:	23,000 lb (10433 kg)
Empty Weight:	11,800 lb (5352 kg)
Height:	16 ft 3 in (4.95 m)
Power Plant:	Two General Electric T700-GE-701C turboshaft engines, each rated at 1,940 shp (1447 kW), driving four-blade main and tail rotors
Maximum Fuel Capacity:	2,550 lb (1157 kg)
Maximum Speed:	143 kts (265 kph)
Operating Range:	257 nm (476 km)
Mission Equipment:	AN/APG-78 Fire Control Radar (FCR), AN/APR-48A Radio Frequency Interferometer (RFI), AN/AAQ-11 PNVS, AN/ASQ-170 TADS

Although AH-64As still spearhead the Army's attack helicopter fleet, over time their prominence will be eclipsed by AH-64D Apache Longbows, as more of the older helicopters are remanufactured to the new configuration.

It entered regular service at Fort Hood, Texas, in 1998, and was declared operational in October of the following year. Deliveries to combat units are continuing at a steady rate.

Instead of new-build aircraft, the AH-64Ds are being remanufactured from AH-64A airframes. Under the current plan, the service will upgrade 748 of these helicopters and equip 227 of them with the Longbow FCR, while the remainder will be made capable of carrying the FCR. However, the Army announced recently it was considering reducing the number of upgraded aircraft to just 530 and having the FCR installed in 500 of them. Under the plan, unmodified AH-64As would be issued to ARNG units still flying AH-1F Cobras.

Boeing is developing a number of new technologies for the AH-64D including a new center fuselage manufactured from composite materials instead of aluminum, and a new electrically powered gun turret to replace the current unit, which is hydraulically operated. The new turret will be lighter and offer improved aiming accuracy. The AH-64D might also be fitted with a new 3,000-shp (2237-kW) engine to be developed under the Army's common engine program (CEP).

US Army South (USARSO) operated its ARLs from Howard AFB, Panama, until closure of the base forced their relocation to Fort Bliss, Texas.

BOMBARDIER AEROSPACE (INCLUDING DE HAVILLAND CANADA AND SHORTS)

de Havilland Canada/Northrop Grumman
RC-7B Airborne Reconnaissance Low-Multimission (ARL-M), EO-5B Airborne Reconnaissance Low-COMINT (ARL-C)

Developed by California Microwave, which is now part of Northrop Grumman, the RC-7B is based on the de Havilland Canada DHC-7 commercial airliner. The aircraft is configured for communications and imagery intelligence (COMINT/IMINT) gathering, known as the airborne reconnaissance low-multimission (ARL-M).

RC-7Bs are assigned to corps-level military intelligence brigades and were operationally deployed in 1997. Currently, however, the platform is operational only in Korea, although an earlier variant, designated the EO-5B (ARL-C), operates in support of US Southern Command. This example is equipped with COMINT systems only. Army requirements call for nine RC-7Bs to be built but just eight have been funded so far and one of these, the Army's sole O-5A imagery intelligence (ARL-I) variant, was lost in a crash in Colombia in 1999. The particular aircraft was believed to have been partially modified to RC-7B (ARL-M) configuration.

Besides these electronic DHC-7 variants, a small number of standard airliners are flown under contract by Raytheon's Range Systems Engineering Division, to support operations at the Army's Kwajalein Atoll Missile Range in the Marshall Islands.

de Havilland Canada UV-18A Twin Otter (DHC-6-200)

Between 1976 and 1982, six de Havilland Canada DHC-6-300 commuter airliners were delivered to the Alaska ARNG. Possessing short takeoff and landing (STOL) capabilities and of being operated with wheels, skis or floats, they have proved extremely useful to operations within the state. Designated the UV-18A, the high-wing monoplane was capable of carrying up to 18 passengers and differed from commercial variants by having military avionics, high-flotation landing gear and a greater capacity for internal fuel.

In 1995, the Army announced plans for a new Alaska Support Aircraft (ASA) and the Twin Otters were replaced by C-23B+ Sherpas two years later, although all six examples remain in the inventory. During 1998, two were transferred to the 'Golden Knights' parachute team to act as support aircraft and two more were transferred to test duties with CECOM's Night Vision Directorate Airborne Applications Division at Fort Belvoir, Virginia. The last two have gone to the US Navy and USAF.

de Havilland Canada UV-18A Twin Otter Specifications

Maximum Takeoff Weight:	12,500 lb (5670 kg)
Empty Weight:	7,415 lb (3363 kg)
Fuselage Length:	49 ft 6 in (15.09 m)
Wingspan:	65 ft 0 in (19.81 m)
Height:	10 ft 6 in (3.20 m)
Power Plant:	Two Pratt & Whitney Canada PT6A-27 turboprop engines, each rated at 652 shp (486 kW), driving three-blade, constant-speed propellers
Maximum Fuel Capacity:	DHC-6 Series 300 – 2,583 lb (1172 kg)
Maximum Speed:	196 kts (363 km/h)
Service Ceiling:	26,700 ft (8138 m)
Operating Range:	775 nm (1435 km)
Crew:	2–3
Armament:	None
Accommodations:	18 passengers, or 8 litters and 3 attendants
Missions:	Parachute team support, test and evaluation

de Havilland Canada RC-7B ARL-M Specifications

Maximum Takeoff Weight:	44,000 lb (19958 kg)
Empty Weight:	27,000 lb (12247 kg)
Fuselage Length:	86 ft 6 in (26.37 m)
Wingspan:	93 ft 0 in (28.35 m)
Height:	26 ft 2 in (7.98 m)
Power Plant:	Four Pratt & Whitney Canada PT6A-50 turboprop engines, each rated at 1,120 shp (835 kW), driving four-blade, constant-speed propellers
Maximum Fuel Capacity:	9,925 lb (4502 kg)
Maximum Speed:	250 kts (463 km/h)
Service Ceiling:	21,000 ft (6401 m)
Operating Range:	1,130 nm (2093 km)
Crew:	6
Armament:	None
Mission Equipment:	Infrared line scanner and daylight television sensors, communications/signals intercept and direction finding (DF) equipment, synthetic aperture radar and moving target indicator (SAR/MTI)
Missions:	Reconnaissance, ELINT

Six UV-18As were originally delivered to the Alaska ARNG's 1-207th AVN, of which four subsequently went to active-component units after being replaced by C-23B+ Sherpas. The "Twotters" serve as systems development and training aircraft.

US Army

Shorts C-23A/B/B+ Sherpa

The Shorts Model SD3-30, designated the C-23A, first entered US service in 1983 when the USAF began receiving 18 of the light transports. In essence, the C-23A was a freighter version of the civil variant. It lacked passenger windows and was equipped with a forward cargo door and an aft cargo ramp. The Army acquired nine examples in 1990, previously operated by the USAFE's 608th Military Airlift Group (MAG) at Ramstein AB, Germany. Although several were assigned to Army depots, most were used in test roles and only a handful still remain in service. One example flies as a dedicated multisensor test bed in connection with the development of UAVs. The Army also obtained four civil SD3-30s for operations on Kwajalein Atoll but they are no longer in service.

In 1988, the C-23B entered the ARNG's inventory, replacing de Havilland Canada C-7A Caribous assigned to AVCRADs. With a different construction from the initial model, the C-23B was built using a Shorts 360 (Model SD3-60) wing fitted to an SD3-30 airframe. It is powered by Pratt & Whitney PT6A-65AR engines. Although similar in appearance to the C-23A, the 'Bravo' has passenger windows and its cargo ramp can be operated when it is airborne.

Production of the SD3-30 had already ended in 1993 when the Army wanted to acquire more C-23Bs. Eager to fill the order, Shorts offered to create 28 aircraft from old SD3-60 airliners. Modification of the SD3-60 to C-23B+ configuration involved adding a 36-inch (0.91-m) section to the fuselage forward of the wing. In addition, the aft fuselage and single vertical tail of the SD3-60 were removed and

The Army is equipping its entire fleet of 16 C-23B and 28 C-23B+ Sherpas with an updated flight management system. However, senior commanders hope to replace the type with another based on the airframe that will be the foundation of the aerial common sensor (ACS) program.

and are assigned to theater aviation companies for the purpose of flying inter-theater and intra-theater general aviation support missions. The entire fleet is now receiving UNS-1K flight management systems from Universal Avionics Systems Corporation. However, plans to redesignate these aircraft as C-23Cs have been shelved.

CESSNA AIRCRAFT

Cessna 182Q Skylane

Although the Army once operated more than 250 Cessna Model 172Es, designated T-41Bs, none remain in service today. However, the service purchased a pair of Model 182Q Skylanes in 1989, which are presently operated by the US Military Academy's 2d Aviation Detachment at Stewart IAP, Newburgh, New York. They are tasked as support aircraft but also serve as proficiency trainers for USMA instructors.

Approaching Baltimore-Washington IAP, this JC-23A is one of nine C-23As acquired from the USAF. It still sports its old European I paint scheme and is assigned to the Army's ATTC at Fort Rucker, Alabama, as an airborne multisensor test bed.

Cessna 182Q Skylane Specifications

Maximum Takeoff Weight:	3,105 lb (1408 kg)
Empty Weight:	1,747 lb (792 kg)
Fuselage Length:	28 ft 0 in (8.53 m)
Wingspan:	35 ft 10 in (10.92 m)
Height:	9 ft 3 in (2.82 m)
Power Plant:	One Textron Lycoming IO-540 turbocharged reciprocating engine rated at 230 shp (172 kW), driving a two-blade, constant-speed propeller
Maximum Speed:	187 kts (346 km/h)
Service Ceiling:	20,000 ft (6096 m)
Operating Range:	1,009 nm (1869 km)
Crew:	2
Armament:	None
Accommodations:	2 passengers
Missions:	Mission support

Serial 89-0266 is one of only two Cessna 182Qs currently flying with the Army. It is operated from Stewart IAP in Newburgh, the former Air Force base that also serves as an annex for the US Military Academy (USMA).

Shorts C-23B+ Sherpa Specifications

Maximum Takeoff Weight:	25,600 lb (11612 kg)
Empty Weight:	16,040 lb (7276 kg)
Fuselage Length:	58 ft 0 in (17.68 m)
Wingspan:	74 ft 10 in (22.81 m)
Height:	16 ft 5 in (5.00 m)
Power Plant:	Two Pratt & Whitney Canada PT6A-65AR turboshaft engines, each rated at 1,424 shp (1062 kW), driving five-blade, constant-speed propellers
Maximum Fuel Capacity:	4,543 lb (2061 kg)
Maximum Speed:	240 kts (444 km/h)
Service Ceiling:	13,950 ft (4252 m)
Operating Range:	1,030 nm (1908 km)
Crew:	3
Armament:	None
Accommodations:	18–20 passengers or 15 litters and 3 attendants or up to 7,275 lb (3300 kg) of cargo
Missions:	Operational support airlift, theater airlift

replaced with a new section that featured a cargo ramp and twin vertical stabilizers from the SD3-30.

The ARNG accepted the first of 28 C-23B+ Sherpas from Bombardier's Shorts Division in Bridgeport, West Virginia, on 25 June 1996. These aircraft now operate alongside 18 earlier C-23Bs

Cessna UC-35A/B Citation Ultra/Citation Encore

The Cessna Model 560 Citation V Ultra was named winner of the Army's C-XX(MR) competition in 1995, and entered service as the UC-35A in 1997. It was needed to meet the service's requirement for a high-priority, mid-range transport, something long-range C-20 Gulfstreams and the short-range Beech C-12 cannot efficiently provide.

The Ultra is equipped with an EFIS cockpit and configured to carry eight passengers or a cargo payload. The type is operated primarily by active-duty and USARC theater aviation companies for the Joint Operational Support Airlift Command (JOSAC), but they are also tasked to support a number of CinCs, including US Army Europe (USAREUR), the Eighth US Army (EUSA), Forces Command (FORSCOM) and the US Army Special Operations Command (USASOC).

Initially, the purchase of 35 UC-35As was envisaged but, after delivery of 20 UC-35As has been made, production will switch to the UC-35B model, which is based on the Citation Encore. The new aircraft will be fitted with Pratt & Whitney Canada PW535A turbofans to provide more power. Delivery of the first of three UC-35Bs ordered is expected by the end of 2000.

Cessna UC-35A Citation Ultra Specifications

Maximum Takeoff Weight:	16,500 lb (7484 kg)
Empty Weight:	9,250 lb (4196 kg)
Fuselage Length:	48 ft 10.75 in (14.90 m)
Wingspan:	52 ft 2.25 in (15.91 m)
Height:	15 ft 2.25 in (4.64 m)
Power Plant:	Two Pratt & Whitney Canada JT15-5D turbofan engines, each rated at 3,045 lb st (13.54 kN)
Maximum Fuel Capacity:	5,529 lb (2508 kg)
Maximum Speed:	430 kts (796 km/h)
Service Ceiling:	45,000 ft (13716 m)
Operating Range:	1,959 nm (3628 km)
Crew:	2
Armament:	None
Accommodations:	8 passengers
Missions:	Operational support airlift, theater airlift

Cessna O-2A Skymaster Specifications

Maximum Takeoff Weight:	5,400 lb (2449 kg)
Empty Weight:	2,848 lb (1292 kg)
Fuselage Length:	29 ft 9 in (9.07 m)
Wingspan:	38 ft 0 in (11.58 m)
Height:	9 ft 4 in (2.84 m)
Power Plant:	Two Continental IO360 reciprocating engines, each rated at 210 hp (157 kW), driving two-blade, constant-speed propellers
Maximum Fuel Capacity:	Approximately 900 lb (408 kg)
Maximum Speed:	173 kts (320 km/h)
Service Ceiling:	10,000 ft (3048 m)
Operating Range:	921 nm (1706 km)
Crew:	2
Armament:	None
Missions:	Test support

UC-35As have replaced C-12 King Airs within several units but it seems unlikely the Army will be able to secure the 35 aircraft it says it needs. Those based within the continental United States primarily serve with the USARC and all are finished in "diplomatic" white, devoid of unit markings.

Serial 67-21349 is flown from Laguna AAF by the Air Operations Division at Yuma Proving Ground. Serving previously with the US Navy and US Air Force, this O-2A Skymaster is one of only two such aircraft still in US military service.

Cessna O-2A Skymaster

Developed from Cessna's Model 337M, O-2A Skymasters were first purchased by the USAF as off-the-shelf observation/forward air control (FAC) aircraft for operations over Southeast Asia. The type served with USAF units in this role from the mid-1960s and was operational elsewhere late into the 1980s.

The O-2A entered the Army's inventory in 1977 but the last few examples served with the US Navy until they were transferred to the Army in 1990. Today, two O-2As are all that remain with the Army and fly from Laguna AAF as part of testing programs carried out at Yuma Proving Ground. Until recently, Skymasters were based at Fort Huachuca, Arizona, supporting electronic tests and UAV development.

FAIRCHILD AEROSPACE

Fairchild C-26B Metroliner (Metro 23)

In 1986, the USAF selected the Fairchild SA-227AC Metro III airliner to meet its ANG requirement for an Operational Support Transport Aircraft (ANGOSTA). C-26As first entered service in 1987 and the ARNG also obtained two aircraft in 1988 that were assigned to units in Colorado and the District of Columbia. Subsequent purchases were of a variant based on the SA-227DC Metro 23, designated the C-26B, and 10 state OSACOM detachments as well as the ARNG training site at Bridgeport, West Virginia, ultimately flew this variant.

Although capable of carrying 19 passengers for more than 1,200 miles (1931 km), Metroliners are configured either with 14 seats or to carry up to 3,900 lb (1769 kg) of cargo. Alternatively, they can be configured for MEDEVAC missions or to fill a combination of roles, simultaneously. No examples serve with active-duty units and aircraft assigned to the ARNG are normally used for joint-service operational support airlift missions.

Fairchild C-26B Metroliner Specifications

Maximum Takeoff Weight:	16,500 lb (7484 kg)
Empty Weight:	9,500 lb (4309 kg)
Fuselage Length:	59 ft 4.25 in (18.09 m)
Wingspan:	57 ft 0 in (17.37 m)
Height:	16 ft 8 in (5.08 m)
Power Plant:	Two Allied Signal (Garrett) TPE331-12-UAR-701G turboprop engines, each rated at 1,119 shp (834 kW), driving four-blade, constant-speed propellers
Maximum Fuel Capacity:	2,309 lb (1047 kg)
Maximum Speed:	313 kts (580 km/h)
Service Ceiling:	25,000 ft (7620 m)
Operating Range:	1,043 nm (1932 km)
Crew:	2
Armament:	None
Accommodations:	19 passengers, or 6 litters and seven passengers
Missions:	Operational support airlift (OSA), theater airlift

OSACOM's operational support airlift Fairchild C-26B Metroliners are finished in a "diplomatic white" paint scheme. The type, which is a development of the Metro III commuter airliner, first entered Army service in 1987

FOKKER AIRCRAFT

Fokker C-31A Troopship

The Army operates two Fokker C-31As (Model F27-400M) that are probably the most often seen of the fixed-wing aircraft in its fleet. Based on the F27 airliner, the type entered service in 1985, equipped with reinforced floors and removable paratroop doors. With the capacity to carry 48 parachutists, the Troopships were initially leased for the US Army 'Golden Knights' Parachute Team, replacing aging C-7A Caribous used in this role. The aircraft received the C-31A designation when they were purchased in 1988, but carried none during the period they were leased. The aircraft are currently based at Simmons AAF at Fort Bragg, North Carolina.

Two C-31A Troopships have served the US Army Parachute Team, the 'Golden Knights,' since replacing C-7A Caribous in 1985.

Fokker C-31A Troopship Specifications

Maximum Takeoff Weight:	45,900 lb (20820 kg)
Empty Weight:	24,720 lb (11213 kg)
Fuselage Length:	77 ft 3.25 in (23.55 m)
Wingspan:	95 ft 2 in (29.01 m)
Height:	27 ft 11 in (8.51 m)
Power Plant:	Two Rolls-Royce Dart Mk 551 turboshaft engines, each rated at 2,330 shp (1738 kW), driving four-blade, constant-speed propellers
Maximum Fuel Capacity:	9,167 lb (4158 kg)
Maximum Speed:	282 kts (522 km/h)
Service Ceiling:	30,000 ft (9144 m)
Operating Range:	2,370 nm (4389 km)
Crew:	3
Armament:	None
Accommodations:	48 parachutists
Missions:	Parachute drops

GENERAL DYNAMICS (INCLUDING GULFSTREAM AEROSPACE AND GULFSTREAM AMERICAN)

Gulfstream American G-1159 Gulfstream II

Although designed and initially built by Grumman Aerospace, the Gulfstream II program was taken over by Gulfstream American. Subsequently, production switched to the Gulfstream III.

When the US Army Corps of Engineers leased a Grumman G-1159 Gulfstream II in 1981, it marked the first time the service had operated a jet aircraft. Designated the VC-11A, it was purchased outright in 1989 and was subsequently redesignated a C-20J. It served with OSACOM until 1998, after which it was sold. Today, a single Gulfstream II operates from Holloman AFB, New Mexico, under contract to the Sensors Directorate of the Space and Missile Defense Command (SMDC). It carries a civil registration, however, and is not listed in the Army's inventory.

Two C-20Es are operated by OSACOM including serial 87-0139, which is seen here at Hickam AFB, Hawaii. It is assigned to the Regional Flight Center.

Gulfstream Aerospace C-20E/F Gulfstream III/IV

The Army's first new Gulfstreams were purchased in 1988 when two G-1159A Gulfstream IIIs were delivered to the Davison Aviation Command. Designated C-20Es, they are currently assigned to OSACOM. The C-20E is longer than its predecessor and has a redesigned wing of slightly longer span. Furthermore, it is equipped with updated avionics and has the capacity to carry more fuel.

In 1991, the service purchased a Gulfstream IV, which carries the designation C-20F and features the same wing as the C-20E. However, it is powered by Rolls-Royce Tay Mk 610 turbofans and has a slightly longer fuselage. The higher thrust and fuel efficiency of the Tay gives the C-20F a range of over 5,000 miles. The aircraft is based at Andrews AFB, Maryland, along with one of the C-20Es. The other E model operates from Hickam AFB, Hawaii.

The Army operates one example of the larger Gulfstream IV model, designated the C-20F. Serial 91-0108 is with OSACOM's Priority Air Transport Detachment at Andrews AFB, Maryland.

Specifications: See US Navy Aircraft section for details.

Missions: Priority airlift.

Gulfstream Aerospace C-37A Gulfstream V

Designated the C-37A, a single Gulfstream V entered service with the Army in late November 1999. It was delivered to Andrews AFB, Maryland, and assigned to OSACOM's Priority Air Transport Detachment to operate on long-range, high priority missions that exceed the capabilities of C-20E/F variants.

Specifications: See USAF Aircraft section for details.

Missions: Long-range priority airlift.

PILATUS AIRCRAFT (Including Britten-Norman)

Pilatus UV-20A Chiricahua

Developed from the piston-engine-powered PC-6 Porter, the first PC-6/A turboprop flew in May 1961, and was followed in May 1964 by the PC-6/B. Besides those built in Switzerland, approximately 100 Turbo Porters were manufactured under license in the United States by Fairchild Hiller. The aircraft built by the company primarily were civil variants but at least 38 were delivered as AU-23A counter-insurgency (COIN) aircraft. Based on the PC-6/C airframe, early AU-23As were originally built for the USAF but were handed over to Thailand's armed forces when American involvement in Southeast Asia ended. That country also obtained additional examples under foreign military sales (FMS) contracts.

In 1979, Switzerland's Pilatus Aircraft delivered two PC-6/B2-H2 Turbo Porters to the Army's Berlin Brigade at Templehof Airport in West Berlin, Germany. Designated the UV-20A, and possessing short takeoff and landing (STOL) capabilities, these aircraft served in aeromedical evacuation and VIP transport roles. After German reunification, they were transferred to Fort Bragg, North Carolina, and assigned in 1991 to the US Army 'Golden Knights' Parachute Team for training purposes and as support aircraft for national competitions.

Pilatus UV-20A Chiricahua Specifications

Maximum Takeoff Weight:	4,850 lb (2200 kg)
Empty Weight:	2,685 lb (1218 kg)
Fuselage Length:	35 ft 9 in (10.90 m)
Wingspan:	49 ft 8 in (15.14 m)
Height:	10 ft 6 in (3.20 m)
Power Plant:	One Pratt & Whitney Canada PT6A-27 turboprop engine, rated at 680 shp (507 kW), driving three-blade, constant-speed propellers
Maximum Fuel Capacity:	1,148 lb (521 kg)
Maximum Speed:	151 kts (280 km/h)
Service Ceiling:	25,000 ft (7620 m)
Operating Range:	739 nm (1369 km)
Crew:	1
Armament:	None
Accommodations:	7–10 passengers or 8 paratroopers
Missions:	Parachute team support

Two Pilatus UV-20As once flew with the Berlin Brigade at Tempelhof Airport. However, no US Army aircraft remain on station in the once divided German city. Today, the Chiricahuas are operated by the aviation detachment of the 'Golden Knights' and carry the markings of the US Army Parachute Team.

Britten-Norman BN.2T Islander

First flown on 13 June 1965, the BN.2 Islander entered civil service in 1967. The Army obtained a single example of the BN.2B-21 variant via the Confiscated/Excessed Aircraft Program (CEAP) in 1988 for operation by the Communications and Electronics Command (CECOM) at NAES Lakehurst, New Jersey. Later, however, it was transferred to CECOM's Night Vision Directorate Airborne Applications Branch at Davison AAF, Fort Belvoir, Virginia, and flew in support of systems development efforts. The Army replaced the aircraft's Textron Lycoming IO540 piston engines with Allison turboprops, which resulted in its change of designation to BN.2T.

PIPER AIRCRAFT

Piper PA-31T Cheyenne

A single Piper Aircraft PA-31T is believed to operate from Simmons AAF at Fort Bragg, North Carolina, in support of US Army Special Operations forces. Although little is known about the aircraft and its role, it is likely the Army acquired it through the CEAP.

RAYTHEON AIRCRAFT (INCLUDING BEECH AIRCRAFT)

Beech 1900D Airliner

A single, nonstandard Model 1900D serves with the Soldier and Biological Chemical Command (SBCCOM) with Army Materiel Command (AMC), at the Aberdeen Proving Ground in Maryland. The aircraft, based at Phillips AAF, is capable of transporting 19 passengers and is there primarily for the use of SBCCOM teams needing to respond to biological and chemical emergencies.

Beech C-12C/D/F/J/R/T Huron (Super King Air 200)

The Army's first Super King Airs included three Model A100-1 (later A200) aircraft, which were acquired in 1972 for the purpose of testing a signals intelligence system (SIGINT). Designated RU-21Js, the aircraft were modified to VIP configuration and redesignated C-12Ls at the conclusion of the program. They were retired from service in 1997.

Beginning in 1974, 60 C-12As were delivered to the Army as staff/utility transports and, although based on the Model A200, these aircraft were powered by Pratt & Whitney Canada PT6A-38 engines. Most of the early examples were then redesignated C-12Cs after receiving uprated PT6A-41 engines. In 1978, 14 production C-12Cs were ordered, followed by the first of 40 C-12D (Model A200CT) aircraft. The latter essentially is a C-12C equipped with a high-flotation landing gear; provision for wingtip-mounted, 52-gallon auxiliary fuel tanks; and a port side cargo door.

Britten-Norman BN.2T Islander Specifications

Maximum Takeoff Weight:	6,600 lb (2994 kg)
Empty Weight:	3,945 lb (1789 kg)
Fuselage Length:	35 ft 7.75 in (10.87 m)
Wingspan:	53 ft 0 in (16.15 m)
Height:	13 ft 8.75 in (4.18 m)
Power Plant:	Two Rolls-Royce Allison 250-C30 turboprop engines, each rated at 320 shp (239 kW), driving three-blade, constant-speed propellers
Maximum Fuel Capacity:	1,440 lb (653 kg)
Maximum Speed:	300 kts (556 km/h)
Service Ceiling:	18,900 ft (5761 m)
Operating Range:	886 nm (1641 km)
Crew:	2
Armament:	None
Accommodations:	2–4 systems operators
Missions:	Test support

BN.2Ts are operated in small numbers by several of the world's air arms. However, the only Islander in US service is assigned to the Army's Night Vision Directorate Airborne Applications Division and is based at Davison AAF at Fort Belvoir, Virginia.

Piper PA-31T Cheyenne Specifications

Maximum Takeoff Weight:	9,000 lb (4082 kg)
Empty Weight:	4,983 lb (2260 kg)
Fuselage Length:	34 ft 8 in (10.57 m)
Wingspan:	42 ft 8 in (13.01 m)
Height:	12 ft 9 in (3.89 m)
Power Plant:	Two Pratt & Whitney Canada PT6A-28 turboprop engines, each rated at 620 shp (462 kW), driving three-blade, constant-speed propellers
Maximum Fuel Capacity:	2,633 lb (1194 kg)
Maximum Speed:	280 kts (519 km/h)
Service Ceiling:	29,000 ft (8839 m)
Operating Range:	839 nm (1554 km)
Crew:	2
Armament:	None
Missions:	Mission support

Beech 1900D Airliner Specifications

Maximum Takeoff Weight:	16,950 lb (7688 kg)
Empty Weight:	10,615 lb (4815 kg)
Fuselage Length:	57 ft 10 in (17.63 m)
Wingspan:	57 ft 11 in (17.65 m)
Height:	14 ft 11 in (4.55 m)
Power Plant:	Two Pratt & Whitney Canada PT6A-67D turboprop engines, each rated at 1,279 shp (954 kW), driving four-blade, constant-speed propellers
Maximum Fuel Capacity:	4,490 lb (2037 kg)
Maximum Speed:	283 kts (524 km/h)
Service Ceiling:	25,000 ft (7620 m)
Operating Range:	1,600 nm (2963 km)
Crew:	2
Armament:	None
Accommodations:	19 passengers
Missions:	Priority airlift

Army C-12s carry very little in the way of markings and it is often difficult to determine the operator simply by looking at the aircraft. Serial 88-0086 is a C-12T assigned to the California ARNG's OSACOM Detachment 32. It is based at Mather Airport, Sacramento.

After obtaining 74 C-12A/C Hurons, the Army began taking delivery of the C-12D variant. Serial 84-24376 is operated by the C/2-228th AVN(TA) at Simmons AAF at Fort Bragg, North Carolina. The 'Deltas' primarily are assigned to OSACOM and theater aviation units.

Of the 40 'Deltas' ordered between 1978 and 1984, 16 were modified for use as Special Electronic Mission Aircraft (see RC-12 entry). Between 1985 and 1987 the Army also purchased 19 C-12Fs, a variant based on the Model B200 version and powered by PT6A-42 engines. Four years later, an order was placed for the first of 29 C-12Rs, an aircraft very similar to the C-12F in most respects. However, it came with four-blade propellers and cockpit avionics that included an electronic flight instrument system (EFIS), digital autopilot and a Global Positioning System (GPS)-equipped flight management system. In September 1995, the Army took delivery of the first of 42 ex-USAF C-12Fs and two C-12Js. The major difference between Air Force and Army F models are their four-blade propellers. The J, on the other hand, is based on the Beech Model 1900C and is equipped with a cargo door and seating for up to 19 passengers.

Roles filled by the King Airs include inter- and intra-theater transport, general support and operational support airlift. They are assigned to active-duty and USARC theater aviation battalions, OSACOM regional flight centers (RFCs) and state flight detachments (SFDs) as well as to major commands in Europe and Japan, directly. Forty C-12Fs with the RFCs and SFDs are being upgraded through installation of an FDS-255 EFIS, a TCAS II and an FMS-800 flight management system. This will make them functionally similar to C-12Rs and examples so modified are being redesignated C-12Ts. With the exception of a small number of aircraft used for flight training, the majority of C-12Cs have been retired.

Beech C-12F Huron Specifications

Maximum Takeoff Weight:	12,500 lb (5670 kg)
Empty Weight:	7,538 lb (3419 kg)
Fuselage Length:	43 ft 9 in (13.34 m)
Wingspan:	54 ft 6 in (16.61 m)
Height:	15 ft 0 in (4.57 m)
Power Plant:	Two Pratt & Whitney Canada PT6A-42 turboprop engines, each rated at 850 shp (634 kW), driving three- or four-blade, constant-speed propellers
Maximum Fuel Capacity:	2,606 lb (1182 kg)
Maximum Speed:	295 kts (546 km/h)
Service Ceiling:	35,000 ft (10668 m)
Operating Range:	1,460 nm (2704 km)
Crew:	2
Armament:	None
Accommodations:	8 passengers
Missions:	Operational support, theater airlift

Beech RC-12D/H/K/N/P/Q Guardrail

Assigned to military intelligence brigades, the RC-12s are referred to as Special Electronic Mission Aircraft. Communications (COMINT) and electronics (ELINT) missions that come under the "umbrella" of signals intelligence (SIGINT) are assigned to six different RC-12 Guardrail variants. Equipped with a variety of antennas, these aircraft carry sophisticated electronics designed to collect, identify and locate enemy command, control and air defense emitters. However, the Guardrails are also capable of providing precision targeting information.

RC-12s began replacing RU-21Hs in the role in the mid-1980s and all are assigned to military intelligence battalions. They are deployed in "packages" of between six and 12 aircraft and, although the RC-12D is based on the A200CT airframe, the other variants are built around B200 airframes. Furthermore, there are major differences in the internal systems carried by Guardrail aircraft, whereby three Guardrail Common Sensor (GR/CS) systems and a single Improved Guardrail V (IGRV) system are currently deployed. Fielding the GR/CS System 3 is the 3rd MI Bn, flying RC-12Hs in Korea. The 1st MI Bn in Germany operates RC-12Ks and fields the GR/CS System 4, whereas the GR/CS System 1 is located at Hunter AAF in Savannah, Georgia, and is operated by the 224th MI Bn. This battalion flies RC-12Ns. The most advanced version is the GR/CS System 2, which will become operational in 2000 under the control of the 15th MI Bn at Fort Hood, Texas. This battalion will operate a mix of nine RC-12P and three RC-12Q platforms that will replace the six RC-12Ds that form part of the last remaining IGRV system. Airborne Guardrail elements are supported by vans on the ground that house computer processing centers. The 304th MI Bn at Fort Huachuca, Arizona, is the Guardrail training organization.

Nine RC-12Ns, including serial 88-0326, are assigned to B Company/224th MI Bn (Aerial Exploitation) at Hunter AAF, Georgia. These aircraft represent the airborne elements of the Guardrail Common Sensor (GR/CS) System 1.

Beech RC-12N Guardrail Specifications

(Largely per C-12F except as shown below)

Maximum Takeoff Weight:	16,200 lb (7348 kg)
Empty Weight:	13,100 lb (5942 kg)
Wingspan:	57 ft 10 in (17.63 m)
Power Plant:	Two Pratt & Whitney Canada PT6A-67 turboprop engines, each rated at 1,100 shp (820 kW), driving three- or four-blade, constant-speed propellers
Maximum Speed:	250 kts (463 km/h)
Operating Range:	1,200 nm (2222 km)
Mission:	ELINT

Beech JU-21H Ute

The Army first received U-21A Utes in 1967 and has operated several variants in utility and ELINT roles in the years since. The unpressurized aircraft was created by mating the fuselage of the Beech Queen Air 65-80 with the wings, tail and undercarriage of the King Air 65-90. In the utility role, the U-21A/G series was capable of carrying up to 12 combat troops, or 3,000 lb (1361 kg) of cargo, or three stretchers and three ambulatory patients, or six staff personnel. In all, 161 examples were procured by the Army in 1966 and 1967 and the last 17 were designated U-21Gs.

Nearly one-third of the U-21 fleet was converted for a variety of ELINT missions. Of these, the last few RU-21Hs assigned for intelligence roles were retired in 1994, and an upgrade program was subsequently initiated to convert cockpits and systems so that 36 aircraft could be used for utility purposes. However, this project was terminated after only about a dozen aircraft were delivered, due to the fact ex-USAF C-12Fs were made available to the Army, instead. Today, only a single JU-21H is assigned for testing duties at Fort Rucker. Four F models based on the A100 version of the King Air, owned by the Army but assigned to the US Naval Test Pilot School at NAS Patuxent River, Maryland, were retired in 1999.

This RC-12K carries the serial number 85-0149 and is operated by Raytheon Aircraft as a development airframe for the Guardrail program. Eight more aircraft are assigned to B Company/1st MI Bn (Aerial Exploitation) at Weisbaden AAF, near Frankfurt in Germany.

Beech T-34C Turbo Mentor

A small number of US Navy-owned Beech T-34Cs are assigned to the Army Aviation Technical Test Center (ATTC) at Fort Rucker, Alabama, and are flown as chase aircraft for testing conducted at Cairns AAF. The Army first bailed six examples from the Navy in 1987 to support its test programs at Edwards AFB, California, and at Pope AFB, North Carolina. However, the Navy reclaimed the three Mentors at Pope in 1990, although those at Edwards were retained by the Army and transferred to Fort Rucker when test activities were relocated to the Alabama facility in 1996. One aircraft has since gone to Pope AFB.

Specifications: See US Navy Aircraft section for details.

Missions: Test support.

Beech U-21F Ute Specifications

Maximum Takeoff Weight	10,600 lb (4808 kg)
Empty Weight	6,405 lb (2905 kg)
Length	39 ft 11.25 in (12.17 m)
Wing Span	45 ft 10.5 in (13.98 m)
Height	15 ft 4.25 in (4.68 m)
Power Plant	Two Pratt & Whitney Canada PT6A-20 turboprop engines, each rated at 680 shp (507 kW), driving four-blade, constant-speed propellers
Maximum Speed	247 kts at 10,000 ft (457 km/h at 3048 m)
Service Ceiling:	28,900 ft (8809 m)
Operating Range	1,286 nm (2382 km)
Crew	2
Armament:	None
Missions:	Training

Two T-34Cs are still assigned to the Army Aviation Technical Training Center, while the third is with the Airborne Special Operations Test Board at Simmons AAF, Pope AFB, North Carolina.

Four U-21F Utes once supported operations at the Naval Test Pilot School at NAS Patuxent River, Maryland. In 1999 they were replaced by C-12Cs.

Sikorsky UH-60 Blackhawks fitted with skis are a regular sight in Alaska, where they serve both with active-duty units and those assigned to the Alaska ARNG's 1-207th AVN (GSAB).

SIKORSKY AIRCRAFT

Sikorsky UH-60A/L/Q, EH-60A/L, HH-60L, MH-60A/K/L Blackhawk

Developed as a replacement for the UH-1H "Huey," the Sikorsky Model S-70 was named winner of the Army's Utility Tactical Transport Aircraft System (UTTAS) competition in December 1976. This followed a competitive fly-off against the Boeing Vertol YUH-61A. Designated UH-60As, the first of the new helicopters entered the Army's inventory in 1979 and almost 1,000 examples were delivered during the 10 years that followed. Production ended in

The EH-60A Quick Fix 2B is readily identified by the antennas mounted on the fuselage boom. This Blackhawk is assigned to C Company, 2d Battalion, 227th Aviation Regiment at Fort Hood, Texas. The command aviation company is with the 1st Cavalry Division.

1989 and switched to the UH-60L the following year. Sikorsky continues to deliver this upgraded variant to the Army today, to serve in a number of roles.

Equipped with more powerful engines, the UH-60L is capable of operating at higher gross weights and introduced a Hover Infrared Suppression System (HIRSS). Together, the old and new variants serve as the Army's primary rotary-wing, transport platform, flying with general support, assault, command and medical battalions assigned to division, corps and theater aviation brigades. Specialized variants include the EH-60A Quick Fix 2B, which is a command and control (C^2) aircraft, and the MH-60A, MH-60K and MH-60L, which are optimized for Special Operations missions. The newest variant is the UH-60Q, a dedicated ambulance variant now being fielded to medical companies, and plans call for as many as 357 UH-60As to be modified to this configuration. New-build HH-60Ls will also be assigned to combat rescue and ambulance duties, and the

Essentially an upgraded UH-60L, the MH-60L is fitted with the External Stores Suspension System (ESSS), a FLIR turret and color weather radar. However, it does not carry an external refueling boom.

Sikorsky UH-60L Blackhawk Specifications

Maximum Takeoff Weight:	17,000 lb (7711 kg)
Empty Weight:	11,500 lb (5216 kg)
Fuselage Length:	50 ft 0.75 in (15.26 m)
Overall Length:	64 ft 10 in (19.76 m)
Main Rotor Diameter:	53 ft 8 in (16.36 m)
Height:	12 ft 4 in (3.76 m)
Power Plant:	Two General Electric T700-GE-701C turboshaft engines, each rated at 1,940 shp (1447 kW), driving four-blade main and tail rotors
Maximum Fuel Capacity:	2,430 lb (1102 kg)
Maximum Speed:	160 kts (296 km/h)
Service Ceiling:	19,000 ft (5791 m)
Operating Range:	300–995 nm (556–1843 km)
Crew:	3
Armament:	M144 armament system consisting of pintle-mounted 7.62-mm M60D machine guns; M139 mine dispensing system; and a number of Special Operations dedicated aircraft are capable of firing a variety of forward-firing weapons
Accommodations:	14 troops, or 6 litters and 3 attendants, or an 8,000-lb (3,629-kg) external sling load
Missions:	Utility, electronic warfare/command and control (C^2) air ambulance, Special Operations gunship

Having an external refueling boom means the MH-60K does not necessarily have to carry auxiliary fuel tanks. This means larger internal loads can be transported.

US Army

EH-60As will be modified to EH-60L Advanced Quick Fix (AQF) configuration. Improved ELINT and COMINT capabilities and new direction-finding (DF) equipment will be among the enhancements.

Beginning in 2002, as many as 613 UH-60As will be brought up to UH-60L+ standard through the fitting of wide-chord rotor blades, a T700-GE-701C engine and a new digital cockpit based on that of the UH-60Q. Thereafter, up to 255 UH-60Ls will be modified to UH-60X configuration and the new variant will share a common cockpit with the UH-60L+. However, it will be powered by a 3,000-shp (2237-kW) engine to be developed under the Army's CEP. The new power plant should allow the UH-60X to carry a 9,000-lb (4082-kg) external payload for a distance of 160 nm (296 km), more than double the UH-60A's range for the same load.

TRW/IAI-MALAT DIVISION

TRW-IAI RQ-5A Hunter

Teamed with the Israeli Aircraft Industries (IAI) Malat Division, TRW was declared the winner of the US Army's Short-Range UAV competition in 1988. Originally intended for service with corps- and division-level military intelligence battalions the RQ-5A Hunter (formerly the BQM-155A) first flew in March 1991. Despite escalating costs and problems with the UAV, LRIP of seven Hunter systems was approved in January 1993, and the first system was delivered in April 1995. However, subsequent testing revealed other deficiencies and

Even though the Army's Hunter UAV program was cancelled in 1996, seven systems were delivered and the type saw service over the Balkans in 1999 with A Company, 15th Military Intelligence Battalion.

TRW-IAI RQ-5A Hunter Specifications

Maximum Takeoff Weight:	1,600 lb (726 kg)
Empty Weight:	1,100 lb (499 kg)
Length:	22 ft 11 in (6.99 m)
Wing Span:	29 ft 2.5 in (8.90 m)
Height:	5 ft 6.5 in (1.69 m)
Power plant:	Two Motto Guzzi 750 cc reciprocating engines, each rated at 64 hp (48 kW), driving two-blade propellers
Maximum Fuel Capacity:	342 lb (155 kg)
Maximum Speed:	106 kts (196 km/h)
Operating Range:	10-hour endurance. Radius limited by communication range of 68 nm (126 km) but can be extended to 162 nm (300 km) with air relay.
Service Ceiling:	16,000 ft (4877 m)
Crew:	None
Armament:	None
Mission Equipment:	Electro-optical/infrared (EO/IR) cameras
Missions:	Reconnaissance

three crashes occurred between August and September 1995, which caused cancellation of full-rate production in January 1996. Seven systems, which included 75 RQ-5As, were eventually delivered to the Army. One was assigned to IIICORPS at Fort Hood, Texas, for concept development and continuation training, whereas another went to Fort Huachuca, Arizona, for training purposes. A third was delivered to the Joint Readiness Training Center (JRTC) at Fort Polk, Louisiana, while the remainder have gone into long-term storage.

NON-DESIGNATED FORMER SOVIET BLOC AIRCRAFT

The Operational Test and Evaluation Command's Threat Support Activity (OTSA) unit, based at Biggs AAF, Fort Bliss, Texas, operates a small number of former Soviet-bloc aircraft. They are used for several purposes, including weapon system test and evaluation and as "aggressor" aircraft during military exercises. Accordingly, they are flown regularly to the Joint Readiness Training Center at Fort Polk, Louisiana; to the National Training Center at Fort Irwin, California; and to Nellis AFB, Nevada. Among these aircraft are two Antonov An-2 'Colt' utility biplanes, the only known fixed-wing type in the group. Helicopters include the Kamov Ka-32T 'Helix,' a utility variant of the naval antisubmarine platform, three transport types that include a Mil Mi-2 'Hoplight,' an Mi-8T 'Hip-C' and an Mi-17 'Hip-H,' plus several Mi-14PL 'Haze-A' antisubmarine helicopters. Also operated are Mi-24D 'Hind-D' and Mi-24P 'Hind-F' gunships. They have been obtained from a variety of sources and some were once in East German service. The Mi-2 and Ka-32T are civil variants and most likely were purchased on the civilian market. Although most

Operational Test and Evaluation Command's OTSA often flies Mil Mi-24s to facilities in Louisiana and Nevada, to serve as opposing forces during training exercises.

of the aircraft still field some of their original equipment, they also have been fitted with American-made systems for air traffic and other communications purposes. In addition, each is equipped with a Multiple Integrated Laser Engagement System (MILES), which is a training system.

Among former Soviet types acquired by the Army, at least two Antonov An-2 'Colts' are operated by OTSA from its home station at Biggs AAF, Texas.

Two attack helicopter battalions are now equipped with the AH-64D Apache Longbow. The Army is currently negotiating a second multi-year contract for the modification of additional AH-64As.

AIRFIELDS AND FACILITIES

MAJOR AVIATION FACILITIES WITHIN THE UNITED STATES

Aberdeen Proving Ground, Maryland
Location: Near Baltimore
Command: AMC
Airfield/Heliport: Phillips AAF and Weide AHP
Organizations & Units: US Army Soldier and Biological Chemical Command (SBCCOM), Developmental Test Command (DTC), SBCCOM Aviation Detachment, units of the Maryland ARNG

Fort Belvoir, Virginia
Established: 1912
Location: Near Alexandria
Command: MDW
Airfield/Heliport: Davison AAF
Named For: Brig. Gen. Donald A. Davison, a noted World War II aviation engineer
Organizations & Units: Headquarters for Operational Support Airlift Command (OSACOM), 12th Aviation Battalion, US Army Communication and Electronic Command's (CECOM's) Night Vision Directorate Airborne Applications Branch (NVDAAB)

Fort Benning, Georgia
Location: Near Columbus
Command: TRADOC
Airfield/Heliport: Lawson AAF supports a single medical company
Organizations & Units: US Army Infantry Center and School

Fort Bliss, Texas
Established: 1854
Location: El Paso
Command: TRADOC
Airfield/Heliport: Biggs AAF supports the 204th Military Intelligence Battalion and the OPTEC Threat Support Activity (OTSA)
Organizations & Units: US Army Air Defense Artillery Center and School

Fort Bragg, North Carolina
Established: 1918
Location: Near Fayetteville
Command: FORSCOM
Airfield/Heliport: Simmons AAF supports corps and division aviation brigades
Organizations & Units: XVIII Airborne Corps and 82d Airborne Division

Fort Campbell, Kentucky
Established: 1942
Location: Near Nashville, Tennessee
Command: FORSCOM
Airfield/Heliport: Campbell AAF and Sabre AHP support division and regiment aviation brigades
Organizations & Units: 101st Airborne Division (Air Assault), 160th Special Operations Aviation Regiment (Airborne)

Fort Carson, Colorado
Established: 1942
Location: Adjacent to Colorado Springs and Peterson AFB
Command: FORSCOM
Airfield/Heliport: Butts AAF supports a regimental aviation squadron
Organizations & Units: 3d Armored Cavalry Regiment

Muir AAF is home to Pennsylvania ARNG AH-1F Cobras assigned to 1-104th Cavalry. The aviation support facility is located at Fort Indiantown Gap.

Fort Drum, New York
Established: 1951
Location: Near Watertown
Command: FORSCOM
Airfield/Heliport: Wheeler Sack AAF supports a divisional aviation brigade
Organizations & Units: 10th Infantry Division (Light) (Mountain Division)

Fort Eustis, Virginia
Established: 1918
Location: Near Newport News
Command: TRADOC
Airfield/Heliport: Felker AAF supports the operations of one USARC helicopter battalion
Organizations & Units: Army Aviation Logistic School

Fort Hood, Texas
Established: 1942
Location: Near Killeen
Command: FORSCOM
Airfield/Heliport: Hood AAF and Robert Gray AAF support aviation units of the commands listed below
Organizations & Units: IIICORPS, 21st Cavalry Brigade (Air Combat), 13th Corps Support Command, 504th Military Intelligence Brigade, 1st Cavalry Division, 4th Infantry Division

Fort Huachuca, Arizona
Established: 1877
Location: Near Sierra Vista
Command: TRADOC
Airfield/Heliport: Libby AAF supports the 111th Military Intelligence Brigade (Training)
Organizations & Units: US Army Intelligence Center and School, Electronic Proving Ground, Test Experimentation Command's Intelligence and Electronic Warfare Test Directorate

Hunter Army Airfield, Georgia
Established: 1941
Location: Near Savannah
Command: FORSCOM
Airfield/Heliport: Hunter AAF supports an aviation brigade and a single battalion
Organizations & Units: 3d Infantry Division, 160th Aviation Regiment

Fort Indiantown Gap, Pennsylvania
Established: 1940
Location: Near Harrisburg
Command: ARNG
Airfield/Heliport: Muir AAF
Organizations & Units: Pennsylvania National Guard units

Fort Irwin, California
Established: 1940
Location: Near Barstow
Command: FORSCOM
Airfield/Heliport: Possesses small airfield for deployed aircraft only and aviation units operate from Barstow Daggett Airport
Organizations & Units: National Training Center (NTC)

Fort Knox, Kentucky
Established: 1918
Location: Near Louisville
Command: TRADOC
Airfield/Heliport: Godman AAF supports USARC units
Organizations & Units: US Army Armor Center and School

Fort Leavenworth, Kansas
Established: 1827
Location: Near Kansas City
Command: TRADOC

Airfield/Heliport: Sherman AAF supports a handful of small aviation units
Organizations & Units: 35th Infantry Division

Fort Lewis, Washington

Established: 1917
Location: Near Tacoma
Command: FORSCOM
Airfield/Heliport: Gray AAF and Lewis AAF support elements of the Washington ARNG and USARC as well as active-duty units
Organizations & Units: ICORPS, 66th Aviation Brigade

Fort Polk, Louisiana

Established: 1941
Location: Near Alexandria
Command: FORSCOM
Airfield/Heliport: Polk AAF supports the 2d ACR's regimental aviation squadron
Organizations & Units: Joint Readiness Training Center (JRTC), 2d Armored Cavalry Regiment (ACR)

Redstone Arsenal, Alabama

Established: 1941
Location: Huntsville
Command: AMC
Airfield/Heliport: Redstone AAF
Organizations & Units: Aviation and Missile Command (AMCOM), Redstone Technical Test Center

Fort Richardson, Alaska

Established: 1940
Location: Anchorage
Command: USARAK
Airfield/Heliport: Bryant AHP supports units of the Alaska ARNG
Organizations & Units: Arctic Support Brigade

Fort Riley, Kansas

Established: 1853
Location: Manhattan
Command: FORSCOM
Airfield/Heliport: Marshall AAF supports a single medical company
Organizations & Units: 24th Infantry Division (Mechanized)

Fort Rucker, Alabama

Established: 1942
Location: Near Montgomery
Command: TRADOC
Airfield/Heliport: Cairns AAF, Hanchey AHP, Knox AHP and Lowe AHP support the base's training units
Organizations & Units: US Army Aviation Center (USAAVNC), Aviation Technical Test Center (ATTC)

Schofield Barracks, Hawaii

Established: 1908
Location: Oahu
Command: USARPAC
Airfield/Heliport: Wheeler AAF supports a division aviation brigade and units of the Hawaii ARNG
Organizations & Units: 25th Infantry Division (Light)

Fort Sill, Oklahoma

Established: 1869
Location: Near Lawton
Command: TRADOC
Airfield/Heliport: Henry Post AAF supports a detachment of air ambulance helicopters
Organizations & Units: US Army Artillery Center and School

Fort Stewart, Georgia

Established: 1940
Location: Near Savannah
Command: FORSCOM
Organizations & Units: 3d Infantry Division (Mechanized)

Fort Wainwright, Alaska

Established: 1961
Location: Fairbanks
Command: USARAK
Airfield/Heliport: Wainwright AAF
Organizations & Units: Arctic Support Brigade

MAJOR ARMY AIRFIELDS WITHIN THE USA

FACILITIES OPERATED BY THE ARNG AND USARC

Location	Branch	Location	Branch
Abrams MAP, Grand Ledge, Michigan	ARNG	Henry Rohlsen Airport, St Croix, USVI	ARNG
Akron - Canton RAP, Greensburg, Ohio	ARNG	Indianapolis IAP, Indiana	ARNG
Albany County Airport, Latham, New York	ARNG	Isla Grande Airport, San Juan, Puerto Rico	ARNG
Alexandria - Esler RAP, Pineville, Louisiana	ARNG	Jefferson City Memorial Airport, Missouri	ARNG
Austin - Bergstrom IAP, Texas	ARNG	Johnson CAP, Olathe, Kansas	USARC
Bangor IAP, Maine	ARNG	Johnstown - Cambria CAP, Pennsylvania	ARNG/USARC
Bethel Airport, Alaska	ARNG	Juneau IAP, Alaska	ARNG
Birmingham IAP, Alabama	ARNG	Key Field, Meridian, Mississippi	ARNG
Bismark MAP, North Dakota	ARNG	Lakefront Airport, New Orleans, Louisiana	ARNG
Boise Air Terminal - Gowen Field, Idaho	ARNG	Lakeland - Linder RAP, Florida	ARNG
Boone MAP, Iowa	ARNG	Las Cruces IAP, New Mexico	ARNG
Bradley IAP, Windsor Locks, Connecticut	ARNG	Lincoln MAP, Nebraska	ARNG
Branson RAP, Springfield, Missouri	ARNG	Long Island Mac Arthur Airport, Ronkonkoma, New York	ARNG
Buckley ANGB, Aurora, Colorado	ARNG	Los Alamitos AAF, California	ARNG/USARC
Burlington IAP, South Burlington, Vermont	ARNG	Lovell Field, Chattanooga, Tennessee	ARNG
Camp Robinson AAF, North Little Rock, Arkansas	ARNG	Martindale AAF, San Antonio, Texas	ARNG
Capital City Airport, Frankfort, Kentucky	ARNG	McCoy AAF, Fort McCoy, Wisconsin	USARC
Capital City Airport, Lansing, Michigan	ARNG	McGhee Tyson ANGB, Knoxville, Tennessee	ARNG
Cheyenne Airport, Wyoming	ARNG	McNary Field, Salem, Oregon	ARNG
Clarksburg Benedum Airport, Bridgeport, West Virginia	ARNG	Mercer CAP, West Trenton, New Jersey	ARNG
Columbia MAP/McEntire ANGS, Eastover, South Carolina	ARNG	Midway Airport, Chicago, Illinois	ARNG
Craig MAP, Jacksonville, Florida	ARNG	Mobile Downtown Airport, Alabama	ARNG
Dane County RAP - Truax Field, Madison, Wisconsin	ARNG	Montgomery CAP, Conroe, Texas	USARC
Davenport MAP, Iowa	ARNG	Montgomery RAP - Dannelly Field, Alabama	ARNG
Decatur Airport, Illinois	ARNG	NAS North Island, California	ARNG
Dobbins ARB, Marietta, Georgia	ARNG/USARC	NAS Willow Grove JRB, Pennsylvania	USARC
Eagle County RAP, Gypsum, Colorado	ARNG	New Castle CAP, Delaware	ARNG
Eastern Oregon RAP, Pendleton, Oregon	ARNG	Nome Airport, Alaska	ARNG
Ellington Field Airport, Houston, Texas	ARNG	Otis ANGB, Falmouth, Massachusetts	ARNG
Elmendorf AFB, Alaska	ARNG	Papago AAF, Phoenix, Arizona	ARNG
Forbes Field Airport, Topeka, Kansas	ARNG	Picatinny Arsenal, Dover, New Jersey	ARNG
Fort Sheridan, Illinois	USARC	Quonset State Airport, North Kingston, Rhode Island	ARNG
Fresno - Yosemite IAP, California	ARNG	Raleigh - Durham IAP, Morrisville, North Carolina	ARNG
Gen. Howell Muldrow Heliport, Lexington, Oklahoma	ARNG	Rapid City RAP, South Dakota	ARNG
General Lyman Field/Hilo IAP, Hawaii	ARNG	Reno/Stead Airport, Nevada	ARNG
Grand Prairie AAF, Texas	ARNG	Richmond IAP, Sandston, Virginia	ARNG
Greater Peoria Airport, Illinois	ARNG	Rickenbacker IAP, Columbus, Ohio	ARNG
Greater Rochester IAP, New York	ARNG	Rowan CAP, Salisbury, North Carolina	ARNG
Groton - New London Airport, Connecticut	ARNG	Sacramento Mather Airport, California	ARNG
Gulfport - Biloxi RAP, Mississippi	ARNG	Salina MAP, Kansas	ARNG
Hawkins Field, Jackson, Mississippi	ARNG	Salt Lake City MAP, West Jordan, Utah	ARNG
Helena RAP, Montana	ARNG	Santa Fe County MAP, New Mexico	ARNG

An AH-64A Apache assigned to the South Carolina ARNG's 1-151st AVN (ATK). The unit is based at Columbia Municipal Airport in Eastover.

UH-1V "Hueys" belonging to the Delaware ARNG's 198th Medical Company (Air Ambulance) stand lined up at New Castle County Airport, Delaware. Detachment 1 of the 198th MEDCO was reassigned to A/3-126th AVN (LUH) in September 1999 but remains stationed at New Castle.

MAJOR ARMY FACILITIES OVERSEAS

Location	Command
Armstrong AHP, Büdingen, Germany	USAREUR
Aviano AB, Italy	USAREUR
Bad Kreuznach, Germany	USAREUR
Camp Casey, Tongduchon, Republic of Korea	EUSA
Camp Doha, Kuwait	THREEUSA
Camp Eagle AAF, Pyongtaeng-ni, Republic of Korea	EUSA
Camp Gary Owen, Munsan, Republic of Korea	EUSA
Camp Page AAF, Chunchon, Republic of Korea	EUSA
Camp Red Cloud, Uijongbu, Republic of Korea	EUSA
Camp Stanley AAF, Uijongbu, Republic of Korea	EUSA
Camp Stanton, Tonggo-ri, Republic of Korea	EUSA
Camp Walker, Taegu, Republic of Korea	EUSA
Chiévres, Casteau, Belgium	USAREUR
Cigli AB, Izmir, Turkey	USAREUR
Coleman AAF, Würzburg, Germany	USAREUR
Darmstadt AHP, Wiesbaden, Germany	USAREUR
Desederio AAF/Camp Humphreys, Seoul, Rep. of Korea	EUSA
Fliegerhorst AAF, Hanau, Germany	USAREUR
Giebelstadt AAF, Germany	USAREUR
Grafenwoehr AAF, Germany	USAREUR
Heidelberg AAF, Germany	USAREUR
Hohenfels AAF, Germany	USAREUR
Kastner AAF/Camp Zama, Japan	USARPAC
Katterbach AHP, Ansbach, Germany	USAREUR
Kitzingen, Germany	USAREUR
Landstuhl AHP, Germany	USAREUR
Leighton Barracks, Würzburg, Germany	USAREUR
NAF Atsugi, Japan	USARPAC
NAVSTA Roosevelt Roads, Puerto Rico	USARSO
Schweinfurt AAF, Germany	USAREUR
Seoul K16 AB, Sung Nam, Republic of Korea	EUSA
Soto Cano AB, Honduras	USARSO
Storck Barracks, Illesheim, Germany	USAREUR
Stuttgart IAP, Germany	USAREUR
Vicenza AB, Italy	USAREUR
Wiesbaden AAF, Germany	USAREUR
Yongsang Barracks, Seoul, Republic of Korea	EUSA

ARNG AND USARC FACILITIES (Continued)

Location	Branch
Shelbyville MAP, Indiana	ARNG
Silver Bell AHP/Pinal Airpark, Marana, Arizona	ARNG
Smyrna Airport, Tennessee	ARNG
Spokane IAP, Washington	ARNG
St. Paul Downtown Airport/Holman Field, Minnesota	ARNG
St. Augustine Airport, Florida	ARNG
State Military Reservation, Concord MAP, New Hampshire	ARNG
Stockton MAP, California	ARNG
Tulsa IAP, Oklahoma	ARNG
Tupelo MAP - C.D. Lemmons Field, Mississippi	ARNG
Univ. Oklahoma Westheimer Airport, Norman, Oklahoma	ARNG
Waterloo MAP, Iowa	ARNG
West Bend MAP, Wisconsin	ARNG
Westover AFB, Chicopee, Massachusetts	ARNG
Wheeling - Ohio CAP, West Virginia	ARNG
Whiteman AFB, Missouri	ARNG
Will Rogers WAP, Oklahoma City, Oklahoma	ARNG
Winder - Barrow Airport, Georgia	ARNG
Wood CAP, Parkersburg, West Virginia	ARNG

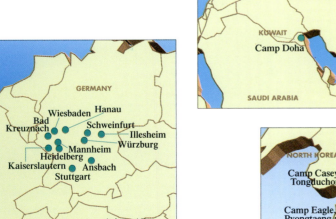

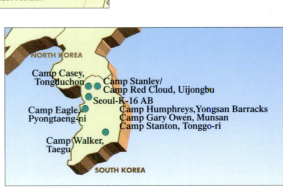

MILITARY AIRCRAFT PROGRAMS UNDER DEVELOPMENT

BuNo 164941 is the third MV-22B engineering and manufacturing development (EMD) Osprey and is now undergoing modification to CV-22B configuration for the Air Force Special Operations Command (AFSOC).

BELL HELICOPTER TEXTRON/ BOEING COMPANY

Bell Boeing CV-22 Osprey

While the MV-22 Osprey is scheduled to become operational with the Marine Corps in 2001, the AFSOC is expected to field the first of 50 CV-22 Ospreys in 2004. In Air Force service, the tilt-rotor promises to enhance military operations through better efficiencies and lower operational costs compared with the platforms it will replace. The new aircraft will demonstrate greater lift capability, improved safety, better range and increased speed.

The CV-22 will be enhanced with many of the high-speed, classified avionics suites and onboard computers that have made the MH-53J Pave Low III and MH-53M Pave Low IV such successful Special Operations platforms. The CV-22 is also expected to replace some HC-130P/N Combat Shadows and MC-130E Combat Talons used for resupply, transport and refueling missions.

For the Air Force, the Osprey is being modified for covert night-time infiltration and extraction of Special Operations forces through the fitting of an AN/APQ-174 terrain-following and terrain-avoidance radar. In addition, it will have an integrated navigation system to allow penetration in all weather conditions at altitudes as low as 100 feet (30 m). The night-vision-goggle (NVG)-compatible cockpit will have a multimission advanced tactical terminal (MATT) integrated with digital map displays scaled down to 0.5 nautical mile, and the CV-22 will be equipped with an AN/ALQ-211 suite of integrated radio frequency countermeasures (SIRFC). Other systems common to the MV-22B include AN/ALE-47 missile-warning and AN/AVR-2A laser-detection sets, and an AN/AAQ-16 FLIR.

Carrying 13,782 lb (6251 kg) of fuel, the aircraft will be capable of inserting or extracting 18 troops over a 500-nautical-mile (926-km) radius without needing to refuel. All variants are to be equipped with an extendible refueling probe that will increase the Osprey's range to about 2,100 nautical miles (3900 km) with a single refueling cycle. Its cruising speed is expected to be 275 knots (509 km/h).

More details about the tilt-rotor, including specifications, can be found on page 164 in the *US Marine Corps* chapter of this book.

BOEING COMPANY/LOCKHEED MARTIN MISSILES & SPACE/TRW

Boeing YAL-1A Attack Laser (747-400F)

A team comprising the Boeing Company, Lockheed Martin and TRW was awarded a $1.1 billion contract by the Air Force in November 1996 to develop an airborne laser (ABL) system. Using a heavily modified Boeing 747-400F as the platform, a high-energy Chemical Oxygen Iodine Laser (COIL), capable of emitting sufficient energy to destroy enemy missiles during the boost phase of their flight, will be fitted into an aimable turret. In the boost stage, such missiles are most vulnerable to attack and have not had an opportunity to release their warheads. As a part of its overall missile defense system, the United States will employ ABL weaponry to meet such threats.

A joint government and industry effort, the project is being led by Boeing and assembly of a prototype began recently at one of its facilities in Washington. That aircraft made its first flight in January 2000 and was delivered to Boeing's Wichita plant to receive the modifications that will allow it to receive the first laser and associated systems. The contractor is responsible for integration of the weapon system and providing the 747-400F, and is to supply the systems collectively referred to as BM/C4I. These comprise battle management, command, control, communications, computers and intelligence. The COIL is being developed by TRW's Space and Electronics Group, along with the necessary ground support equipment. The primary role

The ABL's beam transfer assembly is designed to provide automatic targeting, whereas the fire control assembly will handle target engagement. The turret assembly in the nose houses a 59-in (1.5-m) telescope to be used during target acquisition and for directing the beam.

of Lockheed Martin's Missiles & Space Division is to design and build the beam control/fire control system that will ensure the laser is accurately aligned for firing. In addition, this system will provide target acquisition and tracking, fire control and engagement sequencing, aim-point and kill determination, laser beam wave front and jitter control. It will also handle calibration and diagnostics to allow autonomous operation and provide post mission analysis.

In addition to the high-energy laser beam, the ABL will emit separate illuminator laser beams. This megawatt-class laser weapon can be employed above the cloud layer to detect launchings of hostile theater ballistic missiles, which it then tracks and destroys. In all, a fleet of seven AL-1As is expected to join the Air Force inventory. The first aircraft should be operational between 2006 and 2008.

Boeing YAL-1A Attack Laser Specifications

Maximum Takeoff Weight:	800,000–850,000 lb (362875–385555 kg)
Overall Length:	231 ft 10 in (70.66 m)
Wingspan:	211 ft 5 in (64.44 m)
Height:	63 ft 8 in (19.41 m)
Power Plant:	Four General Electric CF6-80C2B1 high-bypass turbofans, each rated at 56,700 lb st (252.2 kN)
Maximum Fuel Capacity:	386,675 lb (175393 kg)
Maximum Speed:	507 kts (939 km/h)
Operating Range:	4,467 nm (8273 km)
Service Ceiling:	34,700 ft (10577 m)
Crew:	N/A
Mission Equipment:	Turret-mounted, high-energy laser and focusing telescope
Mission:	Antiballistic missile defense

A rendering of the Navy Unique Fleet Essential Airlift (NUFEA) aircraft, which is based on the Boeing 737-700 airframe and designated the C-40A.

BOEING COMPANY

Boeing C-40A (737-700C)

Under development as a replacement for the Navy's C-9 transport aircraft, which have served since the early 1970s, the Boeing C-40A is based on the company's latest B737 variant. Under a $163 million contract that dates from August 1997, Boeing will deliver four C-40As beginning in April 2001 to Commander Fleet Logistics Support Wing, as part of the Navy Unique Fleet Essential Airlift (NUFEA) program.

Referred to as Increased Gross Weight Quick Change (IGW QC), the aircraft is a military freighter derivative of the B737-700 "next-generation" airliner that will feature a B777-style flight deck, updated avionics and more fuel-efficient engines. It will have a payload capacity of 38,500 lb (17463 kg), and a prominent feature of the jet is a newly designed 11-foot by seven-foot (3.35-m x 2.13-m) freight door that will facilitate rapid loading and unloading of cargoes.

The Navy will be able to configure the C-40A either to carry 120 passengers, or as a freighter capable of hauling eight cargo pallets, or as a combination platform capable of accommodating 70 passengers and three pallets.

Boeing C-40A Specifications

Maximum Takeoff Weight:	133,000 lb (60328 kg)
Empty Weight:	83,790 lb (38007 kg)
Overall Length:	110 ft 4 in (33.63 m)
Wingspan:	112 ft 7 in (34.32 m)
Height:	41 ft 2 in (12.55 m)
Power Plant:	Two CFM International CFM-56-7B turbofans, each rated at approximately 24,000 lb st (106.8 kN)
Maximum Fuel Capacity:	46406 lb (21049 kg)
Maximum Speed:	515 kts (954 km/h)
Operating Range:	3302 nm (6115 km)
Service Ceiling:	41,000 ft (12497 m)
Crew:	3
Accommodations:	120 passengers
Missions:	Fleet logistic support

BOEING COMPANY/ SIKORSKY AIRCRAFT

Boeing Sikorsky RAH-66A Comanche

Originally intended as a multiplatform replacement for the Army's AH-1 Cobra, UH-1H Iroquois and OH-58 Kiowa helicopters, the Boeing Sikorsky RAH-66A Comanche is the first helicopter to be developed specifically for the role of armed reconnaissance. Comanches will be assigned to air cavalry troops and attack helicopter battalions, and will be the primary asset within cavalry units as well as light infantry and airborne divisions. It will also supplement AH-64D Apaches in heavy division/corps attack helicopter battalions.

Serving with armored and mechanized infantry (heavy) divisions, the Comanche's primary roles will be to scout for enemy forces and designate targets for Apaches to attack. With light infantry and airborne divisions, however, the RAH-66A will fly both as a scout and an attack platform.

Development of the Comanche began in 1982 when the Army issued a request for Light Helicopter Experimental (LHX) design concepts. At that time, the service was looking for two specific variants capable of separately carrying out light-utility and scout attack (SCAT) missions, and expected to procure more than 4,500 examples for these purposes. Despite the difference in missions, the systems employed by the two variants were expected to demonstrate 70 percent commonality and both aircraft were expected to weigh approximately 8,000 lb (3629 kg). The light-utility variant was to be designed to carry six troops or 2,000 lb (907 kg) of cargo while the SCAT variant was to carry advanced sensors and weapons.

The Army eventually concluded that no single platform could fulfill both of the missions and, in 1987, issued a revised proposal for a scout and attack aircraft. A formal request for proposals (RFP) followed in June 1988, and by October two competing manufacturing teams, Boeing Helicopters/Sikorsky Aircraft and Bell Helicopter/ McDonnell Douglas Helicopter, had been awarded 23-month demonstration/validation contracts valued at $158 million. Both teams proposed advanced designs that incorporated low-observable (stealth) characteristics, but while the Bell/McDonnell Douglas team offered a platform equipped with a bearingless four-blade main rotor and NOTAR (no tail rotor), Boeing and Sikorsky proposed a helicopter with a bearingless five-blade main rotor and shrouded tail rotor (or fantail). Following a period of evaluation, the Boeing/Sikorsky team was declared the winner in April 1991 of the since-renamed "LH" competition.

The first prototype RAH-66A was rolled out at the Sikorsky Aircraft facility in Stratford, Connecticut, on 25 May 1995 and its maiden flight took place on 4 January 1996. The second prototype flew on 30 March 1999 and, although it made a small number of test flights, primarily it will serve to test the Comanche's mission equipment package (MEP) beginning in 2001. Under the terms of the EMD program, the team will produce 13 preproduction prototypes (PPPs) starting in 2003. The first five aircraft will be used for development tests and will participate in digital warfighting experiments, whereas the eight EMD aircraft that follow will be utilized for initial operational test and evaluation (IOT&E) as well as for user evaluations. The first lot of low-rate initial production (LRIP) Comanches will be purchased in Fiscal Year 2005 (FY05) and the type should achieve IOC when it is fielded in 2006. Current plans call for 1,213 examples to be built.

The Comanche's design incorporates a number of stealth features, including a radar cross section reported to be lower than that of the Hellfire missile. It will have internally carried weapons, a retractable landing gear and a stowable cannon. The fuselage, which is made entirely from composite materials, has faceted sensor turrets, flat plate canopies and flared fuselage sides that serve to deflect radar signals away from their source. The five-blade composite main rotor and fantail reduce the aircraft's acoustic signature, while the infrared

Boeing Sikorsky RAH-66A Specifications

Maximum Takeoff Weight:	13,000 lb (5897 kg)
Empty Weight:	9,022 lb (4092 kg)
Overall Length:	46 ft 10.25 in (14.28 m)
Fuselage Length:	43 ft 3.75 in (13.20 m)
Main Rotor Diameter:	40 ft 0 in (12.19 m)
Height:	11 ft 0.75 in (3.37 m)
Power Plant:	Two LHTEC T800-LHT-801 turboshaft engines, each rated at 1,432 shp (1068 kW), driving a five-blade main rotor and an eight-blade shrouded tail rotor (fantail)
Maximum Fuel Capacity:	2,525 lb (1145 kg)
Maximum Speed:	175 kts (324 km/h)
Service Ceiling:	14,000 ft (4267 m)
Maximum Range:	1,260 nm (2334 km)
Operating Range:	150 nm (278 km) mission radius
Crew:	2
Armament:	XM301 20-mm cannon; AGM-114 antitank and AIM-92 air-to-air missiles; 2.75-in (70-mm) cannon carried internally and externally
Mission Equipment:	Night-vision pilotage system (NVPS), FLIR, low-light television (LLTV) laser range finder/designator (LRF/D)
Missions:	Reconnaissance, close air support (CAS)

signature is lessened because heat-producing engine components are located within the fuselage where the exhaust is cooled by mixing it with ambient air before it is ducted out under the tail. As a result, the Comanche is said to radiate 75 percent less heat than military helicopters now in service. Designed for ease of maintenance, the electronic equipment aboard the RAH-66A is carried primarily in two avionics bays running along the sides of the fuselage, plus a third located in the nose. Maintainable in the field and having a built-in diagnostic system, the avionics do not require intermediate-level or the usual in-shop repairs.

Manufactured by the Light Helicopter Turbine Engine Company (LHTEC), a joint venture between Rolls-Royce (Allison) and Allied Signal (Garrett), a pair of T800-LHT-801 turboshaft engines power the RAH-66A. LHTEC was selected in 1988 after competing for the contract against a team from Avco Lycoming and Pratt & Whitney. Besides the two T800s, each of which is rated at 1,432 shp (1068 kW), the Comanche has a small secondary power unit developed by Williams International. Designated the WTS-124, it provides electrical power and compressed air for the engine-start. It also powers the No. 3 hydraulic system and the environmental control system during normal operation of the aircraft.

The Comanche's passive electro-optical sensor (EOS) system comprises two independent turreted subsystems. The target acquisition system (TAS) includes an advanced forward-looking infrared/low-light television (FLIR/LLTV) and a laser range-finder/designator (LFRF/D). Separately, a night-vision pilotage system (NVPS) includes a second and independent FLIR as well as an image intensifier. The aircraft is to be equipped with a version of the AH-64D's AN/APG-78 Longbow millimeter-wave fire-control radar (FCR) and, as on the Apache Longbow, this radar will be installed atop the rotor mast in a redesigned low-observable radome. Originally planned for installation on Lot 6 aircraft procured in FY10, the system will now be deployed with the first operational Comanches in 2006.

Identical front and rear crew stations each include an 8-inch by 6-inch (203-mm x 152-mm) color multifunction display and a 7.8-inch by 5-inch (198-mm x 127-mm) monochrome display. Additionally, the crew will be equipped with a wide-field-of-view, helmet-integrated display-and-sight system (HIDSS), and the avionics incorporate a digital map display, GPS/INS and electronic support measures. The latter include laser and radar warning receivers, and RF and IR jammers.

The Comanche's three-barrel General Dynamics/GIAT XM301 20-mm cannon is equipped with 500 rounds and is capable of firing at rates of 750 and 1,500 rounds per minute. The helicopter is also capable of carrying AGM-114 Hellfire surface-attack missiles, AIM-92 Stinger air-to-air missiles and 2.75-in (70-mm) rockets. The RAH-66A's stealthy configuration allows a mix of Hellfires and Stingers, or rockets to be carried internally on integrated-retractable aircraft munitions system (I-RAMS) panels, each of which is equipped with three hardpoints. They can be used to accommodate a single AGM-114 each, pairs of AIM-92s or rockets in four-tube composite pods. The I-RAMS panels are also designed to act as maintenance stands when the aircraft is on the ground. By installing an external, nonretractable enhanced fuel and armament management system (EFAMS), which can be accomplished in just 15 minutes, the weapon load can be increased further. The EFAMS also can be fitted with 230-gallon (871-lit) or 430-gallon (1628-lit) external fuel tanks that enable the helicopter to self-deploy and fly a maximum distance of 1,260 nautical miles (2334 km).

COMPETING PRIMARY CONTRACTORS:
BOEING COMPANY AND LOCKHEED MARTIN

Joint Strike Fighter (JSF)

In an effort to secure what promises to be the largest tactical aircraft contract ever, the Boeing Company and Lockheed Martin, along with their collaborative partners, are competing to build the Joint Strike Fighter. Conceived as a low-cost, single-engine platform that will be the basis for Air Force, US Navy and US Marine Corps versions with a high degree of commonality, the total order is expected to exceed 2,900 aircraft. The targeted flyaway cost for the conventional takeoff and landing (CTOL) variant, which the USAF plans to begin fielding in 2008, is $28 million. A carrier-capable (CV) variant for the Navy has a target cost of $38 million, whereas the short takeoff and vertical landing (STOVL) variant for the USMC is supposed to be tagged at $35 million. It is estimated the total program will top $200 billion.

By the mid-1990s, a variety of circumstances created the economic, political and military climate that ultimately produced the JSF program. It was initiated after the DoD completed its "Bottom-up Review" and concluded that sweeping change was necessary to maintain viable tactical aircraft programs. It was recognized that it was no longer economically feasible for the three armed services to acquire and maintain nine different tacair platforms, along with all the different models, blocks and upgrades that have created huge supply deficits and training problems in recent years. With escalating life-cycle costs affecting many of the aircraft now in service, and advances in technology quickly negating some of their capabilities, a fundamental reevaluation was inevitable. Joint-service development

was deemed the answer.

Both aerospace contractors are building two demonstrators and selection of the winning platform is expected in 2001. All variants are required to have a maximum takeoff weight of 50,000 lb (22680 kg) and a combat radius of at least 600 nautical miles (1111 km). Furthermore, the USAF version must be able to carry at least 15,000 lb (6804 kg) of fuel internally, and deliver at least 13,000 lb (5897 kg) of ordnance or payload. For the Navy, the carrier variant is viewed as a high-end complement to the F/A-18E/F Super Hornet and will be the heaviest JSF. Strengthened to withstand the rigors of catapult launches and deck landings, it will weigh in 2,000 lb (907 kg) heavier and have a payload 4,000 lb (1814 kg) greater. The Navy views as essential a first-day-of-war strike capability for the JSF. Accordingly, its stealthiness must allow penetration of heavily defended areas for attacks on hardened and mobile targets.

Unlike the Air Force and Navy, which view the JSF as complementary to their F-22 Raptor and Super Hornet programs, respectively, the Marine Corps is relying exclusively on the JSF to be its tacair platform. The aircraft is designed to replace both its Hornet and Harrier fleets and is an important step in the Corps' planned conversion to an all-STOVL force, an objective it hopes to achieve early in the 21st century.

In January 2000, both aerospace companies were close to completing construction of their demonstrators and planned to fly them for the first time during the spring.

Three-view renderings of competing Joint Strike Fighter (JSF) designs released by Boeing and Lockheed Martin. Both the X-32A and X-35A are due to make their maiden flights during early 2000, and the winner will be announced during 2001.

Boeing Company
X-32A/B JSF proposal

Lockheed Martin
X-35A/B JSF proposal

A ... Airborne
AA ... Air Ambulance
AAB ... Army Air Base
AAC ... Army Air Corps
AACS ... Airborne Air Control Squadron
AAF ... Army Airfield
AAFA ... Army Aviation Flight Activity
AAFSS ... Advanced Aerial Fire Support System
AAH ... Advanced Attack Helicopter
AAMP ... Army Aviation Modernization Plan
AAOF ... Army Aviation Operating Facility
AASF ... Army Aviation Support Facility
AASLT ... Air Assault
AATC ... ANG/AFRES Test Center
AATD ... Aviation Applied Test Directorate
AAWWS ... Airborne Adverse Weather Weapons System
AB ... Air Base
ABCCC .. Airborne Battlefield Command and Control Center
ABD ... Airborne Division
ABL ... Airborne Laser
ABN ... Airborne
ABNCP ... Airborne Command Post
ABNSOTD ... Airborne Special Operations Test Directorate
ABU ... Avionics Block Update
ABW ... Air Base Wing
AC ... Air Combat Cavalry Squadron
ACC ... Air Combat Command
ACCS ... Airborne Command Control Squadron
ACE ... Aviation Combat Element
ACF ... Air Combat Fighter
ACG ... Airborne Control Group
ACIS ... Advanced Control Indicator Set
ACM ... Air Combat Maneuvering
ACR ... Armored Cavalry Regiment
ACS ... Aerial Common Sensor
ACT ... Air Cavalry Troop
A-CUPID ... A/OA-10A Combat Upgrade Plan Integrated Details
ACW ... Air Control Wing
AD ... Armored Division
ADD ... Aeroflightdynamics Directorate
ADF ... Air Defense Fighter
ADS ... Air Demonstration Squadron
AE ... Aerial Exploitation
AEESB ... Airborne Engineering Evaluation Support Branch
AEF ... Air Expeditionary Force
AEG ... Air Expeditionary Group
AETC ... Air Education and Training Command
AEW ... Air Expeditionary Wing
AF ... Air Facility *or* Air Force
AFAF ... Air Force Auxiliary Field
AFB ... Air Force Base
AFCENT ... Allied Forces Central Europe
AFCS ... Automatic Flight Control System
AFDD ... Aero Flight Dynamics Directorate
AFFSA ... Air Force Flight Standards Agency
AFFTC ... Air Force Flight Test Center
AFLANDSOUTHEAST ... Allied Forces Land Southeast
AFLC ... Air Force Logistics Command
AFMC ... Air Force Materiel Command
AFNORTHWEST ... Allied Forces Northwest Europe
AFRC ... Air Force Reserve Command *or* Armed Forces Reserve Center
AFSC ... Air Force Systems Command
AFSOC ... Air Force Special Operations Command
AFSOUTH ... Allied Forces Southern Europe
AFSPC ... Air Force Space Command
AG ... Airlift Group
AGR ... Active Guard and Reserve
AHB ... Assault Helicopter Battalion
AHP ... Army Heliport
AIP ... Antisurface Warfare Improvement Plan
AIR ... Air Cavalry Squadron
AIRLANT ... Atlantic Naval Air Force
AIRTEVRON ... Air Test and Evaluation Squadron
ALC ... Air Logistic Center
ALCC ... Airborne Launch Control Center
ALF ... Airlift Flight
ALFS ... Airborne Low Frequency Sonar
ALPAT ... Alaska Patrol
AMARC ... Aerospace Maintenance and Regeneration Ctr.
AMC ... Air Mobility Command *or* Aviation Maintenance Company *or* US Army Materiel Command
AMCM ... Airborne Mine Countermeasures
AMCOM ... Aviation and Missile Command
AMP ... Avionics Modernization Program
AMRAAM ... Advanced Medium Air-to-Air Missile
AMSA ... Advanced Manned Strategic Aircraft
AMW ... Air Mobility Wing
ANG ... Air National Guard
ANGB ... Air National Guard Base
ANGOSTA ... Operational Support Transport Aircraft
ANGS ... Air National Guard Station
ANNUALEX ... Annual Exercise
AO ... Area of Operations
AOD ... Air Operations Division
AOE ... Army of Excellence
AOR ... Area of Responsibility
AP ... Airport
APG ... Aberdeen Proving Ground
APU ... Auxiliary Power Unit
ARB ... Air Reserve Base
ARCENT ... US Army Forces Central Command
ARG ... Air Refueling Group *or* Amphibious Ready Group
ARI ... Aviation Restructure Initiative
ARIA ... Advanced Range Instrumentation Aircraft
ARIES ... Airborne Reconnaissance Integrated Intelligence System
ARL ... Airborne Reconnaissance Low
ARL-C ... Airborne Reconnaissance Low - COMINT
ARL-I ... Airborne Reconnaissance Low - Imagery Intelligence
ARL-M ... Airborne Reconnaissance Low - Multimission
ARNG ... US Army National Guard
ARS ... Air Reserve Station *or* Air Refueling Squadron
ARSC ... Aircraft Repair and Supply Center
ARW ... Air Refueling Wing
AS ... Airlift Squadron *or* Air Station
ASA ... Alaska Support Aircraft
ASE ... Aviation Support Element
ASF ... Aviation Support Facility
ASIP ... Avionics System Improvement Program
ASLT ... Assault Helicopter Company
ASLT L ... Assault Helicopter Company Light
ASOTD ... Airborne Special Operations Test Directorate
ASR ... Armed Surface Reconnaissance
AST ... Airborne Surveillance Testbed
ASU SWA ... Administrative Support Unit Southwest Asia
ASW ... Antisubmarine Warfare
AT ... Airmanship Trainer
ATARS ... Advanced Tactical Air Reconnaissance System
ATB ... Advanced Technology Bomber *or* Aviation Training Brigade
ATC ... Army Training Command
ATCA ... Advanced Tanker/Cargo Aircraft
ATCOM ... Aviation and Troop Command
ATD ... Aviation Test Directorate
ATF ... Advanced Tactical Fighter
ATK ... Attack Helicopter Company or Battalion
ATKHB ... Attack Helicopter Battalion
ATK L ... Attack Helicopter Company Light
ATRS ... Aerial Targets Squadron
ATTC ... Aviation Technical Training Center
AU ... Air University
AUTEC ... Atlantic Underwater Test and Evaluation Center
AVCRAD ... Aviation Classification and Repair Activity Depot
AVIM ... Aviation Intermediate Maintenance Battalion
AVN ... Aviation Battalion or Company
AVNBDE ... Aviation Brigade
AVN DET ... Aviation Detachment
AVTD ... Aviation Test Division
AW ... Airlift Wing
AWACS ... Airborne Warning and Control System
AWC ... Air Warfare Center
BDA ... Battle Damage Assessment
BDE ... Brigade
BIOT ... British Indian Ocean Territory
BMUP ... Block Modification Update Program
BN ... Battalion
BRAC ... Base Realignments and Closures Commission
BS ... Bomb Squadron
BW ... Bomb Wing
CAB ... Command Aviation Battalion
CAG ... Commander Air Wing
CALCM ... Conventional Air-Launched Cruise Missile
CAP ... County Airport *or* Combat Air Patrol
CARAEWRON ... Carrier Airborne Early Warning Squadron
CAS ... Close Air Support
CAV ... Cavalry Squadron
CD ... Cavalry Division
CEAP ... Confiscated/Excessed Aircraft Program
CEC ... Cooperative Engagement Capability
CECAT ... Combat Enhancing Capability Aviation Team
CECOM ... Communication - Electronics Command
CENTCOM ... Central Command
CEP ... Common Engine Program
CEWI ... Combat Electronic Warfare Intelligence
CFCTS ... Contract Flight Crew Training System
CFLSW ... Commander, Fleet Logistic Support Wing
CFT ... Conformal Fuel Tanks
CG ... Coast Guard
CGAF ... Coast Guard Air Facility
CGAS ... Coast Guard Air Station
CGATC ... Coast Guard Aviation Training Center
CGATTC ... Coast Guard Aviation Technical Training Center
CGB ... Coast Guard Base
CGSC ... Coast Guard Support Center
C^4I ... Command, Control, Communications, Computers and Intelligence
CIA ... Central Intelligence Agency
CILOP ... Conversion-In-Lieu-Of-Procurement
CINC *or* CinC ... Commander in Chief
CINCAFSE ... Commander in Chief, Allied Forces Southern Europe
CINCLANTFLT ... Commander in Chief, US Atlantic Fleet
CINCPAC ... Commander in Chief, Pacific
CINCPACFLT ... Commander in Chief, US Pacific Fleet
CINCUSNAVEUR ... Commander in Chief, US Naval Forces Europe
CMD ... Command Aviation Company
CMTC ... Combat Maneuver Training Center
CMUP ... Conventional Mission Upgrade Program
CNATRA ... Chief, Naval Air Training Command
CNET ... Chief of Naval Education and Training
C-NITE ... Cobra NITE sight
CNO ... Chief of Naval Operations
CO ... Company
COD ... Carrier Onboard Delivery
COIL ... Chemical Oxygen Iodine Laser
COIN ... Counterinsurgency
COMAEWWINGLANT ... Commander, Airborne Early Warning Wing Atlantic
COMAEWWINGPAC ... Commander, Airborne Early Warning Wing Pacific
COMFAIRMED ... Commander, Fleet Air Mediterranean
COMFITWINGLANT ... Commander, Fighter Wing Atlantic
COMFITWINGPAC ... Commander, Fighter Wing Pacific
COMFLEETAIRKEF ... Commander, Fleet Air Keflavik
COMFLEETLOGSUPWING ... Commander, Fleet Logistic Support Wing
COMHELRESWING ... Commander, Helicopter Reserve Wing
COMHELTACWINGLANT ... Commander, Helicopter Tactical Wing Atlantic
COMHELTACWINGPAC ... Commander Helicopter Tactical Wing Pacific
COMHSLWINGLANT ... Commander, Helicopter Antisubmarine Light Wing Atlantic
COMHSLWINGPAC ... Commander, Helicopter Antisubmarine Light Wing Pacific
COMHSWINGLANT ... Commander, Helicopter Antisubmarine Wing Atlantic
COMHSWINGPAC ... Commander, Helicopter Antisubmarine Wing Pacific
COMINEWARCOM .. Commander, Mine Warfare Command
COMINT ... Communications Intelligence
COMMARFORLANT ... Commander, US Marine Forces Atlantic
COMMARFORPAC .. Commander, US Marine Forces Pacific
COMMARFORRES ... Commander, Marine Forces Reserve
COMNAVAIRLANT ... Commander, Naval Air Force, US Atlantic Fleet
COMNAVAIRPAC ... Commander, Naval Air Force, US Pacific Fleet
COMNAVAIRRESFOR .. Commander, Naval Reserve Forces
COMNAVAIRSYSCOM ... Commander, Naval Air Systems Command
COMNAVFORCENT ... Commander, US Naval Forces Central Command
COMNAVSEA .. Commander, Naval Sea Systems Command
COMOPTEVFOR ... Commander, Operational Test and Evaluation Force
COMPATRECONFORLANT ... Commander, Patrol and Reconnaissance Force Atlantic
COMPATRECONFORPAC ... Commander, Patrol and Reconnaissance Force Pacific
COMPATRECONWING ... Commander, Patrol and Reconnaissance Wing
COMPTUEX ... Composite Training Unit Exercise
COMRESPATWING ... Commander, Reserve Patrol Wing
COMSEACONWINGLANT ... Commander, Sea Control Wing Atlantic
COMSEACONWINGPAC ... Commander, Sea Control Wing Pacific
COMSTRATCOMWING ... Commander, Strategic Communications Wing
COMSTRIKFIGHTWINGLANT ... Commander, Strike Fighter Wing Atlantic
COMVAQWINGPAC ... Commander, Electronic Attack Wing Pacific
CONUS ... Continental United States
COSCOM ... Corps Support Command
COTS ... Commercial Off-The-Shelf
CRAG ... Compass, Radar and GPS
CRL ... Common Rotary Launcher
CRTC ... Cold Regions Test Center
CSA ... Common Support Aircraft
CSAB ... Combat Support Aviation Battalion
CSAR ... Combat Search and Rescue
CSRL ... Common Strategic Rotary Launcher
CSS ... Coastal Systems Station
CSU ... Communications System Upgrade
CSW ... Capital Support Wing
CT ... Counterterrorism
CTG ... Combat Training Group
CTOL ... Conventional Takeoff and Landing
CTS ... Combat Training Squadron
CV ... Fleet Carrier
CVBG ... Carrier Battle Group
CVE ... Escort Carrier
CVG ... Carrier Air Group
CVHA ... Assault Helicopter Carrier
CVL ... Light Carrier
CVS ... Antisubmarine Carrier
CVSGR ... Carrier Antisubmarine Group Reserve
CVW ... Carrier Air Wing
CVWR ... Carrier Air Wing Reserve
CX-HLS ... Cargo Experimental - Heavy Logistic System
DACT ... Dissimilar Air Combat Training
DAISS ... Digital Airborne Intercommunications Switching System
DARPA ... Defense Advanced Research Projects Agency
DAS ... Defensive Avionics System
DASB ... Division Aviation Support Battalion
DCSA ... Defense Security Cooperation Agency
DCU ... Dynamic Component Update
DECM ... Defensive Electronic Countermeasures
DET *or* Det. ... Detachment
DF ... Direction-Finding
DISCOM ... Division Support Command
DIV *or* Div. ... Division
DoD ... Department of Defense
DPG ... Dugway Proving Ground
DRU ... Direct Reporting Unit
DTC ... Developmental Test Command
EAACS ... Expeditionary Airborne Air Control Squadron
EAATS ... Eastern ARNG Aviation Training Site
EAC ... Echelon Above Corps
EACTAB(P) ... Echelon Above Corps Theater Aviation Brigade (Provisional)
EAF ... Expeditionary Aerospace Force
EARS ... Expeditionary Air Refueling Squadron
EAS ... Expeditionary Airlift Squadron
ECAS ... Enhanced Cobra Armament System
ECM ... Electronic Countermeasures
ECMO ... Electronic Countermeasures Officer
ECS ... Electronic Combat Squadron
EEZ ... Exclusive Economic Zone
EFAMS ... Enhanced Fuel And Armament Management System
EFIS ... Electronic Flight Instrumentation System
EFS ... Expeditionary Fighter Squadron
ELINT ... Electronic Intelligence
EMALS ... Electromagnetic Aircraft Launch System
EMD ... Engineering and Manufacturing Development
EO ... Electro-Optical
EOG ... Expeditionary Operations Group
EOS ... Electro-Optical Sensor
EPG ... Electronic Proving Ground
ERAS ... Electromagnetic Aircraft Recovery System
ERQS ... Expeditionary Rescue Squadron
ERS ... Expeditionary Reconnaissance Squadron
ESM ... Electronic Support Measures
ESRA ... Extended Selected Restricted Availability
ESSS ... External Stores Suspension System
ETD ... Executive Transport Detachment
ETO ... European Theater of Operations
ETS ... External Tank Suspension
EUSA ... Eighth US Army
EW ... Electronic Warfare
EWAT ... Electronic Warfare Advanced Technology
EWWS ... Electronic Warfare Warning Set
FAA ... Federal Aviation Administration
FAC ... Forward Air Control
FADEC ... Full Authority Digital Engine Control
FAIRECONRON ... Fleet Air Reconnaissance Squadron
FBM ... Fleet Ballistic Missile
FCR ... Fire Control Radar
FCTC ... Fleet Combat Training Center
FEMA ... Federal Emergency Management Agency
FFAR ... Folding-Fin Aircraft Rockets
FG ... Fighter Group
FITCOMPRON ... Composite Fighter Squadron
FITRON ... Fighter Squadron
FIVEUSA ... Fifth US Army
FIWC ... Fleet Information Warfare Center
FLECOMPRON ... Fleet Composite Squadron
FLELOGSUPRON ... Fleet Logistic Support Squadron
FLIR ... Forward-Looking Infrared
FLT DET ... Flight Detachment
FLTS ... Flight Test Squadron
FMF ... Fleet Marine Force
FMS ... Foreign Military Sales
FORSCOM ... US Army Forces Command
FRS ... Fleet Readiness Squadron
FS ... Fighter Squadron
FSAT ... Full-Scale Aerial Target
FSD ... Flight Support Detachment *or* Full-Scale Development
FTG ... Flying Training Group
FTS ... Flight Training Squadron
FTU ... Formal Training Unit
FTW ... Flying Training Wing
FW ... Fighter Wing
FWATS ... Fixed-Wing Aviation Training Site
FY ... Fiscal Year
GS ... General Support Aviation Company
GSAB ... General Support Aviation Battalion
GP ... Group *or* General Purpose
GPS ... Global Positioning System
GPWS ... Ground-Proximity Warning System
GR/CS ... Guardrail Common Sensor
GRP ... Group
H&HS ... Headquarters and Headquarters Squadrons
HARM ... High-Speed Antiradiation Missile
HATS ... High-Altitude Training Site
HC ... Combat Support Helicopter Squadron
HCS ... Combat Support Special Helicopter Squadron
HELANTISUBRONLIGHT ... Helicopter Antisubmarine Squadron Light
HELATRARON ... Helicopter Training Squadron
HELMINERON ... Mine Countermeasures Squadron
HELSUPRON ... Combat Support Helicopter Squadron
HELSUPRONSPEC ... Combat Support (Special) Helicopter Squadron
HF ... Helicopter Flight
HH ... Heavy Helicopter Company
HHB ... Heavy Helicopter Battalion
HHC ... Headquarters & Headquarters Company
HHT ... Headquarters & Headquarters Troop
HIDSS ... Helmet-Integrated Display And Sight System
HIRSS ... Hover Infrared Suppression System
HM ... Helicopter Mine Countermeasures Squadron
HMH ... Marine Heavy Helicopter Squadron
HMLA ... Marine Light Attack Helicopter Squadron
HMM ... Marine Medium Helicopter Squadron
HMM(T) ... Marine Medium Helicopter (Training) Squadron
HMMWV ... High Mobility Multipurpose Wheeled Vehicle
HMT ... Marine Helicopter Training Squadron
HQ ... Headquarters
HQDA ... Headquarters Department of the Army
HS ... Helicopter Squadron *or* Helicopter Antisubmarine Warfare Squadron
HSB ... Helicopter School Battalion
HSL ... Helicopter Antisubmarine Squadron (Light)
HT ... Helicopter Training Squadron
HQ ... Headquarters
HUD ... Head-Up Display
IAAFA ... Inter American Air Forces Academy
IAP ... International Airport
IBSU ... Icebreaker Support Unit
ICAP ... Improved Capability
ICBM ... Intercontinental Ballistic Missile
ICH ... Improved Cargo Helicopter
ICORPS ... I Corps
ICS ... Internal Countermeasures Set
ID ... Infantry Division
IERW ... Initial Entry Rotary Wing
IEW ... Intelligence and Electronic Warfare Directorate
IFF ... Introduction to Fighter Fundamentals *or* Identification Friend or Foe
IFR ... Instrument Flight Rules
IFT ... In-flight Trainer
IGRV ... Improved Guardrail V
IGW QC ... Increased Gross Weight Quick Change
IIICORPS ... III Corps
ILS ... Instrument Landing System
IMINT ... Imagery Intelligence
INS ... Inertial Navigation System
INSCOM ... US Army Intelligence and Security Command
IOC ... Initial Operational Capability or Industrial Operations Command (US Army)
IOT&E ... Initial Operational Test and Evaluation
IPE ... Improved Performance Engine
IR ... Infrared
IRADS ... Infrared Acquisition and Designation System
I-RAMS ... Integrated Retractable Aircraft Munitions System
IRDS ... Infrared Detection Set
ISAR ... Inverse Synthetic Aperture Radar
ISD ... Integrated Self-Defense
JASSM ... Joint Air-to-Surface Standoff Missile
JCS ... Joint Chiefs of Staff
JDAM ... Joint Direct Attack Munition
JIATF-E ... Joint Interagency Task Force East
JMSDF ... Japan Maritime Self-Defense Force
JOSAC ... Joint Operational Support Airlift Command
JPATS ... Joint Primary Aircraft Training System
JRB ... Joint Reserve Base
JRTC ... Joint Readiness Training Center
JSAF ... Joint SIGINT Avionics Family
JSF ... Joint Strike Fighter
JSOW ... Joint Standoff Weapon
JTFEX ... Joint Task Force Exercise
JTIDS ... Joint Tactical Information Distribution System
JTRA ... Joint Transport Rotary Aircraft
L ... Light

LAMPS ... Light Airborne Multipurpose System
LANTAREA ... Atlantic Area
LANTIRN ... Low Altitude Navigation and Targeting Infrared for Night
LBHL ... Longbow Hellfire Launcher
LERX ... Leading-Edge Root Extension
LG ... Logistics Group
LGB ... Laser-Guided Bomb
LHA ... General Purpose Amphibious Assault Ship
LHD ... Multipurpose Amphibious Assault Ship
LHTEC ... Light Helicopter Turbine Engine Company
LHX ... Light Helicopter Experimental
LI ... Low Intensity (Warfare) Battalion
LIC ... Low Intensity Conflict
LLLTV ... Low-Light-Level Television
LLTV ... Low-Light Television
LOA ... Length Overall
LOH ... Light Observation Helicopter
LPD ... Amphibious Transport Dock
LPH ... Amphibious Assault Ship (Helicopter)
LRAACA ... Long-Range Air Antisubmarine Warfare Capable Aircraft
LRF/D ... Laser Range Finder/Designator
LRIP ... Low-Rate Initial Production
LSD ... Dock Landing Ship
LSE ... US Army Element Land Southeast
LSI ... Lear Siegler Services
LTD ... Laser Target Designator/Ranger
LTGR ... Laser-Guided Training Round
LUH ... Light Utility Helicopter
LUHB ... Light Utility Helicopter Battalion
LWF ... Lightweight Fighter
M ... Mechanized
MACE ... Mobilization AVCRAD Control Element
MACOM ... Major Command
MAD ... Magnetic Anomaly Detector
MAE ... Medium-Altitude Endurance
MAG ... Marine Air Group *or* Military Airlift Group
MAGTF ... Marine Air-Ground Task Force
MAP ... Municipal Airport *or* Metropolitan Airport
MARFOR ... Marine Force
MARFORLANT ... Marine Forces Atlantic
MARFORPAC ... Marine Forces Pacific
MARFORRES ... Marine Forces Reserve
MASD ... Marine Aviation Support Detachment
MASINT ... Measurements and Signatures Intelligence
MATS ... Materiel Squadron
MATT ... Multimission Advanced Tactical Terminal
MAW ... Marine Air Wing
MAWTS ... Marine Aviation Weapons and Tactics Squadron
MCAAS ... Marine Corps Auxiliary Air Station
MCAF ... Marine Corps Air Facility
MCAGCC ... Marine Corps Air Ground Combat Center
MCALF ... Marine Corps Auxiliary Landing Field
MCAP ... Multimission Capability
MCAS ... Marine Corps Air Station
MCB ... Marine Corps Base
MCM ... Airborne Mine Countermeasures
MCU ... Mission Computer Upgrade
MDW ... Military District of Washington
MDZA ... Maritime Defense Zone Atlantic
MDZP ... Maritime Defense Zone Pacific
MEB ... Medical Evacuation Battalion
Mech ... Mechanized
MEDBDE ... Medical Brigade
MED CO ... Medical Helicopter Company
MEDCOM ... US Army Medical Command
MED DET ... Medical Helicopter Detachment
MEDEVAC ... Medical Evacuation
MEDGRP ... Medical Group
MEF ... Marine Expeditionary Force
MEP ... Mission Equipment Package
MER ... Multiple Ejector Rack
MEU ... Marine Expeditionary Unit
MI ... Military Intelligence
MIBDE ... Military Intelligence Brigade
MICOM ... Missile Command
MIDS ... Multifunction Information Distribution System
MILES ... Multiple Integrated Laser Engagement System
MILSTAR ... Military Strategic and Tactical Relay Satellite System
MMRT ... Modified Miniature Receiver Terminal
MMS ... Mast-Mounted Site
MMW ... Millimeter Wave
MOOTW ... Military Operations Other Than War
MOTT ... Multiservice Operational Test Team
MPRS ... Multipoint Refueling System
MR ... Medium Range
MRR ... Medium-Range Recovery
MRS ... Medium-Range Surveillance
MS ... Missile Squadron
MSIP ... Multistage Improvement Plan
MTI ... Moving Target Indicator
MTPC ... Maintenance Test Pilot Course
MUG ... Midlife Upgrade
MWHS ... Marine Wing Headquarters Squadron
NAAS ... Naval Auxiliary Air Station
NAB ... Naval Amphibious Base
NADEP ... Naval Aviation Depot
NAES ... Naval Air Engineering Station
NAF ... Naval Air Facility
NALF ... Naval Auxiliary Landing Field
NALO ... Naval Aviation Logistics Office
NAOC ... National Airborne Operations Court
NAP ... Naval Aviation Pilot
NAR ... Naval Air Reserve
NAS ... Naval Air Station
NASA ... National Aeronautics and Space Administration
NATO ... North Atlantic Treaty Organization
NAVAIR ... Naval Air Systems Command
NAVAIRLANT ... Naval Air Force, US Atlantic Fleet
NAVAIRPAC ... Naval Air Force, US Pacific Fleet
NAVAIRSYSCOM ... Naval Air Systems Command
NAVSEA ... Naval Sea Systems Command
NAVSTA ... Naval Station
NAWC ... Naval Air Warfare Center
NAWCAD ... Naval Air Warfare Center Aircraft Division
NAWCWD ... Naval Air Warfare Center Weapons Division
NAWS ... Naval Air Weapons Station
NCA ... National Command Authority
NCR ... National Capital Region
NCSC ... Naval Coastal Systems Center
NEADS ... Northeast Air Defense Sector
NFATS ... Naval Force Aircraft Test Squadron
NFDS ... Naval Flight Demonstration Squadron
NFO ... Naval Flight Officer
NGT ... Next-Generation Trainer
NOLF ... Naval Outlying Landing Field
NOLO ... No Live Operator
NORAD ... North American Air Defense Command
NOTAR ... No Tail Rotor
NOTS ... Naval Ordnance Test Station
NRL FSD ... Naval Research Laboratory Flight Support Detachment
NRRF ... Naval Radio Relay Facility
NRWATS ... Naval Rotary-Wing Aircraft Test Squadron
NSA ... Naval Support Activity
NSATS ... Naval Strike Aircraft Test Squadron
NSAWC ... Naval Strike and Air Warfare Center
NSF ... Naval Support Facility
NSTTS ... Navy Standard Tow Target System
NSWC ... Naval Strike Weapons Center
NSWC-DD ... Naval Surface Warfare Center-Dahlgren Division
NTC ... National Training Center
NTH ... New Training Helicopter
NTPS ... Naval Test Pilot School
NTS ... Night Targeting System
NTSU ... Naval Training Support Unit
NUFEA ... Navy Unique Fleet Essential Airlift
NUWC ... Naval Undersea Warfare Center
NVDAAB ... Night Vision Directorate Airborne Applications Branch
NVG ... Night Vision Goggles
NVPS ... Night Vision Pilotage System
NWC ... Naval Weapons Center
NWTS ... Naval Weapons Test Squadron
OCONUS ... Outside the Continental United States
OG ... Operations Group
OL ... Operating Location
OLF ... Outlying field
OMD ... Operations Maintenance Division
ONEUSA ... First US Army
OOTW ... Operations Other Than War
OPBAT ... Operation Bahamas, Turks and Caicos
OPEVAL ... Operational Evaluation
OPFOR ... Opposing Force
OPS GP ... Operations Group
OPTEC ... Operational Test and Evaluation Command
OSA ... Operational Support Airlift
OSAA ... Operational Support Airlift Agency
OSACOM ... Operational Support Airlift Command
OT&E ... Operational Test and Evaluation
OTSA ... OPTEC Threat Support Activity
P ... Provisional
PACAF ... Pacific Air Forces
PACAREA ... Pacific Area
PAI ... Primary Aircraft Inventory
PATD ... Priority Air Transport Detachment
PATRON ... Patrol Squadron
PATWING ... Patrol and Reconnaissance Wing
PDM ... Programmed Depot Maintenance
PIA ... Planned Incremental Availability
PLTN ... Platoon
PMRF ... Pacific Missile Range Facility
PMTC ... Pacific Missile Test Center
PNVS ... Pilots Night-Vision System
POW ... Prisoner of War
PPO ... Presidential Pilot's Office
PRTV ... Production Representative Test Vehicle
R ... Remanufacture
RAF ... Royal Air Force
RAID ... Reconnaissance and Interdiction Detachment
RAP ... Regional Airport
RAS ... Regimental Aviation Squadron
RCOH ... Refueling and Complex Overhaul
R&D ... Research and Development
RDTE ... Research, Development, Test and Evaluation
RECDET ... Reconnaissance Detachment
(RECON) ... Reconnaissance Cavalry Squadron
REGT or Regt. ... Regiment
RF ... Radio Frequency
RFC ... Regional Flight Center
RFI ... Radio Frequency Interferometer
RFP ... Request For Proposals
ROTC ... Reserve Officer Training Corps
RPV ... Remotely Piloted Vehicle
RQF ... Rescue Flight
RQG ... Rescue Group
RQS ... Rescue Squadron
RQW ... Rescue Wing
RS ... Reconnaissance Squadron
RSTA ... Reconnaissance, Surveillance and Target Acquisition
RT ... Refuelable Tanker
RTTC ... Redstone Technical Test Center
RVSR ... Reduced Vertical Separation Requirements
RW ... Reconnaissance Wing
RWR ... Radar Warning Receiver
SAC ... Strategic Air Command
SAR ... Search and Rescue *or* Synthetic Aperture Radar
SAS ... Stability Augmentation System
SATCOM ... Satellite Communications
SBCCOM ... Soldier and Biological Chemical Command
SCAT ... Scout Attack
SCT ... Scout
SEACONRON ... Sea Control Squadron
SEAD ... Suppression of Enemy Air Defenses
SEADS ... Southeast Air Defense Sector
SEAL ... Sea, Air and Land (Special Operations teams)
SECNAV ... Secretary of the Navy
SETAF ... Southern Europe Task Force
SFD ... State Flight Detachment
SFOR ... Stabilization Force
SFWSL ... Strike Fighter Weapons School Atlantic
SHAPE ... Supreme Headquarters Allied Powers Europe
SIGINT ... Signals Intelligence
SINCGARS ... Single Channel Ground and Airborne Radio System
SIRFC ... Suite of Integrated RF Countermeasures
SLAM ... Standard Land Attack Missile
SLAR ... Side-Looking Airborne Radar
SLEP ... Service Life Extension Plan
SMDAC ... Space and Missile Defense Acquistion Center
SMDC ... Space and Missile Defense Command
SMDTC ... Space and Missile Defense Technical Center
SOA ... Special Operations Aviation
SOAR ... Special Operations Aviation Regiment
SOC ... Special Operations Capable
SOF ... Special Operations Forces
SOG ... Special Operations Group
SOLL ... Special Operations Low Level
SOMS ... Station Operations Maintenance Squadron
SOS ... Special Operations Squadron
SOUTHCOM ... Southern Command
SOW ... Special Operations Wing
SPECPROJPATRON ... Special Projects Patrol Squadron
SPW ... Space Wing
Sqn ... Squadron
SRF ... Ship Repair Facility
SRR ... Short-Range Recovery
SSC ... Surface Search and Clarification
S/SEP ... Safety/System Enhancement Program
SSIP ... Sensor System Improvement Program
STARC ... State Area Command
STARS ... Surveillance Target Attack Radar System
STOL ... Short Takeoff and Landing
STOVL ... Short Takeoff and Vertical Landing
STRIKFITRON ... Strike Fighter Squadron
SUBCOM ... Subcommand
SUW ... Surface Warfare
TA ... Theater Aviation Company
TAB ... Theater Aviation Battalion
TAC ... Tactical Air Command *or* Tactical Air Control
TACAMO ... TAke Charge And Move Out
TADS ... Target Acquisition Designation Sight
TAG ... Adjutant General
(TAR) ... Target Acquisition Reconnaissance
TARPS ... Tactical Air Reconnaissance Pod System
TAS ... Target Acquisition System
TAW ... Training Air Wing
TCAS ... Traffic Collision Avoidance System
TDY ... Temporary Duty
TEG ... Test Evaluation Group
TES ... Test and Evaluation Squadron
TESTG ... Test Group
TESTS ... Test Squadron
TEXCOM ... Test and Experimentation Command
TF ... Task Force
THREEUSA ... Third US Army
TIS ... Thermal Imaging Sensor
TJS ... Tactical Jamming System
TOW ... Tube-Launched Optically-Tracked Wire-Guided Missile
TPS ... Test Pilot School
TRADOC ... US Army Training and Doctrine Command
TRARON ... Fixed-Wing Training Squadron
TRG ... Training Group
TRP ... Troop
TRS ... Training Squadron
TRW ... Training Wing
TSTC ... Texas State Technical College
TTTS ... Tanker/Transport Training System
TUAV ... Tactical Unmanned Aerial Vehicle
TVS ... Television Sensor
TW ... Test Wing
UAV ... Unmanned Aerial Vehicle
UDP ... Unit Deployment Program
UFT ... Undergraduate Flying Training
UHF ... Ultra High Frequency
UNTP ... Undergraduate Navigator Training Program
USA ... United States of America *or* United States Army
USAAAD ... US Army Air Ambulance Detachment
USAAF ... US Army Air Forces
USAALS ... US Army Aviation Logistics School
USAAMC ... US Army Aeromedical Center
USAAMC-AAD ... US Army Aeromedical Command-Air Ambulance Division
USAAMCOM ... US Army Aviation and Missile Command
USAARL ... US Army Aeromedical Research Laboratory
USAATCA ... US Army Air Traffic Control Activity
USAAVNC ... US Army Aviation Center
USACECOM ... US Army Communications-Electronics Command
USACOM ... US Atlantic Command
USAENGCS ... US Army Engineer Center and School
USAEUR ... US Army Europe
USAF ... US Air Force
USAFA ... US Air Force Academy
USAFADS ... USAF Air Demonstration Squadron
USAFE ... US Air Forces in Europe
USAFWS ... USAF Weapons School
USAG ... US Army Garrison
USAICS ... US Army Intelligence Center and School
USAINFCS ... US Army Infantry Center and School
USAIOC ... US Army Industrial Operations Command
USAJ ... US Army Japan
USAKA/KMR ... US Army Kwajalein Atoll/Kwajalein Missile Range
USAMEDCOM ... US Army Medical Command
USAPT ... US Army Parachute Team
USARAK ... US Army Alaska
USARC ... US Army Reserve Command
USARCENT ... US Army Forces Central Command
USAREC ... US Army Recruiting Command
USARPAC ... US Army Pacific
USARSO ... US Army South
USASB ... US Army Sinai Battalion
USASBCCOM ... US Army Soldier and Biological Chemical Command
USASMDC ... US Army Space and Missile Defense Command
USASOC ... US Army Special Operations Command
USATACOM ... US Army Tank- Automotive and Armaments Command
USCENTAF ... US Central Command Air Force
USCENTCOM ... US Central Command
USCG ... US Coast Guard
USCGSS ... US Coast Guard Support Center
USEUCOM ... US European Command
USFJ ... US Forces Japan
USJFCOM ... US Joint Forces Command
USMA ... US Military Academy
USMC ... US Marine Corps
USN ... US Navy
USNR ... US Naval Reserve
USNTPS ... US Naval Test Pilot School
USPACOM ... US Pacific Command
USSCOM ... US Strategic Command
USSOCOM ... US Special Operations Command
USSOUTHCOM ... US Southern Command
USSPACECOM ... US Space Command
USSTRATCOM ... US Strategic Command
USTRANSCOM ... US Transportation Command
USW ... Undersea Warfare
UTTAS ... Utility Tactical Transport Aircraft System
UTX ... Utility Trainer Experimental
UV ... Ultraviolet
VAQ ... Electronic Combat Squadron
VAQRON ... Electronic Attack Squadron
VAW ... Airborne Early Warning Squadron
VC ... Fleet Composite Squadron
VCORPS ... V Corps
VERTREP ... Vertical Replenishment
VF ... Fighter Squadron
VFA ... Strike Fighter Squadron
VFAX ... Fighter/Attack Aircraft
VFC ... Fighter Composite Squadron
VFR ... Visual Flight Training
VHF ... Very High Frequency
VLF ... Very Low Frequency
VMA ... Marine Attack Squadron
VMAQ ... Marine Tactical Electronic Warfare Squadron
VMCJ ... Marine Composite Reconnaissance Squadron
VMFA ... Marine Fighter Attack Squadron
VMFA(AW) ... Marine All-Weather Fighter Attack Squadron
VMFAT ... Marine Strike Fighter Training Squadron
VMFT ... Marine Fighter Training Squadron
VMGR ... Marine Aerial Refueler Transport Squadron
VMGRT ... Marine Aerial Refueler Transport Training Squadron
VMR ... Marine Transport Squadron
VMU ... Marine Unmanned Aerial Vehicle Squadron
VP ... Patrol Squadron
VPU ... Special Projects Patrol Squadron
VQ ... Fleet Air Reconnaissance Squadron
VR ... Fleet Logistic Support Squadron
VRC ... Fleet Logistic Support Squadron (Composite)
VS ... Sea Control Squadron
VSTOL ... Vertical and Short Takeoff and Landing
VT ... Training Squadron
VX ... Air Test and Evaluation Squadron
WAATS ... Western ARNG Aviation Training Site
WADS ... Western Air Defense Sector
WCMD ... Wind-Corrected Munitions Dispenser
WEG ... Weapons Evaluation Group
WESTPAC ... Western Pacific
WHCA ... White House Communications Agency
WR-ALC ... Warner Robins Air Logistic Center
WRS ... Weather Reconnaissance Squadron
WSMR ... White Sands Missile Range
XVIIIABNCORPS ... XVIII Airborne Corps
YPG ... Yuma Proving Ground
(-) ... Reinforced *(USMC)*
(-) ... Headquarters With a Detached Platoon *(US Army)*

Appendix II: USAF Aerospace Expeditionary Force Deployments

LEAD WINGS

AEF 1	388th Fighter Wing, Hill AFB, Utah	1 October 1999 - 30 November 1999
AEF 2	7th Bomb Wing, Dyess AFB, Texas	1 October 1999 - 30 November 1999
AEF 3	3rd Wing, Elmendorf AFB, Alaska	1 December 1999 - 28 February 2000
AEF 4	48th Fighter Wing, RAF Lakenheath, UK	1 December 1999 - 28 February 2000
AEF 5	355th Fighter Wing, Davis Monthan AFB, Arizona	1 March 2000 - 31 May 2000
AEF 6	20th Fighter Wing, Shaw AFB, South Carolina	1 March 2000 - 31 May 2000
AEF 7	2nd Bomb Wing, Barksdale AFB, Louisiana	1 June 2000 - 31 August 2000
AEF 8	28th Bomb Wing, Ellsworth AFB, South Dakota	1 June 2000 - 31 August 2000
AEF 9	27th Fighter Wing, Cannon AFB, New Mexico	1 September 2000 - 30 November 2000
AEF 10	1st Fighter Wing, Langley AFB, Virginia	1 September 2000 - 30 November 2000

MOBILITY LEAD WINGS

AEF 1/2	43rd Airlift Wing, Pope AFB, North Carolina	1 October 1999 - 30 November 1999
AEF 3/4	60th Air Mobility Wing, Travis AFB, California	1 December 1999 - 28 February 2000
AEF 5/6	22nd Air Refueling Wing, McConnell AFB, Kansas	1 March 2000 - 31 May 2000
AEF 7/8	319th Air Refueling Wing, Grand Forks AFB, North Dakota	1 June 2000 - 31 August 2000
AEF 9/10	92nd Air Refueling Wing, Fairchild AFB, Washington	1 September 2000 - 30 November 2000

Manufacturer	Type	Operator(s)
Bell Helicopter Textron (Bell)	AH-1F Cobra	USA
	AH-1W/Z* Sea Cobra	USMC
	UH-1H/V Iroquois	USA
	HH-1N, UH-1N Iroquois	USAF/USN USA/USMC
	UH-1Y Iroquois*	USMC
	TH-57B/C Sea Ranger	USN
	OH-58A/C Kiowa	USA/USN
	OH-58D Kiowa Warrior	USA
	TH-67A Creek	USA
Bell Helicopter Textron/Boeing	MV-22B Osprey	USMC
Boeing Company	B767-200	USA
	B-52H Stratofortress	USAF
	EC-18B, TC-18E/F	USAF/USN
	C-22B/C	USAF
	C-25A	USAF
	C-32A	USAF
	C-40A*	USN
	C-135B/C/E Stratolifter	USAF
	OC-135B Open Skies	USAF
	TC-135S/W Stratolifter	USAF
	KC-135D/E/R/T Stratotanker	USAF
	EC-135E/K/N Stratolifter	USAF
	NC-135B/E Stratolifter	USAF
	RC-135S/U/V/W Stratolifter	USAF
	WC-135W Stratolifter	USAF
	VC-137C, EC-137D Stratoliner	USAF
	E-3B/C Sentry	USAF
	E-4B/C* NAOC	USAF
	E-6A/B Mercury	USN
	CH/HH/UH-46D Sea Knight	USN
	CH-46E Sea Knight	USMC
	CH-47D/F* Chinook	USA
	MH-47E Chinook	USA
	T-43A, CT-43A	USAF
	C-17A Globemaster III	USAF
Boeing Company (Hughes Helicopters)	TH-6B Cayuse	USN
Boeing Company (McDonnell Douglas Helicopter)	AH-6J, MH-6J Little Bird	USA
	AH-64A/D Apache/Apache Longbow	USA
Boeing Company (McDonnell Douglas)	TA-4J Skyhawk	USN
	C-9A, C-9B, VC-9C, DC-9 Nightingale/Skytrain II	USAF/USN/USMC
	KC-10A Extender	USAF
	QRF-4C, QF-4E/G/J/N Phantom II	USAF/USN
	F-4F Phantom II	USAF
	F-15A/B/C/D Eagle	USAF
	F-15E Strike Eagle	USAF
	F/A-18A/B/C/D Hornet	USN/USMC
	F/A-18E/F Super Hornet	USN
	T-45A/C Goshawk	USN
	AV-8B, TAV-8B, AV-8B+ Harrier II	USMC
Boeing Company (North American)	NT-39A/B Sabreliner	USAF
Boeing Company (Rockwell International)	B-1B Lancer	USAF
	T-2C Buckeye	USN
	T-38C Talon*	USAF
Boeing Company/Northrop Grumman		
Boeing Company/Sikorsky Aircraft	RAH-66A Comanche*	USA
Bombardier Aerospace (de Havilland Canada)	E-9A	USAF
	NU-1B Otter	USN
	U-6A Beaver	USN
	UV-18A/B Twin Otter	USA/USAF
Bombardier Aerospace (de Havilland Canada/ Northrop Grumman)	EO-5B, RC-7B, DHC-7	USA
Bombardier Aerospace (Learjet Inc.)	C-21A Learjet	USAF
Bombardier Aerospace (Shorts Brothers)	C-23A/B/B+ Sherpa	USA
CASA	CASA 212-200	USAF
Cessna Aircraft	O-2A Skymaster	USA
Cessna Aircraft	T-37B Tweet	USAF
Cessna Aircraft	Cessna 150M	USAF
Cessna Aircraft	T-41D, Cessna 182Q	USA
Cessna Aircraft	UC-35A/B/C/D Citation	USA/USMC
Dassault Aviation (Falcon Jet)	HU-25A/B/C	USCG
Eurocopter (Aerospatiale)	HH-65A Dolphin	USCG
Fairchild Aerospace	C-26A/B, UC-26C, C-26D, SA227 Metroliner	USAF/USA/USN
Fokker Aircraft	C-31A Troopship	USA
General Atomics Aeronautical Systems	RQ-1A Predator	USAF
General Dynamics (Grumman Aerospace)	VC-4A Gulfstream I	USCG
General Dynamics (Grumman Aerospace, Gulfstream Aerospace)	G-1159 Gulfstream II	USA

Company	Type	Operator(s)
General Dynamics (Gulfstream Aerospace)	C-20A/B/C/D/E Gulfstream III	USAF/USCG/ USN/USMC/USA
	C-20F/G/H Gulfstream IV	USAF/USN/ USMC/USA
	C-37A Gulfstream V	USAF/USA
IAI/Galaxy Aircraft	C-38A Astra	USAF
Kaman Aerospace	SH-2G Seasprite	USN
Lockheed Martin	C-5A/B/C Galaxy	USAF
	C-130E/H/J/T, LC-130H Hercules	USAF/USN
	EC-130E/H/J Hercules	USAF
	MC-130E/H Combat Talon I/II	USAF
	MC-130P Combat Shadow	USAF
	KC-130F/J/R/T Hercules	USMC
	TC-130G Hercules	USN
	AC-130H/U Spectre	USAF
	HC-130H/N/P Hercules	USAF/USCG
	NC-130H Hercules	USN
	WC-130H/J Hercules	USAF
	C-141B/C Starlifter	USAF
	F-22A Raptor	USAF
	UP/VP-3A Orion	USN
	(E)P-3B, P-3C, NP-3B/C/D Orion	USN
	EP-3E Orion	USN
	S-3B Viking	USN
	U-2S, TU-2S	USAF
	F-117A Nighthawk	USAF
Lockheed Martin (Fairchild Republic)	OA/A-10A Thunderbolt II	USAF
Lockheed Martin (General Dynamics)	F-16A/B/C/D Fighting Falcon	USAF
	F-16A/B(ADF) Fighting Falcon	USAF
MD Helicopters	MH-90 Enforcer	USCG
Northrop Grumman	TE-8A, E-8C Joint Stars	USAF
Northrop Grumman (Grumman)	EA-6B Prowler	USN/USMC
	C-2A Greyhound	USN
	E-2C Hawkeye	USN
	F-14A/B/D Tomcat	USN
Northrop Grumman (Northrop)	F-5E/F Tiger II	USN/USMC
	T-38, AT-38B, T-38C* Talon	USAF/USN
	B-2A Spirit	USAF
Northrop Grumman (Teledyne Ryan Aeronautical)	RQ-4A Global Hawk	USAF
Pilatus Aircraft	UV-20A Chiricahua	USA
Pilatus Aircraft (Britten Norman)	BN-2T Islander	USA
Pioneer UAV (AAI/IAI)	RQ-2A Pioneer	USN/USMC
Piper Aircraft	PA-31T Cheyenne	USA
Raytheon Aircraft (Beech Aircraft)	B1900D	USN/USA
	UC-12B/F/M	USN/USMC
	TC-12B	USN
	C-12C/D/F/J/R/T Huron	USA/USAF
	RC-12D/H/K/N/P/Q Guardrail	USA
	RC-12F/M	USN
	T-1A Jayhawk	USAF/USN
	T-6A Texan II	USAF/USN
	T-34C Turbo Mentor	USN/USMC/USA
	T-44A Pegasus	USN
	JU-21H Ute	USA
Rockwell Intl. (North American)	CT-39G, T-39G, T-39N Sabreliner	USMC/USN
Schleicher	TG-9A	USAF
Schweizer Aircraft	TG-3A	USAF
	TG-4A	USAF
	TG-7A	USAF
	X-26A	USN
Sikorsky Aircraft	EH-60A/L, HH-60L, MH-60A/L/K, UH-60A/L/Q Blackhawk	USA
	SH-60B/F/R Seahawk	USN
	HH/MH-60G Pavehawk	USAF
	HH-60H/J Seahawk	USN/USCG
	VH-60N Blackhawk	USMC
	CH-60S Knighthawk	USN
	VH-3A, NVH-3A, VH-3D Sea King	USN/USMC
	UH-3H Sea King	USN
	NCH/TH-53A Sea Stallion	USAF
	CH-53D/E Sea Stallion/Super Stallion	USMC
	MH-53E Sea Dragon	USMC/USN
	MH-53J/M Pave Low III/IV	USAF
Slingsby Aviation	T-3A Firefly	USAF
Stemme	TG-11A	USAF
TRW/IAI-Malat Division	RQ-5A Hunter	USA

NON-DESIGNATED FORMER SOVIET BLOC AIRCRAFT

Company	Type	Operator(s)
Antonov	An-2 'Colt'	USA
Kamov	Ka-32 'Helix'	USA
Mil	Mi-2 'Hoplite'	USA
	Mi-8 'Hip'	USA
	Mi-14 'Haze'	USA
	Mi-17 'Hip'	USA
	Mi-24 'Hind'	USA
	Mi-2 'Hoplite'	USA

DESIGNATION ELEMENTS

Since October 1962, the four military services and the US Coast Guard have assigned standardized military designations to their aircraft, missiles and spacecraft in accordance with Department of Defense Directive 4120.15. Such designations are officially referred to as a Mission Design Series (MDS) and, under this system, a series of letters and numbers identify specific characteristics of the aerospace vehicle or weapon system.

Each designation comprises some of the following: Status prefix, modified mission indicator, basic mission indicator, vehicle type, launch environment, design number and series indicator. Some of the foregoing are required, whereas others are optional depending on the nature of the system or vehicle. Although not a part of MDS, additional indicators are assigned to further identify the system or vehicle, including a configuration or component number, block number and serial number.

REQUIRED DESIGNATORS

BASIC MISSION (Required for standard vehicles)
This letter indicates the primary function and capability of a standard aerospace vehicle such as a bomber or fighter, and appears immediately to the left of the design number, separated by a dash. In the case of the B-1B, for instance, the first letter denotes a bomber. However, in the case of nonstandard vehicles like an air-launched weapon, the basic mission identifier appears to the immediate left of that for the vehicle type. In the case of the AGM-88A high-speed antiradiation missile, for instance, M indicates a guided missile whereas G indicates its mission is surface attack.

Aircraft

Identifier	Mission(s)
A	Attack
B	Bomber
C	Transport
D	Drone Director
E	Special Electronics Installation
F	Fighter
O	Observation
P	Maritime Patrol
R	Reconnaissance
S	Antisubmarine
T	Trainer
U	Utility
X	Research (nonoperational test bed)

Missiles, etc.

C	Transport
D	Decoy
E	Electronics/Communications
G	Surface Attack
I	Aerial/Space Intercept
L	Launch Detection/Surveillance
M	Scientific Calibration
N	Navigation
Q	Drone
S	Space Support
T	Training
U	Underwater Attack
W	Weather/Meteorological

VEHICLE TYPE
(Nonstandard vehicles, missiles and spacecraft)
Nonstandard vehicles include helicopters and vertical/short takeoff and landing (VSTOL) aircraft and, like missiles and space vehicles, must carry a basic mission or modified mission identifier along with a vehicle type identifier. It appears immediately to the left of the design number, separated by a dash. In the case of the Apache Longbow, the designator is AH-64D. The H signifies it is a helicopter, while the A indicates its basic mission is attack.

Aircraft

Identifier	Type
G	Glider
H	Helicopter/Rotary Wing
S	Spaceplane
V	VSTOL/STOL/STOVL
Z	Lighter-than-air (Balloons etc.)

Missiles, etc.

B	Booster
M	Guided-Missile or Drone
N	Probe
R	Rocket
S	Satellite

LAUNCH ENVIRONMENT (Rockets and missiles only)
To indicate the launch environment or platform, a letter is placed immediately to the left of the mission identifier. Referring to the AGM-88A again as the example, the fact that it is air-launched is indicated by the letter A.

Identifier	Launch Method
A	Air
B	Multiple (more than one option)
C	Coffin (from ground)
F	Hand (by personnel)
G	Runway
H	Above Ground (silo-stored)
L	Below Ground (silo-stored)
M	Mobile Vehicle
P	Soft Pad
R	Surface Vessel
S	Space
U	Underwater

DESIGN NUMBER
Used to identify major design changes within the same basic mission vehicle or system, consecutive numbers are placed to the immediate right of the basic mission or vehicle-type identifier, separated by a dash. In the case of the F-22A Raptor, the design number is 22, signifying this was the twenty-second MDS requested under the current designation system for an aircraft with a fighter mission.

SERIES
Identifying production models for a particular design number, and representing major modifications that affect logistical support for a vehicle or system, a letter or number is placed immediately to the right of the design number. These run sequentially but, to avoid confusion, 0, 1, O and I are not used. In the case of the F/A-18E, the letter E denotes the vehicle is the fifth production model of the Hornet.

OPTIONAL DESIGNATORS

STATUS PREFIX
This identifier is used to show the vehicle or system is used for nonstandard duties like testing, or when it happens to be a prototype or experimental aircraft. The identifier appears immediately to the left of the modified or basic mission symbol in the case of an aircraft, and immediately to the left of the launch environment or mission identifier for a rocket or missile. The letter Y in the YF-22 designation, for instance, indicates a prototype.

Aircraft

Identifier	Status
G	Permanently Grounded
J	Special Test (Temporary)
N	Special Test (Permanent)
X	Experimental or Under Development
Y	Prototype
Z	Planning or Pre-development

Missiles, etc.

C	Captive
D	Dummy
J	Special Test (Temporary)
N	Special Test (Permanent)
X	Experimental
Y	Prototype
Z	Planning or Pre-development

MODIFIED MISSION (Aircraft only)
Appearing immediately to the left of a basic mission identifier, a letter can be used to denote a change in an aircraft's basic mission. In the case of the QF-4G Phantom II, for instance, the letter Q indicates that an F-4G has been modified for remote or unmanned flight.

Identifier	Modified Mission
A	Attack
C	Transport
D	Drone Director
E	Special Electronics Installation
F	Fighter
H	Search and Rescue
K	Tanker
L	Cold Weather (Arctic Ops., etc.)
M	Multimission
O	Observation
P	Maritime Patrol
Q	Drone/Unmanned
R	Reconnaissance
S	Antisubmarine
T	Trainer
U	Utility
V	Staff
W	Weather/Meteorlogical

NON-MDS IDENTIFIERS

CONFIGURATION OR COMPONENT NUMBER
(Rockets and missiles only)
A configuration change to a weapon system that affects performance, tactics or integral components but does not change its operations or logistics reporting, is indicated by a character placed immediately to the right of the series identifier, separated by a dash.

BLOCK NUMBER
A production group of identically configured aircraft within a particular design series is denoted by a two-digit number that follows the word BLOCK. This is frequently encountered in the case of aircraft with long production runs like the F-16. Intermediate block numbers are sometimes used for field modifications and, as with configuration or component numbers, each military branch has its own system for designating them.

SERIAL NUMBER
Each military branch decides how it assigns its serial numbers, which are unique identifiers assigned to aircraft. Over the years, the USAF and US Army have changed their serial designation systems several times, although both continue to use the last two digits of the fiscal year in which the aircraft was ordered as the first two digits of the serial. This is followed by a dash and a series of sequential numbers starting at 0001 each year. For instance, the first aircraft ordered in Fiscal Year 2000 will carry the serial 00-0001.

In 1989, the serials for both services were integrated, although those for UH-60 Blackhawk helicopters are exceptions. The type's serials are formulated on the Army's previous designation system, which is based on sequential numbers starting at 20000. Air Force HH-60s are integrated into the Army's procurement procedure and thus carry numbers in that service's sequence. Even so, there are many exceptions to the general rule and, on some occasions, the receiving unit's designation or part of the manufacturer's construction number has been incorporated into the serial.

Aircraft temporarily transferred to the Air Force from the Navy usually retain their naval serials but, sometimes, are given USAF serials that include four or more digits after the block number for the year in which they were originally ordered by the Navy. In other instances, the final four digits of the bureau number are added to the fiscal year in which the USAF acquired the aircraft.

The US Navy and the US Marine Corps share an entirely different serialing scheme that is based on progressive numbers allocated by the Naval Air Systems Command. These numbers were originally allocated by the Bureau of Aeronautics and continue to be referred to as Bureau Numbers (BuNos). Today's six-digit system began as a five-digit system with BuNo at 00001 in 1940. The sequence was advanced to a sixth digit in 1945 when Bureau Number 100000 was assigned. As US Marine Corps aircraft are procured by the Navy, they are included within the Navy's series.

Occasionally, aircraft are transferred from the Air Force or Army to the Navy, in which instances new serials are not normally assigned. However, the Navy drops the dash between the fiscal year and sequence number to effectively create a new six-digit number. Aircraft on loan from other services usually retain their original serials.

In the case of the US Coast Guard, aircraft are sometimes procured directly, as was the case with the HH-65A Dolphin, or they are acquired through the Department of Defense. In any event, the service has its own series of numbers that supercede those assigned by the procuring service. The first Coast Guard type to receive numbers under the current system was the HH-60J Jayhawk. That type's serials are based on the series design number followed by sequential numbers that start at 01. The first Jayhawk delivered thus was serialed 6001. Dolphins delivered before the current numbering system went into effect were subsequently re-serialed to conform.

INDEX TO ORGANIZATIONS AND UNITS

PICTURE ACKNOWLEDGEMENTS

Dust Jacket
    Randy Jolly (3), Ted Carlson, Joe Cupido,
    Rick Llinares (2), Dave Mason
Page 6   Rick Llinares
Page 10   USAF, Randy Jolly
Page 11   Rick Llinares, Riccardo Niccoli
Page 13   Robert F. Dorr
Page 14   Ted Carlson (2)
Page 15   Ted Carlson (2), Rick Llinares
Page 16   Ted Carlson (3)
Page 17   Ted Carlson (2), Randy Jolly
Page 18   Rick Llinares, Tom Kaminski
Page 19   Ted Carlson (5)
Page 20   Ted Carlson (2), Pete Becker,
    Tom Kaminski
Page 21   Ted Carlson
Page 22   Bob Greby, USAF
Page 23   Ted Carlson (5)
Page 24   USAF, Lockheed Martin, Ted Carlson (2)
Page 25   USAF, Ted Carlson
Page 26   Dave Mason, USAF (2)
Page 27   Randy Jolly
Page 28   Dave Mason, USAF, Riccardo Niccoli
Page 29   Dave Mason, Ted Carlson (2)
Page 30   Ted Carlson (4), Scott McDowell
Page 31   Jim Dunn, via Tom Kaminski
Page 32   Ted Carlson (3), Jim Dunn
Page 33   Dave Mason, Jim Dunn
Page 34   Ted Carlson (2)
Page 35   Rick Llinares
Page 36   USAF, Randy Jolly
Page 37   Ted Carlson, Robert F. Dorr
Page 38   Scott McDowell, Ted Carlson (2)
Page 39   Ted Carlson (3), Scott McDowell,
    Riccardo Niccoli
Page 40   Riccardo Niccoli, USAF
Page 41   USAF, Rick Llinares, Keith Snyder
Page 42   Randy Jolly, Brian C. Rogers, Ted Carlson
Page 44   Craig Kaston
Page 45   Ted Carlson (2)
Page 46   Jim Dunn
Page 47   Tom Kaminski, Jim Dunn
Page 48   Jim Dunn, Robert F. Dorr
Page 49   John Sheets, Boeing Company
Page 50   Andy Wolfe
Page 51   Ted Carlson, Boeing Company, Dave Mason
Page 52   Dave Mason, via Tom Kaminski
Page 53   Ted Carlson, Jim Dunn
Page 54   Ted Carlson (2)
Page 55   Dave Mason, Randy Jolly
Page 56   Ted Carlson, Brian C. Rogers
Page 57   Bob Greby, Riccardo Niccoli,
    Tom Kaminski
Page 58   Brian C. Rogers, Tom Ring
Page 59   Tom Kaminski (2), Brian C. Rogers
Page 60   Jim Dunn, Brian C. Rogers (2)
Page 61   Robert F. Dorr, Jim Dunn
Page 62   Rick Llinares, Henry B. Ham
Page 64   Dave Mason, Mel Williams
Page 65   Ted Carlson, Randy Jolly
Page 66   Lockheed Martin (2), Dave Mason
Page 68   Jim Dunn

Page 69   Jim Dunn (2)
Page 70   Pete Trafford, Jim Dunn
Page 72   Ted Carlson, Randy Jolly
Page 73   Pete Trafford
Page 74   Jim Dunn, Ted Carlson
Page 75   Ted Carlson, Robert F. Dorr
Page 76   Raytheon Aircraft, Ted Carlson
Page 77   USAFA, via Tom Kaminski
Page 78   Tom Kaminski, Randy Jolly
Page 79   Ted Carlson, Brian C. Rogers
Page 80   Randy Jolly
Page 82   Randy Jolly
Page 83   Ted Carlson
Page 84   Randy Jolly
Page 85   Ted Carlson, Dave Mason
Page 86   Ted Carlson
Page 87   Randy Jolly
Page 88   Tom Kaminski
Page 89   Northrop Grumman
Page 90   Pete Becker
Page 92   US Navy, Riccardo Niccoli
Page 93   Dave Mason, Riccardo Niccoli
Page 95   Mike Anselmo
Page 96   via Tom Kaminski
Page 97   via E. S. Holmberg (2),
    via Tom Kaminski (2)
Page 98   Tom Kaminski, Rick Llinares
Page 99   via Tom Kaminski (3), Ted Carlson,
    via E. S. Holmberg, Tom Kaminski
Page 100   Ted Carlson, via E. S. Holmberg
Page 101   Ted Carlson
Page 102   Ted Carlson, via E. S. Holmberg (3)
Page 103   Ted Carlson (2), via E. S. Holmberg,
    Tom Kaminski
Page 104   Ted Carlson (3)
Page 105   US Navy, Rick Llinares
Page 106   Ted Carlson
Page 107   Ted Carlson (3)
Page 108   Tom Kaminski, Riccardo Niccoli
Page 109   via E. S. Holmberg (2), US Navy,
    Tom Kaminski
Page 110   via E. S. Holmberg (2), Mel Williams,
    Riccardo Niccoli
Page 111   via E. S. Holmberg (2), US Navy/Erik Kenney,
    US Navy/Tom Wynn
Page 112   via E. S. Holmberg (2), US Navy/Mahlon K.
    Miller, US Navy/Edward Berard
Page 113   via E. S. Holmberg (2), US Navy/Matthew J.
    MaGee, US Navy
Page 114   via E. S. Holmberg (2), US Navy/Daniel J.
    Quinajon, US Navy/James Williams
Page 115   Joe Cupido, US Navy
Page 116   Ted Carlson, Norris Graser
Page 117   Mike Anselmo (2)
Page 118   Don Logan, Dave Mason
Page 119   Ted Carlson
Page 120   Joe Cupido, Ted Carlson
Page 122   Tom Kaminski, Rick Llinares
Page 123   Tom Kaminski, Ted Carlson
Page 124   Norris Graser, Ted Carlson, Tom Kaminski
Page 125   Tom Kaminski (2)
Page 126   via Tom Kaminski, Tom Kaminski

Page 127   Mel Williams
Page 128   J. G. Handelman, Ted Carlson (2)
Page 129   Ted Carlson (2)
Page 130   Warren Thompson
Page 132   Jim Dunn
Page 133   Randy Jolly, Ted Carlson
Page 134   Ted Carlson
Page 136   Ted Carlson, Tom Kaminski
Page 137   Tom Kaminski, Tom Ring
Page 138   Riccardo Niccoli, via Tom Kaminski
Page 139   Tom Kaminski, Norris Graser
Page 140   Tom Kaminski, Rick Llinares
Page 141   Ted Carlson
Page 142   via E. S. Holmberg
Page 144   Rick Llinares, via E. S. Holmberg (4)
Page 145   J.G. Handelman, via E. S. Holmberg (2)
Page 148   US Marine Corps (2)
Page 149   US Marine Corps
Page 150   Rick Llinares
Page 151   Randy Jolly
Page 152   Dave Mason, Randy Jolly
Page 153   Ted Carlson, via E. S. Holmberg,
    J. G. Handelman
Page 154   via E. S. Holmberg (3), Rick Llinares
Page 155   via E. S. Holmberg (3), Rick Llinares (2),
    Ted Carlson (2)
Page 156   Ted Carlson (2), via E. S. Holmberg (2)
Page 157   Ted Carlson (4), via E. S. Holmberg (3)
Page 158   via E. S. Holmberg (2), Ted Carlson (2),
    Johnathan Chuck, Rick Llinares
Page 159   via E. S. Holmberg, US Navy (2)
Page 160   Randy Jolly, via E. S. Holmberg (6)
Page 161   Rick Llinares
Page 162   Ted Carlson
Page 163   Tom Kaminski (2)
Page 164   Andy Wolfe
Page 166   Rick Llinares
Page 168   Ted Carlson, Riccardo Niccoli
Page 169   Ted Carlson, Scott McDowell,
    US Marine Corps
Page 170   J. G. Handelman, Ted Carlson, Randy Jolly
Page 171   Ted Carlson, US Marine Corps, Rick Llinares
Page 172   Rick Llinares, US Marine Corps, Ted Carlson
Page 174   Tom Kaminski, Ted Carlson, Norris Graser
Page 176   Chuck Lloyd, Dave Brown
Page 177   Randy Jolly
Page 178   Rick Llinares
Page 180   Rick Llinares
Page 181   Dave Mason
Page 182   US Coast Guard, Ted Carlson
Page 183   Tom Kaminski, Dave Mason
Page 184   Pete Becker
Page 185   Rick Llinares
Page 186   Robert F. Dorr
Page 187   Norris Graser
Page 188   Pete Becker, Ted Carlson
Page 189   Robert F. Dorr, Ted Carlson
Page 190   via Tom Kaminski (2)
Page 191   Jim Dunn, Dave Mason
Page 192   MD Helicopters, Ted Carlson
Page 193   Rick Llinares, Robert F. Dorr
Page 194   Robert F. Dorr, via E. S. Holmberg (2)

Page 195   Tom Hildreth
Page 196   US Army, Ted Carlson
Page 197   Randy Jolly, Tom Kaminski
Page 198   Stephen Miller
Page 199   Ted Carlson
Page 200   Mel Williams
Page 201   Pete Trafford (2), via Bill Barto
Page 202   Don Linn
Page 203   US Army, Ted Carlson
Page 204   Tom Ring, US Army (2), Ted Carlson (3)
Page 205   US Army
Page 206   Ted Carlson, Dave Mason
Page 207   via Tom Kaminski
Page 208   US Army, via Tom Kaminski,
    via Bill Barto, Randy Jolly
Page 209   Norris Graser
Page 210   Boeing Company, Institute of Heraldry
    Dept. of Army, US Army
Page 211   Tom Kaminski, Rick Llinares,
    US Army, via Bill Barto
Page 212   via Bill Barto, Rick Llinares, Don Linn
Page 213   US Army, Bill Shull
Page 214   Bombardier/Shorts
Page 215   Dennis Vink
Page 216   Dave Mason, via Bill Barto
Page 217   US Army, via Tom Kaminski
Page 218   Boeing Company, via Tom Kaminski
Page 219   Boeing Company
Page 220   via Tom Kaminski, Dave Mason
Page 221   Ted Carlson, Norris Graser
Page 222   Ted Carlson (2), Paul Hart,
    via Tom Kaminski
Page 224   Don Linn
Page 225   Ted Carlson, Don Linn
Page 226   Bell Helicopter Textron, Tom Kaminski,
    Boeing Company
Page 227   Ted Carlson (2)
Page 228   Ted Carlson, Rick Llinares
Page 229   Dave Mason, Randy Jolly
Page 230   Ted Carlson, Bill Barbant, Tom Kaminski
Page 231   Brian C. Rogers, Dennis Vink
Page 232   Stephen Harding, Ted Carlson
Page 233   Robert F. Dorr, Brian C. Rogers,
    Stephen Harding
Page 234   Stephen Harding, Ted Carlson
Page 235   Tom Kaminski (2)
Page 236   Raytheon Aircraft, Ted Carlson,
    Tom Kaminski
Page 237   Dave Mason, Keith Snyder,
    Ted Carlson (2)
Page 238   IAI/TRW, Ted Carlson, Dave Brown
Page 239   Rick Llinares
Page 240   Tom Kaminski
Page 242   Pete Becker
Page 243   Don Linn
Page 244   Bell Boeing, USAF (2)
Page 245   Boeing Company (2), US Navy
Page 246   Boeing Sikorsky
Page 247   USAF, US Navy, US Marine Corps,
    Boeing Company, Lockheed Martin